THE COMPLETE GOLFER'S ALMANAC 1996

A COMPENDIUM OF USEFUL GOLFING FACTS AND INFORMATION

by
James M. Lane

A Perigee Book

A Perigee Book
Published by The Berkley Publishing Group
200 Madison Avenue
New York, NY 10016

Copyright © 1996 by James M. Lane

Book design by James M. Lane

Cover illustration by Walt Spitzmiller

All rights reserved. This book, or parts thereof,
may not be reproduced in any form without permission.

First edition: April 1996

Printed simultaneously in Canada.

The Putnam Berkley World Wide Web site address is http://www.berkley.com

Library of Congress Cataloguing-in-Publication Data

Lane, James M. (James Max)
    The complete golfer's almanac 1996/James M. Lane. —1st ed.
       p. cm.
   "A Perigee Book."
   ISBN 0-399-51992-0 (alk. paper)
    1. Golf—Miscellanea. 2. Almanacs, American. I. Title.
GV965.L25 1996
796.352 02—dc20   94-37049
                                                                                           CIP

Printed in the United States of America

10 9 8 7 6 5 4 3 2 1

Quick Index

1996 Majors Preview..4
1996 Calendar..6

1995 in Review
The Major Championships...16
Professional Tour Results...27
Statistical Highlights...58

People
PGA Tour...70
Senior PGA Tour...98
LPGA Tour..116
Prominent Foreign Pros..132
Hall of Fame...137
Teaching Professionals...154

History
Major Championship Results 1860-1995..............................158
International Team Events 1927-1995...................................185
U.S. Club Professional Results 1968-1995............................189
U.S. Amateur Results 1895-1995..193
Tour Event History, 1899-1995...204
U.S. College Results 1897-1995..236
U.S. Junior Results 1948-1995..242
Awards..248
Memorable Dates in Golf History...253

Places
The Top 250 Courses in the World.......................................271
Golf Schools...290
Golf, by Nation...306
Golf, by U.S. State..336

Information
The Golf Economy..355
Associations and Addresses..358
Easy Guide to Golfing Terminology......................................378

General Index...385
Sources...396
Acknowledgments..397

1996
MAJOR CHAMPIONSHIP PREVIEWS

The Masters
Augusta National Golf Club, Augusta, Georgia

Course designed by—*Alister Mackenzie with Robert T. Jones (1932)*
Other course architects—*Perry Maxwell, Robert Trent Jones,*
George Cobb, Jack Nicklaus, Tom Fazio
Defending Champion—*Ben Crenshaw*
Golfer's Almanac Favorite—*Davis Love III*
Also watch—*John Huston, Greg Norman, Tom Watson*
Key holes—*12, 13, 15, 18*
Television—*USA/CBS*

Notes: Despite a reputation as a long-hitter's course, Augusta yields to the Master of the five and fifteen-foot putts. Foreign players have won six of the last eight titles, but Davis Love, John Huston and Tom Watson have been the strongest overall performers of recent years. Don't count out Tom Lehman, who had back-to-back top-three finishes in 1993-94.

The U.S. Open
Oakland Hills Country Club, Birmingham, Michigan

Course designed by—*Donald Ross (1924)*
Other course architect—*Robert Trent Jones, Sr.*
Defending Champion—*Corey Pavin*
Last champion at Oakland Hills—*Andy North*
Golfer's Almanac Favorite—*Colin Montgomerie*
Also watch—*Jay Haas, Greg Norman, Frank Nobilo, Scott Verplank*
Key holes—*14, 15, 16*
Television: *ESPN/NBC*

Notes: Only one golfer, Andy North in 1985, has broken par over 72 holes in an Open played at Oakland Hills since the remodeling by Robert Trent Jones in 1951. Palmer, Nicklaus, Player, Hogan, Littler, and David Graham have won majors here. Oakland Hills last hosted a major in 1991 when Jack Nicklaus won a dramatic U.S. Senior Open over Chi Chi Rodriguez. Jay Haas tied for 7th in the 1979 PGA here, while Frank Nobilo and Greg Norman have both posted consecutive top-ten finishes in the 1994 and 1995 Opens.

British Open
Royal Lytham & St. Anne's, Lytham St. Annes, Lancashire, England

Course designed by—*George Lowe (1886)*
Defending Champion—*John Daly*
Last champion at Royal Lytham & St. Anne's—*Seve Ballesteros*
Golfer's Almanac Favorite—*Corey Pavin*
Also—*David Frost, Greg Norman, Nick Price, Loren Roberts, Constantino Rocca*
Key holes—*7, 13, 14, 17*
Television—*ABC/ESPN*

Notes: "The railway on the right scares us into a hook: and the hook takes us into a bunker, and the bunker loses us the hole." So wrote Bernard Darwin almost sixty years ago about the travails of the early holes in particular, and Royal Lytham & St. Anne's in general, where shotmaking artists such as Seve Ballesteros, Gary Player and Tony Jacklin have taught us that making something out of nothing is the key to victory. Making an astounding number of putts also comes in handy on the renowned greens, bringing Loren Roberts and David Frost as well as Corey Pavin into contention. Nick Price finished runner-up the last outing at Royal Lytham in 1988, and should not be counted out for his major championship comeback after a disappointing 1995 campaign. And after a near-miss in the 1995 Open at the Old Course, Constantino Rocca may find this course more to his liking.

PGA Championship
Valhalla Golf Club, Louisville, Kentucky

Course designed by—*Jack Nicklaus (1986)*
Defending champion—*Steve Elkington*
Golfer's Almanac Favorite—*Lee Janzen*
Also watch—*David Duval, Steve Elkington, Peter Jacobsen, Justin Leonard, Phil Mickelson, Scott Simpson, Payne Stewart*
Key holes—*14, 18*
Television—*USA/CBS*

Notes: Valhalla is a new addition to the PGA Championship rotation, and has not hosted a major championship or a PGA TOUR event. So favorites will be hard to pick, although with the Nicklaus design style of the 1980s featuring tough, intimidating golf holes expect this to be a return to the traditional par scoring of major championships after the birdie festival at Riviera in 1995. Long, accurate driving and precise mid-iron play will reap rewards here, making this a course for Open perennials such as Scott Simpson and Lee Janzen, while forgiving the occasionally wayward putting of Peter Jacobsen and Payne Stewart. The PGA Championship often is the first major won by a young player, so no one should be too surprised to see Justin Leonard, David Duval or Phil Mickelson steal the trophy.

1996 CALENDAR

OVERVIEW: *Includes listing of all major PGA, LPGA, and Senior Tour events. For tournaments, the lead television network is indicated in bold. Television coverage is typically 4:00pm-6:00pm on Saturdays; 3:30pm-6:00pm Sundays, Eastern time. Major championships are typically telecast in their entirety, with the exception of the Masters, which follows a standard network schedule. Secondary networks typically carry the telecast in off-air hours and on Thursday and Friday of the tournament. Tournaments without a network indicated are often televised by regional sports networks and/or via satellite services. Check your local TV, cable, or satellite programming guide for details.*

PGA TOUR

Dates	Network	Tournament, Location
January 4-7	ABC	Mercedes Championships *La Costa Resort—Carlsbad, CA*
January 11-14	ESPN	Northern Telecom Open *Tucson Nat'l Golf Resort—Tucson, AZ*
January 18-21	NBC	Bob Hope Chrysler Classic *Indian Wells, Indian Ridge, Bermuda Dunes, La Quinta—Palm Desert, CA*
January 25-28	ESPN	Phoenix Open *TPC of Scottsdale—Scottsdale, AZ*
February 1-4	CBS	AT&T Pebble Beach National Pro-Am *Pebble Beach, Spyglass Hill, Poppy Hills—Pebble Beach, CA*
February 8-11	NBC	Buick Invitational of California *Torrey Pines—La Jolla, CA*
February 15-18	TBS	United Airlines Hawaiian Open *Waialae Country Club—Honolulu, HI*
February 22-25	CBS	Nissan Open *Riviera Country Club—Pacific Palisades, CA*
February 29-March 3	CBS	Doral-Ryder Open *Doral Resort & Country Club—Miami, FL*
March 7-10	NBC	Honda Classic *TPC at Heron Bay, Coral Springs, FL*
March 14-17	NBC	Bay Hill Invitational *Bay Hill Club & Lodge—Orlando, FL*
March 21-24	NBC	Freeport-McMoRan Classic *English Turn Golf & Country Club—New Orleans, LA*
March 28-31	NBC	THE PLAYERS Championship *TPC at Sawgrass—Ponte Vedra Beach, FL*
April 4-7	CBS	Bell South Classic *Atlanta Country Club—Marietta, GA*

Dates	Network	Tournament, Location
April 11-14	CBS USA	**The Masters** *Augusta National Golf Club—Augusta, GA*
April 18-21	CBS	**MCI Classic—The Heritage of Golf** *Harbour Town Golf Links—Hilton Head Island, SC*
April 25-28	CBS	**Kmart Greater Greensboro Open** *Forest Oaks Country Club—Greensboro, NC*
May 2-5	ABC	**Shell Houston Open** *TPC at The Woodlands—The Woodlands, TX*
May 9-12	ABC	**Byron Nelson Classic** *TPC at Las Colinas—Irving, TX*
May 16-19	CBS	**MasterCard Colonial** *Colonial Country Club—Ft. Worth, TX*
May 23-26	CBS	**Kemper Open** *TPC at Avenel—Potomac, MD*
May 30-June 2	ABC	**Memorial Tournament** *Muirfield Village Golf Club—Dublin, OH*
June 6-9	CBS	**Buick Classic** *Westchester Country Club—Rye, NY*
June 13-16	NBC USA	**United States Open** *Oakland Hills Country Club—Birmingham, MI*
June 20-23	CBS	**FedEx St. Jude Classic** *TPC at Southwind—Memphis, TN*
June 27-30	CBS	**Canon Greater Hartford Open** *TPC at River Highlands—Cromwell, CT*
July 4-7	CBS	**Motorola Western Open** *Cog Hill Golf Club—Lemont, IL*
July 11-14	ESPN	**Anheuser-Busch Golf Classic** *Kingsmill Golf Club—Williamsburg, VA*
July 18-21	ABC ESPN	**British Open** *Royal Lytham & St. Anne's—Lytham, England*
July 18-21	TGC	**Deposit Guaranty Golf Classic** *Annandale Golf Club—Madison, MS*
July 25-28	TGC	**The New England Classic** *Pleasant Valley Country Club—Sutton, MA*
August 1-4	CBS	**Buick Open** *Warwick Hills Golf & Country Club—Grand Blanc, MI*
August 8-11	CBS USA	**PGA Championship** *Valhalla Golf Club—Louisville, KY*
August 15-18	CBS	**The Sprint International** *Castle Pines Golf Club–Castle Rock, CO*
August 22-25	CBS	**NEC World Series of Golf** *Firestone Country Club–Akron, OH*
August 22-25		**Greater Vancouver Open** *Northview Golf & Country Club—Surrey, British Columbia*

Calendar–PGA TOUR

Dates	Network	Tournament, Location
August 29–September 1	ABC	**Greater Milwaukee Open** *Brown Deer Park Golf Course–Milwaukee, WI*
September 5–8	ESPN	**Bell Canadian Open** *Glen Abbey Golf Club–Oakville, Ontario*
September 12–15	TGC	**Quad City Classic** *Oakwood Country Club–Coal Valley, IL*
September 19–22	TGC	**B.C. Open** *En-Joie Golf Club–Endicott, NY*
September 26–29	ESPN	**Buick Challenge** *Callaway Gardens Resort—Pine Mountain, GA*
October 2–6	ESPN	**Las Vegas Invitational** *TPC at Summerlin, Las Vegas CC, Desert Inn CC–Las Vegas, NV*
October 10–13	TGC	**La Cantera Texas Open** *La Cantera Golf Club—San Antonio, TX*
October 17–20	TGC	**Walt Disney World/Oldsmobile Classic** *Lake Buena Vista Golf Club–Orlando, FL*
October 24–27	ABC	**THE TOUR Championship** *Southern Hills Country Club—Tulsa, OK*
November 7–10	ABC	**Lincoln-Mercury Kapalua International** *Kapalua Resort –Lahaina, Maui, HI*
November 14–17	CBS	**Franklin Funds Shark Shootout** *Sherwood Country Club–Thousand Oaks, CA*
November 21–24	NBC	**The World Cup of Golf** *To be announced*
November 30–December 1	ABC	**Skins Game** *To be announced*
December 5–8	ABC	**JCPenney Classic** *Innisbrook Hilton Resort—Tarpon Springs FL*
December 12–15	ABC	**Diners Club Matches** *PGA West, Jack Nicklaus Resort Course–La Quinta, CA*
January 3–5, 1997	ABC	**Anderson Consulting World Championship of Golf** *Grayhawk Golf Club—Scottsdale, AZ*

Senior PGA TOUR

Dates	Network	Tournament, Location
January 15-21	ESPN	Senior Tournament of Champions Hyatt Dorado Beach—Dorado Beach, Puerto Rico
January 22-28	ABC	Senior Skins Game Mauni Lani Resort—Kohala Coast, HI
January 29-February 4	ESPN	Royal Caribbean Classic Links at Key Biscayne—Key Biscayne, FL
February 5-11	ESPN	Greater Naples Challenge The Vineyards—Naples, FL
February 12-18	ESPN	GTE Suncoast Classic TPC at Tampa Bay—Tampa, FL
February 19-25		Senior Golf Classic Sarasota, FL
February 26-March 3	ESPN	FHP Health Care Classic Ojai Valley Inn & Country Club—Ojai, CA
March 4-5	TBS	Senior Slam of Golf To be announced
March 11-17	ESPN	Toshiba Senior Classic Costa Mesa Golf Club—Newport Beach, CA
March 18-24	ABC	Liberty Mutual Legends of Golf Stadium Course at PGA West—La Quinta, CA
March 25-31		SBC presents The Dominion The Dominion Country Club—San Antonio, TX
April 1-7	ESPN	The Tradition Desert Mountain—Scottsdale, AZ
April 15-21	NBC	PGA Seniors Championship PGA National Golf Club—Palm Beach Gardens, FL
April 22-28	ESPN	Las Vegas Senior Classic TPC at Summerlin—Las Vegas, NV
April 29-May 5	ESPN	Charlotte Invitational TPC at Piper Glen—Charlotte, NC
May 6-12	ESPN	Nationwide Championship Golf Club of Georgia—Atlanta, GA
May 13-19	ESPN	Cadillac NFL Golf Classic Upper Montclair Country Club—Clifton, NJ
May 20-26	NBC	BellSouth Senior Classic at Opryland Opryland Golf Club—Nashville, TN
May 27-June 2		Bruno's Memorial Classic Greystone Golf Club—Birmingham, AL
June 3-9		Quicksilver Classic Quicksilver Country Club—Pittsburgh, PA
June 17-23	ESPN	Bell Atlantic Classic Chester Valley Golf Club—Malvern, PA
June 24-30	ESPN	Kroger Senior Classic The Golf Center at Kings Island—Mason, OH

Calendar–Senior PGA TOUR

Dates	Network	Tournament, Location
July 1-7	NBC	US Senior Open Cleveland, OH
July 8-14	ABC	FORD SENIOR PLAYERS Championship TPC of Michigan—Dearborn, MI
July 15-21	ESPN	Burnet Senior Classic Bunker Hills Golf Club—Coon Rapids, MN
July 22-28	CBS	Ameritech Senior Open Stonebridge Country Club—Chicago, IL
July 29-August 4	ESPN	VFW Senior Championship Loch Lloyd Country Club—Belton, MO
August 5-11		First of America Classic Grad Rapids, MI
August 12-18	ESPN	Northville Long Island Classic Meadow Brook Country Club—Jericho, NY
August 19-25	ESPN	Bank of Boston Senior Golf Classic Nashawtuc Country Club—Boston, MA
August 26-September 1		Franklin Quest Championship Park Meadows—Park City, UT
September 2-8		Northwest Classic Inglewood Country Club—Seattle, WA
September 9-15		Bank One Classic Kearney Golf Links—Lexington, KY
September 16-22		Brickyard Crossing Championship Brickyard Crossing—Indianapolis, IN
September 23-29	ESPN	Vantage Championship Tanglewood Park—Clemmons, NC
September 30-October 6		Ralph's Senior Classic Wilshire Country Club—Los Angeles, CA
October 7-13	ESPN	The Transamerica Silverado Country Club—Napa, CA
October 14-20		Raley's Senior Gold Rush Rancho Murieta Country Club—Sacramento, CA
October 21-27	ESPN	Hyatt Regency Maul Kaanapali Classic Royal Kaanapali Golf Club—Maui, HI
October 28-November 3		Emerald Coast Classic The Moors—Pensacola, FL
November 4-10	ESPN	Energizer SENIOR TOUR Championship The Dunes Golf & Beach Club—Myrtle Beach, SC
December 9-15	ABC	Diners Club Matches PGA West—La Quinta, CA
December 16-22	NBC	Lexus Challenge La Quinta, CA

LPGA TOUR

Dates	Network	Tournament, Location
January 11-14		Chrysler-Plymouth Tournament of Champions *Grand Cypress Golf Club—Orlando, FL*
January 19-21	TGC	HEALTHSOUTH Inaugural *Lake Buena Vista Golf Club—Orlando, FL*
February 22-24		Cup Noodles Hawaiian Ladies Open *Kapolei Golf Course—Kapolei, Oahu, HI*
March 14-17	TGC	PING/Welch's Championship *Randolph Park Golf Course—Tucson, AZ*
March 21-24	ESPN	Standard Register PING *Moon Valley Country Club—Phoenix, AZ*
March 28-31	ABC ESPN	Nabisco Dinah Shore *Mission Hills Country Club—Rancho Mirage, CA*
April 4-7		Sacramento LPGA Classic *Twelve Bridges Golf Club—Sacramento, CA*
April 19-21		Chick-Fil-A Charity Championship *Eagle's Landing Country Club—Stockbridge, GA*
April 26-28	TGC	Sara Lee Classic *Hermitage Golf Course—Old Hickory, TN*
May 2-5	CBS	Sprint Titleholders Championship *LPGA International—Daytona Beach, FL*
May 9-12	CBS	McDonald's LPGA Championship *DuPont Country Club—Wilmington, DE*
May 23-26		LPGA Corning Classic *Corning Country Club—Corning, NY*
May 25-26	ABC	JCPenney LPGA Skins Game *Stonebriar Country Club—Frisco, TX*
May 30-June 2	ABC ESPN	United States Women's Open *Pine Needles Lodge and Golf Club—Pinehurst, NC*
June 6-9		Oldsmobile Classic *Walnut Hills Country Club—East Lansing, MI*

Dates	Network	Tournament, Location
June 14-16	TGC	The Edina Realty LPGA Classic *Edinburgh USA Golf Course—Brooklyn Park, MN*
June 20-23	TGC	Rochester International *Locust Hill Country Club—Pittsford, NY*
June 28-30		ShopRite LPGA Classic *Greate Bay Resort & Country Club—Somers Point, NJ*
July 5-7	TGC	Jamie Farr Kroger Classic *Highland Meadows Golf Club—Sylvania, OH*
July 12-14		Youngstown-Warren LPGA Classic *Avalon Lakes—Warren, OH*
July 18-21		Friendly's Classic *Crestview Country Club—Agawam, MA*
July 25-28		Heartland Classic *Forest Hills Country Club—St. Louis, MO*
August 1-4	TGC	du Maurier Ltd. Classic *Edmonton Country Club—Edmonton, AL*
August 8-11	TGC	PING/Welch's Championship *Blue Hill Country Club—Canton, MA*
August 15-18		Weetabix Women's British Open *Woburn Golf & Country Club—Milton Keynes, England*
August 23-25		Star Bank LPGA Classic *Country Club of the North—Dayton, OH*
August 31- September 2		State Farm Rail Classic *Rail Golf Club—Springfield, IL*
September 6-8		PING-AT&T LPGA Golf Championship *Columbia Edgewater Country Club—Portland, OR*
September 12-15		Safeco Classic *Meridian Valley Country Club—Kent, WA*
September 20-22		The Solheim Cup *St. Pierre Hotel Golf & Country Club—Chepstow, Wales*
September 26-29		Fieldcrest Cannon Classic *Peninsula Country Club—Charlotte, NC*

Dates	Network	Tournament, Location
October 3-6	NBC	JAL Big Apple Classic *Wykagyl Country Club—New Rochelle, NY*
October 17-20	TGC	Samsung World Championship of Women's Golf *Paradise Country Club—Cheju Island, South Korea*
October 25-27		Nichirei International *Ami Golf Club—Ibaragi, Japan*
November 1-3		Toray Japan Queens Cup *To be announced*
December 5-8		JCPenney Classic *Innisbrook Hilton Resort—Tarpon Springs, FL*
December 13-15	ABC	Diner's Club Matches *PGA West-Jack Nicklaus Resort Course—La Quinta, CA*
December 21-22	ABC	Wendy's Three-Tour Challenge *Muirfield Village Golf Club—Dublin, OH*

EUROPEAN TOUR

Dates	Network	Tournament, Location
January 25-28	TGC	Johnnie Walker Classic *Tanah Merah Golf Club—Singapore*
February 1-4		Heineken Classic *The Vines—Perth, Australia*
February 8-11		South African National Pro-Am *Sun City—Sun City, South Africa*
February 15-18	TGC	Lexington South African PGA *Houghton—Johannesburg, South Africa*
February 29- March 3	TGC	Open Mediterriania *To be announced*
March 7-10	TGC	Moroccan Open *Golf Royal de Agadir—Agadir, Morocco*
March 14-17	TGC	Dubai Desert Classic *Emirates G.C.—Dubai, United Arab Emirates*

Dates	Network	Tournament, Location
March 21-24		Portuguese Open *Penha Longa G.C.—Sintra, Portugal*
March 28-31		Madeira Island Open *Campo de Golfe—Madeira*
April 18-21	TGC	Cannes Open *Cannes Mougains G.C.—Cannes, France*
April 25-28	TGC	Turespana Masters *To be announced*
May 2-5	TGC	Italian Open *Bergamo—Milan, Italy*
May 9-12	TGC	Peugeot Open de Espana *To be announced*
May 11-14	TGC	Benson and Hedges International Open *To be announced*
May 20-21		Five Tours European qualifying tournament *To be announced*
May 24-27	TGC	PGA Championship *Wentworth Club (West)—Surrey, England*
May 30-June 2	TGC	Tournament Players Championship *Gut Kaden—Hamburg, Germany*
June 6-9	TGC	English Open *Forest of Arden G.C.—Warwickshire, England*
June 13-16		Jersey Open *La Moye (Nicklaus)—St. Brelade, England*
June 20-23	TGC	BMW International Open *To be announced*
June 27-30	TGC	Open de France *Le Golf National—Versailles, France*
July 4-7	TGC	Murphy's Irish Open *To be announced*
July 10-13	TGC	Bell's Scottish Open *Carnoustie—Angus, Scotland*

Dates	Network	Tournament, Location
July 18-21	ABC ESPN	British Open *Royal Lytham & St. Anne's—Lytham, England*
July 25-28	TGC	Dutch Open *Hilversumsche G.C.—Hilversum, Netherlands*
August 1-4	TGC	Scandanavian Masters *Forsgardens—Gothenburg, Sweden*
August 8-10		Austrian Open *G.C. Waldviertal—Litschau, Austria*
August 15-18	TGC	Czech Open *Marianske Lazne G.C.—Czech Republic*
August 22-25	TGC	Volvo German Open *Nippenburg G.C.—Stuttgart, Germany*
August 29- September 1	TGC	European Masters *Crans-sur-Sierre—Switzerland*
September 5-8	TGC	British Masters *Collingtree Park—Northampton, England*
September 12-15	TGC	Trophee Lancome *St. Nom-la-Breteche—Versailles, France*
September 19-22		Loch Lomond World Invitational *Loch Lomond—Loch Lomond, Scotland*
September 26-29	TGC	European Open *Kildare C.C.—Dublin, Ireland*
October 3-6	TGC	German Masters *To be announced*
October 10-13	TGC	Toyota World Match Play Championship *Wentworth Club—Surrey, England*
October 17-20	TGC	Alfred Dunhill Cup *Old Course—St. Andrews, Scotland*
October 24-27	TGC	Volvo Masters *Valderrama—Sotogrande, Spain*
October 31- November 3		World Open *Chateau Élan—Atalnta, U.S.A.*

1995 MAJOR CHAMPIONSHIP RESULTS

OVERVIEW: *Complete scores and prize money for the four major championships on the PGA TOUR, Senior PGA TOUR, and the LPGA Tour. Asterisks denote playoff victories.*

PGA TOUR

THE MASTERS
Augusta National G.C.,
Augusta, Georgia,
Apr. 6-9, 1995

BEN CRENSHAW	$396,000	70-67-69-68	274
DAVIS LOVE III	$237,600	69-69-71-66	275
GREG NORMAN	$127,600	73-68-68-68	277
JAY HAAS	$127,600	71-64-72-70	277
DAVID FROST	$83,600	66-71-71-71	279
STEVE ELKINGTON	$83,600	73-67-67-72	279
PHIL MICKELSON	$70,950	66-71-70-73	280
SCOTT HOCH	$70,950	69-67-71-73	280
CURTIS STRANGE	$63,800	72-71-65-73	281
FRED COUPLES	$57,200	71-69-67-75	282
BRIAN HENNINGER	$57,200	70-68-68-76	282
KENNY PERRY	$48,400	73-70-71-69	283
LEE JANZEN	$48,400	69-69-74-71	283
JOSE MARIA OLAZABAL	$39,600	66-74-72-72	284
TOM WATSON	$39,600	73-70-69-72	284
HALE IRWIN	$39,600	69-72-71-72	284
IAN WOOSNAM	$28,786	69-72-71-73	285
RAYMOND FLOYD	$28,786	71-70-70-74	285
BRAD FAXON	$28,786	76-69-69-71	285
PAUL AZINGER	$28,786	70-72-73-70	285
COLIN MONTGOMERIE	$28,786	71-69-76-69	285
COREY PAVIN	$28,786	67-71-72-75	285
JOHN HUSTON	$28,786	70-66-72-77	285
DUFFY WALDORF	$18,260	74-69-67-76	286
DAVID GILFORD	$18,260	67-73-75-71	286
DAVID EDWARDS	$18,260	69-73-73-71	286
LOREN ROBERTS	$18,260	72-69-72-73	286
NICK FALDO	$18,260	70-70-71-75	286
JUMBO OZAKI	$15,300	70-74-70-73	287
BOB ESTES	$15,300	73-70-76-68	287
BRUCE LIETZKE	$15,300	72-71-71-74	288
PETER JACOBSEN	$15,300	72-73-69-74	288
BERNHARD LANGER	$15,300	71-69-73-75	288
MARK O'MEARA	$15,300	68-72-71-77	288
MARK MCCUMBER	$10,850	73-69-69-79	290
JACK NICKLAUS	$10,850	67-78-70-75	290
DAN FORSMAN	$10,850	71-74-74-71	290
WAYNE GRADY	$10,850	69-73-74-74	290
CHIP BECK	$10,850	68-76-69-77	290
TOM LEHMAN	$9,500	71-72-74-75	292
MARK CALCAVECCHIA	$8,567	70-72-78-73	293
TIGER WOODS	amateur	72-72-77-72	293
JEFF SLUMAN	$8,567	73-72-71-77	293
PAYNE STEWART	$8,567	71-72-72-78	293
JOHN DALY	$7,500	75-69-71-81	296
SEVE BALLESTEROS	$7,500	75-68-78-75	296
RICK FEHR	$6,800	76-69-69-83	297

THE UNITED STATES OPEN
Shinnecock Hills G.C.,
Southampton, New York
June 15-18, 1995

COREY PAVIN	$350,000	72-69-71-68	280
GREG NORMAN	$207,000	68-67-74-73	282
TOM LEHMAN	$131,974	70-72-67-74	283
NEAL LANCASTER	$66,634	70-72-77-65	284
JEFF MAGGERT	$66,634	69-72-77-66	284
BILL GLASSON	$66,634	69-70-76-69	284
JAY HAAS	$66,634	70-73-72-69	284
DAVIS LOVE III	$66,634	72-68-73-71	284
PHIL MICKELSON	$66,634	68-70-72-74	284
FRANK NOBILO	$44,184	72-72-70-71	285
BOB TWAY	$44,184	69-69-72-75	285
VIJAY SINGH	$44,184	70-71-72-72	285

MARK MCCUMBER	$30,934	70-71-77-68	286
DUFFY WALDORF	$30,934	72-70-75-69	286
BRAD BRYANT	$30,934	71-75-70-70	286
JEFF SLUMAN	$30,934	72-69-74-71	286
MARK ROE	$30,934	71-69-74-72	286
LEE JANZEN	$30,934	70-72-72-72	286
STEVE STRICKER	$30,934	71-70-71-74	286
NICK PRICE	$30,934	66-73-73-74	286
FUZZY ZOELLER	$20,085	69-74-76-68	287
PAYNE STEWART	$20,085	74-71-73-69	287
BRETT OGLE	$20,085	71-75-72-69	287
PETE JORDAN	$20,085	74-71-71-71	287
BILLY ANDRADE	$20,085	72-69-74-72	287
SCOTT VERPLANK	$20,085	72-69-71-75	287
IAN WOOSNAM	$20,085	72-71-69-75	287
COLIN MONTGOMERIE	$13,912	71-74-75-68	288
MIGUEL ANGEL JIMENEZ	$13,912	72-72-75-69	288
MIKE HULBERT	$13,912	74-72-72-70	288
JUMBO OZAKI	$13,912	69-68-80-71	288
SCOTT SIMPSON	$13,912	67-75-74-72	288
DAVID DUVAL	$13,912	70-73-73-72	288
JOSE-MARIA OLAZABAL	$13,912	73-70-72-73	288
GARY HALLBERG	$13,912	70-76-69-73	288
BILL PORTER	$9,812	73-70-79-67	289
RAY FLOYD	$9,812	74-72-76-67	289
HAL SUTTON	$9,812	71-74-76-68	289
CURTIS STRANGE	$9,812	70-72-76-71	289
GUY BOROS	$9,812	73-71-74-71	289
STEVE ELKINGTON	$9,812	72-73-73-71	289
CURT BYRUM	$9,812	70-70-76-73	289
BERNHARD LANGER	$9,812	74-67-74-74	289
BARRY LANE	$8,147	74-72-71-73	290
CHRISTIAN PENA	$7,146	74-71-76-70	291
JIM GALLAGHER JR.	$7,146	71-75-77-68	291
JIM MCGOVERN	$7,146	73-69-81-68	291
OMAR URESTI	$7,146	71-74-75-71	291
JOHN DALY	$7,146	71-75-74-71	291
NICK FALDO	$7,146	72-68-79-72	291
BRADLEY HUGHES	$7,146	72-71-75-73	291
BOB BURNS	$5,843	73-72-75-72	292
EDUARDO ROMERO	$5,843	73-71-75-73	292
TED TRYBA	$5,843	71-75-73-73	292
PETER JACOBSEN	$5,843	72-72-74-74	292
MATT GOGEL	$5,843	73-70-73-76	292
BRAD FAXON	$4,834	71-73-77-72	293
TOM WATSON	$4,834	70-73-77-73	293
CHRIS PERRY	$4,834	70-74-75-74	293
STEVE LOWERY	$4,834	69-72-75-77	293
SCOTT HOCH	$4,834	74-72-70-77	293
GREG BRUCKNER	$4,834	70-72-73-78	293
JOHN COOK	$3,969	70-75-76-73	294
BRANDT JOBE	$3,969	71-72-76-75	294
DAVID EDWARDS	$3,969	72-74-72-76	294
PAUL GOYDOS	$3,969	73-73-70-78	294
TOM KITE	$3,349	70-72-80-71	295
MIKE BRISKY	$3,349	71-72-77-75	295
TOMMY ARMOUR III	$3,349	77-69-74-75	295
JOHN CONNELLY	$3,039	75-71-74-76	296
BEN CRENSHAW	$2,807	72-71-79-75	297
JOHN MAGINNES	$2,807	75-71-74-77	297
JOE GULLION	$2,574	70-74-81-76	301

THE BRITISH OPEN
The Old Course,
St. Andrews, Scotland
July 20-23, 1995

*JOHN DALY	$200,000	67-71-73-71	282
COSTANTINO ROCCA	$160,000	69-70-70-73	282
STEVEN BOTTOMLEY	$105,065	70-72-72-69	283
MARK BROOKS	$105,065	70-69-73-71	283
MICHAEL CAMPBELL	$105,065	71-71-65-76	283
VIJAY SINGH	$64,800	68-72-73-71	284
STEVE ELKINGTON	$64,800	72-69-69-74	284
BOB ESTES	$53,333	72-70-71-72	285
COREY PAVIN	$53,333	69-70-72-74	285
MARK JAMES	$53,333	72-75-68-70	285
PAYNE STEWART	$41,600	72-68-75-71	286
BRETT OGLE	$41,600	73-69-71-73	286
SAM TORRANCE	$41,600	71-70-71-74	286
ERNIE ELS	$41,600	71-68-72-75	286
GREG NORMAN	$29,120	71-74-72-70	287
ROBERT ALLENBY	$29,120	71-74-71-71	287
BEN CRENSHAW	$29,120	67-72-76-72	287
PER-ULRIK JOHANSSON	$29,120	69-78-68-72	287
BRAD FAXON	$29,120	71-67-75-74	287
PETER MITCHELL	$21,600	73-74-71-70	288
DAVID DUVAL	$21,600	71-75-70-72	288
ANDREW COLTART	$21,600	70-74-71-73	288
BARRY LANE	$21,600	72-73-68-75	288
LEE JANZEN	$16,506	73-73-71-72	289

18 Major Championships

STEVE WEBSTER	amateur	70-72-74-73	289	GARY PLAYER	$7,960	71-73-77-74	295
BERNHARD LANGER	$16,506	72-71-73-73	289	OLLE KARLSSON	$7,960	71-76-73-75	295
JESPER PARNEVIK	$16,506	75-71-70-73	289	MATS HALLBERG	$7,960	68-76-75-76	295
MARK CALCAVECCHIA	$16,506	71-72-72-74	289	SCOTT HOCH	$7,960	74-72-73-76	295
BILL GLASSON	$16,506	68-74-72-75	289	GARY HALLBERG	$7,960	72-74-72-77	295
KATSUYOSKI TOMORI	$16,506	70-68-73-78	289	JOSE RIVERO	$7,960	70-72-75-78	295
ROSS DRUMMOND	$12,995	74-68-77-71	290	TIGER WOODS	amateur	74-71-72-78	295
JOSE MARIA OLAZABAL	$12,995	72-72-74-72	290	PATRICK BURKE	$7,200	75-72-78-71	296
DAVID FROST	$12,995	72-72-74-72	290	JAY HAAS	$7,200	76-72-70-78	296
HISAYUKI SASAKI	$12,995	74-71-72-73	290	RYOKEN KAWAGASHI	$7,200	72-76-80-68	296
JOHN HUSTON	$12,995	71-74-72-73	290	BOB LOHR	$7,200	76-68-79-73	296
PETER JACOBSEN*	$12,995	71-70-70-73	290	SANDY LYLE	$7,200	71-71-79-75	296
DARREN CLARKE	$12,995	69-77-70-74	290	JACK NICKLAUS	$7,200	78-70-77-71	296
DAVID FEHERTY	$12,995	68-75-71-76	290	JARMO SANDELIN	$7,200	75-71-77-73	296
TOM WATSON	$12,995	67-76-70-77	290	STEVE LOWERY	$7,200	69-74-76-77	296
SEVE BALLESTEROS	$11,280	75-69-76-71	291	DEAN ROBERTON	$7,200	71-73-74-78	296
WARREN BENNETT	$11,280	72-74-73-72	291	MARK DAVIS	$6,600	74-71-76-76	297
PHIL MICKELSON	$11,280	70-71-77-73	291	MIGUEL JIMENEZ	$6,600	75-73-76-73	297
MARK MCNULTY	$11,280	67-76-74-74	291	JAY DELSING	$6,600	72-75-73-77	297
NICK FALDO	$11,280	74-67-75-75	291	EDUARDO ROMERO	$6,600	74-74-72-77	297
BRIAN WATTS	$11,280	72-71-73-75	291	GENE SAUERS	$6,600	69-73-75-80	297
JOHN COOK	$11,280	69-70-75-77	291	WAYNE RILEY	$6,600	70-72-75-80	297
NICK PRICE	$11,280	70-74-70-77	291	JOHN HAWKSWORTH	$6,400	73-74-75-76	298
GORDON SHERRY	amateur	70-71-74-76	291	BILL LONGMUIR	$6,400	72-76-72-78	298
IAN WOOSNAM	$10,160	71-74-76-71	292	JOSE COCERES	$6,400	71-76-78-74	299
ANDERS FORSBRAND	$10,160	70-74-75-73	292	LEE WESTWOOD	$6,400	71-72-82-74	299
MARK O'MEARA	$10,160	72-72-75-73	292	SIMON BURNELL	$6,400	72-76-75-77	300
TOMMY NAKAJIMA	$10,160	73-72-72-75	292	DAVIS LOVE III	$6,400	70-78-74-78	300
BRIAN CLAAR	$10,160	71-75-71-75	292	GARY CLARK	amateur	71-76-80-74	301
KEN GREEN	$10,160	71-72-73-76	292	MARK NICHOLS	$6,400	75-68-78-81	302
JIM GALLAGHER JR.	$9,520	69-76-75-73	293	DON POOLEY	$6,400	76-71-80-75	302
PETER O'MALLEY	$9,520	71-73-74-75	293	PEDRO LINHART	$6,400	72-75-77-79	303
RUSSELL CLAYDON	$9,520	70-74-71-78	293				
PAUL BROADHURST	$8,760	73-72-76-73	294				
DERRICK COOPER	$8,760	71-76-74-73	294				
PETER SENIOR	$8,760	71-75-78-70	294				
EDUARDO HERRERA	$8,760	74-72-73-75	294				
TOM KITE	$8,760	72-76-71-75	294				
PAUL LAWRIE	$8,760	73-71-72-78	294				
MARTIN GATES	$8,760	73-73-72-76	294				
RAYMOND FLOYD	$8,760	72-74-72-76	294				
JUSTIN LEONARD	$8,760	73-67-77-77	294				
DAVID GILFORD	$8,760	69-72-75-78	294				
PETER BAKER	$7,960	70-74-81-70	295				
JONATHAN LOMAS	$7,960	74-73-75-73	295				
JEFF MAGGERT	$7,960	75-70-78-72	295				
FRANK NOBILO	$7,960	70-71-80-74	295				

THE PGA CHAMPIONSHIP
Riviera C.C.,
Los Angeles, California
August 10-13, 1995

*STEVE ELKINGTON	$360,000	68-67-68-64	267
COLIN MONTGOMERIE	$216,000	68-67-67-65	267
ERNIE ELS	$116,000	66-65-66-72	269
JEFF MAGGERT	$116,000	66-69-65-69	269
BRAD FAXON	$80,000	70-67-71-63	271
MARK O'MEARA	$68,500	64-67-69-73	273
BOB ESTES	$68,500	69-68-68-68	273
CRAIG STADLER	$50,000	71-66-66-71	274

STEVE LOWERY	$50,000	69-68-68-69	274
JUSTIN LEONARD	$50,000	68-66-70-70	274
JAY HAAS	$50,000	69-71-64-70	274
JEFF SLUMAN	$50,000	69-67-68-70	274
PAYNE STEWART	$33,750	69-70-69-67	275
KIRK TRIPLETT	$33,750	71-69-68-67	275
JIM FURYK	$33,750	68-70-69-68	275
MIGUEL JIMENEZ	$33,750	69-69-67-70	275
CURTIS STRANGE	$26,000	72-68-68-68	276
MICHAEL CAMPBELL	$26,000	71-65-71-69	276
COSTANTINO ROCCA	$26,000	70-69-68-69	276
JESPER PARNEVIK	$21,000	69-69-70-69	277
GREG NORMAN	$21,000	66-69-70-72	277
DUFFY WALDORF	$21,000	69-69-67-72	277
WOODY AUSTIN	$15,500	70-70-70-68	278
BILLY MAYFAIR	$15,500	68-68-72-70	278
LEE JANZEN	$15,500	66-70-72-70	278
STEVE STRICKER	$15,500	75-64-69-70	278
BRUCE LIETZKE	$15,500	73-68-67-70	278
NOLAN HENKE	$15,500	68-73-67-70	278
PETER JACOBSEN	$15,500	69-67-71-71	278
SAM TORRANCE	$15,500	69-69-69-71	278
FRED COUPLES	$8,906	70-69-74-66	279
GIL MORGAN	$8,906	66-73-74-66	279
PAUL AZINGER	$8,906	70-70-72-67	279
NICK FALDO	$8,906	69-73-70-67	279
D.A. WEIBRING	$8,906	74-68-69-68	279
MARK BROOKS	$8,906	67-74-69-69	279
JOSE MARIA OLAZABAL	$8,906	72-66-70-71	279
JOE OZAKI	$8,906	71-70-65-73	279
PHILLIP WALTON	$6,750	71-70-71-68	280
NICK PRICE	$6,750	71-71-70-68	280
LENNIE CLEMENTS	$6,750	67-71-72-70	280
FRED FUNK	$6,750	70-72-68-70	280
SANDY LYLE	$6,750	67-73-69-71	280
BEN CRENSHAW	$5,600	68-73-73-67	281
PETER SENIOR	$5,600	68-71-74-68	281
CHIP BECK	$5,600	66-74-73-68	281
JIM GALLAGHER JR.	$5,600	64-72-73-72	281
GENE SAUERS	$5,600	69-71-68-73	281
JOHN ADAMS	$4,620	65-76-71-70	282
KENNY PERRY	$4,620	75-67-70-70	282
ROBIN FREEMAN	$4,620	71-69-70-72	282
JUMBO OZAKI	$4,620	73-68-69-72	282
BRIAN CLAAR	$4,620	68-67-73-74	282
HALE IRWIN	$4,050	71-68-71-73	283
MICHAEL BRADLEY	$4,050	63-73-73-74	283
TOM KITE	$4,050	70-69-70-74	283
SCOTT SIMPSON	$4,050	71-67-71-74	283
ED DOUGHERTY	$3,630	68-72-74-70	284
TOM WATSON	$3,630	71-71-72-70	284
LOREN ROBERTS	$3,630	74-68-71-71	284
STEVE PATE	$3,630	71-71-71-71	284
PER-ULRIK JOHANSSON	$3,630	72-69-71-72	284
BARRY LANE	$3,400	74-68-75-68	285
LANNY WADKINS	$3,400	73-69-71-72	285
MIKE SULLIVAN	$3,400	72-69-71-73	285
DILLARD PRUITT	$3,300	73-69-72-72	286
DAVID FROST	$3,263	69-73-72-73	287
JACK NICKLAUS	$3,263	69-71-71-76	287
FUZZY ZOELLER	$3,225	72-69-75-72	288
BRIAN KAMM	$3,200	71-66-74-78	289
CURT BYRUM	$3,163	71-71-78-71	291
WAYNE DEFRANCESCO	$3,163	69-73-74-75	291

LPGA TOUR

NABISCO DINAH SHORE
Mission Hills C.C.,
Rancho Mirage, California
March 23-26, 1995

NANCI BOWEN	**$127,500**	**69-75-71-70**	**285**
SUSIE REDMAN	$79,129	75-70-70-71	286
BRANDIE BURTON	$42,237	76-71-71-69	287
SHERRI TURNER	$42,237	72-74-71-70	287
LAURA DAVIES	$42,237	75-69-70-73	287
NANCY LOPEZ	$42,237	74-71-68-74	287
C. WALKER	$23,738	74-73-69-72	288
T. GREEN	$23,738	71-70-70-77	288
D. COE-JONES	$20,103	71-75-71-72	289
C. PIERCE	$17,964	77-71-73-69	290
BETSY KING	$14,200	77-75-71-68	291
D. MOCHRIE	$14,200	78-73-70-70	291
BARB MUCHA	$14,200	74-74-72-71	291
S. PALMER	$14,200	72-73-74-72	291
D. MASSEY	$14,200	71-75-72-73	291
ALICIA DIBOS	$10,056	77-74-75-66	292
S. STEINHAUER	$10,056	78-74-72-68	292
A. NICHOLAS	$10,056	75-74-73-70	292
PAT BRADLEY	$10,056	74-75-71-72	292
JULI INKSTER	$10,056	76-70-73-73	292

JO MYERS	$10,056	77-68-73-74	292
M. ESTILL	$10,056	72-72-74-74	292
MEG MALLON	$10,056	74-72-71-75	292
A. SORENSTAM	$8,040	76-74-74-69	293
M.SPENCER-DEVIIN	$8,040	69-79-74-71	293
KRISTI ALBERS	$8,040	76-72-72-73	293
JANE GEDDES	$7,014	76-76-74-68	294
KRIS TSCHETTER	$7,014	75-74-73-72	294
LORI WEST	$7,014	74-75-71-74	294
KELLY ROBBI	$7,014	76-67-76-75	294
BARB THOMAS	$7,014	79-69-70-76	294
DALE EGGELING	$5,859	72-78-75-70	295
CINDY RARICK	$5,859	74-73-78-70	295
L. NEUMANN	$5,859	75-74-74-72	295
JULIE LARSEN	$5,859	74-76-72-73	295
KAREN NOBLE	$5,859	71-77-71-76	295
CAROLINE KEGGI	$4,690	78-71-76-71	296
VAL SKINNER	$4,690	80-72-72-72	296
H. KOBAYASHI	$4,690	80-73-70-73	296
A. OKAMOTO	$4,690	75-75-73-73	296
N. RAMSBOTTOM	$4,690	72-74-74-76	296
LAURI MERTEN	$4,690	74-69-73-80	296
PATTY SHEEHAN	$3,763	78-73-76-70	297
AMY BENZ	$3,763	75-76-75-71	297
LISA WALTERS	$3,763	75-74-75-73	297
M.B. ZMMERMAN	$3,763	74-73-77-73	297
D. AMMACCAPANE	$3,002	79-71-77-7l	298
CINDY SCHREYER	$3,002	75-72-79-72	298
ALICE RITZMAN	$3,002	76-77-71-74	298
BETH DANIEL	$3,002	77-74-73-74	298
P. JORDA	$3,002	73-74-72-79	298
ROSIE JONES	$2,309	80-71-76-72	299
F. DESCAMPE	$2,309	77-72-78-72	299
JANE CRATER	$2,309	75-76-74-74	299
J.BRILES-HINTON	$2,309	74-74-77-74	299
M. MCNAMARA	$2,309	79-71-70-79	299
JEAN ZEDLITZ	$1,646	71-80-77-72	300
M. MCGANN	$1,646	77-76-74-73	300
LKUYO SHIOTANI	$1,646	76-77-74-73	300
TRISH JOHNSON	$1,646	74-75-78-73	300
CHRIS JOHNSON	$1,646	72-79-71-78	300
PENNY HAMMEL	$1,646	69-76-77-78	300
K. GUADAGNINO	$1,304	74-79-75-73	301
M. FIGUERAS-DOTTI	$1,304	74-78-75-74	301
LISA KIGGENS	$1,218	75-78-73-76	302
C.JOHNSTON-FORBES	$1,218	73-79-74-76	302
PEARL SINN	$1,155	74-73-78-78	303
A. FINNEY	$1,025	77-76-76-75	304
TINA BARRETT	$1,025	73-80-76-75	304
K.PETERSON-PARKER	$1,025	80-71-78-75	304
S. FAMIG	$1,025	77-72-80-75	304
CAROLYN HILL	$1,025	76-75-77-76	304
JAN STEPHENSON	$898	76-77-80-72	305
MARTHA NAUSE	$898	79-74-75-77	305
DONNA ANDREWS	$898	76-72-79-78	305
M. BERTEOTTI	$859	72-80-78-77	307
JODY ANSCHUTZ	$841	78-75-78-80	311

MCDONALD'S LPGA CHAMPIONSHIP

DuPont C.C., Wilmington, Delaware
May 11-14, 1995

KELLY ROBBINS	**$180,000**	**66-68-72-68**	**274**
LAURA DAVIES	$111,711	68-68-69-70	275
JULIE LARSEN	$65,416	71-68-70-71	280
MARIANNE MORRIS	$65,416	67-71-70-72	280
PATTY SHEEHAN	$65,416	67-68-72-73	280
BARB THOMAS	$38,947	70-66-73-72	281
DOTTIE MOCHRIE	$38,947	67-70-71-73	281
PAT BRADLEY	$29,890	71-70-70-71	282
TAMMIE GREEN	$29,890	69-72-70-71	282
ANNIKA SORENSTAM	$25,362	71-71-72-69	283
KRISTI ALBERS	$20,681	71-71-72-70	284
DALE EGGELING	$20,681	72-72-68-72	284
JOAN PITCOCK	$20,681	75-66-71-72	284
BETSY KING	$20,681	69-71-72-72	284
LISA KIGGENS	$16,504	70-70-75-70	285
MEG MALLON	$16,504	70-72-71-72	285
BARB MUCHA	$16,504	71-69-71-74	285
BETH DANIEL	$13,080	71-73-72-70	286
NANCY SCRANTON	$13,080	71-75-69-71	286
SUSIE REDMAN	$13,080	73-71-71-71	286
LORI GARBACZ	$13,080	71-71-72-72	286
KRIS TSCHETTER	$13,080	73-69-71-73	286
NANCY LOPEZ	$13,080	73-71-68-74	286
COLLEEN WALKER	$13,080	70-70-72-74	286
ALLISON FINNEY	$13,080	71-68-70-77	286
SHERRI TURNER	$10,626	73-74-70-70	287
KATHY GUADAGNINO	$10,626	72-73-68-74	287
NANCI BOWEN	$10,626	71-71-71-74	287
KIM WILLIAMS	$9,374	72-71-75-70	288
MICHELE REDMAN	$9,374	75-68-72-73	288

U.S. WOMEN'S OPEN
The Broadmoor, Colorado Springs, Colorado
July 13-16, 1995

ANNIKA SORENSTAM	$175,000	67-71-72-68	278
MEG MALLON	$103,500	70-69-66-74	279
PAT BRADLEY	$56,238	67-71-72-67	280
BETSY KING	$56,238	72-69-72-70	280
LETA LINDLEY	$35,285	70-68-74-69	281
ROSIE JONES	$35,285	69-70-70-72	281
TAMMIE GREEN	$28,009	68-70-75-69	282
DAWN COE-JONES	$28,009	68-70-74-70	282
JULIE LARSEN	$28,009	68-71-68-75	282
MARIANNE MORRIS	$22,190	73-73-70-67	283
PATTY SHEEHAN	$22,190	70-73-71-69	283
VAL SKINNER	$22,190	68-72-72-71	283
DOTTIE MOCHRIE	$18,007	73-70-69-72	284
KRIS TSCHETTER	$18,007	68-74-69-73	284
KELLY ROBBINS	$18,007	74-68-68-74	284
CHRIS JOHNSON	$14,454	71-70-74-70	285
JILL BRILES-HINTON	$14,454	66-72-74-73	285
DALE EGGELING	$14,454	70-68-73-74	285
TANIA ABITBOL	$14,454	67-72-72-74	285
MICHELE REDMAN	$12,449	70-75-71-70	286
LISELOTTE NEUMANN	$11,154	70-71-75-71	287
AYAKO AKAMOTO	$11,154	70-73-71-73	287
ALICE RITZMAN	$11,154	75-69-69-74	287
JOAN PITCOCK	$9,287	72-73-72-71	288
CAROLYN HILL	$9,287	74-73-70-71	288
LAURA DAVIES	$9,287	72-73-69-74	288
M.B. ZIMMERMAN	$9,287	72-72-68-76	288
NANCY LOPEZ	$6,841	72-73-74-70	289
BRANDIE BURTON	$6,841	72-73-74-70	289
AMY FRUHWIRTH	$6,841	75-72-72-70	289
COLLEEN WALKER	$6,841	69-73-75-72	289
MAYUMI HIRASE	$6,841	70-74-73-72	289
PAMELA WRIGHT	$6,841	72-73-71-73	289
JEAN BARTHOLOMEW	$6,841	67-71-77-74	289
DEBBI KOYAMI	$6,841	74-68-73-74	289
GAIL GRAHAM	$6,841	71-72-71-75	289
SUZANNE STRUDWICK	$5,218	75-70-73-72	290
JULI INKSTER	$5,218	72-73-72-73	290
STACY HOLLINS	$5,218	69-72-75-74	290
HELEN ALFREDSSON	$4,353	69-75-78-69	291
MICHELLE MCGANN	$4,353	73-72-74-72	291
JUDY DICKINSON	$4,353	75-70-64-72	291
CARIN HJALMARSSON	$4,353	70-71-77-73	291
JANE GEDDES	$9,374	71-71-71-75	288
MICHELLE ESTILL	$9,374	72-73-67-76	288
PAT HURST	$7,970	74-72-74-69	289
K. PETERSON-PARKER	$7,970	74-73-71-71	289
VICKI FERGON	$7,970	73-71-74-71	289
ELLIE GIBSON	$7,970	73-69-74-73	289
ROSIE JONES	$7,970	72-71-68-78	289
JOANNE CARNER	$5,957	74-73-73-70	290
SALLY LITTLE	$5,957	73-73-71-73	290
JENNY LIDBACK	$5,957	75-70-71-74	290
RENEE HEIKEN	$5,957	73-71-72-74	290
LISELOTTE NEUMANN	$5,957	70-71-75-74	290
HELEN ALFREDSSON	$5,957	72-74-69-75	290
CHRIS JOHNSON	$5,957	72-69-73-76	290
BECKY IVERSON	$5,957	67-70-77-76	290
TRISH JOHNSON	$5,957	71-71-71-77	290
DAWN COE-JONES	$3,939	73-74-74-70	291
ALISON NICHOLAS	$3,939	76-71-73-71	291
LISA WALTERS	$3,939	72-74-74-71	291
TRACY KERDYK	$3,939	73-70-77-71	291
JULI INKSTER	$3,939	71-74-73-73	291
MITZI EDGE	$3,939	72-72-72-75	291
KAREN NOBLE	$3,939	74-68-72-77	291
VAL SKINNER	$3,939	73-69-69-80	291
ALICE RITZMAN	$2,636	68-75-76-73	292
MISSIE BERTEOTTI	$2,636	72-69-78-73	292
JUDY DICKINSON	$2,636	72-73-73-74	292
CAROLYN HILL	$2,636	71-74-72-75	292
JANE CRAFTER	$2,636	76-69-71-76	292
M. FIGUERAS-DOTTI	$2,636	71-73-69-79	292
CAROLINE PIERCE	$1,908	73-74-74-72	293
MISSIE MCGEORGE	$1,908	73-71-76-73	293
C. JOHNSTON-FORBES	$1,908	72-75-72-74	293
HELEN DOBSON	$1,908	77-70-71-75	293
M.B. ZIMMERMAN	$1,908	74-70-74-75	293
DEBBIE MASSEY	$1,569	74-73-73-74	294
VICKI GOETZE	$1,569	72-74-74-74	294
BARB SCHERBAK	$1,569	72-73-74-75	294
CATHY MOCKETT	$1,569	73-72-72-77	294
AMY BENZ	$1,569	72-75-69-78	294
CINDY RARICK	$1,388	75-71-75-74	295
EMILEE KLEIN	$1,313	77-70-75-74	296
TRACY HANSON	$1,313	69-78-74-75	296
JILL BRILES-HINTON	$1,268	72-73-74-78	297
EVA DAHLLOF	$1,238	73-72-75-78	298
SUZANNE STRUDWICK	$1,213	74-73-76-76	299
LORI TATUM	$1,188	72-74-78-76	300

ALICIA DIBOS	$4,353	73-72-73-73	291	L. RINKER-GRAHAM	$27,928	71-71-70-74	286
JANE GEDDES	$4,353	71-75-68-77	291	HELEN ALFREDSSON	$21,314	76-70-70-71	287
K. PETERSON-PARKER	$3,788	73-71-73-75	292	D. AMMACCAPANE	$21,314	76-71-68-72	287
LAUREL KEAN	$3,452	69-75-76-73	293	HOLLIS STACEY	$21,314	73-73-69-72	287
MISSIE MCGEORGE	$3,452	75-71-73-74	293	DOTTIE MOCHRIE	$16,136	74-73-72-69	288
PAT HURST	$3,452	69-71-78-75	293	MEG MALLON	$16,136	73-72-73-70	288
ALISON NICHOLAS	$3,452	72-71-72-78	293	VAL SKINNER	$16,136	74-72-71-71	288
SHERRI TURNER	$3,091	74-73-75-72	294	KRIS TSCHETTER	$16,136	75-70-71-72	288
JAN STEPHENSON	$3,091	73-75-73-73	294	ROSIE JONES	$13,369	79-70-73-67	289
SARAH INGRAM	amateur	71-70-79-74	294	JOAN PITCOCK	$13,369	76-70-69-74	289
ERIKA HAYASHIDA	$2,829	70-72-78-75	295	EMILEE KLEIN	$11,859	79-71-69-71	290
KATHRYN MARSHALL	$2,829	76-71-73-75	295	CINDY SCHREYER	$11,859	73-74-72-71	290
VICKI GOETZE	$2,829	77-69-73-76	295	HIROMI KOBAYASHI	$11,859	76-70-72-72	290
LAURI RINKER-GRAHAM	$2,508	70-75-76-75	296	DANA DORMANN	$11,859	74-72-72-72	290
WENDY WARD	amateur	72-73-76-75	296	CINDY RARICK	$10,180	73-72-75-71	291
KRISTI ALBERS	$2,508	75-73-73-75	296	TRACY KERDYK	$10,180	76-72-71-72	291
MARTHA NAUSE	$2,508	72-74-74-76	296	PATTY JORDAN	$10,180	72-72-74-73	291
KELLEE BOOTH	amateur	74-73-72-77	296	MICHELE REDMAN	$8,442	75-75-75-67	292
KAREN NOBLE	$2,508	70-75-73-78	296	AMY FRUHWIRTH	$8,442	77-72-75-68	292
GRACE PARK	amateur	69-78-78-72	297	KATHRYN MARSHALL	$8,442	74-75-73-70	292
AMY ALCOTT	$2,109	72-74-77-74	297	ELAINE CROSBY	$8,442	73-72-76-71	292
AMY BENZ	$2,109	71-75-76-75	297	JULIE LARSEN	$8,442	76-72-72-72	292
ELAINE CROSBY	$2,109	74-73-75-75	297	PAT HURST	$8,442	73-72-74-73	292
MAGGIE WILL	$2,109	72-74-75-76	297	BARB SCHERBAK	$8,442	73-74-70-75	292
LENORE RITTENHOUS	$2,109	72-75-72-78	297	PATTY SHEEHAN	$8,442	66-74-74-75	292
MICHELLE ESTILL	$2,109	74-71-73-79	297	ALLISON FINNEY	$6,801	76-74-72-71	293
SHELLY RULE	$1,758	75-73-77-73	298	GAIL GRAHAM	$6,801	74-73-73-73	293
STEPHANIE MAYNORE	$1,758	74-73-74-77	298	AMY ALCOTT	$6,801	75-73-71-74	293
CAROLINE KEGGI	$1,758	71-76-73-78	298	CAROLINE PIERCE	$6,801	72-76-70-75	293
A. ACKER-MACOSKO	$1,563	73-70-79-77	299	MARY ANN LAPOINTE	amateur	72-78-72-71	293
BARB MUCHA	$1,563	73-74-75-77	299	M.B. ZIMMERMAN	$5,329	78-72-73-71	294
MARGARET PLATT	$1,446	73-75-78-77	303	JILL BRILES-HINTON	$5,329	74-75-72-73	294
ALISON MUNT	$1,368	71-76-80-79	306	MELISSA MCNAMARA	$5,329	72-75-73-74	294
				ROBIN WALTON	$5,329	74-72-74-74	294
				JAN STEPHENSON	$5,329	75-72-72-75	294
				ALICIA DIBOS	$5,329	75-69-75-75	294
				PAM WRIGHT	$5,329	75-72-70-77	294
				MITZI EDGE	$5,329	75-70-72-77	294
				MICHELLE BELL	$3,763	77-71-77-70	295
				LORI TATUM	$3,763	71-78-73-73	295
				ANNIKA SORENSTAM	$3,763	76-72-74-73	295
				DALE EGGELING	$3,763	73-74-75-73	295
				BETH DANIEL	$3,763	72-75-75-73	295
				AMY BENZ	$3,763	71-72-78-74	295
				DONNA ANDREWS	$3,763	74-76-70-75	295
				VICKI GOETZE	$2,523	78-72-74-72	296
				MARGARET PLATT	$2,523	75-75-73-73	296

Du MAURIER LTD. CLASSIC
Beaconsfield G.C., Montreal, Quebec, Canada
August 24-27, 1995

JENNY LIDBACK	**$150,000**	**71-69-68-72**	**280**
LISELOTTE NEUMAN	$93,093	71-66-72-72	281
JULI INKSTER	$67,933	72-71-70-70	283
TAMMIE GREEN	$52,837	75-71-68-70	284
BETSY KING	$38,998	76-70-67-72	285
JANE GEDDES	$38,998	71-73-69-72	285
MICHELLE ESTILL	$27,928	73-77-69-67	286

TRACY HANSON	$2,523	75-73-75-73	296
LETA LINDLEY	$2,523	74-76-72-74	296
VICKI FERGON	$2,523	78-71-73-74	296
BRANDIE BURTON	$2,523	76-69-77-74	296
RENEE HEIKEN	$2,523	77-73-71-75	296
PEARL SINN	$2,523	72-78-71-75	296
JODY ANSCHUTZ	$1,668	74-76-77-70	297
MISSIE BERTEOTTI	$1,668	77-73-75-72	297
BARB MUCHA	$1,668	77-72-76-72	297
STEPHANIE FARWIG	$1,668	72-76-77-72	297
LIA BIEHL	$1,668	79-70-74-74	297
M. FIGUERAS-DOTTI	$1,668	72-76-71-78	297
CAROLYN HILL	$1,341	77-73-76-72	298
KRISTI COATS	$1,341	75-71-80-72	298
LORIE KANE	$1,341	78-71-75-74	298
JANE CRAFTER	$1,341	71-72-79-76	298
ELLIE GIBSON	$1,341	77-71-73-77	298
TINA BARRETT	$1,190	76-74-76-74	300
L. MCFADDEN-SHEPHARD	$1,127	74-76-75-76	301
NANCY WHITE-BROPHY	$1,127	75-69-79-78	301

Senior PGA TOUR

THE TRADITION
G.C. at Desert Mountain,
Scottsdale, Arizona
March 30-April 2, 1995

*JACK NICKLAUS	$150,000	69-71-69-67	276
ISAO AOKI	$88,000	71-66-72-67	276
JIM FERREE	$72,000	67-74-69-67	277
JIM COLBERT	$60,000	76-64-70-70	280
JIMMY POWELL	$48,000	75-68-69-69	281
RAY FLOYD	$38,000	70-72-71-69	282
JAY SIGEL	$38,000	70-69-71-72	282
TOM WEISKOPF	$27,500	75-74-67-67	283
DALE DOUGLASS	$27,500	74-74-67-68	283
BRUCE SUMMERHAYS	$27,500	71-77-66-69	283
BOB MURPHY	$27,500	73-71-69-70	283
JIM DENT	$19,200	75-73-68-68	284
DAVE STOCKTON	$19,200	73-68-74-69	284
BOB CHARLES	$19,200	69-76-70-69	284
ROCKY THOMPSON	$19,200	73-71-69-71	284
LARRY GILBERT	$19,200	71-70-71-72	284
GEORGE ARCHER	$15,033	70-72-72-71	285
GRAHAM MARSH	$15,033	72-69-72-72	285
GARY PLAYER	$15,033	69-70-72-74	285
J.C. SNEAD	$11,740	75-70-71-70	286
TOMMY AARON	$11,740	73-69-73-71	286
KERMIT ZARLEY	$11,740	71-74-70-71	286
GARY GROH	$11,740	72-73-70-71	286
LEE TREVINO	$11,740	70-68-74-74	286
TOM SHAW	$9,533	82-70-69-66	287
ARNOLD PALMER	$9,533	71-74-71-71	287
JACK KIEFER	$9,533	74-74-69-70	287
LARRY ZIEGLER	$8,100	72-74-71-71	288
DON BIES	$8,100	73-72-70-73	288
DAVE EICHELBERGER	$8,100	73-72-70-73	288
CALVIN PEETE	$8,100	69-71-73-75	288
BOBBY NICHOLS	$7,050	74-75-71-69	289
HAROLD HENNING	$7,050	75-73-69-72	289
DEWITT WEAVER	$6,600	72-77-70-71	290
BOBBY MITCHELL	$6,300	74-73-72-72	291
JOHN PAUL CAIN	$5,625	73-75-74-70	292
CHARLES COODY	$5,625	72-70-76-74	292
JERRY MCGEE	$5,625	69-76-73-74	292
GIBBY GILBERT	$5,625	71-70-73-76	292
AL GEIBERGER	$5,100	74-74-72-73	293
BOB E. SMITH	$4,900	77-75-72-70	294
KEN STILL	$4,700	75-74-70-76	295
SIMON HOBDAY	$4,400	73-79-77-67	296
LARRY LAORETTI	$4,400	77-76-72-71	296
BUD ALLIN	$3,700	71-75-82-69	297
BOB DICKSON	$3,700	76-76-73-72	297
WALTER ZEMBRISKI	$3,700	78-77-71-71	297
TONY JACKLIN	$3,700	77-74-72-74	297
TOM WARGO	$3,700	76-73-72-76	297
HARRY TOSCANO	$2,800	72-75-81-70	298
WALT MORGAN	$2,800	75-80-70-73	298
ROBERT GAONA	$2,800	74-75-74-75	298
DAVE HILL	$2,800	76-76-71-75	298
JIM ALBUS	$2,350	72-77-77-73	299
DICK GOETZE	$2,350	78-74-75-72	299
LEE ELDER	$2,150	76-77-73-74	300
BRUCE CRAMPTON	$2,150	71-78-73-78	300
GAY BREWER	$2,000	77-74-79-71	301
TERRY DILL	$1,900	75-80-73-74	302
DICK HENDRICKSON	$1,750	78-75-77-73	303
ORVILLE MOODY	$1,750	79-71-74-79	303
ED SNEED	$1,450	80-78-74-73	305
BOB ZIMMERMAN	$1,450	76-81-73-75	305
AL KELLEY	$1,450	77-77-75-76	305
HOMERO BLANCAS	$1,450	77-75-73-80	305

BUTCH BAIRD	$1,200	80-78-78-72	308
BILLY CASPER	$1,050	82-77-73-77	309
BILLY MAXWELL	$1,050	79-78-76-76	309
CHUCK MONTALBANO	$940	79-77-80-74	310
ROBERT LANDERS	$880	79-76-75-82	312
GENE LITTLER	$790	82-75-79-79	315
BEN SMITH	$790	74-80-79-82	315
BRUCE DEVLIN	$700	78-77-82-79	316

PGA SENIORS CHAMPIONSHIP

PGA National G.C.,
Palm Beach Gardens, Florida
April 13-16, 1995

RAY FLOYD	**$180,000**	**70-70-67-70**	**277**
JOHN PAUL CAIN	$75,000	72-71-70-69	282
LARRY GILBERT	$75,000	71-70-72-69	282
LEE TREVINO	$75,000	72-70-69-71	282
GRAHAM MARSH	$40,000	71-71-70-71	283
ISAO AOKI	$40,000	70-69-73-71	283
BOB CHARLES	$40,000	70-75-68-70	283
JACK NICKLAUS	$30,000	76-66-68-74	284
JIM COLBERT	$25,000	69-69-71-76	285
BOB MURPHY	$17,833	71-73-70-72	286
GEORGE ARCHER	$17,833	73-71-68-74	286
JIM ALBUS	$17,833	69-73-69-75	286
GIBBY GILBERT	$15,500	74-73-68-72	287
BOB DICKSON	$14,750	74-73-71-70	288
ED SNEED	$14,750	73-73-69-73	288
DALE DOUGLASS	$13,000	77-70-71-71	289
NOEL RATCLIFFE	$13,000	76-67-74-72	289
J.C. SNEAD	$13,000	71-70-76-72	289
TERRY DILL	$13,000	72-72-71-74	289
DEWITT WEAVER	$13,000	68-73-72-76	289
KERMIT ZARLEY	$10,500	74-73-72-71	290
SEIICHI KANAI	$10,500	73-75-71-71	290
BILL KENNEDY	$10,500	72-70-76-72	290
HARRY TOSCANO	$10,500	68-76-73-73	290
LARRY ZIEGLER	$10,500	73-72-70-75	290
BRUCE SUMMERHAYS	$8,250	71-77-71-72	291
ROCKY THOMPSON	$8,250	74-69-77-71	291
CHI CHI RODRIGUEZ	$8,250	73-73-75-70	291
CALVIN PEETE	$8,250	68-76-70-77	291
JACK KIEFER	$5,281	73-73-75-71	292
LARRY LAORETTI	$5,281	69-76-76-71	292
ORVILLE MOODY	$5,281	71-78-72-71	292
TOMMY HORTON	$5,281	78-69-70-75	292
JAY SIGEL	$5,281	74-75-73-70	292
DICK HENDRICKSON	$5,281	70-73-74-75	292
TOM WARGO	$5,281	72-74-77-69	292
WALTER ZEMBRISKI	$5,281	70-78-76-68	292
DAVE EICHELBERGER	$3,500	74-75-72-72	293
HAROLD HENNING	$2,769	70-80-70-74	294
BUDDY ALLIN	$2,769	74-71-74-75	294
RANDY PETRI	$2,769	72-74-75-73	294
BOB ZIMMERMAN	$2,769	71-75-73-75	294
MALCOLM GREGSON	$2,769	73-75-73-73	294
GAY BREWER	$2,769	71-76-72-75	294
ROGER KENNEDY	$2,769	73-76-72-73	294
MARION HECK	$2,769	72-76-70-76	294
TOM SHAW	$2,300	70-76-74-75	295
RANDY GLOVER	$2,117	71-72-74-79	296
GARY GROH	$2,117	74-71-77-74	296
MIKE JOYCE	$2,117	76-72-76-72	296
RICHIE BASSETT	$1,950	71-74-75-77	297
DICK LOTZ	$1,950	72-73-77-75	297
SIMON HOBDAY	$1,950	76-74-72-75	297
BOB REITH	$1,850	72-75-78-73	298
ROBERT GAONA	$1,750	70-72-79-78	299
WALTER T. MORGAN	$1,750	71-76-76-76	299
BILLY KING	$1,750	72-77-75-75	299
GENE BOREK	$1,663	72-74-74-80	300
JIM DENT	$1,663	75-75-78-72	300
GARY PLAYER	$1,600	72-77-72-80	301
DWIGHT NEVIL	$1,600	73-77-75-76	301
BRUCE CRAMPTON	$1,600	74-74-80-73	301
LEE ELDER	$1,550	76-73-78-75	302
LARRY MANCOUR	$1,502	79-70-74-80	303
JOE HUBER	$1,502	73-73-79-78	303
ANTONIO GARRIDO	$1,502	76-74-78-75	303
BOB CARSON	$1,460	75-75-75-79	304
JIM PETRALIA	$1,440	70-80-79-76	305
MASARU AMANO	$1,420	73-75-80-78	306
HIROSHI ISHII	$1,400	70-77-80-82	309

U.S. SENIOR OPEN

Congressional C.C., Bethesda, Maryland
June 29-July 2, 1995

TOM WEISKOPF	**$175,000**	**69-69-69-68**	**275**
JACK NICKLAUS	$103,500	71-71-70-67	279

BOB MURPHY	$51,998	69-70-71-70	280		BUTCH BAIRD	$3,504	76-73-73-77	299
ISAO AOKI	$51,998	70-68-68-72	280		ARNOLD PALMER	$3,189	72-74-76-78	300
HALE IRWIN	$32,625	72-68-71-71	282		DALE DOUGLASS	$3,189	77-70-73-80	300
J.C. SNEAD	$32,625	68-73-70-71	282		JIM COLBERT	$3,017	73-74-78-76	301
LEE TREVINO	$28,073	73-68-74-68	283		BILL MILLER	$2,909	73-75-75-79	302
GRAHAM MARSH	$24,811	69-70-74-71	284		MIKE BALLO	$2,807	70-79-75-79	303
RAYMOND FLOYD	$24,811	70-72-69-73	284		DENNY LYONS	$2,708	76-72-79-77	304
DEWITT WEAVER	$22,043	73-71-70-71	285		RON SKILES	$2,484	72-74-83-76	305
BOB CHARLES	$19,094	74-70-71-71	286		STEVE SPRAY	$2,484	74-76-77-78	305
BOB BETLEY	$19,094	76-67-71-72	286		BOB HAUER	$2,484	72-75-78-80	305
BRIAN BARNES	$19,094	69-72-71-74	286		BOB MENNE	$2,484	70-74-79-82	305
KERMIT ZARLEY	$15,596	74-69-74-71	288		JACK RULE	$2,241	74-72-82-78	306
ROCKY THOMPSON	$15,596	72-73-69-74	288		MARION HECK	$2,241	76-73-78-79	306
LARRY LAORETTI	$15,596	69-73-71-75	288		TOM SHAW	$2,131	76-74-76-83	309
MIKE JOYCE	$13,331	71-74-74-70	289					
JOHN MORGAN	$13,331	74-68-76-71	289					

FORD SENIOR PLAYERS CHAMPIONSHIP

TPC of Michigan,
Dearborn, Michigan
July 13-16, 1995

GARY PLAYER	$11,851	73-71-75-71	290					
CALVIN PEETE	$11,851	73-71-72-74	290					
HAROLD HENNING	$9,798	76-73-71-71	291					
LARRY RINGER	$9,798	68-80-69-74	291					
MIKE MCCULLOUGH	$9,798	73-76-68-74	291					
JAY SIGEL	$9,798	70-73-73-75	291					
DAVE STOCKTON	$9,798	69-70-74-78	291		*J.C. SNEAD	$225,000	69-68-66-69	272
DON BIES	$8,355	71-72-75-74	292		JACK NICKLAUS	$132,000	71-68-66-67	272
BOB LEAVER	$7,758	73-69-77-74	293		JIM COLBERT	$90,000	70-63-75-68	276
TOM WARGO	$7,758	72-75-71-75	293		JERRY MCGEE	$90,000	68-73-67-68	276
BABE HISKEY	$6,439	72-77-77-68	294		BEN SMITH	$90,000	73-67-67-69	276
CHI CHI RODRIGUEZ	$6,439	73-77-71-73	294		ISAO AOKI	$60,000	71-68-68-70	277
JIM ALBUS	$6,439	73-72-74-75	294		DON BIES	$48,000	74-71-68-65	278
BRUCE SUMMERHAYS	$6,439	72-72-74-76	294		BOB MURPHY	$48,000	71-68-69-70	278
WALTER ZEMBRISKI	$6,439	74-71-73-76	294		DAVE STOCKTON	$48,000	69-69-66-74	278
TOMMY AARON	$6,439	70-68-79-77	294		HALE IRWIN	$34,500	74-69-72-64	279
DICK GOETZ	$5,253	75-71-76-73	295		TOM WEISKOPF	$34,500	70-71-69-69	279
SIMON HOBDAY	$5,253	72-72-75-76	295		AL GEIBERGER	$34,500	71-69-68-71	279
BOB WYNN	$5,253	71-73-73-78	295		RAY FLOYD	$34,500	69-70-66-74	279
JOHN PAUL CAIN	$4,821	76-73-71-76	296		GRAHAM MARSH	$26,250	72-70-70-68	280
BOB HOUSEN	amateur	76-70-73-77	296		LARRY LAORETTI	$26,250	64-69-69-68	280
DAVE OJALA	$4,531	71-75-74-77	297		WALT MORGAN	$26,250	74-67-69-70	280
JIMMY POWELL	$4,531	73-74-72-78	297		KERMIT ZARLEY	$26,250	69-69-67-75	280
CHUCK MONTALBANO	$4,018	71-77-78-72	298		TONY JACKLIN	$19,890	73-71-70-67	281
BOB HULLENDER	$4,018	74-73-77-74	298		JIM DENT	$19,890	75-69-69-68	281
VINNIE GILES	$4,018	74-73-77-74	298		ROCKY THOMPSON	$19,890	70-69-72-70	281
BOB DICKSON	$4,018	73-75-74-76	298		JAY SIGEL	$19,890	69-72-68-72	281
RICHARD BASSETT	$4,018	72-72-77-77	298		MIKE HILL	$19,890	71-69-66-75	281
GIBBY GILBERT	$4,018	76-69-72-81	298		DEWITT WEAVER	$14,379	71-73-70-68	282
RICHIE KARL	$3,504	74-75-77-73	299		BOB CHARLES	$14,379	68-73-73-68	282
DAVE EICHELBERGER	$3,504	70-80-75-74	299		BOB ZIMMERMAN	$14,379	68-74-72-68	282

GIBBY GILBERT	$14,379	73-70-70-69	282	BRUCE CRAMPTON	$3,938	75-72-73-72	292
TOMMY AARON	$14,379	74-72-67-69	282	JOHN PAUL CAIN	$3,938	72-72-78-70	292
DICK RHYAN	$14,379	74-69-69-70	282	MIKE JOYCE	$3,938	81-71-71-69	292
SIMON HOBDAY	$14,379	71-72-69-70	282	DICK GOETZ	$3,300	75-75-74-69	293
TOM WARGO	$10,830	69-74-73-67	283	GAY BREWER	$3,300	76-71-74-72	293
GEORGE ARCHER	$10,830	73-67-75-68	283	TERRY DILL	$3,300	73-71-72-77	293
JIMMY POWELL	$10,830	70-72-71-70	283	CHARLES COODY	$2,925	72-75-70-77	294
LEE TREVINO	$10,830	70-67-74-72	283	WALT ZEMBRISKI	$2,925	70-73-74-77	294
ROBERT GAONA	$10,830	74-67-65-77	283	BOBBY NICHOLS	$2,625	73-72-78-72	295
JIM ALBUS	$9,225	75-69-69-71	284	MARION HECK	$2,625	73-72-75-75	295
JACK KIEFER	$9,225	71-74-68-71	284	ED SNEED	$2,325	77-78-70-71	296
LARRY GILBERT	$8,550	73-74-67-71	285	MILLER BARBER	$2,325	77-69-79-71	296
DAVE EICHELBERGER	$7,650	69-70-75-72	286	GARY GROH	$1,950	80-74-70-73	297
LARRY ZIEGLER	$7,650	71-73-69-73	286	DICK HENDRICKSON	$1,950	72-79-73-73	297
BRUCE SUMMERHAYS	$7,650	72-73-72-69	286	BRUCE DEVLIN	$1,950	76-71-77-73	297
BOB E. SMITH	$7,650	75-70-66-75	286	JOE JIMENEZ	$1,650	83-77-67-71	298
JIM FERREE	$7,650	71-69-71-75	286	DEANE BEMAN	$1,500	70-71-78-80	299
DON JANUARY	$6,450	75-68-71-74	288	HARRY TOSCANO	$1,365	76-72-80-73	301
HAROLD HENNING	$6,450	73-73-67-75	288	ORVILLE MOODY	$1,365	72-73-75-81	301
HOMERO BLANCAS	$6,450	71-72-69-76	288	BABE HISKEY	$1,230	78-75-72-77	302
DAVE HILL	$5,550	76-73-67-74	290	RIVES MCBEE	$1,140	77-81-70-75	303
ARNOLD PALMER	$5,550	73-72-72-73	290	BILL HALL	$1,050	78-79-75-72	304
BUTCH BAIRD	$5,550	75-67-70-78	290	BUD ALLIN	$990	75-78-75-78	306
LARRY MOWRY	$4,800	75-73-69-74	291	BOB BRUE	$930	79-78-72-80	309
BOB DICKSON	$4,800	73-73-74-71	291	TOM SHAW	$870	73-73-85-80	311
DICK LOTZ	$3,938	74-76-70-72	292				

1995 TOUR RESULTS

OVERVIEW: *Top finishers, scores, and prize money for all tournaments (through October 30), on the PGA TOUR, LPGA Tour, Senior PGA TOUR, Nike TOUR, European Tour, Women's European Tour, Asian Tour, Australian Tour, Japanese Tour and Senior Japanese Tour. Asterisks not otherwise noted denote playoff victories.*

PGA TOUR

MERCEDES CHAMPIONSHIP
La Costa C.C.,
Carlsbad, California
January 6-9, 1995

STEVE ELKINGTON	$180,000	69-71-71-67	278
BRUCE LIETZKE	$108,000	71-69-71-67	278
BILL GLASSON	$68,000	70-69-73-67	279
CRAIG STADLER	$48,000	71-65-73-71	280
TOM LEHMAN	$35,250	75-68-72-66	281
RICK FEHR	$35,250	71-74-70-66	281
BEN CRENSHAW	$35,250	71-67-75-68	281
FRED COUPLES	$35,250	73-68-68-72	281
LEE JANZEN	$28,750	72-63-76-71	282
JOHN HUSTON	$28,750	67-66-72-77	282

UNITED AIRLINES HAWAIIAN OPEN
Waialae C.C., Honolulu, Hawaii
January 13-16, 1995

JOHN MORSE	$216,000	71-65-65-68	269
DUFFY WALDORF	$105,600	68-65-71-68	272
TOM LEHMAN	$105,600	68-70-67-67	272
PAUL AZINGER	$49,600	72-67-69-66	274
BILL GLASSON	$49,600	70-70-68-66	274
DAN POHL	$49,600	69-67-69-69	274
JOHN HUSTON	$38,700	72-68-69-66	275
MARK BROOKS	$38,700	68-69-68-70	275
CHIP BECK	$34,800	71-66-66-73	276
DAVID ISHII	$31,200	71-69-68-69	277
GRANT WAITE	$31,200	71-69-66-71	277

NORTHERN TELECOM OPEN
TPC at Starpass and Tucson National,
Tucson, Arizona
January 13-16, 1995

PHIL MICKELSON	$225,000	65-66-70-68	269
SCOTT SIMPSON	$110,000	69-65-68-68	270
JIM GALLAGHER, JR.	$110,000	68-64-69-69	270
BRETT OGLE	$60,000	68-65-68-70	271
JIM FURYK	$50,000	69-69-67-67	272
WOODY AUSTIN	$37,813	68-69-70-67	274
JOE OZAKI	$37,813	68-67-70-69	274
BOB TWAY	$37,813	70-65-69-70	274
DAVID DUVAL	$37,813	67-70-67-70	274
TOM KITE	$37,813	71-66-67-70	274
DON POOLEY	$37,813	71-66-65-72	274
BRANDEL CHAMBLEE	$26,250	70-71-68-66	275
TOM PURTZER	$26,250	65-71-70-69	275
BART BRYANT	$26,250	70-69-67-69	275
HAL SUTTON	$21,875	70-71-69-66	276
NOLAN HENKE	$21,875	70-67-70-69	276
GARY MCCORD	$15,813	72-68-71-66	277
JOHN COOK	$15,813	74-67-70-66	277

PHOENIX OPEN
TPC of Scottsdale, Scottsdale, Arizona
January 27-30, 1995

*VIJAY SINGH	$234,000	70-67-66-66	269
BILLY MAYFAIR	$140,400	69-67-67-66	269
BEN CRENSHAW	$88,400	68-64-70-69	271
PAYNE STEWART	$53,733	71-68-67-66	272
BRUCE LIETZKE	$53,733	72-65-69-66	272
STEVE JONES	$53,733	68-69-68-67	272
JOE OZAKI	$37,830	68-71-67-67	273

Phoenix Open, continued

HALE IRWIN	$37,830	66-66-72-69	273
MARK CALCAVECCHIA	$37,830	72-67-66-68	273
STEVE LOWERY	$37,830	70-68-65-70	273
JOHN ADAMS	$37,830	71-66-66-70	273

AT&T NATIONAL PRO-AM
Pebble Beach G.L., Spyglass Hill G.C., and Poppy Hills G.C.,
Monterey, California
February 3-6, 1995

PETER JACOBSEN	$252,000	67-73-66-65	271
DAVID DUVAL	$151,200	72-67-67-67	273
KENNY PERRY	$81,200	68-68-67-72	275
DAVIS LOVE III	$81,200	65-71-71-68	275
PAYNE STEWART	$56,000	71-67-69-70	277
GUY BOROS	$46,900	69-66-71-72	278
BRAD FAXON	$46,900	70-64-72-72	278
JACK NICKLAUS	$46,900	71-70-67-70	278
EMLYN AUBREY	$36,400	70-69-68-72	279
JOHN ADAMS	$36,400	72-66-71-70	279
MARK O'MEARA	$36,400	73-68-70-68	279
NICK FALDO	$36,400	66-72-69-72	279

BUICK INVITATIONAL OF CALIFORNIA
Torrey Pines G.C., San Diego, California
February 9-12, 1995

PETER JACOBSEN	$216,000	68-65-68-68	269
MARK CALCAVECCHIA	$79,200	71-67-67-68	273
MIKE HULBERT	$79,200	70-65-70-68	273
KIRK TRIPLETT	$79,200	69-69-66-69	273
HAL SUTTON	$79,200	67-69-68-69	273
DILLARD PRUITT	$41,700	69-70-68-68	275
DAN POHL	$41,700	65-74-66-70	275
DAVID OGRIN	$33,600	66-69-74-67	276
NOLAN HENKE	$33,600	68-66-73-69	276
JOHN HUSTON	$33,600	69-71-67-69	276
BRANDEL CHAMBLEE	$33,600	66-66-74-70	276

BOB HOPE CHRYSLER CLASSIC
PGA West (Palmer), Bermuda Dunes C.C., Indian Wells C.C., Tamarisk C.C.,
Palm Desert, California
February 15-19, 1995

KENNY PERRY	$216,000	63-71-64-67-70	335
DAVID DUVAL	$143,000	68-69-65-67-69	336
DILLARD PRUITT	$62,400	65-70-69-68-65	337
TOMMY TOLLES	$62,400	66-69-68-64-70	337
CURTIS STRANGE	$62,400	64-73-67-63-70	337
ROBERT GAMEZ	$43,200	70-68-66-68-66	338
TOMMY ARMOUR III	$34,920	66-67-69-68-69	339
KELLY GIBSON	$34,920	65-71-67-67-69	339
DONNIE HAMMOND	$34,920	67-69-66-69-68	339
MARK BROOKS	$34,920	67-68-69-65-70	339
HARRY TAYLOR	$34,920	66-64-66-71-72	339

NISSAN OPEN
Riviera C.C., Pacific Palisades, California
February 23-26, 1995

COREY PAVIN	$216,000	67-66-68-67	268
JAY DON BLAKE	$105,600	69-67-66-69	271
KENNY PERRY	$105,600	70-62-68-71	271
SCOTT SIMPSON	$52,800	70-66-68-68	272
CRAIG STADLER	$52,800	67-68-67-70	272
JODIE MUDD	$43,200	66-71-69-67	273
JAY HAAS	$38,700	69-70-68-67	274
LANNY WADKINS	$38,700	67-72-66-69	274
BRIAN KAMM	$27,600	67-74-67-68	276
MIKE REID	$27,600	69-69-69-69	276
RONNIE BLACK	$27,600	72-68-66-70	276
MIKE HULBERT	$27,600	71-66-68-71	276
JIM FURYK	$27,600	67-74-65-70	276

DORAL-RYDER OPEN
Doral C.C. (Blue Course), Miami, Florida
March 2-5, 1995

NICK FALDO	$270,000	67-71-66-69	273
PETER JACOBSEN	$132,000	68-69-64-73	274
GREG NORMAN	$132,000	68-68-65-73	274
JUSTIN LEONARD	$62,000	68-68-71-68	275
STEVE ELKINGTON	$62,000	67-72-67-69	275
DAVIS LOVE III	$62,000	65-69-70-71	275
HALE IRWIN	$48,375	70-70-67-69	276
WOODY AUSTIN	$48,375	66-71-68-71	276
STEVE STRICKER	$43,500	70-68-71-68	277

Doral-Ryder Open continued

STEVE LOWERY	$39,000	65-72-73-68	278
MARK O'MEARA	$39,000	69-72-66-71	278

HONDA CLASSIC
Weston Hills C.C., Fort Lauderdale, Florida
March 9-12, 1995

MARK O'MEARA	$216,000	68-65-71-71	275
NICK FALDO	$129,600	67-71-69-69	276
IAN WOOSNAM	$81,600	68-72-69-68	277
ANDREW MAGEE	$57,600	69-67-76-67	279
BLAINE MCCALLISTER	$48,000	70-66-73-71	280
BILL BRITTON	$43,200	71-69-72-69	281
MIKE STANDLY	$40,200	71-66-75-70	282
MICHAEL BRADLEY	$32,400	73-69-73-68	283
SEVE BALLESTEROS	$32,400	70-68-76-69	283
SCOTT VERPLANK	$32,400	74-67-73-69	283
KEITH FERGUS	$32,400	69-72-71-71	283
BRIAN CLAAR	$32,400	69-70-72-72	283

NESTLE INVITATIONAL
Bay Hill Club, Orlando, Florida
March 17-20, 1995

LOREN ROBERTS	$216,000	68-65-68-71	272
BRAD FAXON	$129,000	69-70-64-71	274
PETER JACOBSEN	$81,600	70-68-68-69	275
STEVE STRICKER	$57,600	67-72-69-69	277
NICK FALDO	$39,300	71-73-66-68	278
JAY HAAS	$39,300	72-69-69-68	278
DUFFY WALDORF	$39,300	71-72-70-65	278
MARK MCCUMBER	$39,300	69-70-69-70	278
JESPER PARNEVIK	$39,300	67-72-67-72	278
BOB LOHR	$39,300	69-70-67-72	278

THE PLAYERS CHAMPIONSHIP
TPC at Sawgrass (Stadium),
Ponte Vedra, Florida
March 23-26, 1995

LEE JANZEN	$540,000	69-74-69-71	283
BERNHARD LANGER	$324,000	69-71-71-73	284
GENE SAUERS	$156,000	67-72-78-68	285
PAYNE STEWART	$156,000	69-73-71-72	285
COREY PAVIN	$156,000	66-73-72-74	285
BRAD BRYANT	$104,250	72-71-72-71	286
DAVIS LOVE III	$104,250	73-67-74-72	286
LARRY MIZE	$87,000	69-77-72-69	287
BILLY ANDRADE	$87,000	74-69-73-71	287
JOE OZAKI	$87,000	72-72-75-71	287

FREEPORT-MCMORAN CLASSIC
English Turn G. & C.C.,
New Orleans, Louisiana
March 30-April 2, 1995

*DAVIS LOVE III	$216,000	68-69-66-71	274
MIKE HEINEN	$129,600	66-71-71-66	274
DAVID DUVAL	$81,600	67-68-71-69	275
CRAIG PARRY	$57,600	71-69-66-70	276
JEFF MAGGERT	$43,800	72-66-70-69	277
DAVID PEOPLES	$43,800	70-69-66-72	277
MIKE STANDLY	$43,800	70-65-69-73	277
SCOTT SIMPSON	$36,000	68-70-71-69	278
BRAD BRYANT	$36,000	65-74-69-70	278
DANNY BRIGGS	$27,600	69-71-73-66	279
KIRK TRIPLETT	$27,600	66-73-71-69	279
BRIAN CLAAR	$27,600	68-70-71-70	279
MARK WIEBE	$27,600	70-68-68-73	279
LENNIE CLEMENTS	$27,600	69-68-70-72	279

THE MASTERS
Augusta National G.C., Augusta, Georgia
April 6-9, 1995

BEN CRENSHAW	$396,000	70-67-69-68	274
DAVIS LOVE III	$237,600	69-69-71-66	275
GREG NORMAN	$127,600	73-68-68-68	277
JAY HAAS	$127,600	71-64-72-70	277
DAVID FROST	$83,600	66-71-71-71	279
STEVE ELKINGTON	$83,600	73-67-67-72	279
PHIL MICKELSON	$70,950	66-71-70-73	280
SCOTT HOCH	$70,950	69-67-71-73	280
CURTIS STRANGE	$63,800	72-71-65-73	281
FRED COUPLES	$57,200	71-69-67-75	282
BRIAN HENNINGER	$57,200	70-68-68-76	282

For a complete summary of all players making the cut at The Masters, please refer to "1995 Major Championships"

MCI CLASSIC
Harbour Town G.L.,
Hilton Head Island, South Carolina
April 13-16, 1995

*BOB TWAY	$234,000	67-69-72-67	275
NOLAN HENKE	$114,300	66-72-70-67	275
DAVID FROST	$114,300	71-68-66-70	275
WOODY AUSTIN	$53,733	71-72-69-64	276
NICK FALDO	$53,733	74-64-70-68	276
MARK MCCUMBER	$53,733	70-71-64-71	276
NICK PRICE	$36,508	69-72-71-65	277
ERNIE ELS	$36,508	73-70-64-70	277
STEVE LOWERY	$36,508	68-73-66-70	277
GIL MORGAN	$36,508	73-71-62-71	277
TOM WATSON	$36,508	70-68-68-71	277
DAVID EDWARDS	$36,508	70-69-66-72	277

KMART GREATER GREENSBORO OPEN
Forest Oaks C.C., Greensboro, North Carolina
April 20-23, 1995

JIM GALLAGHER, JR.	$270,000	69-70-69-66	274
JEFF SLUMAN	$132,000	70-65-66-74	275
PETER JACOBSEN	$132,000	69-65-69-72	275
JOHN ADAMS	$72,000	70-66-70-70	276
MARK CALCAVECCHIA	$60,000	68-73-67-69	277
JESPER PARNEVIK	$54,000	70-68-68-72	278
GUY BOROS	$43,650	73-67-70-69	279
TED TRYBA	$43,650	69-70-69-71	279
STEVE STRICKER	$43,650	68-73-66-72	279
BRAD FAXON	$43,650	65-71-71-72	279
VIJAY SINGH	$43,650	65-72-69-73	279

SHELL HOUSTON OPEN
TPC at the Woodlands, The Woodlands, Texas
April 27-30, 1995

*PAYNE STEWART	$252,000	73-65-70-68	276
SCOTT HOCH	$151,200	68-64-69-75	276
CHARLIE RYMER	$95,200	69-69-68-71	277
PAUL STANKOWSKI	$61,600	71-68-71-68	278
TRAY TYNER	$61,600	70-69-68-71	278
BRETT OGLE	$48,650	68-69-71-71	279
BRIAN CLAAR	$48,650	73-68-67-71	279
VIJAY SINGH	$40,600	70-70-70-70	280
JOHN WILSON	$40,600	71-69-68-72	280
STEVE RINTOUL	$40,600	66-70-71-73	280

BELLSOUTH CLASSIC
Atlanta C.C., Marietta, Georgia
May 5-8, 1995

MARK CALCAVECCHIA	$234,000	67-69-69-66	271
JIM GALLAGHER	$140,400	65-70-68-70	273
STEPHEN KEPPLER	$88,400	67-69-67-71	274
CURTIS STRANGE	$53,733	70-71-69-65	275
SCOTT VERPLANK	$53,733	72-67-67-69	275
GUY BOROS	$53,733	71-67-67-70	275
SCOTT HOCH	$37,830	69-71-71-65	276
BILLY ANDRADE	$37,830	72-68-69-67	276
LENNIE CLEMENTS	$37,830	70-66-72-68	276
BRANDEL CHAMBLEE	$37,830	68-70-69-69	276
TOMMY TOLLES	$37,830	70-69-68-69	276

GTE BYRON NELSON CLASSIC
TPC at Los Colinas, Los Colinas, Texas
May 12-15, 1995

ERNIE ELS	$234,000	69-61-65-68	263
D.A. WEIBRING	$97,067	65-69-67-65	266
MIKE HEINEN	$97,067	67-66-67-66	266
ROBIN LEE FREEMAN	$97,067	65-65-68-68	266
JAY DON BLAKE	$45,663	64-69-69-66	268
SCOTT VERPLANK	$45,663	67-69-67-65	268
KENNY PERRY	$45,663	65-66-70-67	268
GIL MORGAN	$45,663	68-66-68-66	268
LOREN ROBERTS	$36,400	68-67-69-65	269
BOB TWAY	$36,400	68-66-69-66	269

MEMORIAL TOURNAMENT
Muirfield Village G.C., Dublin, Ohio
May 19-22, 1995

GREG NORMAN	$306,000	66-70-67-66	269
STEVE ELKINGTON	$126,933	69-68-69-67	273
MARK CALCAVECCHIA	$126,933	69-71-66-67	273
DAVID DUVAL	$126,933	70-71-64-68	273
JAY HAAS	$57,630	72-72-66-65	275
BEN CRENSHAW	$57,630	67-68-71-69	275

Memorial Tournament continued

TOM WATSON	$57,630	67-71-68-69	275
DAVID FROST	$57,630	68-72-65-70	275
ROBERT GAMEZ	$57,630	68-67-69-71	275
NICK PRICE	$45,900	71-71-69-65	276

SOUTHWESTERN BELL COLONIAL
Colonial C.C., Fort Worth, Texas
May 26-29, 1995

TOM LEHMAN	$252,000	67-68-68-68	271
CRAIG PARRY	$151,200	66-65-70-71	272
D.A. WEIBRING	$95,200	66-72-69-67	274
WOODY AUSTIN	$67,200	67-69-66-73	275
BRAD FAXON	$51,100	67-70-75-64	276
JUSTIN LEONARD	$51,100	68-72-68-68	276
MARK MCCUMBER	$51,100	67-73-68-68	276
JEFF MAGGERT	$39,200	66-68-74-69	277
ROCCO MEDIATE	$39,200	69-68-70-70	277
MARK CALCAVECCHIA	$39,200	70-67-68-72	277
BILLY MAYFAIR	$39,200	68-71-68-71	277

KEMPER OPEN
TPC at Avenel, Potomac, Maryland
June 8-11, 1995

*LEE JANZEN	$252,000	68-69-68-67	272
COREY PAVIN	$151,200	73-68-63-68	272
ROBIN LEE FREEMAN	$95,200	70-69-66-68	273
JUSTIN LEONARD	$52,780	71-67-70-67	275
VIJAY SINGH	$52,780	65-71-71-68	275
GREG NORMAN	$52,780	72-66-69-68	275
MARK O'MEARA	$52,780	66-70-69-70	275
DAVIS LOVE III	$52,780	68-63-71-73	275
KENNY PERRY	$35,000	72-68-69-67	276
NICK PRICE	$35,000	70-68-70-68	276
LARRY MIZE	$35,000	67-70-70-69	276
JOHN MAHAFFEY	$35,000	72-69-65-70	276
PAYNE STEWART	$35,000	69-69-65-73	276

BUICK CLASSIC
Westchester C.C., Rye, New York
June 9-12, 1995

*VIJAY SINGH	$216,000	70-69-67-72	278
DOUG MARTIN	$129,600	67-70-72-69	278

BOBBY WADKINS	$81,600	72-66-69-71	279
DILLARD PRUITT	$47,250	72-69-70-69	280
ERNIE ELS	$47,250	68-69-75-68	280
FRED FUNK	$47,250	71-68-71-70	280
NICK FALDO	$47,250	70-70-68-72	280
DAVID DUVAL	$33,600	69-75-67-70	281
BOB GILDER	$33,600	73-70-68-70	281
BLAINE MCCALLISTER	$33,600	69-71-69-72	281
BRUCE FLEISHER	$33,600	68-71-69-73	281

UNITED STATES OPEN
Shinnecock Hills G.C.,
Southampton, New York
June 15-18, 1995

COREY PAVIN	**$350,000**	72-69-71-68	**280**
GREG NORMAN	$207,000	68-67-74-73	282
TOM LEHMAN	$131,974	70-72-67-74	283
NEAL LANCASTER	$66,634	70-72-77-65	284
JEFF MAGGERT	$66,634	69-72-77-66	284
BILL GLASSON	$66,634	69-70-76-69	284
JAY HAAS	$66,634	70-73-72-69	284
DAVIS LOVE III	$66,634	72-68-73-71	284
PHIL MICKELSON	$66,634	68-70-72-74	284
FRANK NOBILO	$44,184	72-72-70-71	285
BOB TWAY	$44,184	69-69-72-75	285
VIJAY SINGH	$44,184	70-71-72-72	285

For a complete summary of all players making the cut at the U.S. Opens, please refer to "1995 Major Championships"

CANON GREATER HARTFORD OPEN
TPC at River Highlands,
Cromwell, Connecticut
June 22-25, 1995

GREG NORMAN	$216,000	67-64-65-71	267
DAVE STOCKTON JR.	$89,600	65-68-68-68	269
GRANT WAITE	$89,600	66-67-67-69	269
KIRK TRIPLETT	$89,600	64-67-69-69	269
BRIAN HENNINGER	$43,800	66-67-72-65	270
DON POOLEY	$43,800	67-72-66-65	270
FUZZY ZOELLER	$43,800	70-63-66-71	270
BOB ESTES	$34,800	64-72-68-67	271
MICHAEL BRADLEY	$34,800	67-66-69-69	271
BILLY ANDRADE	$34,800	74-65-62-70	271

FEDEX ST. JUDE CLASSIC
TPC Southwind, Memphis, Tennessee
June 29-July 2, 1995

JIM GALLAGHER JR.	$225,000	65-62-68-72	267
JAY DELSING	$110,000	69-63-69-67	268
KEN GREEN	$110,000	68-67-65-68	268
GENE SAUERS	$60,000	68-65-63-73	269
BRANDEL CHAMBLEE	$40,938	69-70-65-66	270
ROCCO MEDIATE	$40,938	65-71-67-67	270
JOHN COOK	$40,938	65-70-67-68	270
STEVE JONES	$40,938	68-69-65-68	270
LARRY MIZE	$40,938	69-66-67-68	270
BOB TWAY	$40,938	65-64-70-71	270

MOTOROLA OPEN
Cog Hill (No. 4), Lemont, Illinois
July 6-9, 1995

BILLY MAYFAIR	$360,000	73-70-69-67	279
JEFF MAGGERT	$132,000	74-73-69-64	280
JUSTIN LEONARD	$132,000	70-71-72-67	280
SCOTT SIMPSON	$132,000	71-72-69-68	280
JAY HAAS	$132,000	69-68-73-70	280
JOHN HUSTON	$64,750	73-68-72-68	281
BOB TWAY	$64,750	76-69-68-68	281
BOB ESTES	$64,750	72-73-66-70	281
STEVE LOWERY	$64,750	69-70-70-71	281
SCOTT GUMP	$50,000	74-70-72-66	282
WOODY AUSTIN	$50,000	74-70-69-69	282
SCOTT HOCH	$50,000	73-69-70-70	282

ANHEUSER-BUSCH OPEN
Kingsmill G.C., Williamsburg, Virginia
July 13-16, 1995

TED TRYBA	$198,000	69-67-68-68	272
SCOTT SIMPSON	$118,800	69-69-68-67	273
SCOTT HOCH	$57,200	67-69-71-67	274
LENNIE CLEMENTS	$57,200	68-69-69-68	274
JIM CARTER	$57,200	66-69-68-71	274
MARCO DAWSON	$38,225	68-71-73-63	275
CURTIS STRANGE	$38,225	72-70-65-68	275
JEFF SLUMAN	$31,900	72-69-67-69	277
DAVID OGRIN	$31,900	71-71-66-69	277
FRED FUNK	$31,900	68-68-70-71	277

THE BRITISH OPEN
The Old Course, St. Andrews, Scotland
July 20-23, 1995

*JOHN DALY	$200,000	67-71-73-71	282
COSTANTINO ROCCA	$160,000	69-70-70-73	282
STEVEN BOTTOMLEY	$105,065	70-72-72-69	283
MARK BROOKS	$105,065	70-69-73-71	283
MICHAEL CAMPBELL	$105,065	71-71-65-76	283
VIJAY SINGH	$64,800	68-72-73-71	284
STEVE ELKINGTON	$64,800	72-69-69-74	284
BOB ESTES	$53,333	72-70-71-72	285
COREY PAVIN	$53,333	69-70-72-74	285
MARK JAMES	$53,333	72-75-68-70	285

For a complete summary of all players making the cut at the British Open, please refer to "1995 Major Championships"

DEPOSIT GUARANTY CLASSIC
Annandale G.C., Madison, Mississippi
July 20-23, 1995

ED DOUGHERTY	$126,000	68-68-70-66	272
GIL MORGAN	$75,600	69-69-67-69	274
PETE JORDAN	$47,600	71-67-69-69	275
STEVE RINTOUL	$27,563	73-68-67-68	276
TOM BYRUM	$27,563	69-69-68-70	276
KIRK TRIPLETT	$27,563	66-70-69-71	276
DICKY THOMPSON	$27,563	67-68-68-73	276
ROCKY WALCHER	$20,300	70-68-73-66	277
DICKY PRIDE	$20,300	66-68-70-73	277
BOB GILDER	$20,300	69-66-69-73	277

IDEON CLASSIC
Pleasant Valley G.C., Sutton, Massachusetts
July 27-30, 1995

FRED FUNK	$180,000	66-63-66-73	268
JIM MCGOVERN	$108,000	66-66-67-70	269
DON POOLEY	$68,000	70-64-68-68	270
JOEY SINDELAR	$39,375	69-66-70-66	271
LENNIE CLEMENTS	$39,375	67-68-69-67	271
ROGER MALTBIE	$39,375	68-67-69-67	271
JAY WILLIAMSON	$39,375	67-67-68-69	271
GREG KRAFT	$29,000	70-67-66-69	272
HOWARD TWITTY	$29,000	67-67-68-70	272
DAN FORSMAN	$29,000	69-65-67-71	272

BUICK OPEN
Warwick Hills G. & C.C.,
Grand Blanc, Michigan
August 2-5, 1995

*WOODY AUSTIN	$216,000	63-68-72-67	270
MIKE BRISKY	$129,600	67-68-67-68	270
ERNIE ELS	$62,400	69-68-66-68	271
TOM BYRUM	$62,400	69-67-65-70	271
JEFF SLUMAN	$62,400	66-67-67-71	271
FRED COUPLES	$43,200	68-67-67-70	272
JOEL EDWARDS	$40,200	69-65-68-71	273
PAYNE STEWART	$37,200	65-65-73-71	274
TOM LEHMAN	$33,600	71-66-70-68	275
JONATHAN KAYE	$33,600	69-67-69-70	275

PGA CHAMPIONSHIP
Riviera C.C., Pacific Palisades, California
August 10-13, 1995

*STEVE ELKINGTON	$360,000	68-67-68-64	267
COLIN MONTGOMERIE	$216,000	68-67-67-65	267
ERNIE ELS	$116,000	66-65-66-72	269
JEFF MAGGERT	$116,000	66-69-65-69	269
BRAD FAXON	$80,000	70-67-71-63	271
MARK O'MEARA	$68,500	64-67-69-73	273
BOB ESTES	$68,500	69-68-68-68	273
CRAIG STADLER	$50,000	71-66-66-71	274
STEVE LOWERY	$50,000	69-68-68-69	274
JUSTIN LEONARD	$50,000	68-66-70-70	274
JAY HAAS	$50,000	69-71-64-70	274
JEFF SLUMAN	$50,000	69-67-68-70	274

For a complete summary of all players making the cut at the PGA Championship, please refer to "1995 Major Championships"

THE SPRINT INTERNATIONAL
Castle Pines G.C.,
Castle Pines, Colorado
August 17-20, 1995

The Sprint International uses the Modified Stableford scoring system that places a premium on birdies, eagles, and double eagles.

LEE JANZEN	$270,000	10-9-6-9	34
ERNIE ELS	$162,000	17-0-7-9	33
MARK WIEBE	$87,000	8-15-(-1)-6	28
JAY HAAS	$87,000	3-12-13-0	28
DAVID DUVAL	$60,000	10-9-6-2	27
JOSE MARIA OLAZABAL	$52,125	7-5-6-8	26
TOM WATSON	$52,125	7-8-9-2	26
GREG NORMAN	$43,500	14-3-(-2)-9	24
DAVIS LOVE III	$43,500	11-6-6-1	24
DAN FORSMAN	$43,500	3-10-7-4	24

NEC WORLD SERIES OF GOLF
Firestone C.C. (South), Akron, Ohio
August 24-27, 1995

*GREG NORMAN	$360,000	73-68-70-67	278
NICK PRICE	$176,000	72-69-69-68	278
*BILLY MAYFAIR	$176,000	70-68-70-70	278
PHIL MICKELSON	$88,000	69-74-70-66	279
VIJAY SINGH	$88,000	71-69-65-74	279
FRED COUPLES	$69,500	68-76-68-68	280
JIM GALLAGHER JR.	$69,500	66-71-70-73	280
MIKE SULLIVAN	$62,000	71-67-74-69	281
LOREN ROBERTS	$56,000	72-74-70-66	282
JOSE MARIA OLAZABAL	$56,000	68-70-69-75	282

GREATER MILWAUKEE OPEN
Brown Deer G.C., Milwaukee, Wisconsin
August 31-September 3, 1995

SCOTT HOCH	$180,000	68-71-65-65	269
MARCO DAWSON	$108,000	70-65-70-67	272
JEFF SLUMAN	$52,000	72-71-65-66	274
JIM GALLAGHER JR.	$52,000	68-71-68-67	274
JOE ACOSTA	$52,000	68-69-69-68	274
JOEY SINDELAR	$32,375	74-68-68-65	275
STEVE LOWERY	$32,375	70-69-71-65	275
DUFFY WALDORF	$32,375	69-73-65-68	275
LEE RINKER	$32,375	70-68-67-70	275
BOB ESTES	$22,167	71-70-71-64	276
D.A. WEIBRING	$22,167	70-69-71-66	276
ANDREW MAGEE	$22,167	69-72-69-66	276
JAY HAAS	$22,167	74-68-67-67	276
MARK O'MEARA	$22,167	69-71-68-68	276
ROBERT GAMEZ	$22,167	67-69-70-70	276

BELL CANADIAN OPEN
Glen Abbey G.C., Oakville, Ontario
September 7-10, 1995

*MARK O'MEARA	$234,000	72-67-68-67	274
BOB LOHR	$140,400	68-67-69-70	274
NICK PRICE	$88,400	72-69-68-68	277
HAL SUTTON	$62,400	69-72-68-69	278
BILL GLASSON	$49,400	68-74-68-70	280
ANDREW MAGEE	$49,400	68-68-73-71	280
TONY SILLS	$43,550	72-68-73-69	282
SCOTT DUNLAP	$40,300	71-67-73-72	283
BRIAN KAMM	$36,400	74-71-70-69	284
BOB TWAY	$36,400	69-72-68-75	284

QUAD CITY CLASSIC
Oakwood G.C., Coal Valley, Illinois
September 21-24, 1995

D.A. WEIBRING	$180,000	64-65-68	197
JONATHAN KAYE	$108,000	67-66-65	198
JAY DELSING	$68,000	69-64-67	200
JIM MCGOVERN	$48,000	64-71-66	201
DENNIS PAULSON	$36,500	71-66-65	202
MICHAEL ALLEN	$36,500	66-70-66	202
SCOTT HOCH	$36,500	71-65-66	202
BOB GILDER	$30,000	68-69-66	203
CURT BYRUM	$30,000	66-68-69	203
BRUCE FLEISHER	$26,000	72-66-66	204
SCOTT VERPLANK	$26,000	65-73-66	204

B.C. OPEN
En-Joie G.C., Endicott, New York
September 14-17, 1995

HAL SUTTON	$180,000	71-69-68-61	269
JIM MCGOVERN	$108,000	71-67-69-63	270
KIRK TRIPLETT	$58,000	69-67-69-66	271
CRAIG STADLER	$58,000	67-69-68-67	271
JAY HAAS	$38,000	68-69-71-64	272
STEWART CINK	$38,000	71-70-66-65	272
JOEY SINDELAR	$29,100	68-68-70-67	273
JEFF LEONARD	$29,100	69-66-71-67	273
JAY WILLIAMSON	$29,100	67-68-69-69	273
JEFF SLUMAN	$29,100	67-69-68-69	273
SKIP KENDALL	$29,100	66-69-68-70	273

BUICK CHALLENGE
Callaway Gardens Resort,
Pine Mountain, Georgia
September 21-24, 1995

FRED FUNK	$180,000	69-67-69-67	272
LOREN ROBERTS	$88,000	70-69-67-67	273
JOHN MORSE	$88,000	71-68-67-67	273
GUY BOROS	$41,433	68-69-72-65	274
JEFF SLUMAN	$41,433	67-69-70-68	274
KIRK TRIPLETT	$41,433	71-66-69-68	274
DAVID OGRIN	$33,500	70-68-70-67	275
SCOTT HOCH	$28,000	70-70-69-67	276
JOHN HUSTON	$28,000	67-71-70-68	276
LARRY NELSON	$28,000	71-65-70-70	276
STEVE STRICKER	$28,000	66-67-72-71	276

WALT DISNEY WORLD/ OLDSMOBILE CLASSIC
Walt Disney World Resort, Orlando, Florida
October 5-8, 1995

BRAD BRYANT	$216,000	67-63-68	198
HAL SUTTON	$105,600	67-66-66	199
TED TRYBA	$105,600	69-65-65	199
JOE ACOSTA JR.	$49,600	68-67-66	201
BOB TWAY	$49,600	65-70-66	201
MIKE REID	$49,600	68-66-67	201
CHARLIE RYMER	$31,275	68-68-66	202
LEE RINKER	$31,275	68-67-67	202
JAY WILLIAMSON	$31,275	69-65-68	202
MIKE HULBERT	$31,275	68-64-68	202
RUSS COCHRAN	$31,275	66-67-69	202
MIKE HEINEN	$31,275	65-68-69	202
PATRICK BURKE	$31,275	66-65-71	202
CARL PAULSON	$31,275	62-68-72	202

TEXAS OPEN
LaCantera C.C., San Antonio, Texas
October 6-9, 1995

DUFFY WALDORF	$198,000	66-66-71-65	268
JUSTIN LEONARD	$118,800	67-70-69-68	274
JOHN MORSE	$57,200	70-69-71-70	280
JOHN MAHAFFEY	$57,200	67-71-71-71	280

Texas Open, continued

LOREN ROBERTS	$57,200	64-72-73-71	280
MIKE STANDLY	$38,225	68-71-74-68	281
JAY DON BLAKE	$38,225	67-67-70-77	281
JAY HAAS	$34,100	68-68-74-72	282
MARK WIEBE	$30,800	74-69-70-70	283
LEE RINKER	$30,800	70-66-72-75	283

LAS VEGAS INVITATIONAL
TPC at Summerlin, Las Vegas, Nevada
October 11-15, 1995

JIM FURYK	$270,000	67-65-65-67-67	331
BILLY MAYFAIR	$162,000	66-65-67-66-68	332
SCOTT MCCARRON	$102,000	71-65-69-64-65	334
BRAD BRYANT	$62,000	65-68-67-69-66	335
PHIL BLACKMAR	$62,000	69-66-71-64-65	335
MARK O'MEARA	$62,000	67-67-66-65-70	335
GLEN DAY	$46,750	70-67-65-68-66	336
DAVIS LOVE III	$46,750	67-67-68-67-67	336
DAVID EDWARDS	$46,750	67-66-64-69-70	336
BILL GLASSON	$36,000	68-68-68-65-65	337
KIRK TRIPLETT	$36,000	66-67-69-68-67	337
RICK FEHR	$36,000	64-68-71-67-67	337
JOE OZAKI	$36,000	63-69-71-66-68	337

THE TOUR CHAMPIONSHIP
Southern Hills C.C., Tulsa, Oklahoma
October 26-29, 1995

BILLY MAYFAIR	$540,000	68-70-69-73	280
STEVE ELKINGTON	$265,500	71-72-67-73	283
COREY PAVIN	$265,500	72-70-68-73	283
WOODY AUSTIN	$132,000	71-68-73-72	284
SCOTT SIMPSON	$132,000	71-70-74-69	284
VIJAY SINGH	$108,000	69-71-72-73	285
BRAD BRYANT	$99,000	69-68-73-76	286
JUSTIN LEONARD	$99,000	70-70-72-74	286
DAVID DUVAL	$87,600	74-69-71-73	287
GREG NORMAN	$87,600	72-70-74-71	287

Senior PGA TOUR

TOURNAMENT OF CHAMPIONS
La Costa C.C., Carlsbad, California
January 7-9, 1995

*JIM COLBERT	$148,000	72-66-71	209
JIM ALBUS	$87,000	70-70-69	209
JIM DENT	$65,000	69-72-69	210
LARRY GILBERT	$65,000	73-67-70	210
TOM WARGO	$47,000	73-72-66	211
RAYMOND FLOYD	$35,500	68-71-75	214
DAVE STOCKTON	$35,500	72-71-71	214
LEE TREVINO	$35,500	70-68-76	214
JACK NICKLAUS	$27,500	75-72-68	215
TONY JACKLIN	$24,500	71-70-75	216
JACK KIEFER	$24,500	69-73-74	216

SENIOR SLAM OF GOLF
Cabo del Sol (Ocean), Los Cabos, Mexico
February 11-12, 1995

RAYMOND FLOYD	$250,000	72-67	139
DAVE STOCKTON	$125,000	70-75	145
SIMON HOBDAY	$75,000	70-77	147
LEE TREVINO	$50,000	80-75	155

GTE SUNCOAST CLASSIC
TPC of Tampa at Cheval, Lutz, Florida
February 17-19, 1995

DAVE STOCKTON	$112,500	70-66-68	204
JIM COLBERT	$55,000	71-68-67	206
BOB CHARLES	$55,000	68-69-69	206
J.C. SNEAD	$55,000	68-69-69	206
SIMON HOBDAY	$31,000	68-71-68	207
JACK NICKLAUS	$31,000	69-70-68	207
BRUCE LEHNHARD	$31,000	70-68-69	207
LEE TREVINO	$19,800	69-72-67	208
BOB MURPHY	$19,800	70-69-69	208
RAY FLOYD	$19,800	66-72-70	208
GRAHAM MARSH	$19,800	70-68-70	208

THE INTELLINET CHALLENGE
The Vineyards, Naples, Florida
February 10-12, 1995

BOB MURPHY	$90,000	67-70	137
RAY FLOYD	$52,800	69-69	138
MIKE HILL	$39,600	71-69	140
ROCKY THOMPSON	$39,600	70-70	140
LARRY GILBERT	$22,080	74-67	141
JERRY MCGEE	$22,080	72-69	141
RICHIE KARL	$22,080	71-70	141
BOB CHARLES	$22,080	69-72	141
JIM ALBUS	$22,080	69-72	141
BOB BRUE	$15,600	70-72	142

FHP HEALTH CARE CLASSIC
Ojai Valley Inn & C.C., Ojai, California
March 3-5, 1995

*BRUCE DEVLIN	$112,500	64-66	130
DAVE EICHELBERGER	$66,000	64-66	130
DALE DOUGLASS	$54,000	67-65	132
BUD ALLIN	$34,500	72-61	133
TOM WARGO	$34,500	70-63	133
DAVE HILL	$34,500	68-65	133
DAVE STOCKTON	$34,500	63-70	133
JIM COLBERT	$19,000	68-66	134
LARRY ZIEGLER	$19,000	68-66	134
HARRY TOSCANO	$19,000	67-67	134
JAY SIGEL	$19,000	67-67	134
BOB CHARLES	$19,000	64-70	134
JIM DENT	$19,000	66-68	134

DOMINION SENIOR CLASSIC
Dominion Country Club, San Antonio, Texas
March 10-12, 1995

JIM ALBUS	$97,500	71-65-69	205
JAY SIGEL	$52,000	69-73-66	208
RAYMOND FLOYD	$52,000	72-68-68	208
LEE TREVINO	$39,000	72-67-70	209
DAVE STOCKTON	$28,600	74-69-67	210
TOMMY AARON	$28,600	72-68-70	210
DAVE EICHELBERGER	$22,100	71-70-70	211
DICK HENDRICKSON	$22,100	70-71-70	211
JIM FERREE	$15,058	75-69-68	212
ISAO AOKI	$15,058	74-69-69	212
GAY BREWER	$15,058	72-71-69	212
JOHN PAUL CAIN	$15,058	76-66-70	212
LEE ELDER	$15,058	67-72-73	212
JIM DENT	$15,058	72-67-73	212

TOSHIBA SENIOR CLASSIC
Mesa Verde C.C., Costa Mesa, California
March 17-19, 1995

GEORGE ARCHER	$120,000	67-68-64	199
DAVE STOCKTON	$64,000	69-67-64	200
TOM WARGO	$64,000	65-67-68	200
MARION HECK	$48,000	67-72-63	202
DEWITT WEAVER	$38,400	72-65-66	203
TERRY DILL	$30,400	69-72-64	205
J.C. SNEAD	$30,400	67-70-68	205
BOB MURPHY	$20,266	68-73-65	206
AL GEIBERGER	$20,266	71-69-66	206
ROCKY THOMPSON	$20,266	68-70-68	206
TOM WEISKOPF	$20,266	68-67-71	206
JIM DENT	$20,266	70-66-70	206
BOB E. SMITH	$20,266	70-65-71	206

THE TRADITION
Golf Club at Desert Mountain, Scottsdale, Arizona
March 30-April 2, 1995

*JACK NICKLAUS	$150,000	69-71-69-67	276
ISAO AOKI	$88,000	71-66-72-67	276
JIM FERREE	$72,000	67-74-69-67	277
JIM COLBERT	$60,000	76-64-70-70	280
JIMMY POWELL	$48,000	75-68-69-69	281
RAY FLOYD	$38,000	70-72-71-69	282
JAY SIGEL	$38,000	70-69-71-72	282
TOM WEISKOPF	$27,500	75-74-67-67	283
DALE DOUGLASS	$27,500	74-74-67-68	283
BRUCE SUMMERHAYS	$27,500	71-77-66-69	283
BOB MURPHY	$27,500	73-71-69-70	283

For a complete summary of all scores at The Tradition, please refer to "1995 Major Championships"

PGA SENIORS CHAMPIONSHIP
PGA National G.C., Palm Beach Gardens, Florida
April 13-16, 1995

RAY FLOYD	$180,000	70-70-67-70	277
JOHN PAUL CAIN	$75,000	72-71-70-69	282
LARRY GILBERT	$75,000	71-70-72-69	282
LEE TREVINO	$75,000	72-70-69-71	282

PGA Seniors Championship, continued

GRAHAM MARSH	$40,000	71-71-70-71	283
ISAO AOKI	$40,000	70-69-73-71	283
BOB CHARLES	$40,000	70-75-68-70	283
JACK NICKLAUS	$30,000	76-66-68-74	284
JIM COLBERT	$25,000	69-69-71-76	285
BOB MURPHY	$17,833	71-73-70-72	286
GEORGE ARCHER	$17,833	73-71-68-74	286
JIM ALBUS	$17,833	69-73-69-75	286

For a complete summary of all scores at the PGA Seniors Championship, please refer to "1995 Major Championships"

LIBERTY MUTUAL LEGENDS OF GOLF
PGA West (Stadium), La Quinta, California
April 21-23, 1995

LEE TREVINO/MIKE HILL	$100,000	64-66-65	195
GIBBY GILBERT/J.C. SNEAD	$50,000	65-64-68	197
CHI CHI RODRIGUEZ/JIM DENT	$25,625	64-70-64	198
BOB MURPHY/JIM COLBERT	$25,625	65-67-66	198
BOBBY NICHOLS/DAVE HILL	$25,625	68-63-67	198
TONY JACKLIN/BOB CHARLES	$25,625	66-65-67	198
CHAS. COODY/D. DOUGLASS	$18,500	63-68-68	199
O. MOODY/J. POWELL	$16,500	68-64-68	200
A. GEIBERGER/D. STOCKTON	$16,500	65-65-70	200
H. HENNING/D. EICHELBERGER	$14,000	69-67-65	201

LAS VEGAS SENIOR CLASSIC
TPC at Summerlin, Las Vegas, Nevada
April 28-30, 1995

JIM COLBERT	$150,000	65-71-69	205
JIM DENT	$74,266	67-70-70	207
ROCKY THOMPSON	$74,266	70-65-72	207
RAY FLOYD	$74,266	66-70-71	207
TOM WEISKOPF	$48,800	72-69-67	208
DAVE STOCKTON	$33,280	70-72-68	210
JACK KIEFER	$33,280	73-69-68	210
GIBBY GILBERT	$33,280	72-70-68	210
MIKE HILL	$33,280	75-66-69	210
GRAHAM MARSH	$33,280	73-64-73	210

PAINEWEBBER INVITATIONAL
TPC at Piper Glen, Charlotte, North Carolina
May 5-7, 1995

BOB MURPHY	$120,000	68-66-69	203
RAY FLOYD	$64,000	69-69-67	205
LARRY ZIEGLER	$64,000	66-69-70	205
JIM COLBERT	$43,200	70-71-66	207
GRAHAM MARSH	$43,200	67-68-72	207
LARRY GILBERT	$28,800	74-68-66	208
JERRY MCGEE	$28,800	70-69-69	208
KERMIT ZARLEY	$28,800	73-66-69	208
DAVE STOCKTON	$20,800	72-70-67	209
WALT MORGAN	$20,800	69-72-68	209
TOM SHAW	$20,800	70-68-71	209

CADILLAC NFL GOLF CLASSIC
Upper Montclair C.C., Clifton, New Jersey
May 12-14, 1995

GEORGE ARCHER	$142,500	69-66-70	205
BOB MURPHY	$76,000	65-73-68	206
RAY FLOYD	$76,000	67-71-68	206
LEE TREVINO	$57,000	70-66-71	207
ISAO AOKI	$45,600	68-69-71	208
LARRY ZIEGLER	$36,100	69-69-71	209
DAVE STOCKTON	$36,100	70-67-72	209
JERRY MCGEE	$28,500	70-70-70	210
AL GEIBERGER	$28,500	69-69-72	210
DALE DOUGLASS	$23,750	69-71-71	211
BOB CHARLES	$23,750	69-70-72	211

BELL ATLANTIC CLASSIC
Chester Valley G.C., Malvern, Pennsylvania
May 19-21, 1995

JIM COLBERT	$135,000	68-71-68	207
J.C. SNEAD	$79,200	66-72-70	208
JACK NICKLAUS	$64,800	72-69-68	209
CALVIN PEETE	$54,000	71-73-67	211
ED SNEED	$35,100	72-71-69	212
BRUCE SUMMERHAYS	$35,100	70-70-72	212
CHARLES COODY	$35,100	72-69-71	212
DAVE STOCKTON	$35,100	68-71-73	212
LEE TREVINO	$25,200	69-72-72	213
DEANE BEMAN	$22,500	68-74-72	214
DAVE EICHELBERGER	$22,500	71-71-72	214

QUICKSILVER CLASSIC
Quicksilver C.C., Pittsburgh, Pennsylvania
May 26-28, 1995

DAVE STOCKTON	$165,000	72-69-67	208
ISAO AOKI	$96,800	68-72-69	209

Quicksilver Classic, continued

TOM WARGO	$66,000	71-72-67	210
GEORGE ARCHER	$66,000	69-68-73	210
DAVE EICHELBERGER	$66,000	71-68-71	210
TONY JACKLIN	$44,000	73-69-69	211
J.C. SNEAD	$39,600	69-72-71	212
DEWITT WEAVER	$29,040	71-75-67	213
BUD ALLIN	$29,040	68-76-69	213
JOHN PAUL CAIN	$29,040	71-72-70	213
GRAHAM MARSH	$29,040	70-71-72	213
JERRY MCGEE	$29,040	69-71-73	213

BRUNO'S MEMORIAL CLASSIC
Greystone G.C., Birmingham, Alabama
June 2-4, 1995

GRAHAM MARSH	$157,500	68-63-70	201
J.C. SNEAD	$92,400	71-67-68	206
LARRY LAORETTI	$57,750	70-67-70	207
BUD ALLIN	$57,750	67-70-70	207
TOM WEISKOPF	$57,750	68-68-71	207
BRUCE SUMMERHAYS	$57,750	67-69-71	207
AL GEIBERGER	$37,800	70-68-70	208
TOM WARGO	$33,600	71-67-71	209
RAY FLOYD	$28,350	69-72-69	210
ISAO AOKI	$28,350	72-69-69	210

DALLAS REUNION PRO-AM
Oak Cliff C.C., Dallas, Texas
June 6-8, 1995

TOM WARGO	$82,500	64-64-69	197
DAVE STOCKTON	$44,000	67-68-69	204
DAVE EICHELBERGER	$44,000	66-68-70	204
BRUCE SUMMERHAYS	$27,133	69-70-69	208
JIM ALBUS	$27,133	70-71-67	208
BRIAN BARNES	$27,133	68-70-70	208
JIM DENT	$18,700	72-73-64	209
MARION HECK	$18,700	73-70-66	209
BUD ALLIN	$14,300	69-72-69	210
BEN SMITH	$14,300	71-74-65	210
HAROLD HENNING	$14,300	71-71-68	210

BELLSOUTH SENIOR CLASSIC
Springhouse G.C., Nashville, Tennessee
June 9-11, 1995

JIM DENT	$165,000	66-69-68	203
BOB MURPHY	$96,800	70-66-69	205
DAVE STOCKTON	$79,200	71-67-68	206
DAVE HILL	$59,400	67-74-66	207
HALE IRWIN	$59,400	70-68-69	207
JIM ALBUS	$39,600	69-70-69	208
TOMMY AARON	$39,600	70-68-70	208
ROCKY THOMPSON	$39,600	71-67-70	208
HAROLD HENNING	$30,800	65-74-70	209
ISAO AOKI	$24,420	70-74-66	210
BRUCE SUMMERHAYS	$24,420	73-70-67	210
JAY SIGEL	$24,420	73-68-69	210
KERMIT ZARLEY	$24,420	69-71-70	210
DAVE EICHELBERGER	$24,420	68-70-72	210

NATIONWIDE CHAMPIONSHIP
GC of Georgia, Alpharetta, Georgia
June 23-25, 1995

BOB MURPHY	$180,000	71-64-68	203
HALE IRWIN	$96,000	70-65-70	205
BRUCE SUMMERHAYS	$96,000	63-71-71	205
ISAO AOKI	$72,000	69-70-67	206
TOM WEISKOPF	$52,800	75-66-66	207
GRAHAM MARSH	$52,800	69-67-71	207
JAY SIGEL	$43,200	71-67-70	208
DALE DOUGLASS	$33,000	71-72-66	209
DEANE BEMAN	$33,000	66-73-70	209
TOM WARGO	$33,000	69-69-71	209
LARRY LAORETTI	$33,000	66-68-75	209

U.S. SENIOR OPEN
Congressional C.C., Bethesda, Maryland
June 29-July 2, 1995

TOM WEISKOPF	$175,000	69-69-69-68	275
JACK NICKLAUS	$103,500	71-71-70-67	279
BOB MURPHY	$51,998	69-70-71-70	280
ISAO AOKI	$51,998	70-68-68-72	280
HALE IRWIN	$32,625	72-68-71-71	282
J.C. SNEAD	$32,625	68-73-70-71	282
LEE TREVINO	$28,073	73-68-74-68	283
GRAHAM MARSH	$24,811	69-70-74-71	284
RAYMOND FLOYD	$24,811	70-72-69-73	284
DEWITT WEAVER	$22,043	73-71-70-71	285

For a complete summary of all players making the cut at the Senior Open, please refer to "1995 Major Championships"

KROGER SENIOR CLASSIC
The Golf Center at Kings Island, Mason, Ohio
July 7-9, 1995

MIKE HILL	$135,000	64-66-66	196
ISAO AOKI	$79,200	66-66-65	197
GRAHAM MARSH	$64,800	70-63-65	198
ROCKY THOMPSON	$48,600	70-67-64	201
J.C. SNEAD	$48,600	66-68-67	201
ED SNEED	$36,000	67-70-65	202
LEE TREVINO	$27,450	72-66-65	203
JIM COLBERT	$27,450	69-68-66	203
GIBBY GILBERT	$27,450	70-66-67	203
AL GEIBERGER	$27,450	68-67-68	203

FORD SENIOR PLAYERS CHAMPIONSHIP
TPC of Michigan, Dearborn, Michigan
July 13-16, 1995

*J.C. SNEAD	$225,000	69-68-66-69	272
JACK NICKLAUS	$132,000	71-68-66-67	272
JIM COLBERT	$90,000	70-63-75-68	276
JERRY MCGEE	$90,000	68-73-67-68	276
BEN SMITH	$90,000	73-67-67-69	276
ISAO AOKI	$60,000	71-68-68-70	277
DON BIES	$48,000	74-71-68-65	278
BOB MURPHY	$48,000	71-68-69-70	278
DAVE STOCKTON	$48,000	69-69-66-74	278
HALE IRWIN	$34,500	74-69-72-64	279
TOM WEISKOPF	$34,500	70-71-69-69	279
AL GEIBERGER	$34,500	71-69-68-71	279
RAY FLOYD	$34,500	69-70-66-74	279

For a complete summary of all players making the cut at the Ford Senior Players, please refer to "1995 Major Championships"

FIRST OF AMERICA CLASSIC
Egypt Valley G.C., Ada, Michigan
July 21-23, 1995

JIMMY POWELL	$105,000	68-66-67	201
BABE HISKEY	$61,600	71-65-70	206
LARRY LAORETTI	$50,400	68-69-70	207
DICK RHYAN	$28,467	72-69-67	208
SIMON HOBDAY	$28,467	69-71-68	208
JIM ALBUS	$28,467	69-70-69	208
JIM COLBERT	$28,467	69-70-69	208
WALT MORGAN	$28,467	69-69-70	208
GEORGE ARCHER	$28,467	66-72-70	208
BOB WYNN	$18,200	69-70-70	209

AMERITECH SENIOR OPEN
Stonebridge C.C., Aurora, Illinois
July 28-30, 1995

HALE IRWIN	$127,500	66-63-66	195
KERMIT ZARLEY	$74,800	69-65-68	202
DAVE STOCKTON	$61,200	73-65-66	204
MIKE HILL	$51,000	67-72-66	205
RAY FLOYD	$37,400	69-69-68	206
JIM COLBERT	$37,400	66-68-72	206
GAY BREWER	$25,925	74-68-65	207
BEN SMITH	$25,925	69-68-70	207
JOE JIMENEZ	$25,925	74-62-71	207
DAVE HILL	$25,925	69-68-70	207

VFW SENIOR CHAMPIONSHIP,
Loch Lloyd Country Club, Belton, Maryland.
August 4-6, 1995

BOB MURPHY	$135,000	69-63-63	195
JIM COLBERT	$79,200	68-66-62	196
JAY SIGEL	$64,800	65-66-67	198
SIMON HOBDAY	$48,600	66-68-66	200
BUD ALLIN	$48,600	63-69-68	200
ISAO AOKI	$36,000	68-67-66	201
LEE TREVINO	$26,280	70-68-64	202
DAVE STOCKTON	$26,280	69-68-65	202
LARRY GILBERT	$26,280	70-67-65	202
HALE IRWIN	$26,280	67-68-67	202
BRUCE SUMMERHAYS	$26,280	69-64-69	202

BURNET SENIOR CLASSIC
Bunker Hills G.C., Coon Rapids, Minnesota
August 11-13, 1995

RAY FLOYD	$165,000	68-65-68	201
GRAHAM MARSH	$96,800	64-69-69	202
JIM ALBUS	$72,600	68-69-69	206
GIBBY GILBERT	$72,600	64-70-72	206
DAVE STOCKTON	$45,467	68-71-68	207
KERMIT ZARLEY	$45,467	72-67-68	207
BUTCH BAIRD	$45,467	67-70-70	207
TERRY DILL	$31,533	68-69-71	208
GEORGE ARCHER	$31,533	68-69-71	208
LEE TREVINO	$31,533	68-66-74	208

NORTHVILLE LONG ISLAND CLASSIC
Meadow Brook Club, Jericho, New York
August 18-20, 1995

Northville Long Island Classic, continued

LEE TREVINO	$120,000	67-69-66	202
BUD ALLIN	$70,400	67-69-70	206
JACK KIEFER	$44,000	72-69-66	207
JAY SIGEL	$44,000	68-70-69	207
BEN SMITH	$44,000	68-68-71	207
LARRY GILBERT	$44,000	68-68-71	207
JOHN PAUL CAIN	$28,800	65-69-74	208
LARRY LAORETTI	$20,667	69-71-69	209
BOB MURPHY	$20,667	69-71-69	209
GEORGE ARCHER	$20,667	71-66-72	209
JIM ALBUS	$20,667	68-69-72	209
TONY JACKLIN	$20,667	66-71-72	209
DAVE EICHELBERGER	$20,667	69-66-74	209

BANK OF BOSTON SENIOR GOLF CLASSIC
Nashawtuc C.C., Concord, Massachusetts
August 25-27, 1995

ISAO AOKI	$120,000	69-66-69	204
BOB CHARLES	$64,000	70-67-68	205
HALE IRWIN	$64,000	71-66-68	205
WALTER ZEMBRISKI	$43,200	71-69-67	207
BRUCE SUMMERHAYS	$43,200	72-69-66	207
TERRY DILL	$28,800	75-68-65	208
JAY SIGEL	$28,800	74-68-66	208
GEORGE ARCHER	$28,800	69-70-69	208
BUD ALLIN	$22,400	69-69-71	209
DAVE EICHELBERGER	$19,200	71-72-67	210
BOB MURPHY	$19,200	71-70-69	210
ROCKY THOMPSON	$19,200	69-70-71	210

GTE NORTHWEST CLASSIC
Inglewood G.C., Kenmore, Washington
September 8-10, 1995

WALT MORGAN	$90,000	68-68-67	203
DAVE STOCKTON	$52,800	69-69-68	206
ROCKY THOMPSON	$36,000	71-69-67	207
AL GEIBERGER	$36,000	69-71-67	207
GEORGE ARCHER	$36,000	70-68-69	207
JIMMY POWELL	$21,600	67-72-69	208
BOB E. SMITH	$21,600	68-69-71	208
BRUCE SUMMERHAYS	$21,600	72-66-70	208
BUTCH BAIRD	$16,800	70-71-69	210
JOE JIMENEZ	$12,150	67-77-67	211
BOB DICKSON	$12,150	69-74-68	211
BOB ZIMMERMAN	$12,150	68-73-70	211

BRICKYARD CROSSING CHAMPIONSHIP
Brickyard Crossing G.C., Indianapolis, Indiana
September 15-17, 1995

SIMON HOBDAY	$112,500	71-65-68	204
KERMIT ZARLEY	$46,200	68-70-67	205
ISAO AOKI	$46,200	69-69-67	205
HALE IRWIN	$46,200	70-66-69	205
LEE TREVINO	$46,200	67-69-69	205
BOB MURPHY	$46,200	67-68-70	205
BRUCE SUMMERHAYS	$25,500	69-73-64	206
RAY FLOYD	$25,500	65-72-69	206
JIM ALBUS	$20,250	70-67-70	207
TOM WARGO	$20,250	71-66-70	207

BANK ONE SENIOR CLASSIC
Kearney Hill Links, Lexington, Kentucky
September 22-24, 1995

GARY PLAYER	$90,000	72-75-64	211
JACK KIEFER	$52,800	72-73-68	213
HAROLD HENNING	$33,000	76-70-68	214
J.C. SNEAD	$33,000	72-72-70	214
GEORGE ARCHER	$33,000	73-70-71	214
ISAO AOKI	$33,000	72-71-71	214
DAVE EICHELBERGER	$18,300	72-75-68	215
JOHN PAUL CAIN	$18,300	71-74-71	215
TOM WARGO	$18,300	72-72-71	215
MIKE HILL	$18,300	71-72-72	215

VANTAGE CHAMPIONSHIP
Tanglewood Park, Clemmons, North Carolina
September 29-October 1, 1995

HALE IRWIN	$225,000	66-68-65	199
DAVE STOCKTON	$132,000	68-66-69	203
RAY FLOYD	$108,000	70-69-67	206
ROCKY THOMPSON	$64,800	69-69-69	207
ISAO AOKI	$64,800	68-70-69	207
JIM ALBUS	$64,800	71-66-70	207
GARY PLAYER	$64,800	70-67-70	207
MIKE HILL	$64,800	67-69-71	207
DALE DOUGLASS	$42,000	71-70-67	208
JACK KIEFER	$31,285	71-72-66	209

THE TRANSAMERICA
Silverado C.C., Napa, California
October 6-8, 1995

LEE TREVINO	$97,500	66-69-66	201
BRUCE SUMMERHAYS	$57,200	67-68-69	204
BEN SMITH	$46,800	66-69-70	205
BOB MURPHY	$39,000	66-72-68	206
JIM ALBUS	$26,867	69-69-69	207
WALT MORGAN	$26,867	69-67-71	207
JOHN BLAND	$26,867	65-70-72	207
JIMMY POWELL	$17,875	70-71-68	209
GRAHAM MARSH	$17,875	71-70-68	209
DAVE STOCKTON	$17,875	71-70-68	209
TOMMY AARON	$17,875	71-68-70	209

RALEY'S SENIOR GOLD RUSH
Rancho Murieta C.C., Rancho Murieta, California
October 13-15, 1995

DON BIES	$105,000	69-68-68	205
LEE TREVINO	$61,600	72-65-69	206
BOB MURPHY	$38,500	70-71-67	208
JIM COLBERT	$38,500	69-71-68	208
J.C. SNEAD	$38,500	68-71-69	208
GRAHAM MARSH	$38,500	68-71-69	208
BOB CHARLES	$23,800	69-72-68	209
JAY SIGEL	$23,800	70-71-68	209
RIVES MCBEE	$18,200	72-69-69	210
BUD ALLIN	$18,200	71-67-72	210
TOM WARGO	$18,200	70-68-72	210

RALPH'S SENIOR CLASSIC
Rancho Park G.C., Los Angeles, California
October 20-22, 1995

JOHN BLAND	$120,000	69-67-65	201
JIM COLBERT	$70,400	65-70-67	202
TERRY DILL	$52,800	67-69-67	203
DAVE STOCKTON	$52,800	68-67-68	203
AL GEIBERGER	$38,400	69-69-66	204
CHI CHI RODRIGUEZ	$30,400	68-68-69	205
LARRY GILBERT	$30,400	67-65-73	205
HALE IRWIN	$22,933	70-72-64	206
MILLER BARBER	$22,933	70-68-68	206
BUD ALLIN	$22,933	67-70-69	206

MAUI KAANAPALI SENIOR CLASSIC
Kaanapali Resort, Maui, Hawaii
October 26-29, 1995

*BOB CHARLES	$90,000	69-67-68	204
DAVE STOCKTON	$52,800	65-69-70	204
LEE TREVINO	$43,200	69-66-70	205
HAROLD HENNING	$29,600	67-70-69	206
GRAHAM MARSH	$29,600	68-69-69	206
MIKE MCCULLOUGH	$29,600	66-67-73	206
DON BIES	$21,600	69-70-68	207
BRUCE SUMMERHAYS	$16,500	65-71-72	208
TERRY DILL	$16,500	72-65-71	208
JERRY MCGEE	$16,500	70-67-71	208
BOB MURPHY	$16,500	68-68-72	208

EMERALD COAST CLASSIC
Moors G.C., Milton, Florida
November 3-5, 1995

*RAY FLOYD	$150,000	69-66	135
TOM WARGO	$88,000	71-64	135
BUD ALLIN	$66,000	73-63	136
BOB MURPHY	$66,000	72-64	136
ISAO AOKI	$48,000	68-69	137
JOHN BLAND	$38,000	70-68	138
BRUCE DEVLIN	$38,000	68-70	138
DAVE STOCKTON	$28,666	70-69	139
BOB DICKSON	$28,666	70-69	139
BRUCE SUMMERHAYS	$28,666	70-69	139

SENIOR TOUR CHAMPIONSHIP
The Dunes G. & B.C., Myrtle Beach, South Carolina
November 9-12, 1995

JIM COLBERT	$262,000	68-69-71-74	282
RAYMOND FLOYD	$151,000	71-74-69-69	283
TOM WARGO	$115,000	73-69-73-70	285
ROCKY THOMPSON	$115,000	71-75-68-71	285
DAVE STOCKTON	$83,900	74-71-69-72	286
DAVE EICHELBERGER	$69,800	73-72-70-72	287
BOB CHARLES	$62,800	76-70-69-73	288
MIKE HILL	$48,000	75-74-71-69	289
HALE IRWIN	$48,000	72-70-75-72	289
GEORGE ARCHER	$48,000	72-75-71-71	289
GRAHAM MARSH	$48,000	74-70-71-74	289

LPGA TOUR

HEALTHSOUTH PALM BEACH CLASSIC
Walt Disney World (Eagle Pines),
Orlando, Florida
January 20-22, 1995

PAT BRADLEY	$67,500	71-72-68	211
BETH DANIEL	$41,891	71-70-71	212
VAL SKINNER	$30,569	71-72-70	213
LAURA DAVIES	$23,776	73-69-72	214
JOAN PITCOCK	$19,247	74-71-70	215
MISSIE MCGEORGE	$15,850	72-70-74	216
MEG MALLON	$12,567	70-74-73	217
HELEN ALFREDSSON	$12,567	71-72-74	217
J. GALLAGHER-SMITH	$7,189	68-72-68	218
DAWN COE-JONES	$7,189	75-73-70	218
LAURI MERTEN	$7,189	73-75-70	218
KELLY ROBBINS	$7,189	75-72-71	218
BARB MUCHA	$7,189	73-74-71	218
STEPHANIE MAYNOR	$7,189	75-71-72	218
DALE EGGELING	$7,189	74-72-72	218
MARGARET PLATT	$7,189	74-70-74	218
PAT HURST	$7,189	74-70-74	218
JERILYN BRITZ	$7,189	73-70-75	218
GAIL GRAHAM	$7,189	70-73-75	218
C. JOHNSTON-FORBES	$7,189	70-72-76	218

CUP NOODLES HAWAIIAN LADIES OPEN
Ko Olina G.C.,
Ewa Beach, Hawaii
February 16-18, 1995

BARB THOMAS	$82,500	68-66-70	204
HIROMI KOBAYASHI	$39,208	72-71-66	209
KRIS TSCHETTER	$39,208	69-71-69	209
CHRIS JOHNSON	$39,208	69-68-72	209
BRANDIE BURTON	$17,324	68-74-69	211
COLLEEN WALKER	$17,324	70-70-71	211
DALE EGGELING	$17,324	69-71-71	211
MARIANNE MORRIS	$17,324	71-68-72	211
ANNIKA SORENSTAM	$17,324	69-70-72	211
DENISE BALDWIN	$10,240	69-73-70	212
MITSUYO HIRATA	$10,240	67-75-70	212
BETSY KING	$10,240	70-71-71	212
MICHELE REDMAN	$10,240	69-70-73	212

PING/WELCH'S CHAMPIONSHIP
Randolph North G.C.,
Tucson, Arizona
March 9-12, 1995

DOTTIE MOCHRIE	$67,500	70-68-72-68	278
CINDY RARICK	$36,230	72-74-67-70	283
ANNIKA SORENSTAM	$36,230	70-70-73-70	283
KIM WILLIAMS	$23,776	67-74-75-68	284
ROSIE JONES	$17,548	74-72-70-69	285
AMY ALCOTT	$17,548	70-69-73-73	285
KRIS TSCHETTER	$10,778	74-73-71-69	286
K. PETERSON-PARKER	$10,778	73-73-71-69	286
BARB THOMAS	$10,778	69-74-74-69	286
JULI INKSTER	$10,778	71-71-72-72	286
CAROLINE PIERCE	$10,778	75-67-70-74	286

PINEWILD WOMEN'S CHAMPIONSHIP
Pinewild C.C.,
Pinesurst, North Carolina
March 14-16, 1995

*ROSIE JONES	$97,500	72-70-69	211
DOTTIE MOCHRIE	$60,510	72-69-70	211
MICHELLE MCGANN	$32,299	75-70-67	212
NANCI BOWEN	$32,299	71-72-69	212
ANNIKA SORENSTAM	$32,299	73-69-70	212
BRANDIE BURTON	$32,299	70-71-71	212
HELEN ALFREDSSON	$17,226	71-75-67	213
CARIN HJALMARSSON	$17,226	72-73-68	213
JOAN PITCOCK	$17,226	75-67-71	213
PAGE DUNLAP	$10,999	72-72-70	214
MEG MALLON	$10,999	72-71-71	214
JULI INKSTER	$10,999	70-73-71	214
SALLY LITTLE	$10,999	74-68-72	214
CAROLINE PIERCE	$10,999	69-72-73	214
LISELOTTE NEUMANN	$10,999	70-69-75	214
NICOLE JERAY	$10,999	71-67-76	214

STANDARD REGISTER PING
Moon Valley C.C.,
Phoenix, Arizona
March 16-19, 1995

LAURA DAVIES	$105,000	69-68-70-73	280
BETH DANIEL	$65,165	69-69-71-72	281
K. PETERSON PARKER	$38,159	71-70-73-69	283
ROSIE JONES	$38,159	73-70-70-70	283
JOAN PITCOCK	$38,159	70-70-73-70	283
WENDY WARD	amateur	69-71-71-72	283
MITZI EDGE	$24,656	71-73-68-72	284
ANNIKA SORENSTAM	$19,549	72-71-73-69	285
JANE GEDDES	$19,549	73-75-67-70	285
M. FIGUERAS DOTTI	$14,265	70-76-70-70	286
MARIANNE MORRIS	$14,265	71-72-71-72	286
MICHELE REDMAN	$14,265	71-69-73-73	286
BETSY KING	$14,265	73-71-68-74	286

CHICK FIL-A CHAMPIONSHIP
Eagle's Landing C.C.,
Stockbridge, Georgia
March 21-23, 1995

LAURA DAVIES	$75,000	67-67-67	201
KELLY ROBBINS	$46,546	67-72-66	205
KRISTI ALBERS	$33,966	67-69-70	206
SHERRI TURNER	$21,805	73-71-63	207
VICKI FERGON	$21,805	69-69-69	207
DOTTIE MOCHRIE	$21,805	69-66-72	207
LISELOTTE NEUMANN	$12,579	72-70-67	209
MICHELLE MCGANN	$12,579	70-72-67	209
BRANDIE BURTON	$12,579	72-69-68	209
KAREN WEISS	$12,579	69-72-68	209

NABISCO DINAH SHORE
Mission Hills C.C.,
Rancho Mirage, California
March 23-26, 1995

NANCI BOWEN	$127,500	69-75-71-70	285
SUSIE REDMAN	$79,129	75-70-70-71	286
BRANDIE BURTON	$42,237	76-71-71-69	287
SHERRIE TURNER	$42,237	72-74-71-70	287
LAURA DAVIES	$42,237	75-69-70-73	287
NANCY LOPEZ	$42,237	74-71-68-74	287
COLLEEN WALKER	$23,738	74-73-69-72	288
TAMMIE GREEN	$23,738	71-70-70-77	288
DAWN COE-JONES	$20,103	71-75-71-72	289
CAROLINE PIERCE	$17,964	77-71-73-69	290
BETSY KING	$14,200	77-75-71-68	291
DOTTIE MOCHRIE	$14,200	78-73-70-70	291
BARB MUCHA	$14,200	74-74-72-71	291
SANDRA PALMER	$14,200	72-73-74-72	291
DEBBIE MASSEY	$14,200	71-75-72-73	291

For a complete summary of all players making the cut at the Dinah Shore, please refer to "1995 Major Championships"

SPRINT CHALLENGE
Indigo Lakes G. & T. Resort,
Daytona Beach, Florida
April 27-30, 1995

VAL SKINNER	$180,000	71-65-70-67	273
KRIS TSCHETTER	$111,711	66-67-72-70	275
MICHELLE MCGANN	$81,519	70-65-72-69	276
MEG MALLON	$57,365	69-69-70-69	277
DOTTIE MOCHRIE	$57,365	66-72-69-70	277
DAWN COE-JONES	$36,431	67-68-75-68	278
COLLEEN WALKER	$36,431	66-72-70-70	278
BETH DANIEL	$36,431	72-67-68-71	278
TRISH JOHNSON	$26,871	73-70-70-66	279
KELLY ROBBINS	$26,871	68-75-70-66	279

SARA LEE CLASSIC
Hermitage G.C., Old Hickory, Tennessee
May 5-7, 1995

MICHELLE MCGANN	$78,750	69-65-68	202
DOTTIE MOCHRIE	$37,425	67-71-65	203
KELLY ROBBINS	$37,425	68-67-68	203
LAURA DAVIES	$37,425	64-69-70	203
JANE GEDDES	$22,455	69-70-66	205
HELEN ALFREDSSON	$17,309	70-68-68	206
JENNY LIDBACK	$17,309	69-68-69	206
COLLEEN WALKER	$13,737	67-69-71	207
BETSY KING	$10,699	72-71-65	208
BARB THOMAS	$10,699	71-70-67	208
M. FIGUERAS-DOTTI	$10,699	70-70-68	208
CAROLINE PIERCE	$10,699	68-69-71	208

MCDONALD'S LPGA CHAMPIONSHIP
Du Pont C.C., Wilmington, Delaware
May 11-14, 1995

KELLY ROBBINS	$180,000	66-68-72-68	274
LAURA DAVIES	$111,711	68-68-69-70	275
JULIE LARSEN	$65,416	71-68-70-71	280
MARIANNE MORRIS	$65,416	67-71-70-72	280
PATTY SHEEHAN	$65,416	67-68-72-73	280
BARB THOMAS	$38,947	70-66-73-72	281
DOTTIE MOCHRIE	$38,947	67-70-71-73	281
PAT BRADLEY	$29,890	71-70-70-71	282
TAMMIE GREEN	$29,890	69-72-70-71	282
ANNIKA SORENSTAM	$25,362	71-71-72-69	283

For a complete summary of all players making the cut at the McDonald's LPGA, please refer to "1995 Major Championships."

STAR BANK LPGA CHAMPIONSHIP
C.C. of the North, Beaver Creek, Ohio
May 19-21, 1995

CHRIS JOHNSON	$75,000	68-75-67	210
JULI INKSTER	$46,546	69-68-74	211
MICHELE REDMAN	$33,966	72-70-70	212
DAWN COE-JONES	$26,418	71-75-67	213
PATTY SHEEHAN	$19,499	70-73-71	214
PAT HURST	$19,499	70-70-74	214
JANE GEDDES	$13,250	75-71-69	215
ROSIE JONES	$13,250	71-74-70	215
TAMMIE GREEN	$13,250	71-71-73	215
TRACY KERDYK	$10,064	75-70-71	216
MARDI LUNN	$10,064	70-73-73	216

LPGA CORNING CLASSIC
Corning C.C., Corning, New York
May 25-28, 1995

ALISON NICHOLAS	$82,500	70-67-66-72	275
D. AMMACCAPANE	$44,282	72-67-70-69	278
BARB MUCHA	$44,282	71-69-68-70	278
PAT BRADLEY	$29,060	67-68-70-74	279
MEG MALLON	$21,448	74-70-66-71	281
ROSIE JONES	$21,448	72-66-70-73	281
ANNIKA SORENSTAM	$15,359	70-69-72-71	282
ALICE RITZMAN	$15,359	75-67-67-73	282
LAURI MERTEN	$12,316	71-71-70-71	283
AMY FRUHWIRTH	$12,316	73-68-71-71	283

OLDSMOBILE CLASSIC
Walnut Hills C.C., East Lansing, Michigan
June 1-4, 1995

DALE EGGELING	$90,000	63-69-71-71	274
MEG MALLON	$42,772	71-69-69-67	276
ANNIKA SORENSTAM	$42,772	73-65-70-68	276
ELAINE CROSBY	$42,772	67-68-73-68	276
MICHELLE MCGANN	$23,398	70-69-68-70	277
K. PETERSON-PARKER	$23,398	68-69-70-70	277
D. AMMACCAPANE	$15,901	69-68-71-70	278
KRIS TSCHETTER	$15,901	69-66-72-71	278
JOAN PITCOCK	$15,901	66-69-70-73	278
MICHELE REDMAN	$12,111	69-68-73-69	279
HELEN ALFREDSSON	$12,111	65-74-69-71	279

EDINA REALTY CLASSIC
Edinburgh USA G.C.,
Brooklyn Park, Minnesota
June 9-11, 1995

JULIE LARSEN	$75,000	66-68-71	205
LEIGH ANN MILLS	$46,546	69-69-68	206
NANCY LOPEZ	$24,845	75-67-67	209
LISELOTTE NEUMANN	$24,845	70-71-68	209
MICHELLE MCGANN	$24,845	70-69-70	209
PAT BRADLEY	$24,845	67-70-72	209
BETSY KING	$13,963	70-72-68	210
CINDY RARICK	$13,963	66-71-73	210
AMY FRUHWIRTH	$11,196	69-71-71	211
SHERRI STEINHAUER	$11,196	70-69-72	211

ROCHESTER INTERNATIONAL
Locust Hill C.C.,
Pittsford, New York
June 15-18, 1995

PATTY SHEEHAN	$82,500	73-66-69-70	278

Rochester International, continued

SHERRI STEINHAUER	$51,201	70-67-72-73	282
PAM WRIGHT	$37,363	75-67-74-67	283
HELEN ALFREDSSON	$29,060	69-69-72-75	285
JANE GEDDES	$18,404	69-75-72-70	286
CAROLINE PIERCE	$18,404	74-72-69-71	286
DALE EGGELING	$18,404	69-72-71-74	286
ALICE RITZMAN	$18,404	70-73-67-76	286
MICHELLE ESTILL	$12,316	74-73-68-72	287
JOANNE CARNER	$12,316	68-68-78-73	287

SHOPRITE LPGA CLASSIC
Greate Bay C.C., Somers Point, New Jersey
June 23-25, 1995

BETSY KING	**$97,500**	**66-71-67**	**204**
ROSIE JONES	$52,333	68-71-67	206
BETH DANIEL	$52,333	68-70-68	206
VAL SKINNER	$28,346	72-68-67	207
TAMMIE GREEN	$28,346	69-70-68	207
MICHELE REDMAN	$28,346	68-68-71	207
M. SPENCER-DEVLIN	$17,226	71-67-70	208
DOTTIE MOCHRIE	$17,226	70-68-70	208
BRANDIE BURTON	$17,226	70-67-71	208
HELEN ALFREDSSON	$12,118	75-70-65	210
LISELOTTE NEUMANN	$12,118	73-68-69	210
ALICIA DIBOS	$12,118	71-70-69	210
MICHELLE ESTILL	$12,118	67-69-74	210

YOUNGSTOWN-WARREN LPGA CLASSIC
Avalon Lakes G.C.,
Warren, OH
June 30-July 2, 1995

*MICHELLE MCGANN	$82,500	65-70-70	205
K. PETERSON-PARKER	$51,201	65-69-71	205
NANCY LOPEZ	$37,363	71-66-69	206
TAMMIE GREEN	$29,060	72-68-67	207
MICHELLE BELL	$23,524	70-69-69	208
KELLY ROBBINS	$19,373	69-70-70	209
CATHY MOCKETT	$15,359	70-69-71	210
VAL SKINNER	$15,359	69-70-71	210
ROSIE JONES	$12,316	66-77-68	211
M. SPENCER-DEVLIN	$12,316	69-69-73	211

JAMIE FARR TOLEDO CLASSIC
Highland Meadows G.C.,
Sylvania, Ohio
July 7-9, 1995

KATHRYN MARSHALL	**$75,000**	**67-71-67**	**205**
SHERRI STEINHAUER	$46,546	69-70-67	206
PAM WRIGHT	$33,966	71-66-70	207
PAT BRADLEY	$17,528	71-70-67	208
KELLY ROBBINS	$17,528	69-71-69	208
DEB RICHARD	$17,528	72-67-69	208
BETH DANIEL	$17,528	71-68-69	208
BETSY KING	$17,528	68-71-69	208
BRANDIE BURTON	$17,528	68-71-69	208
LAURA BROWN	$9,309	70-73-66	209
VICKI FERGON	$9,309	73-69-67	209
LENORE RITTENHOUSE	$9,309	68-72-69	209
M. SPENCER-DEVLIN	$9,309	67-71-71	209

U.S. WOMEN'S OPEN
The Broadmoor G.C. (East),
Colorado Springs, Colorado
July 13-16, 1995

ANNIKA SORENSTAM	**$175,000**	**67-71-72-68**	**278**
MEG MALLON	$103,500	70-69-66-74	279
PAT BRADLEY	$56,238	67-71-72-67	280
BETSY KING	$56,238	72-69-72-70	280
LETA LINDLEY	$35,285	70-68-74-69	281
ROSIE JONES	$35,285	69-70-70-72	281
TAMMIE GREEN	$28,009	68-70-75-69	282
DAWN COE-JONES	$28,009	68-70-74-70	282
JULIE LARSEN	$28,009	68-71-68-75	282
MARIANNE MORRIS	$22,190	73-73-70-67	283
PATTY SHEEHAN	$22,190	70-73-71-69	283
VAL SKINNER	$22,190	68-72-72-71	283

For a complete summary of all players making the cut at the U.S. Women's Open, please refer to "1995 Major Championships"

JAL BIG APPLE CLASSIC
Wykagyl C.C.,
New Rochelle, New York
July 20-23, 1995

TRACY KERDYK	**$105,000**	**74-66-66-67**	**273**

JAL Big Apple Classic, continued

ELAINE CROSBY	$44,910	72-71-65-69	277
CAROLINE PIERCE	$44,910	70-68-70-69	277
MICHELLE MCGANN	$44,910	66-68-74-69	277
CARIN HJALMARSSON	$44,910	69-71-65-72	277
KRIS TSCHETTER	$24,656	70-70-69-70	279
PAM WRIGHT	$19,549	70-71-70-69	280
M.B. ZIMMERMAN	$19,549	69-70-71-70	280
STEFANIE CROCE	$16,555	74-69-68-70	281
AMY ALCOTT	$14,794	68-72-73-69	282

PING/WELCH'S CHAMPIONSHIP
Blue Hill C.C.,
Canton, Massachusetts
August 10-14, 1995

BETH DANIEL	$67,500	65-68-69-69	271
MEG MALLON	$36,230	68-68-70-68	274
COLLEEN WALKER	$36,230	67-68-67-72	274
BETSY KING	$21,511	69-72-68-66	275
JANE GEDDES	$21,511	65-71-71-68	275
MAGGIE WILL	$15,850	70-69-68-69	276
ELAINE CROSBY	$13,360	70-70-73-66	279
MISSIE MCGEORGE	$9,691	72-70-70-68	280
DOTTIE MOCHRIE	$9,691	72-71-68-69	280
JILL BRILES-HINTON	$9,691	72-69-70-69	280
SHARON BARRETT	$9,691	70-68-73-69	280
JULIE LARSEN	$9,691	66-72-72-70	280

MCCALL'S LPGA CLASSIC AT STRATTON MOUNTAIN
Stratton Mountain C.C.,
Stratton Mountain, Vermont
August 3-6, 1995

DOTTIE MOCHRIE	$75,000	69-67-68	204
KELLY ROBBINS	$46,546	70-69-68	207
JANE GEDDES	$33,966	71-68-69	208
C. JOHNSTON-FORBES	$20,065	70-70-69	209
KRIS TSCHETTER	$20,065	71-68-70	209
AMY FRUHWIRTH	$20,065	71-66-72	209
PAT BRADLEY	$20,065	69-67-73	209
MISSIE MCGEORGE	$11,825	70-71-69	210
VICKI FERGON	$11,825	70-68-72	210
ROSIE JONES	$11,825	69-69-72	210

WEETABIX WOMEN'S BRITISH OPEN
Woburn G. & C.C., Milton Keynes, England
August 17-20, 1995

KARRIE WEBB	$92,400	69-70-69-70	278
JILL MCGILL	$46,200	71-73-71-69	284
ANNIKA SORENSTAM	$46,200	70-72-71-71	284
MISSIE BERTEOTTI	$22,073	73-71-71-70	285
CAROLINE PIERCE	$22,073	70-70-72-73	285
VAL SKINNER	$22,073	74-68-67-76	285
SUZANNE STRUDWICK	$14,630	73-68-71-74	286
M-L. DE LORENZI	$10,683	68-74-73-73	288
NANCY LOPEZ	$10,683	71-73-70-74	288
WENDY DOOLAN	$10,683	73-71-70-74	288
LISELOTTE NEUMANN	$10,683	67-74-71-76	288

du MAURIER LTD. CLASSIC
Beaconsfield G.C.,
Pointe-Clare, Quebec, Canada
August 24-27, 1995

JENNY LIDBACK	$150,000	71-69-68-72	280
LISELOTTE NEUMAN	$93,093	71-66-72-72	281
JULI INKSTER	$67,933	72-71-70-70	283
TAMMIE GREEN	$52,837	75-71-68-70	284
BETSY KING	$38,998	76-70-67-72	285
JANE GEDDES	$38,998	71-73-69-72	285
MICHELLE ESTILL	$27,928	73-77-69-67	286
L. RINKER-GRAHAM	$27,928	71-71-70-74	286
HELEN ALFREDSSON	$21,314	76-70-70-71	287
D. AMMACCAPANE	$21,314	76-71-68-72	287
HOLLIS STACEY	$21,314	73-73-69-72	287

For a complete summary of all players making the cut at the duMaurier Classic, please refer to "1995 Major Championships"

STATE FARM RAIL CLASSIC
Rail G.C., Springfield, Illinois
September 2-4, 1995

*M.B. ZIMMERMAN	$82,500	72-69-65	206
EMILEE KLEIN	$51,201	67-67-72	206
COLLEEN WALKER	$29,982	71-68-68	207
LETA LINDLEY	$29,982	71-66-70	207
BETSY KING	$29,982	67-67-73	207

Stae Farm Rail Classic, continued

BETH DANIEL	$19,373	69-67-72	208
MICHELLE MCGANN	$16,328	72-68-69	209
NANCY LOPEZ	$14,391	71-69-70	210
STEPHANIE MAYNOR	$12,316	71-71-69	211
MEG MALLON	$12,316	68-71-72	211

PING-CELLULAR ONE GOLF CHAMPIONSHIP
Columbia Edgewater C.C.,
Portland, Oregon
September 8-10, 1995

ALISON NICHOLAS	$75,000	66-73-68	207
KELLY ROBBINS	$46,546	73-67-70	210
VICKI GOETZE	$33,966	73-68-70	211
BETSY KING	$23,902	74-71-67	212
ROSIE JONES	$23,902	68-73-71	212
TRACY HANSON	$15,179	72-71-70	213
LAURIE BROWER	$15,179	72-69-72	213
PATTY SHEEHAN	$15,179	70-69-74	213
LAURA DAVIES	$9,812	75-73-66	214
JOAN PITCOCK	$9,812	70-75-69	214
DALE EGGELING	$9,812	72-71-71	214
HIROMI KOBAYASHI	$9,812	70-73-71	214
ALICIA DIBOS	$9,812	70-70-74	214

SAFECO CLASSIC
Meridian Valley C.C.,
Kent, Washington
September 14-17, 1995

PATTY SHEEHAN	$75,000	68-65-70-71	274
EMILEE KLEIN	$46,546	73-65-71-67	276
ALISON NICHOLAS	$33,966	68-70-70-69	277
LISELOTTE NEUMANN	$26,418	68-69-68-74	279
JANE GEDDES	$21,386	68-72-67-73	280
ANNIKA SORENSTAM	$15,179	76-70-67-68	281
MOIRA DUNN	$15,179	72-74-66-69	281
JULIE LARSEN	$15,179	70-70-69-72	281
ROSIE JONES	$10,651	72-70-72-68	282
PAM WRIGHT	$10,651	73-70-70-69	282
MITZI EDGE	$10,651	67-70-71-74	282

HEARTLAND CLASSIC
Forest Hills C.C., St. Louis, Missouri
September 21-24, 1995

ANNIKA SORENSTAM	$78,750	69-67-70-72	278
JAN STEPHENSON	$48,873	71-76-69-72	288
DALE EGGELING	$35,664	74-74-71-70	289
MICHELE REDMAN	$22,895	73-70-74-73	290
TRACY HANSON	$22,895	68-75-74-73	290
PAT HURST	$22,895	71-74-71-74	290
MITZI EDGE	$15,586	73-72-71-75	291
LETA LINDLEY	$11,821	74-77-69-72	292
NANCY RAMSBOTTOM	$11,821	72-76-72-72	292
MARDI LUNN	$11,821	73-72-75-72	292
TINA BARRETT	$11,821	75-70-73-74	292

FIELDCREST CANNON CLASSIC
Peninsula C.C., Charlotte, North Carolina
September 28-October 1, 1995

GAIL GRAHAM	$75,000	67-68-69-69	273
TAMMIE GREEN	$46,546	67-71-67-70	275
JULI INKSTER	$27,256	67-71-70-69	277
KAREN LUNN	$27,256	70-67-71-69	277
HIROMI KOBAYASHI	$27,256	65-71-69-72	277
HELEN ALFREDSSON	$17,612	66-73-72-68	279
JANE GEDDES	$12,579	72-68-72-68	280
MOIRA DUNN	$12,579	72-69-70-69	280
NANCY LOPEZ	$12,579	68-70-71-71	280
STEPHANIE FARWIG	$12,579	71-72-65-72	280

WORLD CHAMPIONSHIP OF WOMEN'S GOLF
Paradise G.C., Cheju Island, South Korea
October 12-15, 1995

*ANNIKA SORENSTAM	$117,500	72-69-71-70	282
LAURA DAVIES	$65,000	67-71-71-73	282
DOTTIE MOCHRIE	$40,000	72-68-72-72	284
PAT BRADLEY	$30,000	68-70-76-72	286
MEG MALLON	$22,500	73-72-71-71	287
ROSIE JONES	$22,500	67-73-72-75	287
VAL SKINNER	$18,000	70-69-77-72	288

World Championship of Women's Golf, continued

BETSY KING	$17,000	68-70-77-74	289
TAMMIE GREEN	$16,000	69-72-74-75	290
JENNY LIDBACK	$15,000	71-71-74-75	291

NICHIREI CHAMPIONSHIP
Tsukuba C.C., Ibaraki-Ken, Japan
October 27-29, 1995

	USLPGA	JLPGA
FIRST ROUND:	2	6
SECOND ROUND:	3	6
THRID ROUND:	13	4
FINAL RESULTS	19	17

SAMSUNG CHAMPIONSHIP OF WOMEN'S GOLF
Paradise G.C., Cheju Island, South Korea
October 12-15, 1995

*ANNIKA SORENSTAM	$117,500	72-69-71-70	282
LAURA DAVIES	$65,000	67-71-71-73	282
DOTTIE MOCHRIE	$40,000	72-68-72-72	284
PAT BRADLEY	$30,000	68-70-76-72	286
MEG MALLON	$22,500	73-72-71-71	287
ROSIE JONES	$22,500	67-73-72-75	287
VAL SKINNER	$18,000	70-69-77-72	288
BETSY KING	$17,000	68-70-77-74	289
TAMMIE GREEN	$16,000	69-72-74-75	290
JENNY LIDBACK	$15,000	71-71-74-75	291

THE JCPENNEY CLASSIC
Innisbrook Hilton, Tarpon Springs, Florida
November 30-December 3, 1995

D. LOVE III/B. DANIEL	$162,500	66-65-63-63	257
R. GAMEZ/H. ALFREDSSON	$79,000	63-67-65-64	259
J. PARNEVIK/A. SORENSTAM	$52,000	67-66-64-63	260
M. MCCUMBER/L. DAVIES	$39,500	63-65-67-67	262
J. DELSING/V. SKINNER	$29,750	62-67-65-69	263
K. PERRY/M. MCCANN	$22,755	69-63-68-64	264
M. BRADLEY/K. PETERSON-PARKER	$22,755	63-68-64-69	264
B. MAYFAIR/B. BURTON	$14,406	69-60-64-64	265
J. HUSTON/L. NEUMANN	$14,406	66-68-64-67	265
B. ANDRADE/K. TSCHETTER	$14,406	66-65-65-69	265

NIKE TOUR

SAN JOSE OPEN
San Jose, California, February 23-26, 1995

JOHN MAGINNES	277	$36,000

EMPIRE OPEN
Moreno Valley, CA, March 2-5, 1995

JEFF BREHAUT	204	$36,000

MONTERREY OPEN
Monterrey, Mexico, March 16-19, 1995

STUART APPLEBY	273	$40,500

LOUISIANA OPEN
Broussard, LA, March 23-26, 1995

STAN UTLEY	268	$36,000

PENSACOLA CLASSIC
Milton, FL, March 30-April 2, 1995

CLARENCE ROSE	201	$36,000

MISSISSIPPI GULF COAST CLASSIC
Gulfport, MS, April 6-9, 1995

ALLEN DOYLE	273	$36,000

TALLAHASSEE OPEN
Tallahassee, FL, April 13-16, 1995

BILL MURCHISON	276	$36,000

SHREVEPORT OPEN
Shreveport, LA, April 20-23, 1995

BRAD FABEL	131	$36,000

ALABAMA CLASSIC
Huntsville, AL, April 27-30, 1995

JERRY KELLY	273	$36,000

SOUTH CAROLINA CLASSIC
Florence, SC, May 4-7, 1995
JERRY FOLTZ 279 $36,000

CENTRAL GEORGIA OPEN
Macon, GA, May 11-14, 1995
MATT PETERSON 268 $36,000

KNOXVILLE OPEN
Knoxville, TN, May 18-21, 1995
THOMAS SCHERRER 275 $36,000

GREATER GREENVILLE CLASSIC
Greenville, SC, May 25-28, 1995
DAVID TOMS 267 $36,000

DOMINION OPEN
Glen Allen, VA, June 1-4, 1995
HUGH ROYER III 270 $36,000

MIAMI VALLEY OPEN
Springboro, OH, June 8-11, 1995
STAN UTLEY 264 $36,000

CLEVELAND OPEN
Concord, OH, June 15-18, 1995
KARL ZOLLER 274 $36,000

CAROLINA CLASSIC
Cary, NC, June 22-25, 1995
MICHAEL CHRISTIE 266 $36,000

PHILADELPHIA OPEN
Huntingdon Valley, PA, June 29-July 2, 1995
SEAN MURPHY 267 $36,000

BUFFALO OPEN
Hamburg, NY, July 13-16, 1995
JERRY KELLY 274 $36,000

GATEWAY CLASSIC
St. Louis, MO, July 20-23, 1995
CHRIS SMITH 203 $36,000

WICHITA OPEN
Wichita, KS, July 27-30, 1995
DAVID TOMS 269 $36,000

DAKOTA DUNES OPEN
Dakota Dunes, SD, August 3-6, 1995
CHRIS SMITH 272 $36,000

OZARKS OPEN
Springfield, MO, August 10-13, 1995
MIKE SCHUCHART 271 $36,000

PERMIAN BASIN OPEN
Odessa, TX, August 17-20, 1995
HUGH ROYER III 275 $36,000

TEXARKANA OPEN
Texarkana, AR, August 24-27, 1995
ALLEN DOYLE 269 $36,000

NIKE TOUR CHAMPIONSHIP
Roswell, GA, October 19-22, 1995

*ALLEN DOYLE	$45,000	72-68-71-71	283
JOHN MAGINNES	$28,375	68-73-73-69	283
BRAD FABEL	$21,250	69-74-73-69	285
SEAN MURPHY	$16,250	69-73-72-72	286
OLIN BROWNE	$12,500	72-74-73-68	287
JOE DURANT	$12,500	78-66-71-72	287

EUROPEAN TOUR

DUBAI DESERT CLASSIC
Emirates G.C., Dubai, United Arab Emirates
January 27-30, 1995
FRED COUPLES   279

CANARY ISLANDS OPEN
Maspalomas, Gran Canria,
February 9-12, 1995
JARMO SANDELIN   282

TURESPANA OPEN MEDITERRIANIA
Villa Martin G.C., Torrevieja, Spain
February 23-26, 1995
ROBERT KARLSSON   276

PEUGEOT OPEN DE ESPAÑA
Madrid, Spain, February 23-26, 1995
SEVE BALLESTEROS   274   £91,660

CATALAN OPEN
Gerona, Spain, April 14-17, 1995
PHILIP WALTON   281   £50,000

VOLVO CHAMPIONSHIP
Wentworth, England, May 25-28, 1995
BERNHARD LANGER   279   £150,000

MURPHY'S ENGLISH OPEN
Coventry, England, June 1-4, 1995
PHILIP WALTON   279 $173,328

EUROPEAN TOURNAMENT CHAMPIONSHIP
Hamburg, Germany, June 8-11, 1995
BERNHARD LANGER   282 $179,000

JERSEY OPEN
La Moye, St. Brelade, England, June 22-25, 1995
ANDREW OLDCORN   273   £50,000

BMW INTERNATIONAL
Munich, Germany, June 29-July 2, 1995
FRANK NOBILO   272   £91,660

MURPHY'S IRISH OPEN
Thomastown, Ireland, July 6-9, 1995
SAM TORRANCE   277   £111,107

SCOTTISH OPEN
Carnoustie, Scotland, July 12-15, 1995
WAYNE RILEY   276   £91,660

BRITISH OPEN
St. Andrews, Scotland, July 20-23, 1995

*JOHN DALY	$200,000	67-71-73-71	282
COSTANTINO ROCCA	$160,000	69-70-70-73	282
STEVEN BOTTOMLEY	$105,065	70-72-72-69	283
MARK BROOKS	$105,065	70-69-73-71	283
MICHAEL CAMPBELL	$105,065	71-71-65-76	283
VIJAY SINGH	$64,800	68-72-73-71	284
STEVE ELKINGTON	$64,800	72-69-69-74	284
BOB ESTES	$53,333	72-70-71-72	285
COREY PAVIN	$53,333	69-70-72-74	285
MARK JAMES	$53,333	72-75-68-70	285
PAYNE STEWART	$41,600	72-68-75-71	286
BRETT OGLE	$41,600	73-69-71-73	286
SAM TORRANCE	$41,600	71-70-71-74	286
ERNIE ELS	$41,600	71-68-72-75	286
GREG NORMAN	$29,120	71-74-72-70	287
ROBERT ALLENBY	$29,120	71-74-71-71	287
BEN CRENSHAW	$29,120	67-72-76-72	287
PER-ULRIK JOHANSSON	$29,120	69-78-68-72	287
BRAD FAXON	$29,120	71-67-75-74	287
PETER MITCHELL	$21,600	73-74-71-70	288
DAVID DUVAL	$21,600	71-75-70-72	288
ANDREW COLTART	$21,600	70-74-71-73	288
BARRY LANE	$21,600	72-73-68-75	288

For a complete summary of all players making the cut at the British Open, please refer to "1995 Major Championships"

HEINEKEN DUTCH OPEN
Amsterdam, Holland,
July 27-30, 1995
SCOTT HOCH 269 £108,330

SCANDANAVIAN MASTERS
Malmo, Sweden, August 2-5, 1995
JESPER PARNEVIK 270 £91,660

AUSTRIAN OPEN
Litschau, Austria, August 9-12, 1995
ALEXANDER CEJKA 267 £91,660

CZECH REPUBLIC OPEN
Marianske Lazne, August 16-19, 1995
PETER TERAVAINEN 268 £91,660

GERMAN OPEN
Stuttgart, Germany, August 23-26, 1995
COLIN MONTGOMERIE 268 £91,660

EUROPEAN MASTERS
Crans-sur-Serre, Switzerland,
August 30-September 2, 1995
MATHIAS GRONBERG 270 £100,000

TROPHEE LANCOME
Paris, France, September 6-9, 1995
COLIN MONTGOMERIE 269 £100,000

BRITISH MASTERS
Northampton, England,
September 14-17, 1995
SAM TORRANCE 270 £108,330

EUROPEAN OPEN
Dublin, Ireland,
September 27-October 1, 1995
BERNHARD LANGER 280 £100,000

GERMAN MASTERS
Berlin, Germany, October 5-8, 1995
ANDERS FORSBRAND 264 £91,660

WORLD MATCH PLAY
Wentworth, England, October 12-15, 1995
ERNIE ELS DEF. STEVE ELKINGTON, 2 & 1

VOLVO EUROPEAN MASTERS
Sotogrande, Spain, October 26-29, 1995
ALEXANDER CEJKA 282 £125,000

AUSTRALIAN TOUR

FOODLINK QUEENSLAND OPEN
Brisbane, Queensland, Australia
October 20-23, 1994
LUCAS PARSONS 282 $36,000

EPSON SINGAPORE OPEN
Singapore, October 27-30, 1994
KYI HLA HAN 275 $98,287

ALFRED DUNHILL MASTERS
Bali, Indonesia, November 3-6, 1994
JACK KAY 277 $83,918

VICTORIAN OPEN
Melbourne, Victoria, Australia
November 10-13, 1994
PATRICK BURKE 278 $36,000

AUSTRALIAN PGA CHAMPIONSHIP
Sydney, New South Wales, Australia
November 17-20, 1994
ANDREW COLTART 281 $36,000

AUSTRALIAN OPEN
Sydney, New South Wales, Australia
November 24-27, 1994
ROBERT ALLENBY   280 $153,000

GREG NORMAN'S HOLDEN CLASSIC
Melbourne, Victoria, Australia
December 1-4, 1994
ANTHONY GILLIGAN   274 $126,000

AIR NEW ZEALAND SHELL OPEN
Aukland, New Zealand,
December 8-11, 1994
SHANE ROBINSON   274 $43,929

SCHWEPPES COOLUM CLASSIC
Coolum, Queensland, Australia,
December 15-18, 1994
MICHAEL CLAYTON   277 $36,000

NEW ZEALAND OPEN
Aukland, New Zealand,
January 6-9, 1995
LUCAS PARSONS   282 $42,827

FORD OPEN
Sydney, New South Wales, Australia
January 13-16, 1995
TIM ELLIOTT   275 $36,000

OPTUS PLAYERS CHAMPIONSHIP
Kingston Heath, Victoria, Australia
January 20-23, 1995
TIM ELLIOTT   282 $63,000

HEINEKEN CLASSIC
Gold Coast, Queensland, Australia
January 27-30, 1995
ROBERT ALLENBY   278 $72,000

CANON CHALLENGE
Sydney, New South Wales, Australia
February 24-27, 1995
CRAIG PARRY   275 $63,000

VICTORIAN OPEN
Melbourne, Victoria, Australia
November 16-19, 1995
STEPHEN LEANEY   283 $36,000

HEINEKEN AUSTRALIAN OPEN
Melbourne, Victoria, Australia
November 23-26, 1995
GREG NORMAN   278 $153,000

ALFRED DUNHILL MASTERS
Esmerelda, Jakarta, Indonesia
December 15-18, 1994
MICHAEL CAMPBELL   267 $95,541

SCHWEPPES COOLUM CLASSIC
Coolum, Queensland, Australia,
December 14-17, 1995
SHANE ROBINSON   278 $38,000

CANADIAN TOUR

ALBERTA OPEN
Ponoka, Alberta, Canada
June 15-18, 1995
IAN HUTCHINGS   268 $18,000

B.C. TEL PACIFIC OPEN
Richmond, British Columbia, Canada
June 22-25, 1995
NICK GOETZE   270 $22,500

CANADIAN MASTERS
Lancaster, Ontario, Canada
June 29-July 2, 1995
SCOTT DUNLAP   268 $36,000

EXPORT "A" INC. ONTARIO OPEN
London, Ontario, Canada
July 6-9, 1995
RAY FREEMAN   273 $22,500

INFINTI TOURNAMENT PLAYERS' CHAMPIONSHIP
Toronto, Ontario, Canada
July 13-16, 1995
GUY HILL   266 $22,500

KLONDIKE DAYS CLASSIC
Edmonton, Alberta, Canada
July 20-23, 1995
RAY FREMAN   265 $18,000

MONTCLAIR PEI CLASSIC
Lakeside, Prince Edward Island, Canada
July 27-30, 1995
JIM RUTLEDGE   280 $22,500

MORNINGSIDE CLASSIC
August 3-6, 1995
JEFF BLOOM   273 $18,000

PAYLESS OPEN
Vancouver, British Columbia, Canada
August 10-13, 1995
NORM JARVIS   267 $18,000

TRAFALGAR CPGA CHAMPIONSHIP
Manotick, Ontario, Canada
August 17-20, 1995
TREVOR DODDS   276 $22,500

XEROX MANITOBA OPEN
Winnipeg, Manitoba, Canada
August 24-27, 1995
TREVOR DODDS   279 $18,000

BELL CANADIAN OPEN
Glen Abbey G.C., Oakville, Ontario
September 7-10, 1995

*MARK O'MEARA	$234,000	72-67-68-67	274
BOB LOHR	$140,400	68-67-69-70	274
NICK PRICE	$88,400	72-69-68-68	277
HAL SUTTON	$62,400	69-72-68-69	278
BILL GLASSON	$49,400	68-74-68-70	280
ANDREW MAGEE	$49,400	68-68-73-71	280

[PGA TOUR event]

SOUTH AMERICAN TOUR

ECUADORIAN OPEN
Guayaquil C.C., Guayaquil, Ecuador
October 19-22, 1995
FABIAN MONTOVIA   273 $18,000

FARALLONES OPEN
Club Campestre, Farallones
October 5-8, 1995
PEDRO MARTINEZ   272 $14,400

LOS LEONES OPEN
Club de Golf, Los Leones
November 30-December 3, 1995
IAN HUTCHINS   280 $18,000

LOS INKAS PERU OPEN
Los Inkas C.C., Peru
October 26-29, 1995
RAUL FRETES   269 $21,600

LITTORAL OPEN
Rosario G.C., Rosario, Argentina
November 9-12, 1995
ANGEL CABRERA　　　　274　　　　$16,200

SAN ANDRES OPEN
San Andres G.C.,
Buenos Aires, Argentina
October 12-15, 1995
RON WUENSCHE　　　　273　　　　$14,400

ABIERTO DEL URUGUAY
Club de Golf del Uruguay,
Montevideo, Uruguay
November 16-19, 1995
RICARDO GONZALEZ　　　　275　　　　$12,600

PRINCE OF WALES OPEN
Prince of Wales C.C.
November 23-26, 1995
GUILLERMO ENCINA　　　　274　　　　$21,600

OTHER NOTABLE TOURNAMENTS

TOKEN CORPORATION CUP
Kedon, Japan, January 27-30, 1995
TODD HAMILTON　　　　281　　　　¥18,000,000

SOUTH AFRICAN PGA
Johannesburg, South Africa,
February 16-19, 1995
ERNIE ELS　　　　271

ALFRED DUNHILL CHALLENGE
Johannesburg, South Africa,
February 23-26, 1995
SOUTHERN AFRICA 14　　　　AUSTRALASIA 11

PHILIPPINE OPEN
Manila, Philippines, February 23-26, 1995
CARLOS ESPINOSA　　　　282　　　　$49,980

KENYA OPEN
Nairobi, Kenya, March 2-5, 1995
JAMES LEE　　　　265

SHIZUOKA OPEN CUP
Hamaka, Japan, March 16-19, 1995
BRIAN WATTS　　　　280　　　　$49,980

BENSON & HEDGES MALAYSIA OPEN
Royal Selangor G.C.,
Kuala Lumpur, Malaysia
March 17-20, 1995
JOAKIM HAEGGMANN　　　　279　　　　$41,650

VOLVO CHINA OPEN
Beijing International G.C.,
Beijing, China
April 27-30, 1995
CRAIG PARRY　　　　282

PASSPORT OPEN
Seoul, South Korea,
August 31-September 3, 1995
VIJAY SINGH　　　　272

JPGA MATCHPLAY CHAMPIONSHIP
Tomakomai, Japana,
August 31-September 3, 1995
KATSUYOSHI TOMORI
DEF. SHIGEKI MARUYAMA 2&1

SUNTORY OPEN
Narashino, Japan,
September 7-10, 1995
MASAHIRO KURAMOTO　　　　273　　　　$170,500

ANA OPEN
Sapporo, Japan, September 14-17, 1995
MASASHI OZAKI 279

JUN CLASSIC
Ogawa, Japan,
September 21-24, 1995
SATOSHI HIGASHI 270

JAPAN OPEN
Kawagoe, Japan,
September 28-October 1, 1995
TOSHIMITSU IZAWA 277

TOKAI CLASSIC
Miyoshi, Japan, October 5-8, 1995
MASAYUKI KAWAMURA 285

GOLF DIGEST OPEN
Susono, Japan, October 12-15, 1995
STEWART GINN 267

SARAZEN WORLD OPEN
Braselton, Georgia
November 2-5, 1995
FRANK NOBILO 280 $650,000

KAPALUA INVITATIONAL
Kapalua, Maui, Hawaii
November 2-5, 1995
JIM FURYK 271 $180,000

HONG KONG OPEN
Hong Kong, November 16-19, 1995
GARY WEBB 271

DUNLOP PHOENIX OPEN
Miyazaki, Japan, November 16-19
MASASHI OZAKI 273

SHARK SHOOTOUT
Thousand Oaks, California
November 17-19, 1995
MARK CALCAVECCHIA/
STEVE ELKINGTON 184 $300,000

SKINS GAME
Palm Desert, California
November 26, 1995
FRED COUPLES 8 SKINS $270,000
COREY PAVIN 10 SKINS $240,000
PETER JACOBSEN 1 SKIN $30,000
TOM WATSON 0 SKINS $0

DINER'S CLUB MATCHES
PGA West.,
La Quinta, California
December 15-18, 1994

PGA
TOM LEHMAN/DUFFY WALDORF DEF. KENNY PERRY/JOHN HUSTON, 1 UP

LPGA
KELLY ROBBINS/TAMMIE GREEN DEF. LAURA DAVIES/MARDI LUNN, 1 UP

SPGA
JIM COLBERT/BOB MURPHY DEF. DAVE STOCKTON/HALE IRWIN, 1 UP

JOHNNIE WALKER WORLD CHAMPIONSHIP
Tryall Club,
Montego Bay, Jamaica
December 14-17, 1994
FRED COUPLES 279 $550,000

LEXUS CHALLENGE
La Quinta C.C.,
La Quinta, California
December 16, 1995
R. FLOYD/M. CHIKLIS 127 $180,000

1995 QUALIFYING SCHOOL RESULTS

PGA TOUR
Bear Lakes Country Club,
West Palm Beach, FL.
Nov. 29-Dec. 4, 1995

CARL PAULSON	70-65-69-65-69-71	409
OMAR URESTI	70-67-71-67-68-67	410
STEVE HART	67-70-68-69-68-68	410
SHANE BERTSCH	71-68-68-69-69-66	411
JOEY GULLION	71-68-72-64-69-67	411
OLIN BROWNE	70-68-65-68-70-70	411
TOM BYRUM	71-68-68-71-64-69	411
KEVIN SUTHERLAND	70-64-66-68-68-72	411
TIM HERRON	71-69-65-68-69-70	412
RUSS COCHRAN	69-70-69-67-66-71	412
STEVE JURGENSEN	68-70-68-70-67-70	413
CLARENCE ROSE	67-67-68-72-69-74	414
DAVID PEOPLES	69-68-68-67-70-72	414
SCOTT MEDLIN	69-69-69-71-64-72	414
ROBERT WRENN	67-68-70-71-74-65	415
LUCAS PARSONS	69-68-69-68-73-70	415
PAUL STANKOWSKI	66-67-69-77-66-70	415
HISAYUKI SASAKI	74-64-70-69-68-70	415
BRIAN TENNYSON	69-71-68-65-70-72	415
BILLY RAY BROWN	75-68-68-67-71-67	416
FRANK LICKLITER, JR.	73-75-65-67-67-69	416
LEN MATTIACE	71-68-72-69-67-69	416
JEFF GALLAGHER	66-74-66-72-69-69	416
RONNIE BLACK	71-68-70-64-72-71	416
STEVE RINTOUL	72-65-69-70-69-71	416
SCOTT DUNLAP	70-73-68-71-68-67	417
JOE DALEY	67-71-73-69-68-69	417
BART BRYANT	70-68-69-70-69-71	417
JARMO SANDELIN	74-72-67-68-70-67	418
JOHN MAGINNES	71-71-69-68-72-67	418
TAYLOR SMITH	69-69-71-73-69-67	418
GREG KRAFT	71-73-67-67-71-69	418
JEFF JULIAN	73-67-74-67-68-69	418
JAY WILLIAMSON	70-68-68-72-70-70	418
JOEL EDWARDS	67-70-66-70-72-73	418
MIKE SWARTZ	70-65-70-69-71-73	418
JEFF HART	67-73-69-74-67-69	419
ANDY BEAN	74-67-70-68-71-69	419
GARY RUSNAK	73-72-66-72-68-68	419
JOHN ELLIOT	70-69-72-69-70-69	419
RON WHITTAKER	74-68-69-70-71-67	419
BRYAN GORMAN	72-68-67-70-71-71	419

All of the above players received exemptions for the 1996 PGA TOUR.

LPGA TOUR

LU BENVENUTI	74-69-72-68	283
KARRIE WEBB	73-71-72-68	284
WENDY WARD	75-72-70-70	287
ALISON MUNT	70-77-71-72	290
ESTAFANIA KNUTH	72-73-77-69	291
CATRIN NILSMARK	74-72-77-69	292
KIM SHIPMAN	73-75-73-71	292
SUSAN VEASEY	73-73-75-71	292
ROBIN WALTON	75-75-72-71	293
JILL MCGILL	75-73-74-71	293
PATTI BERENDT	69-76-77-71	293
KRISTAL PARKER-GREGORY	74-75-72-72	293
KAREN DAVIES	77-68-76-72	293
MAYUMI HIRASE	74-73-73-74	294
EVA DAHLLOF	72-74-73-75	294
STEPHANIE FARWIG	80-68-77-70	295
MICHELLE DOBEK	75-78-69-73	295
PATTI LISCIO	78-72-72-73	295
KIM BAUER	74-75-73-73	295
LESLIE SPALDING	76-72-73-74	295
WENDY DOOLAN	76-77-73-70	296

All of the above players received full exemptions for the 1996 LPGA TOUR.

TINA TOMBS	76-75-74-71	296
DEBORAH VIDAL	Medical Exemption	
DALE REID	75-75-74-72	296
TARA FLEMING	74-75-75-72	296
KAY COCKERILL	73-73-78-72	296
DINA AMMACCAPANE	75-76-72-73	296
TINA PATERNOSTRO	75-72-73-76	296
JEAN BARTHOLOMEW	81-74-73-69	297
CHRISTA TENO	81-73-71-72	297
KELLY LEADBETTER	73-71-80-73	297
PAM KOMETANI	71-72-79-75	297
ANGIE RIDGEWAY	73-75-73-76	297
KIM CATHREIN	76-73-78-71	298

CORINNE DIBNAH	73-76-78-71	298
DEBORAH LEE	76-73-77-72	298
RENEE HEIKEN	78-78-72-71	299
JANICE GIBSON	75-75-78-71	299
CINDY HALEY	77-76-74-72	299
KATE GOLDEN	79-73-75-72	299
SUZY GREEN	75-75-73-76	299
LIZ EARLEY	72-75-76-76	299
NOELLE OAGHE	79-73-76-72	300
TISH CERTO	80-74-73-73	300
SUE THOMAS	76-74-76-74	300
LAURA BAUGH	77-72-77-74	300
MARTHA RICHARDS	76-71-77-76	300
ANNETTE DELUCA	75-74-71-80	300
LORIE KANE	76-78-74-73	301
LA REE PEARL SUGG	79-74-73-75	301
RHONDA REILLY	76-76-74-75	301
LAURA WITVOET	74-76-76-75	301
ANNA ACKER-MACOSKO	76-73-76-76	301
SHANI WAUGH	79-70-75-77	301

All of the above players received conditional exemptions for the 1996 LPGA TOUR.

JANE EGAN	77-80-72-73	302
CAROLINE PEEK	81-74-74-73	302
VICKI SUHOCKI	78-72-78-74	302
LORETTA ALDERETE	74-76-78-74	302
STEPHANIE COMSTOCK	76-77-74-75	302
TONYA GILL	76-72-79-75	302
DEBORAH ECKROTH	75-74-77-76	302
KAREN LUNN	72-74-78-78	302
SARAH MCGUIRE	77-76-75-75	303
LISA GRIMES	75-75-72-81	303
AMY DUBOIS	76-72-81-75	304
LISA DEPAULO	76-77-75-76	304
LORI ATSEDES	79-73-76-76	304
LAURA BROWN	77-76-74-77	304
JULIE HENNESSY	81-73-75-76	305
JEAN ZEDLITZ	76-76-77-76	305
ELIZABETH BOWMAN	75-74-79-78	306
LIA BIEHL	72-76-80-78	306
LORI TATUM	79-74-76-78	307

SENIOR PGA TOUR

Pete Dye Resort Course at
The Westin Mission Hill
Rancho Mirage, California
November 28-December 1, 1995

MASARU AMANO	71-68-65-66	**270**
JOHN JACOBS	67-70-68-67	272
BOBBY STROBLE	69-67-68-68	272
FRANK CONNER	72-66-68-71	274
RICK ACTON	66-73-67-68	274
BUNKY HENRY	70-69-69-66	274
JIM WILKINSON	69-71-65-71	276
JOHN SCHRODER	70-67-69-71	276
ROBERT LANDERS	67-74-66-70	277
BOB CARSON	72-67-68-70	277
HARRY TOSCANO	73-68-67-69	277
DENNIS COSCINA	72-70-68-68	278
ED SNEED	69-69-69-72	279
BOB BETLEY	73-68-68-70	279
TERRY CARLSON	68-71-72-68	279
MIKE MCCULLOUGH	67-74-69-70	280

All of the above players received exemptions for the 1996 Senior PGA TOUR.

TOUR PRIZE MONEY & STATISTICS FOR 1995

OVERVIEW: *Key statistics and the official money lists for the PGA TOUR, Senior PGA TOUR, LPGA, the PGA European Tour, plus the PING and Sony world professional golf rankings.*

1995 LPGA TOUR

ROLEX PLAYER OF THE YEAR
1	ANNIKA SORENSTAM	43
2	LAURA DAVIES	35
3	DOTTIE MOCHRIE	33
4	MICHELLE MCGANN	32
5	KELLY ROBBINS	31
6	BETH DANIEL	27
7	PAT BRADLEY	26
8	BETSY KING	25
9	ROSIE JONES	22
9	PATTY SHEEHAN	22

ROLEX ROOKIE OF THE YEAR
1	PAT HURST	527
2	TRACY HANSON	522
3	EMILEE KLEIN	515
4	LETA LINDLEY	434
5	CARIN HJALMARSSON	423
6	MOIRA DUNN	236
7	RENEE HEIKEN	182
8	CATRIONA MATTHEW	168
9	CATRIN NILSMARK	129
10	DENISE PHILBRICK	107

SCORING AVERAGE (VARE TROPHY)
1	ANNIKA SORENSTAM	70.96
2	DOTTIE MOCHRIE	71.00
3	BETSY KING	71.24
4	LAURA DAVIES	71.26
5	MEG MALLON	71.29
6	BETH DANIEL	71.35
7	COLLEEN WALKER	71.38
8	MICHELLE MCGANN	71.56
9	TAMMIE GREEN	71.57
10	ROSIE JONES	71.64

BIRDIES
1	BETSY KING	317
2	JANE GEDDES	301
3	KRIS TSCHETTER	281
4	BRANDI BURTON	275
5	ROSIE JONES	272
6	BETH DANIEL	266
7	VAL SKINNER	258
8	COLLEEN WALKER	257
9	MICHELLE MCGANN	255
9	KELLY ROBBINS	255

DRIVING DISTANCE
1	LAURA DAVIES	265.2 YDS
2	KELLY ROBBINS	261.6
3	MICHELLE MCGANN	256.1
4	KAREN LUNN	252.5
5	JANE GEDDES	252.4
6	JILL BRILES-HINTON	252.2
7	BETH DANIEL	252.1
8	FLORENCE DESCAMPS	251.2
9	MICHELLE ESTILL	250.9
10	SHERRI TURNER	250.4

PUTTING AVERAGE
1	KAY COCKERILL	29.57
2	STEPHANIE MAYNOR	29.63
3	PAGE DUNLAP	29.67
4	ROSIE JONES	29.76
4	ANNIKA SORENSTAM	29.76
6	COLLEEN WALKER	29.79
7	LAURI MERTEN	29.81
7	DEB RICHARD	29.81
9	ELLIE GIBSON	29.82
10	LAURA DAVIES	29.84

1995 LPGA MONEY LEADERS

#	Name	Earnings	#	Name	Earnings
1	SORENSTAM, ANNIKA	$660,224	59	MCGEORGE, MISSIE	$92,885
2	DAVIES, LAURA	$527,995	60	DIBOS, ALICIA	$89,070
3	ROBBINS, KELLY	$527,655	61	FINNEY, ALLISON	$87,620
4	MOCHRIE, DOTTIE	$521,000	62	RITZMAN, ALICE	$85,294
5	KING, BETSY	$481,149	63	EDGE, MITZI	$84,374
6	DANIEL, BETH	$466,622	64	RAMSBOTTOM, NANCY	$81,610
7	MCGANN, MICHELLE	$449,296	65	MAYNOR, STEPHANIE	$78,384
8	MALLON, MEG	$421,484	66	STACY, HOLLIS	$76,840
9	SKINNER, VAL	$419,963	67	JOHNSON, TRISH	$75,798
10	JONES, ROSIE	$418,856	68	WALTERS, LISA	$75,087
11	BRADLEY, PAT	$368,904	69	STEPHENSON, JAN	$72,822
12	TSCHETTER, KRIS	$362,216	70	BRILES-HINTON, JILL	$71,376
13	GREEN, TAMMIE	$334,017	71	ALCOTT, AMY	$70,883
14	SHEEHAN, PATTY	$333,147	72	JOHNSTON-FORBES, C.	$69,475
15	GEDDES, JANE	$308,618	73	BERTEOTTI, MISSIE	$68,406
16	NEUMANN, LISELOTTE	$281,734	74	WILLIAMS, KIM	$66,119
17	COE-JONES, DAWN	$268,665	75	MILLS, LEIGH ANN	$62,722
18	WALKER, COLLEEN	$263,391	76	RICHARD, DEB	$62,658
19	LIDBACK, JENNY	$259,386	77	GOETZE, VICKI	$62,060
20	EGGELING, DALE	$256,839	78	FIGUERAS-DOTTI, M.	$60,214
21	LARSEN. JULIE	$256,248	79	CRAFTER, JANE	$60,133
22	ALFREDSSON, HELEN	$252,495	80	LUNN, MARDI	$57,936
23	NICHOLAS, ALISON	$225,351	81	KIGGENS, LISA	$57,361
24	BOWEN, NANCI	$223,224	82	LITTLE, SALLY	$56,186
25	BURTON, BRANDIE	$214,455	83	RITTENHOUSE, L.	$54,081
26	STEINHAUER, SHERRI	$213,657	84	WILL, MAGGIE	$53,289
27	LOPEZ, NANCY	$210,882	85	BARRETT, TINA	$52,251
28	PITCOCK, JOAN	$203,421	86	STRUDWICK, S.	$50,310
29	THOMAS, BARB	$201,087	87	DUNN, MOIRA	$50,158
30	JOHNSON, CHRIS	$200,418	88	WEST, LORI	$49,877
31	INKSTER, JULI	$195,739	89	NAUSE, MARTHA	$49,525
32	PIERCE, CAROLINE	$195,085	90	MCNAMARA, M.	$49,262
33	REDMAN, MICHELE	$190,338	91	WEISS, KAREN	$48,141
34	PETERSON-PARKER, KATIE	$188,570	92	MERTEN, LAURI	$47,520
35	MORRIS, MARIANNE	$182,949	93	CROCE, STEFANIA	$42,915
36	CROSBY, ELAINE	$182,383	94	SCHREYER, CINDY	$42,688
37	AMMACCAPANE, DANIELLE	$181,560	95	HILL, CAROLYN	$41,753
38	KERDYK, TRACY	$181,403	96	MOCKETT, CATHY	$39,454
39	KOBAYASHI, HIROMI	$176,766	97	RINKER-GRAHAM, L.	$38,740
40	KLEIN, EMILEE	$173,494	98	CARNER, JOANNE	$38,033
41	ZIMMERMAN, MARY BETH	$156,741	99	MYERS, TERRY-JO	$37,887
42	MUCHA, BARB	$156,527	100	MATTHEW, C.	$37,832
43	GRAHAM, GAIL	$142,346	101	JERAY, NICOLE	$37,477
44	WRIGHT, PAM	$139,939	102	GIBSON, ELLIE	$37,396
45	ESTILL, MICHELLE	$135,455	103	BELL, MICHELLE	$37,312
46	REDMAN, SUSIE	$132,251	104	DUNLAP, PAGE	$36,603
47	RARICK, CINDY	$128,437	105	HARVEY, NANCY	$36,147
48	HJALMARSSON, CARIN	$126,959	106	HEIKEN, RENEE	$35,773
49	HURST, PAT	$124,989	107	BENZ, AMY	$35,572
50	MARSHALL, KATHRYN	$124,888	108	PLATT, MARGARET	$34,787
51	HANSON, TRACY	$121,287	109	NOBLE, KAREN	$34,086
52	FERGON, VICKI	$114,038	110	BROWER, LAURIE	$33,633
53	LINDLEY, LETA	$109,975	111	SCRANTON, N.	$33,188
54	FRUHWIRTH, AMY	$109,229	112	BALDWIN, DENISE	$31,363
55	TURNER, SHERRI	$107,324	113	LUNN, KAREN	$31,333
56	IVERSON, BECKY	$105,285	114	WALTON, ROBIN	$29,769
57	ALBERS, KRISTI	$105,016	115	SAIKI, KIM	$29,760
58	SPENCER-DEVLIN, MUFFIN	$98,098	116	MASSEY, DEBBIE	$29,465
			117	DORMANN, DANA	$28,582

118	FARWIG, STEPHANIE	$28,070		25	COE-JONES, DAWN	$1,529,175.57
119	HAMMEL, PENNY	$27,490		26	STEINHAUER, SHERRI	$1,468,046.00
120	ZEDLITZ, JEAN	$27,295		27	CAPONI, DONNA	$1,387,919.73
121	DAHLLOF, EVA	$26,939		28	POSTLEWAIT, KATHY	$1,381,510.27
122	SMYERS, SHERRIN	$26,477		29	NEUMANN, LISELOTTE	$1,364,478.00
123	ANDREWS, D.	$25,346		30	RITZMAN, ALICE	$1,362,909.32
124	NILSMARK, CATRIN	$25,329		31	RARICK, CINDY	$1,346,633.50
125	DESCAMPE, F.	$24,324		32	PALMER, SANDRA	$1,331,999.86
126	DICKINSON, JUDY	$23,602		33	BLALOCK, JANE	$1,290,943.62
127	ANDERSON, JANET	$23,020		34	BURTON, BRANDIE	$1,286,545.00
128	MILLER, ALICE	$22,970		35	MASSEY, DEBBIE	$1,267,042.13
129	BARRETT, SHARON	$22,924		36	SKINNER, VAL	$1,262,355.75
130	GIBSON, JANICE	$22,427		37	TURNER, SHERRI	$1,196,401.78
131	JORDAN, PATTY	$22,079		38	ANDREWS, DONNA	$1,189,041.00
132	PHILBRICK, DENISE	$21,865		39	EGGELING, DALE	$1,175,799.00
133	HAMLIN, SHELLEY	$20,504		40	CROSBY, ELAINE	$1,171,983.00
134	PALMER, SANDRA	$20,035		41	FERGON, VICKI	$1,113,341.59
135	OKAMOTO, AYAKO	$19,951		42	NAUSE, MARTHA	$1,112,525.96
136	KEAN, LAUREL	$19,710		43	MERTEN, LAURI	$1,112,217.65
137	SINN, PEARL	$19,391		44	BENZ, AMY	$1,104,176.15
138	RENNER, JODI	$19,215		45	RIZZO, PATTI	$1,072,650.75
139	WYATT, JENNIFER	$18,419		46	SCRANTON, NANCY	$1,057,097.00
140	CHILLEMI, CONNIE	$17,997		47	HAYNIE, SANDRA	$1,055,874.57
141	TATUM, LORI	$17,879		48	FIGUERAS-DOTTI, M.	$1,044,475.00
142	ANSCHUTZ, JODY	$17,672		49	MILLER, ALICE	$1,025,608.72
143	KEGGI, CAROLINE	$17,235		50	MCGANN, MICHELLE	$993,107.00
144	GUADAGNINO, K.	$16,458				
145	SCHERBAK, BARB	$16,138				
146	PARKER-GREGORY, K.	$15,768				
147	MACKALL, M.	$15,493				
148	KOYAMA, DEBBI	$15,437				
149	ABITBOL, TANIA	$14,454				
150	RICHARDS, M.	$14,296				

PGA TOUR

CAREER EARNINGS

1	KING, BETSY	$4,892,873.50
2	BRADLEY, PAT	$4,772,115.03
3	DANIEL, BETH	$4,492,091.80
4	SHEEHAN, PATTY	$4,455,399.01
5	LOPEZ, NANCY	$4,064,802.83
6	ALCOTT, AMY	$3,064,889.14
7	CARNER, JOANNE	$2,840,071.63
8	OKAMOTO, AYAKO	$2,715,678.85
9	MOCHRIE, DOTTIE	$2,574,716.00
10	STEPHENSON, JAN	$2,275,075.00
11	GEDDES, JANE	$2,269,254.30
12	JONES, ROSIE	$2,193,048.97
13	INKSTER, JULI	$2,070,418.23
14	STACY, HOLLIS	$2,005,087.99
15	WALKER, COLLEEN	$1,991,323.71
16	DICKINSON, JUDY	$1,990,807.92
17	MALLON, MEG	$1,862,059.00
18	WHITWORTH, K.	$1,726,597.01
19	GREEN, TAMMIE	$1,715,863.00
20	DAVIES, LAURA	$1,685,657.00
21	RICHARD, DEB	$1,674,690.00
22	LITTLE, SALLY	$1,648,210.80
23	AMMACCAPANE, D.	$1,631,836.00
24	JOHNSON, CHRIS	$1,553,666.50

ALL-AROUND

1	JUSTIN LEONARD	323
2	JEFF SLUMAN	326
3	KIRK TRIPLETT	339
4	DAVID DUVAL	348
5	MARK CALCAVECCHIA	350
6	JIM GALLAGHER, JR.	353
7	SCOTT VERPLANK	378
8	JOHN ADAMS	381
9	STEVE LOWERY	395
10	BRAD BRYANT	397
10	DUFFY WALDORF	397

BIRDIE LEADERS

1	STEVE LOWERY	410
2	WOODY AUSTIN	404
2	JIM FURYK	404
4	KIRK TRIPLETT	399
5	JUSTIN LEONARD	386
6	CURT BYRUM	380
6	FRED FUNK	380
8	MARK CALCAVECCHIA	372
9	SCOTT HOCH	371
10	PAUL GOYDOS	366

DRIVING DISTANCE
1	JOHN DALY	289.0 YDS.
2	DAVIS LOVE III	284.6
3	DENNIS PAULSON	284.1
4	VIJAY SINGH	283.5
5	KELLY GIBSON	280.2
6	JOHN ADAMS	278.9
6	BRETT OGLE	278.9
8	CARL PAULSON	278.2
9	WOODY AUSTIN	277.5
10	FRED COUPLES	276.3

DRIVING ACCURACY
1	FRED FUNK	81.3%
2	DOUG TEWELL	80.3
3	LARRY MIZE	79.6
4	DAVID EDWARDS	79.1
5	BRUCE LIETZKE	78.8
6	BRUCE FLEISHER	78.7
7	LENNIE CLEMENTS	78.3
8	CURTIS STRANGE	77.9
9	NICK FALDO	77.8
9	BILL PORTER	77.8

EAGLE LEADERS
1	KELLY GIBSON	16
2	PAUL AZINGER	15
3	DAVIS LOVE III	14
4	JOHN ADAMS	13
5	WOODY AUSTIN	12
5	MICHAEL BRADLEY	12
5	MARK CALCAVECCHIA	12
5	JIM GALLAGHER, JR.	12
5	JAY HAAS	12
5	MIKE STANDLY	12
5	TOMMY TOLLES	12

GREENS IN REGULATION
1	LENNIE CLEMENTS	72.3%
2	BART BRYANT	71.4
3	CRAIG STADLER	71.3
3	GRANT WAITE	71.3
5	DAVE BARR	70.9
6	SCOTT GUMP	70.7
7	SCOTT SIMPSON	70.6
8	MARK O'MEARA	70.5
9	TOM LEHMAN	70.4
9	TOM PURTZER	70.4

PUTTING LEADERS
1	JIM FURYK	1.708
2	SCOTT HOCH	1.737
3	GENE SAUERS	1.740
4	PETE JORDAN	1.744
5	BRAD FAXON	1.749
6	PAYNE STEWART	1.750
7	PAUL AZINGER	1.751
7	BOB ESTES	1.751
7	JAY HAAS	1.751
7	STEVE LOWERY	1.751
7	FUZZY ZOELLER	1.751

SAND SAVES
1	BILLY MAYFAIR	68.6%
2	STEVE ELKINGTON	68.2
3	DAVID FROST	66.9
4	DAVID FEHERTY	64.1
5	DAVID OGRIN	62.5
6	BEN CRENSHAW	61.4
7	BILL BRITTON	61.3
7	ERNIE ELS	61.3
9	GREG NORMAN	61.0
10	JEFF SLUMAN	60.8

SCORING LEADERS
1	GREG NORMAN	69.06
2	STEVE ELKINGTON	69.59
3	ERNIE ELS	69.81
3	NICK PRICE	69.81
5	NICK FALDO	69.85
5	TOM LEHMAN	69.85
7	VIJAY SINGH	69.92
8	BOB TWAY	69.93
9	SCOTT SIMPSON	69.99
10	PETER JACOBSEN	70.03

TOTAL DRIVING
1	NICK PRICE	40
2	HAL SUTTON	58
3	PETER JACOBSEN	60
4	GREG NORMAN	63
5	GRANT WAITE	73
6	BILL GLASSON	82
7	BRUCE LIETZKE	83
8	TOM WATSON	87
9	DAVID DUVAL	102
10	CRAIG STADLER	103

1995 PGA TOUR MONEY LEADERS
1	NORMAN, GREG	$1,654,959
2	MAYFAIR, BILLY	$1,543,192
3	JANZEN, LEE	$1,378,966
4	PAVIN, COREY	$1,340,079
5	ELKINGTON, STEVE	$1,254,352
6	LOVE III, DAVIS	$1,111,999
7	JACOBSEN, PETER	$1,075,057
8	GALLAGHER, JR., JIM	$1,057,241
9	SINGH, VIJAY	$1,019,713
10	O'MEARA, MARK	$914,129
11	DUVAL, DAVID	$881,436
12	STEWART, PAYNE	$866,219
13	CALCAVECCHIA, MARK	$843,552

#	Name	Earnings	#	Name	Earnings
14	ELS, ERNIE	$842,590	73	MORGAN, GIL	$255,565
15	LEHMAN, TOM	$831,231	74	ADAMS, JOHN	$243,366
16	HAAS, JAY	$822,259	75	CLAAR, BRIAN	$241,107
17	SIMPSON, SCOTT	$795,798	76	WAITE, GRANT	$240,722
18	HOCH, SCOTT	$792,643	77	MCCALLISTER, BLAINE	$238,847
19	FALDO, NICK	$790,961	78	HENKE, NOLAN	$237,141
20	TWAY, BOB	$787,348	79	JONES, STEVE	$234,749
21	PERRY, KENNY	$773,368	80	DELSING, JAY	$230,769
22	LEONARD, JUSTIN	$748,793	81	MARTIN, DOUG	$227,463
23	CRENSHAW, BEN	$737,475	82	POOLEY, DON	$226,804
24	AUSTIN, WOODY	$736,497	83	EDWARDS, DAVID	$225,857
25	BRYANT, BRAD	$723,834	84	PARNEVIK, JESPER	$222,458
26	FUNK, FRED	$717,232	85	BRADLEY, MICHAEL	$214,469
27	ROBERTS, LOREN	$678,335	86	CHAMBLEE, BRANDEL	$213,796
28	MICKELSON, PHIL	$655,777	87	OLAZABAL, JOSE-MARIA	$213,415
29	TRIPLETT, KIRK	$644,607	88	PRUITT, DILLARD	$210,453
30	PRICE, NICK	$611,700	89	GAMEZ, ROBERT	$206,588
31	SLUMAN, JEFF	$563,681	90	SINDELAR, JOEY	$202,896
32	SUTTON, HAL	$554,733	91	DAY, GLEN	$201,809
33	FURYK, JIM	$535,380	92	BRISKY, MIKE	$194,874
34	MAGGERT, JEFF	$527,952	93	FORSMAN, DAN	$194,539
35	WALDORF, DUFFY	$525,622	94	KAYE, JONATHAN	$191,883
36	WEIBRING, D.A.	$517,065	95	IRWIN, HALE	$190,961
37	FAXON, BRAD	$471,887	96	RINKER, LEE	$187,065
38	LOWERY, STEVE	$463,858	97	COOK, JOHN	$186,977
39	TRYBA, TED	$451,983	98	ROCCA, COSTANTINO	$185,500
40	STRICKER, STEVE	$438,931	99	GUMP, SCOTT	$184,828
41	ESTES, BOB	$433,992	100	AZINGER, PAUL	$182,595
42	MORSE, JOHN	$416,803	101	LANCASTER, NEAL	$182,219
43	GLASSON, BILL	$412,094	102	CARTER, JIM	$180,664
44	MCGOVERN, JIM	$402,587	103	RYMER, CHARLIE	$180,401
45	STADLER, CRAIG	$402,316	104	KITE, TOM	$178,580
46	LANGER, BERNHARD	$394,877	105	STANDLY, MIKE	$177,920
47	MCCUMBER, MARK	$375,923	106	WOOSNAM, IAN	$174,464
48	BROOKS, MARK	$366,860	107	BYRUM, CURT	$173,838
49	STRANGE, CURTIS	$358,175	108	GREEN, KEN	$173,577
50	FROST, DAVID	$357,658	109	GIBSON, KELLY	$173,425
51	CLEMENTS, LENNIE	$355,130	110	ZOELLER, FUZZY	$170,706
52	HEINEN, MIKE	$350,920	111	BECK, CHIP	$170,081
53	MONTGOMERIE, COLIN	$335,617	112	WIEBE, MARK	$168,832
54	BLAKE, JAY DON	$333,551	113	SULLIVAN, MIKE	$167,486
55	VERPLANK, SCOTT	$332,886	114	HENNINGER, BRIAN	$166,730
56	OGLE, BRETT	$326,932	115	WADKINS, BOBBY	$166,527
57	DALY, JOHN	$321,748	116	TOLLES, TOMMY	$166,431
58	WATSON, TOM	$320,785	117	POHL, DAN	$166,219
59	LOHR, BOB	$314,947	118	KAMM, BRIAN	$165,235
60	SAUERS, GENE	$311,578	119	BURKE, PATRICK	$162,892
61	HULBERT, MIKE	$311,055	120	MAHAFFEY, JOHN	$156,608
62	BOROS, GUY	$303,654	121	BLACKMAR, PHIL	$154,801
63	COUPLES, FRED	$299,259	122	DOUGHERTY, ED	$154,007
64	HUSTON, JOHN	$294,574	123	OGRIN, DAVID	$151,419
65	PARRY, CRAIG	$293,413	124	STOCKTON, JR., DAVE	$149,579
66	OZAKI, JOE	$290,001	125	WILSON, JOHN	$149,280
67	MIZE, LARRY	$289,576	126	FEHR, RICK	$147,766
68	FREEMAN, ROBIN	$283,756	127	ACOSTA, JR., JOE	$147,745
69	ANDRADE, BILLY	$276,494	128	MCCARRON, SCOTT	$147,371
70	LIETZKE, BRUCE	$269,394	129	GOYDOS, PAUL	$146,423
71	DAWSON, MARCO	$261,214	130	FERGUS, KEITH	$146,359
72	MAGEE, ANDREW	$256,918	131	COCHRAN, RUSS	$145,663

Statistics and Money Lists

132	BYRUM, TOM	$145,427		191	BURNS, BOB	$59,243
133	STANKOWSKI, PAUL	$144,558		192	CINK, STEWART	$58,426
134	JORDAN, PETE	$143,936		193	JIMENEZ, MIGUEL	$57,196
135	CAMPBELL, MIKE	$141,388		194	TORRANCE, SAM	$56,970
136	HAMMOND, DONNIE	$141,150		195	COTNER, KAWIKA	$56,625
137	TWITTY, HOWARD	$140,695		196	BROWN, BILLY RAY	$56,111
138	GILDER, BOB	$139,361		197	ALLEN, MICHAEL	$55,825
139	KRAFT, GREG	$137,655		198	SPRINGER, MIKE	$55,146
140	AUBREY, EMLYN	$137,020		199	ALLEM, FULTON	$54,239
141	ARMOUR III, T.	$134,407		200	LEONARD, JEFF	$53,444
142	TYNER, TRAY	$126,339				
143	BLACK, RONNIE	$122,188				
144	PURTZER, TOM	$120,717		**ALL-TIME PGA TOUR MONEY LEADERS**		
145	WILLIAMSON, JAY	$120,180		1	GREG NORMAN	$9,592,829
146	BRYANT, BART	$119,201		2	TOM KITE	$9,337,998
147	BARR, DAVE	$118,218		3	PAYNE STEWART	$7,389,479
148	HART, DUDLEY	$116,334		4	NICK PRICE	$7,338,119
149	EDWARDS, JOEL	$114,285		5	FRED COUPLES	$7,188,408
150	PERRY, CHRIS	$113,632		6	COREY PAVIN	$7,175,523
151	SILLS, TONY	$113,186		7	TOM WATSON	$7,072,113
152	RINTOUL, STEVE	$112,877		8	PAUL AZINGER	$6,957,324
153	HAYES, J.P.	$111,696		9	BEN CRENSHAW	$6,845,235
154	FLEISHER, BRUCE	$108,830		10	CURTIS STRANGE	$6,791,618
155	MEDIATE, ROCCO	$105,618		11	MARK O'MEARA	$6,126,466
156	URESTI, OMAR	$104,876		12	LANNY WADKINS	$6,028,855
157	BOTTOMLEY, STEVEN	$104,738		13	CRAIG STADLER	$6,008,753
158	PAULSON, DENNIS	$103,411		14	MARK CALCAVECCHIA	$5,866,716
159	REID, MIKE	$102,809		15	HALE IRWIN	$5,845,024
160	HALLBERG, GARY	$99,332		16	CHIP BECK	$5,755,844
161	PRIDE, DICKY	$97,712		17	BRUCE LIETZKE	$5,710,262
162	WADKINS, LANNY	$97,485		18	DAVIS LOVE III	$5,623,890
163	TAYLOR, HARRY	$94,265		19	SCOTT HOCH	$5,465,898
164	KENDALL, SKIP	$93,606		20	DAVID FROST	$5,458,172
165	DENNIS, CLARK	$92,077		21	JACK NICKLAUS	$5,440,357
166	FEHERTY, DAVID	$90,274		22	JAY HAAS	$5,426,821
167	KEPPLER, STEPHEN	$90,040		23	RAY FLOYD	$5,194,044
168	PATE, STEVE	$89,756		24	GIL MORGAN	$4,991,433
169	PEOPLES, DAVID	$86,679		25	FUZZY ZOELLER	$4,918,771
170	FIORI, ED	$83,852		26	MARK MCCUMBER	$4,799,702
171	HAAS, JERRY	$78,769		27	SCOTT SIMPSON	$4,768,955
172	HUMENIK, ED	$78,150		28	LARRY MIZE	$4,584,287
173	VAUGHAN, BRUCE	$77,561		29	JIM GALLAGHER, JR.	$4,583,940
174	DIMARCO, CHRIS	$74,698		30	PETER JACOBSEN	$4,547,564
175	BRITTON, BILL	$73,574		31	STEVE ELKINGTON	$4,525,487
176	ALLENBY, ROBERT	$73,288		32	HAL SUTTON	$4,486,587
177	GOTSCHE, STEVE	$70,425		33	JOHN COOK	$4,461,954
178	PORTER, BILL	$68,390		34	WAYNE LEVI	$4,237,387
179	NICKLAUS, JACK	$68,180		35	LEE JANZEN	$3,910,397
180	FLOYD, RAY	$65,031		36	JEFF SLUMAN	$3,860,431
181	MCNULTY, MARK	$64,795		37	JOHN MAHAFFEY	$3,828,008
182	WOOD, WILLIE	$64,697		38	BOB TWAY	$3,815,540
183	PAULSON, CARL	$64,501		39	LOREN ROBERTS	$3,809,733
184	BALLESTEROS, SEVE	$64,345		40	STEVE PATE	$3,661,591
185	CARNEVALE, MARK	$62,206		41	DAVID EDWARDS	$3,646,275
186	PATE, JERRY	$62,001		42	D.A. WEIBRING	$3,612,373
187	MALTIE, ROGER	$61,664		43	JOEY SINDELAR	$3,565,399
188	OZAKI, JUMBO	$60,292		44	BRAD FAXON	$3,537,539
189	WURTZ, MARK	$59,949		45	LEE TREVINO	$3,478,450
190	LEWIS, J.L.	$59,750		46	JOHN HUSTON	$3,408,018

47	BILLY MAYFAIR	$3,397,626
48	TIM SIMPSON	$3,351,476
49	KEN GREEN	$3,347,802
50	LARRY NELSON	$3,313,938
51	MARK BROOKS	$3,300,176
52	TOM PURTZER	$3,250,834
53	ANDY BEAN	$3,250,480
54	BILL GLASSON	$3,230,227
55	MIKE REID	$3,131,821
56	DAN FORSMAN	$3,040,150
57	GENE SAUERS	$3,002,576
58	DAN POHL	$2,909,071
59	TOM LEHMAN	$2,902,257
60	MIKE HULBERT	$2,878,027
61	BRAD BRYANT	$2,866,233
62	KENNY PERRY	$2,844,072
63	ANDREW MAGEE	$2,832,873
64	DON POOLEY	$2,811,123
65	JODIE MUDD	$2,806,955
66	JEFF MAGGERT	$2,753,797
67	JOHNNY MILLER	$2,746,425
68	BLAINE MCCALLISTER	$2,678,444
69	RUSS COCHRAN	$2,668,983
70	HOWARD TWITTY	$2,665,173
71	BOB GILDER	$2,636,473
72	RICK FEHR	$2,620,197
73	HUBERT GREEN	$2,586,664
74	D. HAMMOND	$2,567,729
75	BOBBY WADKINS	$2,448,213
76	DOUG TEWELL	$2,424,476
77	ROCCO MEDIATE	$2,367,238
78	BOB ESTES	$2,332,399
79	BILLY ANDRADE	$2,311,290
80	MARK WIEBE	$2,305,739
81	CALVIN PEETE	$2,302,363
82	BOB LOHR	$2,287,789
83	JAY DON BLAKE	$2,276,989
84	DAVE BARR	$2,270,323
85	TOM WEISKOPF	$2,241,688
86	J.C. SNEAD	$2,219,171
87	NOLAN HENKE	$2,215,189
88	PHIL MICKELSON	$2,204,542
89	FRED FUNK	$2,191,458
90	ROGER MALTBIE	$2,164,079
91	STEVE JONES	$2,129,428
92	GARY HALLBERG	$2,128,311
93	DUFFY WALDORF	$2,113,447
94	MIKE SULLIVAN	$2,077,400
95	KEITH CLEARWATER	$2,056,142
96	FULTON ALLEM	$2,031,256
97	VIJAY SINGH	$2,002,503
98	IAN BAKER-FINCH	$1,998,078
99	NICK FALDO	$1,977,198
100	MIKE DONALD	$1,938,765

SENIOR TOUR

ALL-AROUND

1	ISAO AOKI	82
2	RAY FLOYD	101
3	DAVE STOCKTON	113
4	JIM COLBERT	122
5	GRAHAM MARSH	141
6	JAY SIGEL	157
7	BOB MURPHY	159
8	BRUCE SUMMERHAYS	161
9	J.C. SNEAD	177
10	LEE TREVINO	178

BIRDIE LEADERS

1	BRUCE SUMMERHAYS	393
2	DAVE STOCKTON	391
3	JIM COLBERT	365
4	DAVE EICHELBERGER	364
5	JIM ALBUS	355
5	LEE TREVINO	355
7	JACK KIEFER	340
8	BUD ALLIN	337
9	LARRY LAORETTI	329
10	ROCKY THOMPSON	328
10	KERMIT ZARLEY	328

DRIVING ACCURACY

1	DEANE BEMAN	80.4%
1	CHARLES SIFFORD	80.4
3	JOHN PAUL CAIN	77.5
4	BOB CHARLES	76.7
5	DICK RHYAN	75.9
6	CALVIN PEETE	75.8
7	BOB SMITH	75.7
8	GRAHAM MARSH	75.6
9	WALTER ZEMBRISKI	75.4
10	RAY FLOYD	74.8

DRIVING DISTANCE

1	JAY SIGEL	279.3 YDS
2	JIM DENT	275.4
3	DAVE EICHELBERGER	274.6
4	TERRY DILL	274.1
5	MIKE STILL	273.1
6	TOM WEISKOPF	271.8
7	RAY FLOYD	269.8
8	JIM ALBUS	269.2
9	BRUCE SUMMERHAYS	268.8
10	DICK GOETZ	267.7

EAGLE LEADERS

1	DAVE EICHELBERGER	13

2	TONY JACKLIN	11
2	JAY SIGEL	11
4	ISAO AOKI	10
4	TERRY DILL	10
4	BRUCE SUMMERHAYS	10
7	GEORGE ARCHER	8
7	DAVE STOCKTON	8
7	ROCKY THOMPSON	8
7	TOM WARGO	8
7	DEWITT WEAVER	8

GREENS IN REGULATION

1	RAY FLOYD	76.2%
2	TOM WEISKOPF	74.1
3	MIKE HILL	73.6
4	BOB MURPHY	73.3
5	GRAHAM MARSH	73.1
6	ISAO AOKI	73.0
7	J.C. SNEAD	72.9
7	DAVE STOCKTON	72.9
9	KERMIT ZARLEY	72.8
10	JIM ALBUS	72.1

PUTTING LEADERS

1	ISAO AOKI	1.736
2	LEE TREVINO	1.738
3	DAVE STOCKTON	1.742
4	GEORGE ARCHER	1.751
4	GRAHAM MARSH	1.751
6	HAROLD HENNING	1.752
7	BOB MURPHY	1.757
8	RAY FLOYD	1.758
9	BOB CHARLES	1.760
10	ROCKY THOMPSON	1.761

SAND SAVES

1	GEORGE ARCHER	57.6%
2	DAVE STOCKTON	57.0
3	MARION HECK	55.6
4	ISAO AOKI	55.2
5	SIMON HOBDAY	55.1
6	JIM COLBERT	54.2
7	HAROLD HENNING	53.8
8	JIMMY POWELL	53.0
9	DON DAVIS	52.9
10	ROCKY THOMPSON	52.2

SCORING LEADERS

1	RAY FLOYD	69.45
2	ISAO AOKI	69.52
3	BOB MURPHY	69.78
4	DAVE STOCKTON	69.79
5	LEE TREVINO	69.83
6	GRAHAM MARSH	70.01
7	BOB CHARLES	70.16
8	JIM COLBERT	70.31

| 9 | J.C. SNEAD | 70.43 |
| 9 | TOM WEISKOPF | 70.43 |

TOTAL DRIVING

1	RAY FLOYD	17
2	JAY SIGEL	30
3	ISAO AOKI	34
4	GRAHAM MARSH	40
5	WALTER MORGAN	43
6	JACK KIEFER	45
7	MIKE HILL	48
7	J.C. SNEAD	48
9	JIM ALBUS	49
10	JIM COLBERT	52

PGA SENIOR TOUR MONEY LEADERS

1	DAVE STOCKTON	$1,303,280
2	JIM COLBERT	$1,167,352
3	BOB MURPHY	$1,146,591
4	RAY FLOYD	$1,118,545
5	ISAO AOKI	$964,833
6	J.C. SNEAD	$956,937
7	LEE TREVINO	$909,010
8	GRAHAM MARSH	$790,178
9	HALE IRWIN	$751,175
10	JIM ALBUS	$708,711
11	GEORGE ARCHER	$698,787
12	B. SUMMERHAYS	$671,421
13	TOM WARGO	$641,187
14	BOB CHARLES	$589,832
15	JAY SIGEL	$541,707
16	JACK NICKLAUS	$538,800
17	R. THOMPSON	$533,021
18	JIM DENT	$527,531
19	TOM WEISKOPF	$525,237
20	MIKE HILL	$523,136
21	D. EICHELBERGER	$519,066
22	BUD ALLIN	$501,092
23	KERMIT ZARLEY	$499,939
24	LARRY GILBERT	$456,728
25	JACK KIEFER	$437,508
26	SIMON HOBDAY	$429,767
27	WALTER MORGAN	$404,456
28	JOHN PAUL CAIN	$382,421
29	JIMMY POWELL	$376,339
30	JERRY MCGEE	$366,697
31	TONY JACKLIN	$366,114
32	LARRY LAORETTI	$366,049
33	GIBBY GILBERT	$359,278
34	AL GEIBERGER	$358,835
35	DALE DOUGLASS	$334,654
36	DON BIES	$320,500
37	BEN SMITH	$307,798
38	DEWITT WEAVER	$301,919
39	GARY PLAYER	$287,251
40	TERRY DILL	$282,361
41	TOMMY AARON	$281,474
42	BOB SMITH	$279,807

#	Name	Money
43	LARRY ZIEGLER	$246,131
44	H. HENNING	$234,697
45	BOB DICKSON	$233,223
46	BUTCH BAIRD	$227,377
47	BRUCE DEVLIN	$224,143
48	HARRY TOSCANO	$216,297
49	ED SNEED	$206,021
50	CALVIN PEETE	$199,067
51	DAVE HILL	$197,466
52	WALTER ZEMBRISKI	$194,157
53	C. RODRIGUEZ	$179,889
54	RIVES MCBEE	$170,044
55	TOM SHAW	$169,122
56	JIM FERREE	$166,917
57	D. HENDRICKSON	$165,222
58	CHARLES COODY	$155,862
59	DEANE BEMAN	$153,811
60	MARION HECK	$153,558
61	DICK RHYAN	$152,054
62	CHUCK MONTALBANO	$149,370
63	JOHN BLAND	$146,867
64	GAY BREWER	$142,752
65	R. ZIMMERMAN	$139,168
66	JOE JIMENEZ	$131,461
67	MILLER BARBER	$129,108
68	DICK GOETZ	$126,111
69	BOB BETLEY	$103,486
70	M. MCCULLOUGH	$101,692
71	BOBBY MITCHELL	$98,188
72	HOMERO BLANCAS	$98,006
73	GARY GROH	$95,559
74	DON JANUARY	$91,717
75	BABE HISKEY	$89,279
76	BOBBY NICHOLS	$88,669
77	ROBERT LANDERS	$74,078
78	B. CRAMPTON	$73,404
79	ORVILLE MOODY	$69,021
80	MIKE STILL	$66,118
81	BOB BRUE	$61,596
82	ROBERT GAONA	$57,114
83	BRIAN BARNES	$56,717
84	MIKE JOYCE	$53,186
85	BOB WYNN	$52,729
86	ARNOLD PALMER	$51,526
87	BILLY CASPER	$50,982
88	LARRY MOWRY	$47,343
89	KEN STILL	$47,041
90	RICHIE KARL	$46,906
91	LEE ELDER	$43,796
92	BOB CARSON	$42,183
93	ROGER KENNEDY	$41,869
94	GENE LITTLER	$41,506
95	B. LEHNHARD	$41,329
96	DICK LOTZ	$34,194
97	JOHN BRODIE	$32,785
98	DON DAVIS	$25,066
99	BOB TOSKI	$22,155
100	AL KELLEY	$22,055
101	CHARLES SIFFORD	$20,541
102	D. MASSENGALE	$20,394
103	TOM ULOZAS	$18,961
104	BOB LEAVER	$17,999
105	TED HAYES	$17,470
106	RON SKILES	$17,427
107	JOHN MORGAN	$16,674
108	BOB MENNE	$14,240
109	SNELL LANCASTER	$14,181
110	BOB THATCHER	$14,177
111	BILL KENNEDY	$13,942
112	DENNY SPENCER	$13,488
113	ROGER STERN	$13,272
114	TOM JOYCE	$13,262
115	NOEL RATCLIFFE	$13,000
116	BOB IRVING	$12,688
117	JOHN JACOBS	$12,603
118	AGIM BARDHA	$12,552
119	ROY ABRAMEIT	$12,384
120	LARRY RINGER	$12,030
121	BILL HALL	$12,005
122	W. ARMSTRONG	$11,645
123	SEIICHI KANAI	$10,500
124	BOB LUNN	$10,463
125	ROBERT RAWLINS	$10,364
126	MARTY BOHEN	$10,350
127	BOB HAUER	$9,191
128	STEVE ROBBINS	$9,062
129	BOBBY STROBLE	$8,980
130	LOU GRAHAM	$8,920
131	BOB REITH	$8,423
132	T. HORTON	$7,601
133	RON WIDBY	$6,668
134	R. BASSETT	$6,276
135	MIKE FETCHICK	$6,168
136	BILL TINDALL	$5,975
137	DWIGHT NEVIL	$5,780
138	CHARLIE EPPS	$5,640
139	GARY COWAN	$5,463
140	BILLY MAXWELL	$5,122
141	JIM WILKINSON	$4,920
142	DAVE OJALA	$4,879
143	JOE HUBER	$4,622
144	FRED RUIZ	$4,500
145	RANDY GLOVER	$4,232
146	BILL LYTLE	$4,190
147	JESSE VAUGHN	$4,180
148	BOB GOALBY	$3,855
149	BILL MILLER	$3,703
150	ROD CURL	$3,587

ALL-TIME SR. PGA TOUR MONEY LEADERS

#	Name	Money
1	LEE TREVINO	$5,784,327
2	BOB CHARLES	$5,640,898
3	CHI CHI RODRIGUEZ	$5,244,386
4	MIKE HILL	$4,994,635
5	GEORGE ARCHER	$4,967,092
6	JIM COLBERT	$4,532,856
7	DALE DOUGLASS	$4,380,971
8	DAVE STOCKTON	$4,283,149
9	JIM DENT	$4,121,862

Statistics and Money Lists

10	BRUCE CRAMPTON	$3,666,812
11	GARY PLAYER	$3,578,363
12	RAY FLOYD	$3,531,105
13	MILLER BARBER	$3,493,553
14	AL GEIBERGER	$3,399,205
15	JIM ALBUS	$3,179,736
16	ORVILLE MOODY	$3,116,776
17	HAROLD HENNING	$3,095,542
18	DON JANUARY	$2,904,155
19	CHARLES COODY	$2,811,306
20	ROCKY THOMPSON	$2,744,364
21	BOB MURPHY	$2,657,346
22	J.C. SNEAD	$2,652,598
23	WALTER ZEMBRISKI	$2,549,442
24	SIMON HOBDAY	$2,451,656
25	ISAO AOKI	$2,382,324
26	GIBBY GILBERT	$2,326,989
27	JIM FERREE	$2,286,348
28	DAVE HILL	$2,254,218
29	JIMMY POWELL	$2,151,327
30	TOM WARGO	$2,133,846
31	DON BIES	$2,080,513
32	GENE LITTLER	$2,077,672
33	TOMMY AARON	$1,853,207
34	DEWITT WEAVER	$1,836,042
35	JACK NICKLAUS	$1,782,388
36	LARRY GILBERT	$1,760,766
37	KERMIT ZARLEY	$1,760,633
38	GAY BREWER	$1,753,865
39	BUTCH BAIRD	$1,734,347
40	LARRY LAORETTI	$1,723,278
41	BOBBY NICHOLS	$1,719,024
42	BEN SMITH	$1,701,061
43	BILLY CASPER	$1,664,210
44	LARRY MOWRY	$1,643,813
45	TOM SHAW	$1,641,082
46	ARNOLD PALMER	$1,577,609
47	JACK KIEFER	$1,541,749
48	RIVES MCBEE	$1,486,167
49	DICK HENDRICKSON	$1,477,593
50	LEE ELDER	$1,458,226

PGA EUROPEAN TOUR

PGA EUROPEAN TOUR MONEY LEADERS

1	TORRANCE, SAM	£630,481
2	MONTGOMERIE, COLIN	£626,651
3	LANGER, BERNHARD	£570,174
4	ROCCA, C.	£459,945
5	CAMPBELL, MICHAEL	£361,267
6	JAMES, MARK	£265,827
7	LANE, BARRY	£259,196
8	FORSBRAND, A.	£242,046
9	O'MALLEY, PETER	£237,951
10	RILEY, WAYNE	£237,951
11	WALTON, PHILIP	£218,056
12	CLARK, HOWARD	£215,168
13	CLARKE, DARREN	£208,675
14	BROADHURST, PAUL	£194,942
15	PARNEVIK, JESPER	£194,879
16	RIVERO, JOSE	£185,558
17	NOBILO, FRANK	£173,456
18	SANDELIN, JARMO	£169,306
19	GRONBERG, M.	£167,488
20	GILFORD, DAVID	£167,323
21	JOHANSSON, PER-ULRIK	£165,179
22	JIMENEZ, M. ANGEL	£160,921
23	CEJKA, ALEXANDER	£157,114
24	TERAVAINEN, PETER	£155,497
25	TURNER, GREG	£153,144
26	RAFFERTY, RONAN	£149,570
27	BAKER, PETER	£147,286
28	BALLESTEROS, SEVE	£145,285
29	GARRIDO, IGNACIO	£143,838
30	COLTART, ANDREW	£141,359
31	SPENCE, JAMIE	£140,537
32	STRUVER, SVEN	£138,546
33	MITCHELL, PETER	£137,289
34	LYLE, SANDY	£136,644
35	OLDCORN, A.	£135,269
36	JONZON, MICHAEL	£133,559
37	COOPER, DERRICK	£131,542
38	LUNA, SANTIAGO	£129,189
39	CLAYDON, RUSSELL	£128,049
40	KARLSSON, ROBERT	£127,599
41	HAEGGMAN, JOAKIM	£127,491
42	CAGE, STUART	£125,867
43	TOWNSEND, JAY	£124,795
44	ALLENBY, ROBERT	£120,005
45	HEDBLOM, PETER	£119,361
46	COCERES, JOSE	£116,215
47	CHAPMAN, ROGER	£114,263
48	LANNER, MATS	£113,712
49	EALES, PAUL	£112,719
50	KARLSSON, OLLE	£109,648

1995 SONY RANKINGS

1	NORMAN, GREG, AUS	22.21
2	LANGER, BERNHARD, EUR	16.01
3	PRICE, NICK, ZIM	15.83
4	ELS, ERNIE, AFR	15.81
5	FALDO, NICK, ENG	14.42
6	MONTGOMERIE, COLIN, EUR	14.29
7	PAVIN, COREY, USA	12.69
8	COUPLES, FRED, USA	12.23
9	ELKINGTON, STEVE, AUS	10.72
10	OZAKI, JUMBO, JPN	10.47
11	LEHMAN, TOM, USA	9.74
12	OLAZABAL, JOSE MARIA, SP	9.73
13	SINGH, VIJAY, ASA	8.68
14	TORRANCE, SAM, EUR	8.33
15	JANZEN, LEE, USA	8.29
16	ROBERTS, LOREN, USA	8.23
17	MCCUMBER, MARK, USA	8.18
18	LOVE III, DAVIS, USA	7.98
19	FROST, DAVID, SA	7.67
20	JACOBSEN, PETER, USA	7.64
21	CRENSHAW, BEN, USA	7.27

22	HOCH, SCOTT, USA	7.17		82	CEJKA, ALEXANDER, EUR	3.49
23	ROCCA, COSTANTINO, EUR	7.14		83	MORGAN, GIL, USA	3.39
24	MICKELSON, PHIL, USA	7.10		84	OZAKI, JOE, JPN	3.38
25	BALLESTEROS, SEVE, SP	7.01		85	JOBE, BRANDT, USA	3.33
26	ZOELLER, FUZZY, USA	6.90		86	HAEGGMAN, JOAKIM, EUR	3.29
27	GALLAGHER JR., JIM, USA	6.65		87	ROMERO, EDUARDO, SAM	3.15
28	HAAS, JAY, USA	6.63		88	HAMILTON, TODD, USA	3.14
29	FAXON, BRAD, USA	6.25		89	RILEY, WAYNE, ANZ	3.08
30	MCNULTY, MARK, ZIM	6.23		90	COOK, JOHN, USA	3.04
31	MAGGERT, JEFF, USA	6.07		91	CLEMENTS, LENNIE, USA	3.01
32	STEWART, PAYNE, USA	6.06		92	TURNER, GREG, ANZ	3.00
33	WATSON, TOM, USA	5.97		93	RIVERO, JOSE, EUR	2.94
34	CALCAVECCHIA, MARK, USA	5.96		94	FEHR, RICK, USA	2.93
35	WOOSNAM, IAN, EUR	5.87		95	ROE, MARK, EUR	2.91
36	SIMPSON, SCOTT, USA	5.75		96	O'MALLEY, PETER, ANZ	2.89
37	MAYFAIR, BILLY, USA	5.72		97	BAKER, PETER, EUR	2.83
38	PARNEVIK, JESPER, EUR	5.68		98	JOHNSTONE, TONY, ZIM	2.81
39	GLASSON, BILL, USA	5.61		99	FURYK, JIM, USA	2.76
40	DUVAL, DAVID, USA	5.46		100	KURAMOTO, WASAH'O, JPN	2.75
41	CAMPBELL, MICHAEL, AUS	5.26				
42	O'MEARA, MARK, USA	5.13				
43	ESTES, BOB, USA	5.11				

PING LEADERBOARD

44	DALY, JOHN, USA	4.85				
45	MIZE, LARRY, USA	4.83				
46	KITE, TOM, USA	4.82		1	DAVIES, LAURA, ENG	369.98
47	PERRY, KENNY, USA	4.81		2	SORENSTAM, ANNIKA, SWE	269.80
48	GILFORD, DAVID, EUR	4.80		3	DANIEL, BETH, USA	209.11
49	JAMES, MARK, EUR	4.76		4	MOCHRIE, DOTTIE, USA	197.65
50	NOBILO, FRANK, ANZ	4.72		5	NEUMANN, L., SWE	186.61
51	STADLER, CRAIG, USA	4.70		6	KING, BETSY, USA	168.37
52	WATTS, BRIAN, USA	4.67		7	ROBBINS, KELLY, USA	165.09
53	AZINGER, PAUL, USA	4.61		8	MCGANN, MICHELLE, USA	145.83
54	ALLENBY, ROBERT, ANZ	4.52		9	MALLON, MEG, USA	139.64
55	SENIOR, PETER, AUS	4.50		10	GREEN, TAMMIE, USA	126.68
56	PARRY, CRAIG, AUS	4.49		11	SHEEHAN, PATTY, USA	123.71
57	IRWIN, HALE, USA	4.49		12	ALFREDSSON, HELEN, SWE	122.44
58	JIMENEZ, MIGUEL A., EUR	4.47		13	BRADLEY, PAT, USA	116.06
59	LANE, BARRY, EUR	4.46		14	JONES, ROSIE, USA	115.63
60	TWAY, BOB, USA	4.31		15	NICHOLAS, ALISON, ENG	114.75
61	LIETZKE, BRUCE, USA	4.22		16	GEDDES, JANE, USA	114.63
62	STRANGE, CURTIS, USA	4.20		17	SKINNER, VAL, USA	110.89
63	LEONARD, JUSTIN, USA	4.11		18	HIRASE, MAYUMI, JPN	110.73
64	TRIPLETT, KIRK, USA	4.11		19	SHIOTANI, IKUYO, JPN	102.60
65	OGLE, BRETT, AUS	4.08		20	DE LORENZI, MARIE., FRA	97.15
66	WALDORF, DUFFY, USA	4.05		21	STEINHAUER, SHERRI, USA	88.74
67	FORSBRAND, ANDERS, EUR	4.03		22	FUKUSHIMA, AKIKO, JPN	87.63
68	NAKAJIMA, TOMMY, JPN	3.99		23	TSCHETTER, KRIS, USA	86.17
69	FUNK, FRED, USA	3.98		24	EGGELING, DALE USA	84.96
70	AUSTIN, WOODY, USA	3.95		25	KOBAYASHI, HIROMI, JPN	83.54
71	HUSTON, JOHN, USA	3.92		26	COE-JONES, DAWN, CAN	82.35
72	WEIBRING, D.A., USA	3.90		27	CROSBY, ELAINE, USA	82.15
73	BRYANT, BRAD, USA	3.85		28	FAIRLOUGH, LORA, ENG	79.00
74	LOWERY, STEVE, USA	3.76		29	MCGUIRE, MARNIE, NZ	75.38
75	CLARK, HOWARD, EUR	3.75		30	DIBNAH, CORINNE, AUS	73.73
76	JOHANSSON, P., EUR	3.73		31	LARSEN, JULIE, USA	70.88
77	EDWARDS, DAVID, USA	3.69		32	ANDREWS, DONNA, USA	68.59
78	STRICKER, STEVE, USA	3.67		33	WALKER, COLLEEN, USA	65.91
79	CLARKE, DARREN, EUR	3.63		34	BURTON, BRANDIE, USA	65.82
80	SLUMAN, JEFF, USA	3.63		35	HIGO, KAORI, JPN	64.10
81	SUTTON, HAL, USA	3.57		36	INKSTER, JULI, USA	61.69

37	BOWEN, NANCI, USA	60.05	69	STEPHENSON, JAN, AUS	34.65
38	LOPEZ, NANCY, USA	59.95	70	YASUI, JANKO, JPN	34.37
39	HUANG, BIE-SHYUN, TWN	59.13	71	MARSHALL, KATHRYN., SCOT	34.08
40	JOHNSON, CHRIS, USA	58.74	72	KIMURA, TOSHIMI, JPN	33.50
41	MORIGUCHI, YUKO, JPN	55.86	72	WRIGHT, PAM, SCOT	33.50
42	WEBB, KARRIE, AUS	52.73	74	YOSHIKAWA, NAYOKO, JPN	33.40
43	LIDBACK, JENNY, PER	52.45	75	YAMAOKA, AYEMI, JPN	32.85
44	PIERCE, CAROLINE, ENG	52.25	76	IVERSON, BECKY, USA	32.75
45	LEE, YOUNG-ME, KOR	52.15	77	RITZMAN, ALICE, USA	32.40
46	WON, JAE-SOOK, KOR	52.08	78	RAMSBOTTOM, N., USA	32.00
47	PITCOCK, JOAN, USA	52.02	79	KU, OK-HEE, KOR	31.75
48	HASHIMOTO, AIKO, JPN	49.33	80	RARICK, CINDY, USA	31.61
49	HETHERINGTON, RACHEL, AUS	49.08	81	MCGEORGE, MISSIE USA	30.55
50	HATTORI, MICHIKO, JPN	48.80	82	KIGGENS, LISA, USA	29.30
51	JOHNSON, TRISH, ENG	47.53	83	DICKINSON, JUDY, USA	29.07
52	HANSON, TRACY, USA	47.04	84	NAUSE, MARTHA, USA	28.91
53	KERDYK, TRACY, USA	46.12	85	HACKNEY, LISA, ENG	28.80
54	REDMAN, MICHELE, USA	45.04	86	ZIMMERMAN, MARY BETH, USA	28.63
55	RICHARD, DEB, USA	43.49	87	REDMAN, SUSIE, USA	28.25
56	GRAHAM, GAIL, CANADA	43.47	88	MERTEN, LAURI, USA	27.82
57	OKAMOTO, AYAKO, JPN	41.98	89	LUNN, MARDI, AUS	27.70
58	KO, WOO SOON, SKO	41.25	90	KARINA ORUM, DEN	27.68
59	THOMAS, BARB, USA	40.77	91	DIBOS, ALICIA, PER	27.15
60	NAKANO, AKI, JPN	40.73	92	DASSU, FEDERICA, ITL	27.00
61	TAKAMURA, AKI, JPN	39.75	93	HIYOSHI, KUMIKO, JPN	26.15
62	MUCHA, BARB, USA	39.16	94	TURNER, SHERRI, USA	26.10
63	KLEIN, EMILEE, USA	38.56	95	MEUNIER, PATRICIA, FRA	25.30
64	PETERSON-PARKER, K., USA	38.10	95	ALCOTT, AMY, USA	25.30
65	AMMACCAPANE, D., USA	35.80	97	DESCAMPE, F., BEL	24.80
66	HJALMARSSON, C., SWE	35.16	98	HALL, CAROLINE, ENG	24.25
67	ESTILL, MICHELLE, USA	34.95	98	REID, DALE, SCOT	24.25
68	MORRIS, MARIANNE, USA	34.80	100	FORBES, JULIE, SCOT	24.24

PGA TOUR PERSONALITIES

OVERVIEW: *Biographies and career summaries of leading PGA Tour personalities.*

FULTON ALLEM
Birthdate: September 15, 1957
Birthplace: Kroonstad, South Africa
PGA TOUR Victories: (3) 1991 Independent Insurance Agent Open. 1993 Southwestern Bell Colonial, NEC World Series of Golf.
Other Victories: None.
National/International Teams: None.

PGA TOUR CAREER SUMMARY
Year	Money	Rank
1987	$88,734	105
1988	$163,911	73
1989	$134,706	104
1990	$134,493	116
1991	$229,702	71
1992	$208,981	74
1993	$851,345	9
1994	$166,144	109
1995	$54,239	199
Career	$2,031,256	96

BILLY ANDRADE
Birthdate: January 25, 1964
Birthplace: Fall River, MA
PGA TOUR Victories: 1991 Kemper Open, Buick Classic.
Other Victories: None.
National/International Teams: 1986 World Amateur Cup. 1987 Walker Cup.

PGA TOUR CAREER SUMMARY
Year	Money	Rank
1988	$74,950	134
1989	$202,242	69
1990	$231,362	64
1991	$615,765	14
1992	$202,509	76
1993	$365,759	40
1994	$342,208	48
1995	$276,494	69
Career	$2,311,290	79

WOODY AUSTIN
Birthdate: January 27, 1964
Birthplace: Tampa, FL
PGA TOUR Victories: (1) 1995 Buick Open
Other Victories: None.
National/International Teams: None.

PGA TOUR CAREER SUMMARY
Year	Money	Rank
1995	$736,497	24
Career	$736,497	NR

PAUL AZINGER
Birthdate: January 6, 1960
Birthplace: Holyoke, MA
PGA TOUR Victories: (11) 1987 Phoenix Open, Panasonic-Las Vegas Invitational, Canon-Sammy Davis Jr. Greater Hartford Open. 1988 Hertz Bay Hill Classic. 1989 Canon Greater Hartford Open. 1990 MONY Tournament of Champions. 1991 AT&T Pebble Beach National Pro-Am. 1992 Tour Championship. 1993 Memorial Tournament, New England Classic, PGA Championship.
Other Victories: 1988 Fred Meyer Challenge (with Bob Tway), 1990 BMW Open, 1991 Fred Meyer Challenge (with Ben Crenshaw). 1992 BMW Open.
National/International Teams: 1989 Ryder Cup, World Cup. 1991 Ryder Cup. 1993 Ryder Cup.

PGA TOUR CAREER SUMMARY
Year	Money	Rank
1982	$10,655	171
1983	DNP	---
1984	$27,821	144
1985	$81,179	93
1986	$254,019	29
1987	$822,481	2
1988	$594,850	11
1989	$951,649	3
1990	$944,731	4
1991	$685,603	9
1992	$929,863	7

Year	Money	Rank
1993	$1,458,456	2
1994	$13,422	242
1995	$182,595	100
Career	$6,957,324	8

DAVE BARR

Birthdate: March 1, 1952
Birthplace: Kelowna, British Columbia
PGA TOUR Victories: (2) **1981** Quad Cities Open. **1987** Georgia-Pacific Atlanta Golf Classic.
Other Victories: 1983 World Cup Individual Title. **1985** World Cup Team Title (with Dan Halldorson). **1994** Alfred Dunhill Cup.
National/International Teams: 1972 Canadian World Amateur Cup. **1977, 1978, 1982, 1983, 1984, 1985, 1987, 1988, 1989, 1990, 1991, 1993** World Cup. **1986, 1987, 1988, 1989, 1990, 1993, 1994** Dunhill Cup.

PGA TOUR CAREER SUMMARY

Year	Money	Rank
1978	$11,897	133
1979	$13,022	142
1980	$14,664	141
1981	$46,214	90
1982	$12,474	166
1983	$52,800	96
1984	$113,336	62
1985	$126,177	65
1986	$122,181	70
1987	$202,241	54
1988	$291,244	33
1989	$190,480	75
1990	$197,979	80
1991	$144,389	108
1992	$118,859	119
1993	$179,264	96
1994	$314,885	53
1995	$118,218	147
Career	$2,270,323	84

CHIP BECK

Birthdate: September 12, 1956
Birthplace: Fayetteville, NC
PGA TOUR Victories: (4) **1988** Los Angeles Open, USF&G Classic. **1990** Buick Open. **1992** Freeport-McMoran Classic.
Other Victories: 1989, 1992 Merrill Lynch Shoot-Out Championships.
National/International Teams: 1988 KirinCup. **1989** Asahi Glass Four Tours World Championship of Golf. **1989, 1991, 1993** Ryder Cup.

PGA TOUR CAREER SUMMARY

Year	Money	Rank
1980	$17,109	131
1981	$30,034	110
1982	$57,608	76
1983	$149,909	33
1984	$177,289	34
1985	$76,036	97
1986	$215,140	39
1987	$523,003	9
1988	$918,818	2
1989	$894,087	9
1990	$571,816	17
1991	$578,535	16
1992	$689,703	17
1993	$803,376	25
1994	$281,131	68
1995	$170,081	111
Career	$5,755,844	16

JAY DON BLAKE

Birthdate: October 28, 1958
Birthplace: St. George, UT
PGA TOUR Victories: 1991 Shearson Lehman Brothers Open.
Other Victories: None.
National/International Teams: None.

PGA TOUR CAREER SUMMARY

Year	Money	Rank
1987	$ 87,634	106
1988	$131,937	90
1989	$200,499	71
1990	$148,384	106
1991	$563,854	21
1992	$299,298	51
1993	$202,482	86
1994	$309,351	55
1995	$333,551	54
Career	$2,276,989	90

GUY BOROS

Birthdate: September 4, 1964
Birthplace: Ft. Lauderdale, FL
PGA TOUR Victories: None.
National/International Teams: None.

PGA TOUR CAREER SUMMARY

Year	Money	Rank
1995	$303,654	62
Career	$303,654	NR

MICHAEL BRADLEY
Birthdate: July 17, 1966
Birthplace: Largo, FL
PGA TOUR Victories: None.
National/International Teams: None.

PGA TOUR CAREER SUMMARY
Year	Money	Rank
1993	$126,160	121
1994	$175,137	104
1995	$214,469	85
Career	$515,766	NR

MARK BROOKS
Birthdate: March 25, 1961
Birthplace: Fort Worth, TX
PGA TOUR Victories: (4) 1988 Canon Sammy Davis, Jr. Greater Hartford Open. 1991 Kmart Greater Greensboro Open, Greater Milwaukee Open. 1994 Kemper Open.
Other Victories: None.
National/International Teams: None.

PGA TOUR CAREER SUMMARY
Year	Money	Rank
1984	$40,438	122
1985	$32,094	141
1986	$47,264	140
1987	$42,100	165
1988	$280,636	36
1989	$112,834	115
1990	$307,948	45
1991	$667,263	11
1992	$629,754	21
1993	$249,697	66
1994	$523,285	31
1995	$366,860	48
Career	$3,300,176	51

BRAD BRYANT
Birthdate: December 11, 1954
Birthplace: Amarillo, TX
PGA TOUR Victories: (1) 1995 Walt Disney World Oldsmobile Classic.
Other Victories: 1988 Utah State Open.
National/International Teams: None.

PGA TOUR CAREER SUMMARY
Year	Money	Rank
1978	$4,350	173
1979	$63,013	67
1980	$56,115	68
1981	$52,070	80
1982	$99,576	37
1983	$93,021	61
1984	$36,605	127
1985	$1,683	231
1986	$11,290	202
1987	$17,090	191
1988	$62,614	141
1989	$174,393	84
1990	$189,795	86
1991	$152,202	99
1992	$227,529	69
1993	$230,139	74
1994	$687,803	18
1995	$723,834	25
Career	$2,866,233	61

BOB BURNS
Birthdate: May 5, 1968
Birthplace: Mission Hills, CA
PGA TOUR Victories: None.
Other Victories: 1990 NCAA Division II Championship.
National/International Teams: None.

PGA TOUR CAREER SUMMARY
Year	Money	Rank
1994	$178,168	101
1995	$59,243	191
Career	$237,411	NR

CURT BYRUM
Birthdate: December 29, 1958
Birthplace: Onida, SD
PGA TOUR Victories: (1) 1989 Hardee's Golf Classic.
National/International Teams: None.

PGA TOUR CAREER SUMMARY
Year	Money	Rank
1983	$30,772	130
1984	$27,836	143
1985	$6,943	193
1986	$79,454	108
1987	$212,450	46
1988	$208,853	55
1989	$221,702	64
1990	$117,134	129
1991	$78,125	148
1992	$31,450	194
1993	—	—
1994	$137,587	128
1995	$173,838	107
Career	$1,326,743	NR

MARK CALCAVECCHIA
Birthdate: June 12, 1960

Birthplace: Laurel, NE
PGA TOUR Victories: (7) **1986** Southwest Golf Classic. **1987** Honda Classic. **1988** Bank of Boston Classic. **1989** Phoenix Open, Nissan Los Angeles Open. **1992** Phoenix Open. **1995** Bell South Classic.
Other Victories: **1988** Australian Open.
National/International Teams: **1987** Kirin Cup. **1987, 1989, 1991** Ryder Cup. **1989, 1990** Asahi Glass Four Tours World Championship of Golf. **1989, 1990** Dunhill Cup.

PGA TOUR CAREER SUMMARY

Year	Money	Rank
1981	$404	253
1982	$25,064	134
1983	$16,313	161
1984	$29,660	140
1985	$15,957	162
1986	$155,012	58
1987	$522,423	10
1988	$751,912	6
1989	$807,741	5
1990	$834,281	7
1991	$323,621	50
1992	$377,234	39
1993	$630,366	21
1994	$533,201	30
1995	$843,552	13
Career	$5,866,716	14

MARK CARNEVALE

Birthdate: May 21, 1960
Birthplace: Annapolis, MD
PGA TOUR Victories: (1) **1992** Chattanooga Classic.
Other Victories: **1984** Virginia Open. **1990** Utah Open.
National/International Teams: None.

PGA TOUR CAREER SUMMARY

Year	Money	Rank
1992	$220,921	70
1993	$100,046	145
1994	$192,653	93
1995	$62,206	185
Career	$575,827	NR

BRIAN CLAAR

Birthdate: July 29, 1959
Birthplace: Santa Monica, CA
PGA TOUR Victories: None.
Other Victories: **1989** Hong Kong Open, Thailand Open.
National/International Teams: None.

PGA TOUR CAREER SUMMARY

Year	Money	Rank
1986	$117,355	7
1987	$43,111	162
1988	$30,276	172
1989	$88,010	133
1990	$161,356	98
1991	$251,309	67
1992	$192,255	78
1993	$202,624	85
1994	$165,370	110
1995	$241,107	75
Career	$1,462,496	NR

LENNIE CLEMENTS

Birthdate: January 20, 1957
Birthplace: Cherry Point, NC
PGA TOUR Victories: None.
Other Victories: **1982** Timex Open. **1983** Sahara Nevada Open. **1988** Spalding Invitational.
National/International Teams: None.

PGA TOUR CAREER SUMMARY

Year	Money	Rank
1981	$7,786	178
1982	$44,796	97
1983	$44,455	110
1984	$25,712	146
1985	$49,383	120
1986	$112,642	79
1987	$124,989	83
1988	$86,332	120
1989	$69,399	147
1990	$80,095	146
1991	$62,827	163
1992	$30,121	198
1993	$141,526	115
1994	$416,880	39
1995	$355,130	51
Career	$1,652,055	NR

RUSS COCHRAN

Birthdate: October 31, 1958
Birthplace: Paducah, KY
PGA TOUR Victories: (1) **1991** Western Open.
Other Victories: **1983** Magnolia Classic, Greater Baltimore Open.
National/International Teams: None.

PGA TOUR CAREER SUMMARY

Year	Money	Rank
1983	$7,986	188

Year	Money	Rank
1984	$133,342	51
1985	$87,331	87
1986	$89,817	92
1987	$148,110	74
1988	$148,960	80
1989	$132,678	107
1990	$230,278	65
1991	$684,851	10
1992	$326,290	46
1993	$293,868	59
1994	$239,827	77
1995	$145,663	131
Career	$2,668,983	69

JOHN COOK
Birthdate: October 2, 1957
Birthplace: Toledo, OH
PGA TOUR Victories: (6) **1981** Bing Crosby National Pro-Am. **1983** Canadian Open. **1987** The International. **1992** Bob Hope Chrysler Classic, United Airlines Hawaiian Open, Las Vegas Invitational.
Other Victories: 1978 U.S. Amateur. **1982** Sao Paulo Brazilian Open. **1983** World Cup Team Title (with Rex Caldwell).
National/International Teams: 1979 World Amateur Cup. **1983** World Cup. **1993** Ryder Cup.

PGA TOUR CAREER SUMMARY
Year	Money	Rank
1980	$43,316	78
1981	$127,608	25
1982	$57,483	77
1983	$216,868	16
1984	$65,710	89
1985	$53,573	106
1986	$255,126	27
1987	$333,184	29
1988	$139,916	84
1989	$39,445	172
1990	$448,112	28
1991	$646,984	26
1992	$1,165,606	3
1993	$342,321	45
1994	$429,725	37
1995	$186,977	97
Career	$4,461,954	33

FRED COUPLES
Birthdate: October 3, 1959
Birthplace: Seattle, WA
PGA TOUR Victories: (10) **1983** Kemper Open. **1984** Tournament Players Championship. **1987** Byron Nelson Golf Classic. **1990** Nissan Los Angeles Open. **1991** Federal Express St. Jude Classic, B.C. Open. **1992** Nissan Los Angeles Open, Nestle Invitational, Masters. **1993** Honda Classic.
Other Victories: 1991 Johnnie Walker World Championship of Golf in Jamaica. **1990** RMCC invitational (with Ray Floyd), Sazale Classic (with Mike Donald). **1992, 1993, 1994** World Cup (with Davis Love III). **1995** Dubai Desert Classic, Johnnie Walker Classic.
National/International Teams: 1984 U.S. vs. Japan. **1989, 1991, 1993** Ryder Cup. **1990, 1991** Asahi Glass Four Tours World Championship of Golf. **1992, 1993** Dunhill Cup. **1992, 1993, 1994, 1995** World Cup.

PGA TOUR CAREER SUMMARY
Year	Money	Rank
1981	$78,939	53
1982	$77,606	53
1983	$209,733	19
1984	$334,573	7
1985	$171,272	38
1986	$116,065	76
1987	$441,025	19
1988	$489,822	21
1989	$693,944	11
1990	$757,999	9
1991	$791,749	3
1992	$1,364,188	1
1993	$796,579	10
1994	$625,654	23
1995	$299,259	63
Career	$7,188,408	5

BEN CRENSHAW
Birthdate: January 11, 1952
Birthplace: Austin, TX
PGA TOUR Victories: (18) **1973** San Antonio-Texas Open. **1976** Bing Crosby National Pro-Am, Hawaiian Open, Kings Island Open. **1977** Colonial National Invitational. **1979** Phoenix Open, Walt Disney World Team Championship (with George Burns). **1980** Anheuser-Busch Classic. **1983** Byron Nelson Classic. **1984** Masters. **1986** Buick Open, Vantage Championship. **1987** USF&G Classic. **1988** Doral Ryder Open. **1990** Southwestern Bell Colonial. **1992** Centel Western Open. **1993** Nestle Invitational. **1995** Masters.
Other Victories: 1976 Irish Open. **1980** Texas State Open. **1988** World Cup Individual Title.
National/International Teams: 1981, 1983, 1987 Ryder Cup. **1983** U.S. vs. Japan. **1987, 1988** World Cup. **1988** Kirin Cup. **1995** Dunhill Cup.

PGA TOUR CAREER SUMMARY

Year	Money	Rank
1980	$237,727	8
1981	$151,038	20
1982	$54,277	83
1983	$275,474	7
1984	$270,989	16
1985	$25,814	149
1986	$388,169	8
1987	$638,194	3
1988	$696,895	8
1989	$433,095	21
1990	$351,193	33
1991	$224,563	75
1992	$439,071	31
1993	$318,605	51
1994	$659,252	21
1995	$737,475	23
Career	$6,845,235	8

JOHN DALY

Birthdate: April 28, 1966
Birthplace: Sacramento, CA
PGA TOUR Victories: (3) 1991 PGA Championship. 1992 B.C. Open. 1994 Bell South Classic.
Other Victories: 1987 Missouri Open. 1990 Ben Hogan Utah Classic. 1995 British Open.
National/International Teams: 1992, 1993, 1994 Dunhill Cup.

PGA TOUR CAREER SUMMARY

Year	Money	Rank
1991	$574,783	17
1992	$387,455	37
1993	$225,591	76
1994	$340,034	49
1995	$321,748	57
Career	$1,849,961	NR

GLEN DAY

Birthdate: November 16, 1965
Birthplace: Mobile, AL
PGA TOUR Victories: None.
Other Victories: 1989 Malaysian Open.
National/International Teams: None.

PGA TOUR CAREER SUMMARY

Year	Money	Rank
1994	$357,236	45
1995	$201,809	91
Career	$559,045	NR

JAY DELSING

Birthdate: October 17, 1960
Birthplace: St. Louis, MO
PGA TOUR Victories: None.
Other Victories: None.
National/International Teams: None.

Year	Money	Rank
1985	$46,480	125
1986	$65,407	123
1987	$58,657	136
1988	$45,504	152
1989	$26,565	187
1990	$207,740	74
1991	$149,775	100
1992	$296,740	52
1993	$233,484	71
1994	$143,738	124
1995	$230,769	80
Career	$1,505,302	NR

ED DOUGHERTY

Birthdate: November 4, 1947
Birthplace: Chester, PA
PGA TOUR Victories: (1) 1995 Deposit Guaranty Classic.
Other Victories: 1985 PGA Club Pro Championship.
National/International Teams: None.

PGA TOUR CAREER SUMMARY

Year	Money	Rank
1975	$9,374	129
1976	$17,333	113
1977	$17,606	113
1978	$9,936	141
1979	$24,802	115
1980	$9,113	168
1981	DNP	---
1982	$27,948	128
1983-86	DNP	---
1987	$76,705	115
1988	$22,455	195
1989	$1,800	267
1990	$124,505	123
1991	$201,958	82
1992	$237,525	66
1993	$167,651	99
1994	$97,137	157
1995	$154,007	122
Career	$1,229,423	NR

DAVID DUVAL
Birthdate: February 9, 1971
Birthplace: Jacksonville, FL
PGA TOUR Victories: None
Other Victories: 1993 NIKE Wichita Open, NIKE TOUR Championship.
National/International Teams: None.

PGA TOUR CAREER SUMMARY
Year	Money	Rank
1993	$27,180	180
1994	$44,006	195
1995	$881,436	11
Career	$952,622	NR

DAVID EDWARDS
Birthdate: April 18, 1956
Birthplace: Neosho, MO
PGA TOUR Victories: (4) 1980 Walt Disney World Team Championship. 1984 Los Angeles Open. 1992 Memorial Tournament. 1993 MCI Heritage Classic.
Other Victories: 1978 NCAA Championship.
National/International Teams: None.

PGA TOUR CAREER SUMMARY
Year	Money	Rank
1980	$35,810	93
1981	$68,211	65
1982	$49,896	91
1983	$114,037	48
1984	$236,061	23
1985	$21,506	157
1986	$122,079	71
1987	$148,217	73
1988	$151,513	76
1989	$239,906	57
1990	$166,028	95
1991	$396,695	38
1992	$515,070	27
1993	$653,087	20
1994	$458,845	34
1995	$225,857	83
Career	$3,646,275	41

STEVE ELKINGTON
Birthdate: December 8, 1962
Birthplace: Inverell, Australia
PGA TOUR Victories: (5) 1990 Kmart Greater Greensboro Open. 1991 The Players Championship. 1992 Infiniti Tournament of Champions. 1995 Mercedes Championships, PGA Championship.
Other Victories: 1992 Australian Open.
National/International Teams: None.

PGA TOUR CAREER SUMMARY
Year	Money	Rank
1987	$75,738	118
1988	$149,972	79
1989	$231,062	61
1990	$548,564	18
1991	$549,120	25
1992	$746,352	12
1993	$675,383	17
1994	$294,943	62
1995	$1,254,352	5
Career	$4,525,487	31

ERNIE ELS
Birthdate: October 17, 1969
Birthplace: Johannesburg, South Africa
PGA TOUR Victories: (2) 1994 U.S. Open. 1995 Byron Nelson Classic.
Other Victories: 1995 South African PGA.
National/International Teams: None.

PGA TOUR CAREER SUMMARY
Year	Money	Rank
1991	$2,647	274
1992	$18,420	213
1993	$38,185	190
1994	$684,440	19
1995	$842,590	14
Career	$1,527,090	NR

BOB ESTES
Birthdate: February 2, 1966
Birthplace: Graham, TX
PGA TOUR Victories: None
Other Victories: 1988 Bogey Hills Invitational.
National/International Teams: None.

PGA TOUR CAREER SUMMARY
Year	Money	Rank
1988	$5,968	237
1989	$135,628	102
1990	$212,090	69
1991	$147,364	105
1992	$190,778	80
1993	$447,187	32
1994	$765,360	14
1995	$433,992	41
Career	$2,332,399	78

NICK FALDO
Birthdate: July 18, 1957
Birthplace: Hertfordshire, England
PGA TOUR Victories: (4) 1984 Sea Pines Heritage

Classic. **1989** Masters. **1990** Masters. **1995** Doral-Ryder Open.
Other Victories: **1987** British Open. **1990** British Open. **1992** British Open. **1993** Johnnie Walker World Championship.
National/International Teams: **1977, 1979, 1981, 1985, 1987, 1989, 1991, 1993, 1995** Ryder Cup. **1977, 1991** World Cup. **1985, 1988, 1987, 1991** Dunhill Cup. **1986** Nissan Cup. **1987** Kirin Cup. **1990** Four Tours Championship.

PGA TOUR CAREER SUMMARY

Year	Money	Rank
1981	$23,320	119
1982	$56,667	79
1983	$67,851	79
1984	$116,845	38
1985	$54,060	117
1986	$52,965	135
1987	$36,281	169
1988	$179,120	84
1989	$327,981	31
1990	$345,262	37
1991	$127,156	117
1992	$345,188	41
1993	$188,886	91
1994	$221,146	83
1995	$790,961	19
Career	$2,933,669	78

BRAD FAXON

Birthdate: August 1, 1961
Birthplace: Oceanport, NJ
PGA TOUR Victories: (4) **1986** Provident Classic. **1991** Buick Open. **1992** New England Classic, The International.
Other Victories: **1979, 1980** Rhode Island Amateur.
National/International Teams: **1983** Walker Cup.

PGA TOUR CAREER SUMMARY

Year	Money	Rank
1984	$71,688	82
1985	$46,813	124
1986	$92,716	90
1987	$113,534	90
1988	$162,656	74
1989	$222,076	63
1990	$197,118	81
1991	$422,088	34
1992	$812,093	8
1993	$312,023	55
1994	$612,847	24
1995	$471,887	37
Career	$3,537,539	44

RICK FEHR

Birthdate: August 28, 1962
Birthplace: Seattle, WA
PGA TOUR Victories: (3) **1986** B.C. Open. **1994** B.C. Open, Walt Disney World/Oldsmobile.
Other Victories: **1982** Western Amateur.
National/International Teams: **1983** Walker Cup.

PGA TOUR CAREER SUMMARY

Year	Money	Rank
1985	$40,101	133
1986	$151,162	61
1987	$106,808	94
1988	$79,080	130
1989	$93,142	131
1990	$149,867	105
1991	$288,983	55
1992	$433,003	33
1993	$556,322	28
1994	$573,963	27
1995	$147,766	126
Career	$2,620,197	72

DAN FORSMAN

Birthdate: July 15, 1958
Birthplace: Rhinelander, WI
PGA TOUR Victories: (4) **1985** Quad Cities Open. **1986** Bay Hill Classic. **1990** Shearson Lehman Hutton Open. **1992** Buick Open.
Other Victories: None.
National/International Teams: None.

PGA TOUR CAREER SUMMARY

Year	Money	Rank
1983	$37,859	118
1984	$52,152	105
1985	$150,334	53
1986	$169,445	54
1987	$157,727	63
1988	$269,440	40
1989	$141,174	99
1990	$319,160	43
1991	$214,175	78
1992	$763,190	10
1993	$410,150	36
1994	$160,805	112
1994	$194,539	93
Career	$3,040,150	56

DAVID FROST

Birthdate: September 11, 1959
Birthplace: Cape Town, South Africa
PGA TOUR Victories: (8) **1988** Southern Open, Tucson Open. **1989** NEC World Series of Golf.

1990 USF&G Classic. **1992** Buick Classic, Hardee's Golf Classic. **1993** Canadian Open, Hardee's Golf Classic.
Other Victories: 1983 Gordon's Gin Classic. **1984** Cannes Open. **1987** South African Masters. **1989** Sun City Million Dollar Challenge. **1990** Sun City Million Dollar Challenge. **1994** Hong Kong Open
National/International Teams: 1994 Presidents Cup.

PGA TOUR CAREER SUMMARY

Year	Money	Rank
1985	$118,537	70
1986	$187,944	48
1987	$518,072	11
1988	$691,500	9
1989	$620,430	11
1990	$372,485	32
1991	$171,262	93
1992	$717,884	15
1993	$1,030,717	5
1994	$671,683	20
1994	$357,658	50
Career	$5,458,172	20

FRED FUNK
Birthdate: June 14, 1956
Birthplace: Takoma Park, MD
PGA TOUR Victories: (3) 1992 Shell Houston Open. **1995** Ideon Classic, Buick Challenge.
Other Victories: 1993 Mexican Open.
National/International Teams: None.

PGA TOUR CAREER SUMMARY

Year	Money	Rank
1989	$59,695	157
1990	$179,346	91
1991	$226,915	73
1992	$416,930	34
1993	$309,435	56
1994	$281,905	67
1995	$717,232	26
Career	$2,191,458	89

JIM FURYK
Birthdate: May 12, 1970
Birthplace: West Chester, PA
PGA TOUR Victories: (1) 1995 Las Vegas Invitational.
Other Victories: 1993 NIKE Bakersfield Classic. **1995** Kapalua Invitational.
National/International Teams: None.

PGA TOUR CAREER SUMMARY

Year	Money	Rank
1994	$236,603	78
1995	$535,380	33
Career	$771,983	NR

JIM GALLAGHER, JR.
Birthdate: March 24, 1961
Birthplace: Johnstown, PA
PGA TOUR Victories: (5) 1990 Greater Milwaukee Open. **1993** Anheuser-Busch Golf Classic, TOUR Championship. **1995** KMart Greater Greensboro Open, FedEx St. Jude Classic.
Other Victories: 1982 Indiana State Open. **1983** Indiana State Open.
National/International Teams: 1991 Four Tours World Championship of Golf. **1993-95** Ryder Cup.

PGA TOUR CAREER SUMMARY

Year	Money	Rank
1984	$22,249	148
1985	$19,061	159
1986	$79,967	107
1987	$39,402	166
1988	$83,766	124
1989	$265,809	50
1990	$476,706	25
1991	$570,627	18
1992	$638,314	19
1993	$1,078,870	4
1994	$325,976	51
1995	$1,057,241	8
Career	$4,583,940	29

ROBERT GAMEZ
Birthdate: July 21, 1968
Birthplace: Las Vegas, NV
PGA TOUR Victories: (2) 1990 Northern Telecom Tucson Open, Nestle Invitational.
Other Victories: 1989 Porter Cup.
National/International Teams: 1989 Walker Cup.

PGA TOUR CAREER SUMMARY

Year	Money	Rank
1989	$4,827	237
1990	$461,407	27
1991	$280,349	59
1992	$215,648	72
1993	$236,458	70
1994	$380,353	44
1995	$206,588	89
Career	$1,790,802	NR

BOB GILDER
Birthdate: December 31, 1950
Birthplace: Corvallis, OR
PGA TOUR Victories: (6) **1976** Phoenix Open. **1980** Canadian Open. **1982** Byron Nelson Classic, Manufacturers Hanover Westchester Classic, Bank of Boston Classic. **1983** Phoenix Open.
Other Victories: **1974** New Zealand Open. **1982** Bridgestone International. **1988** Kapakua International, Acom Team Title (with Doug Tewell).
National/International Teams: **1982** World Cup, U.S. vs. Japan. **1983** Ryder Cup.

PGA TOUR CAREER SUMMARY

Year	Money	Rank
1976	$101,262	24
1977	$36,844	72
1978	$72,515	36
1979	$134,428	22
1980	$152,597	19
1981	$74,756	59
1982	$308,648	6
1983	$139,125	39
1984	$23,313	147
1985	$47,152	123
1986	$98,181	85
1987	$94,310	100
1988	$144,523	82
1989	$187,910	78
1990	$154,934	102
1991	$251,683	66
1992	$170,761	91
1993	$148,496	108
1994	$154,868	118
1995	$139,361	138
Career	$2,636,473	66

BILL GLASSON
Birthdate: April 29, 1960
Birthplace: Fresno, CA
PGA TOUR Victories: (6) **1985** Kemper Open. **1988** B.C. Open, Centel Classic. **1989** Doral-Ryder Open. **1992** Kemper Open. **1994** Phoenix Open.
Other Victories: None.
National/International Teams: None.

PGA TOUR CAREER SUMMARY

Year	Money	Rank
1984	$17,845	162
1985	$195,449	29
1986	$121,516	72
1987	$151,701	69
1988	$380,651	30
1989	$474,511	19
1990	$156,791	100
1991	$46,995	178
1992	$283,765	54
1993	$299,799	57
1994	$689,110	17
1995	$412,094	43
Career	$3,230,227	54

KEN GREEN
Birthdate: July 23, 1958
Birthplace: Danbury, CT
PGA TOUR Victories: (5) **1985** Buick Open. **1986** The International. **1988** Canadian Open, Greater Milwaukee Open. **1989** Greater Greensboro Open.
Other Victories: **1985** Connecticut Open. **1988** Dunlop Phoenix in Japan. **1990** Hong Kong Open. **1992** Connecticut Open.
National/International Teams: **1989** Ryder Cup, Four Tours World Championship of Golf.

PGA TOUR CAREER SUMMARY

Year	Money	Rank
1982	$11,899	167
1983	$40,263	114
1984	$20,160	158
1985	$151,355	52
1986	$317,835	16
1987	$237,271	36
1988	$779,181	4
1989	$304,754	37
1990	$267,172	54
1991	$263,034	65
1992	$360,398	41
1993	$229,750	75
1994	$155,156	116
1995	$173,577	108
Career	$3,347,802	49

JAY HAAS
Birthdate: December 2, 1953
Birthplace: St. Louis, MO
PGA TOUR Victories: (9) **1978** San Diego Open. **1981** Greater Milwaukee Open, B.C. Open. **1982** Hall of Fame Classic, Texas Open. **1987** Houston Open. **1988** Bob Hope Chrysler Classic. **1992** Federal Express St. Jude Classic. **1993** Texas Open.
Other Victories: **1991** Mexican Open.
National/International Teams: **1975** Walker Cup. **1983** Ryder Cup.

PGA TOUR CAREER SUMMARY

Year	Money	Rank
1980	$114,102	35
1981	$181,894	15
1982	$229,748	13

Year	Money	Rank
1983	$191,735	23
1984	$148,514	45
1985	$121,488	69
1986	$189,204	45
1987	$270,347	37
1988	$490,409	20
1989	$248,830	54
1990	$180,023	89
1991	$200,637	84
1992	$632,627	20
1993	$601,603	26
1994	$593,386	25
1995	$822,259	16
Career	$5,426,821	22

GARY HALLBERG

Birthdate: May 31, 1958
Birthplace: Berwyn, IL
PGA TOUR Victories: (3) 1983 Andy Williams-San Diego Open. 1987 Greater Milwaukee Open. 1992 Buick Southern Open.
Other Victories: 1982 Chunichi Crowns. 1986 Chrysler Team Championship. 1988 Jerry Ford Invitational.
National/International Teams: None.

PGA TOUR CAREER SUMMARY

Year	Money	Rank
1980	$64,244	63
1981	$45,793	91
1982	$36,192	111
1983	$120,140	45
1984	$187,260	30
1985	$108,872	75
1986	$68,479	121
1987	$210,786	48
1988	$28,551	179
1989	$146,833	95
1990	$128,954	121
1991	$273,546	62
1992	$236,629	67
1993	$147,706	111
1994	$224,965	82
1995	$99,332	160
Career	$2,128,311	92

DONNIE HAMMOND

Birthdate: April 1, 1957
Birthplace: Frederick, MD
PGA TOUR Victories: (2) 1986 Bob Hope Chrysler Classic. 1989 Texas Open
Other Victories: 1989, 1990 Jerry Ford Invitational.
National/International Teams: None.

PGA TOUR CAREER SUMMARY

Year	Money	Rank
1983	$41,336	112
1984	$67,874	86
1985	$102,709	77
1986	$254,987	28
1987	$157,480	64
1988	$256,019	44
1989	$458,741	20
1990	$151,811	104
1991	$102,668	135
1992	$197,065	77
1993	$340,432	47
1994	$295,436	61
1995	$141,150	136
Career	$2,567,729	74

MIKE HEINEN

Birthdate: January 17, 1967
Birthplace: Rayne, LA
PGA TOUR Victories: (3) 1990 B.C. Open. 1991 Phoenix Open. 1993 Bell South Classic.
Other Victories: None.
National/International Teams: None.

PGA TOUR CAREER SUMMARY

Year	Money	Rank
1994	$390,963	40
1995	$350,920	52
Career	$741,883	NR

NOLAN HENKE

Birthdate: November 25, 1964
Birthplace: Battle Creek, MI
PGA TOUR Victories: (3) 1990 B.C. Open. 1991 Phoenix Open. 1993 Bell South Classic.
Other Victories: None.
National/International Teams: None.

PGA TOUR CAREER SUMMARY

Year	Money	Rank
1989	$59,465	159
1990	$294,592	48
1991	$518,811	28
1992	$326,387	45
1993	$502,375	31
1994	$278,419	70
1995	$237,141	78
Career	$2,215,189	87

BRIAN HENNINGER

Birthdate: October 19, 1963
Birthplace: Sacramento, CA

PGA TOUR Victories: (1) 1994 Deposit Guaranty Classic.
Other Victories: 1992 Ben Hogan South Texas, Ben Hogan Macon Open, Ben Hogan Knoxville Open.
National/International Teams: None.

PGA TOUR CAREER SUMMARY

Year	Money	Rank
1993	$112,811	130
1994	$294,075	63
1995	$166,730	114
Career	$473,616	NR

SCOTT HOCH
Birthdate: November 24, 1955
Birthplace: Raleigh, NC
PGA TOUR Victories: (5) 1980 Quad Cities Open. 1982 USF&G Classic. 1984 Lite Quad Cities Open. 1989 Las Vegas Invitational. 1994 Bob Hope Chrysler. 1995 Greater Milwaukee Open.
Other Victories: 1982 Pacific Masters, Casio World Open. 1986 Casio World Open. 1990 Korean Open. 1991 Korean Open. 1995 Dutch Open.
National/International Teams: 1978 World Amateur Cup. 1979 Walker Cup.

PGA TOUR CAREER SUMMARY

Year	Money	Rank
1980	$45,800	75
1981	$49,606	85
1982	$193,882	16
1983	$144,605	37
1984	$224,345	27
1985	$186,020	35
1986	$222,077	36
1987	$391,747	20
1988	$397,599	26
1989	$670,680	10
1990	$333,978	40
1991	$520,038	27
1992	$84,798	146
1993	$403,742	37
1994	$804,559	11
1995	$792,643	18
Career	$5,465,898	19

MIKE HULBERT
Birthdate: April 14, 1958
Birthplace: Elmira, NY
PGA TOUR Victories: (3) 1986 Federal Express-St. Jude Classic. 1989 B.C. Open. 1991 Anheuser Busch Golf Classic.
Other Victories: None.
National/International Teams: None.

PGA TOUR CAREER SUMMARY

Year	Money	Rank
1985	$18,368	161
1986	$276,687	21
1987	$204,375	49
1988	$127,752	94
1989	$477,621	16
1990	$216,002	67
1991	$551,750	24
1992	$279,577	55
1993	$193,833	89
1994	$221,007	84
1995	$311,055	61
Career	$2,878,027	60

JOHN HUSTON
Birthdate: June 1, 1961
Birthplace: Mt. Vernon, IL
PGA TOUR Victories: (2) 1990 Honda Classic. 1992 Walt Disney World/Oldsmobile Classic.
Other Victories: 1988 JC Penney Classic (with Amy Benz). 1985 Florida Open.
National/International Teams: None.

PGA TOUR CAREER SUMMARY

Year	Money	Rank
1988	$150,301	78
1989	$203,207	68
1990	$435,690	30
1991	$395,853	40
1992	$515,452	26
1993	$681,441	15
1994	$731,499	16
1995	$294,574	64
Career	$3,408,018	46

HALE IRWIN
Birthdate: June 3, 1945
Birthplace: Joplin, MO
PGA TOUR Victories: (19) 1971 Heritage Classic. 1973 Heritage Classic. 1974 U.S. Open. 1975 Western Open, Atlanta Classic. 1976 Glen Campbell Los Angeles Open, Florida Citrus Open. 1977 Atlanta Classic, Hall of Fame Classic, San Antonio Texas Open. 1979 U.S. Open. 1981 Hawaiian Open, Buick Open. 1982 Honda Inverrary Classic. 1983 Memorial Tournament. 1984 Bing Crosby Pro-Am. 1985 Memorial Tournament. 1990 U.S. Open, Buick Classic.
Other Victories: 1978 Australian PGA. 1979 South African PGA, World Cup Individual Title. 1981 Bridgestone Classic. 1982 Brazilian Open. 1986 Bahamas Classic. 1987 Fila Classic.
National/International Teams: 1974, 1979 World

Cup. **1975, 1977, 1979, 1981, 1991** Ryder Cup. **1983** U.S. vs. Japan.

PGA TOUR CAREER SUMMARY

Year	Money	Rank
1980	$109,810	38
1981	$276,499	7
1982	$173,719	19
1983	$232,567	13
1984	$183,364	31
1985	$195,007	31
1986	$59,983	128
1987	$100,825	96
1988	$164,996	72
1989	$150,977	93
1990	$836,249	6
1991	$422,652	33
1992	$98,208	131
1993	$252,686	65
1994	$814,436	10
1995	$190,961	95
Career	$5,845,024	15

PETER JACOBSEN

Birthdate: March 4, 1954
Birthplace: Portland, OR
PGA TOUR Victories: (6) **1980** Buick-Goodwrench Open. **1984** Colonial National Invitational, Sammy Davis Jr. Greater Hartford Open. **1990** Bob Hope Chrysler Classic. **1995** AT&T National Pro-Am, Buick Invitational.
Other Victories: **1976** Oregon Open, Northern California Open. **1979** Western Australian Open. **1981** Johnny Walker Cup. **1982** Johnny Walker Cup. **1986** Fred Meyer Challenge (with Curtis Strange).
National/International Teams: **1985, 1995** Ryder Cup. **1995** Dunhill Cup.

PGA TOUR CAREER SUMMARY

Year	Money	Rank
1980	$138,562	26
1981	$85,624	50
1982	$145,832	25
1983	$158,765	29
1984	$295,025	10
1985	$214,959	23
1986	$112,984	78
1987	$79,924	111
1988	$526,765	16
1989	$267,241	48
1990	$547,280	19
1991	$263,180	84
1992	$106,100	127
1993	$222,291	77
1994	$211,762	88
1995	$1,075,057	7
Career	$4,547,564	30

LEE JANZEN

Birthdate: August 28, 1964
Birthplace: Austin, MN
PGA TOUR Victories: (7) **1992** Northern Telecom Open. **1993** Phoenix Open, U.S. Open. **1994** Buick Westchester Classic. **1995** The Players' Championship, Kemper Open, Sprint International.
Other Victories: None.
National/International Teams: **1993** Ryder Cup. **1995** Dunhill Cup.

PGA TOUR CAREER SUMMARY

Year	Money	Rank
1990	$132,986	115
1991	$228,242	72
1992	$795,279	9
1993	$932,335	7
1994	$442,588	35
1995	$1,378,966	3
Career	$3,910,397	35

BRIAN KAMM

Birthdate: September 3, 1961
Birthplace: Rochester, NY
PGA TOUR Victories: None.
Other Victories: None.
National/International Teams: None.

PGA TOUR CAREER SUMMARY

Year	Money	Rank
1990	$8,775	237
1991	$81,932	146
1992	$20,020	211
1993	$183,185	94
1994	$181,884	98
1995	$165,235	118
Career	$641,031	NR

TOM KITE

Birthdate: December 9, 1949
Birthplace: Austin, TX
PGA TOUR Victories: (19) **1976** IVB-Bicentennial Golf Classic. **1978** B.C. Open. **1981** American Motors-Inverrary Classic. **1982** Bay Hill Classic. **1983** Bing Crosby National Pro-Am. **1984** Doral-Eastern Open, Georgia-Pacific Atlanta Classic. **1985** MONY Tournament of Champions. **1986** Western Open. **1987** Kemper Open. **1989** Nestle Invitational, The Players Championship, Nabisco

Championships. **1990** Federal Express St. Jude Classic. **1991** Infiniti Tournament of Champions. **1992** BellSouth Classic, U.S. Open. **1993** Bob Hope Chrysler Classic, Nissan Los Angeles Open.
Other Victories: 1980 European Open.
National/International Teams: 1981, 1983, 1985, 1987, 1989, 1993 Ryder Cup.

PGA TOUR CAREER SUMMARY

Year	Money	Rank
1980	$152,490	20
1981	$375,699	1
1982	$341,061	3
1983	$257,086	9
1984	$348,840	5
1985	$258,793	14
1986	$394,184	7
1987	$525,516	8
1988	$760,405	5
1989	$1,395,27	8
1990	$658,202	15
1991	$396,580	39
1992	$957,444	6
1993	$887,811	8
1994	$658,689	22
1995	$178,580	104
Career	$9,337,998	2

GREG KRAFT
Birthdate: April 4, 1964
Birthplace: Detroit, MI
PGA TOUR Victories: None.
Other Victories: 1993 Deposit Guaranty Golf Classic.
National/International Teams: None.

PGA TOUR CAREER SUMMARY

Year	Money	Rank
1992	$88,824	140
1993	$290,581	60
1994	$279,901	69
1995	$137,655	139
Career	$796,961	NR

NEAL LANCASTER
Birthdate: September 13, 1960
Birthplace: Smithfield, NC
PGA TOUR Victories: None.
Other Victories: 1989 Pine Tree Open, Utah State Open.
National/International Teams: None.

PGA TOUR CAREER SUMMARY

Year	Money	Rank
1990	$85,769	142
1991	$180,037	90
1992	$146,967	103
1993	$149,381	107
1994	$305,038	58
1995	$182,219	101
Career	$1,049,311	NR

TOM LEHMAN
Birthdate: March 7, 1959
Birthplace: Austin, MN
PGA TOUR Victories: (2) **1994** Memorial. **1995** Colonial Invitational.
Other Victories: 1991 South Carolina Classic.
National/International Teams: 1994 Presidents Cup. **1995** Ryder Cup.

PGA TOUR CAREER SUMMARY

Year	Money	Rank
1983	$9,413	183
1984	$9,382	184
1985-91	DNP	---
1992	$579,093	24
1993	$422,761	33
1994	$1,031,144	4
1995	$831,231	15
Career	$2,902,257	59

JUSTIN LEONARD
Birthdate: June 15, 1972
Birthplace: Dallas, TX
PGA TOUR Victories: None.
Other Victories: 1993 NCAA Championship.
National/International Teams: None.

PGA TOUR CAREER SUMMARY

Year	Money	Rank
1994	$140,413	126
1995	$748,793	22
Career	$889,206	NR

BRUCE LIETZKE
Birthdate: July 18, 1951
Birthplace: Kansas City, KS
PGA TOUR Victories: (12) **1977** Tucson Open, Hawaiian Open. **1978** Canadian Open. **1979** Tucson Open. **1980** Colonial. **1981** Bob Hope Desert Classic, San Diego Open, Byron Nelson Classic. **1982** Canadian Open. **1984** Honda Classic. **1988** Byron Nelson Classic. **1992** Colonial.
Other Victories: 1971 Texas State Amateur.
National/International Teams: 1981 Ryder Cup. **1984** U.S. vs. Japan.

PGA TOUR CAREER SUMMARY

Year	Money	Rank

PGA TOUR CAREER SUMMARY

Year	Money	Rank
1980	$183,884	16
1981	$343,446	4
1982	$217,447	14
1983	$153,255	32
1984	$342,853	6
1985	$136,992	59
1986	$183,761	47
1987	$154,383	68
1988	$500,815	19
1989	$307,987	36
1990	$329,294	41
1991	$568,272	19
1992	$703,605	16
1993	$163,241	101
1994	$564,926	28
1995	$269,394	70
Career	$5,710,262	17

ROBERT LOHR

Birthdate: November 2, 1960
Birthplace: Cincinnati, OH
PGA TOUR Victories: (1) **1988** Walt Disney World Oldsmobile Classic.
Other Victories: **1990** Mexican Open.
National/International Teams: None.

PGA TOUR CAREER SUMMARY

Year	Money	Rank
1985	$93,651	81
1986	$85,949	99
1987	$137,108	80
1988	$315,536	32
1989	$144,242	98
1990	$141,260	109
1991	$386,759	41
1992	$128,307	112
1993	$314,982	54
1994	$225,048	80
1995	$314,947	59
Career	$2,287,789	82

DAVIS LOVE III

Birthdate: April 13, 1964
Birthplace: Charlotte, NC
PGA TOUR Victories: (9) **1987** MCI Heritage Classic. **1990** The International. **1991** MCI Heritage Classic. **1992** The Players Championship, MCI Heritage Classic, Kmart Greater Greensboro Open. **1993** Infiniti Tournament of Champions, Las Vegas Invitational. **1995** Freeport McMoRan Classic.
Other Victories: **1992, 1993, 1994, 1995** World Cup (with Fred Couples). **1995** World Cup

Individual Title. **1994** Lincoln-Mercury Kapalua Invitational.
National/International Teams: **1985** Walker Cup. **1992** Dunhill Cup. **1992, 1993, 1995** World Cup. **1993, 1995** Ryder Cup.

PGA TOUR CAREER SUMMARY

Year	Money	Rank
1986	$113,245	77
1987	$297,378	33
1988	$156,068	75
1989	$278,760	44
1990	$537,172	20
1991	$686,360	8
1992	$1,191,630	2
1993	$777,059	12
1994	$474,219	33
1995	$1,111,999	6
Career	$5,623,890	19

STEVE LOWERY

Birthdate: October 12, 1960
Birthplace: Birmingham, AL
PGA TOUR Victories: (1) **1994** Sprint International.
Other Victories: **1992** Ben Hogan Tulsa Open.
National/International Teams: None.

PGA TOUR CAREER SUMMARY

Year	Money	Rank
1988	$44,327	157
1989	$38,699	174
1990	$68,524	159
1991	$87,597	143
1992	$22,608	207
1993	$188,287	92
1994	$794,048	12
1995	$463,858	38
Career	$1,669,249	NR

ANDREW MAGEE

Birthdate: May 22, 1962
Birthplace: Paris, France
PGA TOUR Victories: (4) **1988** Pensacola Open. **1991** Nestle Invitational, Las Vegas Invitational. **1995** Northern Telecom Open.
Other Victories: None.
National/International Teams: None.

PGA TOUR CAREER SUMMARY

Year	Money	Rank
1985	$75,593	99
1986	$69,478	120
1987	$94,598	99

Year	Money	Rank
1988	$261,954	43
1989	$126,770	109
1990	$210,507	71
1991	$750,082	5
1992	$285,947	53
1993	$269,988	62
1994	$431,041	25
1995	$256,918	72
Career	$2,832,873	63

JEFF MAGGERT
Birthdate: February 20, 1964
Birthplace: Columbia, MO
PGA TOUR Victories: (1) **1993** Walt Disney World/Oldsmobile Classic.
Other Victories: 1990 Ben Hogan Knoxville Open, Ben Hogan Buffalo Open.
National/International Teams: 1994 President's Cup. **1995** Ryder Cup.

PGA TOUR CAREER SUMMARY
Year	Money	Rank
1990	$2,080	277
1991	$240,940	68
1992	$377,408	38
1993	$793,023	11
1994	$814,475	8
1995	$527,952	34
Career	$2,753,797	66

ROGER MALTBIE
Birthdate: June 30, 1951
Birthplace: Modesto, CA
PGA TOUR Victories: (5) **1975** Quad Cities Open, Pleasant Valley Classic. **1976** Memorial Tournament. **1985** Manufacturers Hanover Westchester Classic, NEC World Series of Golf.
Other Victories: 1980 Magnolia Classic.
National/International Teams: None.

PGA TOUR CAREER SUMMARY
Year	Money	Rank
1975	$81,035	23
1976	$117,736	18
1977	$51,727	59
1978	$12,440	129
1979	$9,796	155
1980	$38,626	84
1981	$75,009	58
1982	$77,067	55
1983	$75,751	70
1984	$118,128	56

Year	Money	Rank
1985	$360,554	8
1986	$213,206	40
1987	$157,023	65
1988	$150,602	77
1989	$134,333	105
1990	$58,536	169
1991	$37,962	188
1992	$109,742	125
1993	$155,454	103
1994	$67,686	174
1995	$61,664	187
Career	$2,164,079	90

BILLY MAYFAIR
Birthdate: August 6, 1966
Birthplace: Phoenix, AZ
PGA TOUR Victories: (3) **1993** Greater Milwaukee Open. **1995** Western Open, TOUR Championship.
Other Victories: None.
National/International Teams: None.

PGA TOUR CAREER SUMMARY
Year	Money	Rank
1989	$111,996	116
1990	$893,658	12
1991	$185,668	89
1992	$191,878	79
1993	$513,072	30
1994	$158,159	113
1995	$1,543,192	2
Career	$3,397,626	47

BLAINE McCALLISTER
Birthdate: October 17, 1958
Birthplace: Fort Stockton, TX
PGA TOUR Victories: (5) **1988** Hardee's Golf Classic. **1989** Honda Classic, Bank of Boston Classic. **1991** H-E-B Texas Open. **1993** B.C. Open.
Other Victories: None.
National/International Teams: None.

PGA TOUR CAREER SUMMARY
Year	Money	Rank
1982	$7,894	80
1983	$5,218	201
1984-85	DNP	---
1986	$88,732	94
1987	$120,005	87
1988	$225,680	49
1989	$593,891	15
1990	$152,048	103
1991	$412,975	36
1992	$261,187	59
1993	$290,434	61

Year	Money	Rank
1994	$351,554	47
1995	$238,847	77
Career	$2,678,444	68

MARK McCUMBER
Birthdate: September 7, 1951
Birthplace: Jacksonville, FL
PGA TOUR Victories: (9) 1979 Doral-Eastern Open. 1983 Western Open, Pensacola Open. 1985 Doral-Eastern Open. 1987 Anheuser-Busch Classic. 1988 The Players Championship. 1989 Western Open. 1994 Anheuser-Busch Classic, TOUR Championship.
Other Victories: None.
National/International Teams: 1988, 1989 World Cup. 1989 Ryder Cup.

PGA TOUR CAREER SUMMARY
Year	Money	Rank
1980	$38,985	86
1981	$33,363	103
1982	$31,684	119
1983	$288,294	8
1984	$133,445	50
1985	$192,752	32
1986	$110,442	80
1987	$390,865	22
1988	$559,111	13
1989	$548,587	14
1990	$163,413	97
1991	$173,852	92
1992	$136,653	108
1993	$363,289	41
1994	$1,208,209	3
1995	$375,923	47
Career	$4,799,702	26

JIM McGOVERN
Birthdate: February 2, 1965
Birthplace: Teaneck, NJ
PGA TOUR Victories: (1) 1993 Shell Houston Open.
Other Victories: 1990 Hogan Lake City Classic, Texarkana Open, New Haven Open.
National/International Teams: None.

PGA TOUR CAREER SUMMARY
Year	Money	Rank
1991	$88,867	141
1992	$169,889	92
1993	$587,495	27
1994	$227,764	79
1995	$402,587	44
Career	$1,476,602	NR

MARK McNULTY
Birthdate: October 25, 1953
Birthplace: Bindwa, Zimbabwe
PGA TOUR Victories: None.
Other Victories: 1994 BMW International.
National/International Teams: 1993, 1994 World Cup.

PGA TOUR CAREER SUMMARY
Year	Money	Rank
1982	$50,322	90
1983	$40,062	115
1984	$5,382	198
1985	$3,600	217
1986	$6,170	225
1987	$4,165	243
1988	$39,481	159
1989	DNP	---
1990	$34,375	188
1991	$34,321	194
1992	$46,171	181
1994	$157,700	114
1995	$64,795	181
Career	$486,544	NR

ROCCO MEDIATE
Birthdate: December 17, 1962
Birthplace: Greensburg, PA
PGA TOUR Victories: (2) 1991 Doral-Ryder Open. 1993 Kmart Greater Greensboro Open.
Other Victories: 1992 Perrier French Open.
National/International Teams: None.

PGA TOUR CAREER SUMMARY
Year	Money	Rank
1986	$20,670	174
1987	$112,099	91
1988	$129,829	92
1989	$132,501	108
1990	$240,825	62
1991	$597,438	15
1992	$301,896	49
1993	$680,623	16
1994	$45,940	193
1995	$105,618	155
Career	$2,367,238	77

PHIL MICKELSON
Birthdate: June 16, 1970
Birthplace: San Diego, CA
PGA TOUR Victories: (5) 1991 Northern Telecom

Open. **1993** Buick Invitational of California, The International. **1994** Mercedes Championships. **1995** Northern Telecom Open.
Other Victories: 1990 U.S. Amateur.
National/International Teams: 1989, 1991 Walker Cup. **1995** Ryder Cup.

PGA TOUR CAREER SUMMARY

Year	Money	Rank
1991	$0	---
1992	$171,713	90
1993	$628,735	22
1994	$748,316	15
1995	$655,777	28
Career	$2,204,542	88

LARRY MIZE
Birthdate: September 23, 1958
Birthplace: Augusta, GA
PGA TOUR Victories: (4) **1983** Danny Thomas-Memphis Classic. **1987** Masters. **1993** Northern Telecom Open, Buick Open.
Other Victories: 1993 Johnny Walker World Championship.
National/International Teams: 1987 Ryder Cup.

PGA TOUR CAREER SUMMARY

Year	Money	Rank
1982	$28,787	124
1983	$146,325	35
1984	$172,513	36
1985	$231,041	17
1986	$314,051	17
1987	$561,407	6
1988	$187,823	62
1989	$278,388	45
1990	$668,198	14
1991	$279,081	60
1992	$316,428	47
1993	$724,680	12
1994	$386,029	42
1995	$289,576	67
Career	$4,584,287	28

GIL MORGAN
Birthdate: September 25, 1946
Birthplace: Wewoka, OK
PGA TOUR Victories: (7) **1977** B.C. Open. **1978** Los Angeles Open, World Series of Golf. **1979** Memphis Classic. **1983** Tucson Open, Los Angeles Open. **1990** Kemper Open.
Other Victories: 1978 Pacific Masters.
National/International Teams: 1979-1983 Ryder Cup.

PGA TOUR CAREER SUMMARY

Year	Money	Rank
1980	$135,308	28
1981	$171,184	18
1982	$139,652	26
1983	$306,133	5
1984	$281,948	13
1985	$133,941	62
1986	$98,770	84
1987	$133,980	81
1988	$286,002	34
1989	$300,395	39
1990	$702,629	11
1991	$232,912	70
1992	$272,959	56
1993	$810,312	24
1994	$309,690	54
1995	$255,565	73
Career	$4,991,433	24

JOHN MORSE
Birthdate: February 16, 1958.
Birthplace: Marshall, MI
PGA TOUR Victories: (1) **1995** Hawaiian Open.
Other Victories: None
National/International Teams: None.

PGA TOUR CAREER SUMMARY

Year	Money	Rank
1994	$146,137	122
1995	$416,803	42
Career	$562,940	NR

GREG NORMAN
Birthdate: February 10, 1955
Birthplace: Queensland, Australia
PGA TOUR Victories: (15) **1984** Kemper Open, Canadian Open. **1986** Panasonic Las Vegas Invitational, Kemper Open. **1988** MCI Heritage Classic. **1989** The International, Greater Milwaukee Open. **1990** Doral-Ryder Open, The Memorial. **1992** Canadian Open. **1993** Doral-Ryder Open. **1994** The Players Championship. **1995** The Memorial, Canon Greater Hartford Open, NEC World Series of Golf.
Other Victories: 1976 Lakes Classic. **1977** Martini International. **1978** New South Wales Open, Fiji Open. **1979** Martini International, Hong Kong Open. **1980** French Open, World Match Play, Scandanavian Enterprise Open, Australian Open, Australian Masters. **1981** Martini International, Dunlop Masters, Australian Masters. **1982** Dunlop Masters, State Express Classic, Benson & Hedges International Open. **1983** Australian Masters,

Queensland Open, New South Wales Open, Cannes Invitational, Kapalua International, Hong Kong Open, World Match Play. **1984** Australian Masters, Victoria Open. **1986** British Open, European Open, Suntory World Match Play, Queensland Open, New South Wales Open, South Australian Open, Western Australian Open. **1987** Australian Open, Australian Masters. **1993** British Open, PGA Grand Slam of Golf. **1994** Johnnie Walker Classic. **1995** Heineken Classic, Australian Open.
National/International Teams: 1976, 1978 World Cup. 1985, 1986 Nissan Cup. 1985, 1986, 1987, 1988, 1989, 1990, 1992 Dunhill Cup. 1987 Kirin Cup. 1989 Four Tours World Championship.

PGA TOUR CAREER SUMMARY

Year	Money	Rank
1983	$71,411	74
1984	$310,230	9
1985	$165,458	42
1986	$653,296	1
1987	$535,450	7
1988	$514,854	17
1989	$835,096	4
1990	$1,165,477	1
1991	$320,196	53
1992	$876,443	18
1993	$1,359,653	3
1994	$1,330,307	2
1995	$1,654,959	1
Career	$9,592,829	1

BRETT OGLE
Birthdate: July 14, 1964
Birthplace: Paddington, Australia
PGA TOUR Victories: (2) **1993** AT&T Pebble Beach National Pro-Am. **1994** Hawaiian Open.
Other Victories: **1985** Australian Junior Championship. **1989** Mirage Queensland Open. **1990** Australian Open.
National/International Teams: 1992, 1995 World Cup.

PGA TOUR CAREER SUMMARY

Year	Money	Rank
1993	$337,373	49
1994	$284,495	66
1995	$326,932	56
Career	$948,800	NR

JOSE-MARIA OLAZABAL
Birthdate: February 5, 1966
Birthplace: Fuentenabia, Spain
PGA TOUR Victories: (4) **1990** NEC World Series of Golf. **1991** The International. **1994** Masters, NEC World Series of Golf.
Other victories: **1983** Italian Amateur, Spanish Amateur. **1986** European Masters, Swiss Open, Sanyo Open. **1988** Belgian Open, German Masters. **1989** Tenerife Open, Dutch Open. **1990** Benson & Hedges International, Irish Open, Lancome Trophy, Visa Taiheyo Club Masters. **1991** Catalonia Open. **1992** Turespana Open de Tenerife, Open Mediterrania. **1994** Volvo PGA..
National/International Teams: 1986, 1987, 1988, 1989, 1992 Dunhill Cup. 1987, 1989, 1991, 1993 Ryder Cup. 1989 World Cup. 1987 Kirin Cup. 1989, 1990 Four Tours World Championship.

PGA TOUR CAREER SUMMARY

Year	Money	Rank
1987	$7,470	215
1988	DNP	---
1989	$56,039	160
1990	$337,837	38
1991	$382,124	43
1992	$63,429	161
1993	$60,160	174
1994	$969,900	7
1995	$213,415	87
Career	$2,090,374	NR

MARK O'MEARA
Birthdate: January 13, 1957
Birthplace: Goldsboro, NC
PGA TOUR Victories: (10) **1984** Greater Milwaukee Open. **1985** Bing Crosby Pro-Am, Hawaiian Open. **1989** AT&T Pebble Beach National Pro-Am. **1990** AT&T Pebble Beach National Pro-Am, H-E-B Texas Open. **1991** Walt Disney World/Oldsmobile Classic. **1992** AT&T Pebble Beach National Pro-Am. **1995** Honda Classic, Bell Canadian Open.
Other Victories: None.
National/International Teams: 1984 U.S. vs. Japan. 1985 Nissan Cup. 1985, 1989, 1991 Ryder Cup.

PGA TOUR CAREER SUMMARY

Year	Money	Rank
1981	$76,083	55
1982	$31,711	118
1983	$69,354	76
1984	$465,873	2
1985	$340,840	10
1986	$252,827	30
1987	$327,250	30
1988	$438,311	22
1989	$815,804	13
1990	$707,175	10

Year	Money	Rank
1991	$583,896	20
1992	$759,648	11
1993	$349,516	43
1994	$214,070	86
1995	$914,129	10
Career	$6,126,466	11

CRAIG PARRY

Birthdate: December 1, 1966
Birthplace: Sunshine, Australia
PGA TOUR Victories: None.
Other Victories: 1987 Canadian Tournament Players Championship. 1989 Wang Four Stars National Pro-Celebrity, German Open, Bridgestone ASO. 1991 Lancia Martini Italian Open, Bell's Scottish Open. 1994 Australian Masters.
National/International Teams: 1988 Kirin Cup. 1989, 1990, 1991 Four Tours World Championship of Golf.

PGA TOUR CAREER SUMMARY

Year	Money	Rank
1989	$1,650	282
1990	$43,351	181
1991	$83,767	162
1992	$241,901	64
1993	$323,068	50
1994	$354,602	46
1995	$293,413	65
Career	$1,212,984	NR

STEVE PATE

Birthdate: May 26, 1961
Birthplace: Ventura, CA
PGA TOUR Victories: (5) 1987 Southwest Classic. 1988 MONY Tournament of Champions, Shearson Lehman Hutton Andy Williams Open. 1991 Honda Classic. 1992 Buick Invitational of California.
Other Victories: None.
National/International Teams: 1988 Kirin Cup. 1991 Ryder Cup.

PGA TOUR CAREER SUMMARY

Year	Money	Rank
1985	$89,358	86
1986	$176,100	51
1987	$335,728	26
1988	$582,473	12
1989	$306,554	35
1990	$334,505	39
1991	$727,997	6
1992	$472,626	30
1993	$254,841	84
1994	$291,651	64
1995	$89,756	168
Career	$3,661,591	40

COREY PAVIN

Birthdate: November 16, 1959
Birthplace: Oxnard, CA
PGA TOUR Victories: (13) 1984 Houston Coca-Cola Open. 1985 Colonial National Invitation. 1986 Hawaiian Open, Greater Milwaukee Open. 1987 Bob Hope Chrysler Classic, Hawaiian Open. 1988 Texas Open presented by Nabisco. 1991 Bob Hope Chrysler Classic, BellSouth Atlanta Classic. 1992 Honda Classic. 1994 Nissan Los Angeles Open. 1995 Nissan Open, U.S. Open.
Other Victories: 1993 Toyota World Match Play.
National/International Teams: 1981 Walker Cup. 1985 Nissan Cup. 1991, 1993, 1995 Ryder Cup.

PGA TOUR CAREER SUMMARY

Year	Money	Rank
1984	$250,536	18
1985	$387,508	6
1986	$304,558	19
1987	$498,406	15
1988	$216,768	50
1989	$177,084	82
1990	$468,830	26
1991	$979,430	1
1992	$980,934	5
1993	$675,087	18
1994	$906,305	8
1995	$1,340,079	4
Career	$7,175,523	6

KENNY PERRY

Birthdate: August 10, 1960
Birthplace: Elizabethtown, KY
PGA TOUR Victories: (3) 1991 Memorial Tournament. 1994 New England Classic. 1995 Bob Hope Chrysler Desert Classic.
Other Victories: None.
National/International Teams: None.

PGA TOUR CAREER SUMMARY

Year	Money	Rank
1987	$107,239	93
1988	$139,421	85
1989	$202,099	70
1990	$279,881	50
1991	$368,784	44
1992	$190,455	81
1993	$196,863	88
1994	$585,941	26
1995	$773,368	21
Career	$2,844,072	62

NICK PRICE

Birthdate: January 28, 1957
Birthplace: Durban, South Africa
PGA TOUR Victories: (14) **1983** World Series of Golf. **1991** GTE Byron Nelson Classic, Canadian Open. **1992** PGA Championship, H-E-B Texas Open. **1993** The Players Championship, Canon Greater Hartford Open, Sprint Western Open, Federal Express St. Jude Classic. **1994** Honda Classic, Southwestern Bell Colonial, Motorola Open, PGA Championship, Canadian Open.
Other Victories: **1980** Swiss Open. **1981** South African Masters, Italian Masters. **1982** Vaal Reefs Open. **1985** Lancome Trophy, ICL International. **1992** PGA Grand Slam of Golf, Air New Zealand Shell Open. **1993** ICL International. **1994** British Open.
National/International Teams: **1993** Dunhill Cup. **1978, 1993** World Cup.

PGA TOUR CAREER SUMMARY

Year	Money	Rank
1983	$49,435	103
1984	$109,480	66
1985	$96,069	80
1986	$225,373	35
1987	$334,169	28
1988	$266,300	42
1989	$296,170	42
1990	$520,777	22
1991	$714,389	7
1992	$1,135,773	4
1993	$1,478,557	1
1994	$1,499,927	1
1995	$611,700	30
Career	$7,338,119	4

DICKY PRIDE

Birthdate: July 15, 1969
Birthplace: Tuscaloosa, AL
PGA TOUR Victories: (1) **1994** Fedex St. Jude Memorial Classic.
Other Victories: None.
National/International Teams: None.

PGA TOUR CAREER SUMMARY

Year	Money	Rank
1994	$305,769	57
1995	$97,712	161
Career	$403,481	NR

TOM PURTZER

Birthdate: Dec. 5, 1951
Birthplace: Des Moines, IA
PGA TOUR Victories: (5) **1977** Los Angeles Open. **1984** Phoenix Open. **1988** Southwest Classic. **1991** Colonial, NEC World Series of Golf.
Other Victories: None.
National/International Teams: **1979** U.S. vs. Japan.

PGA TOUR CAREER SUMMARY

Year	Money	Rank
1975	$2,093	194
1976	$26,682	82
1977	$79,337	37
1978	$58,618	55
1979	$113,270	30
1980	$118,185	34
1981	$122,812	27
1982	$100,118	36
1983	$103,261	55
1984	$164,244	39
1985	$49,979	119
1986	$218,281	37
1987	$123,287	85
1988	$197,740	5
1989	$154,868	8
1990	$285,176	49
1991	$750,568	4
1992	$166,722	9
1993	$107,570	136
1994	$187,307	94
1995	$120,717	144
Career	$3,250,834	52

LOREN ROBERTS

Birthdate: June 24, 1955
Birthplace: San Luis Obispo, CA
PGA TOUR Victories: (2) **1994** Nestle Bay Hill Invitational. **1995** Nestle Bay Hill Invitational.
Other Victories: None.
National/International Teams: None.

PGA TOUR CAREER SUMMARY

Year	Money	Rank
1981	$8,935	172
1982	DNP	---
1983	$7,724	189
1984	$87,515	87
1985	$92,761	83
1986	$53,655	133
1987	$87,489	138
1988	$138,890	89
1989	$275,862	46
1990	$478,522	24
1991	$281,173	56
1992	$338,673	43
1993	$316,508	53
1994	$1,015,671	6
1995	$678,335	27
Career	$3,809,733	39

GENE SAUERS

Birthdate: August 22, 1962
Birthplace: Savannah, GA
PGA TOUR Victories: (2) **1986** Bank of Boston Classic. **1989** Hawaiian Open.
Other Victories: None.
National/International Teams: None.

PGA TOUR CAREER SUMMARY

Year	Money	Rank
1984	$36,537	128
1985	$48,526	121
1986	$199,044	42
1987	$244,655	38
1988	$280,719	35
1989	$303,669	38
1990	$374,485	31
1991	$400,535	37
1992	$434,566	32
1993	$117,608	128
1994	$250,654	73
1995	$311,578	60
Career	$3,002,576	57

SCOTT SIMPSON

Birthdate: September 17, 1955
Birthplace: San Diego, CA
PGA TOUR Victories: (6) **1980** Western Open. **1984** Westchester Classic. **1987** Greater Greensboro Open, U.S. Open. **1989** BellSouth Atlanta Classic. **1993** GTE Byron Nelson Classic.
Other Victories: None.
National/International Teams: **1977** Walker Cup. **1987** Ryder Cup.

PGA TOUR CAREER SUMMARY

Year	Money	Rank
1979	$53,084	74
1980	$141,323	24
1981	$108,793	34
1982	$146,903	24
1983	$144,172	38
1984	$248,581	22
1985	$171,245	39
1986	$202,223	41
1987	$621,032	4
1988	$108,301	106
1989	$298,920	40
1990	$235,309	63
1991	$322,936	51
1992	$155,284	97
1993	$707,166	14
1994	$307,884	56
1995	$795,798	17
Career	$4,768,955	27

VIJAY SINGH

Birthdate: February 22, 1963
Birthplace: Lautoka, Fiji
PGA TOUR Victories: (3) **1993** Buick Westchester Classic. **1995** Phoenix Open, Buick Westchester Classic.
Other Victories: **1984** Malaysian PGA Championship. **1984** Volvo German Open. **1988, 1989** Nigerian Open. **1990** Turespana Masters. **1992** Volvo German Open. **1994** Trophee Lancome, Scandanavian Masters
National/International Teams: None.

PGA TOUR CAREER SUMMARY

Year	Money	Rank
1993	$657,831	19
1994	$325,959	52
1995	$1,019,713	9
Career	$2,002,503	97

MIKE SPRINGER

Birthdate: November 3, 1965
Birthplace: San Francisco, CA
PGA TOUR Victories: (1) **1994** Greater Milwaukee Open.
Other Victories: None.
National/International Teams: None.

PGA TOUR CAREER SUMMARY

Year	Money	Rank
1991	$178,587	91
1992	$144,316	104
1993	$214,729	79
1994	$770,717	13
1995	$55,146	198
Career	$1,363,495	NR

JEFF SLUMAN

Birthdate: September 11, 1957
Birthplace: Rochester, NY
PGA TOUR Victories: (1) **1988** PGA Championship.
Other Victories: **1985** Tallahassee Open.
National/International Teams: None.

PGA TOUR CAREER SUMMARY

Year	Money	Rank
1983	$13,643	171
1984	$603	281
1985	$100,523	78
1986	$154,129	60
1987	$335,590	27
1988	$503,321	18
1989	$154,507	89

Year	Money	Rank
1990	$264,012	56
1991	$552,979	23
1992	$729,027	14
1993	$187,841	93
1994	$301,178	59
1995	$563,681	31
Career	$3,860,431	36

CRAIG STADLER

Birthdate: June 2, 1953
Birthplace: San Diego, CA
PGA TOUR Victories: (11) **1980** Bob Hope Desert Classic, Greater Greensboro Open. **1981** Kemper Open. **1982** Joe Garagiola Tucson Open, The Masters, Kemper Open, World Series of Golf. **1984** Byron Nelson Classic. **1991** The TOUR Championship. **1992** NEC World Series of Golf. **1994** Buick Invitational of California.
Other Victories: None.
National/International Teams: **1975** Walker Cup. **1983, 1985** Ryder Cup.

PGA TOUR CAREER SUMMARY

Year	Money	Rank
1980	$206,291	8
1981	$218,829	8
1982	$446,462	1
1983	$214,496	17
1984	$324,241	8
1985	$297,926	11
1986	$170,076	53
1987	$235,831	39
1988	$276,313	37
1989	$409,419	25
1990	$278,482	52
1991	$827,628	2
1992	$487,460	28
1993	$553,622	29
1994	$474,831	32
1995	$402,316	45
Career	$6,008,753	13

MIKE STANDLY

Birthdate: May 19, 1964
Birthplace: Abilene, TX
PGA TOUR Victories: (1) **1993** Freeport-McMoRan Classic.
Other Victories: **1984** Boone Links Invitational.
National/International Teams: None.

PGA TOUR CAREER SUMMARY

Year	Money	Rank
1991	$55,846	171
1992	$213,712	73
1993	$323,886	49
1994	$179,850	99
1995	$177,920	105
Career	$951,214	NR

PAYNE STEWART

Birthdate: January 30, 1957
Birthplace: Springfield, MO
PGA TOUR Victories: (9) **1982** Quad Cities Open. **1983** Walt Disney World Classic. **1987** Hertz Bay Hill Classic. **1989** MCI Heritage Classic, PGA Championship. **1990** MCI Heritage Classic, GTE Byron Nelson Classic. **1991** U.S. Open. **1995** Shell Houston Open.
Other Victories: **1981** India Open.
National/International Teams: **1986** Nissan Cup. **1987** Kirin Cup. **1987, 1989, 1991, 1993** Ryder Cup. **1987, 1990** World Cup. **1989, 1990** Asahi Glass Four Tours World Championship of Golf.

PGA TOUR CAREER SUMMARY

Year	Money	Rank
1981	$13,400	157
1982	$98,686	38
1983	$178,809	25
1984	$288,795	11
1985	$225,729	19
1986	$535,389	3
1987	$511,026	12
1988	$553,571	14
1989	$1,201,301	2
1990	$976,281	3
1991	$476,971	31
1992	$334,738	44
1993	$982,876	6
1994	$145,687	123
1995	$866,219	12
Career	$7,389,479	3

DAVE STOCKTON, JR.

Birthdate: July 31, 1968
Birthplace: Redlands, CA
PGA TOUR Victories: None.
Other Victories: None.
National/International Teams: None.

PGA TOUR CAREER SUMMARY

Year	Money	Rank
1994	$185,205	96
1995	$149,579	124
Career	$334,784	NR

CURTIS STRANGE
Birthdate: January 30, 1955
Birthplace: Norfolk, VA
PGA TOUR Victories: (17) **1979** Pensacola Open. **1980** Michelob-Houston Open, Westchester Classic. **1983** Sammy Davis, Jr. Greater Hartford Open. **1984** LaJet Classic. **1985** Honda Classic, Panasonic Las Vegas Inv., Canadian Open. **1986** Houston Open. **1987** Canadian Open, FedEx St. Jude Classic, NEC World Series of Golf. **1988** Independent Insurance Agent Open, Memorial Tournament, U.S. Open, Nabisco Championships. **1989** U.S. Open.
Other Victories: 1989, 1993 Holden Classic.
National/International Teams: 1974 World Amateur Cup. **1975** Walker Cup. **1983, 1985, 1987, 1989, 1995** Ryder Cup. **1985** Nissan Cup. **1987, 1988** Kirin Cup. **1987, 1988, 1989, 1991** Dunhill Cup. **1989** Four Tours Championship.

PGA TOUR CAREER SUMMARY
Year	Money	Rank
1980	$271,888	3
1981	$201,513	9
1982	$263,378	10
1983	$200,116	21
1984	$276,773	14
1985	$542,321	1
1986	$237,700	32
1987	$925,941	1
1988	$1,147,644	1
1989	$752,587	7
1990	$277,172	53
1991	$336,333	48
1992	$150,639	99
1993	$262,697	63
1994	$390,881	41
1995	$358,175	49
Career	$6,791,618	10

STEVE STRICKER
Birthdate: February 23, 1967
Birthplace: Edgerton, WI
PGA TOUR Victories: None.
Other Victories: 1993 Canadian PGA.
National/International Teams: None.

PGA TOUR CAREER SUMMARY
Year	Money	Rank
1990	$3,973	255
1991	DNP	---
1992	$5,550	261
1993	$46,171	186
1994	$334,409	50
1995	$438,931	40
Career	$829,555	NR

HAL SUTTON
Birthdate: April 28, 1958
Birthplace: Shreveport, LA
PGA TOUR Victories: (8) **1982** Walt Disney World Golf Classic. **1983** Tournament Players Championship, PGA Championship. **1985** St. Jude Memphis Classic, Southwest Classic. **1986** Phoenix Open, Memorial Tournament. **1995** B.C. Open.
Other Victories: 1985 Chrysler Team Championship (with Ray Floyd).
National/International Teams: 1983 U.S. vs. Japan. **1985, 1987** Ryder Cup.

PGA TOUR CAREER SUMMARY
Year	Money	Rank
1982	$237,434	11
1983	$426,668	1
1984	$227,949	26
1985	$365,340	7
1986	$429,434	6
1987	$477,996	16
1988	$137,296	88
1989	$422,703	23
1990	$207,084	75
1991	$346,411	47
1992	$39,234	185
1993	$74,144	161
1994	$540,162	29
1995	$554,733	32
Career	$4,486,587	32

DOUG TEWELL
Birthdate: August 27, 1949
Birthplace: Baton Rouge, LA
PGA TOUR victories: (2) **1986** Los Angeles Open. **1987** Pensacola Open.
Other Victories: 1988 Acom Team title (with Bob Gilder). **1978** South Central PGA.
National/International Teams: None.

PGA TOUR CAREER SUMMARY
Year	Money	Rank
1975	$1,812	201
1976	$3,640	185
1977	$33,162	76
1978	$16,629	113
1979	$84,500	43
1980	$161,684	17
1981	$41,540	94
1982	$78,770	52
1983	$112,367	49
1984	$117,988	57
1985	$137,426	58
1986	$310,285	18
1987	$150,116	71

Year	Money	Rank
1988	$209,196	53
1989	$174,607	83
1990	$137,795	112
1991	$137,360	111
1992	$159,856	96
1993	$132,478	117
1994	$177,388	102
1995	$45,878	226
Career:	$2,424,476	76

KIRK TRIPLETT
Birthdate: March 29, 1962
Birthplace: Moses Lake, WA
PGA TOUR Victories: None.
Other Victories: 1988 Alberta Open, Nevada Open, Ft. McMurray Classic.
National/International Teams: None.

PGA TOUR CAREER SUMMARY
Year	Money	Rank
1990	$183,464	88
1991	$137,302	112
1992	$175,868	85
1993	$189,418	90
1994	$422,171	38
1995	$644,607	29
Career	$1,752,829	NR

TED TRYBA
Birthdate: January 15, 1967
Birthplace: Wilkes-Barre, PA
PGA TOUR Victories: (1) 1995 Anheuser-Busch Classic.
Other Victories: None.
National/International Teams: None.

PGA TOUR CAREER SUMMARY
Year	Money	Rank
1990	$ 10,708	226
1991-92	DNP	---
1993	$136,670	116
1994	$246,481	74
1995	$451,983	39
Career	$845,842	NR

BOB TWAY
Birthdate: May 4, 1959
Birthplace: Oklahoma City, OK
PGA TOUR Victories: (7) 1986 Shearson Lehman Open, Westchester Classic, Atlanta Classic, PGA Championship. **1989** Memorial Tournament. **1990** Las Vegas Invitational. **1995** MCI Classic.
Other Victories: 1983 Sandpiper Santa Barbara Open. **1986** Fred Meyer Challenge (with Paul Azinger). **1987** Oklahoma State Open, Chrysler Team Championship (with Mike Hulbert).
National/International Teams: 1980 World Amateur Cup. **1986** Nissan Cup.

PGA TOUR CAREER SUMMARY
Year	Money	Rank
1985	$164,023	45
1986	$652,780	2
1987	$212,362	47
1988	$381,966	29
1989	$488,340	17
1990	$495,862	23
1991	$322,931	52
1992	$47,632	179
1993	$148,120	109
1994	$114,176	114
1995	$787,348	20
Career	$3,815,540	38

HOWARD TWITTY
Birthdate: January 15, 1949
Birthplace: Phoenix, AZ
PGA TOUR Victories: (3) 1979 B.C. Open. **1980** Sammy Davis Jr. Greater Hartford Open. **1993** United Airlines Hawaiian Open.
Other Victories: None.
National/International Teams: None.

PGA TOUR CAREER SUMMARY
Year	Money	Rank
1980	$165,190	14
1981	$52,183	79
1982	$57,355	78
1983	$20,000	150
1984	$51,971	106
1985	$92,958	82
1986	$156,119	57
1987	$169,442	61
1988	$87,985	119
1989	$107,200	119
1990	$129,444	120
1991	$226,426	74
1992	$284,042	57
1993	$416,833	34
1994	$131,408	130
1995	$140,695	137
Career	$2,665,173	70

SCOTT VERPLANK
Birthdate: July 9, 1964
Birthplace: Dallas, TX

PGA TOUR Victories: (2) 1985 Western Open. 1988 Buick Open.
Other Victories: None.
National/International Teams: None.

PGA TOUR CAREER SUMMARY

Year	Money	Rank
1986	$19,575	177
1987	$34,136	173
1988	$366,045	31
1989	$82,345	141
1990	$303,589	47
1991	$3,195	266
1992	$1,760	309
1994	$183,015	97
1995	$332,886	55
Career	$1,326,546	NR

BOBBY WADKINS

Birthdate: July 26, 1951
Birthplace: Richmond, VA
PGA TOUR Victories: None.
Other Victories: None.
National/International Teams: None.

PGA TOUR CAREER SUMMARY

Year	Money	Rank
1975	$23,330	90
1976	$23,510	93
1977	$20,867	103
1978	$70,426	41
1979	$121,373	28
1980	$56,728	67
1981	$58,346	73
1982	$69,400	59
1983	$56,363	92
1984	$108,335	67
1985	$84,542	90
1986	$226,079	33
1987	$342,173	25
1988	$193,022	59
1989	$152,184	91
1990	$190,613	85
1991	$206,503	81
1992	$30,382	197
1993	$39,153	189
1994	$208,358	89
1995	$166,527	115
Career	$2,448,213	75

LANNY WADKINS

Birthdate: December 5, 1949
Birthplace: Richmond, VA
PGA TOUR Victories: (21) 1972 Sahara Invitational. 1973 Byron Nelson Classic, USI Classic. 1977 PGA Championship, World Series of Golf. 1979 Glen Campbell Los Angeles Open, Tournament Players Championship. 1982 Phoenix Open, MONY Tournament of Champions, Buick Open. 1983 Greater Greensboro Open, MONY Tournament of Champions. 1985 Bob Hope Classic, Los Angeles Open, Walt Disney World/Oldsmobile Classic. 1987 Doral-Ryder Open. 1988 Hawaiian Open, Colonial . 1990 Anheuser-Busch Golf Classic. 1991 United Hawaiian Open. 1992 Canon Greater Hartford Open.
Other Victories: 1970 U.S. Amateur, Western Amateur. 1978 Canadian PGA. 1979 Bridgestone Open. 1984 World Nissan Championship. 1990 Fred Meyer Challenge.
National/International Teams: 1969, 1971 Walker Cup. 1970 World Amateur Cup. 1982, 1983 U.S. vs. Japan. 1985 Nissan Cup. 1987 Kirin Cup.1977, 1979, 1983, 1985, 1987, 1989, 1991, 1993 , 1995 (Captain) Ryder Cup. 1977, 1984, 1985 World Cup.

PGA TOUR CAREER SUMMARY

Year	Money	Rank
1971	$15,291	111
1972	$116,616	10
1973	$200,455	5
1974	$51,124	54
1975	$23,582	88
1976	$42,849	64
1977	$244,882	3
1978	$53,811	61
1979	$195,710	10
1980	$67,778	58
1981	$51,704	81
1982	$306,827	7
1983	$319,271	3
1984	$198,996	29
1985	$446,893	2
1986	$264,931	23
1987	$501,727	13
1988	$616,596	10
1989	$233,363	60
1990	$673,433	13
1991	$651,495	12
1992	$366,837	40
1993	$244,643	68
1994	$54,114	185
1995	$97,485	162
Career	$6,028,855	12

GRANT WAITE

Birthdate: August 11, 1964
Birthplace: Palmerston, New Zealand

PGA TOUR Victories: (1) 1993 Kemper Open.
Other Victories: 1992 New Zealand Open.
National/International Teams: None.

PGA TOUR CAREER SUMMARY

Year	Money	Rank
1990	$60,076	177
1991-92	DNP	---
1993	$411,405	35
1994	$71,695	172
1995	$240,722	76
Career	$773,898	NR

DUFFY WALDORF

Birthdate: August 20, 1962
Birthplace: Los Angeles, CA
PGA TOUR Victories: (1) 1995 Texas Open.
Other Victories: 1984 California State Amateur.
1984 Broadmoor Invitational. 1985 Rice Planters.
National/International Teams: None.

PGA TOUR CAREER SUMMARY

Year	Money	Rank
1987	$53,175	148
1988	$55,221	143
1989	$149,945	94
1990	$71,673	157
1991	$196,081	86
1992	$582,120	23
1993	$202,638	84
1994	$274,971	71
1995	$525,622	35
Career	$2,113,447	93

TOM WATSON

Birthdate: September 4, 1949
Birthplace: Kansas City, MO
PGA TOUR Victories: (32) 1974 Western Open. 1975 Byron Nelson Golf Classic. 1977 Bing Crosby National Pro-Am, Wickes Andy Williams San Diego Open, Masters, Western Open. 1978 Joe Garagiola Tucson Open, Bing Crosby National Pro-Am, Byron Nelson Golf Classic, Colgate Hall of Fame Classic, Anheuser-Busch Classic. 1979 Sea Pines Heritage Classic, Tournament of Champions, Byron Nelson Golf Classic, Memorial Tournament, Colgate Hall of Fame Classic. 1980 Andy Williams San Diego Open, Glen Campbell Los Angeles Open, MONY Tournament of Champions, New Orleans Open, Byron Nelson Classic, World Series of Golf. 1981 Masters, USF&G New Orleans Open, Atlanta Classic. 1982 Glen Campbell Los Angeles Open, Sea Pines Heritage Classic, U.S. Open. 1984 Seiko-Tucson Match Play, MONY Tournament of Champions, Western Open. 1987 Nabisco Championships of Golf.
Other Victories: 1975 British Open. 1977 British Open. 1980 Dunlop Phoenix, British Open. 1982 British Open. 1983 British Open. 1992 Hong Kong Open.
National/International Teams: 1977, 1981, 1983, 1989 Ryder Cup. 1982, 1984 USA vs. Japan.

PGA TOUR CAREER SUMMARY

Year	Money	Rank
1971	$2,185	224
1972	$31,081	79
1973	$74,973	35
1974	$135,474	10
1975	$153,795	7
1976	$138,202	12
1977	$310,653	1
1978	$382,429	1
1979	$462,636	1
1980	$530,808	1
1981	$347,660	3
1982	$316,483	5
1983	$237,519	12
1984	$476,260	1
1985	$226,778	18
1986	$278,338	20
1987	$616,351	5
1988	$273,216	39
1989	$185,398	80
1990	$213,988	88
1991	$364,877	45
1992	$299,818	50
1993	$342,023	46
1994	$380,378	43
1995	$320,785	58
Career	$7,072,113	7

D.A. WEIBRING

Birthdate: May 25, 1953
Birthplace: Quincy, IL
PGA TOUR Victories: (4) 1979 Quad Cities Open. 1987 Beatrice Western Open. 1991 Hardee's Golf Classic. 1995 Quad City Open.
Other Victories: 1985 Polaroid Cup, Shell-Air New Zealand Open. 1989 Family House Invitational.
National/International Teams: None.

PGA TOUR CAREER SUMMARY

Year	Money	Rank
1980	$78,611	53
1981	$92,388	45
1982	$117,941	31
1983	$61,831	84
1984	$110,325	65

Year	Money	Rank
1985	$153,079	50
1986	$167,602	55
1987	$391,363	21
1988	$186,677	63
1989	$98,688	127
1990	$156,235	101
1991	$558,648	22
1992	$253,018	62
1993	$299,294	58
1994	$255,757	72
1995	$517,065	36
Career	$3,612,373	42

MARK WIEBE

Birthdate: September 13, 1957
Birthplace: Denver, CO
PGA TOUR Victories: (2) **1985** Anheuser-Busch Classic. **1986** Hardee's Golf Classic.
National/International Teams: None.

PGA TOUR CAREER SUMMARY

Year	Money	Rank
1984	$16,257	166
1985	$181,894	36
1986	$260,180	25
1987	$128,651	82
1988	$392,166	28
1989	$296,269	41
1990	$210,435	72
1991	$100,046	136
1992	$174,763	86
1993	$360,213	42
1994	$16,033	229
1995	$168,832	112
Career	$2,305,739	80

IAN WOOSNAM

Birthdate: March 2, 1958
Birthplace: Oswestry, Wales
PGA TOUR Victories: (2) **1991** USF&G Classic, Masters.
Other Victories: 1988 Volvo PGA Championship, Carrol's Irish Open, Panasonic European Open. **1989** Carrolls Irish Open. **1990** Amex Mediterranean Open, Monte Carlo Open, Bell's Scottish Open, Epson Grand Prix, Suntory World Match Play Championship. **1991** Mediterranean Open, Monte Carlo Open, PGA Grand Slam. **1992** European Monte Carlo. **1993** Murphy's English Open, Trophee Lancome. **1994** Air France Cannes Open.
National/International Teams: 1980, 1982, 1983, 1984, 1985, 1987, 1990, 1991, 1992, 1993 World Cup. 1983, 1985, 1987, 1989, 1991, 1993, 1995 Ryder Cup. **1985, 1986, 1988, 1989, 1990, 1991, 1993** Dunhill Cup. **1985, 1986** Nissan Cup. **1987** Kirin Cup. **1989, 1993** Four Tours World Championship of Golf.

PGA TOUR CAREER SUMMARY

Year	Money	Rank
1986	$4,000	233
1987	$3,980	236
1988	$8,464	219
1989	$146,323	97
1990	$72,138	156
1991	$485,023	23
1992	$52,046	171
1993	$55,426	176
1995	$174,464	106
Career	$1,001,864	NR

FUZZY ZOELLER

Birthdate: November 11, 1951
Birthplace: New Albany, IN
PGA TOUR Victories: (10) **1979** Andy Williams-San Diego Open, Masters. **1981** Colonial National Invitational. **1983** Sea Pines Heritage Classic, Las Vegas Pro-Celebrity Classic. **1984** U.S. Open. **1985** Bay Hill Classic. **1986** AT&T Pebble Beach National Pro-Am, Sea Pines Heritage Classic, Anheuser-Busch Golf Classic.
Other Victories: 1985-86 Skins Game.
National/International Teams: 1979, 1983, 1985 Ryder Cup.

PGA TOUR CAREER SUMMARY

Year	Money	Rank
1975	$7,318	146
1976	$52,557	56
1977	$76,417	40
1978	$109,055	20
1979	$196,951	9
1980	$95,531	46
1981	$151,571	19
1982	$128,512	28
1983	$417,597	2
1984	$157,460	40
1985	$244,003	15
1986	$358,115	13
1987	$222,921	44
1988	$209,584	51
1989	$217,742	65
1990	$199,629	79
1991	$385,139	42
1992	$125,003	114
1993	$378,175	39
1994	$1,016,804	5
1995	$170,706	110
Career	$4,918,771	25

SENIOR PGA TOUR PERSONALITIES

OVERVIEW: *Biographies and career summaries of leading Senior PGA TOUR players, including 1995 statistical summaries and career highlights.*

TOMMY AARON
Birthdate: February 22, 1937
Birthplace: Gainesville, GA
PGA TOUR Victories: (2) 1970 Atlanta Classic. 1973 Masters.
Senior PGA TOUR Victories: (1) 1992 Kaanapali Classic.
Other Victories: 1969 Canadian Open. 1960 Western Amateur.
National/International Teams: 1959 Walker Cup. 1969, 1973 Ryder Cup.

SENIOR PGA TOUR CAREER SUMMARY

Year	Money	Rank
1987	$98,421	29
1988	$81,829	41
1989	$51,800	60
1990	$107,651	46
1991	$152,443	43
1992	$459,230	12
1993	$266,611	34
1994	$397,515	26
1995	$281,474	41
Sr. Career	$1,853,207	33

JIM ALBUS
Birthdate: June 18, 1940
Birthplace: Staten Island, NY
PGA TOUR Victories: None
Senior PGA TOUR Victories: (4) 1991 MAZDA Presents THE SENIORS PLAYERS Championship. 1993 GTE Suncoast Classic. 1994 Vantage at the Dominion, Bank of Boston Senior Golf Classic.
Other Victories: 1970 Metropolitan Open Championship. 1985 Metropolitan Open Championship.
National/International Teams: None.

SENIOR PGA TOUR CAREER SUMMARY

Year	Money	Rank
1990	$14,433	95
1991	$301,406	20
1992	$404,693	16
1993	$627,883	12
1994	$1,237,128	3
1995	$708,711	10
Sr. Career	$3,179,736	15

BUDDY ALLIN
Birthdate: October 13, 1944
Birthplace: Bremerton, WA
PGA TOUR Victories: (5) 1971 Greater Greensboro Open. 1973 Florida Citrus Open. 1974 Doral-Eastern Open, Byron Nelson Golf Classic. 1976 Pleasant Valley Classic.
Senior PGA TOUR Victories: None
Other Victories: 1980 New Zealand Open.
National/International Teams: None.

SENIOR PGA TOUR CAREER SUMMARY

Year	Money	Rank
1994	$1,100	196
1995	$501,092	22
Sr. Career	$502,192	NR

ISAO AOKI
Birthdate: August 31, 1942
Birthplace: Abiko, Chiba, Japan
Senior PGA TOUR Victories: (4) 1992 Nationwide Championship. 1994 Bank One Senior Classic, Brickyard Crossing Championship. 1995 Bank of Boston Classic.
Other Victories: 1991 Bridgestone Tournament.
National/International Teams: 1982, 1983, 1984 Japanese National Team. 1985, 1987, 1988 Kirin Cup.

SENIOR PGA TOUR CAREER SUMMARY

Year	Money	Rank
1992	$324,650	26
1993	$557,667	15

Year	Money	Rank
1994	$632,975	11
1995	$964,833	5
Sr. Career	$2,383,324	25

GEORGE ARCHER
Birthdate: October 1, 1939
Birthplace: San Francisco, CA
PGA TOUR Victories: (12) **1965** Lucky International. **1967** Greensboro. **1968** Pensacola, New Orleans. **1969** Williams San Diego, Hartford. **1972** Glen Campbell Los Angeles, Greensboro Open. **1976** Del Webb Sahara Invitational. **1984** Bank of Boston Classic.
Senior PGA TOUR Victories: (19) **1989** Gatlin Brothers Southwest Classic. **1990** MONY Tournament of Champions, Northville Long Island Classic, GTE Northwest Classic, Gold Rush at Rancho Mudeta. **1991** Northville Long Island Classic, GTE North Classic, Raley's Senior Gold Rush. **1992** Murata Reunion Pro-Am, Northville Long Island Classic, Bruno's Memorial Classic. **1993** Ameritech Senior Open, First of America Classic, Raley's Senior Gold Rush, PING Kaanapali Classic. **1994** The Chrysler Cup. **1995** Vantage Championship, Cadillac NFL Golf Classic, Toshiba Senior Classic.
Other Victories: **1963** Trans-Mississippi Amateur. **1963** Northern California Open. **1968** PGA National Team Championship (with Bobby Nichols). **1969** Argentine Masters. **1981** Colombian Open. **1982** Philippines Open.
National/International Teams: 1990, 1991, 1992, 1993 U.S. DuPont Cup Team.

SENIOR PGA TOUR CAREER SUMMARY
Year	Money	Rank
1989	$ 98,063	45
1990	$749,691	4
1991	$963,455	2
1992	$860,175	2
1993	$963,124	3
1994	$684,944	10
1995	$698,787	11
Sr. Career	$4,967,092	5

BUTCH BAIRD
Birthdate: July 20, 1936
Birthplace: Chicago, IL
PGA Tour Victories: (2) **1961** Waco Turner Open. **1976** San Antonio-Texas Open
PGA Tour Career Earnings: $329,789
Senior PGA Tour Victories: (2) **1986** Cuyahoga Seniors International. **1989** Northville Long Island Classic.
Other Victories: **1965** PGA National Four-Ball Championship (with Gay Brewer). **1968** Texas PGA. **1974** Florida PGA.
National/International Teams: None.

SENIOR PGA TOUR CAREER SUMMARY
Year	Money	Rank
1986	$101,686	20
1987	$249,731	10
1988	$138,193	24
1989	$234,963	21
1990	$150,313	39
1991	$160,131	41
1992	$169,202	41
1993	$150,038	55
1994	$177,031	49
1995	$227,377	43
Sr. Career	$1,734,347	39

MILLER BARBER
Birthdate: March 31, 1931
Birthplace: Shreveport, LA
PGA TOUR Victories: (11) **1964** Cajun Classic. **1967** Oklahoma City Open. **1968** Byron Nelson Classic. **1969** Kaiser International. **1970** New Orleans Open, Phoenix Open. **1972** Tucson Open. **1973** World Open. **1974** Ohio Kings Island Open. **1977** Anheuser-Busch Classic. **1978** Phoenix Open.
Senior PGA TOUR Victories: (24) **1981** Peter Jackson Champ., Suntree Senior Classic, PGA Seniors Championship. **1982** U.S. Senior Open, Suntree Senior Classic, Hilton Head Senior, International. **1983** Senior TPC, Merrill Lynch/ Golf Digest Commemorative, United Virginia Bank, Hilton Head Seniors International. **1984** Roy Clark Senior Challenge, U.S. Senior Open, Greater Syracuse Seniors, Denver Post Championship. **1985** Sunrise Senior Classic, U.S. Senior Open, PaineWebber World Seniors Invitational. **1986** MONY Tournament of Champions. **1987** Showdown Classic, Newport Cup. **1988** Showdown Classic, Fairfield-Barnett Classic. **1989** MONY Tournament of Champions, Vintage Chrysler Invitational.
Other Victories: **1985** Shootout at Jeremy Ranch (with Ben Crenshaw). **1985** Coca Cola Grand Slam. **1987** Mazda Championship (with Nancy Lopez). **1991** Fuji Electric Grandslam.

National/International Teams: **1969, 1971** Ryder Cup. **1991, 1992** Chrysler Cup. **1991, 1992** DuPont Cup.

SENIOR PGA TOUR CAREER SUMMARY

Year	Money	Rank
1981	$83,136	1
1982	$106,890	1
1983	$231,008	2
1984	$299,099	2
1985	$241,999	4
1986	$204,837	9
1987	$347,571	5
1988	$329,833	9
1989	$370,229	11
1990	$274,184	21
1991	$288,753	21
1992	$170,798	40
1993	$318,986	30
1994	$126,327	60
1995	$129,108	67
Sr. Career	$3,493,553	13

BOB BETLEY

Birthdate: February 1, 1940
Birthplace: Butte, MT
PGA TOUR Victories: None.
Senior PGA TOUR Victories: (1) **1993** Bank of Boston Senior Golf Classic.
Other Victories: **1972** Nevada Open. **1974** Idaho Open. **1976** Frontier Airlines Invitational, Arizona Open. **1977** Nevada Open, Utah Open. **1978** Frontier Airlines Invitational, Izod International, Arizona Open. **1990** Colorado Open.
National/International Teams: None.

SENIOR PGA TOUR CAREER SUMMARY

Year	Money	Rank
1991	$ 84,262	59
1992	$ 78,012	70
1993	$407,300	24
1994	$42,683	84
1995	$103,486	69
Sr. Career	$815,246	NR

DON BIES

Birthdate: December 10, 1937
Birthplace: Cottonwood, ID
PGA TOUR Victories: (2)**1975** Sammy Davis, Jr. Greater Hartford Open.
SENIOR PGA TOUR Victories: (7) **1988** Northville Invitational, GTE Kaanapali Classic. **1989** Murata Seniors Reunion, The Traditional Desert Mountain, GTE Kaanapali Classic. **1992** PaineWebber Invitational. **1995** Raley's Senior Gold Rush.
Other Victories: **1989** Air New Zealand Shell Open.
National/International Teams: None.

SENIOR PGA TOUR CAREER SUMMARY

Year	Money	Rank
1988	$293,552	11
1989	$421,769	8
1990	$265,275	2
1991	$191,174	3
1992	$352,618	21
1993	$239,781	36
1994	$137,185	56
1995	$320,500	36
Sr. Career	$2,080,513	31

JOHN BLAND

Birthdate: March 6, 1945
Birthplace: Cape Town, South Africa
PGA TOUR Victories: None.
Senior PGA Tour Victories: (1) **1995** Raley's Senior Classic.
National/International Teams: **1992** Dunhill Cup.

SENIOR PGA TOUR CAREER SUMMARY

Year	Money	Rank
1995	$146,867	63
Sr. Career	$146,867	63

JOHN PAUL CAIN

Birthdate: January 14, 1936
Birthplace: Sweetwater, TX
PGA TOUR Victories: None.
Senior PGA Tour Victories: (2) **1989** Greater Grand Rapids Open. **1994** Ameritech Senior Open.
Other Victories: **1959** Texas Amateur Championship.
National/International Teams: None

SENIOR PGA TOUR CAREER SUMMARY

Year	Money	Rank
1989	$146,763	30
1990	$208,759	29
1991	$149,002	44
1992	$148,058	44
1993	$ 92,873	66
1994	$291,868	31
1995	$382,421	28
Sr. Career	$1,419,744	NR

BOB CHARLES

Birthdate: March 14, 1936
Birthplace: Carterton, New Zealand
PGA TOUR Victories: (5) **1963** Houston Open. **1965** Tucson Open. **1967** Atlanta Classic. **1968** Canadian Open. **1974** Greater Greensboro Open.
Senior PGA TOUR Victories: (21) **1987** Vintage Chrysler Invitational, GTE Classic, Sunwest Bank/Charley Pride Golf Classic. **1988** NYNEX/Golf Digest Commemorative, Sunwest Bank/Charley Pride Classic, Rancho Murieta Senior Gold Rush, Vantage Presents Bank One Classic, Pepsi Senior Challenge. **1989** GTE Suncoast Classic, NYNEX/Golf Digest Commemorative, Digital Seniors Classic, Sunwest Bank/Charley Pride Classic, Fairfield Barnett Space Coast Classic. **1990** Digital Seniors Classic, GTE Kaanapali Classic. **1991** GTE Suncoast Classic. **1992** Raley's Senior Gold Rush, Transamerica Senior Golf Classic. **1993** Doug Sanders Celebrity Classic, Bell Atlantic Classic, Quicksilver Classic.
Other Victories: 1954, 1966, 1970, 1973 New Zealand Open. 1961, 1979, 1980 New Zealand PGA. 1962, 1974 Swiss Open. 1963 British Open. 1969 Picadilly Match Play. 1972 Dunlop Masters. 1972 John Player Classic. 1973 Scandinavian Open, South African Open. 1978 Air New Zealand Shell open. 1983 Tallahassee Open.
National/International Teams: None.

SENIOR PGA TOUR CAREER SUMMARY

Year	Money	Rank
1986	$261,160	7
1987	$389,437	3
1988	$533,929	1
1989	$725,887	1
1990	$584,318	7
1991	$673,910	6
1992	$473,903	1
1993	$1,046,823	2
1994	$473,237	23
1995	$589,832	14
Sr. Career	$5,640,898	2

JIM COLBERT

Birthdate: March 9, 1941
Birthplace: Elizabeth, NJ
PGA TOUR Victories: (8) **1969** Monsanto Open. **1972** Greater Milwaukee Open. **1973** Greater Jacksonville Open. **1974** American Golf Classic. **1975** Walt Disney World Team Championship (with Dean Refram). **1980** Joe Garagiola Tucson Open. **1983** Colonial National Invitation, Texas Open.
Senior PGA TOUR Victories: (13) **1991** Southwestern Bell Classic, Vantage Championship, First Development Kaanapali Classic. **1992** GTE Suncoast Classic, Vantage Championship. **1993** Royal Caribbean Classic, Ford Senior Players Championship. **1994** Kroger Senior Classic, Southwestern Bell Classic. **1995** Tournament of Champions, Las Vegas Senior Classic, Bell Atlantic Senior Classic, Senior TOUR Championship.
Other Victories: 1987 Jerry Ford Invitational.
National/International Teams: 1992, 1993 DuPont Cup.

SENIOR PGA TOUR CAREER SUMMARY

Year	Money	Rank
1991	$880,749	3
1992	$825,768	3
1993	$779,889	7
1994	$996,615	5
1995	$1,167,352	2
Sr. Career	$4,532,856	6

CHARLES COODY

Birthdate: July 13, 1937
Birthplace: Stamford, TX
PGA TOUR Victories: (3) **1964** Dallas Open. **1969** Cleveland Open. **1971** Masters.
Senior PGA TOUR Victories: (4) **1989** General Tire Las Vegas Classic. **1990** Vantage Championship. **1991** NYNEX Commemorative, Transamerica Senior Golf Championship.
Other Victories: 1971 World Series of Golf. 1973 John Player Classic. 1994 Liberty Mutual Legends of Golf (with Dale Douglass).
National/International Teams: 1971 Ryder Cup. 1989, 1990 DuPont Cup.

SENIOR PGA TOUR CAREER SUMMARY

Year	Money	Rank
1987	$93,064	31
1988	$161,286	20
1989	$403,880	10
1990	$762,901	3
1991	$543,326	8
1992	$286,294	28
1993	$221,982	37
1994	$219,215	39
1995	$155,862	58
Sr. Career	$2,811,306	19

BRUCE CRAMPTON

Birthdate: September 28, 1935
Birthplace: Sydney, Australia
PGA TOUR Victories: (14) **1961** Milwaukee Open. **1962** Motor City Open. **1964** Texas Open.**1965** Bing Crosby National Pro Am, Colonial Invitaional, "500" Festival Open. **1969** Hawaiian Open. **1970** Westchester Classic. **1971** Western Open. **1973** Phoenix Open, Tucson Open, Houston Open, American Golf Classic. **1976** Houston Open.
Senior PGA TOUR Victories: (19) **1986** Benson & Hedges Invitational at the Dominion, MONY Syracuse Senior Classic, GTE Northwest Classic, PaineWebber World Seniors Invitational, Pepsi Senior Challenge, Las Vegas Senior Classic, Shearson Lehman Brothers Seniors. **1987** Denver Champions of Golf, Greenbrier/American Express Championship, MONY Syracuse Seniors Classic, Vantage Presents Bank One Seniors. **1988** United Hospitals Classic, GTE Northwest Classic. **1989** MONY Arizona Classic, Ameritech Senior Open. **1990** PaineWebber Invitational, Gatlin Brothers Southwest Senior Classic. **1991** Infiniti Senior Tournament of Champions. **1992** GTE West Classic.
Other Victories: **1956** Australian Open. **1959** Far East Open. **1961** Milwaukee Open. **1987, 1988** Liberty Mutual Legends of Golf (with Orville Moody).
National/International Teams: None.

SENIOR PGA TOUR CAREER SUMMARY

Year	Money	Rank
1985	$14,250	57
1986	$454,299	1
1987	$437,904	2
1988	$332,927	8
1989	$443,582	7
1990	$464,569	11
1991	$514,509	11
1992	$471,873	11
1993	$366,762	25
1994	$103,860	65
1995	$73,404	78
Sr. Career	$3,666,812	10

JIM DENT

Birthdate: May 9, 1939
Birthplace: Augusta, GA
Senior PGA TOUR Victories: (9) **1989** MONY Syracuse Senior Classic, Newport Cup. **1990** Vantage at The Dominion, MONY Syracuse Senior Classic, Kroger Senior Classic, Crestar Classic. **1992** Newport Cup. **1994** Bruno's Memorial Classic. **1995** Bruno's Memorial Senior Classic.
Other Victories: **1976, 1977, 1978** Florida PGA Championship.
National/International Teams: **1990, 1991** DuPont Cup.

SENIOR PGA TOUR CAREER SUMMARY

Year	Money	Rank
1989	$337,691	12
1990	$693,214	6
1991	$529,315	9
1992	$593,979	9
1993	$513,515	1
1994	$854,891	8
1995	$527,531	18
Sr. Career	$4,121,862	9

BRUCE DEVLIN

Birthdate: October 10, 1937
Birthplace: Armidale, Australia
PGA Tour Victories: (8) **1964** St Petersburg Open. **1966** Colonial National Invitation, Carling Open. **1969** Byron Nelson Classic. **1970** Bob Hope Desert Classic, Cleveland Open. **1972** Houston Open, U.S.I. Classic.
PGA Tour Career Earnings: $907,069
Senior PGA Tour Victories: (1) FHP Health Care Senior Classic.
Other Victories: **1959** Australian Amateur. **1960** Australian Open. **1963** French Open, New Zealand Open; **1966** Australian PGA. **1969** Australian PGA. **1970** Alcan, Australian PGA.
National/International Teams: **1970** World Cup

SENIOR PGA TOUR CAREER SUMMARY

Year	Money	Rank
1987	$ 30,771	64
1988	$125,660	26
1989	$121,585	37
1990	$ 83,761	54
1991	$132,607	49
1992	$ 74,498	71
1993	$ 65,383	74
1994	$ 40,224	87
1995	$224,143	47
Sr. Career	$898,632	NR

TERRY DILL
Birthdate: May 13, 1939
Birthplace: Forth Worth, TX
PGA Tour Victories: None
PGA Tour Career Earnings: $250,289
Senior PGA Tour Victories: (1) 1992 Bank One Senior Classic
National/International Teams: None.

SENIOR PGA TOUR CAREER SUMMARY
Year	Money	Rank
1989	$ 82,332	50
1990	$278,372	19
1991	$242,191	31
1992	$211,998	34
1993	$179,976	50
1994	$224,885	36
1995	$282,361	40
Sr. Career	$1,502,114	NR

DALE DOUGLASS
Birthdate: March 5, 1936
Birthplace: Wewoka, OK
PGA TOUR Victories: (3) 1969 Azalea Open, Kemper Open. 1970 Phoenix Open.
Senior PGA TOUR Victories: (10) 1986 Vintage Invitational, Johnny Mathis Senior Classic, U.S. Senior Open, Fairfield Barnett Senior Classic. 1988 GTE Suncoast Classic. 1990 Bell Atlantic Classic. 1991 Showdown Classic. 1992 NYNEX Commemorative, Ameritech Senior Open. 1993 Ralphs Senior Classic.
Other Victories: 1990 Liberty Mutual Legends of Golf (with Charles Coody). 1994 Liberty Mutual Legends of Golf (with Charles Coody).
National/International Teams: 1969 Ryder Cup. 1989, 1990, 1991, 1992 DuPont Cup.

SENIOR PGA TOUR CAREER SUMMARY
Year	Money	Rank
1986	$309,760	3
1987	$296,429	7
1988	$280,457	12
1989	$313,275	14
1990	$568,198	8
1991	$606,949	7
1992	$694,564	6
1993	$499,858	19
1994	$518,186	18
1995	$334,654	35
Sr. Career	$4,380,971	7

DAVE EICHELBERGER
Birthdate: September 3, 1943
Birthplace: Waco, TX
PGA TOUR Victories: (4) 1971 Greater Milwaukee Open. 1977 Greater Milwaukee Open. 1980 Bay Hill Classic. 1981 Tallahassee Open.
PGA TOUR Career Earnings: $1,174,354
Senior PGA Tour Victories: (1) 1994 Quicksilver Classic
Other Victories: 1979 J.C Penny Mixed Team Classic (with Murle Breer.) 1994 Diner's Club Matches (with Raymond Floyd).
National/International Teams: None.

SENIOR PGA TOUR CAREER SUMMARY
Year	Money	Rank
1993	$11,927	100
1994	$535,087	20
1995	$519,066	21
Sr. Career	$1,066,080	NR

JIM FERREE
Birthdate: June 10, 1931
Birthplace: Pine Bluff, NC
PGA TOUR Victories: (1) 1958 Vancouver Centennial.
Senior PGA TOUR Victories: (2) 1986 Greater Grand Rapids Open. 1991 Bell Atlantic Classic.
Other Victories: 1961 Jamaica Open. 1962 Panama Open. 1963 Maracaibo Open. 1964 Children's Memorial Hospital Classic. 1981, 1982 Tri-State Senior PGA.
National/International Teams: 1993 DuPont Cup.

SENIOR PGA TOUR CAREER SUMMARY
Year	Money	Rank
1981	$16,694	15
1982	$16,455	30
1983	$69,547	11
1984	$103,717	13
1985	$153,087	9
1986	$184,667	11
1987	$111,858	23
1988	$112,137	30
1989	$194,992	24
1990	$144,680	40
1991	$279,384	23
1992	$194,633	37
1993	$424,333	22
1994	$119,963	63
1995	$166,917	56
Sr. Career	$2,286,348	27

RAYMOND FLOYD
Birthdate: September 4, 1942
Birthplace: Fort Bragg, NC
PGA TOUR Victories: (22) **1963** St. Petersburg Open. **1966** St. Paul Open. **1969** Jacksonville Open, American Golf Classic, PGA Championship. **1975** Kemper Open. **1976** Masters, World Open. **1977** Byron Nelson Classic, Pleasant Valley Classic. **1979** Greensboro Open. **1980** Doral Eastern Open. **1981** Doral Eastern Open, Tournament Players Championship, Manufacturers Hanover Western Classic. **1982** Memorial Tournament, Danny Thomas Memphis Classic, PGA Championship. **1985** Houston Open. **1986** U.S. Open, Walt Disney/Oldsmobile Classic. **1992** Doral-Ryder Open.
Senior PGA TOUR Victories: (12) **1992** GTE North Classic, Ralphs Senior Classic, Senior TOUR Championship. **1993** Gulfstream Aerostream Invitational, Northville Long Island Classic. **1994** The Tradition, Las Vegas Senior Classic, Cadillac NFL Golf Classic. **1995** Senior Slam, PGA Seniors Championship, Burnet Senior Classic, Emerald Coast Senior Classic.
Other Victories: **1978** Brazilian Open. **1979** Costa Rica Cup. **1981** Canadian PGA. **1985** Chrysler Team Championship (with Hal Sutton). **1988** Skins game. **1990** RMCC Invitational (with Fred Couples). **1993** Franklin Funds Shark Shootout (with Steve Elkington). **1995** Lexus Challenge (with Michael Chiklis).
National/International Teams: **1969, 1975, 1977, 1981, 1983, 1985, 1991, 1993** Ryder Cup.

SENIOR PGA TOUR CAREER SUMMARY
Year	Money	Rank
1992	$436,991	14
1993	$713,168	9
1994	$1,142,762	3
1995	$1,118,545	4
Sr. Career	$3,531,105	12

AL GEIBERGER
Birthdate: September 1, 1937
Birthplace: Red Bluff, CA
PGA TOUR Victories: (11) **1962** Ontario Open. **1963** Almaden Open. **1965** American Golf Classic. **1966** PGA Championship. **1974** Sahara Invitational. **1975** Tournament of Champions, Tournament Players Championship. **1976** Greater Greensboro Open, Western Open. **1977** Danny Thomas Memphis Classic. **1979** Colonial National Invitational.
Senior PGA TOUR Victories: (9) **1987** Vantage Championship, Hilton Head Seniors International, Las Vegas Senior Classic. **1988** Pointe/Del E. Webb Arizona Classic. **1989** GTE Northwest Classic. **1991** Kroger Senior Classic. **1992** Infinite Tournament of Champions. **1993** Infiniti Tournament of Champions, GTE West Classic.
Other Victories: **1989** Liberty Mutual Legends of Golf (with Harold Henning).
National/International Teams: **1967, 1975** Ryder Cup. **1991, 1993** DuPont Cup.

SENIOR PGA TOUR CAREER SUMMARY
Year	Money	Rank
1987	$264,798	9
1988	$348,735	6
1989	$527,033	3
1990	$373,624	1
1991	$519,926	10
1992	$385,339	19
1993	$608,877	13
1994	$72,729	69
1995	$358,835	34
Sr. Career	$3,399,205	14

GIBBY GILBERT
Birthdate: January 14, 1941
Birthplace: Chattanooga, TN
PGA TOUR Victories: (3) **1970** Houston Champions International. **1976** Danny Thomas Memphis Classic. **1977** Walt Disney World National Team Championship (with Grier Jones).
Senior PGA TOUR Victories: (4) **1992** Southwestern Bell Classic, First of America Classic, Kroger Senior Classic. **1993** Las Vegas Senior Classic.
Other Victories: **1988, 1989, 1990** Tennessee Opens.
National/International Teams: **1993** DuPont Cup.

SENIOR PGA TOUR CAREER SUMMARY
Year	Money	Rank
1991	$392,351	14
1992	$603,630	8
1993	$661,378	11
1994	$324,242	27
1995	$359,278	33
Sr. Career	$2,326,989	26

LARRY GILBERT
Birthdate: November 19, 1942
Birthplace: Fort Knox, KY

PGA TOUR Victories: None.
Senior PGA TOUR Victories: (2) **1994** Dallas Reunion Pro-Am, Vantage Championship.
Other victories: **1981, 1982, 1991** PGA Club Professional Championship.
National/International Teams: None.

SENIOR PGA TOUR CAREER SUMMARY

Year	Money	Rank
1993	$515,790	17
1994	$831,244	9
1995	$456,728	24
Sr. Career	$1,760,766	36

DICK HENDRICKSON

Birthdate: January 22, 1935
Birthplace: St. Louis, MO
PGA TOUR Victories: None
Senior PGA TOUR Victories: None.
Other Victories: **1972** Philadelphia PGA Championship, Mini Byron.
National/International Teams: None.

SENIOR PGA TOUR CAREER SUMMARY

Year	Money	Rank
1985	$1,463	114
1986	$5,069	79
1988	$83,076	38
1989	$144,739	31
1990	$159,070	34
1991	$281,863	22
1992	$270,025	31
1993	$243,262	35
1994	$153,155	53
1995	$165,222	57
Sr. Career	$1,510,858	49

HAROLD HENNING

Birthdate: October 3, 1934
Birthplace: Johannesburg, South Africa
PGA TOUR Victories: (1) **1966** Texas Open
Senior PGA TOUR Victories: (3) **1985** Seiko/Tucson Match Play Championship. **1988** GTE Classic. **1991** First of America Classic.
Other Victories: **1989** Liberty Mutual Legends of Golf. **1970** Tallahassee Open. **1965** World Cup (with Gary Player).
National/International Teams: **1961, 1965, 1966, 1967, 1970, 1971** World Cup.

SENIOR PGA TOUR CAREER SUMMARY

Year	Money	Rank
1984	$6,500	72
1985	$197,624	6
1986	$173,034	12
1987	$151,986	17
1988	$366,230	5
1989	$453,163	6
1990	$409,879	12
1991	$394,803	13
1992	$347,857	22
1993	$314,104	31
1994	$126,894	59
1995	$234,697	44
Sr. Career	$3,095,542	17

MIKE HILL

Birthdate: January 27, 1939
Birthplace: Jackson, MI
PGA TOUR Victories: (3) **1970** Doral Eastern Open. **1972** San Antonio Texas Open. **1977** Ohio Kings Island Open.
Senior PGA TOUR Victories: (18) **1990** GTE Suncoast Classic, GTE North Classic, Fairfield Barnett Space Coast Classic, Security Pacific Senior Classic, New York Life Championship. **1991** Doug Sanders Kingwood Celebrity Classic, Ameritech Senior Open, GTE Northwest Classic, Nationwide Championship, New York Life Championship. **1992** Vintage ARCO Invitational, Doug Sanders Kingwood Celebrity Classic. **1994** The Intellinet Challenge. **1995** Liberty Mutual Legends of Golf (with Lee Trevino), Kroger Senior Classic.
Other Victories: **1989** Mazda Championship (with Patti Rizzo).
National/International Teams: **1990, 1991, 1992, 1993** DuPont Cup.

SENIOR PGA TOUR CAREER SUMMARY

Year	Money	Rank
1989	$412,104	9
1990	$895,678	2
1991	$1,065,657	1
1992	$802,423	4
1993	$798,116	6
1994	$532,521	16
1995	$523,136	20
Sr. Career	$4,994,635	4

SIMON HOBDAY

Birthdate: June 23, 1940
Birthplace: Mareking, South Africa
Senior PGA TOUR Victories: (5) **1993** Senior Classic, Hyatt Senior TOUR Championship. **1994** U.S. Senior Open, GTE Northwest Classic. **1995**

Brickyard Senior Classic.
Other Victories: 1971 South African Open. 1976 German Open, Rhodesian Open. 1977 Rhodesian Open. 1979 Madrid Open. 1985 TrustBank Tournament.
National/International Teams: 1966 Eisenhower Trophy (representing Zambia).

SENIOR PGA TOUR CAREER SUMMARY

Year	Money	Rank
1991	$353,654	16
1992	$397,382	18
1993	$670,417	1
1994	$606,621	12
1995	$429,767	26
Sr. Career	$2,451,656	24

HALE IRWIN
Birthdate: June 3, 1945
Birthplace: Joplin, MO
PGA Tour Victories: (20) 1971 Heritage Classic. 1973 Heritage Classic. 1974 U.S. Open. 1975 Werstern Open, Atlanta Classic. 1976 Glen Campbell Los Angeles Open, Florida Citrus Open. 1977 Atlanta Classic, Hall of Fame Classic, San Antonio-Texas Open. 1979 U.S. Open. 1981 Hawaiian Open, Buick Open. 1982 Honda-Inverrary Classic. 1983 Memorial Tournament. 1984 Bing Crosby Pro-Am. 1985 Memorial Tournament. 1990 U.S. Open, Buick Classic. 1994 MCI Heritage Classic.
Senior PGA TOUR Victories: (2) Ameritech Senior Open, Vantage Championship.
Other Victories: 1974 Picadilly World Match Play Championship. 1978 Australian PGA, 1979 South African PGA. 1981 Bridgestone Classic (Japan). 1982 Brazilian Open. 1986 Bahamas Classic, 1987 Fila Classic.
National/International Teams: 1974, 1979 World Cup. 1975, 1977, 1979, 1981, 1991 Ryder Cup. 1983 U.S. vs. Japan. 1994 President's Cup (captain).

SENIOR PGA TOUR CAREER SUMMARY

Year	Money	Rank
1995	$751,175	9
Sr. Career	$751,175	NR

TONY JACKLIN
Birthdate: July 7, 1944
Birthplace: Scunthorpe, England
PGA Tour Victories: 1968 Greater Jacksonville Open. 1970 U.S. Open. 1972 Greater Jacksonville
PGA Tour Career Earnings: $352,179
Senior PGA Tour Victories: (1) 1994 First of America Classic
Other Victories: 1965 Gor-Ray Assistants Championship. 1966 Kimberly Tournament (South Africa). 1967 Pringle Tournament, Dunlop Masters, Forrest Products Open, New Zealand PGA Championship. 1969 British Open Championship. 1970 WD & HO Wills Open, Lancome Tournament. 1971 Benson & Hedges Festival. 1972 Dunlop International (Australia), Viyella PGA Championship. 1973 Italian Open, Dunlop Masters, Bogota Open. 1974 Scandinavian Enterprise Open, Los Lagartos Open. 1976 Kerrygold International Classic. 1979 German Open, Venezuela Open. 1981 Billy Butlin Jersey Open. 1982 Sun Alliance PGA Championship.

SENIOR PGA TOUR CAREER SUMMARY

Year	Money	Rank
1994	$221,384	37
1995	$366,697	31
Sr. Career	$588,081	NR

DON JANUARY
Birthdate: November 20, 1929
Birthplace: Plainview, TX
PGA TOUR Victories: (10) 1956 Dallas Centennial Open. 1960 Tucson Open. 1961 St. Paul Open. 1963 Tucson Open. 1966 Philadelphia Classic. 1967 PGA Championship. 1968 Tournament of Champions, Jacksonville Open. 1975 San Antonio Texas Open. 1976 MONY Tournament of Champions.
Senior PGA TOUR Victories: (22) 1980 Atlantic City Senior International. 1981 Michelob-Egypt Temple, Eureka Federal Savings. 1982 Michelob Classic, PGA Seniors Championship. 1983 Gatlin Brothers Senior Classic, Peter Jackson Champions, Marlboro Classic, Denver Post Champions, Citizen's Union Senior Classic, Suntree Seniors Classic. 1984 Vintage Invitational, du Maurier Champions, Digital Middlesex Classic. 1985 Senior TOUR Roundup, The Dominion Seniors, United Hospitals Senior Golf Championship, Greenbrier/American Express Championship. 1986 Senior Players Reunion Pro-Am, Greenbrier/American Express Championship, Seiko/Tucson Match Play Championship. 1987 MONY Senior Tournament of Champions.
Other Victories: 1956 Apple Valley Clambake. 1959 Valencia Open. 1979 PGA Seniors Championship. 1980 Australian Seniors. 1984 Shootout at Jeremy Ranch. 1985 Legends of Golf, Mazda Champions

(with Alice Miller). **1986** Legends of Golf.
National/International Teams: 1965, 1977 Ryder Cup.

SENIOR PGA TOUR CAREER SUMMARY

Year	Money	Rank
1981	$68,075	2
1982	$99,508	2
1983	$237,671	1
1984	$328,597	1
1985	$247,006	3
1986	$299,795	4
1987	$116,685	21
1988	$82,013	40
1989	$59,813	58
1990	$216,243	28
1991	$262,437	28
1992	$328,896	25
1993	$274,338	33
1994	$147, 976	55
1995	$91,717	74
Sr. Career	$2,904,155	18

JACK KIEFER

Birthdate: January 1, 1940
Birthplace: Columbia, PA
SENIOR PGA TOUR Victories: (1) **1994** Ralph's Senior Classic.
Other Victories: 1971 Pennsylvania State Open. **1975** New Jersey Open. **1976** New Jersey Open. **1983** New Jersey Open. **1985** Dodge Open. **1990** New Jersey Senior Open, New Jersey Senior PGA Championship.
National/International Teams: None.

SENIOR PGA TOUR CAREER SUMMARY

Year	Money	Rank
1990	$21,930	87
1991	$119,453	54
1992	$203,095	36
1993	$333,511	27
1994	$509,117	21
1995	$437,508	25
Sr. Career	$1,541,749	47

LARRY LAORETTI

Birthdate: July 11, 1939
Birthplace: Mahopac, NY
Senior PGA TOUR Victories: (1) **1992** U.S. Senior Open.
Other Victories: None.
National/International Teams: 1992 DuPont Cup.

SENIOR PGA TOUR CAREER SUMMARY

Year	Money	Rank
1989	$3,025	110
1990	$165,339	32
1991	$371,097	15
1992	$444,385	13
1993	$183,694	46
1994	$220,001	38
1995	$366,049	32
Sr. Career	$1,723,278	40

DICK LOTZ

Birthdate: October 15, 1942
Birthplace: Oakland, CA
PGA TOUR Victories: (3) **1969** Alameda Open. **1970** Kemper Open, Pensacola Open.
Senior PGA TOUR Victories: None.
Other Victories: None.
National/International Teams: None.

SENIOR PGA TOUR CAREER SUMMARY

Year	Money	Rank
1993	$199,244	44
1994	$167,152	51
1995	$34,194	96
Sr. Career	$403,265	NR

GRAHAM MARSH

Birthdate: January 14, 1944
Birthplace: Kalgoorlie, Australia
PGA Tour Victories: (1) **1977** Heritage Classic
PGA Tour Career Earnings: $199,386
Senior PGA Tour Victories: (1) **1995** Bruno's Memorial Senior Classic.
Other Victories: 1970 Watties Tournament, Swiss Open. **1971** Spalding Masters, Indian Open. **1972** Swiss Open, German Open, Dunlop International. **1973** Sunbeam Electric Scottish Open, Thailand Open, Indian Open, Fuji Sankei Classic. **1974** Malaysian Open, Fuji Sankei Classic, Dunlop Wizard, Tokyo Open, Pepsi-Wilson. **1975** Dunlop Wizard, Tokyo Open, Malaysian Open. **1976** Benson & Hedges International, Dunlop Open, Suntory Open, Dunlop Phoenix, KBC Augusta, Dunhill Match Play, Western Australia Open. **1977** Lancome Trophy, Colgate World Match-Play Championship, Dunhill Match-Play, Suntory Open, Dunlop Wizard, Chunichi Crowns. **1978** Western Australia PGA. **1979** Dutch Open, ANA Sapporo Open,

Dunlop Masters. **1980** Benson & Hedges International. **1981** European Open, Chunichi Crowns, Pepsi-Wilson. **1982** Ford Dealers South Australian Open, Australian Masters, Mayn Nickless Australian PGA Championship, Dunhill Queensland Open, Mitsubishi Galant. **1983** Yomiuri Open, Resch's Pilsner Tweed Classic, New Zealand PGA Championship. **1985** Lawrence Batley International, KLM Dutch Open, Tokai Classic. **1986** Suntory Open. **1987** Visa Taiheiyo Pacific Masters. **1989** Sapporo Tokyo Open. **1990** Tokai Classic.

SENIOR PGA TOUR CAREER SUMMARY
Year	Money	Rank
1994	$492,402	24
1995	$790,178	8
Sr. Career	$1,282,580	NR

RIVES McBEE
Birthdate: October 31, 1938
Birthplace: Denton, TX
PGA TOUR Victories: None
Senior PGA TOUR Victories: (3) **1989** RJR Bank One Classic. **1990** Showdown Classic, Vantage Bank One Classic.
Other Victories: 1973 PGA Club Professional Championship.
National/International Teams: 1989, 1990 DuPont Cup.

SENIOR PGA TOUR CAREER SUMMARY
Year	Money	Rank
1989	$258,487	18
1990	$480,329	10
1991	$141,745	47
1992	$128,862	42
1993	$181,803	47
1994	$166,177	52
1995	$170,044	54
Sr. Career	$1,486,167	48

JERRY McGEE
Birthdate: July 21, 1943
Birthplace: New Lexingon, OH
PGA Tour Victories: (4) **1975** Pensacola Open. **1977** IVB-Philadelphia Classic. **1979** Kemper Open, Sammy Davis, Jr.-Greater Hartford Open.
PGA Tour Career Earnings: $871,545
Senior PGA Tour Victories: None

SENIOR PGA TOUR CAREER SUMMARY
Year	Money	Rank
1993	$113,191	63
1994	$398,219	25
1995	$366,697	30
Sr. Career	$878,107	NR

ORVILLE MOODY
Birthdate: December 9, 1933
Birthplace: Chickasha, OK
PGA TOUR Victories: (1) **1969** U.S. Open.
Senior PGA TOUR Victories: (11) **1984** Daytona Beach Seniors Classic, MONY Tournament of Champions. **1987** Rancho Murieta Senior Gold Rush, GTE Kaanapali Classic. **1988** Vintage Chrysler Invitational, Senior Players Reunion, Greater Grand Rapids Open. **1989** Mazda Senior TPC, U.S. Senior Open. **1991** PaineWebber Invitational. **1992** Franklin Showdown Classic.
Other Victories: 1958 All-Army Championship. **1962** All-Service Championship. **1969** World Cup (with Lee Trevino), World Series of Golf. **1971** Hong Kong Open, Morocco Grand Prix. **1977** International Caribbean Open. **1984** Viceroy Panama Open. **1986** Australian PGA. **1987** Australian PGA, Liberty Mutual Legends of Golf (with Bruce Crampton). **1988** Liberty Mutual Legends of Golf (with Bruce Crampton).
National/International Teams: 1969 World Cup (with Trevino).

SENIOR PGA TOUR CAREER SUMMARY
Year	Money	Rank
1984	$183,920	5
1985	$134,643	12
1986	$128,755	16
1987	$355,793	16
1988	$411,859	4
1989	$647,985	2
1990	$273,224	22
1991	$227,826	3
1992	$288,263	2
1993	$196,565	4
1994	$208,490	42
1995	$69,021	79
Sr. Career	$3,116,776	16

WALTER MORGAN
Birthdate: May 31, 1941
Birthplace: Haddock, GA
PGA Tour Victories: None
PGA Tour Career Earnings: None

Senior PGA Tour Victories: (1) **1995** GTE Northwest Classic.
Other Victories: None
National/International Teams: None.

SENIOR PGA TOUR CAREER SUMMARY

Year	Money	Rank
1991	$10,430	100
1992	$101,037	59
1993	$138,700	57
1994	$27,444	93
1995	$404,456	27
Sr. Career	$682,067	NR

LARRY MOWRY
Birthdate: October 20, 1936
Birthplace: San Diego, CA
PGA TOUR Victories: None.
Senior PGA TOUR Victories: (5) **1987** Crestar Classic, Pepsi Senior Challenge. **1988** General Tire Las Vegas Classic. **1989** General Foods PGA Seniors Championship, RJR at The Dominion.
Other Victories: **1968** Rebel Yell Classic. **1969** Magnolia Classic. **1979** Florida Open, Florida PGA, Colorado Open. **1983** Florida Open.
National/International Teams: None.

SENIOR PGA TOUR CAREER SUMMARY

Year	Money	Rank
1986	$2,563	96
1987	$200,151	13
1988	$275,466	13
1989	$322,788	13
1990	$314,657	17
1991	$67,899	62
1992	$96,322	60
1993	$180,703	49
1994	$135,923	57
1995	$47,343	88
Sr. Career	$1,643,813	44

BOB MURPHY
Birthdate: February 14, 1943
Birthplace: Brooklyn, NY
PGA TOUR Victories: (5) **1968** Philadelphia Classic, Thunderbird Classic. **1970** Greater Hartford Open. **1975** Jackie Gleason Inverrary Classic. **1986** Canadian Open.
Senior PGA TOUR Victories: (7) **1993** Bruno's Memorial Classic, GTE North Classic. **1994** Raley's Senior Gold Rush, Kaanapali Classic. **1995** Intellinet Senior Challenge, PaineWebber Senior Invitational, Nationwide Championship.
Other Victories: **1965** U.S. Amateur. **1966** NCAA. **1967** Florida Open. **1979** Jerry Ford Invitational.
National/International Teams: **1966** Eisenhower Trophy. **1967** Walker Cup. **1975** Ryder Cup. **1993** DuPont Cup.

SENIOR PGA TOUR CAREER SUMMARY

Year	Money	Rank
1993	$768,743	8
1994	$855,862	7
1995	$1,146,591	3
Sr. Career	$2,657,346	21

BOBBY NICHOLS
Birthdate: April 14, 1936
Birthplace: Louisville, KY
PGA TOUR Victories: (11) **1962** St. Petersburg Open, Houston Classic. **1963** Seattle Open. **1964** PGA Championship, Carling World Open. **1965** Houston Classic, **1966** Minnesota Classic. **1970** Dow Jones Open. **1973** Westchester Classic. **1974** Andy Williams San Diego Open, Canadian Open.
Senior PGA TOUR Victories: (1) **1989** Southwestern Bell Classic.
Other Victories: **1968** PGA Team Championship (with George Archer). **1986** Showdown Classic (with Curt Byrum).
National/International Teams: **1967** Ryder Cup.

SENIOR PGA TOUR CAREER SUMMARY

Year	Money	Rank
1986	$56,676	36
1987	$196,698	14
1988	$226,936	14
1989	$210,097	22
1990	$158,144	35
1991	$252,764	29
1992	$223,218	32
1993	$181,433	48
1994	$131,695	58
1995	$88,669	76
Sr. Career	$1,719,024	41

JACK NICKLAUS
Birthdate: January 21, 1940
Birthplace: Columbus, OH
PGA TOUR Victories: (70) **1962** U.S.Open, Seattle World's Fair, Portland. **1963** Palm Springs, Masters, Tournament of Champions, PGA Championship, Sahara. **1964** Portland, Tournament of Champions, Phoenix, Whitemarsh. **1965** Portland,

Masters, Memphis, Thunderbird, Philadelphia. **1966** Masters, Sahara. **1967** U.S. Open, Sahara, Bing Crosby, Western, Westchester. **1968** Western, American Golf Classic. **1969** Sahara, Kaiser, San Diego. **1970** Byron Nelson, National Four Ball (with Arnold Palmer). **1971** PGA Championship, Tournament of Champions, Byron Nelson, National Team (with Arnold Palmer), Disney World. **1972** Bing Crosby, Doral Eastern, Masters, U.S. Open, Westchester, Match Play, Disney. **1973** Bing Crosby, New Orleans, Tournament of Champions, Atlanta, PGA Championship, Ohio Kings Island, Walt Disney. **1974** Hawaii, Tournament Players Championship. **1975** Doral Eastern, Heritage, Masters, PGA Championship, World Open. **1976** Tournament Players Championship, World Series of Golf. **1977** Gleason Inverrary, Tournament of Champions, Memorial. **1978** Gleason Inverrary, Tournament Players Championship, IVB Philadelphia. **1980** U.S. Open, PGA Championship. **1982** Colonial National Invitation. **1984** Memorial. **1986** Masters.
Senior PGA TOUR Victories: (7) **1990** The Tradition at Desert Mountain, Mazda Senior TPC. **1991** The Tradition at Desert Mountain, PGA Seniors Championship, U.S. Senior Open. **1993** U.S. Senior Open. **1994** Mercedes Championships. **1995** The Tradition.
Other Victories: **1959** U.S. Amateur. **1961** U.S. Amateur, NCAA. **1962** World Series of Golf. **1963** World Series of Golf, World Cup, International Trophy (World Cup individual). **1964** Australian Open, World Cup (with Arnold Palmer), International Trophy (World Cup individual). **1966** World Cup (with Arnold Palmer). **1967** World Cup (with Arnold Palmer). **1971** World Cup (with Lee Trevino), International Trophy (World Cup individual). **1973** World Cup (with Johnny Miller). **1983** Chrysler Team (with Johnny Miller).
National/International Teams: **1959**, **1961** Walker Cup. **1963**, **1964**, **1966**, **1967**, **1971**, **1973** World Cup. **1969**, **1971**, **1973**, **1975**, **1977**, **1981**, **1983**, **1987** Ryder Cup.

SENIOR PGA TOUR CAREER SUMMARY

Year	Money	Rank
1990	$340,000	15
1991	$343,734	17
1992	$114,548	53
1993	$206,028	42
1994	$239,278	34
1995	$538,800	16
Sr. Career	$1,782,388	35

CALVIN PEETE
Birthdate: July 18, 1943
Birthplace: Detroit, MI
PGA Tour Victories: (12) **1979** Greater Milwaukee Open. **1982** Greater Milwaukee Open, Anheuser-Bush Classic, B.C. Open, Pensacola Open. **1983** Georgia-Pacific Atlanta Classic, Anheuser-Bush Classic. **1984** Texas Open. **1985** Phoenix Open, Tournament Players Championship. **1986** MONY Tournament of Champions, USF&G Classic.
PGA Tour Career Earnings: $2,302,363
Senior PGA Tour Victories: None

SENIOR PGA TOUR CAREER SUMMARY

Year	Money	Rank
1993	$6,976	120
1994	$175,432	50
1995	$199,067	50
Sr. Career	$381,475	NR

GARY PLAYER
Birthdate: November 1, 1935
Birthplace: Johannesburg, South Africa
PGA TOUR Victories: (21) **1958** Kentucky Derby Open. **1961** Lucky International, Sunshine, Masters. **1962** PGA Championship. **1963** San Diego. **1964** "500" Festival, Pensacola. **1965** U.S. Open. **1969** Tournament of Champions. **1970** Greater Greensboro. **1971** Jacksonville, Tournament National Airlines. **1972** New Orleans, PGA Championship. **1973** Southern. **1974** Masters, Danny Thomas Memphis. **1978** Masters, Tournament of Champions, Houston Open.
Senior PGA TOUR Victories: (18) **1985** Quadel Seniors Classic. **1986** General Foods PGA Seniors Championship, United Hospital Classic, Denver Post Championship. **1987** Mazda Senior TPC, U.S. Senior Open, PaineWebber World Seniors Invitational. **1988** General Foods PGA Seniors Championship, Aetna Challenge, Southwestern Bell Classic, U.S. Senior Open, GTE North Classic. **1989** GTE North Classic, RJR Championship. **1990** PGA Seniors Championship. **1991** Royal Caribbean Classic, **1993** Bank One Classic. **1995** Bank One Senior Classic.
Other Victories: South African Open (13 times). Australian Open (7 times). **1957** Australian PGA. **1959** British Open. **1965** Suntory World Match Play, World Cup (with Harold Henning), International Trophy (World Cup individual), World Series of Golf. **1966** Suntory World Match Play. **1968** British Open, Suntory World Match Play, World Series of Golf. **1971** Suntory World Match

Play. **1972** World Series of Golf, Brazilian Open. **1973** Suntory World Match Play. **1974** Brazilian Open. **1976** South African Dunlop Masters. **1977** International Trophy (World Cup individual). **1980** Chile Open. **1984** Johnnie Walker.
National/International Teams: 1956, 1957, 1958, 1959, 1960, 1962, 1963, 1964, 1965, 1966, 1967, 1968, 1971, 1972, 1973, 1977 World Cup.

SENIOR PGA TOUR CAREER SUMMARY

Year	Money	Rank
1985	$30,000	44
1986	$291,190	5
1987	$333,439	6
1988	$435,914	2
1989	$514,116	4
1990	$507,268	9
1991	$337,253	18
1992	$346,798	23
1993	$360,272	26
1994	$309,776	28
1995	$287,251	39
Sr. Career	$3,578,363	11

JIMMY POWELL

Birthdate: January 17, 1935
Birthplace: Dallas, TX
PGA Tour Victories: None
PGA Tour Career Earnings: $27,796
Senior PGA Tour Victories: (3) **1990** Southwestern Bell Classic. **1992** Aetna Challenge. **1995** First of America Senior Classic.
Other Victories: 1968, 1970 and 1975 Southern California PGA Champion, 1975 California Open.
National/International Teams: None.

SENIOR PGA TOUR CAREER SUMMARY

Year	Money	Rank
1985	$ 45,465	36
1986	$ 44,211	43
1987	$ 58,707	41
1988	$106,300	31
1989	$178,998	26
1990	$208,183	30
1991	$153,605	42
1992	$274,371	29
1993	$164,255	54
1994	$588,378	14
1995	$376,339	29
Sr. Career	$2,151,327	29

DICK RHYAN

Birthdate: November 28, 1934
Birthplace: Columbus, OH
PGA TOUR Victories: None.
Senior PGA TOUR Victories: None.
Other Victories: 1966 Northern Ohio PGA Section, North Florida PGA Seniors.
National/International Teams: None.

SENIOR PGA TOUR CAREER SUMMARY

Year	Money	Rank
1987	$1,300	150
1988	$147,423	23
1989	$109,933	41
1990	$156,868	37
1991	$179,486	36
1992	$131,013	48
1993	$203,374	41
1994	$210,183	41
1995	$152,054	61
Sr. Career	$1,296,634	NR

CHI CHI RODRIGUEZ

Birthdate: October 23, 1935
Birthplace: Bayamon, Puerto Rico
PGA TOUR Victories: (8) **1963** Denver Open. **1964** Lucky International, Western Open. **1967** Texas Open. **1968** Sahara Invitational. **1972** Byron Nelson Classic. **1973** Greater Greensboro Open. **1979** Tallahassee Open.
Senior PGA TOUR Victories: (22) **1986** Senior TPC, Digital Seniors Classic, United Virginia Bank Seniors. **1987** General Foods PGA Seniors Championship, Vantage at The Dominion, United Hospitals Classic, Silver Pages Classic, Senior Players Reunion, Digital Seniors Classic, GTE Northwest Classic. **1988** Doug Sanders Kingwood Classic, Digital Seniors Classic. **1989** Crestar Classic. **1990** Las Vegas Sr. Classic, Ameritech Sr. Open, Sunwest Bank/Charley Pride Senior Golf Classic. **1991** GTE West Classic, Vintage ARGO Invitational, Las Vegas Senior Classic, Murata Reunion Pro-Am. **1992** Ko Olina Senior Invitational, **1993** Burnet Sr. Classic.
Other Victories: 1976 Pepsi Mixed Team Championship (with JoAnn Washam).
National/International Teams: 1961, 1962, 1963, 1964, 1965, 1966, 1967, 1968, 1971, 1974, 1976 World Cup. 1973 Ryder Cup.

SENIOR PGA TOUR CAREER SUMMARY

Year	Money	Rank
1985	$7,700	71

Year	Money	Rank
1986	$399,172	2
1987	$509,145	1
1988	$313,940	10
1989	$275,414	17
1990	$729,788	5
1991	$794,013	4
1992	$711,095	5
1993	$798,857	5
1994	$556,098	14
1995	$179,889	53
Sr. Career	$5,244,386	3

TOM SHAW

Birthdate: December 13, 1938
Birthplace: Wichita, KS
PGA TOUR Victories: (5) 1969 Doral Open, AVCO Golf Classic. 1971 Bing Crosby National Pro Am, Hawaiian Open.
Senior PGA TOUR Victories: (3) 1989 Showdown Classic. 1993 The Tradition. 1994 Sr. Slam of Golf.
Other Victories: None.
National/International Teams: 1989 DuPont Cup.

SENIOR PGA TOUR CAREER SUMMARY

Year	Money	Rank
1989	$281,393	16
1990	$235,683	26
1991	$278,103	24
1992	$144,821	45
1993	$324,385	29
1994	$169,122	55
Sr. Career	$1,641,082	45

JAY SIGEL

Birthdate: November 13, 1943
Birthplace: Narberth, PA
PGA Tour Victories: None
PGA TOUR Career Earnings: None.
Senior PGA Tour Victories: (1) 1994 GTE West Classic.
Other Victories: 1975 Porter Cup. 1979 British Amateur. 1981 Porter Cup. 1982 U.S. Amateur. 1983 U.S. Amateur, U.S. Mid-Amateur. 1985 U.S. Mid-Amateur. 1987 U.S. Mid-Amateur. 1987 Porter Cup.
National/International Teams: Walker Cup 1973, 1977, 1979, 1981, 1983, 1985, 1987, 1989, 1991, 1993.

SENIOR PGA TOUR CAREER SUMMARY

Year	Money	Rank
1994	$634,130	12
1995	$541,707	15
Sr. Career	$1,175,837	NR

BEN SMITH

Birthdate: May 7, 1934
Birthplace: Atlanta, GA
Senior PGA TOUR Victories: None.
Other Victories: 1982 Center Invitational.
National/International Teams: None.

SENIOR PGA TOUR CAREER SUMMARY

Year	Money	Rank
1984	$3,475	87
1985	$78,303	17
1986	$103,863	18
1987	$93,227	30
1988	$160,363	22
1989	$133,920	34
1990	$201,223	31
1991	$178,258	37
1992	$121,138	50
1993	$209,427	40
1994	$180,943	48
1995	$307,798	37
Sr. Career	$1,701,061	42

BOB E. SMITH

Birthdate: December 2, 1942
Birthplace: Sacramento, CA
PGA Tour Victories: None
PGA Tour Career Earnings: $382,786
Senior PGA Tour Victories: None
Other Victories: 1965 Western Amateur. 1966 Porter Cup. 1967 NCAA Small College Championship, Porter Cup, Western Amateur, California State Amateur. 1993 Yanase Cup
National/International Teams: None.

SENIOR PGA TOUR CAREER SUMMARY

Year	Money	Rank
1993	$10,375	107
1994	$123,957	62
1995	$279,807	42
Sr. Career	$414,139	NR

J.C. SNEAD

Birthdate: October 14, 1940
Birthplace: Hot Springs, VA
PGA TOUR Victories: (8) 1971 Tucson Open, Doral Eastern Open. 1972 Philadelphia Classic.

1975 Wickes Andy Williams San Diego Open. 1976 Andy Williams San Diego Open, Kaiser International. 1981 Southern Open. 1987 Manufacturers Hanover Westchester Classic.
Senior PGA TOUR Victories: (2) 1993 Vantage Championship. 1995 Ford Senior Players Championship.
Other Victories: 1973 Australian Open. 1980 Jerry Ford Invitational (co-winner).
National/International Teams: 1971, 1973, 1975 Ryder cup.

SENIOR PGA TOUR CAREER SUMMARY

Year	Money	Rank
1990	$47,494	74
1991	$302,287	19
1992	$383,698	2
1993	$487,500	2
1994	$564,314	13
1995	$956,937	6
Sr. Career	$2,652,598	22

DAVE STOCKTON
Birthdate: November 2, 1941
Birthplace: San Bernardino, CA
PGA TOUR Victories: (11) 1967 Colonial National Foursome (with Laurie Hammer). 1968 Cleveland Open, Greater PGA Championship. 1971 Massachusetts Classic. 1973 Greater Milwaukee Open. 1974 Glen Campbell Los Angeles Open, Quad Cities Open, Sammy Davis Jr. Greater Hartford Open. 1976 PGA Championship.
Senior PGA TOUR Victories: (11) 1992 Senior Players Championship. 1993 Muratec Reunion Pro Am, Southwestern Bell Classic, Franklin Quest Championship, GTE Northwest Classic, The Transamerica. 1994 Nationwide Championship, Ford Senior Players Championship, Burnet Senior Classic. 1995 GTE Suncoast Classic, Quicksilver Classic.
National/International Teams: 1970, 1976 World Cup. 1971, 1977, 1991 Ryder Cup. 1993 DuPont Cup.

SENIOR PGA TOUR CAREER SUMMARY

Year	Money	Rank
1991	$12,965	94
1992	$656,458	7
1993	$1,175,944	1
1994	$1,338,419	1
1995	$1,303,280	1
Sr. Career	$4,283,149	8

BRUCE SUMMERHAYS
Birthdate: February 14, 1944
Birthplace: St. Louis, MO
PGA Tour Victories: None
PGA Tour Career Earnings: None
Senior PGA Tour Victories: None
Other Victories: 1976 Northern California Open. 1966, 1991, 1993 Provo Open. 1975, 1977 Northern California Match Play. 1974, 1977 Northern California Medal Play. 1979, 1981, 1986 Wasatch Open. 1981, 1982 Rocky Mountain Section Champ. 1991 Utah PGA Section. 1992 Dixie Open. 1992 Wendover Open.
National/International Teams: None.

SENIOR PGA TOUR CAREER SUMMARY

Year	Money	Rank
1994	$20,711	96
1995	$671,421	12
Sr. Career	$692,132	NR

ROCKY THOMPSON
Birthdate: October 14, 1939
Birthplace: Shreveport, LA
Senior PGA TOUR Victories: (3) 1991 MONY Syracuse Senior Classic, Digital Seniors Classic. 1994 GTE Suncoast Classic.
Other Victories: None.
National/International Teams: 1991 DuPont Cup.

SENIOR PGA TOUR CAREER SUMMARY

Year	Money	Rank
1989	$17,300	84
1990	$308,915	18
1991	$435,794	12
1992	$432,778	15
1993	$571,844	14
1994	$487,373	22
1995	$533,021	17
Sr. Career	$2,744,364	20

HARRY TOSCANO
Birthdate: April 1, 1942
Birthplace: New Castle, PA
PGA TOUR Victories: None.
Senior PGA TOUR Victories: None.
National/International Teams: None.

SENIOR PGA TOUR CAREER SUMMARY

Year	Money	Rank
1992	$11,849	98
1993	$201,150	43
1994	$207,508	43
1995	$216,297	48
Sr. Career	$636,804	NR

LEE TREVINO
Birthdate: December 1, 1939
Birthplace: Dallas, TX
PGA TOUR Victories: (27) **1968** U.S. Open, Hawaiian Open. **1969** Tucson Open. **1970** Tucson Open, National Airlines Open. **1971** Tallahassee Open, Danny Thomas Memphis Classic, U.S. Open, Canadian Open, Sahara Invitational. **1972** Danny Thomas Memphis Classic, Greater Hartford Open, Greater St. Louis Classic. **1973** Jackie Gleason Inverrary, Doral Eastern Open. **1974** New Orleans Open, PGA Championship. **1975** Florida Citrus Open. **1976** Colonial National Invitational. **1977** Canadian Open. **1978** Colonial National Invitational. **1979** Canadian Open. **1980** Tournament Players Championship, Danny Thomas Memphis Classic, San Antonio Texas Open. **1981** MONY Tournament of Champions. **1984** PGA Championship.
Senior PGA TOUR Victories: (27) **1990** Royal Caribbean Classic, Aetna Challenge, Vintage Chrysler Invitational, Doug Sanders Kingwood Celebrity Classic, NYNEX Commemorative, U.S. Senior Open, Transamerica Senior Golf Championship. **1991** Aetna Challenge, Vantage at The Dominion, Sunwest Bank/Charley Pride Senior Classic. **1992** Vantage at The Dominion, The Tradition, PGA Seniors Championship, Las Vegas Senior Classic, Bell Atlantic Classic. **1993** Cadillac NFL Classic, Nationwide Championship, Vantage Championship.**1994** Royal Caribbean Classic, PGA Seniors Championship, PaineWebber Invitational, Bell Atlantic Classic, Senior Classic at Opryland, Northville Long Island Classic. **1995** Liberty Mutual Legends of Golf (with Mike Hill), Northville Long Island Classic, Transamerica Senior Championship.
Other Victories: **1969** International Trophy (World Cup individual). **1971** British Open. **1972** British Open. **1974** World Series of Golf. **1975** Mexican Open. **1977** Morocco Grand Prix. **1978** Benson & Hedges, Lancome Trophy. **1979** Canadian PGA. **1983** Canadian PGA. **1987** Skins Game.
National/International Teams: **1968, 1969, 1970, 1971, 1974** World Cup. **1969, 1971, 1973, 1975, 1979, 1981, 1985** Ryder Cup.

SENIOR PGA TOUR CAREER SUMMARY

Year	Money	Rank
1989	$9,258	93
1990	$1,190,518	1
1991	$723,163	5
1992	$1,027,000	2
1993	$956,591	4
1994	$1,202,369	2
1995	$909,010	7
Sr. Career	$5,784,327	1

TOM WARGO
Birthdate: September 16, 1942
Birthplace: Marlette, MI
PGA TOUR Victories: None.
PGA TOUR Career Earnings: None.
Senior PGA TOUR Victories: (3) **1993** PGA Senior's Championship. **1994** Doug Sanders Celebrity Classic. **1995** Dallas Reunion Pro-Am.
Other Victories: **1990** PGA Club Professional Stroke Play Championship. **1992** Gateway PGA Sectional Championship.
National/International Teams: None.

SENIOR PGA TOUR CAREER SUMMARY

Year	Money	Rank
1993	$557,270	16
1994	$928,344	6
1995	$641,187	13
Sr. Career	2,133,846	30

DEWITT WEAVER
Birthdate: September 14, 1939
Birthplace: Danville, KY
PGA TOUR Victories: (2) **1971** U.S. Professional Match Play. **1972** Southern Open.
Senior PGA TOUR Victories: (1) **1991** Bank One Senior Classic.
Other Victories: Georgia Open (4).
National/International Teams: None.

SENIOR PGA TOUR CAREER SUMMARY

Year	Money	Rank
1989	$4,133	105
1990	$118,555	45
1991	$264,569	27
1992	$399,155	17
1993	$472,220	21
1994	$295,037	30
1995	$301,919	38
Sr. Career	$1,836,042	34

TOM WEISKOPF

Birthdate: November 9, 1942
Birthplace: Massillon, OH
PGA TOUR Victories: (15) **1968** Andy Williams San Diego Open, Buick Open. **1971** Kemper Open, IVB Philadelphia Classic. **1972** Jackie Gleason Inverarry Classic. **1973** Colonial National Invitation, Kemper Open, IVS Philadelphia Classic, Canadian Open. **1976** Greater Greensboro Open, Canadian Open. **1977** Kemper Open. **1978** Doral Eastern Open. **1981** LaJet Classic. **1982** Western Open.
Senior PGA TOUR Victories: (2) **1994** Franklin Quest Championship. **1995** U.S. Senior Open.
Other Victories: 1972 Picadilly World Match Play. **1973** British Open, World Series of Golf, South African PGA. **1979** Argentina Open.
National/International Teams: 1972 World Cup. **1973, 1975** Ryder Cup.

SENIOR PGA TOUR CAREER SUMMARY

Year	Money	Rank
1992	$15,296	221
1993	$296,528	32
1994	$298,624	29
1995	$525,237	19
Sr. Career	$1,120,389	NR

KERMIT ZARLEY

Birthdate: September 29, 1941
Birthplace: Seattle, WA
PGA TOUR Victories: (2) **1968** Kaiser International. **1970** Canadian Open.
Senior PGA TOUR Victories: (1) **1994** The Transamerica.
Other Victories: 1972 National team championship (with Babe Hiskey).
National/International Teams: None.

SENIOR PGA TOUR CAREER SUMMARY

Year	Money	Rank
1991	$6,858	113
1992	$341,647	24
1993	$414,715	23
1994	$517,724	19
1995	$499,939	23
Sr. Career	$1,760,633	37

WALT ZEMBRISKI

Birthdate: May 24, 1935
Birthplace: Mahwah, NJ
Senior PGA TOUR Victories: (3) **1988** Newport Cup, Vantage Championship. **1989** GTE West Classic.
Other Victories: 1965 New Jersey Amateur.
National/International Teams: None.

SENIOR PGA TOUR CAREER SUMMARY

Year	Money	Rank
1985	$47,023	35
1986	$103,551	19
1987	$189,403	15
1988	$348,531	7
1989	$291,861	15
1990	$276,292	20
1991	$265,951	26
1992	$273,087	30
1993	$331,960	28
1994	$246,412	33
1995	$194,157	52
Sr. Career	$2,549,442	23

LARRY ZIEGLER

Birthdate: August 12, 1939
Birthplace: St. Louis, MO
PGA TOUR Victories: (3) **1969** Michigan Classic. **1975** Greater Jacksonville Open. **1976** First NBC New Orleans Open.
Senior PGA TOUR Victories: (1) **1991** Newport Cup.
Other Victories: 1974 Morocco International Grand Prix. **1978** South and Central American Open.
National/International Teams: None.

SENIOR PGA TOUR CAREER SUMMARY

Year	Money	Rank
1989	$133,339	35
1990	$102,152	49
1991	$169,686	38
1992	$135,015	47
1993	$216,073	38
1994	$185,644	46
1995	$246,131	43
Sr. Career	$1,188,041	NR

LPGA PERSONALITIES

OVERVIEW: *Career victories, earnings, and current playing status for the leading members of the LPGA Tour Division.*

KRISTI ALBERS
Birthdate: December 7, 1963
Birthplace: El Paso, TX
LPGA Victories: (1) **1993** Sprint Classic.
Other Victories: None.

LPGA TOUR CAREER SUMMARY
Year	Money	Rank
1986	$9,230	122
1987	$17,569	104
1988	$27,609	81
1989	$72,900	44
1990	$111,515	35
1991	$139,982	31
1992	$173,189	30
1993	$815,477	17
1994	$136,834	38
1995	$105,106	57
Career	$1,057,417	NR

HELEN ALFREDSSON
Birthdate: April 9, 1965
Birthplace: Goteborg, Sweden
LPGA Victories: (2) **1993** Nabisco Dinah Shore. **1994** Ping/Welch's Championship.
Other Victories: None.

LPGA TOUR CAREER SUMMARY
Year	Money	Rank
1992	$262,115	16
1993	$402,685	5
1994	$247,444	17
1995	$252,495	22
Career	$1,166,974	NR

DANIELLE AMMACCAPANE
Birthdate: November 27, 1965
Birthplace: Babylon, NY
LPGA Victories: (4) **1991** Standard Register Ping. **1992** Standard Register Ping, Centel Classic, Lady Keystone Open.
Other Victories: None.

LPGA TOUR CAREER SUMMARY
Year	Money	Rank
1988	$71,105	44
1989	$135,109	23
1990	$300,231	9
1991	$361,925	6
1992	$513,639	3
1993	$187,862	28
1994	$61,964	76
1995	$181,560	37
Career	$1,631,836	23

DONNA ANDREWS
Birthdate: April 12, 1967
Birthplace: Lynchburg, VA
LPGA Victories: (4) **1993** Ping-Cellular One LPGA Golf Championship. **1994** Ping/Welch's Championship, Nabisco Dinah Shore, ShopRite LPGA Classic.
Other Victories: None.

LPGA TOUR CAREER SUMMARY
Year	Money	Rank
1990	$52,430	75
1991	$73,472	65
1992	$299,839	13
1993	$334,285	9
1994	$429,015	5
1995	$25,346	122
Career	$1,189,041	38

TINA BARRETT
Birthdate: June 5, 1966
Birthplace: Baltimore, MD
LPGA Victories: (1) **1989** Mitsubishi Motors Ocean State Open.
Other Victories: None.

LPGA TOUR CAREER SUMMARY
Year	Money	Rank
1989	$39,776	69
1990	$17,867	121

LPGA Personalities

Year	Money	Rank
1991	$138,232	32
1992	$184,719	28
1993	$261,491	19
1994	$84,729	63
1995	$52,251	85
Career	$778,706	NR

AMY BENZ

Birthdate: May 12, 1962
Birthplace: Rochester, NY
LPGA Victories: None
Other Victories: (1) **1988** JCPenney Classic (with John Huston).

LPGA TOUR CAREER SUMMARY

Year	Money	Rank
1983	$13,143	95
1984	$41,014	54
1985	$62,260	31
1986	$72,407	31
1987	$42,870	57
1988	$117,059	24
1989	$98,129	35
1990	$128,216	29
1991	$96,248	51
1992	$141,673	40
1993	$166,968	35
1994	$118,742	43
1995	$35,572	107
Career	$1,104,176	44

MISSIE BERTEOTTI

Birthdate: September 22, 1963
Birthplace: Pittsburgh, PA
LPGA Victories: (1) **1993** PING/Welch's Championship.
Other Victories: None.

LPGA TOUR CAREER SUMMARY

Year	Money	Rank
1986	$34,092	65
1987	$62,446	45
1988	$69,441	45
1989	$38,493	71
1990	$107,030	38
1991	$106,459	47
1992	$213,720	22
1993	$184,553	31
1994	$121,856	39
1995	$68,406	73
Career	$1,006,596	NR

PAT BRADLEY

Birthdate: March 24, 1951
Birthplace: Westford, MA
LPGA Victories: (31) **1976** Girl Talk Classic. **1977** Bankers Trust Classic. **1978** Lady Keystone, Hoosier Classic, Rail Charity Classic. **1980** Greater Baltimore Classic, Peter Jackson Classic. **1981** Women's Kemper Open, U.S. Women's Open. **1983** Mazda Classic of Deer Creek, Chrysler-Plymouth Charity Classic, Columbia Savings Classic, Mazda Japan Classic. **1985** Rochester International, du Maurier Classic, LPGA National Pro-Am. **1986** Nabisco Dinah Shore, S&H Golf Classic, LPGA Championship, du Maurier Classic, Nestle World Championship. **1987** Standard Register Turquoise Classic. **1989** Al Star/Centinela Hospital Classic. **1990** Oldsmobile LPGA Classic, Standard Register Turquoise Classic, LPGA Corning Classic. **1991** Centel Classic, Rail Charity Golf Classic, SAFECO Classic, MBS LPGA Classic. **1995** HealthSouth Palm Beach Classic.
Other Victories: (4) **1975** Colgate Far East Open. **1978** JCPenney Classic (with Lon Hinkle). **1989** JCPenney Classic (with Bill Glasson). **1992** JCPenney/LPGA Skins Game.

LPGA TOUR CAREER SUMMARY

Year	Money	Rank
1974	$10,839	39
1975	$28,293	14
1976	$84,288	6
1977	$78,709	8
1978	$118,057	2
1979	$132,428	4
1980	$183,377	6
1981	$197,050	3
1982	$113,089	11
1983	$240,207	3
1984	$220,478	4
1985	$387,378	2
1986	$492,021	1
1987	$140,132	15
1988	$15,965	109
1989	$423,714	4
1990	$480,018	5
1991	$763,118	1
1992	$238,541	19
1993	$188,135	27
1994	$236,274	19
1995	$368,904	11
Career	$4,772,115	2

BARB BUNKOWSKY

Birthdate: October 13, 1958
Birthplace: Toronto, Ontario
LPGA Victories: (1) **1984** Chrysler-Plymouth Charity Classic.
Other Victories: None.

LPGA TOUR CAREER SUMMARY

Year	Money	Rank
1983	$28,747	60
1984	$71,682	24
1985	$28,887	76
1986	$25,295	80
1987	$64,365	42
1988	$35,989	71
1989	$4,648	154
1990	$48,064	79
1991	$150,719	28
1992	$79,424	64
1993	$142,907	39
1994	$167,039	31
1995	DNP	--
Career	$835,652	NR

BRANDIE BURTON

Birthdate: January 8, 1972
Birthplace: San Bernardino, CA
LPGA Victories: (4) **1992** Ping/Welch's Championship. **1993** Jamie Farr Toledo Classic, du Maurier Ltd. Classic, SAFECO Classic.
Other Victories: None.

LPGA TOUR CAREER SUMMARY

Year	Money	Rank
1991	$176,412	22
1992	$419,571	4
1993	$517,741	3
1994	$172,821	30
1995	$214,455	25
Career	$1,286,545	34

JOANNE CARNER

Birthdate: April 4, 1939
Birthplace: Kirkland, WA
LPGA Victories: (42) **1970** Wendell West Open. **1971** U.S. Women's Open, Bluegrass Inv. **1974** Bluegrass Inv., Hoosier Classic, Desert Inn Classic, St. Paul Open, Dallas Civitan, Portland Classic. **1975** American Defender Classic, All-American Classic, Peter Jackson Classic. **1976** Orange Blossom Classic, Lady Tara Classic, Hoosier Classic, U.S. Women's Open. **1977** Talk Tournament, Borden Classic, National Jewish Hospital Open. **1978** Peter Jackson Classic, Borden Classic. **1979** Honda Civic Classic, Women's Kemper Open. **1980** Whirlpool Champ., Bent Tree Ladies Classic, Sunstar '80, Honda Civic Classic, Lady Keystone Open. **1981** S&H Golf Classic, Lady Keystone Open, Columbia Savings LPGA Classic, Rail Charity Golf Classic. **1982** Elizabeth Arden Classic, McDonald's LPGA Kids' Classic, Chevrolet World Champ. of Women's Golf, Henredon Classic, Rail Charity Golf Classic. **1983** Chevrolet World Champ. of Women's Golf, Portland Ping Championship. **1984** Corning Classic. **1985** Elizabeth Arden Classic, SAFECO Classic.
Other Victories: (4) **1977** LPGA Team Championship (with Judy Rankin). **1978** Colgate Triple Crown. **1979** Colgate Triple Crown. **1982** JCPenney Classic (with John Mahaffey).

LPGA TOUR CAREER SUMMARY

Year	Money	Rank
1970	$14,551	11
1971	$21,604	6
1972	$18,902	15
1973	$19,688	25
1974	$87,094	1
1975	$64,843	2
1976	$103,275	3
1977	$113,712	2
1978	$108,093	4
1979	$98,219	9
1980	$185,916	5
1981	$206,648	2
1982	$310,399	1
1983	$291,404	1
1984	$144,900	9
1985	$141,941	11
1986	$82,802	26
1987	$66,601	41
1988	$121,218	21
1989	$97,888	36
1990	$87,218	48
1991	$86,874	56
1992	$175,880	29
1993	$134,956	41
1994	$55,474	86
1995	$38,033	98
Career	$2,840,071	7

DAWN COE-JONES

Birthdate: October 19, 1960
Birthplace: Campbell River, B.C.
LPGA Victories: (2) **1992** Women's Kemper Open. **1994** Healthsouth Palm Beach Classic.
Other Victories: (1) **1992** Pizza-La LPGA Matchplay Championship.

LPGA TOUR CAREER SUMMARY

Year	Money	Rank
1984	$19,603	91
1985	$34,864	68
1986	$54,332	47
1987	$72,045	33
1988	$52,659	58
1989	$143,423	19
1990	$240,478	11
1991	$158,013	25
1992	$251,392	17
1993	$271,978	16
1994	$223,696	20
1995	$268,665	17
Career	$1,529,175	25

JANE CRAFTER

Birthdate: December 14, 1955
Birthplace: Perth, Australia
LPGA Victories: (1) **1990** Phar-Mor at Inverrary.
Other Victories: (1) **1987** JCPenney Classic (with Steve Jones).

LPGA TOUR CAREER SUMMARY

Year	Money	Rank
1981	$1,617	135
1982	$7,472	108
1983	$37,433	43
1984	$48,729	46
1985	$60,884	32
1986	$79,431	28
1987	$59,876	48
1988	$32,733	73
1989	$35,086	77
1990	$112,840	34
1991	$34,168	101
1992	$155,485	35
1993	$187,190	29
1994	$65,730	75
1995	$60,133	79
Career	$978,192	NR

ELAINE CROSBY

Birthdate: June 6, 1958
Birthplace: Birmingham, MI
LPGA Victories: (2) **1989** Mazda Japan Classic. **1994** Lady Keystone Open.
Other Victories: None.

LPGA TOUR CAREER SUMMARY

Year	Money	Rank
1985	$10,133	122
1986	$5,533	146
1987	$31,024	74
1988	$15,655	112
1989	$126,899	28
1990	$169,543	18
1991	$181,610	21
1992	$109,125	50
1993	$177,726	33
1994	$338,043	10
1995	$182,383	36
Career	$1,171,983	40

BETH DANIEL

Birthdate: October 14, 1956
Birthplace: Charleston, SC
LPGA Victories: (33) **1979** Patty Berg Classic. **1980** Golden Lights Champ., Patty Berg Classic, Columbia Savings Classic, Chevrolet World Champ. of Women's Golf. **1981** Florida Lady Citrus, Chevrolet World Champ. **1982** Bent Tree Ladies Classic, Amex Sun City Classic, Birmingham Classic, Columbia Sav. Classic, WUI Classic. **1983** McDonald's LPGA Kids Classic. **1985** Kyocera Inamori Classic. **1989** Gr. Washington Open, Rail Charity Golf Classic, SAFECO Classic, Konica Classic. **1990** Orix Hawaiian Open, Women's Kemper Open, Phar-Mor, Mazda LPGA Champ., Northgate Classic, Rail Charity Golf Classic, Centel Classic. **1991** Phar-Mor, McDonald's Champ. **1994** LPGA Corning Classic, Oldsmobile Classic, JAL Big Apple Classic, World Champ. of Women's Golf. **1995** Ping/Welch's Champ., JCPenney Classic.
Other Victories: (4) **1979** World Ladies. **1981** JCPenney Classic (with Tom Kite). **1988** Nichirei Ladies Cup US-Japan Team Championship. **1990** JCPenney Classic (with Davis Love III). **1991** Konica World Ladies.

LPGA TOUR CAREER SUMMARY

Year	Money	Rank
1979	$97,027	10
1980	$231,000	1
1981	$206,977	1
1982	$223,634	5
1983	$167,403	6
1984	$94,284	16
1985	$177,235	8
1986	$103,547	21
1987	$83,308	29
1988	$140,635	17
1989	$504,851	2
1990	$863,578	1
1991	$469,501	4
1992	$329,681	11
1993	$140,001	40
1994	$656,687	2
1995	$466,622	6
Career	$4,492,091	3

LAURA DAVIES
Birthdate: October 5, 1973
Birthplace: Coventry, England
LPGA Victories: (8) **1988** Circle K Tucson Open, Jamie Farr Toledo Classic. **1989** Lady Keystone Open. **1991** Inamori Classic. **1993** McDonald's Champ. **1994** Standard Register Ping, Sara Lee Classic, McDonald's LPGA Champ. **1995** Chick-Fil-A LPGA Classic.
Other Victories: None.
National/International Teams: 1990, 1992, 1994 Solheim Cup.

LPGA TOUR CAREER SUMMARY
Year	Money	Rank
1988	$160,382	15
1989	$181,574	13
1990	$64,863	64
1991	$200,831	20
1992	$150,163	39
1993	$240,643	20
1994	$667,652	1
1995	$527,995	2
Career	$2,194,103	NR

ALICIA DIBOS
Birthdate: March 1, 1960
Birthplace: Lima, Peru
LPGA Victories: None.
Other Victories: None.

LPGA TOUR CAREER SUMMARY
Year	Money	Rank
1993	$28,721	117
1994	$180,374	28
1995	$89,070	60
Career	$298,165	NR

JUDY DICKINSON
Birthdate: May 4, 1950
Birthplace: Akron, OH
LPGA Victories: (4) **1985** Boston Five Classic. **1986** Rochester Int., Safeco Classic. **1992** Inamori Classic.
Other Victories: None.

LPGA TOUR CAREER SUMMARY
Year	Money	Rank
1978	$5,330	83
1979	$24,561	48
1980	$30,648	46
1981	$42,570	36
1982	$47,187	29
1983	$69,091	23
1984	$85,479	18
1985	$167,809	9
1986	$195,834	10
1987	$19,602	96
1988	$160,440	14
1989	$23,460	96
1990	$80,784	52
1991	$251,018	14
1992	$351,559	10
1993	$186,317	30
1994	$246,879	18
1995	$23,602	126
Career	$1,990,807	16

DALE EGGELING
Birthdate: April 21, 1954
Birthplace: Statesboro, GA
LPGA Victories: (2) **1980** Boston Five Classic. **1995** Oldsmobile LPGA Classic.
Other Victories: None.

LPGA TOUR CAREER SUMMARY
Year	Money	Rank
1976	$321	113
1977	$5,859	70
1978	$9,690	68
1979	$21,333	55
1980	$45,335	27
1981	$50,594	23
1982	$57,691	26
1983	$52,967	29
1984	$53,355	37
1985	$34,894	67
1986	$52,684	50
1987	$33,203	71
1988	$32,203	74
1989	$56,108	55
1990	$147,990	24
1991	$78,386	61
1992	$138,781	41
1993	$145,789	38
1994	$157,196	32
1995	$256,839	20
Career	$1,175,799	39

JANE GEDDES
Birthdate: February 5, 1960
Birthplace: Huntington, NY
LPGA Victories: (11) **1986** U.S. Open, Boston Five Classic. **1987** Kemper Open, Glendale Fed. Classic, Mazda LPGA Champ., Jamie Farr Toledo Classic, Boston 5 Classic. **1991** Jamaica Classic, Atlantic City Classic. **1993** Olds. Classic. **1994** Chicago Challenge.
Other Victories: None.

LPGA TOUR CAREER SUMMARY

Year	Money	Rank
1983	$13,7559	4
1984	$53,682	3
1985	$108,971	17
1986	$221,255	5
1987	$396,818	3
1988	$90,298	33
1989	$186,485	12
1990	$181,874	16
1991	$315,240	10
1992	$164,127	32
1993	$263,149	18
1994	$257,045	15
1995	$308,618	15
Career	$2,269,254	11

GAIL GRAHAM

Birthdate: January 16, 1964
Birthplace: Vanderhoof, BC
LPGA Victories: (1) **1995** Fieldcrest Classic.
Other Victories: None.

LPGA TOUR CAREER SUMMARY

Year	Money	Rank
1990	$10,948	143
1991	$46,386	90
1992	$58,938	79
1993	$126,048	45
1994	$121,812	40
1995	$142,346	43
Career	$406,478	NR

TAMMIE GREEN

Birthdate: December 17, 1959
Birthplace: Somerset, OH
LPGA Victories: (4) **1989** du Maurier Ltd. Classic. **1993** HealthSouth Palm Beach Classic, Rochester International. **1994** Youngstown-Warren LPGA Classic.
Other Victories: None.

LPGA TOUR CAREER SUMMARY

Year	Money	Rank
1987	$68,346	39
1988	$120,271	22
1989	$204,143	8
1990	$155,756	22
1991	$237,073	15
1992	$154,717	37
1993	$356,579	7
1994	$418,969	6
1995	$334,017	13
Career	$1,715,863	19

SHELLEY HAMLIN

Birthdate: May 28, 1949
Birthplace: San Mateo, CA
LPGA Victories: (3) **1978** Patty Berg Classic. **1992** The Phar-Mor at Inverrary. **1993** ShopRite LPGA Classic.
Other Victories: (1) **1975** Japan Classic.

LPGA TOUR CAREER SUMMARY

Year	Money	Rank
1972	$12,845	24
1973	$22,831	19
1974	$28,276	18
1975	$15,980	27
1976	$14,960	43
1977	$12,069	55
1978	$34,494	29
1979	$41,739	26
1980	$50,843	23
1981	$32,798	46
1982	$32,878	47
1983	$19,486	77
1984	$9,923	120
1985	$18,564	94
1986	$20,035	93
1987	$85,466	26
1988	$28,521	77
1989	$47,254	61
1990	$17,701	122
1991	$16,170	138
1992	$157,327	34
1993	$129,447	44
1994	$71,864	72
1995	$20,504	133
Career	$941,964	NR

JULI INKSTER

Birthdate: June 24, 1960
Birthplace: Santa Cruz, CA
LPGA Victories: (15) **1983** Safeco Classic. **1984** Nabisco Dinah Shore, du Maurier Classic. **1985** Lady Keystone Open. **1986** Women's Kemper Open, McDonald's Championship, Lady Keystone Open, Atlantic City Classic. **1988** Crestar Classic, Atlantic City Classic, Safeco Classic. **1989** Nabisco Dinah Shore, Crestar Classic. **1991** LPGA Bay State Classic. **1992** JAL Big Apple Classic.
Other Victories: (1) **1986** JCPenney Classic (with Tom Purtzer).

LPGA TOUR CAREER SUMMARY

Year	Money	Rank
1983	$52,220	30
1984	$186,501	6

Year	Money	Rank
1985	$99,651	19
1986	$285,293	3
1987	$140,739	14
1988	$235,344	10
1989	$180,848	14
1990	$54,251	73
1991	$213,096	17
1992	$392,063	7
1993	$116,583	47
1994	$113,829	45
1995	$195,739	31
Career	$2,070,418	13

CHRIS JOHNSON
Birthdate: April 25, 1958
Birthplace: Arcata, CA
LPGA Victories: (7) 1984 Samaritan Classic, Tucson Conquistadores Open. 1986 Glendale Federal Classic. 1987 Columbia Savings National Pro-Am. 1990 Atlantic City Classic. 1991 PING/Welch's Championship. 1995 Star Bank Classic.
Other Victories: None.

LPGA TOUR CAREER SUMMARY
Year	Money	Rank
1980	$2,827	123
1981	$25,182	55
1982	$60,449	24
1983	$37,967	42
1984	$70,979	25
1985	$67,123	29
1986	$200,648	8
1987	$197,722	8
1988	$46,219	61
1989	$97,195	37
1990	$187,486	14
1991	$135,416	33
1992	$105,197	53
1993	$111,027	50
1994	$205,489	22
1995	$200,418	30
Career	$1,553,666	24

TRISH JOHNSON
Birthdate: January 17, 1966
Birthplace: Bristol, England
LPGA Victories: (2) 1993 Las Vegas LPGA at Canyon Gate, Atlanta Women's Championship.
Other Victories: None.

LPGA TOUR CAREER SUMMARY
Year	Money	Rank
1988	$23,972	89
1989	$17,215	115
1990	$58,729	71
1991	$85,639	57
1992	$33,103	112
1993	$331,745	10
1994	$42,750	102
1995	$75,798	67
Career	$668,941	NR

ROSIE JONES
Birthdate: November 13, 1959
Birthplace: Santa Ana, CA
LPGA Victories: (6) 1987 Rail Charity Golf Classic. 1988 USX Golf Classic, Nestle World Championship, Santa Barbara Open. 1991 Rochester International. 1995 Pinewild Women's Championship.
Other Victories: None.

LPGA TOUR CAREER SUMMARY
Year	Money	Rank
1982	$2,869	127
1983	$64,955	27
1984	$81,793	19
1985	$66,665	30
1986	$71,399	33
1987	$188,000	10
1988	$323,392	3
1989	$110,671	32
1990	$353,832	6
1991	$281,089	12
1992	$204,096	25
1993	$320,964	11
1994	$115,166	44
1995	$418,856	10
Career	$2,193,048	12

TRACY KERDYK
Birthdate: March 5, 1966
Birthplace: Coral Gables, FL
Career Victories: (1) 1995 JAL Big Apple Classic.
Other Victories: 1982 American Junior Golf Classic. 1983 PGA Junior Championship, Junior Orange Bowl, Doral Junior Championship. 1987 Canadian Amateur and Public Links
National/International teams: 1988 Curtis Cup.

LPGA TOUR CAREER SUMMARY
Year	Money	Rank
1989	$64,644	51
1990	$35,199	96
1991	$59,122	78
1992	$63,732	72
1993	$64,908	71

Year	Money	Rank
1994	$84,145	65
1995	$181,403	38
Career	$553,153	NR

LISA KIGGENS
Birthdate: August 13, 1972
Birthplace: Salinas, CA
LPGA Victories: None.
Other Victories: None.

LPGA TOUR CAREER SUMMARY

Year	Money	Rank
1992	$5,401	171
1993	$64,851	72
1994	$183,279	26
1995	$57,361	81
Career	$310,892	NR

BETSY KING
Birthdate: August 13, 1955
Birthplace: Reading, PA
LPGA Victories: (30) **1984** Women's Kemper Open, Freedom Orlando Classic, Columbia Savings Classic. **1985** Samaritan Turquoise Classic, Rail Charity Classic. **1986** Henredon Classic, Rail Charity Classic. **1987** Circle K LPGA Tucson Open, Nabisco Dinah Shore, McDonald's Champ., Atlantic City Classic. **1988** Women's Kemper Open, Rail Charity Golf Classic, Cellular One Ping Golf Championship. **1989** Jamaica Classic, Women's Kemper Open, USX Golf Classic, McDonald's Champ., U.S. Women's Open, Nestle World Champ. **1990** Nabisco Dinah Shore, U.S. Women's Open, JAL Big Apple Classic. **1991** LPGA Corning Classic, JAL Big Apple Classic. **1992** Mazda LPGA Champ., The Phar-Mor in Youngstown, Mazda Japan Classic. **1993** Toray Japan Queens Cup. **1995** Shoprite LPGA Classic.
Other Victories: (4) **1981** Itsuki Charity Classic (Japan). **1985** Ladies British Open. **1990** Itoman World Match Play Championship. **1993** JCPenney/LPGA Skins Game.

LPGA TOUR CAREER SUMMARY

Year	Money	Rank
1977	$4,008	83
1978	$44,092	20
1979	$53,900	19
1980	$28,480	50
1981	$51,029	22
1982	$50,563	28
1983	$94,767	14
1984	$266,771	1
1985	$214,411	6
1986	$290,195	2
1987	$460,385	2
1988	$256,957	8
1989	$654,132	1
1990	$543,844	3
1991	$341,784	9
1992	$551,320	2
1993	$595,992	1
1994	$325,074	10
1995	$481,149	5
Career	$4,892,873	1

EMILEE KLEIN
Birthdate: June 11, 1974
Birthplace: Santa Monica, CA
LPGA victories: None
Other victories: **1991** U.S. Junior Girls. **1993** Broadmoor, North/South Amateur.
National/international teams: Curtis Cup **1994**.

LPGA TOUR CAREER SUMMARY

Year	Money	Rank
1995	$173,494	40
Career	$173,494	NR

HIROMI KOBAYASHI
Birthdate: January 8, 1963
Birthplace: Fukushima, Japan
LPGA Victories: (2) **1993** JAL Big Apple Classic, Minnesota LPGA Classic.
Other Victories: None.

LPGA TOUR CAREER SUMMARY

Year	Money	Rank
1990	$66,325	60
1991	$76,582	63
1992	$58,851	80
1993	$347,060	8
1994	$222,774	21
1995	$176,766	39
Career	$948,358	NR

JULIE LARSEN
Birthdate: September 16, 1962
Birthplace: Westchester, NY
LPGA Victories: None
Other victories: **1982** Metropolitan Junior Championship.

LPGA TOUR CAREER SUMMARY

Year	Money	Rank
1995	$256,248	21
Career	$256,248	NR

JENNY LIDBACK
Birthdate: March 30, 1963
Birthplace: Lima, Peru
LPGA Victories: (1) 1995 DuMaurier Classic.
Other victories: 1978 USGA Junior Girls Championship. 1981, Future Legends, Tournament of Champions; All-American Junior Classic.
National/International teams: 1985 World Cup.

LPGA TOUR CAREER SUMMARY

Year	Money	Rank
1989	$42,418	68
1990	$42,063	89
1991	$58,362	80
1992	$26,065	124
1993	$82,136	60
1994	$75,036	68
1995	$259,386	19
Career	$586,466	NR

NANCY LOPEZ
Birthdate: January 6, 1957
Birthplace: Torrance, CA
LPGA Victories: (47) 1978 Bent Tree Ladies Classic, Sunstar Classic, Greater Baltimore Classic, Coca-Cola Classic, Golden Lights Champ., LPGA Champ., Bankers Trust Classic, Colgate European Open, Colgate Far East Open. 1979 Sunstar Classic, Sahara National Pro-Am, Women's International, Coca-Cola Classic, Golden Lights Champ., Lady Keystone Open, Colgate European Open, Mary Kay Classic. 1980 Kemper Open, Sarah Coventry, Rail Charity Classic. 1981 Arizona Copper Classic, Colgate Dinah Shore, Sarah Coventry. 1982 J&B Scotch Pro-Am, Mazda Japan Classic. 1983 Elizabeth Arden Classic, J&B Scotch Pro-Am. 1984 Uniden LPGA Invitational, Chevrolet World Champ. of Women's Golf. 1985 Chrysler/ Plymouth Classic, LPGA Champ. , Mazda Hall of Fame Champ., Henredon Classic, Portland Ping Champ. 1987 Sarasota Classic, Cellular One/PING Golf Champ. 1988 Mazda Classic, Centinela Hospital Classic, Chrysler Plymouth Classic. 1989 LPGA Champ., Atlantic City Classic, Nippon Travel/MBS Classic. 1990 MBS LPGA Classic. 1991 Sara Lee Classic. 1992 Rail Charity Golf Classic, Ping Cellular One LPGA Golf Champ. 1993 Youngstown-Warren LPGA Classic.
Other Victories: (3) 1980 JCPenney Classic 1987 Mazda Champions 1992 Wendy's Three-Tour Challenge.

LPGA TOUR CAREER SUMMARY

Year	Money	Rank
1977	$23,138	31
1978	$189,813	1
1979	$197,488	1
1980	$209,078	4
1981	$165,679	6
1982	$166,474	6
1983	$91,477	15
1984	$183,756	7
1985	$416,472	1
1986	$67,700	35
1987	$204,823	7
1988	$322,154	4
1989	$487,153	3
1990	$301,262	8
1991	$153,772	26
1992	$382,128	8
1993	$304,480	14
1994	$150,399	33
1995	$210,882	27
Career	$4,064,802	5

MEG MALLON
Birthdate: April 14, 1963
Birthplace: Natick, MA
LPGA Victories: (6) 1991 Oldsmobile LPGA Classic, LPGA Champ, U.S. Open, Dakyo World Champ. 1993 PING/Welch's Champ, Sara Lee Classic.
Other Victories: 1983 Michigan Amateur.
National/International Teams: None.

LPGA TOUR CAREER SUMMARY

Year	Money	Rank
1987	$1,572	175
1988	$25,002	87
1989	$42,574	67
1990	$129,381	27
1991	$633,802	2
1992	$400,052	6
1993	$276,291	15
1994	$341,627	9
1995	$421,484	8
Career	$1,862,059	17

KATHRYN MARSHALL
Birthdate: June 8, 1967
Birthplace: Rochford, England
LPGA Victories: (1) 1995 Jamie Farr Toledo Classic.
Other Victories: 1985 Scottish Junior.
National/International teams: Curtis Cup 1990. Solheim Cup 1994.

LPGA TOUR CAREER SUMMARY

Year	Money	Rank
1993	$13,111	134

Year	Money	Rank
1994	DNP	--
1995	$124,888	50
Career	$187,999	NR

MICHELLE McGANN
Birthdate: December 30, 1969
Birthplace: West Palm Beach, FL
LPGA Victories: (1) **1995** Youngstown LPA Classic.
Other Victories: **1988** Doherty Cup Championship

LPGA TOUR CAREER SUMMARY
Year	Money	Rank
1989	$11,679	130
1990	$34,846	98
1991	$121,663	40
1992	$239,062	18
1993	$315,921	12
1994	$269,936	14
1995	$449,296	7
Career	$993,107	50

MISSIE McGEORGE
Birthdate: August 20, 1959
Birthplace: Pueblo, CO
LPGA Victories: (1) **1994** Ping Cellular One Golf Championship.
Other Victories: None.
National/International teams: None.

LPGA TOUR CAREER SUMMARY
Year	Money	Rank
1983	$4,596	133
1984	$20,117	89
1985	$21,563	87
1986	$23,436	83
1987	$63,259	44
1988	$93,397	31
1989	$68,493	48
1990	$93,721	45
1991	$113,959	46
1992	$30,248	118
1993	$180,311	32
1994	$181,281	27
1995	$92,885	59
Career	$894,381	NR

LAURI MERTEN
Birthdate: July 6, 1960
Birthplace: Waukesha, WI
LPGA Victories: (3) **1983** Rail Charity Golf Classic. **1984** Jamie Farr Toledo Classic. **1993** U.S. Women's Open.
Other Victories: None.

LPGA TOUR CAREER SUMMARY
Year	Money	Rank
1983	$51,930	31
1984	$108,920	13
1985	$39,597	55
1986	$45,967	55
1987	$63,492	43
1988	$36,772	70
1989	$42,832	66
1990	$47,263	82
1991	$25,494	112
1992	$53,204	86
1993	$394,744	6
1994	$202,002	24
1995	$47,520	92
Career	$1,112,217	41

DOTTIE MOCHRIE
Birthdate: August 17, 1965
Birthplace: Saratoga Springs, NY
LPGA Victories: (10) **1989** Oldsmobile LPGA Classic. **1990** Crestar Classic. **1992** Nabisco Dinah Shore, Sega Women's Championship, Welch's Classic, Sun-Times Challenge. **1993** World Championship of Women's Golf. **1995** Ping/Welch's Champ., McCall's Classic.
Other Victories: **1992** JCPenney Classic (with Dan Forsman), Wendy's Three-Tour Challenge (with Patty Sheehan and Nancy Lopez). **1994** Chrysler-Plymouth Tournament of Champions.

LPGA TOUR CAREER SUMMARY
Year	Money	Rank
1988	$137,293	20
1989	$130,830	27
1990	$231,410	12
1991	$477,767	3
1992	$693,335	1
1993	$429,118	4
1994	$472,728	4
1995	$521,000	4
Career	$2,574,716	9

MARIANNE MORRIS
Birthdate: March 15, 1965
Birthplace: Middletown, OH
LPGA Victories: None.
Other Victories: **1986** Cincinatti Metropolitan.

LPGA TOUR CAREER SUMMARY
Year	Money	Rank
1990	$13,511	133

Year	Money	Rank
1991	DNP	---
1992	$31,733	117
1993-94	DNP	---
1995	$182,949	35
Career	$228,193	NR

BARB MUCHA
Birthdate: December 1, 1961
Birthplace: Parma, OH
LPGA Victories: (3) **1990** Boston Five Classic. **1992** Oldsmobile Classic. **1994** State Farm Rail Classic.
Other Victories: None.

LPGA TOUR CAREER SUMMARY
Year	Money	Rank
1987	$6,657	140
1988	DNP	---
1989	$47,849	60
1990	$149,972	23
1991	$54,085	83
1992	$190,519	27
1993	$91,806	56
1994	$152,685	36
1995	$156,527	42
Career	$850,100	NR

MARTHA NAUSE
Birthdate September 10, 1954
Birthplace: Sheboygan, WI
LPGA Victories: (1) **1994** Du Maurier Ltd. Classic.
Other Victories: None.

LPGA TOUR CAREER SUMMARY
Year	Money	Rank
1978	$2,646	99
1979	$5,151	97
1980	$10,019	82
1981	$30,866	47
1982	$27,206	57
1983	$41,760	37
1984	$39,169	55
1985	$25,211	79
1986	$37,850	63
1987	$69,412	38
1988	$138,490	19
1989	$138,639	21
1990	$83,383	50
1991	$143,702	30
1992	$64,810	71
1993	$42,090	94
1994	$210,825	24
1995	$49,525	89
Career	$1,112,525	42

LISELOTTE NEUMANN
Birthdate: May 20, 1966
Birthplace: Finspang, Sweden
LPGA Victories: (1) **1994** Minnesota LPGA Classic.
Other Victories: None.
National/International teams: Solheim Cup 1992-94.

LPGA TOUR CAREER SUMMARY
Year	Money	Rank
1988	$188,729	12
1989	$119,915	30
1990	$82,323	51
1991	$151,367	27
1992	$225,667	21
1993	$90,776	57
1994	$505,701	3
1995	$281,734	16
Career	**$1,364,478**	29

ALISON NICHOLAS
Birthdate: March 6, 1962
LPGA Victories: (2) **1995** LPGA Corning Classic, Ping/Cellular One Championship.
Other Victories: **1983** Northern Girls Amateur Open, British Amateur Stroke Play Championship. Yorkshire Ladies County Championship. **1987** Women's British Open. **1989** German Open, Swedish Open.
National/International teams: Solheim Cup **1994**.

LPGA TOUR CAREER SUMMARY
Year	Money	Rank
1990	$11,608	139
1991	DNP	---
1992	DNP	---
1993	$101,203	51
1994	$37,651	111
1995	$225,351	23
Career	**$375,813**	NR

KATIE PETERSON-PARKER
Birthdate: January 26, 1967
Birthplace: Bethesda, MD
LPGA Victories: None.
Other Victories: **1988** North-South, Memphis Invitational.
National/International teams: Curtis Cup **1990**. Doherty Cup **1990**.

LPGA TOUR CAREER SUMMARY
Year	Money	Rank
1991	$33,710	102
1992	$76,174	66
1993	$33,385	111

Year	Money	Rank
1994	$85,684	59
1995	$188,570	34
Career	$427,623	NR

CAROLINE PIERCE
Birthdate: August 2, 1963
Birthplace: Cheshire, England
LPGA Victories: None
Other Victories: None.

LPGA TOUR CAREER SUMMARY

Year	Money	Rank
1988	$1,153	176
1989	$24,545	94
1990	$23,944	111
1991	$56,813	82
1992	$46,767	96
1993	$33,978	109
1994	$84,756	64
1995	$195,085	32
Career	$466,861	NR

JOAN PITCOCK
Birthdate: July 12, 1967
Birthplace: Fresno, CA
LPGA Victories: None
Other Victories: 1983 California State Junior.

LPGA TOUR CAREER SUMMARY

Year	Money	Rank
1988	$22,766	93
1989	$18,284	110
1990	$44,067	88
1991	$79,837	60
1992	$91,359	58
1993	$66,622	67
1994	$114,735	47
1995	$203,421	28
Career	$641,091	NR

NANCY RAMSBOTTOM
Birthdate: August 19, 1962
Birthplace: Birmingham, AL
LPGA Victories: None.
Other Victories: None.

LPGA TOUR CAREER SUMMARY

Year	Money	Rank
1985	$16,997	97
1986	$17,300	98
1987	$24,490	83
1988	$10,834	131
1989	$16,493	116
1990	$31,974	101
1991	$22,294	120
1992	$63,385	73
1993	$93,354	55
1994	$179,325	29
1995	$81,610	64
Career	$558,056	104

CINDY RARICK
Birthdate: September 12, 1959
Birthplace: Glenwood, MN
LPGA Victories: (5) **1987** Tsumura Hawaiian Ladies Open, LPGA Corning Classic. **1989** Chrysler-Plymouth Classic. **1990** Planters Pat Bradley International. **1991** Northgate Computer Classic.
Other Victories: None.

LPGA TOUR CAREER SUMMARY

Year	Money	Rank
1985	$22,094	86
1986	$29,093	72
1987	$162,073	11
1988	$63,699	49
1989	$196,611	11
1990	$259,163	10
1991	$201,342	19
1992	$155,303	36
1993	$174,407	34
1994	$81,923	66
1995	$128,437	47
Career	$1,346,633	31

SUSIE REDMAN
Birthdate: April 17, 1966
Birthplace: Salem, OH
LPGA Victories: None
Other Victories: 1984 National High School All-American Tournament.

LPGA TOUR CAREER SUMMARY

Year	Money	Rank
1985	$1,492	165
1986	$2,593	163
1987	DNP	---
1988	$21,736	97
1989	$28,413	89
1990	$24,574	110
1991	$33,623	103
1992	$88,041	61
1993	$36,426	102
1994	$53,168	89
1995	$132,251	46
Career	$422,317	NR

DEB RICHARD
Birthdate: June 3, 1963
Birthplace: Abbeville, LA
LPGA Victories: (3) **1987** Rochester International. **1991** Women's Kemper Open, The Phar-Mor in Youngstown. **1994** Safeco Classic.
Other Victories: **1991** JBP Cup Match Play.

LPGA TOUR CAREER SUMMARY
Year	Money	Rank
1986	$98,451	22
1987	$83,225	30
1988	$112,647	26
1989	$70,594	47
1990	$186,464	15
1991	$376,640	5
1992	$266,427	15
1993	$223,282	22
1994	$251,513	16
1995	$62,658	76
Career	$1,674,690	21

ALICE RITZMAN
Birthdate: March 1, 1952
Birthplace: Kalispell, MT
LPGA Victories: None
Other Victories: None.

LPGA TOUR CAREER SUMMARY
Year	Money	Rank
1978	$2,504	102
1979	$24,647	47
1980	$38,024	38
1981	$44,664	33
1982	$31,406	49
1983	$39,285	41
1984	$33,604	60
1985	$47,046	50
1986	$84,443	25
1987	$62,312	46
1988	$59,420	53
1989	$177,507	15
1990	$112,840	33
1991	$102,576	49
1992	$201,922	26
1993	$113,992	48
1994	$186,715	25
1995	$85,274	62
Career	$1,362,909	30

KELLY ROBBINS
Birthdate: September 29, 1969
Birthplace: Mt. Pleasant, MI
LPGA Victories: (2) **1993** LPGA Corning Classic. **1994** Jamie Farr Toledo Classic.
Other Victories: None.

LPGA TOUR CAREER SUMMARY
Year	Money	Rank
1992	$90,405	59
1993	$200,744	24
1994	$396,778	7
1995	$527,655	3
Career	$1,215,582	NR

PATTY SHEEHAN
Birthdate: October 27, 1956
Birthplace: Middlebury, VT
LPGA Victories: (34) **1981** Mazda Japan Classic. **1982** Orlando Lady Classic, SAFECO Classic, Inamori Classic. **1983** Corning Classic, LPGA Championship, Henredon Classic, Inamori Classic. **1984** Elizabeth Arden Classic, LPGA Championship, McDonald's Kids Classic, Henredon Classic. **1985** Sarasota Classic, J&B Scotch Pro-Am. **1986** Sarasota Classic, Kyocera Inamori Classic, Konica San Jose Classic. **1988** Sarasota Classic, Mazda Japan Classic. **1989** Rochester International. **1990** The Jamaica Classic, McDonald's Championship, Rochester International, Ping Cellular One Golf Championship, SAFECO Classic. **1991** Orix Hawaiian Ladies Open. **1992** Rochester International, Jamie Farr Toledo Classic, U.S. Women's Open. **1993** Standard Register Ping, Mazda LPGA Championship.**1994** U.S. Women's Open. **1995** Rochester International, Safeco Classic.
Other Victories: (2) **1992** Weetabix Women's British Open, Wendy's Three-Tour Challenge (with Dottie Mochrie and Nancy Lopez).
National/International teams: Solheim Cup 1990, 1992.

LPGA TOUR CAREER SUMMARY
Year	Money	Rank
1980	$17,139	63
1981	$118,463	11
1982	$225,022	4
1983	$250,399	2

Year	Money	Rank
1984	$255,185	2
1985	$227,908	5
1986	$214,281	7
1987	$208,107	6
1988	$326,171	2
1989	$253,605	5
1990	$732,618	2
1991	$342,204	8
1992	$418,622	5
1993	$540,547	2
1994	$323,563	11
1995	$333,147	14
Career	$4,455,399	4

VAL SKINNER

Birthdate: October 16, 1960
Birthplace: Hamilton, MT
LPGA Victories: (5) **1985** Konica San Jose Classic. **1986** Mazda Classic. **1987** MasterCard International. **1993** Lady Keystone Open. **1994** Atlanta Women's Championship.
Other Victories: None.

LPGA TOUR CAREER SUMMARY

Year	Money	Rank
1983	$29,485	57
1984	$23,021	79
1985	$132,307	14
1986	$165,243	11
1987	$122,039	18
1988	$60,334	52
1989	$102,089	34
1990	$66,577	59
1991	$61,923	74
1992	$41,651	100
1993	$129,665	43
1994	$297,494	13
1995	$419,963	9
Career	$1,262,355	36

ANNIKA SORENSTAM

Birthdate: October 9, 1970
Birthplace: Stockholm, Sweden
LPGA Victories: (4) **1995** U.S. Open, Heartland LPGA Classic, World Championship of Women's Golf, Samsung Women's Championship.
Other victories: **1991** NCAA Championship.

LPGA TOUR CAREER SUMMARY

Year	Money	Rank
1994	$127,451	39
1995	$660,224	1
Career	$787,675	NR

HOLLIS STACY

Birthdate: March 16, 1954
Birthplace: Savannah, GA
LPGA Victories: (18) **1977** Rail Charity Golf Classic, Lady Tara Classic, U.S. Women's Open. **1978** U.S. Women's Open, Birmingham Classic. **1979** Mayflower Classic. **1980** CPC International. **1981** West Virginia LPGA Classic, Inamori Classic. **1982** Whirlpool Championship of Deer Creek, S&H Golf Classic, West Virginia LPGA Classic. **1983** S&H Golf Classic, CPC International, Peter Jackson Classic. **1984** U.S. Women's Open. **1985** Mazda Classic of Deer Creek. **1991** Crestar-Farm Fresh Classic.
Other Victories: None.

LPGA TOUR CAREER SUMMARY

Year	Money	Rank
1974	$5,071	60
1975	$14,409	33
1976	$34,842	16
1977	$89,155	5
1978	$95,800	6
1979	$81,265	11
1980	$89,913	11
1981	$138,908	9
1982	$161,379	8
1983	$149,036	9
1984	$87,106	17
1985	$100,592	18
1986	$104,286	19
1987	$86,261	24
1988	$34,091	72
1989	$134,460	24
1990	$64,074	65
1991	$114,731	45
1992	$132,323	44
1993	$191,257	26
1994	$95,146	56
1995	$76,840	66
Career	$2,005,087	14

SHERRI STEINHAUER

Birthdate: December 27, 1962
Birthplace: Madison, WI
LPGA Victories: (2) **1992** du Maurier Ltd. Classic. **1994** Sprint Championship.
Other Victories: None.

LPGA TOUR CAREER SUMMARY

Year	Money	Rank
1986	$7,733	131
1987	$45,741	54
1988	$54,262	57

Year	Money	Rank
1989	$44,825	64
1990	$109,407	37
1991	$165,568	24
1992	$315,145	12
1993	$311,967	13
1994	$398,604	8
1995	$213,657	26
Career	$1,468,046	26

JAN STEPHENSON
Birthdate: December 22, 1951
Birthplace: Sydney, Australia
LPGA Victories: (16) 1976 Sarah Coventry Naples Classic, Birmingham Classic. 1978 Women's International. 1980 Sun City Classic. 1981 Peter Jackson Classic, Mary Kay Classic, United Virginia Bank Classic. 1982 LPGA Championship, Lady Keystone. 1983 Tucson Conquistadores LPGA Open, Lady Keystone Open, U.S. Women's Open. 1985 GNA Classic. 1987 Santa Barbara Open, SAFECO Classic, Konica San Jose Classic.
Other Victories: (7) 1973 Australian Open. 1977 Australian Open. 1981 World Ladies. 1983 JCPenney Mixed Team (with Fred Couples). 1985 Nichirei Ladies Cup, Hennessy French Open. 1990 JCPenney/LPGA Skins Game.
Other victories: None.

LPGA TOUR CAREER SUMMARY
Year	Money	Rank
1974	$16,270	28
1975	$20,066	21
1976	$64,827	8
1977	$65,820	11
1978	$66,033	13
1979	$69,519	15
1980	$41,318	34
1981	$180,528	5
1982	$133,212	10
1983	$193,364	4
1984	$101,215	14
1985	$148,030	10
1986	$165,238	12
1987	$227,303	4
1988	$236,739	9
1989	$71,550	45
1990	$31,070	105
1991	$49,467	88
1992	$132,634	42
1993	$161,123	36
1994	$99,766	54
1995	$72,822	69
Career	$2,275,075	10

BARB THOMAS
Birthdate: January 22, 1961
Birthplace: Sibley, IA
LPGA Victories: (1) 1995 Cup Noodles Hawaiian Ladies Open.
Other Victories: None.

LPGA TOUR CAREER SUMMARY
Year	Money	Rank
1984	$19,698	90
1985	$38,285	59
1986	$44,239	56
1987	$7,777	133
1988	$12,697	126
1989	$31,403	84
1990	$19,616	116
1991	$21,524	123
1992	$15,575	138
1993	$63,052	74
1994	$42,769	101
1995	$201,087	29
Career	$517,713	NR

KRIS TSCHETTER
Birthdate: December 30, 1964
Birthplace: Detroit, MI
LPGA Victories: (1) 1992 Northgate Computer Classic.
Other Victories: (1) 1991 JCPenney Classic (with Billy Andrade).

LPGA TOUR CAREER SUMMARY
Year	Money	Rank
1988	$7,590	145
1989	$18,315	109
1990	$39,469	91
1991	$129,532	38
1992	$157,436	33
1993	$196,913	25
1994	$111,180	47
1995	$362,216	12
Career	$1,022,651	NR

COLLEEN WALKER
Birthdate: August 16, 1966
Birthplace: Jacksonville, FL
LPGA Victories: (7) 1987 Mayflower Classic. 1988 Boston Five Classic. 1990 Circle K Tucson Open. 1991 Lady Keystone Open. 1992 Oldsmobile LPGA Classic, LPGA Corning Classic, SAFECO Classic.
Other Victories: 1988 Mazda Champions (with Dave Hill).

LPGA TOUR CAREER SUMMARY

Year	Money	Rank
1982	$5,393	115
1983	$6,708	122
1984	$22,265	82
1985	$43,999	52
1986	$73,314	31
1987	$190,315	9
1988	$318,116	5
1989	$204,666	7
1990	$225,518	13
1991	$294,845	11
1992	$368,600	9
1993	$96,384	53
1994	$141,200	37
1995	$263,391	18
Career	$1,991,323	15

LISA WALTERS

Birthdate: January 9, 1960
Birthplace: Prince Rupert, B.C.
LPGA Victories: (2) **1992** Itoki Hawaiian Ladies Open. **1993** Itoki Hawaiian Ladies Open.
Other Victories: None.

LPGA TOUR CAREER SUMMARY

Year	Money	Rank
1984	$37,568	56
1985	$32,080	70
1986	$53,411	48
1987	$72,024	34
1988	$22,665	94
1989	$21,979	100
1990	$36,047	94
1991	$32,380	105
1992	$108,157	51
1993	$149,260	37
1994	$71,732	73
1995	$75,087	68
Career	$637,303	NR

PAMELA WRIGHT

Birthdate: June 26, 1964
Birthplace: Scotland
LPGA Victories: None
Other Victories: None
National/International teams: Solheim Cup 1994.

LPGA TOUR CAREER SUMMARY

Year	Money	Rank
1989	$77,951	39
1990	$96,817	44
1991	$96,904	50
1992	$116,775	48
1993	$57,888	81
1994	$35,561	113
1995	$139,939	44
Career	$621,835	NR

FOREIGN PLAYERS

OVERVIEW: *Biographies and career summaries of leading foreign players, including Tour currently played, and career highlights.*

ROBERT ALLENBY
Birthdate: July 12, 1971
Birthplace: Melbourne, Australia
Tour: Australia/New Zealand
Career Highlights: Leader of Australian Order of Merit **1992, 1993. 1993** Optus Players Championship. **1992** Johnnie Walker Classic (Aus), Perak Masters (Malaysia). **1991** Victoria Open. **1990** Victoria Amateur.
National/International Teams: 1993 World Cup, Dunhill Cup.

PETER BAKER
Birthdate: October 7, 1967
Birthplace: Shifnal, England
Tour: Europe
Career Highlights: 1988 Benson & Hedges International. **1990** UAP under-25 Championship. **1993** Dunhill British Masters, Scandinavian Masters. Seventh, **1993** PGA European Tour Order of Merit.
National/International Teams: **1985** Walker Cup. **1993** Ryder Cup, Dunhill Cup.

SEVE BALLESTEROS
Birthdate: April 9, 1957
Birthplace: Pedrena, Santander, Spain
Career Highlights: 1976 Swiss Open, Japanese Open, Dunlop Phoenix (Japan), Lancome Trophy, Swiss Open. **1977** French Open. **1978** Swiss Open, German Open, Japanese Open, Kenya Open, Lancome Trophy. **1980** Dutch Open, Madrid Open, Masters. **1981** World Match Play, Madrid Open, Dunlop Phoenix (Japan), Australian PGA, Spanish Open. **1982** World Match Play, French Open. **1983** Irish Open, Masters, British PGA, Lancome Trophy. **1984** British Open, World Match Play. **1985** USF&G Classic, French Open, World Match Play, Spanish Open, Irish Open. **1986** French Open, Irish Open, British Masters, Dutch Open, Lancome Trophy. **1988** Taiheiyo Masters (Japan), British Open, German Open, Dunlop Phoenix (Japan), Lancome Trophy. **1989** Swiss Open, Madrid Open. **1991** Volvo PGA, British Masters. **1992** Dubai Desert Classic, Turespana Open de Balearas.
National/International Teams: 1975, 1976, 1977, 1992 World Cup. **1979, 1983, 1985, 1987, 1989, 1991, 1993** Ryder Cup. **1986, 1988** Dunhill Cup.

RODGER DAVIS
Birthdate: May 18, 1951
Birthplace: Sydney, Australia
Career Highlights: 1978 West Australia Open, Netherlands Masters. **1979** Victoria Open. **1981** State Express Classic. **1985** Victoria PGA Championship. **1986** PGA Championship, New Zealand Open, Air New Zealand Open, Australian Open. **1988** Bi-Centennial Classic, Wang Pro-Celebrity. **1989** New South Wales Open. **1990** Wang Pro-Celebrity, Spanish Open, Palm Meadows Cup. **1991** Volvo Masters, New Zealand Open, Sanctuary Cove Classic. **1992** Sanctuary Cove Classic. **1993** Air France Cannes Open.

ERNIE ELS
Birthdate: October 17, 1969
Birthplace: Johannesburg, South Africa
Career Highlights: 1986 South African Amateur Championship. **1989** South African Stroke Play Championship (AM). **1990** Amatola Sun Classic. **1992** Protea Assurance South African Open, Lexington PGA Championship, South African Masters, Hollard Royal Swazi Sun Classic, First National Bank Players Championship and Goodyear Classic. **1991-1992** Leader, Sunshine Tour Order of Merit.
National/International Teams: 1992 Dunhill Cup. **1993** World Cup.

NICK FALDO
Birthdate: July 18, 1957
Birthplace: Hertfordshire, England
Career Highlights: 1977 European Tour Rookie of the Year. 1978 British PGA Championship Winner. 1984 Car Care Plan International (England). 1980 British PGA Championship. 1981 British PGA Championship. 1984 Sea Pines Heritage Classic. 1987 British Open, Peugeot Spanish Open, named Member of the British Empire. 1988 Volvo Masters, Peugeot French Open. 1989 Suntory World Match-Play Championship, Peugeot French Open, Dunhill British Masters, Volvo PGA Championship, Masters. 1990 Johnnie Walker Classic British Open, Masters. 1991 Carroll's Irish Open. 1992 Johnnie Walker World Championship, Toyota World Match-Play Championship, PGA European Open, Scandinavian Masters, Open Championship, Carroll's Irish Open. 1993 Johnnie Walker Classic (Singapore), Carroll's Irish Open (play-off).
National/International Teams: 1977, 1979, 1981, 1985, 1987, 1989, 1991, 1993 Ryder Cup. 1977, 1991 World Cup. 1985, 1988, 1987, 1991 Dunhill Cup. 1986 Nissan Cup. 1987 Kirin Cup. 1990 Four Tours Championship.

ANDERS FORSBRAND
Birthdate: April 1, 1961
Birthplace: Filipstad, Sweden
Career Highlights: 1982 Swedish PGA Championship. 1983 Stiab GP. 1984 Swedish International, Gevalia Open. 1987 Ebel European Masters-Swiss Open. 1991 Volvo Open di Firenze, Benson & Hedges Trophy (with Helen Alfredsson). 1992 Volvo Open di Firenze, Credit Lyonnais Cannes Open, Equity & Law Challenge.
National/International Teams: 1984, 1985, 1988, 1991, 1993 World Cup. 1984 Kirin Cup. 1985, 1986, 1987, 1991 Dunhill Cup.

JOAKIM HAEGGMAN
Birthdate: August 28, 1969
Birthplace: Kalmar, Sweden
Career Highlights: Placed 15th on 1993 PGA European Tour Order of Merit. 1990 Wermland Open. 1992 SI Compaq Open. 1993 Peugeot Spanish Open.
National/International Teams: 1993 Ryder Cup, World Cup, Dunhill Cup.

MARK JAMES
Birthdate: October 28, 1953
Birthplace: Manchester
Career Highlights: 1988 Peugeot Spanish Open, South African TPC. 1989 NM English Open, AGF Open, Karl Litten Desert Classic. 1990 NM English Open, Dunhill British Masters. 1993 Madeira Island Open, Turespana Iberia-Open de Canarias.

BARRY LANE
Birthdate: June 21, 1960
Birthplace: Hayes, England
Career Highlights: 5th, European Tour Order of Merit, 1992. 10th, 1993. 1983 Jamaica Open. 1987 Equity & Law Challenge. 1988 Bell's Scottish Open. 1992 Mercedes German Masters. 1993 Canon European Masters.
National/International Teams: 1988 World Cup, Dunhill Cup. 1993 Ryder Cup.

BERNHARD LANGER
Birthdate: August 27, 1957
Birthplace: Anhausen, Germany
Career Highlights: Leader, European Tour Order of Merit, 1981 and 1984. 1980 Dunlop Masters, Colombian Open. 1981 German Open, Bob Hope British Classic. 1982 German Open. 1983 Italian Open, Glasgow Classic, TPC at St. Mellion, Johnnie Walker Tournament, Caslo World (Japan). 1984 Irish Open, Dutch Open, French Open. 1985 German Open, Australian Masters, The Masters, European Open, Sun City Challenge, Lancome Trophy. 1986 German Open. 1987 Irish Open, Co-winner Lancome Trophy, British PGA Championship, Belgian Classic. 1988 European Epson Match Play. 1989 Peugeot Spanish Open, German Masters. 1990 Madrid Open, Austrian Open. 1991 Sun City Million Dollar Challenge, Mercedes German Masters, Hong Kong Open, Benson & Hedges Open. 1992 Heineken Dutch Open, Honda Open. 1993 Volvo PGA Championship, Masters, Volvo German Open.
National/International Teams: 1976, 1977, 1978, 1979, 1980, 1990, 1991 World Cup. 1981, 1983, 1985, 1987, 1989, 1991, 1993 Ryder Cup. 1986, 1993 Nissan Cup (captain both years). 1987 Kirin Cup (captain). 1989 Four Tours World Championship (captain).

LIANG-HSI CHEN
Birthdate: October 18, 1959
Birthplace: Tamsui, Taiwan
Career Highlights: Leader, Taiwan Order of Merit, 1989, 1990. 1986 Johor Classic, Taiwan Linkou Open. 1987 Mercuries Cup of Taiwan Master, Korea Open, Sarak Open. 1988 Taiwan 747 Classic, Hwa Lain Open, Kaohsiung Open. 1989 Taiwan Yuan An Open. 1990 Republic of China PGA Championship, Peral Height Open, Tamsui Open. 1991 Indonesia Open. 1992 Taiwan Chang Hwa Open.
National/International Teams: 1990, 1993 World Cup.

SANDY LYLE
Birthdate: February 9, 1958
Birthplace: Shrewsbury, England
Career Highlights: 1978 Nigerian Open. 1979 Scandinavian Open, European Open. 1981 French Open. 1983 Madrid Open. 1984 Italian Open, Lancome Trophy, Kapalua International, Casio World (Japan). 1985 British Open. 1987 German Masters, Masters. 1988 Dunhill Masters, Suntory World Match Play. 1991 BMW International Open. 1992 Lancia Martini Italian Open.
National/International Teams:
1977 Walker Cup. 1979, 1981, 1983, 1985, 1987 Ryder Cup. 1979, 1980, 1987 World Cup (medalist in 1980). 1985, 1986, 1987, 1988, 1989, 1990 Dunhill Cup. 1985, 1986 Nissan Cup (medalist in 1985). 1987, 1988 Kirin Cup.

MARK McNULTY
Birthdate: October 25, 1953
Birthplace: Zimbabwe
Career Highlights: Twice finished runner-up in the PGA European Tour Order of Merit, in 1987 and 1990. 1987 Million Dollar Challenge, German Open, Dunhill British Masters, London Standard 4-Stars Pro Celebrity, Trustbank Tournament of Champions, Swazi Sun Pro-Am, AECI Charity Classic, South African Open. 1988 Benson & Hedges Trophy (with Marie Laure de Lorenzi), Cannes Open. 1989 Torras Monte Carlo Open. 1990 Volvo German Open, Credit Lyonnais Cannes Open. 1991 Volvo German Open. 1992 Zimbabwe Open. 1993 Lexington PGA Championship.
National/International Teams: 1993 World Cup.

COLIN MONTGOMERIE
Birthdate: June 23, 1963
Birthplace: Glasgow, Scotland
Career Highlights: 1988 European Tour Rookie of the Year. Leader, 1993 Europeon Tour Order of Merit. 1985 Scottish Stroke Play. 1987 Scottish Amateur Championship. 1989 Portuguese Open. 1991 Scandinavian Masters. 1993 Heineken Dutch Open, Volvo Masters.
National/International Teams:
1985, 1987 Walker Cup. 1988, 1991 World Cup. 1988, 1991, 1992 Dunhill Cup. 1991, 1993 Ryder Cup.

TOMMY NAKAJIMA
Birthdate: October 24, 1954
Birthplace: Gunma, Japan
Career Highlights: 1992 Pepsi Ube Kusan, NST Niigata Open, Japan Match Play Championship. Four Japan Opens, three Japan PGA Championships, three Japan Match Play Championships and one Japan Series Championship.

NAM-SIN PARK
Birthdate: April 14, 1959
Birthplace: Kyungki-Do, Korea
Career Highlights: 1986 Fantom Seoul Open. 1987 Que-Nam Open. 1988 Que-Nam Open, Korea Dong-Hae Open. 1990 Astra Korean PGA Championship, Cambridge Members Open. 1992 Fantom Seoul Open. 1993 Maekyung Korea Open, Fantom Open.
National/International Teams: 1988, 1989, 1990, 1991, 1992, 1993 World Cup.

FRANK NOBILO
Birthdate: May 14, 1960
Birthplace: Auckland, New Zealand
Career Highlights: 1978 New Zealand Amateur. 1979 New Zealand Under-25 Stroke Play Championship. 1982 New South Wales PGA. 1985 New Zealand PGA. 1987 New Zealand PGA. 1988 PLM Open. 1991 Lancome Trophy. 1993 Turespana Mediterranean Open.
National/International Teams: 1978 World Amateur Team. 1982, 1987, 1988, 1990, 1991, 1992, 1993 World Cup. 1985, 1986, 1987, 1989, 1990, 1992, 1993 Dunhill Cup.

JOSE-MARIA OLAZABAL
Birthdate: February 5, 1966
Birthplace: Fuenterrabia, Spain
PGA TOUR Victories: (2) **1990** NEC World Series of Golf. **1991** The International.
Career Highlights:
1983 Italian Amateur, Spanish Amateur. **1986** European Masters, Swiss Open, Sanyo Open. **1988** Belgian Open, German Masters. **1989** Tenerife Open, Dutch Open. **1990** Benson & Hedges International, Irish Open, Lancome Trophy, Visa Taiheyo Club Masters. **1990** NEC World Series of Golf. **1991** Catalonia Open, The International. **1992** Turespana Open de Tenerife, Open Mediterrania. **1994** Masters, NEC World Series of Golf.
National/International Teams: **1986, 1987, 1988, 1989, 1992** Dunhill Cup. **1987, 1989, 1991, 1993** Ryder Cup. **1989** World Cup. **1987** Kirin Cup. **1989, 1990** Four Tours World Championship.

MASASHI "JUMBO" OZAKI
Birthdate: January 27,1947
Birthplace: Tokushima, Japan
Career Highlights: Six-time leading money winner, JPGA. **1990** Yonex Hiroshima Open, Maruman Open, Daiwa KBC Augusta. **1992** Dunlop Open, Chunichi Crowns, Philanthropy Cup, All Nippon Airways Open, Japan Open, Visa Taiheyo Masters.

RONAN RAFFERTY
Birthdate: January 13, 1964
Birthplace: Newry, N. Ireland
Career Highlights: Leader, **1989** PGA European Tour Order of Merit. **1979** British Boys Championship. **1980** English Open Amateur Strokeplay Championship. **1982** Venezuelan Open, Daiko Palm Meadows Cup, Portuguese Open. **1987** South Australian Open, New Zealand Open. **1988** Australian Match-Play Championship, Equity & Law Challenge. **1989** Lancia Italian Open, Scandinavian Enterprise Open, Volvo Masters. **1990** Melbourne Classic, PLM Open, Ebel European Masters. **1992** Portuguese Open, Daikyo Palm Meadows Cup. **1993** Austrian Open.
National/International Teams: **1983, 1984, 1987, 1988, 1990, 1991** World Cup. **1986, 1987, 1988, 1989, 1990, 1991, 1992** Dunhill Cup. **1988** Kirin Cup. **1989** Ryder Cup. **1989, 1990, 1991** Four Tours World Championship of Golf.

STEVEN RICHARDSON
Birthdate: July 24, 1966
Birthplace: Windsor, England
Career Highlights: **1989** English Amateur Championship. **1991** Girona Open, Portuguese Open. **1993** German Masters.
National/International Teams:
1989 Walker Cup. **1991** Ryder Cup. **1991, 1992** Dunhill Cup. **1991** Four Tours World Championship of Golf.

JOSE RIVERO
Birthdate: September 20, 1955
Birthplace: Madrid, Spain
Career Highlights:
1984 Lawrence Batley International. **1987** Peugeot French Open. **1988** Monte Carlo Open. **1992** Open Catalonia.
National/International Teams:
1984, 1987, 1988, 1990, 1991, 1992, 1993 World Cup.

CONSTANTINO ROCCA
Birthdate: December 4, 1956
Birthplace: Bergamo, Italy
Career Highlights: **1988** Rolex Pro-Am. **1989** Index Open (Italy), Italian Native, Italian PGA Championship.**1993** Open V33 du Grand Lyon, Peugeot French Open.
National/International Teams:
1988, 1990, 1991, 1992, 1993 World Cup. **1993** Ryder Cup.

EDUARDO ROMERO
Birthdate: July 12, 1954
Birthplace: Cordoba, Argentina
Career Highlights: **1983** Argentine PGA. **1984** Chile Open. **1986** Argentine PGA, Chile Open. **1989** Argentine Open, Lancome Trophy. **1990** Volvo Open di Firenze. **1991** Peugeot Spanish Open, Peugeot French Open.
National/International Teams: **1983, 1984, 1987, 1988, 1991, 1993** World Cup.

ANDERS SORENSEN
Birthdate: June 20, 1962
Birthplace: Helsingor, Denmark
Career Highlights: **1982** Danish Amateur Stroke-Play Championship. **1985** Danish Open. **1986**

Toms Open, Amateur Stroke-Play Championship. 1987 Nescafe Cup (Sweden), Volvo Albatross Open.
National/International Teams: 1987, 1988, 1989, 1990, 1991, 1992, 1993 World Cup.

STEEN TINNING
Birthdate: October 7, 1962
Birthplace: Copenhagen, Denmark
Career Highlights: 1983 Danish Amateur Close Championship. 1986 European Junior Championship. 1989 Tomj Open (Denmark).
National/International Teams: 1987, 1988, 1989, 1990, 1993 World Cup.

SAM TORRANCE
Birthdate: August 24, 1953
Birthplace: Largs, Scotland
Career Highlights: 1980 Scottish PGA Championship, Australian PGA Championship. 1981 Carroll's Irish Open. 1982 Portuguese Open, Spanish Open. 1983 Portuguese Open, Scandinavian Enterprise Open. 1984 Sanyo Open, Benson & Hedges International, Tunisian Open. 1985 Johnnie Walker Monte Carlo Open, Scottish PGA Championship. 1987 Lancia Italian Open. 1990 German Masters. 1991 Jersey European Airways Open, Scottish PGA Championship. 1993 Honda Open, Scottish PGA Championship, Open Catatonia, Kronenbourg Open.
National/International Teams: 1976, 1978, 1982, 1984, 1985, 1987, 1989, 1990, 1991, 1993 World Cup. 1981, 1983, 1985, 1987, 1989, 1991, 1993, 1995 Ryder Cup.

JEAN VAN DE VELDE
Birthdate: May 29, 1966
Birthplace: Mont de Marsan, France
Career Highlights: 1985 French Youth Championship. 1986 French Amateur Championship, French Youth Championship. 1988 UAP Under-25s European Open Championship. 1993 Rome Masters.
National/International Teams: 1989, 1990, 1991, 1992, 1993 World Cup.

IAN WOOSNAM
Birthdate: March 2, 1958
Birthplace: Oswestry, Wales
Career Highlights: 1979 News of the World Under-23 Match-play Championship. 1982 Swiss Open, Cacherel Under-25 Championship. 1983 Silk Cut Masters. 1984 Scandinavian Enterprise Open. 1985 Zambian Open. 1986 Lawrence Batley TPC, "555" Kenya Open. 1987 Jersey Open, Cespa Madrid Open, Bell's Scottish Open, Lancome Trophy, Million Dollar Challenge, Suntory World Match Play Championship, Hong Kong Open, International Trophy (World Cup individual). 1988 Volvo PGA Championship, Carroll's Irish Open, Panasonic European Open. 1989 Carroll's Irish Open. 1990 Amex Mediterranean Open, Monte Carlo Open, Bell's Scottish Open, Epson Grand Prix, Suntory World Match Play Championship. 1991 Mediterranean Open, Monte Carlo Open, USF&G Classic, Masters, PGA Grand Slam. 1992 European Monte Carlo. 1993 Murphy's English Open, Lancome Trophy.
National/International Teams: 1980, 1982, 1983, 1984, 1985, 1987, 1990, 1991, 1992, 1993 World Cup. 1983, 1985, 1987, 1989, 1991, 1993 Ryder Cup. 1985, 1986, 1988, 1989, 1990, 1991, 1993 Dunhill Cup. 1985, 1986 Nissan Cup. 1987 Kirin Cup. 1989, 1993 Four Tours World Championship of Golf.

YU-SHU HSIEH
Birthdate: November 5, 1960
Birthplace: Taiwan
Career Highlights: Winner Taiwan Circuit Order of Merit 1991, 1988, 1987, 1986, 1985. 1985 Taiwan Taichung Open, Linkou Open. 1986 Taiwan King Grapes Open. 1988 General Choutze-Jou Memorial Open, Taiwan Open, Chia Yi Open, Miller Beer Open, Taiwan BMW Open, Indonesia Open. 1991 Taiwan Chanh-Hwa Open. 1993 Taiwan Taichung Open, Mercuries Cup of Taiwan Master.

HALL OF FAME

OVERVIEW: *Dates and short career biographies of the leading players of the past (omitting those covered in the Personalities chapters) since 1870, including the British and European tours, the PGA TOUR, the LPGA, as well as prominent professionals from Asia, Africa, and Australia/New Zealand.*

WILLIE ANDERSON
1878-1910
Emigrant to the United States became the first to win four U.S. Opens (1901, 1903, 1904, 1905).

TOMMY ARMOUR
1896-1968
Won the 1927 U.S. Open, 1930 PGA Championship, and the 1931 British Open. His brilliant 1930 campaign was overshadowed by Bobby Jones' Grand Slam, and Armour has been unjustly overlooked. His *How to Play Your Best Golf All the Time* became a best-seller and for many years was the biggest-selling book ever authored on golf.

JOHN BALL
Dec. 24, 1861-1940
Prominent English amateur of the late 19th and early 20th century. After winning the British Amateur in 1888, Ball became the first English-born player to win the British Open in 1890, and in the same year won his second Amateur, the first to win both titles in the same year. Ball subsequently won the 1892, 1894, 1899, 1907, 1910, and 1912 Amateurs, a record seven titles in all in addition to two runner-up finishes. Ball was also runner-up in the 1892 British Open.

JIM BARNES
April 8, 1886 -May 26, 1966
Won 1916, 1919 PGA Championship; 1921 U.S. Open, 1925 British Open.

PATTY BERG
Born Feb. 13, 1918
Leading player on the LPGA Tour during the 1940s, 1950s and 1960s. Patty Berg first came to national attention by reaching the final of the 1935 U.S. Women's Amateur, losing to Glenna Collett Vare in Vare's final Amateur victory. Berg reached the final in 1937 and won the Amateur in 1938 at Westmoreland. A fixture on the fledgling Women's Professional Golf Association circuit, she won the inaugural U.S. Women's Open. Berg, a founder of the LPGA, won a total of 41 events on the LPGA and WPGA circuit, and was runner-up in the 1957 Open at Winged Foot. She was runner-up in the 1956 and 1959 LPGA Championships. In addition, Berg won the 1953, 1957, and 1958 Western Opens, the 1955 and 1957 Titleholders, both considered majors at the time. Her last victory came in 1962.

JULIUS BOROS
Born March 3, 1920
Won 18 PGA Tour events, including 1952, 1963 U.S. Open, 1968 PGA Championship. Oldest player ever to win a major championship. Member, Ryder Cup team 1959, 1963, 1965, 1967. PGA Player of Year, 1952, 1963. Career PGA Tour earnings, $1,004,861.

JAMES BRAID
Feb. 6, 1870-Nov. 27, 1950
The Scottish-born member of the Great Triumvirate of Braid, Taylor and Vardon—Braid won five British Opens in all and was the first to achieve this feat. His victories came in 1901, 1905, 1906, 1908, and 1910. In addition Braid won four Brish PGA championships in 1903, 1905, 1907 and 1911 as well as the 1910 French Open title. Braid was runner-up in the British Open in 1897 and 1909.

MIKE BRADY
April 15, 1887 -Dec. 3, 1972
Lost to Walter Hagen in a celebrated playoff in the 1919 U.S. Open. Also was runner-up in 1911. Hagen promptly resigned his club pro job after winning in 1919 and Oakland Hills promptly hired Brady. Brady subsequently won the 1922 Western Open at Oakland Hills.

BILLY BURKE
Dec. 14, 1902 -April 19, 1972
Greatest season was 1931, when he won the U.S. Open, reached the semi-finals of the PGA Championship, and won four events on the professional circuit, plus appeared on the Ryder Cup team where he was undefeated in two matches. Subsequently selected for the 1933 Ryder Cup team and won his only match.

JACK BURKE, JR.
Born Jan. 29, 1923
First rose to prominence with two lopsided victories in the 1951 Ryder Cup matches. Subsequently selected for the 1953 and 1955 sides, and in 1957 was named captain of the team. Also served as non-playing captain in the 1973 matches. Won 15 PGA tournaments in his career, including the 1956 Masters and PGA Championships. Perhaps his most famous match was his nine-hour, 40-hole quarterfinal loss to Cary Middlecoff in the 1955 PGA. Selected PGA Player of the Year in 1956, and subsequently challenged in the PGA Championship (fourth, 1958).

WILLIAM C. CAMPBELL
Born 1929
Perhaps the quintessential modern amateur golfer, Campbell nearly made golfing history when he finished runner-up to Roberto deVicenzo in the 1980 U.S. Senior Open. A prominent amateur of the 1950s and 60s, Campbell was selected eight times in all for the Walker Cup team and won the Amateur in 1964. He made an even stronger mark as a senior, winning the Senior Amateur twice in addition to his runner-up finish in the Open. Campbell is one of the few Americans to serve as Captain of the Royal & Ancient Golf Club.

JOANNE CARNER
Born April 4, 1939
Prominent LPGA professional of the 1970s and 1980s following an outstanding amateur career in the 1950s and 1960s. Carner first broke into the headlines in 1956 when, as a 17-year-old, she reached the finals of the U.S. Women's Amateur in the same year she won the Girls Junior Amateur. She went on to win the Amateur five times (in 1957, 1960, 1962, 1966, and 1968) and reach the final round a total of seven times. Carner competed four times on the Curtis Cup team (1958, 1960, 1962, and 1964) and was undefeated in five singles matches. After winning the Burdine's Invitational on the LPGA Tour as an amateur in 1969, Carner made the decision to turn pro in 1970 and has since won an astonishing 42 victories on the LPGA Tour, including the U.S. Women's Open in 1971 and 1976. Carner led the money list in 1974, 1982, and in 1983 at the age of 44.

BILLY CASPER
Born June 31, 1931
One of the top golfers of the 1960s, he was considered just a slight notch below Nicklaus, Player and Palmer, but nevertheless won 51 Tour events and three majors on the circuit. He engineered perhaps the most spectacular comeback of all time when he came from seven strokes back with nine to play to tie Arnold Palmer in the 1966 U.S. Open, winning the playoff on the following day. He won five tournaments in all that year and took PGA Player of the Year honors, repeating in 1970 when he won four tournaments including the Masters. In 1968 he became the first player to top $200,000 in single-season prize money. Casper won the coveted Vardon Trophy for lowest scoring average five times in his career and was selected for eight Ryder Cup teams in all. He won his final Tour victory in 1975, but after a stint as Ryder Cup captain in 1979 he found significant success in the early years of the Senior Tour, winning nine tournaments in all including the 1983 U.S. Senior Open. His career faded in the 1990s but he remains competitive in the Super Seniors bracket, as well as a popular figure on the Senior Tour.

HARRY COOPER
Born August 6, 1904
Prominent PGA Tour professional of the 1920s and 1930s. Perennial U.S. Open contender (with seven top ten finishes and second place in 1927 and 1936), he also placed second in the 1936 Masters as well as reaching the quarterfinals of the PGA on several occasions. His greatest successes were across the border— he won the Canadian Open in 1932 and 1937. Cooper won 321 PGA Tour titles in all and the inaugural Vardon Trophy in 1937. Subsequently was active as a senior golfer, placing sixth in the 1955 PGA Seniors Championship.

HENRY COTTON
Born Jan. 26, 1907

Prominent English player of the 1930s. Cotton almost single-handedly upheld the prestige of British golf in the 1930s with three victories in the British Open (1934, 1937, and 1948). In addition he captured many titles on the European Continent in the 1930s. His greatest year was 1937 when he won the British, French and Czechoslovakian Opens and was selected for the 1937 Ryder Cup matches. Cotton served as captain of the Ryder Cup team in 1947 and 1953.

BOBBY CRUICKSHANK
Nov 16. 1894-Aug. 27, 1975

Prominent player on the PGA circuit from the early 1920s to the early 1930s. Of Scottish birth, he first rose to prominence in reaching the finals of the 1922 and 1923 PGA Championships, losing both times to eventual champion Gene Sarazen. Also was runner-up in the 1923 and 1932 U.S. Opens, and won 20 tour events in his career. His greatest year was 1927, when he won the Los Angeles and Texas Opens and finished as the leading money winner for the year. He last won on tour in 1935.

JIMMY DEMARET
May 24, 1910-Dec. 28, 1983

Perhaps the all-time character of the PGA Tour, he also won 31 events in a long career between 1935 and 1957 and was the first three-time winner of the Masters. Demaret reached his peak in the late 1940s with wins in the Masters in 1947, runner-up to Ben Hogan in both the 1948 U.S. Open and PGA Championship, and leading money winner status in 1947. He reached the the semi-finals of the PGA Championship four times in all but never won. Selected on the 1951 Ryder Cup team, his career declined in the 1950s although he managed several key wins including the 1952 Crosby. Known for his outrageous humor and outrageously colorful outfits, he was the original host of Shell's Wonderful World of Golf in the early 1960s, and was introduced to a new generation of golf fans. The over-70s groupings on the PGA Senior Tour are known as the Friends of Demaret in his honor.

ROBERTO DE VICENZO
Born April 14, 1923

Perhaps the archetypal international golfer of the 1950s, he won an astonishing 230 tournaments worldwide in his career, including four on the PGA Tour and the 1967 British Open. The Argentine-born golfer had the misfortune to sign an incorrect scorecard in the 1968 Masters (after tying Bob Goalby), and was disqualified. DeVicenzo subsequently found great success in the early days of the PGA Senior Tour, winning the Liberty Mutual Legends of Golf three times and the inaugural U.S. Senior Open in 1980. Also won the 1974 PGA Seniors Championship, and represented Argentina 17 times in the Canada and World Cups (leading Argentina to victory in 1953).

LEO DIEGEL
April 27, 1899-May 5, 1951

Prominent player of the 1920s and early 1930s who won 11 PGA Circuit events, and was a four-time winner of the Canadian Open (1924-25, 1928-29). Selected for the inaugural 1927 Ryder Cup team and went on to play on the 1929, 1931 and 1933 teams as well. Diegel's great year was 1928 when he won the Canadian Open and, in winning the 1928 PGA Championship, stopped the four-year winning streak of Walter Hagen (defeating him in the quarter-final to avenge defeats by Hagen in the 1925 quarter-finals and the 1926 final). Diegel achieved the rare double of defending both titles successfully in 1929, this time defeating Hagen in the semi-finals and finishing off The Haig's career. Diegel was runner-up to Bobby Jones at the British Open in 1930, but subsequently did not challenge at major championships.

ED DUDLEY
Feb. 19, 1901-Oct. 25, 1963

Leading tour player of the late 1920s and 1930s, Dudley was a 13-time winner on the Tour. After winning both the Los Angeles and Western Opens in 1931, Dudley had his best year in 1933 when he was a quarter-finalist in the PGA Championship and won selection to the Ryder Cup team. Won two key matches in the 1937 Ryder Cup matches to help the United States win for the first time in England.

OLIN DUTRA
Jan. 17, 1901-May 5, 1983

Played on the PGA Tour in the late 1920s and 1930s, winning 19 tournaments in all. Was most prominent in the early 1930s, winning the 1932 PGA Championship, the 1934 U.S. Open at Merion and playing in the 1933 and 1935 Ryder Cup matches. In the 1932 PGA Championship, Dutra played 196 holes and finished an astounding 19 under par, including finishing as low qualifier and winning his matches 9&8, 5&3, 5&4, 3&2, and 4&3.

CHICK EVANS
July 18, 1890-Nov. 6, 1979
Ranked just below Bobby Jones among U.S. Amateur golfers of the 1920s. Evans was the first amateur to win the U.S. Open and U.S. Amateur in one year, a feat he achieved in 1916 . Evans went on to win the U.S. Amateur in 1920, while finishing runner-up three times. Selected to the Walker Cup team in 1922, 1924, and 1928, Evans competed in a record 50 consecutive U.S. Amateurs in his long career.

JOHNNY FARRELL
Born April 1, 1901
Prominent PGA Tour player of the 1920s and early 1930s who won 22 events in his career. Reached the semi-finals of the 1926 PGA Championship, but his best year was 1927 when he won eight tournaments in all. In 1928 he won the U.S. Open at Olympia Fields by defeating Bobby Jones in a 36-hole playoff. In 1929 he was runner-up at both the British Open and the PGA Championship. Farrell was a key member of the first Ryder Cup team in 1927, and subsequently played in the 1929 and 1931 Matches. His career declined in the 1930s, but Farrell reappeared in the 1950s when he competed in several PGA Seniors Championships.

RAYMOND FLOYD
Born September 4, 1932
Outstanding contemporary golfer especially noted for his longevity, Floyd won PGA Tour events 29 years apart (the 1963 St. Petersburg Open and the 1992 Dorel-Ryder Open), in a career which included 22 victories in all and four majors. The victory at St. Petersburg in 1963 was his PGA Tour debut. Only the British Open title eluded him in a quest for a career Grand Slam, (he was runner up in 1978 at the Old Course). His 1976 victory in the Masters was a modern classic, finishing with a winning margin of eight strokes. Floyd hails from a prominent golfing family, including father L.B. (a noted instructor) and sister Marlene (an LPGA veteran). Floyd was selected to eight Ryder Cup teams in all and was a key player in the 1991 and 1993 victories after serving as non-playing captain in 1989. He became the first player to win on the Senior Tour and the PGA Tour in the same year (1992), and found great success playing both circuits in 1992-93. Since 1994 he has largely confined his activities to the Senior Tour, winning nine victories to date and finishing second on the money list for 1994.

DOUG FORD
Born August 6, 1922
Top-ranked player of the 1950s and early 1960s, Ford won 19 PGA Tour titles in his career including the 1955 PGA Championship and the 1957 Masters. Ford had his greatest year in 1957, winning the Los Angeles Open, the Western Open, and a spot on the Ryder Cup team in addition to the Masters. Ford continued to be a strong threat on Tour through the early 1960s, winning the Canadian Open in 1959 and 1963, the 1962 Crosby, and finishing fifth in the 1961 and 1962 PGA Championships. Ford was on the Ryder Cup team between 1955-61, and was named PGA Player of the Year in 1955. Ford managed several top-20 finishes in the PGA Seniors Championship in the 1970s and won two unofficial Seniors events in 1981, but by the mid-80s was finding only limited success on Tour.

VIC GHEZZI
Oct. 19, 1912-May 30, 1976
Top-ranked PGA Tour player of the late 1930s and 1940s. First rose to prominence at 22 with a victory in the 1935 Los Angeles Open. Ghezzi won the 1941 PGA Championship at Cherry Hills, and after World War II made a brief comeback, finishing runner-up in the 1946 U.S. Open and reaching the semi-finals of the 1947 PGA Championship. Ghezzi was selected for the 1939 and 1941 Ryder Cup teams but the matches were cancelled due to the war. Ghezzi played in the PGA Seniors Championship in the 1960s, finishing as high as seventh in 1964.

RALPH GULDAHL
Born Nov. 22, 1911
Leading player on the PGA Tour in the 1930s and early 1940s, winning 14 tournaments overall. He first rose to prominence with a runner-up finish in the 1933 U.S. Open at the age of 20 (losing to Johnny Goodman, also 20 at the time). His career reached a peak in the late 1930s when he won three consecutive Western Opens (considered a quasi-major championship at the time) in 1936-38, and then won back-to-back U.S. Opens in 1937 and 1938. Guldahl also was a key member of the 1937

Ryder Cup team in winning both his matches. Guldahl also had a stellar 1939 campaign winning the Masters and the Greensboro Open and reached the semi-finals of the PGA Championship in 1940. But after reaching the quarter-finals in the 1941 PGA Championship he did not have significant success in major golf tournaments.

WALTER HAGEN
Dec. 21, 1892-Oct. 6, 1969

One of the great characters of golf and the greatest professional player of the 1920s, Hagen is known today not only for his eleven major championships but his successful efforts to raise the status of the touring golf professional. Hagen first came to national attention as a minor-league baseball pitching prospect but turned to golf full-time after his astonishing victory in the 1914 U.S. Open (at the age of 21). Hagen won the Western Open in 1916 and reached the semi-finals of the inaugural PGA Championship that year at Siwanoy, and returned to the victor's circle at the U.S. Open in 1919 when it resumed following the First World War. But his successes of the 1910s are overshadowed by his play in the 1920s. A runner-up finish in the 1921 U.S. Open, plus victories in the Western Open and that year's PGA Championship touched off a fabulous decade in which he won nine major championships, numerous tournaments on the PGA Circuit, and earned riches giving golf exhibitions worldwide. Hagen won an incredible 33 consecutive matches in the PGA Championship between 1924 and 1928 in winning four consecutive PGA Championships. Walter Hagen also became the first American to win the British Open, and won the affection of the British public in four dashing championships won in 1922, 1924, 1928 and 1929. Hagen was the first American golfer to earn a living as a touring professional, and it was the respect in which golfers such as Hagen and Harry Vardon were held that led the Inverness Club to open the clubhouse to professionals in the 1920 U.S. Open. Hagen was also the first professional golfer to found his own equipment company, and started his own informal tour of exhibition matches and appearances. One of his most celebrated triumphs was a 12 and 11 victory over Bobby Jones in a 72-hole exhibition in 1926, but he could be beaten quite handily as well, losing 18 and 17 to an unknown British professional at the start of one of his exhibition tours. His manager Bob Harlow became the first manger of the PGA Tour Circuit in the 1930s, after The Haig's career went into eclipse. But Hagen continued to be a force throughout the 1930s, winning the 1932 Western Open and serving as captain of the U.S. Ryder Cup team between 1927-37.

CHICK HARBERT
Born Feb. 20, 1915

Prominent PGA Tour pro in the 1940s and 1950s. Masterful match player, Harbert first rose to prominence with a victory in the 1942 Texas Open, but became a leading player after the Second World War by reaching the final of the 1947 PGA Championship. He earned a slot on the 1949 Ryder Cup team and won his only match. After another loss in the finals of the 1952 PGA, Harbert finally broke through with a victory in 1954, which included match victories over Jerry Barber, Tommy Bolt, and defending champion Walter Burkemo. Harbert, who won a total of nine PGA Tour titles between 1941 and 1958, was named captain of the victorious 1955 Ryder Cup team. He continued to compete in the PGA Championship throughout the 1960s, but switched to the Senior circuit in the late 1960s and finished in the top five of the PGA Seniors Championships several times.

CHANDLER HARPER
Born March 10, 1914.

Leading player on the PGA Tour in the 1940s and 1950s, amassing a total of 20 PGA Tour victories including the 1950 PGA Championship. Harper finished fifth in the 1946 U.S. Open but had his greatest success in the 1950s, with a career best in 1955 when he won the Colonial and was selected to the Ryder Cup team. After concluding his Tour career, Harper had great success as a senior golfer, winning the U.S. National Senior Open and the 1968 PGA Seniors Championship.

E.J. (DUTCH) HARRISON
March 29, 1910-June 19, 1982

Feared competitor on Tour from the 1930s to the 1950s. Harrison first rose to prominence by reaching the semi-finals of the 1939 PGA Championship. Harrison won fifteen events between 1937 and 1958, including the 1949 Canadian Open, the 1953 Western Open, and the 1954 Crosby. Harrison was a regular in the Ryder Cup line-up after the Second World War, and finished third in the U.S. Open as late as 1960. Harrison went on to even greater success as a senior, winning the U.S. National Senior Open four times in a row between 1962 and 1965, as well as managing four top-five finishes in the PGA Seniors Championship.

SANDRA HAYNIE
Born June 4, 1943

Leading LPGA player of the 1960s and 1970s. Haynie won the 1957 and 1958 Texas amateurs, and the 1960 Trans-Mississippi as an amateur, and turned pro in 1961. Haynie won the U.S. Women's Open in 1974 and the LPGA Championship in 1965 and 1974. As there were only two designated major championships in 1974, Haynie is considered along with Babe Zaharias to have achieved the LPGA Grand Slam. Haynie won a total of 42 LPGA tournaments in her career, including a final major championship in the 1982 Peter Jackson Classic. Haynie led the Tour in victories in 1974 and 1975.

BEN HOGAN
Born Aug. 13, 1912

The leading PGA Tour professional of the 1940s and 1950s, and some still call Hogan the greatest player of all time. Won a total of 62 PGA Tour events between 1938 and 1953, including victories in every major championship. Hogan was plagued by a snap-hook early in his career and was overshadowed in major championship play by fellow Texan Byron Nelson despite leading the Tour in prize money 1940-42 and winning the Vardon Trophy in 1940 and 1941. In 1942 Hogan won six Tour victories and finished runner-up in the Masters, but it was immediately after the war that he made his mark, with 13 victories in 1946 including the PGA Championship, his first major. Hogan dominated golf in the late 1940s, with victories in the 1948 PGA Championship and U.S. Open, and a leading role in the 1947 Ryder Cup victory in Portland. Hogan suffered massive injuries in a near-fatal auto accident in 1949 and his career was thought to be finished. But after serving as non-playing captain in the 1949 Ryder Cup matches, he staged the most spectacular comeback in the history of golf by achieving even greater success in the 1950s, including a victory in the 1950 U.S. Open just weeks after returning to competitive golf. His injuries prevented him from competing in the PGA Championship, but Hogan still amassed nine major championships in all, including the first three legs of the modern Grand Slam in 1953. He won the U.S. Open four times in all, a record never bettered, and wrote one of the enduring classics of golf instruction in *Five Lessons*. Hogan finished runner-up in the 1955 and 1956 U.S. Opens and finished third in 1960, but after that his career went into decline (except for a spectacular run at the 1967 Masters). He did not choose to compete on the Senior circuit, but instead concentrated on the management of the fabulously successful Ben Hogan Co., a major golf equipment manufacturing concern. Hogan has served as host at Colonial since the 1940s and continues to fulfill that function today. Hogan served as non-playing captain of the 1967 Ryder Cup team.

DOROTHY CAMPBELL HURD HOWE
1883-1946

Prominent amateur golfer of the early 20th centruy. The Scot first gained notice as a three-time winner of the Scottish amateur from 1903 to 1905. Her finest year was 1909 when she won both the U.S. and British amateur titles. She successfully defended in the U.S. Women's Amateur in 1910 and added the Canadian Ladies Amateur—becoming the first woman to win these three national amateur championships. She continued to be a force in amateur golf in the 1910s, winning the 1911 British and Canadian titles and the 1912 Canadian championship. After the First World War she reached the finals of the U.S. Women's Amateur in 1920, losing to Alexa Stirling, but came back to win the title a third time in 1924.

JOCK HUTCHINSON
June 6, 1884-Sept. 28, 1977

Scottish-born, Hutchinson achieved his greatest successes in the United States, first breaking through with runner-up finishes in both the 1916 PGA and U.S. Open. His most successful campaign was 1920, when he won the PGA Championship and the Western Open, and finished runner-up to Ted Ray in the U.S. Open. Hutchinson went on to win the 1921 British Open at St. Andrews, his hometown. Hutchinson became the dominant player in the early years of the PGA Seniors Championship, winning victories in 1937 and 1947, and finishing runner-up six times.

HALE IRWIN
Born June 3, 1945

Very successful PGA Tour star of the 1970s, noted for three victories in the U.S. Open (1974, 1979 and a dramatic playoff victory in 1990 after sinking a 60-foot putt on the final hole to force the playoff). Irwin won eleven tournaments in the 1970s, but is best-known for his astonishing golf from 1990-94 when, between the ages of 45 and 49 he finished twice in the top-10 for earnings, won the U.S. Open and qualified for the 1991 Ryder Cup team. Irwin played on five Ryder Cup teams in all as well as two World Cup teams (winning the individual title in

1979). Captained the inaugural President's Cup team in 1994 before moving to the Senior Tour in 1995.

BETTY JAMESON
Born May 19, 1919

A prominent amateur of the 1930s and 1940s and a leading LPGA/WPGA player of the 1940s. Jameson won back-to-back titles in the U.S. Women's Amateur in 1939 and 1940. Jameson won ten LPGA titles in the 1940s and 1950s after turning professional in 1945. Her biggest triumph was a victory in the 1947 U.S. Women's Open. Jameson was much less prominent during the 1950s but did finish runner-up in the 1952 Open and as victor in the 1954 Western Open, considered a major championship at the time. After winning three titles in 1955, she did not figure prominently in LPGA events.

ROBERT T. JONES
March 17, 1902-Dec. 18, 1971

A golfing prodigy who, after conquering a terrific temper, went on to become the most popular golfer of his time as well as a celebrated author and founder of both the Augusta National Golf Club and the Masters. Jones was a teenage golfing phenomenon the likes of which golf had not yet seen, winning entry into the U.S. Amateur at 14 years, five months in 1916. The USGA did not stage competitions in 1917-18 due to the First World War, but in 1919 Jones reached the final of the Amateur, and in 1920 was medalist in the stroke-play phase of the Amateur as well as winner of the Southern Amateur. By 1922 Jones' game had blossomed and he finished runner-up in the U.S. Open at Skokie, and then won his first U.S. Open in 1923 at Inwood. His 1924 campaign brought him the Amateur Championship at Merion and a runner-up finish in the Open at Oakland Hills. By 1925 Jones was regarded as the finest golfer in the country with the possible exception of Walter Hagen (and this at 23 years of age), and he solidified his reputation with another Amateur Championship and second-place in the Open. In 1926 Jones had his greatest year to date, winning the U.S. and British Opens before losing in the final of the U.S. Amateur to George Von Elm at Baltusrol. Jones, a lifelong amateur, began a career as an Atlanta lawyer, but continued his assault on golf's records each summer, winning the British Open at St. Andrews and storming to an 8 & 7 victory over Charles Evans in the final of the U.S. Amateur at Minkahda. His 1928 campaign was likewise successful, with a runner-up finish in the U.S. Open followed by a smashing 10 & 9 victory in the Amateur over Phillip Perkins. His 1929 campaign brought him a victory in the U.S. Open at Winged Foot, where after finishing in a tie after 72 holes he proceeded to defeat Al Espinosa by 23 strokes in a 36-hole playoff—but Jones did not fare well in the British Open and after finishing as medalist in the Amateur at Pebble Beach lost to 19-year-old Johnny Goodman in the first round of match play. He made use of the time by playing the new Cypress Point course and, impressed with the design, asked architect Alister MacKenzie to collaborate with him on the design for the Augusta National Golf Club. Jones' final summer of major championship golf, in 1930, was a frank assault on the "Impregnable Quadrilateral," the Open and Amateur Championships of the United States and Great Britain. He defeated Mac Smith by two strokes in both the U.S. Open at Interlachen and the British Open ay Hoylake. He faltered somewhat at St. Andrews in his first British Amateur, winning a fourth-round match over Cyril Tolley with the aid of a crucial stymie before cruising to victory in the final. He completed the Grand Slam, as it became known, by finishing as medallist at the Amateur and cruising to victory including an 8 & 7 margin in the final over Eugene Homans. Jones subsequently retired from competitive golf, although he continued to write, and played exhibitions as late as the Second World War to raise money for the war effort. He founded Augusta National Golf Club in 1932 and the Masters in 1933. He suffered from a crippling disease for the last 20 years of his life, but continued to play host at the Masters through 1967. His book *Down the Fairway* is considered one of the game's enduring classics.

LAWSON LITTLE
June 23, 1910-Feb. 1, 1968

The leading amateur of the 1930s and later a successful touring professional. Little rose to prominence in 1934 by winning both the British and U.S. Amateur Championships, and by the astounding feat of defending both titles successfully in 1935. After 1935 Little joined the PGA Tour circuit as a professional—the first prominent amateur to turn professional and presaging prominent defections by Arnold Palmer and Jack Nicklaus from the amateur ranks in later years. Little's decision paid off immediately with a victory in the 1936 Canadian Open, but he did not fulfill the expectations of many despite winning the 1940 U.S. Open and several PGA Tour events, including the 1940 Los Angeles Open and the 1941 Texas Open.

BOBBY LOCKE
Born 1917

Prominent South African golfer of the 1940s and 1950s. Locke first gained attention before the Second World War in winning the New Zealand Open, but after the war quickly established himself as a force in the United States and Europe with a runner-up finish in the 1946 British Open to Sam Snead, a third place finish in the 1947 U.S. Open, and victory in the 1949 British Open. Locke also won 11 events on the PGA Tour between 1947-50, including the 1947 Tournament of Champions and Canadian Open and the 1948 Phoenix Open. In maintaining a presence on the PGA Tour, in South African golf, and in Britain, Locke became the first golfer to fashion his own world-wide tour, presaging the career of Gary Player in the 1960s and 1970s, and Greg Norman in the 1980s and 1990s. Locke's career continued to blossom in the 1950s, crowned by three more victories in the British Open in 1950, 1952 and 1957. He also took home the national championships of South Africa, Germany, France, Switzerland and Egypt during this decade. He was allowed to compete for England in the 1953 Canada Cup, but afterwards represented South Africa and was not allowed to compete on the Ryder Cup team. His final Canada Cup appearance was in 1960, after which he ceased to be a prominent figure in golf.

NANCY LOPEZ
Born Jan. 6, 1957

Dominant LPGA player of the late 1970s, and a prominent player of the 1980s and 1990s. Lopez won the 1972 and 1974 U.S. Girls Junior Amateur, the 1976 Women's NCAA Championship and was undefeated on the 1976 Curtis Cup team, but her career took off in the late 1970s after she turned professional. After winning Rookie of the Year honors in 1977, Lopez won nine tournaments in 1978 including five out of six and a total of seven by mid-June. She won another eight in 1979 and three more in 1980. She has won the LPGA Championship three times (1978, 1985 and 1990), and her 47 career wins place her sixth on the all-time LPGA list.

LLOYD MANGRUM
Aug. 1, 1914-Nov. 17, 1973

Prominent member of the PGA Tour from the 1930s to the 1950s who enjoyed his greatest success in the ten years after the Second World War. Mangrum first won on the Tour in 1940 and gained notice with a runner-up finish in the Masters that year, but after reaching the semi-finals of the 1941 PGA and winning the New Orleans Open and the Crosby in 1942 he was considered one of the leading golfers in the country. Mangrum won the 1946 U.S. Open at Canterbury in a celebrated playoff with Vic Ghezzi and Byron Nelson in which all three tied after the eighteen-hole playoff—Mangrum went on to shoot 72 in the second playoff to win by one. In the late 1940s Mangrum was, after Hogan and Snead, the leading golfer on the Tour, winning a spot on the 1947 and 1949 Ryder Cup teams. In 1951 he finished as leading money-winner and won the Vardon Trophy, and had another outstanding season in 1953 winning four tournaments and the Vardon Trophy. He served as non-playing captain of the victorious 1955 Ryder Cup team, after which his career declined, although he won the 1956 Los Angeles Open and had a Tour victory as late as 1958.

CAROL MANN
Born February 3, 1941

Leading LPGA Tour player of the 1960s and 1970s. Mann started out on the junior amateur circuit, and turned professional in the early 1960s. She won 38 tournaments in all, including the 1965 U.S. Women's Open. Her greatest year was in 1968, when she won ten tournaments (including three consecutive weeks). She led the Tour in victories two other times (1969 and 1975) and won the 1968 Vare Trophy. She won the 1958 Western and Chicago Juniors and the 1960 Chicago Amateur.

JOHN McDERMOTT
Aug. 12, 1891-Aug. l, 1971

McDermott, rather than Francis Ouimet, was the first American-born golfer to win the U.S. Open, a feat he achieved in 1911 at Chicago Golf Club, in a playoff with Mike Brady and George Smith. McDermott had lost a playoff to Alex Smith for the Open title in 1910. McDermott successfully defended his title in 1912, the last American professional to do so until Ralph Guldahl in 1938.

FRED McLEOD
April 25, 1882-May 5, 1976

Prominent player of the 1900s to the 1920s, McLeod won the U.S. Open in a playoff with Willie Smith in 1908 at Myopia Hunt Club. After the First World War he returned to prominence, finishing as runner-up in the 1921 U.S. Open and the 1919 PGA Championship. McLeod was a leading figure in the early days of senior competition, finishing runner-up in the 1937 PGA Seniors Championship, and returning to win the 1938 title at Augusta National.

CARY MIDDLECOFF
Born Jan. 6, 1921

Leading player of the late 1940s and 1950s. Middlecoff began his Tour career with a bang, winning his first tournament in 1947, finishing runner-up in the Masters in 1948, and winning the U.S. Open and seven Tour events in 1949. In 1951 he won another six tournaments including Colonial, and by 1953 he was a member of the Ryder Cup squad. Middlecoff had his best year in 1955, winning six tournaments including the Masters and the Western Open, reached the finals of the PGA Championship, and again won a spot on the Ryder Cup team. In 1956 he won his second U.S. Open, and finished runner-up in 1957, but by the late 50s his game was in decline and, despite a selection to the 1959 Ryder Cup team, he had lost his spot in the forefront of golf to the likes of Palmer and Nicklaus. His final Tour victory was at Memphis in 1961, giving him a career total of 40 titles.

TOM MORRIS, JR.
1851-Dec. 25, 1875

Dominant player of the late 1860s and early 1870s. Young Tom, son of St. Andrews greenkeeper Old Tom Morris, not only dominated golf—he practically re-invented it as well as setting new standards of achievement. Morris won the first of four successive British Open Championships in 1868 at the age of 17. His streak included an 11-stroke victory in 1869 and a 12-stroke victory in 1870 (in a 36-hole format). His 149 in the 1870 British Open over 36 holes was a stroke average that was not equalled until the invention of the rubber-cored ball. After his third consecutive victory, the Championship Belt became his property and the Open was discontinued until a cup was offered as a prize in 1872, whereupon Morris promptly won a fourth consecutive championship. Young Tom introduced the use of the niblick (five-iron) for approach shots. But Young Tom's career was cut tragically short when he died on Christmas Day, 1875, shortly after the death of his young wife in childbirth.

TOM MORRIS, SR.
June 16, 1821-1908

Leading professional, greenkeeper, and course architect of the mid-to-late 19th century. Father of Young Tom Morris, Old Tom was the proprietor of the St. Andrews golf shop, greenkeeper (professional and superintendent), as well as a club maker, course architect, and like son Tom a four-time winner of the British Open. Morris was famous in golf from the early 1840s due to a series of great victories paired with his mentor Allen Robertson against Willie and Jamie Dunn. After serving as apprentice to Robertson, Morris became the greenkeeper at Prestwick in 1851 and remained there through his first three Open Championships, returning to become greenkeeper at St. Andrews where he remained the rest of his life. After the death of Robertson in 1859, Morris became the dominant player in the early years of the British Open, with victories in 1861, 1862, 1864, and 1871. In addition to his four victories, he was four times runner-up in the Open, including finishing second to his son in 1868-69, a unique achievement in golf. Morris laid out many golf courses of the late 19th century and remodeled others, including Royal Dornoch. His apprentices included Donald Ross and Charles Balir Macdonald, and thus his influence has been felt in American golf course architecture.

BYRON NELSON
Born Feb. 4, 1912

The dominant player of the mid-1940s, Nelson won 53 titles in all during his short career on the Tour, which lasted only from 1935-1946. Nelson shot to stardom in 1937 when he won the Masters in the spring and defeated major championship winners Leo Diegel, Johnny Farrell, and Craig Wood at the PGA Championship before losing in the quarterfinals. He also was selected for the 1937 Ryder Cup team which was the first to win on British soil. After a quiet 1938, Nelson won the U.S. Open in 1939, in addition to several Tour victories including the Phoenix and Western Opens. Nelson continued his strong play into the 1940s with wins in the 1940 PGA Championship and the 1942 Masters. Not eligible for military service, Nelson devoted the war years to golf (including a number of war-bond rally exhibitions), and was the dominant player of the time, winning eight tournaments in 1944 and a PGA Tour record 18 in 1945, including the PGA Championship and a record 11 straight tournaments during the winter and spring. Nelson won the Vardon Trophy in 1945 and was voted Athlete of the Year by the Associated Press in recognition of his achievement. Nelson reduced his schedule in 1946 and retired from full-time competition after the 1946 season, although he played on the 1947 Ryder Cup team and occasionally appeared in Tour events during the 1950s (such as his victory in the 1951 Crosby). He did not compete on the Senior circuit, restricting himself to serving as non-playing captain of the 1965 Ryder Cup team, and hosting the Byron Nelson Classic annually since 1968.

JACK NICKLAUS
Born Jan. 21, 1940

Dominant PGA Tour player of the late 1960s and early 1970s. Nicklaus was a golfing prodigy in his native Ohio, playing at Scioto, and under the tutelage of Jack Grout rose rapidly to the front rank of American golf, finishing as runner-up in the U.S. Open at the age of 20, and winning both the NCAA Championship and the U.S. Amateur at 21. He closed his amateur career with his second Walker Cup appearance in 1961.

The second phase of his career began with his decision to turn professional in 1962, and his subsequent victory in the 1962 U.S. Open. Nicklaus' crewcut and chubby features proved unpopular with golfers when he defeated all the crowd favorites in tournament after tournament and, by 1966, had supplanted Arnold Palmer as the leading golfer of the day. But seven major championship victories in the 1960s (the 1962 and 1967 U.S. Opens, the 1966 British Open, the 1963-64 and 1966 Masters, and the 1963 PGA) and several popular victories in the Canada and World Cups (paired with Arnold Palmer) earned Nicklaus the respect of golf fans everywhere. Nicklaus closed his decade with his first Ryder Cup appearance in 1969. His concession of Tony Jacklin's two-foot putt gave Britain a tie in the matches (after five straight losses) and showed the public a magnanimous side of his personality.

The third phase of his career began with a British Open victory in 1970, and during a decade when many golfers expect their games to go into steep decline, Nicklaus won eight more major championships, including his historic 1972 run at the Grand Slam, where he took the first two legs of the Slam at Augusta and Pebble Beach before finishing second to Lee Trevino at Muirfield in the British Open. Nicklaus added two more World Cup appearances, four Ryder Cups, four Australian Opens and the 1970 World Match Play Championship to his portfolio.

The fourth phase of his career began in 1980 with Nicklaus winning both the U.S. Open and the PGA Championship and silencing critics who had begun to suggest that Nicklaus' best days were gone. With golf fans now on his side, he won a hugely popular eighteenth major championship and sixth Masters title in 1986, and continued to show flashes of his old form. He also captained two Ryder Cup teams in 1983 and 1987 to take a spectator's role for the first time in golf.

Although his Tour career had faded by 1990, he proved reluctant to play the PGA Senior Tour and instead has played a limited schedule on both the Senior and regular Tours. Since then, he has had very conspicuous success on the Senior Tour with victories in the Senior Open, the Senior Players Championship, and The Tradition.

FRANCIS OUIMET
May 8, 1893-Sept. 2, 1967

The first American golf celebrity and the dominant amateur until the rise of Bobby Jones. Ouimet was assured of a place in golf's annals after his astonishing playoff victory in the 1913 U.S. Open over Harry Vardon and Ted Ray, considered the best players in the world at the time. Ouimet followed up his upset of the century with a victory in the 1914 Amateur before having his amateur status revoked because of a business association with a sporting goods concern. The outcry over Ouimet's banishment forced the USGA to rescind the ban in 1918, and Ouimet returned to amateur competition. He reached the finals of the Amateur in 1920 and won the Amateur a second time in 1931. In addition, Ouimet played on eight Walker Cup teams between 1922 and 1934, and served as non-playing captain of the Walker Cup team five times between 1936 and 1949. Ouimet subsequently was elected captain of the Royal & Ancient, the first American to hold the post.

ARNOLD PALMER
Born September 10, 1929

Dominant PGA Tour professional of the early 1960s. Palmer first appeared on the national golfing map in 1954 when he captured the U.S. Amateur. Promptly turning professional, he struggled in his early years but captured key championships such as the 1955 Canadian Open and the 1956 Eastern Open before winning the Masters and his first money-title in 1958.

After a solid campaign in 1959 with three victories, Palmer began to dominate the Tour in 1960 when he won eight tournaments (six before July) including the Masters and the U.S. Open before finishing second in the British Open to Kel Nagle, foiling his bid for the Grand Slam. Palmer's commitment to the British Open is credited with reviving interest in the championship in the United States. Palmer continued to dominate the headlines from 1961-64, winning two more Masters titles and two British Opens in addition to two Ryder Cups and four World Cup selections. In the second half of the decade he continued to be successful on Tour with 12 more wins, although he did not secure a major championship despite several runner-up finishes including three in the PGA Championship, the one major he never won.

In the 1970s Palmer faded as a major championship contender after a third-place finish at the 1973 U.S. Open, but he continued to win infrequently in the United States and more so in foreign tournaments (he won the Spanish Open and the British PGA, for example, in this period).

In 1980 Palmer became eligible for the fledgling PGA Senior Tour and promptly recaptured the public's imagination in winning the PGA Seniors Championship in 1980, the U.S. Senior Open in 1981, a second PGA Seniors Championship and the Senior TPC in 1983, and a Senior TPC in 1985. In addition to these major senior titles, Palmer won five other titles between 1981 and 1988.

Palmer continues to compete in Senior and regular Tour events in the 1990s, and has had conspicuous success in the unofficial Senior Skins match, which he has won three times in this decade.

HENRY PICARD
Born Nov. 28, 1907
Prominent PGA Tour player of the late 1930s. Picard was a leading Tour player by the mid-1930s, winning five tournaments in 1935, but he turned in his first outstanding major championship performance with a fifth-place finish in the 1936 U.S. Open, and subsequently won two key points in the 1937 Ryder Cup matches. He broke into the front-rank of American golfers in 1938 with a victory in the Masters in addition to reaching the semi-finals in the PGA Championship. He followed 1938 with a better 1939, winning the PGA Championship in addition to seven other Tour titles and another Ryder Cup appearance. Picard's career quickly declined thereafter and he won his last PGA Tour title in 1941, bringing his career total to 26.

GARY PLAYER
Born November 1, 1935
One of golf's Big Three of the 1960s along with Arnold Palmer and Jack Nicklaus, Gary Player was the first of them to win a career Grand Slam when he won the U.S. Open in 1965. Beginning in the 1950s as a virtually penniless golfer on the European circuit, Player broke through with a win in the 1959 British Open. Although he never played the PGA Tour full-time, he amassed $1.8 million in Tour earnings and was the leading money-winner for 1961. The most-travelled golfer of all time, Player has won tournaments in an astonishing range of countries as well as 13 South African Opens and seven Australian Open titles. Player won eight majors in all, his final victory a stellar come-from-behind victory in the Masters. He followed with two consecutive victories on the regular Tour, which forever put to rest the assertion, made by his detractors, that Player's limited number of Tour victories did not merit him a place in the Big Three. In fact Player was in many ways the finest pressure-player of the three, if lacking Palmer's audacity and Nicklaus' supreme shotmaking. It's characteristic of the man that he won eight majors and yet had only five runner-up finishes (Palmer finished second 11 times and Nicklaus 19 times). Player has also had great success on the Senior Tour, with 18 victories to date including six Senior majors. Like his contemporaries Arnold Palmer and Jack Nicklaus, Player has become involved with international golf course design, and has almost 100 courses to his credit.

BETSY RAWLS
Born May 4, 1928
Prominent LPGA Tour player of the 1950s, 1960s, and 1970s. Rose through the amateur ranks in the late 1940s and after winning the 1949 Trans-National she finished runner-up to Babe Zharias in the 1950 U.S. Women's Open. Turning pro in 1951, she won her first Open Championship. By 1952 she was in the top rank of the LPGA, winning the Western Open in addition to five other tournaments.

Throughout the 1950s she was a consistent winner on the Tour, with major championship victories in the 1953 Open and the 1957 Open, and closed out the decade with victories in the 1959 Western Open and LPGA Championship.

After a strong start in the 1960s with a record fourth win in the Open in 1960, Rawls was not able to continue her blazing 1950s form. Yet she managed to regain her form to win another major championship in the 1969 LPGA Championship.

JOHNNY REVOLTA
Born April 5, 1911
Prominent PGA Tour player of the 1930s and 1940s, later renowned as an instructor. Revolta burst onto the PGA Tour circuit with a splash, winning five tournaments in 1935 (at age 24) including the PGA Championship. He was the leading money-winner in 1935 and played in the Ryder Cup. Revolta never equalled 1935, although he played on the 1937 Ryder Cup team and won tournaments as late as 1947. Revolta wrote golf instruction books and became a celebrated teacher later in life, and sev-

eral present-day LPGA players including Marlene Floyd are former students.

PAUL RUNYAN
Born July 12, 1908
Prominent PGA Tour player of the 1930s. Runyan was a young phenom in the early 30s, winning the PGA Championship by the age of 24 (in 1933) and making the Ryder Cup team. Runyan won nine events in total during 1933, and seven more in 1934, when he finished as leading money-winner for the Tour. Runyan's career declined in the mid-30s, but revived on the strength of his victory in the 1938 PGA Championship, which led to selection for the phantom 1939 and 1941 Ryder Cup teams. Runyan had a fine run as a senior player, finishing runner-up in the PGA Seniors in 1959-1960, and winning in 1961-62.

GENE SARAZEN
Born Feb. 27, 1902
One of the youngest players ever to win the U.S. Open, Sarazen arrived with a thump in international golf with victories in the 1922 U.S. Open and PGA, plus a successful title defense in 1923 of his PGA crown. Sarazen, in the 1923 PGA, was the last golfer to beat Hagen in a PGA Championship match until 1928. Sarazen's fine play in the 1920s was overshadowed by the successes of Bobby Jones and Walter Hagen, but Sarazen did finish as runner-up in the 1928 British Open in addition to many Tour victories in the period. Following the retirement of Jones and the aging of Hagen, Sarazen emerged as a dominant player, winning eight Tour events in 1930, as well as the British and U.S. Opens in 1932. Sarazen also won the 1933 PGA Championship at Blue Mound for a sixth major championship. Sarazen's final total became seven majors after he won the 1935 Masters with "The shot heard round the world," a double-eagle on the 15th hole that is still considered one of the most exciting events in the modern game. With his victory in the Masters Sarazen also became the first golfer to win the career Grand Slam. Sarazen was a steady Tour circuit player during these years, winning 15 other tournaments and the 1930 leading money-winner title. Sarazen repeated as British Open champion in 1932 and was selected for the Ryder Cup team six consecutive times between 1927 and 1937. In later years Sarazen was an active golf personality, winning fame with a new generation of golfers via his role as host of Shell's Wonderful World of Golf—and through his senior play. Sarazen won the 1954 and 1958 PGA Seniors Championship. Late in life, in 1973 at Troon, The Squire, as he was known for his courtly manner, managed to score a rare hole-in-one at the famed Postage Stamp hole, a feat discussed even more than the plus-fours he continued to wear for golf attire. In the early 1990s he became associated with the Sarazen World Championship of Golf, a tournament played at Chateau Elan in Georgia, where he is a course design consultant.

DENNY SHUTE
Oct. 25, 1904-May 13, 1974
Leading PGA Tour player of the 1930s. Shute had a meteoric career on the Tour circuit, winning selection to the Ryder Cup team in 1931 and subsequently taking the British Open title in 1933 in addition to serving again on the Ryder Cup squad. Shute's career rose to a crescendo in 1936-38, winning the 1936 PGA Championship and defending the title successfully in 1937, as well as winning selection to the Ryder Cup team. As late as 1939 Shute was still a major force in professional golf, losing in a play-off for the U.S. Open. He had a successful run in senior golf, finishing runner-up in the 1955 and 1959 PGA Seniors Championship.

ALEX SMITH
1880-April 20, 1931
Prominent professional of the early 20th century and older brother of Mac Smith. The Scottish native moved to the United States in his teens and at the age of 18 he finished runner-up in the first 72-hole U.S. Open at Myopia Hunt Club. During the early 1900s he was consistently on the leaderboard at the U.S. Open, finishing as runner-up again in 1902 and 1905 before winning in 1906 at Onwentsia and in 1910 at Philadelphia Cricket Club. Also finished third in the U.S. Open three times in addition to victories in the 1903 and 1906 Western Opens.

HORTON SMITH
May 22, 1908-Oct. 15, 1963
Leading player on the embryonic PGA Tour Circuit of the 1930s. Grabbed the attention of the golfing world when he reached the semi-finals of the 1928 PGA Championship as a 20-year-old. Smith won eight Tour events in 1929 and qualified for the

Ryder Cup team where he was one of two Americans to win a singles match. Smith finished third in the 1930 U.S. Open, and reached the quarterfinals of the PGA Championship. In 1931 Smith again reached the quarters of the PGA and played on the Ryder Cup team. In late 1933 Smith entered the peak of his career with a key win in the Ryder Cup singles, followed by a victory in the inaugural Masters in spring 1934. Smith had his greatest year in 1936, leading the PGA Tour money list, reaching the quarterfinals of the PGA and winning a second Masters Championship. In all Smith won 31 tournaments, his last great season coming in 1940 when he had his last victory and finished third in the U.S. Open. He was selected to eight Ryder Cup teams in all (three series were cancelled due to the Second World War) and remained undeafeated in Ryder Cup play.

MAC SMITH

March 18, 1890-Nov. 3, 1949

Widely regarded as the greatest player never to win a major, Smith was a perennial contender from the 1910s to the 1930s who managed many classic victories. The younger brother of U.S. Open champion Alex Smith, Mac first gained notice when he tied his brother (along with John J. McDermott) in the 1910 U.S. Open at Philadelphia Cricket Club, only to lose in the play-off. Smith won the 1912 Western Open, but disappeared from the leaderboards for several years, only to come roaring back during the golf boom of the Roaring 20s. Smith won the 1925 Western Open, and had an outstanding season in 1926 when he won five tournaments highlighted by victory in the Texas and Canadian Opens. Smith won the lucrative Los Angeles Open four times, in 1928, 1929, 1932, and 1934, but perhaps his great claim to fame was as an asterisk to history, since he finished as runner-up to Bobby Jones on both legs of Jones' 1930 Grand Slam that were open to professionals—the British and U.S. Opens. Smith had success in the early 1930s but by 1940 his star had dimmed.

SAM SNEAD

Born May 27, 1912

The all-time leading tournament winner for the PGA Tour (81 in all, and a total of 135 tournaments worldwide) who was a leading player from the 1930s to the 1970s on the Tour. Snead was a late bloomer for the period, winning his first tournament in 1936 and joining the Tour in 1937. He won five victories in all in 1937 including the Crosby, played on the Ryder Cup team and finished third on the money-winning list. His 1938 campaign was even more spectacular, with eight victories including the Crosby and the Canadian Open, and the first of four runner-up finishes in the U.S. Open. Snead won the Vardon Trophy and was the leading money-winner for the year. His career took a backseat to the meteoric rise of Byron Nelson and Ben Hogan in the late 1930s and early 1940s, but he won twelve more tournaments in 1939-41, including another Crosby and two Canadian Opens. Snead finally won a major championship in 1942 with a victory in the PGA, but his appearances were limited throughout the War.

In 1945 Snead returned to an active schedule and he won six tournaments in 1945 and another five in 1946 plus the only British Open he ever competed in, at St. Andrews. After off-years in 1947 and 1948, Snead shook off his slump with the finest year of his career in 1949, winning the Vardon Trophy, playing on the winning Ryder Cup team, and winning two major championships (his first Masters and second PGA Championship) in addition to a runner-up finish in the U.S. Open and victories in four regular Tour events. He continued his strong form into 1950 with 11 Tour victories (a total not equaled since), including his fourth Crosby and runner-up finish in the PGA Championship.

He remained at the pinnacle of golf throughout the 1950s, especially with the fading of such longtime rivals as Ben Hogan and Byron Nelson. Snead took the 1951 PGA as well as the 1952 and 1954 Masters to reach a total of seven major championship victories. He represented the United States in the 1953 and 1955 Ryder Cup matches and paired with Ben Hogan to win the 1956 Canada Cup. By the late 1950s, however, his age was beginning to show in the week-to-week Tour grind as he slipped to 45th on the money list by the end of the decade. Snead also captained the winning 1959 Ryder Cup team and was undeafeated in two matches.

Snead's place in golf during the 1960s was very unusual, as he became the first golfer to maintain an active and successful presence in both senior and regular competition. He scored a PGA Tour-record eighth victory in the Greater Greensboro Open in 1965, fully six months after his first senior victories in the PGA Senior Championship and the World Seniors. Snead also represented the United States in three consecutive Canada Cup victories in 1960-1962, winning the individual title at Dorado in Puerto Rico in 1961. Later in the decade Snead won two more PGA Seniors Championships in 1965 and 1967, and he captained the United States team to the historic tie in the 1969 Ryder Cup matches.

In the 1970s, Snead did not play a major role on the world golfing scene, but he continued to make headlines with several outstanding performances. In 1973 he won the PGA Seniors Championship by an amazing fifteen strokes over Julius Boros, and in 1974 finished third in the PGA Championship behind Lee Trevino and Jack Nicklaus. In 1979 he shot his age in the Quad Cities Open (67), and then bettered it in the next round with a 66. But 1979 was the last year he won money in a Tour event.

Snead was active in the early years of the 1980s on the fledgling PGA Senior Tour, and won the 1980 Golf Digest Commemorative and the 1982 Legends of Golf paired with Don January. During the late 1980s his appearances were limited to the Senior Tour and the Masters. Snead surprised crowds with a playoff loss in the par-three tournament at the 1992 Masters, at the age of 80.

LOUISE SUGGS
Born Sept. 7, 1923

Prominent amateur of the late 1940s and a leading LPGA Tour player of the 1950s and 1960s. Suggs shocked women's golf in 1946 by winning two major championships—the Titleholders and the Western Open—as an 18-year-old amateur. She won the 1947 Women's Amateur after finishing as medalist in qualifying and, after three North and South Amateur titles, decided to try her luck in the pro ranks. She found almost immediate success in the embryonic WPGA with major championships in the 1947 and 1949 Western Opens and became a founder of the LPGA after winning the 1949 Open.

Suggs hit a peak in the 1950s with six more major championships (the 1952 Open, 1957 LPGA, 1953 Western, and the 1954, 1956, and 1959 Titleholders). During the decade she was also a three-time runner-up in the Open, and a multiple tournament winner on the regular LPGA Tour circuit, in addition to taking the Vare Trophy in 1957.

Suggs was one of the few 1950s standouts to build a successful career in the 1960s—Suggs won an average of two tournaments a year for the first half of the decade. Her career dwindled in the late 1960s and by the 1970s she was rarely in contention.

JOHN H. TAYLOR
March 19, 1871-February, 1963.

Leading British professional of the 1890s, 1900s and 1910s. Taylor was one of the Great Triumvirate of Harry Vardon, Taylor and James Braid that dominated golf between 1900 and the First World War. Taylor was the first of the trio to achieve national golfing success, winning the 1894 British Open and repeating his success in 1895. He finished runner-up to Harry Vardon in 1896 and did not challenge for the title in the remainder of the decade.

In the 1900s Taylor found his greatest success—despite the vigorous competition between Braid, Vardon and Taylor, J.H. won the 1900 and 1909 championships and was runner-up four times, from 1904-07. In addition he won the 1904 and 1907 British PGA as well as the 1907 and 1909 French Open.

In the 1910s Taylor's age began to tell, but he managed to win the 1913 British Open and finish runner-up to Vardon in the 1914 events. He also won the 1912 German Open. He concluded his active career as a player with the First World War.

PETER THOMSON
Born Aug. 23, 1929

Prominent Australian golfer of the 1950s and 1960s, active on both the PGA and European Tours. Thomson's great achievement was in the British Open, where he first leapt into the spotlight in 1952, at the age of 22, with a runner-up finish to Bobby Locke. After another runner-up finish in 1953, Thomson won the first of his Open titles at Royal Birkdale. After successfully defending his crown at St. Andrews in 1955, Thomson became the first player in 70 years to win three consecutive titles with an Open title in 1956. Thomson also won the Texas Open in 1956 and had a career-best fourth-place finish in the U.S. Open. After a runner-up finish in 1957, Thomson won a fourth title in 1958 at Royal Lytham.

Thomson's career slowed significantly in the 1960s, but Thomson managed a fifth victory in the British Open with a 1965 win at Southport. He was not heard much of after this time except as an administrator, until the birth of the Senior Tour.

He joined the Tour soon after turning 50 but waited until 1985 and age 55 to have his greatest year, with a record nine victories. In addition to his major championship and Senior victories, Thomson won three Australian Opens, nine New Zealand Opens, and the national championships of an assortment of colonies and nations, including Germany, Hong Kong, Holland, Spain and Italy.

JEROME S. TRAVERS
May 19, 1887-March 30, 1951

Leading amateur of the 1900s and 1910s. Travers had his first successes in the U.S. Amateur, winning in 1907 and 1908 at Euclid and Garden City, respectively. Travers won back-to-back Amateurs again in 1912-13, becoming the first player to win four Amateur titles. After losing in the final of the 1914 Amateur to Francis Ouimet, Travers had his greatest season in golf in 1915 when he became one of the few amateurs ever to win the U.S. Open. Travers set a record for widest victory margin in the first round of the 1915 Amateur (14&13 over 36 holes) but could not complete the rare Amateur/Open double.

WALTER TRAVIS
1862-1927

Australian-born amateur who was the dominant force in amateur golf during the 1900s. Travis won the 1900, 1901 and 1903 Amateurs to become the first player to ever win the title three times. Travis finished second to Laurie Aucterlonie in the 1902 U.S. Open, just missing that rare double. But Travis achieved a rare double of his own by becoming the first golfer to win the British and U.S. Amateurs with his British Amateur victory in 1904.

LEE TREVINO
Born December 1, 1939

Leading PGA Tour golfer of the 1970s who has become the most recognizable and successful golfer on the Senior Tour. Trevino was a golf-range assistant pro in Texas who made a living with golf hustling before breaking through with an astonishing victory in the 1968 U.S. Open at Oak Hill. Subsequently joining the Tour full-time, Trevino went on to record six major championships and 27 Tour victories, including the British, Canadian and U.S. Opens in 1971 (a record never equalled). Trevino broke up Jack Nicklaus' bid for the Grand Slam in 1972 by winning the British Open at Muirfield, and won the 1974 and 1984 PGA Championships. In addition to his individual accomplishments, Trevino was selected to six Ryder Cup teams and was non-playing captain in 1985, as well as playing in five World Cups (and winning the individual title in 1969). Trevino moved to the Senior Tour and lit up the circuit with eight victories in 1990 including the U.S. Senior Open. Trevino has won four Senior majors in all and 27 Senior Tour titles to date.

HARRY VARDON
May 9, 1870-March 20, 1937

Leading British professional of the 1890s, 1900s, and 1910s. Vardon was the best player and best known of the Great Triumvirate that dominated golf between 1900 and 1914.

Vardon became well-known after breaking J.H. Taylor's lock on the British Open with a victory in 1896. He continued his great success with back-to-back victories in the 1898-99 British Open, and crowned his success by taking the 1900 U.S. Open title during an exhibition tour of the United States.

Vardon became the first professional golfer to attract such a following that he could sustain himself as a full-time professional and live off his prize earnings and exhibition fees throughout the world. In this respect he presaged the globe-trotting Walter Hagen and wandering foreign players such as Bobby Locke, Peter Thomson, and Gary Player. Vardon popularized the modern overlapping grip (usually known as the Vardon grip) and the modern golf swing that took fullest advantage of the flight characteristics of the rubber-cored ball.

After two more British Open Championships in 1900 and 1903 plus runner-up finishes in 1901-02, Vardon was severely affected by a bout of tuberculosis and by the putting yips (so severe that he once whiffed a putt in competition), and he was not a factor for the remainder of the decade. But he regained his health and form in the 1910s and won two more British Opens (in 1911 and 1914) and had runner-up finishes in the 1912 British Open and the 1913 U.S. Open. After the War, Vardon made only one run at a major championship, finishing runner-up in the 1920 U.S. Open.

GLENNA COLLETT VARE

Born June 20, 1903

Dominant woman player in the United States during the 1920s and early 1930s. She began her career in the 1920s with four U.S. Women's Amateurs, in 1922, 1925, 1928, and 1929 and also won the 1923 and 1924 Canadian Ladies.

In the 1930s she continued to win championships, with two more victories in the U.S. Women's Amateur (the last in 1935), as well as three appearances for the USA on the Curtis Cup squad.

In addition to these national championships, Vare was a six-time champion of the prestigious North and South championship, and served as captain of the Curtis Cup team in 1948 and as non-playing captain in 1950.

TOM WATSON

Born September 4, 1949

The dominant PGA Tour player of the late 1970s and early 1980s, Watson was a little known college golfer noted more for a wild swing than success. He broke through with the British Open title in 1975 and proceeded to topple Jack Nicklaus as the game's greatest player. Defeating Nicklaus at Turnberry in 1977 in what has been called "the most exciting tournament ever played," Watson went on to collect an astonishing five British Open titles in all as well as two PGA titles and the 1982 U.S. Open. Watson's bold putting skills disappeared rapidly and mysteriously after the 1984 season. After winning 29 titles between 1975 and 1984, Watson has won only once in the twelve campaigns since, although he remains highly competitive with the best in the world from tee to green.

JOYCE WETHERED

Born Nov. 7, 1901

Dominant English female amateur of the early 1920s. Wethered had a brief but extremely active career in golf, first winning the English Ladies Championship in 1920. In 1921 she repeated her victory in the English Amateur, but had her greatest success in 1922 and 1924 when she won both the British Ladies Amateur and the English Ladies Amateur. Wethered won two more British Ladies Amateurs in 1925 and 1929 in addition to the 1923 English Ladies Amateur.

KATHY WHITWORTH

Born Sept. 27, 1939

Dominant player of the 1960s and 1970s on the LPGA Tour. After a solid amateur career in the 1950s, Whitworth turned pro at age 19 in 1958 and won her first LPGA victory in 1962. From 1965 until the end of the decade, Whitworth was the dominant player on the Tour, never winning fewer than seven tournaments in a year and taking home four major championships, including the 1965-66 Titleholders, and the 1967 Western Open and LPGA Championship. She also won the 1965-67 and 1969 Vare Trophies.

Whitworth picked up in 1970 where she left off in 1969 and steamrolled to twenty-eight Tour victories in the decade, including the 1970 and 1975 LPGA Championships. After winning the Vare Trophy from 1970-72, however, Whitworth's successes began to be spaced further and further apart.

The 1980s began strongly for Whitworth with at least one victory per season from 1981-85. In addition, Whitworth became the first woman to earn $1 million in prize money, one of two women selected for the Legends of Golf, and a Hall of Famer. She has not won since 1985 but her LPGA-sanctioned victories totaled eighty-eight wins, a record that still stands in all of professional golf.

CRAIG WOOD

Nov. 18, 1901-May 8, 1968

Prominent PGA Tour player of the 1930s and 1940s, Wood still holds the record for the longest drive ever hit in major championship play (430 yards on the fifth hole at St. Andrews in the British Open). Wood arrived late on the Tour but gained attention in 1929 when he reached the quarterfinals of the PGA Championship. Wood earned a selection to the victorious 1931 Ryder Cup team. He won 3 tournaments in 1932 and in 1933 lost the British Open in a playoff to Denny Shute. His 1934 season was his most successful to date. Wood played Ryder Cup and repeated his runner-up finish at Augusta in the 1935 Masters, while in 1936 he reached the semi-finals of the 1936 PGA—but he didn't recapture top form until 1941, when he won the U.S. Open. In 1942 he won his second major, the Masters, as well as the 1942 Canadian Open. After the war Wood disappeared from the Tour golfing scene, and did not play on any Senior circuit.

MICKEY WRIGHT

Born Feb. 14, 1935

Dominant LPGA Tour player of the early 1960s. Wright first gained attention for winning the 1952 U.S. Girls Junior Amateur. After losing in the finals of the 1954 Women's Amateur, Wright turned professional in 1956 and won a total of 82 LPGA events in her career. She won the 1958 Women's Open and the LPGA Championship to enter the front rank of LPGA players, and closed out the 1950s with five wins in 1959 including a second U.S. Open.

Her greatest years were in the 1960s, however, and she began the decade with six wins in 1960 including the LPGA Championship. In 1961 she was the leading money-winner and won three of the four major championships, failing to win only the LPGA. In 1962 she won the money-title and an astonishing ten events, including four in a row, and her eighth and ninth majors in the Titleholders and the Western Open. Her 1963 campaign was the most spectacular of all, with thirteen wins and two more majors in the LPGA and the Western Open. Her 1964 results were only slightly less spectacular, with the money-title, eleven victories, and a twelfth major at the U.S. Women's Open. Wright tied Betsy Rawls' record for most victories in the Open. Plagued by injuries, she sharply reduced her schedule in 1965 and never again played more than 22 events on Tour in a year. Consequently she was less of a dominant player, although a thirteenth major victory in the 1967 Western Open plus at least one win per year throughout the decade proved she was still a force to be reckoned with.

Beginning in 1970, Wright became a part-time player on Tour—hence, she rarely won, although she stayed in the top-50 on the money list as late as 1977. In 1979 she made one last run at a title but lost to Nancy Lopez in the Coca-Cola Classic.

Wright's playing schedule in the 1980s was limited to just three official events, and she did not play a decisive role in any of them. But her U.S. Open record of four wins still stands, and her record of 82 wins has been eclipsed to date only by Kathy Whitworth.

BABE ZAHARIAS

June 26, 1911-September 27, 1956

America's first female golf celebrity and leading player of the 1940s and 1950s. Zaharias first came to national attention as a track and field star, winning a record five gold medals at the 1932 Olympic Games in Los Angeles. Turning to golf, her national fame as an athlete brought a new level of awareness to women's golf. Although originally classified as a professional, she won back her amateur status during the Second World War and won the 1946-47 U.S. Women's Amateur as well as the 1947 British Amateur and three Western Open victories. Formally turning professional in 1947, she dominated the WPGA and later the LPGA (of which she was a founding member) until illness shortened her career in the mid-1950s. She won the 1947 Titleholders and the 1948 U.S. Women's Open for her fourth and fifth major championships.

Zaharias had her greatest year in 1950 when she completed the Grand Slam of the Women's Open, the Titleholders, and the Western Open, in addition to leading the money-list. She was the leading money-winner again in 1951 and in 1952 took another major with a Titleholders victory, but illness prevented her from playing a full schedule in 1952-53. She made a comeback in 1954 and took the Vare Trophy and her tenth and final major with a U.S. Women's Open championship. She fell ill again in 1955 and limited her schedule to eight events, but she managed two wins which were her final ones in competitive golf. Cancer took its toll and Zaharias died in 1956 while still in the top rank of female American golfers.

GOLF INSTRUCTORS

OVERVIEW: *Biographies of leading golf instructors associated with the major national golf schools. Source: Peterson's Golf Schools and Resorts*

JIMMY BALLARD

The one, the only, the inimitable Jimmy Ballard—he swept into national recognition on the basis of his articles on the "Seven Common Denominators" of the golf swing and instruction's "Misleading Terms," which gained a certain notoriety in the late 1970s and are widely accepted today. Jimmy's two early innovations were an emphasis on videotaped swing analysis instead of stop-action photography and his expansion of the definition of great ball strikers beyond golf—identifying great "golf" swings by looking at Joe DiMaggio and Arthur Ashe, for instance. After teaching amateurs for several years, Ballard leapt into national prominence on the basis of his reconstruction of Mac McLendon's swing in the late 1970s which led to three Tour victories for the veteran pro. Since then almost 200 Tour professionals have made the trek to Jimmy's teaching facilities in Alabama, Florida and South Carolina. Curtis Strange, Seve Ballesteros, Hal Sutton, Jerry Pate, Johnny Miller, Hubert Green, and Sandy Lyle are among his major championship winning students. Ballard is also the "guru" who has worked consistently with Jesper Parnevik in helping the unknown Swede to a runner-up finish in the British Open. Ballard is the author of How to Perfect Your Golf Swing as well as a former ESPN swing analyst.

PEGGY KIRK BELL

Peggy Kirk Bell is one of the legends of twentieth century golf, no question about it. Bell was one of the founders of the LPGA Tour and has been recognized by Golf Digest as one of the five most influential women in the game. She was recently honored with the Richardson Award for Distinguished Service, the highest award given by the Golf Writers' Association of America. Bell also received the LPGA Teacher of the Year award, was a two-time Curtis Cup member, the first LPGA Senior champion, winner of many titles including one profesional major championship and is author of "Women's Way to Better Golf" and many articles for national golf publications.

PAUL BERTHOLY

Bob Toski, who would know, calls Bertholy "unquestionably the finest teacher of the golf swing that I have encountered." Leo Fraser, the legendary PGA President, agrees. So did Money Magazine in a two-year study. Bertholy is now 80 years of age but remains an active teacher and a force in the game. Since he has taught legions of PGA teaching professionals in addition to over 100,000 students, his system may well have the most adherents among teaching professionals of any in the country save perhaps Jimmy Ballard's.

KEN BLANCHARD

"Do you want to know the secret about golf?" asks Ken Blanchard in his advertisements—well, the big secret about this school is that...hmmn, Ken Blanchard isn't really much of a golfer compared to most of his colleagues in the golf school game. Blanchard is widely-known as the co-author of *The One-Minute Manager* and *Situational Leadership*. One of his most recent books is *Playing the Great Game of Golf*, which is actually quite good and won him speaking engagements with the National Golf Foundation and a column in LINKS Magazine. In the book, Blanchard applies his innovative management ideas to golf in a way that enhances performance and enjoyment of the game, and The Golf University is designed as an extension of those ideas. To handle the actual instruction, Blanchard has smartly surrounded himself with a capable staff of actual golf instructors under Tom Wischmeyer, but

Blanchard's lack of actual experience in the field and particularly in tournament play makes this school a question mark for serious low-hansicappers and professionals—but excellent for beginners through mid-handicappers.

JIM FLICK

Jim Flick has been one of the nation's top instructors for many years, and Jack Nicklaus needs little introduction either as a player or communicator within the game; but they teamed up late in their careers after Flick's advice had resulted in some noticeable improvements in the Nicklaus game. Flick has trained probably more PGA TOUR pros that any contemporary instructor except perhaps Jimmy Ballard, and has written scores of articles for magazines over the years.

MARLENE FLOYD

Marlene is the younger sister of PGA TOUR star Raymond Floyd, the daughter of influential instructor L.B. Floyd, and an LPGA veteran in her own right who led the LPGA in lowest putting average in 1980 and 1981. Floyd is best known to golfers as a 17-year veteran of golf broadcasts, most recently with NBC. Marlene teaches and plays golf with Fortune 500 executives in numerous corporate outings, and gives many clinics for charity organizations. Aside from her professional credentials, Marlene Floyd is also one of the nicest people in the game.

SHELBY FUTCH

Shelby Futch is John Jacobs' American partner who serves as President and CEO of the Jacobs empire. Shelby is the driving force behind the phenomenal success that the schools have enjoyed. Voted one of the Best 50 Teachers in America by GOLF Magazine, Futch has been published in articles appearing in magazines throughout the world. As a player he is best known for professional tournament play on the Far East and South American Tours and as a past winner of the Illinois PGA Championship.

CHUCK HOGAN

Hogan, president of Sports Enhancements Associates, has taught more than 60 PGA and LPGA tour players, including Johnny Miller, Peter Jacobsen and Colleen Walker. He has produced videos such as "Nice Shot!" and "Aim to Win." He has written five books, is a contributing writer for more than ten magazines (including Golf Magazine and Golf for Women) and has worked with professional athletes in baseball, tennis, gymnastics and track and field. Hogan is a consultant to the golf teams at the University of Arizona, Arizona State and UCLA among others.

JOHN JACOBS

John Jacobs, called "the father of European golf," is one of the most widely known and respected golf instructors in the world. Born in Yorkshire, England, he is well known throughout Europe and is recognized in the United States as "Doctor Golf." His most famous pupil in recent years is Jose-Maria Olazabal. As a player, Jacobs won the Dutch Open, and the South Africa Match Play Championship (defeating Gary Player in the final). Jacobs has captained two Ryder Cup teams and coached a Walker Cup team to victory.

DAVID LEADBETTER

David Leadbetter has built his reputation over the past ten years on the basis of his outstanding success as a pro's pro—first with Nick Price, later with Nick Faldo, and today with practically everyone, it seems. Leadbetter is a native of England who played on the African mini- and junior circuits years ago and became noted among the players for his ferocious interest in swing theory and mechanics. He met Nick Price during this period, who remembers him as always having his head in a book. It was Price's slump in the mid-1980s that marked Leadbetter's rise to prominence as an instructor, as Price has always given great credit to Leadbetter for the improvements in his swing. Leadbetter was also behind the much-vaunted re-building of Nick Faldo's swing and was criticized for his suggestion to Faldo that he should embark on a weight-training program to build the large upper-body muscles.

Leadbetter's book *Faults and Fixes* is one of the minor classics of instruction, and since the late 1980s he has been associated with International Management Group to expand the scope of his activities into the golf school, an expanded publishing schedule, and also into broadcast. Leadbetter was perhaps the first instructor to be retained as a color commentator for a major golf broadcast when he worked the 1993 World Cup at Lake Nona.

Leadbetter makes his home at Lake Nona Golf

Club and the school is headquartered there. But rapid expansion has brought his Academy to nine locations in six countries to date.

JIM MCLEAN

Jim McLean, called "one of the top three teachers in the game today" by PGA TOUR veteran Peter Jacobsen, is one of the 300 Master PGA Professionals out of 22,500 PGA members, and has taught a large number of successful touring professionals and prominent amateurs over the years, including Steve Elkington, Bill Murray, Tom Kite and Bruce Lietzke. Brad Faxon relates that "Jim has taught me more about golf than any other teacher," and 1993 U.S. Women's Open champion Laurie Merten says "Jim and his staff helped me with my attitude while reinforcing the mechanics I needed to succeed on Tour."

JAY OVERTON

Jay Overton founded the Innisbrook Golf Institute in 1979 and might still be running it today if not for his playing schedule—he is one of the elite club professional players winning any number of PGA sectional events and in 1993 playing the PGA TOUR full-time after becoming the oldest player ever to qualify for the TOUR via the grueling Q-School experience.

DAVE PELZ

After 14 years as a NASA research scientist at Goddard Space Center, Dave re-committed his career to the science of golf. For the past 16 years, he has studied the game full-time, from testing and developing equipment, to manufacturing and teaching the finest players in the world. To his successful students such as Tom Kite, D.A Weibring, Tom Sieckmann, Beth Daniel and many others, Dave Pelz is known as "Professor Putt." His book "Putt Like the Pros" is considered the definitive book on putting in the world. Prior to 1985, Pelz worked primarily with PGA and LPGA tour professionals, but in the past ten years has restructured his short game instruction to include small groups of amateurs.

KIP PUTERBAUGH

Kip Puterbaugh has been named by GOLF Magazine as one of the top 50 teaching pros in the country on the strength of his programs at Aviara. Puterbaugh is a noted student of the game apt to quote swing gurus from an earlier era such as Harvey Penick, Norm von Nida and George Knudsen in the course of his sessions. Puterbaugh has authored many articles on golf instruction, including a recent cover story for Golf Digest. He is author of "The Body Swing," published in Japan and Korea, and has created a three-part video series with NBC commentator Charlie Jones. Among his students are PGA TOUR players Dennis Paulson and Scott Simpson.

PHIL RODGERS

Phil Rodgers has been recognized by GOLF Magazine as one of the 50 best instructors in America, making Grand Cypress one of a handful of schools with two top-ranked teachers. Rodgers has been a Class A PGA professional for over 25 years, and prior to his teaching career was a noted touring professional with six PGA victories and a second-place finish in the 1963 British Open, losing in a playoff to Bob Charles at Royal Lytham. Like Charles, Rodgers has gone on to a successful career on the Senior Tour—but in recent years he has become best known as an instructor, with several PGA and LPGA players among his students, most notably Jack Nicklaus. Nicklaus, in fact, recommended Rodgers to the Academy, where he serves as an advisor and instructor for the occasional Phil Rodgers series of advanced instruction.

RICK SMITH

One of the newest of the golf gurus, Smith is a three-time Michigan PGA Teacher of the Year, who doubles as the Director of Golf at the Treetops resort, and triples as a golf course architect with the third (Rick Smith Signature) course at Treetops to his credit. Smith's students run the gamut from beginners to over 100 TOUR players including Lee Janzen, Rocco Mediate and Billy Andrade. Smith was recognized as one of GOLF Magazine's 50 best golf instructors and is a former Spalding National Teacher of the Year.

ROLAND STAFFORD

Stafford has been playing and teaching golf since 1959. A graduate of Northwestern University, he holds a masters in Music Education from the University of Arizona. He has had a successful playing career including several top-10 finishes on the

Senior PGA TOUR, plus victories in the Pennsylvania Open, the Grand Bahama Island Open and three PGA section championships. Stafford has his own line of golf clubs, "The Stafford Legato," and is author of the instructional book and tape "Roland Stafford's Golf Course."

BEN SUTTON

Ben Sutton's philosophy (1908-1991) remains the driving force behind the Ben Sutton golf schools. His primary innovation was to take golf instruction off the driving range and onto the golf course, noting that range-based instruction often failed to translate into real scoring improvements in actual playing conditions. Sutton was also the first to commit to a practice facility larger than the usual assortment of range, practice greens and practice bunkers. Golf course architects such as Jack Nicklaus, Tom Fazio, Arnold Palmer and Ed Seay are now intimately involved with the design and construction of practice holes and facilities as a result of Sutton's influence and success.

DON TRAHAN

A PGA Master Professional and rated one of the top 50 instructors in the country by GOLF Magazine, Trahan became known as "The Swing Surgeon" for his ability to dissect swing problems and instantly offer prescriptions and cures. A PGA professional since 1972, Trahan is a GOLF Magazine teaching editor as well as the author of several books, a video and the computer program Compu-Golf. Don has worked with several touring professionals, but his most remarkable work may well be with his own son, D.J. Trahan, who in 1994 became the youngest player ever to qualify for the U.S. Junior Amateur (at the ripe old age of 13, ahead of the pace set by Jack Nicklaus, Phil Mickelson and Tiger Woods, among others).

KEN VENTURI

Ken Venturi hardly needs an introduction as the CBS Sports golf analyst for the past 28 years. But he's been so long in the broadcast booth that perhaps a few words of introduction to Ken Venturi the golfer would be appropriate. Venturi was one of the leading young amateurs of the early 1950s and turned professional in 1956 after finishing runner-up at The Masters. He won 14 PGA TOUR events in his storied career, including a dramatic victory in the 1964 U.S. Open at Congressional, when the mercury passed 100 degrees in the final round and Venturi overcame heat exhaustion in the final holes to score one of the most dramtic Open victories ever. *Sports Illustrated* named Venturi its Sportsman of the Year for 1964. Venturi went on to play on the 1965 Ryder Cup team and, after joining CBS Sports in the late 1960s, began to build a considerable reputation as a golf analyst and teacher. He was named one of the Ten Living Legends of Golf Instruction by the PGA of America in 1992.

CARL WELTY

Carl Welty is something of a Mad Scientist when it comes to golf instruction—but in the best sense of the term. He has assembled the world's largest collection of videotapes of the world's great golf swings. When he founded the La Costa Golf School in 1964 he had already been working with video golf instruction for over 20 years. As of this writing Welty now has 160 miles of tape on players' golf swings dating back 15 years. My favorite Welty story is his analysis of touring pro Peter Jacobsen. He freeze-framed Jake's five-iron swing at impact, placed a protractor on the screen and measured the angle formed by the five-iron and the ground. The angle was 61 degrees, while Welty's notes show that the angle for tournament winners falls between 53 and 55 degrees. He made notes for Jacobsen's improvement.

Now, that's swing analysis.

PENNY ZAVICHAS

"We didn't just get into women's golf. We helped elevate it and encourage it." So reports owner Penny Zavichas—who is the niece of women's golfing pioneer and Olympic champion Babe Didrickson Zaharias. Zavichas was introduced by Zaharias to golf in the 1950s and since then has amassed a pile of credentials, including a Master Professional rating from the LPGA and the LPGA Teacher of the Year Award. She's taught now since 1959—36 years in the business, and has certainly found her way around a golf swing. Zavichas still makes cameo appearances at most of the LPGA and PGA Teaching Summits as one of the two or three leading golf teachers for women. Zavichas has one of the most credible endorsements in golf—from Karsten Solheim, designer of PING Golf equipment and founder of Karsten Manufacturing.

MAJOR CHAMPIONSHIP WINNERS OF THE PAST

OVERVIEW: *Winners, runners-up and prize money for the four major championships on the PGA TOUR, Senior PGA TOUR, and the LPGA Tour.*

Men's Major Championships

THE MASTERS

Augusta National Golf Club, Augusta, GA

YEAR	WINNER	SCORE	RUNNER-UP
1934	Horton Smith	284	Craig Wood
1935	*Gene Sarazen	282	Craig Wood
1936	Horton Smith	285	Harry Cooper
1937	Byron Nelson	283	Ralph Guldahl
1938	Henry Picard	285	Ralph Guldahl
			Harry Cooper
1939	Ralph Guldahl	279	Sam Snead
1940	Jimmy Demaret	280	Lloyd Mangrum
1941	Craig Wood	280	Byron Nelson
1942	*Byron Nelson	280	Ben Hogan
1943	*No Tournament*	—	————
1944	*No Tournament*	—	————
1945	*No Tournament*	—	————
1946	Herman Keiser	282	Ben Hogan
1947	Jimmy Demaret	281	Byron Nelson
			Frank Stranahan
1948	Claude Harmon	279	Cary Middlecoff
1949	Sam Snead	282	Johnny Bulla
			Lloyd Mangrum
1950	Jimmy Demaret	283	Jim Ferrier
1951	Ben Hogan	280	Skee Riegel
1952	Sam Snead	286	Jack Burke, Jr.
1953	Ben Hogan	274	Ed Oliver, Jr.
1954	*Sam Snead	289	Ben Hogan
1955	Cary Middlecoff	279	Ben Hogan
1956	Jack Burke, Jr.	289	Ken Venturi
1957	Doug Ford	282	Sam Snead
1958	Arnold Palmer	284	Doug Ford
			Fred Hawkins

* *Won in playoff*

YEAR	WINNER	SCORE	RUNNER-UP
1959	Art Wall, Jr.	284	Cary Middlecoff
1960	Arnold Palmer	282	Ken Venturi
1961	Gary Player	280	Charles Coe
			Arnold Palmer
1962	*Arnold Palmer	280	Gary Player
			Dow Finsterwald
1963	Jack Nicklaus	286	Tony Lema
1964	Arnold Palmer	276	Dave Marr
			Jack Nicklaus
1965	Jack Nicklaus	271	Arnold Palmer
			Gary Player
1966	*Jack Nicklaus	288	Tommy Jacobs
			Gay Brewer, Jr.
1967	Gay Brewer, Jr.	280	Bobby Nichols
1968	Bob Goalby	277	Roberto DeVicenzo
1969	George Archer	281	Billy Casper
			George Knudson
			Tom Weiskopf
1970	*Billy Casper	279	Gene Littler
1971	Charles Coody	279	Johnny Miller
			Jack Nicklaus
1972	Jack Nicklaus	286	Bruce Crampton
			Bobby Mitchell
			Tom Weiskopf
1973	Tommy Aaron	283	J.C. Snead
1974	Gary Player	278	Tom Weiskopf
			Dave Stockton
1975	Jack Nicklaus	276	Johnny Miller
			Tom Weiskopf
1976	Ray Floyd	271	Ben Crenshaw
1977	Tom Watson	276	Jack Nicklaus
1978	Gary Player	277	Hubert Green
			Rod Funseth
			Tom Watson
1979	*Fuzzy Zoeller	280	Ed Sneed
			Tom Watson
1980	Seve Ballesteros	275	Gibby Gilbert
			Jack Newton
1981	Tom Watson	280	Johnny Miller
			Jack Nicklaus
1982	*Craig Stadler	284	Dan Pohl
1983	Seve Ballesteros	280	Ben Crenshaw
			Tom Kite
1984	Ben Crenshaw	277	Tom Watson

* Won in playoff

YEAR	WINNER	SCORE	RUNNER-UP
1985	Bernhard Langer	282	Curtis Strange
			Seve Ballesteros
			Ray Floyd
1986	Jack Nicklaus	279	Greg Norman
			Tom Kite
1987	*Larry Mize	285	Seve Ballesteros
			Greg Norman
1988	Sandy Lyle	281	Mark Calcavecchia
1989	*Nick Faldo	283	Scott Hoch
1990	*Nick Faldo	278	Ray Floyd
1991	Ian Woosnam	277	Jose-Maria Olazabal
1992	Fred Couples	275	Ray Floyd
1993	Bernhard Langer	277	Chip Beck
1994	Jose-Maria Olazabal	279	Tom Lehman
1995	Ben Crenshaw	274	Davis Love III

The United States Open Championship

DATE	WINNER	SCORE	RUNNER-UP	SITE
1895	Horace Rawlins	173	Willie Dunn	Newport G. C., Newport, RI
1896	James Foulis	152	Horace Rawlins	Shinnecock Hills G. C., Southampton, NY
1897	Joe Lloyd	162	Willie Anderson	Chicago G. C., Wheaton, IL
1898	Fred Herd	328	Alex Smith	Myopia Hunt Club, S. Hamilton, MA
1899	Willie Smith	315	George Low	Baltimore C. C.
			Val Fitzjohn	(Roland Park Course),
			W.H. Way	Baltimore, MD
1900	Harry Vardon	313	J.H. Taylor	Chicago G. C., Wheaton, IL
1901	*Willie Anderson	331	Alex Smith	Myopia Hunt Club, S. Hamilton, MA
1902	Laurence Auchterlonie	307	Stewart Gardner	Garden City G. C.,
			Walter J. Travis	Garden City, NY
1903	*Willie Anderson	307	David Brown	Baltusrol G. C. (original course), Springfield, NJ
1904	Willie Anderson	303	Gilbert Nicholls	Glen View Club, Golf, IL
1905	Willie Anderson	314	Alex Smith	Myopia Hunt Club, S. Hamilton, MA
1906	Alex Smith	295	William Smith	Onwentsia Club, Lake Forest, IL

*Won in playoff

DATE	WINNER	SCORE	RUNNER-UP	SITE
1907	Alex Ross	302	Gilbert Nicholls	Philadelphia Cricket C. (St. Martin's Course), Philadelphia, PA
1908	*Fred McLeod	322	Willie Smith	Myopia Hunt Club, S. Hamilton, MA
1909	George Sargent	290	Tom McNamara	Englewood G. C., Englewood, NJ
1910	*Alex Smith	298	John J. McDermott Macdonald Smith	Philadelphia Cricket C. (St. Martin's Course), Philadelphia, PA
1911	*John J. McDermott	307	Michael J. Brady George O. Simpson	Chicago G. C., Wheaton, IL
1912	John J. McDermott	294	Tom McNamara	C. C. of Buffalo, Buffalo, NY
1913	*Francis Ouimet	304	Harry Vardon Edward Ray	The Country Club (Original Course), Brookline, MA
1914	Walter Hagen	290	Charles Evans, Jr.	Midlothian C. C., Blue Island, IL
1915	Jerome D. Travers	297	Tom McNamara	Baltusrol G. C., (Revised Course), Springfield, NJ
1916	Charles Evans, Jr.	286	Jock Hutchison	Minikahda Club, Minneapolis, MN
1917	*No Championship*			
1918	*No Championship*			
1919	*Walter Hagen	301	Michael J. Brady	Brae Burn C. C., West Newton, MA
1920	Edward Ray	295	Harry Vardon Jack Burke, Sr. Leo Diegel Jock Hutchison	Inverness Club, Toledo, OH
1921	James M. Barnes	289	Walter Hagen Fred McLeod	Columbia C. C., Chevy Chase, MD
1922	Gene Sarazen	288	Robert T. Jones, Jr John L. Black	Skokie C. C., Glencoe, IL
1923	*Robert T. Jones, Jr.	296	Bobby Cruickshank	Inwood C. C., Inwood, NY
1924	Cyril Walker	297	Robert T. Jones, Jr.	Oakland Hills C. C. (South Course), Birmingham, MI
1925	William Macfarlane	291	Robert T. Jones, Jr.	Worcester C. C., Worcester, MA
1926	Robert T. Jones, Jr.	293	Joe Turnesa	Scioto C. C., Columbus, OH

*Won in playoff

Major Championship Results—The U.S. Open

DATE	WINNER	SCORE	RUNNER-UP	SITE
1927	*Tommy Armour	301	Harry Cooper	Oakmont C. C., Oakmont, PA
1928	*Johnny Farrell	294	Robert T. Jones, Jr.	Olympia Fields C. C. (North Course), Matteson, IL
1929	*Robert T. Jones, Jr.	294	Al Espinosa	Winged Foot G. C. (West Course), Mamaroneck, NY
1930	Robert T. Jones, Jr.	287	Macdonald Smith	Interlachen C. C., Minneapolis, MN
1931	*Billy Burke	292	George Von Elm	Inverness Club, Toledo, OH
1932	Gene Sarazen	286	Bobby Cruickshank T. Philip Perkins	Fresh Meadow C. C., Flushing, NY
1933	John Goodman	287	Ralph Guldahl	North Shore G. C., Glenview, IL
1934	Olin Dutra	293	Gene Sarazen	Merion Cricket C. (East Course), Ardmore, PA
1935	Sam Parks, Jr.	299	Jimmy Thomson	Oakmont C. C., Oakmont, PA
1936	Tony Manero	282	Harry Cooper	Baltusrol G. C. (Upper Course), Springfield, NJ
1937	Ralph Guldahl	281	Sam Snead	Oakland Hills C. C. (South Course), Birmingham, MI
1938	Ralph Guldahl	284	Dick Metz	Cherry Hills Club, Englewood, CO
1939	*Byron Nelson	284	Craig Wood Denny Shute	Philadelphia C. C. (Spring Mill Course), West Conshohocken, PA
1940	*Lawson Little	287	Gene Sarazen	Canterbury G. C., Cleveland, OH
1941	*Craig Wood	284	Denny Shute	Colonial Club, Fort Worth, TX
1942	No championship			
1943	No championship			
1944	No championship			
1945	No championship			
1946	*Lloyd Mangrum	284	Byron Nelson Vic Ghezzi	Canterbury G. C., Cleveland, OH
1947	*Lew Worsham	282	Sam Snead	St. Louis C. C., Clayton, MO

*Won in playoff

Major Championship Results—The U.S. Open

DATE	WINNER	SCORE	RUNNER-UP	SITE
1948	Ben Hogan	276	Jimmy Demaret	Riviera C. C., Los Angeles, CA
1949	Cary Middlecoff	286	Sam Snead Clayton Heafner	Medinah C. C. (No. 3 Course), Medinah, IL
1950	*Ben Hogan	287	Lloyd Mangrum George Fazio	Merion G. C. (East Course), Ardmore, PA
1951	Ben Hogan	287	Clayton Heafner	Oakland Hills C. C. (South Course), Birmingham, MI
1952	Julius Boros	281	Ed S. Oliver	Northwood Club, Dallas, TX
1953	Ben Hogan	283	Sam Snead	Oakmont C. C., Oakmont, PA
1954	Ed Furgol	284	Gene Littler	Baltusrol G. C. (Lower Course), Springfield, NJ
1955	*Jack Fleck	287	Ben Hogan	Olympic Club (Lake Course), San Francisco, CA
1956	Cary Middlecoff	281	Julius Boros Ben Hogan	Oak Hill C. C. (East Course), Rochester, NY
1957	*Dick Mayer	282	Cary Middlecoff	Inverness Club, Toledo, OH
1958	Tommy Bolt	283	Gary Player	Southern Hills C. C., Tulsa, OK
1959	Bill Casper, Jr.	282	Bob Rosburg	Winged Foot G. C. (West Course), Mamaroneck, NY
1960	Arnold Palmer	280	Jack Nicklaus	Cherry Hills C. C., Englewood, CO
1961	Gene Littler	281	Doug Sanders Bob Goalby	Oakland Hills C. C. (South Course), Birmingham, MI
1962	*Jack Nicklaus	283	Arnold Palmer	Oakmont C. C., Oakmont, PA
1963	*Julius Boros	293	Jacky Cupit Arnold Palmer	The Country Club (Championship Course), Brookline, MA
1964	Ken Venturi	278	Tommy Jacobs	Congressional C. C. (Composite Course), Washington, D.C.

* Won in playoff

DATE	WINNER	SCORE	RUNNER-UP	SITE
1965	*Gary Player	282	Kel Nagle	Bellerive C. C., St. Louis, MO
1966	*Bill Casper, Jr.	278	Arnold Palmer	Olympic Club (Lake Course), San Francisco, CA
1967	Jack Nicklaus	275	Arnold Palmer	Baltusrol G. C. (Lower Course), Springfield, NJ
1968	Lee Trevino	275	Jack Nicklaus	Oak Hill C. C. (East Course), Rochester, NY
1969	Orville Moody	281	Deane Beman Al Geiberger Bob Rosburg	Champions G. C. (Cypress Creek Course), Houston, TX
1970	Tony Jacklin	281	Dave Hill	Hazeltine National G. C., Chaska, MN
1971	*Lee Trevino	280	Jack Nicklaus	Merion G. C. (East Course), Ardmore, PA
1972	Jack Nicklaus	290	Bruce Crampton	Pebble Beach G. L., Pebble Beach, CA
1973	John Miller	279	John Schlee	Oakmont C. C., Oakmont, PA
1974	Hale Irwin	287	Forrest Fezler	Winged Foot G. C. (West Course), Mamaroneck, NY
1975	*Lou Graham	287	John Mahaffey	Medinah C. C. (No. 3 Course), Medinah, IL
1976	Jerry Pate	277	Tom Weiskopf Al Geiberger	Atlanta Athletic C. (Highlands Course), Duluth, GA
1977	Hubert Green	278	Lou Graham	Southern Hills C. C., Tulsa, OK
1978	Andy North	285	J.C. Snead Dave Stockton	Cherry Hills C. C., Englewood, CO
1979	Hale Irwin	284	Gary Player Jerry Pate	Inverness Club, Toledo, OH
1980	Jack Nicklaus	272	Isao Aoki	Baltusrol G. C. (Lower Course), Springfield, NJ
1981	David Graham	273	Bill Rogers George Burns	Merion G. C. (East Course), Ardmore, PA

*Won in playoff

Major Championship Results—U.S. Open / The British Open

DATE	WINNER	SCORE	RUNNER-UP	SITE
1982	Tom Watson	282	Jack Nicklaus	Pebble Beach G. L., Pebble Beach, CA
1983	Larry Nelson	280	Tom Watson	Oakmont C. C., Oakmont, PA
1984	*Fuzzy Zoeller	276	Greg Norman	Winged Foot G. C. (West Course), Mamaroneck, NY
1985	Andy North	279	Denis Watson Dave Barr	Oakland Hills C. C. (South Course), Birmingham, MI
1986	Raymond Floyd	279	Lanny Wadkins Chip Beck	Shinnecock Hills G. C., Southampton, NY
1987	Scott Simpson	277	Tom Watson	The Olympic Club (Lake Course), San Francisco, CA
1988	*Curtis Strange	278	Nick Faldo	The Country Club (Championship Course), Brookline, MA
1989	Curtis Strange	278	Ian Woosnam Mark McCumber Chip Beck	Oak Hill C. C. (East Course), Rochester, NY
1990	*Hale Irwin	280	Mike Donald	Medinah C. C. (No. 3 Course), Medinah, IL
1991	*Payne Stewart	282	Scott Simpson	Hazeltine National G. C., Chaska, MN
1992	Tom Kite	285	Jeff Sluman	Pebble Beach G. L., Pebble Beach, CA
1993	Lee Janzen	272	Payne Stewart	Baltusrol G. C. (Lower Course), Springfield, NJ
1994	*Ernie Els	279	Colin Montgomerie Loren Roberts	Oakmont C. C., Oakmont, PA
1995	Corey Pavin	280	Greg Norman	Shinnecock Hills G.L., Southampton, NY

The Open Championship (British Open)

Rotates annually between (at present) The Old Course at St. Andrews (Scotland), Muirfield (Scotland), Royal Troon (Scotland), Turnberry (Scotland), Royal Birkdale (England), Royal Lytham & St. Anne's (England), and Royal St. George's (England).

DATE	WINNER	SCORE	RUNNER-UP	SITE
1860	Willie Park	174	Tom Morris, Sr.	Prestwick
1861	Tom Morris, Sr.	163	Willie Park	Prestwick

* Won in playoff

Major Championship Results—The British Open

DATE	WINNER	SCORE	RUNNER-UP	SITE
1862	Tom Morris, Sr.	163	Willie Park	Prestwick
1863	Willie Park	168	Tom Morris, Sr.	Prestwick
1864	Tom Morris, Sr.	160	Andrew Strath	Prestwick
1865	Andrew Strath	162	Willie Park	Prestwick
1866	Willie Park	169	David Park	Prestwick
1867	Tom Morris, Sr.	170	Willie Park	Prestwick
1868	Tom Morris, Jr.	154	Tom Morris, Sr.	Prestwick
1869	Tom Morris, Jr.	157	Tom Morris, Sr.	Prestwick
1870	Tom Morris, Jr.	149	David Strath Bob Kirk	Prestwick
1871	*No Championship*			
1872	Tom Morris, Jr.	166	David Strath	Prestwick
1873	Tom Kidd	179	Jamie Anderson	St. Andrews
1874	Mungo Park	159	Unknown	Musselburgh
1875	Willie Park	166	Bob Martin	Prestwick
1876	Bob Martin	176	David Strath	St. Andrews
1877	Jamie Anderson	160	R. Pringle	Musselburgh
1878	Jamie Anderson	157	Robert Kirk	Prestwick
1879	Jamie Anderson	169	A. Kirkaldy J. Allan	St. Andrews
1880	Robert Ferguson	162	Unknown	Musselburgh
1881	Robert Ferguson	170	Jamie Anderson	Prestwick
1882	Robert Ferguson	171	Willie Fernie	St. Andrews
1883	*Willie Fernie	159	Robert Ferguson	Musselburgh
1884	Jack Simpson	160	D. Rolland Willie Fernie	Prestwick
1885	Bob Martin	171	Archie Simpson	St. Andrews
1886	David Brown	157	Willie Campbell	Musselburgh
1887	Willie Park, Jr.	161	Bob Martin	Prestwick
1888	Jack Burns	171	B. Sayers D. Anderson	St. Andrews
1889	*Willie Park, Jr.	155	Andrew Kirkaldy	Musselburgh
1890	John Ball	164	Willie Fernie	Prestwick
1891	Hugh Kirkaldy	166	Andrew Kirkaldy Willie Fernie	St. Andrews
1892	Harold H. Hilton	305	John Ball Hugh Kirkaldy	Muirfield
1893	William Auchterlonie	322	John E. Laidlay	Prestwick
1894	John H. Taylor	326	Douglas Rolland	Royal St. George's
1895	John H. Taylor	322	Alexander Herd	St. Andrews
1896	*Harry Vardon	316	John H. Taylor	Muirfield
1897	Harold H. Hilton	314	James Braid	Hoylake
1898	Harry Vardon	307	Willie Park, Jr.	Prestwick
1899	Harry Vardon	310	Jack White	Royal St. George's
1900	John H. Taylor	309	Harry Vardon	St. Andrews

* Won in playoff

DATE	WINNER	SCORE	RUNNER-UP	SITE
1901	James Braid	309	Harry Vardon	Muirfield
1902	Alexander Herd	307	Harry Vardon	Hoylake
1903	Harry Vardon	300	Tom Vardon	Prestwick
1904	Jack White	296	John H. Taylor	Royal St. George's
1905	James Braid	318	John H. Taylor Rolland Jones	St. Andrews
1906	James Braid	300	John H. Taylor	Muirfield
1907	Arnaud Massy	312	John H. Taylor	Hoylake
1908	James Braid	291	Tom Ball	Prestwick
1909	John H. Taylor	295	James Braid Tom Ball	Deal
1910	James Braid	299	Alexander Herd	St. Andrews
1911	Harry Vardon	303	Arnaud Massy	Royal St. George's
1912	Edward (Ted) Ray	295	Harry Vardon	Muirfield
1913	John H. Taylor	304	Edward Ray	Hoylake
1914	Harry Vardon	306	John H. Taylor	Prestwick
1915	*No Championship*			
1916	*No Championship*			
1917	*No Championship*			
1918	*No Championship*			
1919	*No Championship*			
1920	George Duncan	303	Alexander Herd	Deal
1921	*Jock Hutchison	296	Roger Wethered	St. Andrews
1922	Walter Hagen	300	George Duncan James M. Barnes	Royal St. George's
1923	Arthur G. Havers	295	Walter Hagen	Troon
1924	Walter Hagen	301	Ernest Whitcombe	Hoylake
1925	James M. Barnes	300	Archie Compston Ted Ray	Prestwick
1926	Robert T. Jones, Jr.	291	Al Watrous	Royal Lytham
1927	Robert T. Jones, Jr.	285	Aubrey Boomer	St. Andrews
1928	Walter Hagen	292	Gene Sarazen	Royal St. George's
1929	Walter Hagen	292	Johnny Farrell	Muirfield
1930	Robert T. Jones, Jr.	291	Macdonald Smith Leo Diegel	Hoylake
1931	Tommy D. Armour	296	J. Jurado	Carnoustie
1932	Gene Sarazen	283	Macdonald Smith	Prince's
1933	*Denny Shute	292	Craig Wood	St. Andrews
1934	Henry Cotton	283	S. F. Brews	Royal St. George's
1935	Alfred Perry	283	Alfred Padgham	Muirfield
1936	Alfred Padgham	287	James Adams	Hoylake
1937	Henry Cotton	290	R. A. Whitcombe	Carnoustie
1938	R. A. Whitcombe	295	James Adams	Royal St. George's
1939	Richard Burton	290	Johnny Bulla	St. Andrews
1940	*No Championship*			

* Won in playoff

DATE	WINNER	SCORE	RUNNER-UP	SITE
1941	*No Championship*			
1942	*No Championship*			
1943	*No Championship*			
1944	*No Championship*			
1945	*No Championship*			
1946	Sam Snead	290	Bobby Locke	St. Andrews
			Johnny Bulla	
1947	Fred Daly	293	R. W. Horne	Hoylake
			Frank Stranahan	
1948	Henry Cotton	294	Fred Daly	Muirfield
1949	*Bobby Locke	283	Harry Bradshaw	Royal St. George's
1950	Bobby Locke	279	Roberto DeVicenzo	Troon
1951	Max Faulkner	285	A. Cerda	Portrush
1952	Bobby Locke	287	Peter Thomson	Royal Lytham
1953	Ben Hogan	282	Frank Stranahan	Carnoustie
			Dai Rees	
			Peter Thomson	
			A. Cerda	
1954	Peter Thomson	283	S.S. Scott	Royal Birkdale
			Dai Rees	
			Bobby Locke	
1955	Peter Thomson	281	John Fallon	St. Andrews
1956	Peter Thomson	286	Flory Van Donck	Hoylake
1957	Bobby Locke	279	Peter Thomson	St. Andrews
1958	*Peter Thomson	278	Dave Thomas	Royal Lytham
1959	Gary Player	284	Fred Bullock	Muirfield
			Flory Van Donck	
1960	Kel Nagle	278	Arnold Palmer	St. Andrews
1961	Arnold Palmer	284	Dai Rees	Royal Birkdale
1962	Arnold Palmer	276	Kel Nagle	Troon
1963	*Bob Charles	277	Phil Rodgers	Royal Lytham
1964	Tony Lema	279	Jack Nicklaus	St. Andrews
1965	Peter Thomson	285	Brian Huggett	Southport
			Christy O'Connor	
1966	Jack Nicklaus	282	Doug Sanders	Muirfield
			Dave Thomas	
1967	Roberto DeVicenzo	278	Jack Nicklaus	Hoylake
1968	Gary Player	289	Jack Nicklaus	Carnoustie
			Bob Charles	
1969	Tony Jacklin	280	Bob Charles	Royal Lytham
1970	*Jack Nicklaus	283	Doug Sanders	St. Andrews
1971	Lee Trevino	278	Lu Liang Huan	Royal Birkdale
1972	Lee Trevino	278	Jack Nicklaus	Muirfield
1973	Tom Weiskopf	276	Johnny Miller	Troon
1974	Gary Player	282	Peter Oosterhuis	Royal Lytham

*Won in playoff

DATE	WINNER	SCORE	RUNNER-UP	SITE
1975	*Tom Watson	279	Jack Newton	Carnoustie
1976	Johnny Miller	279	Jack Nicklaus Seve Ballesteros	Royal Birkdale
1977	Tom Watson	268	Jack Nicklaus	Turnberry
1978	Jack Nicklaus	281	Ben Crenshaw Tom Kite Ray Floyd Simon Owen	St. Andrews
1979	Seve Ballesteros	283	Ben Crenshaw Jack Nicklaus	Royal Lytham
1980	Tom Watson	271	Lee Trevino	Muirfield
1981	Bill Rogers	276	Bernhard Langer	Royal St. George's
1982	Tom Watson	284	Nick Price Peter Oosterhuis	Royal Troon
1983	Tom Watson	275	Andy Bean	Royal Birkdale
1984	Seve Ballesteros	276	Tom Watson Bernhard Langer	St. Andrews
1985	Sandy Lyle	282	Payne Stewart	Royal St. George's
1986	Greg Norman	280	Gordon Brand	Turnberry
1987	Nick Faldo	279	Paul Azinger Rodger Davis	Muirfield
1988	Seve Ballesteros	273	Nick Price	Royal Lytham
1989	*Mark Calcavecchia	275	Wayne Grady Greg Norman	Royal Troon
1990	Nick Faldo	270	Payne Stewart Mark McNulty	St. Andrews
1991	Ian Baker-Finch	272	Mike Harwood	Royal Birkdale
1992	Nick Faldo	272	John Cook	Muirfield
1993	Greg Norman	267	Nick Faldo	Royal St. George's
1994	Nick Price	268	Jesper Parnevik	Turnberry
1995	*John Daly	282	Constantino Rocca	St. Andrews

The PGA Championship

DATE	WINNER	SCORE	RUNNER-UP	SITE
1916	James M. Barnes	1 up	Jock Hutchison	Siwanoy C. C., Bronxville, NY
1917	*No Championship*			
1918	*No Championship*			
1919	James M. Barnes	6 & 5	Fred McLeod	Engineers C. C., Roslyn, NY
1920	Jock Hutchison	1 up	J. Douglas Edgar	Flossmoor C. C., Flossmoor, IL
1921	Walter Hagen	3 & 2	James M. Barnes	Inwood C. C., Far Rockaway, NY

*Won in playoff

DATE	WINNER	SCORE	RUNNER-UP	SITE
1922	Gene Sarazen	4 & 3	Emmet French	Oakmont C. C., Oakmont, PA
1923	Gene Sarazen	1 up	Walter Hagen	Pelham C. C., Pelham, NY
1924	Walter Hagen	2 up	James M. Barnes	French Lick C. C., French Lick, IN
1925	Walter Hagen	6 & 5	William Mehlhorn	Olympia Fields C. C., Olympia Fields, IL
1926	Walter Hagen	5 & 3	Leo Diegel	Salisbury G. C., Westbury, NY
1927	Walter Hagen	1 up	Joe Turnesa	Cedar Crest C. C., Dallas, TX
1928	Leo Diegel	6 & 5	Al Espinosa	Baltimore C. C., Baltimore, MD
1929	Leo Diegel	6 & 4	Johnny Farrell	Hillcrest C. C., Los Angeles, CA
1930	Tommy Armour	1 up	Gene Sarazen	Fresh Meadow C. C., Flushing, NY
1931	Tom Creavy	2 &1	Denny Shute	Wannamoisett C. C., Rumford, RI
1932	Olin Dutra	4 & 3	Frank Walsh	Keller G. C., St. Paul, MN
1933	Gene Sarazen	5 & 4	Willie Goggin	Blue Mound C. C., Milwaukee, WI
1934	Paul Runyan	1 up	Craig Wood	Park C. C., Williamsville, NY
1935	Johnny Revolta	5 & 4	Tommy Armour	Twin Hills C. C., Oklahoma City, OK
1936	Denny Shute	3 & 2	Jimmy Thomson	Pinehurst C. C., Pinehurst, NC
1937	Denny Shute	1 up	Harold McSpaden	Pittsburg G. C., Aspinwall, PA
1938	Paul Runyan	8 & 7	Sam Snead	Shawnee C. C., Shawnee, Pa.
1939	Henry Picard	1 up	Byron Nelson	Pomonok C. C., Flushing, NY
1940	Byron Nelson	1 up	Sam Snead	Hershey C. C., Hershey, PA
1941	Vic Ghezzi	1 up	Byron Nelson	Cherry Hills C. C., Denver, CO
1942	Sam Snead	2 & 1	Jim Turnesa	Seaview C. C., Atlantic City, NJ
1943	No Championship			
1944	Bob Hamilton	1 up	Byron Nelson	Manito G. & C. C., Spokane, WA

*Won in playoff

DATE	WINNER	SCORE	RUNNER-UP	SITE
1945	Byron Nelson	4 & 3	Sam Byrd	Morraine C. C., Dayton, OH
1946	Ben Hogan	6 & 4	Ed Oliver	Portland G. C., Portland, OR
1947	Jim Ferrier	2 & 1	Chick Harbert	Plum Hollow C. C., Detroit, MI
1948	Ben Hogan	7 & 6	Mike Turnesa	Norwood Hills C. C., St. Louis, MO
1949	Sam Snead	3 & 2	Johnny Palmer	Hermitage C. C., Richmond, VA
1950	Chandler Harper	4 & 3	Henry Williams, Jr.	Scioto C. C., Columbus, OH
1951	Sam Snead	7 & 6	Walter Burkemo	Oakmont C. C., Oakmont, PA
1952	Jim Turnesa	1 up	Chick Harbert	Big Spring C. C., Louisville, KY
1953	Walter Burkemo	2 & 1	Felice Torza	Birmingham C. C., Birmingham, MI
1954	Chick Harbert	4 & 3	Walter Burkemo	Keller G. C., St. Paul, MN
1955	Doug Ford	4 & 3	Cary Middlecoff	Meadowbrook C. C., Detroit, MI
1956	Jack Burke, Jr.	3 & 2	Ted Kroll	Blue Hill C. C., Boston, MA
1957	Lionel Hebert	2 & 1	Dow Finsterwald	Miami Valley C. C., Dayton, OH
1958	Dow Finsterwald	276	Billy Casper	Llanerch C. C., Havertown, PA
1959	Bob Rosburg	277	Jerry Barber, Doug Sanders	Minneapolis G. C., St. Paul, MN
1960	Jay Hebert	281	Jim Ferrier	Firestone C. C., Akron, OH
1961	*Jerry Barber	277	Don January	Olympia Fields C. C., Olympia Fields, IL
1962	Gary Player	278	Bob Goalby	Aronomink G. C., Newtown Square, PA
1963	Jack Nicklaus	279	Dave Ragan, Jr.	Dallas A. C., Dallas, TX
1964	Bobby Nichols	271	Jack Nicklaus, Arnold Palmer	Columbus C. C., Columbus, OH
1965	Dave Marr	280	Billy Casper, Jack Nicklaus	Laurel Valley C. C., Ligonier, PA
1966	Al Geiberger	280	Dudley Wysong	Firestone C. C., Akron, OH

*Won in playoff

Major Championship Results—The PGA Championship

DATE	WINNER	SCORE	RUNNER-UP	SITE
1967	*Don January	281	Don Massengale	Columbine C. C., Littleton, CO
1968	Julius Boros	281	Bob Charles Arnold Palmer	Pecan Valley C. C., San Antonio, TX
1969	Ray Floyd	276	Gary Player	NCR C. C., Dayton, OH
1970	Dave Stockton	279	Arnold Palmer Bob Murphy	Southern Hills C. C., Tulsa, OK
1971	Jack Nicklaus	281	Billy Casper	PGA National G. C., Palm Beach Gdns, FL
1972	Gary Player	281	Tommy Aaron Jim Jamieson	Oakland Hills C. C., Birmingham, MI
1973	Jack Nicklaus	277	Bruce Crampton	Canterbury G. C., Cleveland, OH
1974	Lee Trevino	276	Jack Nicklaus	Tanglewood G. C., Winston-Salem, NC
1975	Jack Nicklaus	276	Bruce Crampton	Firestone C. C., Akron, OH
1976	Dave Stockton	281	Ray Floyd Don January	Congressional C. C., Bethesda, MD
1977	*Lanny Wadkins	282	Gene Littler	Pebble Beach G. L., Pebble Beach, CA
1978	*John Mahaffey	276	Jerry Pate Tom Watson	Oakmont C. C., Oakmont, PA
1979	*David Graham	272	Ben Crenshaw	Oakland Hills C. C., Birmingham, MI
1980	Jack Nicklaus	274	Andy Bean	Oak Hill C. C., Rochester, NY
1981	Larry Nelson	273	Fuzzy Zoeller	Atlanta A. C., Duluth, GA
1982	Raymond Floyd	272	Lanny Wadkins	Southern Hills C. C., Tulsa, OK
1983	Hal Sutton	274	Jack Nicklaus	Riviera C. C., Pacific Palisades, CA
1984	Lee Trevino	273	Gary Player Lanny Wadkins	Shoal Creek C. C., Birmingham, AL
1985	Hubert Green	278	Lee Trevino	Cherry Hills C. C., Denver, CO
1986	Bob Tway	276	Greg Norman	Inverness C. C., Toledo, OH
1987	*Larry Nelson	287	Lanny Wadkins	PGA National G. C., Palm Beach Grdns, FL
1988	Jeff Sluman	272	Paul Azinger	Oak Tree G. C., Edmond, OK
1989	Payne Stewart	276	Mike Reid	Kemper Lakes G. C., Hawthorn Woods, IL

*Won in playoff

DATE	WINNER	SCORE	RUNNER-UP	SITE
1990	Wayne Grady	282	Fred Couples	Shoal Creek C. C., Birmingham, AL
1991	John Daly	276	Bruce Lietzke	Crooked Stick G. C., Carmel, IN
1992	Nick Price	278	John Cook Jim Gallagher Gene Sauers Nick Faldo	Bellerive C. C., St. Louis, MO
1993	*Paul Azinger	272	Greg Norman	Inverness Club, Toledo, OH
1994	Nick Price	269	Corey Pavin	Southern Hills C.C., Tulsa, OK
1995	*Steve Elkington	267	Colin Montgomerie	Riviera C.C., Los Angeles, CA

Women's Major Championships

The United States Women's Open Championship

DATE	WINNER	SCORE	RUNNER-UP	SITE
1946	Patty Berg	5 & 4	Betty Jameson	Spokane C. C., Spokane, WA
1947	Betty Jameson	295	Sally Sessions Polly Riley	Starmount Forest C. C., Greensboro, NC
1948	Babe Zaharias	300	Betty Hicks	Atlantic City C. C., Northfield, NJ
1949	Louise Suggs	291	Babe Zaharias	Prince Georges G. & C. C., Landover, MD
1950	Babe Zaharias	291	Betsy Rawls	Rolling Hills C. C., Wichita, KS
1951	Betsy Rawls	293	Louise Suggs	Druid Hills G. C., Atlanta, GA
1952	Louise Suggs	284	Marlene Bauer Betty Jameson	Bala G. C., Philadelphia, PA
1953	*Betsy Rawls	302	Jacqueline Pung	C. C. of Rochester, Rochester, NY
1954	Babe Zaharias	291	Betty Hicks	Salem C. C., Peabody, MA
1955	Fay Crocker	299	Louise Suggs Mary Lena Faulk	Wichita C. C., Wichita, KS
1956	*Kathy Cornelius	302	Barbara McIntire	Northland C. C., Duluth, MN
1957	Betsy Rawls	299	Patty Berg	Winged Foot G. C. (East Course), Mamaroneck, NY

*Won in playoff

Major Championship Results—U.S. Women's Open

DATE	WINNER	SCORE	RUNNER-UP	SITE
1958	Mickey Wright	290	Louise Suggs	Forest Lake C. C., Bloomfield Hills, MI
1959	Mickey Wright	287	Louise Suggs	Churchill Valley C. C., Pittsburgh, PA
1960	Betsy Rawls	292	Joyce Ziske	Worcester C. C., Worcester, MA
1961	Mickey Wright	293	Betsy Rawls	Baltusrol G.C. (Lower Course), Springfield, NJ
1962	Murle Lindstrom	301	Ruth Jessen, JoAnn Prentice	Dunes G. & B. Club, Myrtle Beach, SC
1963	Mary Mills	289	Sandra Haynie, Louise Suggs	Kenwood C. C., Cincinnati, OH
1964	*Mickey Wright	290	Ruth Jessen	San Diego C. C., Chula Vista, CA
1965	Carol Mann	290	Kathy Cornelius	Atlantic City C. C., Northfield, NJ
1966	Sandra Spuzich	297	Carol Mann	Hazeltine Nat. G. C., Chaska, MN
1967	Catherine Lacoste	294	Susie Maxwell, Beth Stone	Virginia Hot Springs G. & T. C. (Cascades), Hot Springs, VA
1968	Susie Maxwell Berning	289	Mickey Wright	Moselem Springs G. C., Fleetwood, PA
1969	Donna Caponi	294	Peggy Wilson	Scenic Hills C. C., Pensacola, FL
1970	Donna Caponi	287	Sandra Haynie, Sandra Spuzich	Muskogee C. C., Muskogee, OK
1971	JoAnne Carner	288	Kathy Whitworth	Kahkwa Club, Erie, PA
1972	Susie Maxwell Berning	299	Kathy Ahern, Pam Barnett, Judy Rankin	Winged Foot G. C. (East Course), Mamaroneck, NY
1973	Susie Maxwell Berning	290	Shelly Hamlin, Gloria Ehret	C. C. of Rochester, Rochester, NY
1974	Sandra Haynie	295	Beth Stone, Carol Mann	La Grange C. C., La Grange, IL
1975	Sandra Palmer	295	Nancy Lopez, JoAnne Carner, Sandra Post	Atlantic City C. C., Northfield, NJ
1976	*JoAnne Carner	292	Sandra Palmer	Rolling Green G. C., Springfield, PA
1977	Hollis Stacy	292	Nancy Lopez	Hazeltine Nat. G. C., Chaska, MN
1978	Hollis Stacy	289	JoAnne Carner, Sally Little	C. C. of Indianapolis, Indianapolis, IN

*Won in playoff

Major Championship Results—U.S. Women's Open

DATE	WINNER	SCORE	RUNNER-UP	SITE
1979	Jerilyn Britz	284	Debbie Massey Sandra Palmer	Brooklawn C. C., Fairfield, CT
1980	Amy Alcott	280	Hollis Stacy	Richland C. C., Nashville, TN
1981	Pat Bradley	279	Beth Daniel	La Grange C. C., La Grange, IL
1982	Janet Alex	283	Sandra Haynie Donna H. White JoAnne Carner Beth Daniel	Del Paso C.C., Sacramento, CA
1983	Jan Stephenson	290	JoAnne Carner Patty Sheehan	Cedar Ridge C. C., Tulsa, OK
1984	Hollis Stacy	290	Rosie Jones	Salem C. C., Peabody, MA
1985	Kathy Guadagnino	280	Judy Clark	Baltusrol G. C. (Upper Course), Springfield, NJ
1986	*Jane Geddes	287	Sally Little	NCR C. C., Kettering, OH
1987	*Laura Davies	285	Ayako Okamoto JoAnne Carner	Plainfield C. C., Edison, NJ
1988	Liselotte Neumann	277	Patty Sheehan	Baltimore C. C. (Five Farms East), Baltimore, MD
1989	Betsy King	278	Nancy Lopez	Indianwood G. & C. C. (Old/East Course), Lake Orion, MI
1990	Betsy King	284	Patty Sheehan	Atlanta A. C. (Riverside Course), Duluth, GA
1991	Meg Mallon	283	Pat Bradley	Colonial C. C., Fort Worth, TX
1992	*Patty Sheehan	280	Juli Inkster	Oakmont C. C., Oakmont, PA
1993	Laurie Merten	280	Helen Alfredsson	Crooked Stick G. C., Carmel, IN
1994	Patty Sheehan	277	Tammie Green	Indianwood G. & C. C. (Old/East Course), Lake Orion, MI
1995	Annika Sorenstam	278	Meg Mallon	The Broadmoor C.C. (East Course), Colorado Springs, CO

*Won in playoff

Mazda LPGA Championship

DATE	WINNER	SCORE	RUNNER-UP	SITE
1955	Beverly Hanson	220 (4 &3)	Louise Suggs	Orchard Ridge C. C., Ft. Wayne, IN
1956	Marlene Hagge	291	Patty Berg	Forest Lake C. C., Detroit, MI
1957	Louise Suggs	285	Wiffi Smith	Churchill Valley C. C., Pittsburgh, PA
1958	Mickey Wright	288	Fay Crocker	Churchill Valley C. C., Pittsburgh, PA
1959	Betsy Rawls	288	Patty Berg	Sheraton Hotel C. C., French Lick, IN
1960	Mickey Wright	292	Louise Suggs	Sheraton Hotel C. C., French Lick, IN
1961	Mickey Wright	287	Louise Suggs	Stardust C. C., Las Vegas, NV
1962	Judy Kimball	282	Shirley Spork	Stardust C. C., Las Vegas, NV
1963	Mickey Wright	294	Mary Lena Faulk Mary Mills Louise Suggs	Stardust C. C., Las Vegas, NV
1964	Mary Mills	278	Mickey Wright	Stardust C. C., Las Vegas, NV
1965	Sandra Haynie	279	Clifford A. Creed	Stardust C. C., Las Vegas, NV
1966	Gloria Ehret	282	Mickey Wright	Stardust C. C., Las Vegas, NV
1967	Kathy Whitworth	284	Shirley Englehorn	Pleasant Valley C. C., Sutton, MA
1968	*Sandra Post	294	Kathy Whitworth	Pleasant Valley C. C., Sutton, MA
1969	Betsy Rawls	293	Susie Berning Carol Mann	Concord G. C., Kiamesha Lake, NY
1970	Shirley Englehorn	285	Kathy Whitworth	Pleasant Valley C. C., Sutton, MA
1971	Kathy Whitworth	288	Kathy Ahern	Pleasant Valley C. C., Sutton, MA
1972	Kathy Ahern	293	Jane Blalock	Pleasant Valley C. C., Sutton, MA
1973	Mary Mills	288	Betty Burfeindt	Pleasant Valley C. C., Sutton, MA
1974	Sandra Haynie	288	JoAnne Carner	Pleasant Valley C. C., Sutton, MA
1975	Kathy Whitworth	288	Sandra Haynie	Pine Ridge G. C., Baltimore, MD

*Won in playoff

DATE	WINNER	SCORE	RUNNER-UP	SITE
1976	Betty Burfeindt	287	Judy Rankin	Pine Ridge G. C., Baltimore, MD
1977	Chako Higuchi	279	Pat Bradley Sandra Post Judy Rankin	Bay Tree Golf Plantation, N. Myrtle Beach, SC
1978	Nancy Lopez	275	Amy Alcott	Jack Nicklaus G. C., Kings Island, OH
1979	Donna Caponi	279	Jerilyn Britz	Jack Nicklaus G. C., Kings Island, OH
1980	Sally Little	285	Jane Blalock	Jack Nicklaus G. C., Kings Island, OH
1981	Donna Caponi	280	Jerilyn Britz	Jack Nicklaus G. C., Kings Island, OH
1982	Jan Stephenson	279	JoAnne Carner	Jack Nicklaus G. C., Kings Island, OH
1983	Patty Sheehan	279	Sandra Haynie	Jack Nicklaus G. C., Kings Island, OH
1984	Patty Sheehan	272	Beth Daniel Pat Bradley	Jack Nicklaus G. C., Kings Island, OH
1985	Nancy Lopez	273	Alice Miller	Jack Nicklaus G. C., Kings Island, OH
1986	Pat Bradley	277	Patty Sheehan	Jack Nicklaus G. C., Kings Island, OH
1987	Jane Geddes	275	Betsy King	Jack Nicklaus G. C., Kings Island, OH
1988	Sherri Turner	281	Amy Alcott	Jack Nicklaus G. C., Kings Island, OH
1989	Nancy Lopez	274	Ayako Okamoto	Bethesda C. C., Bethesda, MD
1990	Beth Daniel	280	Rosie Jones	Bethesda C. C., Bethesda, MD
1991	Meg Mallon	274	Pat Bradley Ayako Okamoto	Bethesda C. C., Bethesda, MD
1992	Betsy King	267	JoAnne Carner Karen Noble Liselotte Neumann	Bethesda C. C., Bethesda, MD
1993	Patty Sheehan	275	Laurie Merten	Bethesda C. C., Bethesda, MD
1994	Laura Davies	279	Alice Ritzman	DuPont C. C., Wilmington, DE
1995	Kelly Robbins	274	Laurie Davies	DuPont C.C., Wilmington, DE

*Won in playoff

NABISCO Dinah Shore

Mission Hills Country Club, Rancho Mirage, CA
Previously known as the Colgate Dinah Shore (1972-1981)
(Designated Major Commencing 1983.)

DATE	WINNER	SCORE	RUNNER-UP
1972	Jane Blalock	213	Carol Mann
			Judy Rankin
1973	Mickey Wright	284	Joyce Kazmierski
1974	*Jo Ann Prentice	289	Jane Blalock
			Sandra Haynie
1975	Sandra Palmer	283	Kathy McMullen
1976	Judy Rankin	285	Betty Burfeindt
1977	Kathy Whitworth	289	JoAnne Carner
			Sally Little
1978	*Sandra Post	283	Penny Pulz
1979	Sandra Post	276	Nancy Lopez
1980	Donna Caponi	275	Amy Alcott
1981	Nancy Lopez	277	Carolyn Hill
1982	Sally Little	278	Hollis Stacy
			Sandra Haynie
1983	Amy Alcott	282	Beth Daniel
			Kathy Whitworth
1984	*Juli Inkster	280	Pat Bradley
1985	Alice Miller	275	Jan Stephenson
1986	Pat Bradley	280	Val Skinner
1987	*Betsy King	283	Patty Sheehan
1988	Amy Alcott	274	Colleen Walker
1989	Juli Inkster	279	Tammie Green
	JoAnne Carner		
1990	Betsy King	283	Kathy Postlewait
			Shirley Furlong
1991	Amy Alcott	273	Dottie Mochrie
1992	*Dottie Mochrie	279	Juli Inkster
1993	Helen Alfredsson	284	Amy Benz
			Tina Barrett
1994	Donna Andrews	276	Laura Davies
1995	Nanci Bowen	285	Susie Redman

*Won in playoff

Du Maurier Ltd. Classic

(Previously known as La Canadienne (1973), and the Peter Jackson Classic (1974-1982). Designated Major commencing 1979.)

DATE	WINNER	SCORE	RUNNER-UP	SITE
1973	*Jocelyne Bourassa	214	Sandra Haynie Judy Rankin	Montreal G. C., Montreal
1974	Carole Jo Callison	208	JoAnne Carner	Candiac G. C., Montreal
1975	*JoAnne Carner	214	Carol Mann	St. George's C. C., Toronto
1976	*Donna Caponi	212	Judy Rankin	Cedar Brae G. & C. C., Toronto
1977	Judy Rankin	214	Pat Meyers Sandra Palmer	Lachute G. & C. C., Montreal
1978	JoAnne Carner	278	Hollis Stacy	St. George's C. C., Toronto
1979	Amy Alcott	285	Nancy Lopez	Richelieu Valley C. C., Montreal
1980	Pat Bradley	277	JoAnne Carner	St. George's C. C., Toronto, Ontario
1981	Jan Stephenson	278	Nancy Lopez	Summerlea C. C., Dorion, Quebec
1982	Sandra Haynie	280	Beth Daniel	St. George's C. C., Toronto, Ontario
1983	Hollis Stacy	277	JoAnne Carner Alice Miller	Beaconsfield G. C., Montreal, Quebec
1984	Juli Inkster	279	Ayako Okamoto	St. George's G. & C. C., Toronto, Ontario
1985	Pat Bradley	278	Jane Geddes	Beaconsfield C. C., Montreal, Quebec
1986	*Pat Bradley	276	Ayako Okamoto	Board of Trade C. C., Toronto, Ontario
1987	Jody Rosenthal	272	Ayako Okamoto	Islemere G. C., Laval, Quebec
1988	Sally Little	279	Laura Davies	Vancouver G. C., Coquitlam, B.C.
1989	Tammie Green	279	Pat Bradley Betsy King	Beaconsfield G. C., Montreal, Quebec
1990	Cathy Johnston	276	Patty Sheehan	Westmount G. & C. C., Kitchener, Ontario
1991	Nancy Scranton	279	Debbie Massey	Vancouver G. C., Coquitlam, B. C.
1992	Sherri Steinhauer	277	Judy Dickinson	St. Charles C. C., Winnipeg, Manitoba

*Won in playoff

DATE	WINNER	SCORE	RUNNER-UP	SITE
1993	*Brandie Burton	277	Betsy King	London Hunt and C. C., London, Ontario
1994	Martha Nause	279	Michelle McGann	Ottawa Hunt & G. C., Ottawa, Ontario
1995	Jenny Lidback	280	Liselotte Neumann	Beaconsfield G.C., Pointe-Claire, Quebec

Senior Men's Major Championships

The United States Senior Open

DATE	WINNER	SCORE	RUNNER-UP	SITE
1980	Roberto De Vicenzo	285	William C. Campbell	Winged Foot G. C. (East Course), Mamaroneck, NY
1981	*Arnold Palmer	289	Bob Stone / Billy Casper	Oakland Hills C. C. (South Course), Birmingham, MI
1982	Miller Barber	282	Gene Littler / Dan Sikes	Portland G. C., Portland, OR
1983	*Billy Casper	288	Rod Funseth	Hazeltine National G. C., Chaska, MN
1984	Miller Barber	286	Arnold Palmer	Oak Hills C. C. (East Course), Rochester, NY
1985	Miller Barber	285	Roberto DeVicenzo	Edgewood Tahoe G. C., Stateline, NV
1986	Dale Douglass	279	Gary Player	Scioto C. C., Columbus, OH
1987	Gary Player	270	Doug Sanders	Brooklawn C. C., Fairfield, CT
1988	*Gary Player	288	Bob Charles	Medinah C. C. (No. 3 Course), Medinah, IL
1989	Orville Moody	279	Frank Beard	Laurel Valley G. C., Ligonier, PA
1990	Lee Trevino	275	Jack Nicklaus	Ridgewood C. C. (Center and West nines), Paramus, NJ
1991	*Jack Nicklaus	282	Chi Chi Rodriguez	Oakland Hills C. C. (South Course), Birmingham, MI

*Won in playoff

DATE	WINNER	SCORE	RUNNER-UP	SITE
1992	Larry Laoretti	275	Jim Colbert	Saucon Valley C. C. (Old Course), Bethlehem, PA
1993	Jack Nicklaus	278	Tom Weiskopf	Cherry Hills C. C., Englewood, CO
1994	Simon Hobday	274	Graham Marsh	Pinehurst C. C., Pinehurst, NC
1995	Tom Weiskopf	275	Jack Nicklaus	Congressional C.C., Bethesda, MD

Senior PGA Championship

(Played at Augusta National G.C., 1937-38; North Shore C. C. & Bobby Jones G. C., 1940; Sarasota Bay C. C. & Bobby Jones G. C., 1941; Ft. Myers G. & C. C., 1942; PGA National, 1945-62 [Dunedin], 1964, 1966-1973 [JDM CC], 1982-present [Champions Course]; Port St. Lucie C. C., 1963, 1974; Ft. Lauderdale C. C., 1965; Walt Disney World [Magnolia], 1975-79; Turnberry Isle C. C. [South Course], 1979-1981.)

DATE	WINNER	SCORE	RUNNER-UP
1937	Jock Hutchinson	223	George Gordon
1938	*Fred McLeod	154	Otto Hackbarth
1939	*No Championship*		
1940	*Otto Hackbarth	146	Jock Hutchinson
1941	Jack Burke, Sr.	142	Eddie Williams
1942	Eddie Williams	138	Jock Hutchinson
1943	*No Championship*		
1944	*No Championship*		
1945	Eddie Williams	148	Jock Hutchinson
1946	*Eddie Williams	146	Jock Hutchinson
1947	Jock Hutchinson	145	Ben Richter
1948	Charles McKenna	141	Ben Richter
1949	Marshall Crichton	145	Louis Chiapetta
			Jock Hutchinson
			George Smith
1950	Al Watrous	142	Bill Jeliffe
1951	*Al Watrous	142	Jock Hutchinson
1952	Ernie Newnham	146	Al Watrous
1953	Harry Schwab	142	Charles McKenna

* *Won in playoff*   Gene Sarazen

DATE	WINNER	SCORE	RUNNER-UP
1954	Gene Sarazen	214	Perry Del Vecchio
			Al Watrous
1955	Mortie Dutra	213	Mike Murra
			Gene Sarazen
			Denny Shute
1956	Pete Burke	215	Ock Willoweit
1957	*Al Watrous	210	Bob Stupple
1958	Gene Sarazen	288	Charles Sheppard
1959	Willie Goggin	284	Leland Gibson
			Paul Runyan
			Denny Shute
1960	Dick Metz	284	Tony Longo
			Paul Runyan
1961	Paul Runyan	278	Jimmy Demaret
1962	Paul Runyan	278	Errie Ball
			Dutch Harrison
			Joe Brown
1963	Herman Barron	272	John Barnum
1964	Sam Snead	279	John Barnum
1965	Sam Snead	278	Joe Lopez, Sr.
1966	Freddie Haas	286	John Barnum
			Dutch Harrison
1967	Sam Snead	279	Bob Hamilton
1968	Chandler Harper	279	Sam Snead
1969	Tommy Bolt	278	Pete Fleming
1970	Sam Snead	290	Freddie Haas
1971	Julius Boros	285	Tommy Bolt
1972	Sam Snead	286	Tommy Bolt
			Julius Boros
1973	Sam Snead	268	Julius Boros
1974	Roberto DeVicenzo	273	Julius Boros
			Art Wall
1975	*Charlie Sifford	280	Fred Wampler
1976	Pete Cooper	283	Fred Wampler
1977	Julius Boros	283	Freddie Haas
1978	*Joe Jimenez	286	Joe Cheves
			Manuel de la Torre

* *Won in playoff*

DATE	WINNER	SCORE	RUNNER-UP
1979	*Jack Fleck	289	Bob Erickson
			Bill Johnson
1979	Don January	270	George Bayer
1980	*Arnold Palmer	289	Paul Harney
1981	Miller Barber	281	Arnold Palmer
1982	Don January	288	Julius Boros
1983	No Championship		
1984	Arnold Palmer	282	Don January
1984	Peter Thomson	286	Don January
1985	No Championship		
1986	Gary Player	281	Lee Elder
1987	Chi Chi Rodriguez	282	Dale Douglass
1988	Gary Player	284	Chi Chi Rodriguez
1989	Larry Mowry	281	Miller Barber
			Al Geiberger
1990	Gary Player	281	Chi Chi Rodriguez
1991	Jack Nicklaus	271	Bruce Crampton
1992	Lee Trevino	278	Mike Hill
1993	*Tom Wargo	275	Bruce Crampton
1994	Lee Trevino	279	Jim Colbert
1995	Ray Floyd	277	John Paul Cain

The Tradition

(Played at Desert Mountain G. C.—Cochise Course.)

DATE	WINNER	SCORE
1989	Don Bies	275
1990	Jack Nicklaus	206
1991	Jack Nicklaus	277
1992	Lee Trevino	274
1993	Tom Shaw	269
1994	*Raymond Floyd	271
1995	Jack Nicklaus	276

Won in playoff

FORD Senior Players Championship

(Previously known as the Senior Tour Players Championship, 1983-86; and the Mazda Senior Tournament Players Championship. Played at: Canterbury G.C., Cleveland, Ohio, 1983-1986; Sawgrass C.C., Ponte Vedra, Fla., 1986; Players Club at Sawgrass (Valley), Ponte Vedra, Fla., 1988-89; and Dearborn C.C., Dearborn, Mich., 1990-present.)

DATE	WINNER	SCORE
1983	Miller Barber	278
1984	Arnold Palmer	276
1985	Arnold Palmer	274
1986	Chi Chi Rodriguez	206
1987	Gary Player	280
1988	Billy Casper	278
1989	Orville Moody	271
1990	Jack Nicklaus	261
1991	Jim Albus	279
1992	Dave Stockton	277
1993	Jim Colbert	278
1994	Dave Stockton	271
1995	J.C. Snead	272

TEAM EVENTS— PROFESSIONAL INTERNATIONALS

OVERVIEW: *Prominent international team events involving touring professionals.*

THE RYDER CUP

USA vs. Great Britain through 1971. USA vs. Great Britain & Ireland through 1977. USA vs. Europe since 1979. 12-man teams in a three-day format with foursome, best ball, and singles play.

YEAR	WINNER	SCORE	SITE
1927	USA	9.5-2.5	Worcester C. C., USA
1929	Great Britain	7-5	Moortown G. C., England
1931	USA	9-3	Scioto C. C., USA
1933	Great Britain	6.5-5.5	Southport & Ainsdale G. C., England
1935	USA	9-3	Ridgewood C. C., USA
1937	USA	8-4	Southport & Ainsdale G. C., England
1947	USA	11-1	Portland G. C., USA
1949	USA	7-5	Ganton G. C., England
1951	USA	9.5-2.5	Pinehurst C. C., USA
1953	USA	6.5-5.5	Wentworth G. C., England
1955	USA	8-4	Thunderbird G. & C. C., USA
1957	Great Britain	7.5-4.5	Lindrick G. C., England
1959	USA	8.5-3.5	Eldorado C. C., USA
1961	USA	14.5-9.5	Royal Lytham & St. Anne's, England
1963	USA	23-9	East Lake C. C., USA
1965	USA	19.5-12.5	Royal Birkdale G. C., England
1967	USA	23.5-8.5	Champions G. C., USA
1969	Tie	16-16	Royal Birkdale G. C., England
1971	USA	18.5-13.5	Old Warson C. C., USA
1973	USA	19-13	Muirfield, Scotland
1975	USA	21-11	Laurel Valley G. C., USA
1977	USA	12.5-7.5	Royal Lytham & St. Anne's, England
1979	USA	17-11	The Greenbrier, USA
1981	USA	18.5-9.5	Walton Heath G. C., England
1983	USA	14.5-13.5	PGA National G. C., USA
1985	Europe	16.5-11.5	The Belfry, England
1987	Europe	15-13	Muirfield Village G. C., USA
1989	Tie	14-14	The Belfry, England
1991	USA	14.5-13.5	The Ocean Course, USA
1993	USA	15-13	The Belfry, England
1995	Europe	14.5-13.5	Oak Hill G.C., USA

The Solheim Cup

USA vs. Europe. 10-woman teams in a three-day format with foursome, best ball, and singles play.

YEAR	WINNER	SCORE	LOSER	SITE
1990	USA	284	Europe	Lake Nona G. C., Orlando, Florida, USA
1992	Europe	282	USA	Dalmahoy G. & C. C., Edinburgh, Scotland
1994	USA	13-7	Europe	The Greenbrier G. C., White Sulphur Springs, West Virginia, USA

The World Cup

Two-man national teams competing in a combined stroke-play championship. Known as the Canada Cup until 1966.

—TEAM TROPHY—

YEAR	WINNER	TEAM MEMBERS	SITE
1953	**Argentina**	Roberto de Vicenzo/Antonio Cerda	Montreal
1954	**Australia**	Peter Thompson/Kel Nagle	Canada
1955	**United States**	Ed Furgol/Chick Harbert	Washington, DC
1956	**United States**	Ben Hogan/Sam Snead	Wentworth (UK)
1957	**Japan**	Torakichi Nakamura/Koichi Ono	Tokyo
1958	**Ireland**	Harry Bradshaw/Christy O'Connor	Mexico City
1959	**Australia**	Peter Thompson/Kel Nagle	Melbourne
1960	**United States**	Sam Snead/Arnold Palmer	Dublin
1961	**United States**	Sam Snead/Jimmy Demaret	Dorado (Puerto Rico)
1962	**United States**	Sam Snead/Arnold Palmer	Buenos Aires
1963	**United States**	Jack Nicklaus/Arnold Palmer	Paris
1964	**United States**	Jack Nicklaus/Arnold Palmer	Maui
1965	**South Africa**	Gary Player/Harold Henning	Madrid
1966	**United States**	Jack Nicklaus/Arnold Palmer	Tokyo
1967	**United States**	Jack Nicklaus/Arnold Palmer	Mexico City
1968	**Canada**	Al Balding/George Knudson	Rome
1969	**United States**	Lee Trevino/Orville Moody	Singapore
1970	**Australia**	David Graham/Bruce Devlin	Buenos Aires
1971	**United States**	Jack Nicklaus/Lee Trevino	Palm Beach (USA)
1972	**Rep. of China**	Hsieh Min-Nan/Lu Liang-Huan	Melbourne
1973	**United States**	Johnny Miller/Jack Nicklaus	Marbella, Spain
1974	**South Africa**	Bobby Cole/Dale Hayes	Caracas
1975	**United States**	Johnny Miller/Lou Graham	Bangkok
1976	**Spain**	Manuel Pinero/Seve Ballesteros	Palm Springs
1977	**Spain**	Antonio Garrido/Seve Ballesteros	Manila
1978	**United States**	John Mahaffey/Andy North	Kauai
1979	**United States**	John Mahaffey/Hale Irwin	Athens
1980	**Canada**	Dan Halldorson/Jim Nelford	Bogota
1981	**No Tournament**		

YEAR	WINNER	TEAM MEMBERS	SITE
1982	Spain	Manuel Pinero/Jose Canizares	Acapulco
1983	United States	Rex Caldwell/John Cook	Jakarta
1984	Spain	Jose Canizares/Jose Rivero	Rome
1985	Canada	Dave Barr/Dan Halldorson	La Quinta
1986	No Tournament		
1987	Wales	Ian Woosnam/David Llewellyn	Maui
1988	United States	Ben Crenshaw/Mark McCumber	Melbourne
1989	Australia	Peter Fowler/Wayne Grady	Marbella, Spain
1990	Germany	Bernhard Langer/Torsten Giedeon	Orlando
1991	Sweden	Per-Ulrik Johansson/Anders Forsbrand	Rome
1992	United States	Fred Couples/Davis Love III	Madrid
1993	United States	Fred Couples/Davis Love III	Orlando
1994	United States	Fred Couples/Davis Love III	France
1995	United States	Fred Couples/Davis Love III	Beijing

—INTERNATIONAL (INDIVIDUAL TITLE) TROPHY—

YEAR	WINNER	COUNTRY
1953	Antonio Cerda	Argentina
1954	Stan Leonard	Canada
1955	Ed Furgol	United States
1956	Ben Hogan	United States
1957	Torakichi Nakamura	Japan
1958	Angel Miguel	Spain
1959	Stan Leonard	Canada
1960	Flory Van Donck	Belgium
1961	Sam Snead	United States
1962	Roberto de Vicenzo	Argentina
1963	Jack Nicklaus	United States
1964	Jack Nicklaus	United States
1965	Gary Player	South Africa
1966	George Knudson	Canada
1967	Arnold Palmer	United States
1968	Al Balding	Canada
1969	Lee Trevino	United States
1970	Roberto de Vicenzo	Argentina
1971	Jack Nicklaus	United States
1972	Hsieh Min-Nan	Rep. of China
1973	Johnny Miller	United States
1974	Bobby Cole	South Africa
1975	Johnny Miller	United States
1976	Ernesto Acosta	Mexico
1977	Gary Player	South Africa
1978	John Mahaffey	United States
1979	Hale Irwin	United States
1980	Sandy Lyle	Scotland

YEAR	WINNER	COUNTRY
1981	No Tournament	
1982	Manuel Pinero	Spain
1983	Dave Barr	Canada
1984	Jose Canizares	Spain
1985	Howard Clark	England
1986	No Tournament	
1987	Ian Woosnam	Wales
1988	Ben Crenshaw	United States
1989	Peter Fowler	Australia
1990	Payne Stewart	United States
1991	Ian Woosnam	Wales
1992	Brett Ogle	Australia
1993	Bernhard Langer	Germany
1994	Fred Couples	USA
1995	Davis Love III	USA
	Hisayuki Sasahi	Japan

THE ALFRED DUNHILL CUP
The Old Course at St. Andrews, Scotland

Three-man national teams competing in round-robin matches.

YEAR	WINNER	RUNNER-UP
1985	Australia	USA
1986	Australia	Japan
1987	England	Scotland
1988	Ireland	Australia
1989	USA	Japan
1990	Ireland	England
1991	Sweden	South Africa
1992	England	Scotland
1993	USA	England
1994	Canada	USA
1995	Scotland	England

THE PRESIDENT'S CUP
USA vs. an International team from Asia, Africa, and Australasia.
12-man teams in a three-day format with foursome, best ball, and signles play.

YEAR	WINNER	SCORE	RUNNER-UP	SITE
1994	USA	20-12	International	Robert Trent Jones G. C., Manssas, Virginia, USA

CLUB PRO CHAMPIONS

OVERVIEW: *Top-five finishers, scores and prize money for the primary club professional tournaments. Club pros have had their own "Tour" for many years, featuring winter tournaments (typically in Florida around the time of the PGA Merchandise Show); prize money is low but the quality of competition often high with several former and future PGA TOUR players competing. Although no full-time club pro has won a major championship since Claude Harmon in the 1948 Masters, several club professionals such as Jim Albus, Larry Laoretti and Tom Wargo have found fame and fortune on the PGA Senior TOUR.*

Titleist/Foot-Joy PGA Assistant Professional Championship

PGA West—Nicklaus Private (Par 72), La Quinta, California, Nov. 29-Dec. 2, 1994

Wes Short	1	68-71-72-72	283	$6,000
Rob McNamara	T2	69-71-73-73	286	$3,750
Carlton Blewett	T2	70-70-71-75	286	$3,750
Craig Reed	4	73-71-77-67	288	$3,000
Steve Brady	T5	76-71-73-70	290	$2,758
Tim Hobby	T5	69-73-75-73	290	$2,758

Langert PGA Stroke Play Championship

PGA National GC (Par 72)
Palm Beach Gardens, Florida, Jan. 22-25

Bruce Zabriski	1	75-71-68-69	283	$5,000
Jim Estes	2	66-74-70-75	285	$3,000
Mike San Fillipo	T3	69-73-75-69	286	$1,900
Frank Dobbs	T3	69-74-73-70	286	$1,900
Gene Fieger	T3	72-70-72-72	286	$1,900

Langert PGA Match Play Championship

PGA National GC (Par 72)
Miami, Florida, Mar 2-5

QUARTER-FINALS
Jim Estes def. Tom McGinnis, 6 and 5
Craig Thomas def. Frank Dobbs, 1-up
Gene Fieger def. Jeff Foxx, 3 and 2
Gregory Baker def. Craig Murray, 4 and 3

SEMI-FINALS
Fieger def. Estes, 1-up
Thomas def. Baker, 1-up

FINALS
Fieger def. Thomas, 3 and 1

Langert PGA Quarter Century Championship

PGA National G.C. (Estate—Par 72)
Palm Beach Gardens, Florida, Jan.3-4

Under 50			
Jim Gerring	72-82	154	$150
Age 50-54			
Dave Philo	66-73	139	$2,700
Age 55-59			
Art Proctor	70-71	141	$900
Age 60-64			
Larry Mancour	72-70	142	$700
Age 65-69			
Walker Inman Jr.	73-71	144	$700

Age 70-74
Jack Fleck	72-76	148	$700

Age 75-79
Henry Williams	81-78	159	$700

Age 80-84
Skee Riegel	80-83	163	$390

Age 85-89
Edward Locke	88-87	176	$300

Langert PGA Senior-Junior Championship

PGA National G.C.
(Haig and Estate—Par 72)
Palm Beach Gardens, Florida, Jan. 15-17

B. Kennedy/T. Hughes	1	199	$10,000
Lynn Rosley/Randy McGohan	T2	205	$4333
Ken Burnette/Steve Madsen	T2	205	$4,333
John Frillman/Mark Kirk	T2	205	$4,333
Bob Leaver/Earl Svenningsen	5	206	$2,400

Langert PGA Senior Stroke Play Championship

PGA National G.C. (Par 72)
Palm Beach Gardens, Florida, Jan. 6-8

Age 50-54
Bill Kennedy	72-76-75	223	$700

Age 55-59
Carl Lohren	72-71-75	218	$800

Age 60-64
Steve Bull	72-73-74	219	$700

Age 65-69
Charlie Smith	73-70	143	$700

Age 70-74
Ray Montgomery	70-76	146	$600

Age 75-79
Bob Hendricks	78-77	155	$600

Age 80-84
Ralph Bond	78-82	160	$460

Age 85-89
Ted Lockie	85-93	178	$383

PGA Cup Matches

1973	USA 7, Great Britain & Ireland 1	Pinehurst No. 2, USA
1974	USA 11-1/2, Great Britain & Ireland 4-1/2	Pinehurst No. 2, USA
1975	USA 9-1/2, Great Britain & Ireland 6-1/2	Hillside G.C., England
1976	USA 9-1/2, Great Britain & Ireland 6-1/2	Moortown G.C., England
1977	USA 8-1/2, Great Britain & Ireland 8-1/2	Mission Hills C.C., USA
1978	Great Britain & Ireland 10-1/2, USA 6-1/2	St. Mellion G. & C.C., England
1979	Great Britain & Ireland 12-1/2, USA 4-1/2	Castletown Links, Isle of Man
1980	USA 15, Great Britain & Ireland 6	Oak Tree G.C., USA
1981	USA 10-1/2, Great Britain & Ireland 10-1/2	Turnberry Isle C.C., USA
1982	USA 13-1/2, Great Britain & Ireland 7-1/2	Halston Hills Club, USA
1983	Great Britain & Ireland 14-1/2, USA 6-1/2	Muirfield, Scotland

1984	Great Britain & Ireland 12-1/2, USA 8-1/2	Turnberry, Scotland
1986	USA 16, Great Britain & Ireland 9	Knollwood C.C., USA
1988	USA 15-1/2, Great Britain & Ireland 10-1/2	The Belfry, England
1990	USA 19, Europe 7	Turtle Point G.C., USA
1992	USA 12, Europe 11	Kildare C.C., Ireland
1994	USA 15, Europe 11	PGA National G.C., USA

PGA Tournament Series (Florida), 1994-95

Dates	Winner	Score	Money	Site
Nov. 14	Bruce Zabriski Greg Cerulli Ray Cragun	71	$2,600	Cobblestone CC, Palm City
Nov. 21-22	John Reeves	135	$3,300	Wellington Club West, Wellington
Nov. 28-29	Darrell Kestner	137	$3,250	St. Lucie West C.C., Port St. Lucie
Dec. 1-2	George Bowman	137	$3,400	Winston Trails C.C., Lake Worth
Dec. 5-6	Jim Estes	67	$3,500	The Reserve G. & T.C., Ft. Pierce
Dec. 5-6	(Sr.) Gary Wiren	66	$1,800	PGA National Resort, Palm Beach Gardens
Dec. 8-9	Todd M. Smith	134	$3,500	Breakers West C.C, West Palm Beach
Dec. 8-9	Carl Lohren	140	$1,800	St. Lucie West C.C., Port St. Lucie
Dec. 12-13	Jim Estes	138	$3,500	Champions Club at Summerfield, Stuart
Dec. 12-13	(Sr.) Austin Straub	134	$3,400	Palm Beach Gardens M.G.C
Dec. 15-16	Jim Curran	140	$3,500	Binks Forest C.C., Wellington
Dec. 15-16	(Sr.) Larry Mancour	139	$1,750	Club Med at Sandpiper, Port St. Lucie
Feb. 8-9	(Sr.) Bruce Lenhardi	143	$1,850	PGA National Resort, Palm Beach Gardens
Feb. 10-11	Frank Dobbs	138	$3,500	PGA National Resort, Palm Beach Gardens
Feb. 13-14	Mike San Filippo	133	$3,500	PGA National Resort, Palm Beach Gardens
Feb. 13-14	John Frillman	137	$1,850	PGA National Resort, Palm Beach Gardens
Feb 16-17	Gene Fieger	137	$3,250	PGA National Resort, Palm Beach Gardens
Feb. 16-17	(Sr.) Gene Borek	142	$1,800	PGA National Resort, Palm Beach Gardens
Feb. 20-21	Greg Cerullii	136	$3,200	Club Med at Sandpiper, Port St. Lucie
Feb. 20-21	(Sr.) Carl Lohren	141	$1,750	Binks Forest C.C., Wellington

PGA Club Professional Tournament

Year	Winner	Score	Money	Site
1968	Howell Fraser	272	$8,000	Century C.C.
1969	Bob Rosburg	275	$8,000	San Marcos C.C.
1970	Rex Baxter	285	$8,000	Sunol Valley C.C.
1971	Sam Snead	275	$15,000	Pinehurst C.C.
1972	Don Massengale	280	$15,000	Pinehurst C.C.
1973	Rives McBee	282	$16,500	Pinehurst C.C.
1974	Roger Watson	284	$16,500	Pinehurst C.C.
1975	Roger Watson	279	$16,500	Callaway Gardens Resort
1976	Bob Galloway	280	$16,500	Callaway Gardens Resort
1977	Laurie Hammer	282	$16,500	Callaway Gardens Resort
1978	John Gentile	276	$17,000	Callaway Gardens Resort
1979	Buddy Whitten	278	$20,000	Callaway Gardens Resort
1980	John Traub	283	$20,000	PGA National G.C.
1981	Larry Gilbert	285	$20,000	PGA National G.C.
1982	Larry Gilbert	284	$20,000	PGA National G.C.
1983	Larry Webb	283	$20,000	La Quinta Hotel G.C.
1984	Bill Schumaker	284	$25,000	PGA National G.C.
1985	Ed Dougherty	277	$27,500	La Quinta Hotel G.C./Mission Hills
1986	Bob Lendzion	284	$30,000	PGA West/La Quinta Hotel/Mission Hills
1987	Jay Lumpkin	279	$30,000	PGA West/La Quinta Hotel/Mission Hills
1988	Bob Boyd	287	$30,000	Pinehurst C.C.
1989	Bruce Fleisher	277	$30,000	PGA West/La Quinta Hotel/Mission Hills
1990	Brett Upper	275	$32,000	PGA West/La Quinta Hotel/Mission Hills
1991	Larry Gilbert	267	$32,000	Doral C.C.
1992	Ron McDougal	273	$32,000	PGA West/La Quinta Hotel/Mission Hills
1993	Jeffrey Roth	275	$32,000	PGA National G.C.
1994	Sammy Rachels	284	$32,000	Osage Beach and Lake Ozark, MO

AMATEUR GOLF

OVERVIEW: *Winners of national amateur championships since inception, plus annual amateur rankings, Curtis and Walker Cup results through the years and prominent 1994 amateur results.*

U.S. Men's Amateur

Year	Winner	Site	Year	Winner	Site
1895	Charles Blair MacDonald	Newport	1939	Marvin H. Ward	North Shore
1896	H.J. Whigham	Shinnecock	1940	Richard D. Chapman	Winged Foot (West)
1897	H.J. Whigham	Chicago	1941	Marvin H. Ward	Omaha Field
1898	Findlay S. Douglas	Morris County	1942	*No tournament*	
1899	H.M. Harriman	Onwentsia	1943	*No tournament*	
1900	Walter J. Travis	Garden City	1944	*No tournament*	
1901	Walter J. Travis	CC of Atlantic City	1945	*No tournament*	
1902	Louis N. James	Glen View	1946	Ted Bishop	Baltusrol (Lower)
1903	Walter J. Travis	Nassau	1947	Skee Riegel	Pebble Beach
1904	H. Chandler Egan	Baltusrol	1948	William P. Turnesa	Memphis
1905	H. Chandler Egan	Chicago	1949	Charles R. Coe	Oak Hill (East)
1906	Eben M. Byers	Englewood	1950	Sam Urzetta	Minneapolis
1907	Jerome D. Travers	Euclid	1951	Billy Maxwell	Saucon Valley (Old)
1908	Jerome D. Travers	Garden City	1952	Jack Westland	Seattle
1909	Robert A. Gardner	Chicago	1953	Gene Littler	Oklahoma City
1910	Wiliam C. Fownes Jr.	The Country Club	1954	Arnold Palmer	CC of Detroit
1911	Harold H. Hilton	Apawamis	1955	E. Harvie Ward Jr.	CC of Virginia (James R.)
1912	Jerome D. Travers	Chicago	1956	E. Harvie Ward Jr.	Knollwood
1913	Jerome D. Travers	Garden City	1957	Hillman Robbins Jr.	The Country Club
1914	Francis Ouimet	Ekwanok	1958	Charles R. Coe	Olympic (Lake)
1915	Robert A. Gardner	CC of Detroit	1959	Jack Nicklaus	Broadmoor (East)
1916	Chick Evans	Merion	1960	Deane Beman	St. Louis
1917	*No tournament*		1961	Jack Nicklaus	Pebble Beach
1918	*No tournament*		1962	Labron E. Harris Jr.	Pinehurst (No.2)
1919	S. Davidson Herron	Oakmont	1963	Deane Beman	Wakonda
1920	Chick Evans	Engineers	1964	William C. Campbell	Canterbury
1921	Jesse P. Guilford	St. Louis	1965	Robert J. Murphy Jr.	Southern Hills
1922	Jess W. Sweetser	The Country Club	1966	Gary Cowan	Merion (East)
1923	Max R. Marston	Rossmoor	1967	Robert B. Dickson	Broadmoor (West)
1924	Robert T. Jones Jr.	Merion	1968	Bruce Fleisher	Scioto
1925	Robert T. Jones Jr.	Oakmont	1969	Steven N. Melnyk	Oakmont
1926	George Von Elm	Baltusrol	1970	Lanny Wadkins	Waverly
1927	Robert T. Jones Jr.	Minikahda	1971	Gary Cowan	Wilmington (South)
1928	Robert T. Jones Jr.	Brae Burn	1972	Marvin Giles III	Charlotte
1929	Harrison R. Johnston	Pebble Beach	1973	Craig Stadler	Inverness
1930	Robert T. Jones Jr.	Merion	1974	Jerry Pate	Ridgewood
1931	Francis Ouimet	Beverly	1975	Fred Ridley	CC of Virginia (James R.)
1932	C. Ross Somerville	Baltimore	1976	Bill Sander	Bel Air
1933	George T. Dunlap Jr.	Kenwood	1977	John Fought	Aronimink
1934	W. Lawson Little Jr.	The Country Club	1978	John Cook	Plainfield
1935	W. Lawson Little Jr.	The Country Club (O.)	1979	Mark O'Meara	Canterbury
1936	John W. Fischer	Garden City	1980	Hal Sutton	CC of N. Carolina
1937	John Goodman	Alderwood	1981	Nathaniel Crosby	Olympic (Lake)
1938	William P. Turnesa	Oakmont	1982	Jay Sigel	The Country Club

Year	Winner	Site	Year	Winner	Site
1983	Jay Sigel	North Shore	1977	Dale Morey	Salem
1984	Scott Verplank	Oak Tree	1978	Keith K. Compton	Pine Tree
1985	Sam Randolph	Montclair	1979	William C. Campbell	Chicago
1986	Buddy Alexander	Shoal Creek	1980	William C. Campbell	Va. Hot Springs
1987	Bill Mayfair	Jupiter Hills	1981	Edgar R. Updegraff	Seattle
1988	Eric Meeks	Va. Hot Spr. (Cascades)	1982	Alton Duhon	Tucson
1989	Chris Patton	Merion (East)	1983	William Hyndman III	Crooked Stick
1990	Phil Mickelson	Cherry Hills	1984	Robert Rawlins	Birmingham
1991	Mitch Voges	The Honors	1985	Lewis W. Oehmig	Wild Dunes
1992	Justin Leonard	Muirfield Village	1986	R.S. Williams	Interlachen
1993	John Harris	Champions (Cypress Cr.)	1987	John Richardson	Saucon Valley
1994	Eldrick (Tiger) Woods	TPC at Sawgrass	1988	Clarence Moore	Milwaukee
1995	Eldrick (Tiger) Woods	Newport	1989	R.S. Williams	Lochinvar
			1990	Jackie Cummings	Desert Forest
			1991	Bill Bosshard	Crystal Downs

U.S. Men's Mid-Amateur

Year	Winner	Site
1981	Jim Holtgrieve	Bellerive
1982	William Hoffer	Knollwood
1983	Jay Sigel	Cherry Hills
1984	Michael Podolak	Atlanta A.C.
1985	Jay Sigel	The Vintage C.
1986	Bill Loeffler	Annandale
1987	Jay Sigel	Brook Hollow
1988	David Eger	Prairie Dunes
1989	James Taylor	Crooked Stick
1990	Jim Stuart	Troon
1991	Jim Stuart	Long Cove
1992	Danny Yates	Detroit
1993	Jeff Thomas	Eugene
1994	Tim Jackson	Hazeltine National
1995	Jerry Courville	Caves Valley

(continued U.S. Men's Mid-Amateur / Senior list)

1992	Clarence Moore	Loxahatchee
1993	Joe Ungvary	Farmington
1994	O. Gordon Brewer	Champions
1995	James Stahl, Jr.	Prairie Dunes

U.S. Men's Amateur Public Links

Year	Winner	Site
1922	Edmund R. Held	Ottawa Park
1923	Richard J. Walsh	E. Potomac Park
1924	Joseph Coble	Community
1925	Raymond J. McAuliffe	Salisbury
1926	Lester Bolstad	Grover Cleveland Pk.
1927	Carl F. Kauffman	Ridgewood
1928	Carl F. Kauffman	Cobb's Creek
1929	Carl F. Kauffman	Forest Park
1930	Robert E. Wingate	Jacksonville Muni.
1931	Charles Ferrara	Keller
1932	R.L. Miller	Shawnee
1933	Charles Ferrara	Eastmoreland
1934	David A. Mitchell	S. Park Allegheny
1935	Frank Strafaci	Coffin Muni.
1936	B. Patrick Abbott	Bethpage
1937	Bruce N. McCormick	Harding Park
1938	Al Leach	Highland Park
1939	Andrew Swedko	Mt. Pleasant Pk.
1940	Robert C. Clark	Rackham
1941	William M. Welch Jr.	Indian Canyon
1942	*No tournament*	
1943	*No tournament*	
1944	*No tournament*	
1945	*No tournament*	
1946	Smiley L. Quick	Wellshire
1947	Wilfred Crossley	Meadowbrook
1948	Michael Ferentz	N. Fulton Park
1949	Kenneth J. Towns	Rancho
1950	Stan Bielat	Seneca
1951	Dave Stanley	Brown Deer Park
1952	Omer L. Bogan	Miami
1953	Ted Richards Jr.	West Seattle
1954	Gene Andrews	Cedar Crest
1955	Sam Kocsis	Coffin Muni.
1956	James H. Buxbaum	Harding Park

U.S. Men's Senior Amateur

Year	Winner	Site
1955	J. Wood Platt	Belle Meade
1956	Frederick J. Wright	Somerset
1957	J. Clark Espie	Ridgewood
1958	Thomas C. Robbins	Monterey Peninsula
1959	J. Clark Espie	Memphis
1960	Michael Cestone	Oyster Harbours
1961	Dexter H. Dabiels	Southern Hills
1962	Merrill L. Carlsmith	Evanston
1963	Merrill L. Carlsmith	Sea Island
1964	William D. Higgins	Waverly
1965	Robert B. Kiersky	Fox Chapel
1966	Dexter H. Daniels	Tucson National
1967	Ray Palmer	Shinnecock Hills
1968	Curtis Person Sr.	Atlanta C.C.
1969	Curtis Person Sr.	Wichita
1970	Gene Andrews	California
1971	Tom Draper	Sunnybrook
1972	Lewis W. Oehmig	Sharon
1973	William Hyndman III	Onwentsia
1974	Dale Morey	Harbour Town
1975	William F. Colm	Carmel Valley
1976	Lewis W. Oehmig	Cherry Hills

Year	Winner	Site
1957	Don Essig III	Hershey Park
1958	Daniel D. Sikes Jr.	Silver Lake
1959	William A. Wright	Wellshire
1960	Verne Callison	Ala Wai
1961	Richard H. Sikes	Rackham
1962	Richard H. Sikes	Sheridan Park
1963	Robert Lunn	Haggin Oaks
1964	William McDonald	Francis A. Gross
1965	Arne Dokka	North Park
1966	Lamont Kaiser	Brown Deer Park
1967	Verne Callsion	Jefferson Park
1968	Gene Towry	Tenison Memorial
1969	John M. Jackson Jr.	Downing
1970	Robert Risch	Cog Hill (No. 4)
1971	Fred Haney	Papago
1972	Bob Allard	Coffin Muni.
1973	Stan Stopa	Flanders Valley
1974	Charles Barenaba Jr.	Brookside
1975	Randy Barenaba	Wailua
1976	Eddie Mudd	Bunker Hills
1977	Jerry Vidovic	Brown Deer Park
1978	Dean Prince	Bangor Muni.
1979	Dennis Walsh	West Delta
1980	Jodie Mudd	Edgewood Tahoe
1981	Jodie Mudd	Bear Creek Golf World
1982	Billy Tuten	Eagle Creek
1983	Billy Tuten	Hominy Hill
1984	Bill Malley	Indian Canyon
1985	Jim Sorenson	Wailua
1986	Bill Mayfair	Tanglewood Park
1987	Kevin Johnson	Glenview
1988	Ralph Howe III	Jackson Hole
1989	Tim Hobby	Cog Hill (No. 4)
1990	Michael Combs	Eastmoreland
1991	David Berganio Jr.	Otter Creek
1992	Warren Schutte	Edinburgh USA
1993	David Berganio Jr.	Riverside Dunes
1994	Guy Yamamoto	Eagle Bend
1995	Chris Wollman	Stow Acres

Walker Cup

Bi-annual amateur men's competition between the United States and Great Britain & Ireland

Year	Score, Site
1922	USA 8, Great Britain & Ireland 4
	National Golf Links of America
1923	USA 6, Great Britain 5
	St. Andrews (Old)
1924	USA 9, Great Britain & Ireland 3
	Garden City G.C.
1926	USA 6, Great Britain & Ireland 5
	St. Andrews (Old)
1928	USA 11, Great Britain & Ireland 1
	Chicago G.C.
1930	USA 10, Great Britain & Ireland 2
	Royal St. George's G.C.
1932	USA 8, Great Britain 1
	The Country Club (Mass.)
1934	USA 9, Great Britain & Ireland 2
	St. Andrews (Old)
1936	USA 9, Great Britain & Ireland 0
	Pine Valley G.C.
1938	Great Britain & Ireland 7, USA 4
	St. Andrews (Old)
1940-46	*No competition*
1947	USA 8, Great Britain & Ireland 4
	St. Andrews (Old)
1949	USA 10, Great Britain & Ireland 2
	Winged Foot G.C. (West)
1951	USA 6, Great Britain & Ireland 3
	Birkdale G.C.
1953	USA 9, Great Britain & Ireland 3
	The Kittansett Club
1955	USA 10, Great Britain & Ireland 2
	St. Andrews (Old)
1957	USA 8, Great Britain & Ireland 3
	Minikahda Club
1959	USA 9, Great Britain & Ireland 3
	Muirfield
1961	USA 11, Great Britain & Ireland 1
	Seattle G.C.
1963	USA 12, Great Britain & Ireland 8
	Turnberry (Ailsa)
1965	USA 11, Great Britain & Ireland 11
	Baltimore C.C. (Five Farms)
1967	USA 13, Great Britain & Ireland 7
	Royal St. George's G.C.
1969	USA 10, Great Britain & Ireland 8
	Milwaukee C.C.
1971	Great Britain & Ireland 13, USA 11
	St. Andrews (Old)
1973	USA 14, Great Britain & Ireland 10
	The Country Club (Mass.)
1975	USA 15-1/2, Great Britain & Ireland 8-1/2
	St. Andrews (Old)
1977	USA 16, Great Britain & Ireland 8
	Shinnecock Hills
1979	USA 15-1/2, Great Britain & Ireland 8-1/2
	Muirfield
1981	USA 15, Great Britain & Ireland 9
	Cypress Point Club
1983	USA 13-1/2, Great Britain & Ireland 10-1/2
	Royal Liverpool G.C.
1985	USA 13, Great Britain & Ireland 11
	Pine Valley G.C.
1987	USA 16-1/2, Great Britain & Ireland 7-1/2
	Sunningdale G.C.
1989	Great Britain & Ireland 12-1/2, USA 11-1/2
	Peachtree G.C.
1991	USA 14, Great Britain & Ireland 10
	Portmarnock G.C.

1993 USA 19, Great Britain & Ireland 5
      Interlachen C.C.
1995 Great Britain & Ireland 14, United States 10
      Royal Porthcawl

U.S. Men's Amateur Rankings

1955
1. Harvie Ward
2. Joe Conrad
3. Doug Sanders
4. Hillman Robbins
5. Eddie Merrins

1956
1. Harvie Ward
2. Ken Venturi
3. Arnold Blum
4. Doug Sanders
5. Billy Joe Patton

1957
1. Hillman Robbins
2. Dr. F. Taylor
3. Rex Baxter
4. Billy Joe Patton
5. Billy Campbell

1958
1. Charles Coe
2. Bill Hyndman
3. Dick Chapman
4. Billy Joe Patton
5. Phil Rodgers

1959
1. Jack Nicklaus
2. Charles Coe
3. Deane Beman
4. Bill Hyndman
5. Dick Crawford

1960
1. Jack Nicklaus
2. Deane Beman
3. Charlie Smith
4. Bob Cochran
5. Tommy Aaron

1961
1. Jack Nicklaus
2. Bill Hyndman
3. Charles Coe
4. Deane Beman
5. Bob Gardner

1962
1. Labron Harris
2. Billy Joe Patton
3. R.H. Sikes
4. Deane Beman
5. Dr. Ed Updegraff

1963
1. Deane Beman
2. R.H. Sikes
3. George Archer
4. Charles Coe
5. Billy Joe Patton

1964
1. Bill Campbell
2. Deane Beman
3. Dale Morey
4. Ed Tutwiler
5. Steve Opperman

1965
1. George Bouteil
2. Bob Murphy
3. Don Allen
4. Jim Wiechers
5. Deane Beman

1966
1. Gary Cowan
2. Jim Wiechers
3. Marty Fleckman
4. Ron Cerrudo
5. Deane Beman

1967
1. Bob Dickson
2. Bob Smith
3. Hal Underwood
4. Marty Fleckman
5. Bill Campbell

1968
1. Vinny Giles
2. Jack Lewis
3. Bruce Fleisher
4. Bill Hyndman
5. Bill Barbarossa

1969
1. Steve Melnyk
2. Allen Miller
3. Vinny Giles
4. Joe Inman
5. Lanny Wadkins

1970
1. Lanny Wadkins
2. Allen Miller
3. Howard Twitty
4. Gary Cowan
5. Tom Kite

1971
1. Gary Cowan
2. Eddie Pearce
3. Ben Crenshaw
4. Vinny Giles
5. Allen Miller

1972
1. Ben Crenshaw
2. Vinny Giles
3. Mark Hayes
4. Danny Edwards
5. Gary Sanders

1973
1. Ben Crenshaw
2. Vinny Giles
3. Craig Stadler
4. Gary Koch
5. Dick Siderowf

1974
1. Jerry Pate
2. Curtis Strange
3. George Burns
4. Bill Hyndman
5. Gary Koch

1975
1. Andy Bean
2. Fred Ridley
3. Curtis Strange
4. Vinny Giles
5. Phil Hancock

1976
1. Scott Simpson
2. Bob Byman
3. Bill Sander
4. Jay Sigel
5. Dick Siderowf

1977
1. John Fought
2. Gary Hallberg
3. Jim Nelford
4. Scott Simpson
5. John Cook

1978
1. Bobby Clampett
2. John Cook
3. Vance Heafner
4. Scott Hoch
5. Jay Sigel

1979
1. John Cook
2. Mark O'Meara
3. Hal Sutton
4. Rafael Alarcon
5. Jay Sigel

1980
1. Hal Sutton
2. Jay Sigel
3. Fred Couples
4. Jay Don Blake
5. Bobby Clampett

1981
1. Jodie Mudd
2. Frank Fuhrer
3. Nathaniel Crosby
4. Corey Pavin
5. Jay Sigel

1982
1. Jay Sigel
2. Rick Fehr
3. Nathaniel Crosby
4. Brad Faxon
5. John Slaughter

1983
1. Jay Sigel
2. Billy Tuten
3. Scott Verplank
4. Brandel Chamblee
5. Dillard Pruitt

1984
1. Scott Verplank
2. John Inman
3. Jay Sigel
4. Davis Love III
5. Danny Mijovic

1985
1. Scott Verplank
2. Sam Randolph
3. Jay Sigel
4. Clark Burroughs
5. Peter Persons

1986
1. Stewart Alexander
2. Scott Verplank
3. Sam Randolph
4. Chris Kite
5. Bill Andrade

1987
1. Bill Mayfair
2. Jay Sigel
3. Brian Watts
4. Kevin Johnson
5. Hugh Royer

1988
1. Eric Meeks
2. Jay Sigel
3. Ralph Howe
4. David Eger
5. Bill Mayfair

1989-1991
Not available

1992
1. Justin Leonard
2. David Duval
3. Allen Doyle
4. David Howser
5. John Harris

1993
1. Justin Leonard
2. Todd Demsey
3. John Harris
4. Allen Doyle
5. Brian Gay

1994
1. Allen Doyle
2. Eldrick (Tiger) Woods
3. Chris Riley
4. Gary Simpson
5. Alan Bratton

1995
1. Eldrick (Tiger) Woods
2. Tim Jackson
3. Darron Stiles
4. Notah Begay III
5. Paul Simpson

U.S. Women's Amateur

Year	Winner	Site
1895	Mrs. Charles S. Brown	Meadow Brook
1896	Beatrix Hoyt	Morris County
1897	Beatrix Hoyt	Essex County
1898	Beatrix Hoyt	Ardsley
1899	Ruth Underhill	Philadelphia
1900	Frances C. Griscom	Shinnecock Hills
1901	Genevieve Hecker	Baltusrol
1902	Genevieve Hecker	The Country Club
1903	Bessie Anthony	Chicago
1904	Georgianna M. Bishop	Merion
1905	Pauline Mackay	Morris County
1906	Harriot S. Curtis	Brae Burn
1907	Margaret Curtis	Midlothian
1908	Katherine C. Harley	Chevy Chase
1909	Dorothy I. Campbell	Merion
1910	Dorothy I. Campbell	Homewood
1911	Margaret Curtis	Baltusrol
1912	Margaret Curtis	Essex County
1913	Gladys Ravenscroft	Wilmington
1914	Katherine Jackson	Nassau
1915	Florence Vanderbeck	Onwentsia
1916	Alexa Stirling	Belmont Springs
1917	*No tournament*	
1918	*No tournament*	
1919	Alexa Stirling	Shawnee
1920	Alexa Stirling	Mayfield
1921	Marion Hollins	Hollywood
1922	Glenna Collett	Greenbrier
1923	Edith Cummings	Westchester-Biltmore
1924	Dorothy C. Hurd	Rhode Island
1925	Glenna Collett	St. Louis
1926	Helen Stetson	Merion
1927	Miriam Burns Horn	Cherry Valley
1928	Glenna Collett	Va. Hot Springs
1929	Glenna Collett	Oakland Hills
1930	Glenna Collett	Los Angeles
1931	Helen Hicks	CC of Buffalo
1932	Virginia Van Wie	Salem
1933	Virginia Van Wie	Exmoor
1934	Virginia Van Wie	Whitemarsh Valley
1935	Glenna Collett Vare	Interlachen
1936	Pamela Barton	Canoe Brook
1937	Estelle Lawson Page	Memphis
1938	Patty Berg	Westmoreland
1939	Betty Jameson	Wee Burn
1940	Betty Jameson	Pebble Beach
1941	Elizabeth Hicks Newell	The Country Club
1942-5	*No tournament*	
1946	Babe Zaharias	Southern Hills
1947	Louise Suggs	Franklin Hills
1948	Grace S. Lenczyk	Pebble Beach
1949	Dorothy Porter	Merion
1950	Beverly Hanson	Atlanta A.C.
1951	Dorothy Kirby	Town & Country
1952	Jacqueline Pung	Waverly
1953	Mary Lena Faulk	Rhode Island
1954	Barbara Romack	Allegheny
1955	Patricia Lesser	Myers Park
1956	Marlene Stewart	Meridian Hills
1957	JoAnne Gunderson	Del Paso

Year	Winner	Site
1958	Anne Quast	Wee Burn
1959	Barbara McIntire	Congressional
1960	JoAnne Gunderson	Tulsa
1961	Anne Quast Decker	Tacoma
1962	JoAnne Gunderson	C.C. of Rochester
1963	Anne Quast Welts	Taconic
1964	Barbara McIntire	Prairie Dunes
1965	Jean Ashley	Lakewood
1966	JoAnne Carner	Birmingham
1967	Mary Lou Dill	Annandale
1968	JoAnne Carner	Birmingham
1969	Catherina Lacoste	Las Colinas
1970	Martha Wilkinson	Wee Burn
1971	Laura Baugh	Atlanta C.C.
1972	Mary Budke	St. Louis
1973	Carol Semple	Montclair
1974	Cynthia Hill	Broadmoor
1975	Beth Daniel	Brae Burn
1976	Donna Horton	Del Paso
1977	Beth Daniel	Cincinatti
1978	Cathy Sherk	Sunnybrook
1979	Carolyn Hill	Memphis
1980	Juli Inkster	Prairie Dunes
1981	Juli Inkster	Waverly
1982	Juli Inkster	Broadmoor
1983	Joanne Pacillo	Canoe Brook
1984	Deb Richard	Broadmoor
1985	Mickiko Hattori	Fox Chapel
1986	Kay Cockerill	Pasatiempo
1987	Kay Cockerill	Rhode Island
1988	Pearl Sinn	Minikahda
1989	Vicki Goetze	Pinehurst No. 2
1990	Pat Hurst	Canoe Brook
1991	Amy Fruhwirth	Prairie Dunes
1992	Vicki Goetze	Kemper Lakes
1993	Jill McGill	San Diego
1994	Wendy Ward	Cascades
1995	Kelli Kuehne	The Country Club

1964	Lorna Smith	Del Paso
1965	Lorna Smith	Exmoor
1966	Maureen Orcutt	Lakewood
1967	Marge Mason	Atlantic City
1968	Carolyn Cudone	Monterey Peninsula
1969	Carolyn Cudone	Ridgelea
1970	Carolyn Cudone	Coral Ridge
1971	Carolyn Cudone	Sea Island
1972	Carolyn Cudone	Manufacturers'
1973	Gwen Hibbs	San Marcos
1974	Justine B. Cushing	Lakewood
1975	Alberta Bower	Rhode Island
1976	Cecile Maclaurin	Monterey Peninsula
1977	Dorothy Porter	Dunes Club
1978	Alice Dye	Rancho Bernardo
1979	Alice Dye	Herdscrabble
1980	Dorothy Porter	Sea Island
1981	Dorothy Porter	Spring Lake
1982	Edean Ihlanfeldt	Kissing Camels
1983	Dorothy Porter	Gulph Mills
1984	Constance Guthrie	Tacoma
1985	Marlene Street	Sheraton Savannah
1986	Constance Guthrie	Lakewood
1987	Anne Sander	Manufacturers'
1988	Lois Hodge	Sea Island
1989	Anne Sander	TPC at The Woodlands
1990	Anne Sander	Del Rio
1991	Phyllis Preuss	Pine Needles
1992	Rosemary Thompson	Tucson
1993	Anne Sander	Preakness Hills
1994	Nancy Fitzgerald	Sea Island
1995	Jean Smith	Somerset

U.S. Women's Mid-Amateur

1987	Cindy Scholefield	Southern Hills
1988	Martha Lang	Amelia Island
1989	Robin Weiss	The Hills of Lakeway
1990	Carol Semple Thompson	Allegheny
1991	Sarah LeBrun Ingram	Desert Highlands
1992	Marion Maney-McInerny	Old Marsh
1993	Sarah LeBrun Ingram	Rochester
1994	Maria Jemsek	Tacoma
1995	Ellen Port	Essex

U.S. Women's Senior Amateur

1962	Maureen Orcutt	Manufacturers'
1963	Marion Choate	CC of Florida

U.S. Women's Amateur Public Links

1977	Kelly Fuiks	Yahara Hills
1978	Kelly Fuiks	Myrtlewood
1979	Lori Castillo	Braemar
1980	Lori Castillo	Center Square
1981	Mary Enright	Emerald Valley
1982	Nancy Taylor	Alvamar
1983	Kelli Antolock	Ala Wai
1984	Heather Farr	Meadowbrook
1985	Danielle Ammaccapane	Flanders Valley
1986	Cindy Schreyer	SentryWorld
1987	Tracy Kerdyk	Cog Hill No. 4
1988	Pearl Sinn	Page Belcher
1989	Pearl Sinn	Indian Canyon
1990	Cathy Mockett	Hyland Hills
1991	Tracy Hanson	Birdwood
1992	Amy Fruwirth	Haggin Oaks
1993	Connie Masterson	Jackson Hole
1994	Jill McGill	Tam O'Shanter
1995	Jo Jo Robertson	Hominy Hill

Curtis Cup

Bi-annual amateur women's competition between the United States and Great Britain & Ireland

Year   Score, Site
1932   USA 5-1/2, Great Britain & Ireland 3-1/2
       Wentworth
1934   USA 6-1/2, Great Britain & Ireland 2-1/2
       Chevy Chase
1936   USA 4-1/2, Great Britain & Ireland 4-1/2
       Gleneagles
1938   USA 5-1/2, Great Britain & Ireland 3-1/2
       Essex
1940-46   *No competition*
1948   USA 6-1/2, Great Britain & Ireland 2-1/2
       Birkdale
1950   USA 7-1/2, Great Britain & Ireland 1-1/2
       C.C. of Buffalo
1952   USA 5, Great Britain & Ireland 4
       Muirfield
1954   USA 6, Great Britain & Ireland 3
       Merion
1956   USA 5, Great Britain & Ireland 4
       Prince's
1958   USA 4-1/2, Great Britain & Ireland 4-1/2
       Brae Burn
1960   USA 6-1/2, Great Britain & Ireland 2-1/2
       Lindrick
1962   USA 8, Great Britain & Ireland 1
       Broadmoor
1964   USA 10-1/2, Great Britain & Ireland 7-1/2
       Royal Porthcawl
1966   USA 13, Great Britain & Ireland 5
       Virginia Hot Springs
1968   USA 10-1/2, Great Britain & Ireland 7-1/2
       Royal County Down
1970   USA 11-1/2, Great Britain & Ireland 6-1/2
       Brae Burn
1972   USA 10, Great Britain & Ireland 8
       Western Gailes
1974   USA 13, Great Britain & Ireland 5
       San Francisco
1976   USA 11-1/2, Great Britain & Ireland 6-1/2
       Royal Lytham & St. Anne's
1978   USA 12, Great Britain & Ireland 6
       Apawamis Club
1980   USA 13, Great Britain & Ireland 5
       St. Pierre
1982   USA 14-1/2, Great Britain & Ireland 3-1/2
       Denver
1984   USA 9-1/2, Great Britain & Ireland 8-1/2
       Muirfield
1986   Great Britain & Ireland 13, USA 5
       Prairie Dunes
1988   Great Britain & Ireland 11, USA 7
       Royal St. George's
1990   USA 14, Great Britain 4
       Somerset Hills
1992   Great Britain & Ireland 10, USA 8
       Royal Liverpool
1994   United States 13, Great Britain & Ireland 5
       The Honors Course

U.S. Women's Amateur Rankings

1955
1. Pat Lesser
2. Wiffi Smith
3. Jackie Yates
4. Polly Riley
5. Barbara Romack

1956
1. Marlene Stewart
2. JoAnne Gunderson
3. Wiffi Smith
4. Anne Quast
5. Wanda Sanches

1957
1. JoAnne Gunderson
2. Ann C. Johnstone
3. Barabara McIntire
4. Anne Richardson
5. Mary Ann Downey

1958
1. Anne Quast
2. Barbara McIntire
3. Barbara Romack
4. JoAnne Gunderson
5. Carolyn Cudone

1959
1. Barbara McIntire
2. Ann C. Johnstone
3. Joanne Goodwin
4. JoAnne Gunderson
5. Anne Quast

1960
1. JoAnne Gunderson
2. Barbara McIntire
3. Ann C. Johnstone
4. Judy Eller
5. Anne Quast

1961
1. Anne Quast Decker
2. Barbara McIntire
3. Phyllis Preuss
4. Judy Bell
5. Barbara Williams

1962
1. JoAnne Gunderson
2. Clifford Ann Creed
3. Phyllis Preuss
4. Ann C. Johnstone
5. Carol Sorenson

1963
1. Anne Quast Welts
2. Nancy Roth
3. JoAnne Gunderson
4. Peggy Conley
5. Janis Ferraris

1964
1. Barbara McIntire
2. Carol Sorenson
3. Barbara Boddie
4. Nancy Roth
5. Phyllis Preuss

1965
1. Nancy Roth Syms
2. Marlene Streit
3. Jean Ashley
4. Phyllis Preuss
5. Barbara McIntire

1966
1. JoAnne Carner
2. Nancy Roth
3. Shelley Hamlin
4. Roberta Albers
5. Dorothy Porter

1967
1. Mary Lou Dill
2. Phyllis Preuss
3. Jane Bastanchury
4. Martha Wilkinson
5. Dorothy Porter

1968
1. JoAnne Carner
2. Catherina LaCoste
3. Alice Dye
4. Jane Bastanchury
5. Phyllis Preuss

1969
1. Catherine LaCoste
2. Jane Bastanchury
3. JoAnne Carner
4. Barbara McIntire
5. Phyllis Preuss

1970
1. Martha Wilkinson
2. Jane Bastanchury
3. Cynthia Hill
4. Lancy Smith
5. Hollis Stacy

1971
1. Laura Baugh
2. Beth Barry
3. Phyllis Preuss
4. Lancy Smith
5. Barbara McIntire

1972
1. Jane Booth
2. Mary Budke
3. Mickey Walker
4. Debbie Massey
5. Beth Barry

1973
1. Carol Semple
2. Jane Booth
3. Beth Barry
4. Liana Zambresky
5. Anne Sander

1974
1. Debbie Massey
2. Cynthia Hill
3. Lancy Smith
4. Carol Semple
5. Marlene Streit

1975
1. Debbie Massey
2. Beth Daniel
3. Cynthia Hill
4. Nancy Lopez
5. Nancy Roth Syms

1976
1. Nancy Lopez
2. Donna Horton
3. Debbie Massey
4. Carol Semple
5. Marianne Bretton

1977
1. Beth Daniel
2. Cathy Reynolds
3. Cynthia Hill
4. Marcia Dolan
5. Lancy Smith

1978
1. Cathy Sherk
2. Beth Daniel
3. Nancy Syms
4. Judith Oliver
5. Carolyn Hill

1979
1. Carolyn Hill
2. Lancy Smith
3. Brenda Goldsmith
4. Mary Hafeman
5. Julie Gumlia

1980
1. Patti Rizzo
2. Juli Inkster
3. Carol Semple
4. Lori Castillo
5. Kathy Baker

1981
1. Juli Inkster
2. Patti Rizzo
3. Amy Benz
4. Leslie Shannon
5. Mary Hafeman

1982
1. Juli Inkster
2. Kathy Baker
3. Amy Benz
4. Cathy Hanlon
5. Anne Sander

1983
1. Penny Hammel
2. Jody Rosenthal
3. Joanne Pacillo
4. Anne Sander
5. Tammy Wellborn

1984
1. Claire White
2. Leslie Shannon
3. Deb Richard
4. Jody Rosenthal
5. Danielle Ammaccapane

1985
1. Danielle Ammaccapane
2. Kim Williams
3. Michiko Hattori
4. Kathleen McCarthy
5. Leslie Shannon

1986
1. Leslie Shannon
2. Kay Cockerill
3. Carol Semple Thompson
4. Lancy Smith
5. Cindy Scholefield

1987
1. Kay Cockerill
2. Cindy Scholefield
3. Tracy Kerdyk
4. Carol Semple Thompson
5. Caroline Keggi

1988
1. Pearl Sinn
2. Caroline Keggi
3. Anne Sander
4. Michiko Hattori
5. Tracy Kerdyk

1989-1991
Not available.

1992
1. Vicki Goetze
2. Carol Semple Thompson
3. Sarah Ingram
4. Robin Weiss
5. Moira Dunn

1993
1. Sarah Ingram
2. Emilee Klein
3. Carol Semple Thompson
4. Jill McGill
5. Stephanie Sparks

1994
1. Stephanie Neill
2. Sarah Ingram
3. Wendy Ward
4. Robin Weiss
5. Page Marsh Lea

1995
1. Kellee Booth
2. Anne-Marie Knight
3. Maria Jemsek
4. Cristie Kerr
5. Brenda Kuehn

Men's World Amateur Team Championship

Bi-annual amateur men's competition between 4-man national teams.

Year	Winner, Site
1958	Australia St. Andrews, Scotland
1960	USA Merion G.C., USA
1962	USA Fuji G.C., Japan
1964	Gr. Britain & Ireland Olgiata G.C., Italy
1966	Australia Club de Golf, Mexico
1968	USA Royal Melbourne, Australia
1970	USA Real Club de la Purta de Hierro, Spain
1972	USA Olivos G.C., Argentina
1974	USA Campo de Golf, Dominican Rep.
1976	Gr. Britain & Ireland Pennina G.C., Portugal
1978	USA Pacific Harbour G.&C.C., Fiji
1980	USA Pinehurst, USA
1982	USA Lausanne G.C., Switzerland
1984	Japan Royal Hong Kong G.C., Hong Kong
1986	Canada Laguinta, Venezuela
1988	Gr. Britain & Ireland Ullna G.C., Sweden
1990	Sweden Christchurch G.C., New Zealand
1992	New Zealand Capilano G.&C.C., Canada
1994	USA La Boulie

Women's World Amateur Team Championship

Bi-annual amateur women's competition between 4-woman national teams.

Year	Winner, Site
1964	France St. Germain G.C., France
1966	USA Mexico City C.C., Mexico
1968	USA Victoria G.C., Australia.
1970	USA RSHE Club de Campo, Spain
1972	USA The Hindu C.C., Argentina
1974	USA Campo de Golf, Dominican Rep.
1976	USA Vilamoura G.C., Portugal
1978	Australia Pacific Harbour G.&C.C.
1980	USA Pinehurst, USA
1982	USA Geneva G.C., Switzerland
1984	USA Royal Hong Kong G.C., Hong Kong
1986	Spain Lagunita C.C., Venezuela
1988	USA Drottningholm G.C., Sweden
1990	USA Russley G.C., New Zealand
1992	Spain Marine Drive G.C., Canada
1994	USA La Boulie, France

TOUR WINNERS OF THE PAST

OVERVIEW: *Past winners, locations, and winning scores of all current PGA TOUR, LPGA Tour, and Senior PGA TOUR events. Winners of major championships are not included. Playoff winners are marked with an asterisk.*

PGA TOUR

MERCEDES CHAMPIONSHIPS
(Formerly the Tournament of Champions)
Desert Inn C.C., Las Vegas, NV (1953-1966); Stardust C.C., Las Vegas, NV (1967-68); LaCosta C.C., Carlsbad, CA (1969-present).

Year	Winner	Score
1953	Al Besselink	280
1954	Art Wall	278
1955	Gene Littler	280
1956	Gene Littler	281
1957	Gene Littler	285
1958	Stan Leonard	275
1959	Mike Souchak	281
1960	Jerry Barber	268
1961	Sam Snead	273
1962	Arnold Palmer	276
1963	Jack Nicklaus	273
1964	Jack Nicklaus	279
1965	Arnold Palmer	277
1966	*Arnold Palmer	283
1967	Frank Beard	278
1968	Don January	276
1969	Gary Player	284
1970	Frank Beard	273
1971	Jack Nicklaus	279
1972	*Bobby Mitchell	280
1973	Jack Nicklaus	276
1974	Johnny Miller	280
1975	*Al Geiberger	277
1976	Don January	277
1977	*Jack Nicklaus	281
1978	Gary Player	281
1979	Tom Watson	275
1980	Tom Watson	276
1981	Lee Trevino	273
1982	Lanny Wadkins	280
1983	Lanny Wadkins	280
1984	Tom Watson	274
1985	Tom Kite	275
1986	Calvin Peete	267
1987	Mac O'Grady	278
1988	Steve Pate	202
1989	Steve Jones	279
1990	Paul Azinger	272
1991	Tom Kite	272
1992	*Steve Elkington	279
1993	Davis Love III	272
1994	Phil Mickelson	276
1995	Steve Elkington	278

UNITED AIRLINES HAWAIIAN OPEN
Waialae C.C., Honolulu, HI (1965-present).

Year	Winner	Score
1965	*Gay Brewer	281
1966	Ted Makalena	271
1967	*Dudley Wysong	284
1968	Lee Trevino	272
1969	Bruce Crampton	274
1970	No Tournament	
1971	Tom Shaw	273
1972	*Grier Jones	274
1973	John Schlee	273
1974	Jack Nicklaus	271
1975	Gary Groh	274
1976	Ben Crenshaw	270
1977	Bruce Lietzke	273
1978	*Hubert Green	274
1979	Hubert Green	267
1980	Andy Bean	266
1981	Hale Irwin	265
1982	Wayne Levi	277

United Airlines Hawaiian Open continued

1983	Isao Aoki	268
1984	*Jack Renner	271
1985	Mark O'Meara	267
1986	Corey Pavin	272
1987	*Corey Pavin	270
1988	Lanny Wadkins	271
1989	Gene Sauers	197
1990	David Ishii	279
1991	Lanny Wadkins	270
1992	John Cook	265
1993	Howard Twitty	269
1994	Brett Ogle	269
1995	John Morse	269

NORTHERN TELECOM OPEN
(Formerly the Tucson Open)
El Rio G. & C.C., Tucson, AZ (1945-62); 49er C.C., Tucson, AZ (1963-64); Tucson National G.C. (1965-78, 1980, 1991-present); Randolph Park M.G.C. (1979, 1981-1986, 1990); TPC at StarPass, Tucson, AZ (1987-present).

1945	Ray Mangrum	268
1946	Jimmy Demaret	268
1947	Jimmy Demaret	264
1948	Skip Alexander	264
1949	Lloyd Mangrum	263
1950	Chandler Harper	267
1951	Lloyd Mangrum	269
1952	Henry Williams	274
1953	Tommy Bolt	265
1954	No Tournament	
1955	Tommy Bolt	265
1956	Ted Kroll	264
1957	Dow Finsterwald	269
1958	Lionel Hebert	265
1959	Gene Littler	266
1960	Don January	271
1961	*Dave Hill	269
1962	Phil Rodgers	263
1963	Don January	266
1964	Jack Cupit	274
1965	Bob Charles	271
1966	*Joe Campbell	278
1967	Arnold Palmer	273
1968	George Knudson	273
1969	Lee Trevino	271
1970	*Lee Trevino	275
1971	J.C. Snead	273
1972	Miller Barber	273
1973	Bruce Crampton	277
1974	Johnny Miller	272
1975	Johnny Miller	263
1976	Johnny Miller	274
1977	*Bruce Lietzke	275
1978	Tom Watson	276
1979	Bruce Lietzke	265
1980	Jim Colbert	270
1981	Johnny Miller	265
1982	Craig Stadler	266
1983	*Gil Morgan	271
1984	Tom Watson	2&1
1985	Jim Thorpe	4&3
1986	Jim Thorpe	67
1987	Mike Reid	268
1988	David Frost	266
1989	No Tournament	
1990	Robert Gamez	270
1991	Phi Mickelson	272
1992	Lee Janzen	270
1993	Larry Mize	271
1994	Andrew Magee	270
1995	Phil Mickelson	269

PHOENIX OPEN
Phoenix C.C., Phoenix, AZ (1935-86); Arizona C.C., Phoenix, AZ (1955-73); TPC of Scottsdale, Scottsdale, AZ (1987-present).

1935	Ky Laffoon	281
1936	No Tournament	
1937	No Tournament	
1938	No Tournament	
1939	Byron Nelson	198
1940	Ed Oliver	205
1941	No Tournament	
1942	No Tournament	
1943	No Tournament	
1944	*Harold McSpaden	273
1945	Byron Nelson	274
1946	*Ben Hogan	273
1947	Ben Hogan	270
1948	Bobby Locke	268
1949	*Jimmy Demaret	278
1950	Jimmy Demaret	269
1951	Lew Worsham	272
1952	Lloyd Mangrum	274

Phoenix Open continued

Year	Winner	Score
1953	Lloyd Mangrum	272
1954	*Ed Furgol	272
1955	Gene Littler	275
1956	Cary Middlecoff	276
1957	Billy Casper	271
1958	Ken Venturi	274
1959	Gene Littler	268
1960	*Jack Fleck	273
1961	*Arnold Palmer	270
1962	Arnold Palmer	269
1963	Arnold Palmer	273
1964	Jack Nicklaus	271
1965	Rod Funseth	274
1966	Dudley Wysong	278
1967	Julius Boros	272
1968	George Knudson	272
1969	Gene Littler	263
1970	Dale Douglass	271
1971	Miller Barber	261
1972	Homero Blancas	273
1973	Bruce Crampton	268
1974	Johnny Miller	271
1975	Johnny Miller	260
1976	Bob Gilder	268
1977	*Jerry Pate	277
1978	Miller Barber	272
1979	Ben Crenshaw	199
1980	Jeff Mitchell	272
1981	David Graham	268
1982	Lanny Wadkins	263
1983	*Bob Gilder	271
1984	Tom Purtzer	268
1985	Calvin Peete	270
1986	Hal Sutton	267
1987	Paul Azinger	268
1988	*Sandy Lyle	269
1989	Mark Calcavecchia	263
1990	Tommy Armour III	267
1991	Nolan Henke	268
1992	Mark Calcavecchia	264
1993	Lee Janzen	273
1994	Bill Glasson	268
1995	Vijah Singh	269

AT&T PEBBLE BEACH NATIONAL PRO-AM

(Formerly the Bing Crosby National Professional Amateur or Crosby Clambake)

Rancho Santa Fe C.C., San Diego, CA (1937-42); Cypress Point C.C., Pebble Beach, CA (1947-1990); Monterey Peninsula C.C., Monterey Peninsula, CA (1947-66); Pebble Beach G.L., Pebble Beach, CA (1947-present); Spyglass Hill G.C., Pebble Beach, CA (1967-present); Poppy Hills G.C., Monterey Peninsula (1991-present).

Year	Winner	Score
1937	Sam Snead	68
1938	Sam Snead	139
1939	Dutch Harrison	138
1940	Ed Oliver	135
1941	Sam Snead	136
1942	Lloyd Mangrum	
	Leland Gibson	133
1943	No Tournament	
1944	No Tournament	
1945	No Tournament	
1946	No Tournament	
1947	Ed Furgol	
	George Fazio	213
1948	Lloyd Mangrum	205
1949	Ben Hogan	208
1950	Sam Snead	
	Jack Burke, Jr.	
	Smiley Quick	
	Dave Douglas	214
1951	Byron Nelson	209
1952	Jimmy Demaret	145
1953	Lloyd Mangrum	204
1954	Dutch Harrison	210
1955	Cary Middlecoff	209
1956	Cary Middlecoff	202
1957	Jay Hebert	213
1958	Billy Casper	277
1959	Art Wall	279
1960	Ken Venturi	286
1961	Bob Rosburg	282
1962	*Doug Ford	286
1963	Billy Casper	285
1964	Tony Lema	284
1965	Bruce Crampton	284
1966	Don Massengale	283
1967	Jack Nicklaus	284
1968	*Johnny Pott	285
1969	George Archer	283
1970	Bert Yancey	278
1971	Tom Shaw	278

AT&T National Pro-Am continued

1972	*Jack Nicklaus	284
1973	*Jack Nicklaus	282
1974	Johnny Miller	208
1975	Gene Littler	280
1976	Ben Crenshaw	281
1977	Tom Watson	273
1978	*Tom Watson	280
1979	Lon Hinkle	284
1980	George Burns	280
1981	*John Cook	209
1982	Jim Simons	274
1983	Tom Kite	276
1984	*Hale Irwin	278
1985	Mark O'Meara	283
1986	Fuzzy Zoeller	205
1987	Johnny Miller	278
1988	*Steve Jones	280
1989	Mark O'Meara	277
1990	Mark O'Meara	281
1991	Paul Azinger	274
1992	*Mark O'Meara	275
1993	Brett Ogle	276
1994	Johnny Miller	281
1995	Peter Jacobsen	271

BUICK INVITATIONAL OF CALIFORNIA

(Formerly the San Diego Open)

San Diego C.C., San Diego, CA (1952-53); Rancho Santa Fe C.C., Sam Diego, CA (1954); Mission Valley C.C., San Diego, CA (1955, 1957-61); Singing Hills G.C., San Diego, CA (1956); Stardust C.C., San Diego, CA (1962-63, 1965-67); Rancho Bernardo C.C., San Diego, CA (1964); Torrey Pines G.C., San Diego, CA (1968-present).

1952	Ted Kroll	276
1953	Tommy Bolt	274
1954	Gene Littler	274
1955	Tommy Bolt	274
1956	Bob Rosburg	270
1957	Arnold Palmer	271
1958	No Tournament	
1959	Marty Furgol	274
1960	Mike Souchak	269
1961	*Arnold Palmer	271
1962	*Tommy Jacobs	277
1963	Gary Player	270
1964	Art Wall	274
1965	*Wes Ellis	267
1966	Billy Casper	268
1967	Bob Goalby	269
1968	Tom Weiskopf	273
1969	Jack Nicklaus	284
1970	*Pete Brown	275
1971	George Archer	272
1972	Paul Harney	275
1973	Bob Dickson	278
1974	Bobby Nichols	275
1975	*J. C. Snead	279
1976	J. C. Snead	272
1977	Tom Watson	269
1978	Jay Haas	278
1979	Fuzzy Zoeller	282
1980	*Tom Watson	275
1981	*Bruce Lietzke	278
1982	Johnny Miller	270
1983	Gary Hallberg	271
1984	*Gary Koch	272
1985	*Woody Blackburn	269
1986	*Bob Tway	204
1987	George Burns	266
1988	Steve Pate	269
1989	Greg Twiggs	271
1990	Dan Forsman	275
1991	Jay Don Blake	268
1992	Steve Pate	200
1993	Phil Mickelson	278
1994	Craig Stadler	268
1995	Peter Jacobsen	269

BOB HOPE CHRYSLER CLASSIC

Bermuda Dunes C.C., Palm Springs, CA (1960-present); Indian Wells C.C., Indian Wells, CA, (1960-present); Tamarisk C.C. Palm Springs, CA, (1960-63, 1969, 1971, 1973, 1975, 1977, 1979, 1981, 1983, 1985, 1987, 1990, 1993); Thunderbird C.C., Palm Springs, CA (1960-62); Eldorado C.C., Palm Springs, CA (1961-68, 1970, 1972, 1974, 1976, 1978, 1980, 1982, 1984, 1986, 1989); La Quinta C.C., La Quinta, CA (1964-88, 1991-92); TPC at PGA West (Stadium), La Quinta, CA (1987); PGA West (Palmer Course), La Quinta, CA (1989-present); Indian Ridge C.C., La Quinta, CA (1994-present).

Bob Hope Chrysler Classic continued

1960	Arnold Palmer	338
1961	Billy Maxwell	345
1962	Arnold Palmer	342
1963	*Jack Nicklaus	345
1964	*Tommy Jacobs	348
1965	Billy Casper	348
1966	*Doug Sanders	349
1967	Tom Nieporte	349
1968	*Arnold Palmer	348
1969	Billy Casper	345
1970	Bruce Devlin	339
1971	Arnold Palmer	342
1972	Bob Rosburg	344
1973	Arnold Palmer	343
1974	Hubert Green	341
1975	Johnny Miller	339
1976	Johnny Miller	344
1977	Rik Massengale	337
1978	Bill Rogers	339
1979	John Mahaffey	343
1980	Craig Stadler	343
1981	Bruce Lietzke	335
1982	*Ed Fiori	335
1983	*Keith Fergus	335
1984	*John Mahaffey	340
1985	*Lanny Wadkins	333
1986	*Donnie Hammond	335
1987	Corey Pavin	341
1988	Jay Haas	338
1989	*Steve Jones	343
1990	Peter Jacobsen	339
1991	*Corey Pavin	331
1992	*John Cook	336
1993	Tom Kite	325
1994	Scott Hoch	334
1995	Kenny Perry	335

NISSAN OPEN
(Formerly the Los Angeles Open)

Los Angeles C.C., Los Angeles, CA (1926, 1934-36, 1940); El Caballero C.C., Los Angeles, CA (1927); Wilshire C.C., Los Angeles, CA (1928, 1933, 1944); Riviera C.C., Pacific Palisades, CA (1929-1930, 1941, 1945-1953, 1973-present); Hillcrest C.C., Los Angeles, CA (1932, 1942); Griffith Park, Los Angeles, CA (1937-39); Fox Hills C.C., Culver City, CA (1954); Inglewood C.C., Inglewood, CA (1955); Rancho M.G.C., Los Angeles, CA (1956-1967, 1969-1972); Brookside G.C., Pasadena, CA (1968).

1926	Harry Cooper	279
1927	Bobby Cruikshank	282
1928	Mac Smith	284
1929	Mac Smith	285
1930	Densmore Shute	296
1931	Ed Dudley	285
1932	Mac Smith	281
1933	Craig Wood	281
1934	Mac Smith	280
1935	*Vic Ghezzi	285
1936	Jimmy Hines	280
1937	Harry Cooper	274
1938	Jimmy Thomson	273
1939	Jimmy Demaret	274
1940	Lawson Little	282
1941	Johnny Bulla	281
1942	*Ben Hogan	282
1943	No Tournament	
1944	Harold McSpaden	278
1945	Sam Snead	283
1946	Byron Nelson	284
1947	Ben Hogan	280
1948	Ben Hogan	275
1949	Lloyd Mangrum	284
1950	*Sam Snead	280
1951	Lloyd Mangrum	280
1952	Tommy Bolt	289
1953	Lloyd Mangrum	280
1954	Fred Wampler	281
1955	Gene Littler	276
1956	Lloyd Mangrum	272
1957	Doug Ford	280
1958	Frank Stranahan	275
1959	Ken Venturi	278
1960	Dow Finsterwald	280
1961	Bob Goalby	275
1962	Phil Rodgers	268
1963	Arnold Palmer	274
1964	Paul Harney	280
1965	Paul Harney	276
1966	Arnold Palmer	273
1967	Arnold Palmer	269
1968	Billy Casper	274
1969	*Charles Sifford	276
1970	*Billy Casper	276

Nissan Open continued

1971	*Bob Lunn	274
1972	*George Archer	270
1973	Rod Funseth	276
1974	Dave Stockton	276
1975	Pat Fitzsimons	275
1976	Hale Irwin	272
1977	Tom Purtzer	273
1978	Gil Morgan	278
1979	Lanny Wadkins	276
1980	Tom Watson	276
1981	Johnny Miller	270
1982	*Tom Watson	271
1983	Gil Morgan	270
1984	David Edwards	279
1985	Lanny Wadkins	264
1986	Doug Tewell	270
1987	*Tze-Chung Chen	275
1988	Chip Beck	267
1989	Mark Calcavecchia	272
1990	Fred Couples	266
1991	Ted Schulz	272
1992	*Fred Couples	269
1993	Tom Kite	206
1994	Corey Pavin	271
1995	Corey Pavin	268

DORAL RYDER OPEN
(Formerly the Doral-Eastern Open)
Doral C.C. (Blue), Miami, FL (1962-present).

1962	Billy Casper	283
1963	Dan Sikes	283
1964	Billy Casper	277
1965	Doug Sanders	274
1966	Phil Rodgers	278
1967	Doug Sanders	275
1968	Gardner Dickinson	275
1969	Tom Shaw	276
1970	Mike Hill	279
1971	J.C. Snead	275
1972	Jack Nicklaus	276
1973	Lee Trevino	276
1974	Brian Allin	272
1975	Jack Nicklaus	276
1976	Hubert Green	270
1977	Andy Bean	277
1978	Tom Weiskopf	272
1979	Mark McCumber	279
1980	*Raymond Floyd	279
1981	Raymond Floyd	273
1982	Andy Bean	278
1983	Gary Koch	271
1984	Tom Kite	272
1985	Mark McCumber	284
1986	*Andy Bean	276
1987	Lanny Wadkins	277
1988	Ben Crenshaw	274
1989	Bill Glasson	275
1990	*Greg Norman	273
1991	*Rocco Mediate	276
1992	Raymond Floyd	271
1993	Greg Norman	265
1994	John Huston	274
1995	Nick Faldo	273

HONDA CLASSIC
(Formerly the Jackie Gleason Inverrary Classic)
Inverrary G. & C.C., Lauderrhill, FL (1972-1983);
TPC at Eagle Trace, Coral Springs, FL (1984-1991);
Weston Hills G. & C.C., Fort Lauderdale, FL (1992-present).

1972	Tom Weiskopf	278
1973	Lee Trevino	279
1974	Leonard Thompson	278
1975	Bob Murphy	273
1976	Hosted TPC	
1977	Jack Nicklaus	275
1978	Jack Nicklaus	276
1979	Larry Nelson	274
1980	Johnny Miller	274
1981	Tom Kite	274
1982	Hale Irwin	269
1983	Johnny Miller	278
1984	*Bruce Lietzke	280
1985	*Curtis Strange	275
1986	Kenny Knox	287
1987	Mark Calcavecchia	279
1988	Joey Sindelar	276
1989	Blaine McCallister	266
1990	John Huston	282
1991	Steve Pate	279
1992	*Corey Pavin	273
1993	*Fred Couples	207
1994	Nick Price	276
1995	Mark O'Meara	275

BAY HILL INVITATIONAL
(Formerly The Nestle Invitational)
Rio Pinar C.C., Orlando, FL (1965-78); Bay Hill Club, Orlando, FL (1979-present).

1966	Lionel Hebert	279
1967	Julius Boros	274
1968	Dan Sikes	274
1969	Ken Still	278
1970	Bob Lunn	271
1971	Arnold Palmer	270
1972	Jerry Heard	276
1973	Brian Allin	265
1974	Jerry Heard	273
1975	Lee Trevino	276
1976	*Hale Irwin	270
1977	Gary Koch	274
1978	Mac McLendon	271
1979	*Bob Byman	278
1980	Dave Eichelberger	279
1981	Andy Bean	266
1982	*Tom Kite	278
1983	*Mike Nicolette	283
1984	*Gary Koch	272
1985	Fuzzy Zoeller	275
1986	Dan Forsman	202
1987	Payne Stewart	264
1988	Paul Azinger	271
1989	*Tom Kite	278
1990	Robert Gamez	274
1991	Andrew Magee	203
1992	Fred Couples	269
1993	Ben Crenshaw	280
1994	Loren Roberts	275
1995	Loren Roberts	272

THE PLAYERS CHAMPIONSHIP
Atlanta C.C., Atlanta, GA (1974); Colonial C.C., Ft. Worth, TX (1975); Inverrary G.& C.C.. (1976); Sawgrass C.C., Ponte Vedra, FL (1977-81); TPC at Sawgrass, Ponte Vedra, FL (1982-present).

1974	Jack Nicklaus	272
1975	Al Geiberger	270
1976	Jack Nicklaus	269
1977	Mark Hayes	289
1978	Jack Nicklaus	289
1979	Lanny Wadkins	283
1980	Lee Trevino	278
1981	*Raymond Floyd	285
1982	Jerry Pate	280
1983	Hal Sutton	283
1984	Fred Couples	277
1985	Calvin Peete	274
1986	John Mahaffey	275
1987	*Sandy Lyle	274
1988	Mark McCumber	273
1989	Tom Kite	279
1990	Jodie Mudd	278
1991	Steve Elkington	276
1992	Davis Love III	273
1993	Nick Price	270
1994	Greg Norman	264
1995	Lee Janzen	283

FREEPORT-MCMORAN CLASSIC
(Formerly the New Orleans Open)
City Park G.C., New Orleans, LA (1938-62); Lakewood C.C., New Orleans, LA (1963-88); English Turn G. & C.C., New Orleans, LA (1989-present).

1938	Harry Cooper	285
1939	Henry Picard	284
1940	Jimmy Demaret	286
1941	Henry Picard	276
1942	Lloyd Mangrum	281
1943	No Tournament	
1944	Sammy Byrd	285
1945	*Byron Nelson	284
1946	Byron Nelson	277
1947	No Tournament	
1948	Bob Hamilton	280
1949-57	No Tournaments	
1958	*Billy Casper	278
1959	Bill Collins	280
1960	Dow Finsterwald	270
1961	Doug Sanders	272
1962	Bo Wininger	281
1963	Bo Wininger	279
1964	Mason Rudolph	283
1965	Dick Mayer	273
1966	Frank Beard	276
1967	George Knudson	277
1968	George Archer	271
1969	*Larry Hinson	275
1970	*Miller Barber	278
1971	Frank Beard	276
1972	Gary Player	279

Freeport-McMoRan Classic continued

1973	*Jack Nicklaus	280
1974	Lee Trevino	267
1975	Billy Casper	271
1976	Larry Ziegler	274
1977	Jim Simons	273
1978	Lon Hinkle	271
1979	Hubert Green	273
1980	Tom Watson	273
1981	Tom Watson	270
1982	Scott Hoch	206
1983	Bill Rogers	274
1984	Bob Eastwood	272
1985	Seve Ballesteros	205
1986	Calvin Peete	269
1987	Ben Crenshaw	268
1988	Chip Beck	262
1989	Tim Simpson	274
1990	David Frost	276
1991	*Ian Woosnam	275
1992	Chip Beck	276
1993	Mike Standly	281
1994	Ben Crenshaw	273
1995	Davis Love III	274

MCI CLASSIC

(Formerly The Heritage Classic)
Harbour Town G.L.,
Hilton Head, SC (1969-present).

1969	Arnold Palmer	283
1970	Bob Goalby	280
1971	Hale Irwin	279
1972	Johnny Miller	281
1973	Hale Irwin	272
1974	Johnny Miller	276
1975	Jack Nicklaus	271
1976	Hubert Green	274
1977	Graham Marsh	273
1978	Hubert Green	277
1979	Tom Watson	270
1980	*Doug Tewell	280
1981	Bill Rogers	278
1982	*Tom Watson	280
1983	Fuzzy Zoeller	275
1984	Nick Faldo	270
1985	*Bernhard Langer	273
1986	Fuzzy Zoeller	276

1987	Davis Love III	271
1988	Greg Norman	271
1989	Payne Stewart	268
1990	*Payne Stewart	276
1991	Davis Love III	271
1992	Davis Love III	269
1993	David Edwards	273
1994	Hale Irwin	266
1995	Bob Tway	275

KMART GREATER GREENSBORO OPEN

Starmount Forest C.C., Greensboro, NC (1938-45, 1947, 1949, 1951-52, 1954, 1956, 1958-60); Sedgefield C.C., Greensboro, NC (1938-41, 1946, 1948, 1950, 1953, 1955, 1957, 1961-76); Forest Oaks C.C., Greensboro, NC (1977-present).

1938	Sam Snead	272
1939	Ralph Guldahl	280
1940	Ben Hogan	270
1941	Byron Nelson	276
1942	Sam Byrd	279
1943	No Tournament	
1944	No Tournament	
1945	Byron Nelson	271
1946	Sam Snead	270
1947	Vic Ghezzi	286
1948	Lloyd Mangrum	278
1949	*Sam Snead	276
1950	Sam Snead	269
1951	Art Doering	279
1952	Dave Douglas	277
1953	*Earl Stewart	275
1954	*Doug Ford	283
1955	Sam Snead	273
1956	*Sam Snead	279
1957	Stan Leonard	276
1958	Bob Goalby	275
1959	Dow Finsterwald	278
1960	Sam Snead	270
1961	Mike Souchak	276
1962	Billy Casper	275
1963	Doug Sanders	270
1964	*Julius Boros	277
1965	Sam Snead	273
1966	*Doug Sanders	276

KMART Greater Greensboro Open continued

1967	George Archer	267
1968	Billy Casper	267
1969	*Gene Littler	274
1970	Gary Player	271
1971	*Bud Allin	275
1972	*George Archer	272
1973	Chi Chi Rodriguez	267
1974	Bob Charles	270
1975	Tom Weiskopf	275
1976	Al Geiberger	268
1977	Danny Edwards	276
1978	Seve Ballesteros	282
1979	Raymond Floyd	282
1980	Craig Stadler	275
1981	*Larry Nelson	281
1982	Danny Edwards	285
1983	Lanny Wadkins	275
1984	Andy Bean	280
1985	Joey Sindelar	285
1986	Sandy Lyle	275
1987	Scott Simpson	282
1988	*Sandy Lyle	271
1989	Ken Green	277
1990	Steve Elkington	282
1991	*Mark Brooks	275
1992	Davis Love III	272
1993	*Rocco Mediate	281
1994	Mike Springer	275
1995	Jim Gallagher, Jr.	274

SHELL HOUSTON OPEN

River Oaks C.C., Houston, TX (1946); Memorial Park G.C., Houston, TX (1947, 1951-63); Pine Forest C.C., Houston, TX (1949); Brae Burn C.C., Houston, TX (1950); Sharpstown C.C., Houston, TX (1964-65); Champions G.C., Houston, TX (1966-71); Westwood C.C., Houston, TX (1972); Quail Valley G.C., Houston, TX (1973-74); Woodlands C.C., The Woodlands, TX (1974-1984); TPC at The Woodlands (1985-present).

1946	Byron Nelson	274
1947	Bobby Locke	277
1948	No Tournament	
1949	John Palmer	272
1950	Cary Middlecoff	277
1951	Marty Furgol	277
1952	Jack Burke, Jr.	277
1953	*Cary Middlecoff	283
1954	Dave Douglas	277
1955	Mike Souchak	273
1956	Ted Kroll	277
1957	Arnold Palmer	279
1958	Ed Oliver	281
1959	*Jack Burke, Jr.	277
1960	*Bill Collins	280
1961	*Jay Hebert	276
1962	*Bobby Nichols	278
1963	Bob Charles	268
1964	Mike Souchak	278
1965	Bobby Nichols	273
1966	Arnold Palmer	275
1967	Frank Beard	274
1968	Roberto De Vicenzo	274
1969	Hosted U.S. Open	
1970	*Gibby Gilbert	282
1971	*Hubert Green	280
1972	Bruce Devlin	278
1973	Bruce Crampton	277
1974	Dave Hill	276
1975	Bruce Crampton	273
1976	Lee Elder	278
1977	Gene Littler	276
1978	Gary Player	270
1979	Wayne Levi	268
1980	*Curtis Strange	266
1981	Ron Streck	198
1982	*Ed Sneed	275
1983	David Graham	275
1984	Corey Pavin	274
1985	Raymond Floyd	277
1986	*Curtis Strange	274
1987	*Jay Haas	276
1988	*Curtis Strange	270
1989	Mike Sullivan	280
1990	*Tony Sills	204
1991	Fulton Allem	273
1992	Fred Funk	272
1993	*Jim McGovern	199
1994	Mike Heinen	272
1995	Payne Stewart	276

BELLSOUTH CLASSIC

(Formerly the Atlanta Classic)
Atlanta C.C., Marietta, GA (1967-present).

1967	Bob Charles	282

The BellSouth Classic continued

1968	Bob Lunn	280
1969	*Bert Yancey	277
1970	Tommy Aaron	275
1971	*Gardner Dickinson	275
1972	Bob Lunn	275
1973	Jack Nicklaus	272
1974	Hosted TPC	
1975	Hale Irwin	271
1976	Hosted U.S. Open	
1977	Hale Irwin	273
1978	Jerry Heard	269
1979	Andy Bean	265
1980	Larry Nelson	270
1981	*Tom Watson	277
1982	*Keith Fergus	273
1983	*Calvin Peete	206
1984	Tom Kite	269
1985	*Wayne Levi	273
1986	Bob Tway	269
1987	Dave Barr	265
1988	Larry Nelson	268
1989	*Scott Simpson	278
1990	Wayne Levi	275
1991	*Corey Pavin	272
1992	Tom Kite	272
1993	Nolan Henke	271
1994	John Daly	274
1995	Mark Calcavecchia	271

GTE BYRON NELSON CLASSIC

Lakewood C.C., Dallas, TX (1944); Dallas C.C., Dallas, TX (1945); Brook Hollow C.C., Dallas, TX (1946); Preston Hollow C.C., Dallas, TX (1955-56); Glen Lakes C.C., Dallas, TX (1957); Oak Cliffs C.C., Dallas TX (1958--67); Preston Trail G.C., Dallas, TX (1968-82); Las Colinas Sports Club, Irving, TX (1983-85); Cottonwood Valley Course, Irving, TX (1994); TPC at Las Colinas, Irving, TX (1986-present).

1944	Byron Nelson	276
1945	Sam Snead	276
1946	Ben Hogan	284
1947-55	No Tournaments	
1956	Don January	268
1956A	*Peter Thomson	267
1957	Sam Snead	264
1958	*Sam Snead	272

1959	Julius Boros	274
1960	*Johnny Pott	275
1961	Earl Stewart, Jr.	278
1962	Billy Maxwell	277
1963	No Tournament	
1964	Charles Coody	271
1965	No Tournament	
1966	Roberto De Vicenzo	276
1967	Bert Yancey	274
1968	Miller Barber	270
1969	Bruce Devlin	277
1970	*Jack Nicklaus	274
1971	Jack Nicklaus	274
1972	*Chi Chi Rodriguez	273
1973	*Lanny Wadkins	277
1974	Brian Allin	269
1975	Tom Watson	269
1976	Mark Hayes	273
1977	Raymond Floyd	276
1978	Tom Watson	272
1979	*Tom Watson	275
1980	Tom Watson	274
1981	*Bruce Lietzke	281
1982	Bob Gilder	266
1983	Ben Crenshaw	273
1984	Craig Stadler	276
1985	*Bob Eastwood	272
1986	Andy Bean	269
1987	*Fred Couples	266
1988	*Bruce Lietzke	271
1989	*Jodie Mudd	265
1990	Payne Stewart	202
1991	Nick Price	270
1992	*Billy Ray Brown	199
1993	Scott Simpson	270
1994	Neal Lancaster	132
1995	Ernie Els	263

BUICK CLASSIC

(Formerly the Westchester Classic)

Westchester C.C., Harrison, NY (1967-present).

1967	Jack Nicklaus	272
1968	Julius Boros	272
1969	Frank Beard	275
1970	Bruce Crampton	273
1971	Arnold Palmer	270
1972	Jack Nicklaus	270
1973	*Bobby Nichols	272

Buick Classic continued

1974	Johnny Miller	269
1975	*Gene Littler	271
1976	David Graham	272
1977	Andy North	272
1978	Lee Elder	274
1979	Renner Jack	277
1980	Curtis Strange	273
1981	Raymond Floyd	275
1982	Bob Gilder	261
1983	Seve Ballesteros	276
1984	Scott Simpson	269
1985	*Roger Maltbie	275
1986	Bob Tway	272
1987	*J.C. Snead	276
1988	*Seve Ballesteros	276
1989	*Wayne Grady	277
1990	Hale Irwin	269
1991	Billy Andrade	273
1992	David Frost	268
1993	Vijay Singh	280
1994	Lee Janzen	268
1995	Vijah Singh	278

COLONIAL INVITATIONAL

Colonial C.C., Fort Worth, TX (1946-present).

1946	Ben Hogan	279
1947	Ben Hogan	279
1948	Clayton Heafner	272
1949	No Tournament	
1950	Sam Snead	277
1951	Cary Middlecoff	282
1952	Ben Hogan	279
1953	Ben Hogan	282
1954	Johnny Palmer	280
1955	Chandler Harper	276
1956	Mike Souchak	280
1957	Roberto DeVicenzo	284
1958	Tommy Bolt	282
1959	*Ben Hogan	285
1960	Julius Boros	280
1961	Doug Sanders	281
1962	*Arnold Palmer	281
1963	Julius Boros	279
1964	Billy Casper	279
1965	Bruce Crampton	276
1966	Bruce Devlin	280
1967	Dave Stockton	278
1968	Billy Casper	275
1969	Gardner Dickinson	278
1970	Homero Blancas	273
1971	Gene Littler	283
1972	Jerry Heard	275
1973	Tom Weiskopf	276
1974	Rod Curl	276
1975	Hosted TPC	
1976	Lee Trevino	273
1977	Ben Crenshaw	272
1978	Lee Trevino	268
1979	Al Geiberger	274
1980	Bruce Lietzke	271
1981	Fuzzy Zoeller	274
1982	Jack Nicklaus	273
1983	*Jim Colbert	278
1984	*Peter Jacobsen	270
1985	Corey Pavin	266
1986	*Dan Pohl	205
1987	Keith Clearwater	266
1988	Lanny Wadkins	270
1989	Ian Baker-Finch	270
1990	Ben Crenshaw	272
1991	Tom Purtzer	267
1992	*Bruce Lietzke	267
1993	Fulton Allem	264
1994	Nick Price	266
1995	Tom Lehman	271

THE MEMORIAL TOURNAMENT

Muirfield Village G.C.,
Dublin, OH (1976-present).

1976	*Roger Maltbie	288
1977	Jack Nicklaus	281
1978	Jim Simons	284
1979	Tom Watson	285
1980	David Graham	280
1981	Keith Fergus	284
1982	Raymond Floyd	281
1983	Hale Irwin	281
1984	*Jack Nicklaus	280
1985	Hale Irwin	281
1986	Hal Sutton	271
1987	Don Pooley	272
1988	Curtis Strange	274
1989	Bob Tway	277
1990	Greg Norman	216
1991	*Kenny Perry	273

The Memorial continued

1992	*David Edwards	273
1993	Paul Azinger	274
1994	Tom Lehman	268
1995	Greg Norman	269

KEMPER OPEN

Pleasant Valley C.C., Sutton, MA (1968); Quial Hollow C.C., Charlotte, NC (1969-79); Congressional C.C., Bethesda, MD (1980-86); TPC at Avenel, Potomac, MD (1987-present).

1968	Arnold Palmer	276
1969	Dale Douglass	274
1970	Dick Lotz	278
1971	*Tom Weiskopf	277
1972	Doug Sanders	275
1973	Tom Weiskopf	271
1974	*Bob Menne	270
1975	Raymond Floyd	278
1976	Joe Inman	277
1977	Tom Weiskopf	277
1978	Andy Bean	273
1979	Jerry McGee	272
1980	John Mahaffey	275
1981	Craig Stadler	270
1982	Craig Stadler	275
1983	*Fred Couples	287
1984	Greg Norman	280
1985	Bill Glasson	278
1986	*Greg Norman	277
1987	Tom Kite	270
1988	*Morris Hatalsky	274
1989	Tom Byrum	268
1990	Gil Morgan	274
1991	*Billy Andrade	263
1992	Bill Glasson	276
1993	Grant Waite	275
1994	Mark Brooks	271
1995	Lee Janzen	272

CANON GREATER HARTFORD OPEN

(Formerly the Sammy Davis Jr. Gr. Hartford Open)
Wethersfield C.C., Hartford, CT (1952-1983); TPC of Connecticut, Cromwell, CT (1984-present).

1952	Ted Kroll	273
1953	Bob Toski	269
1954	*Tommy Bolt	271
1955	Sam Snead	269
1956	*Arnold Palmer	274
1957	Gardner Dickinson	272
1958	Jack Burke, Jr.	268
1959	Gene Littler	272
1960	*Arnold Palmer	270
1961	*Billy Maxwell	271
1962	*Bob Goalby	271
1963	Billy Casper	271
1964	Ken Venturi	273
1965	*Billy Casper	274
1966	Art Wall	266
1967	Charlie Sifford	272
1968	Billy Casper	266
1969	*Bob Lunn	268
1970	Bob Murphy	267
1971	*George Archer	268
1972	*Lee Trevino	269
1973	Billy Casper	264
1974	Dave Stockton	268
1975	*Don Bies	267
1976	Rik Massengale	266
1977	Bill Kratzert	265
1978	Rod Funseth	264
1979	Jerry McGee	267
1980	*Howard Twitty	266
1981	Hubert Green	264
1982	Tim Norris	259
1983	Curtis Strange	268
1984	Peter Jacobsen	269
1985	*Phil Blackmar	271
1986	*Mac O'Grady	269
1987	Paul Azinger	269
1988	*Mark Brooks	269
1989	Paul Azinger	267
1990	Wayne Levi	267
1991	*Billy Ray Brown	271
1992	Lanny Wadkins	274
1993	Nick Price	271
1994	David Frost	268
1995	Greg Norman	267

FEDEX ST. JUDE CLASSIC

Formerly the Danny Thomas Memphis Classic
Colonial C.C., Memphis TN (1958-88); TPC at Southwind, Germantown, TN (1989-present).

| 1958 | Billy Maxwell | 267 |
| 1959 | *Don Whitt | 272 |

Fedex St. Jude Classic continued

Year	Player	Score
1960	*Tommy Bolt	273
1961	Cary Middlecoff	266
1962	*Lionel Hebert	267
1963	*Tony Lema	270
1964	Mike Souchak	270
1965	*Jack Nicklaus	271
1966	Bert Yancey	265
1967	Dave Hill	272
1968	Bob Lunn	268
1969	Dave Hill	265
1970	Dave Hill	267
1971	Lee Trevino	268
1972	Lee Trevino	281
1973	Dave Hill	283
1974	Gary Player	273
1975	Gene Littler	270
1976	Gibby Gilbert	273
1977	Al Geiberger	273
1978	*Andy Bean	277
1979	*Gil Morgan	278
1980	Lee Trevino	272
1981	Jerry Pate	274
1982	Raymond Floyd	271
1983	Larry Mize	274
1984	Bob Eastwood	280
1985	*Hal Sutton	279
1986	Mike Hulbert	280
1987	Curtis Strange	275
1988	Jodie Mudd	273
1989	John Mahaffey	272
1990	*Tom Kite	269
1991	Fred Couples	269
1992	Jay Haas	263
1993	Nick Price	266
1994	Dicky Pride	267
1995	Jim Gallagher, Jr.	267

MOTOROLA WESTERN OPEN

Formerly the Western Open

Glenview G.C., Chicago, IL (1899); Midlothian C.C., Chicago, IL (1901, 1969, 1973); Euclid Club, Cleveland, OH (1902); Milwaukee C.C. (1903); Kent C.C., Grand Rapids, MI (1904, 1911); Cincinatti G.C., Cincinatti, OH (1905); Homewood C.C., Chicago, IL (1906); Hinsdale G.C., Hinsdale, IL (1907); Normandie G.C., St. Louis, MO (1908); Skokie C.C., Chicago, IL (1909); Beverly C.C., Chicago, IL (1910, 1963-, 1967, 1970); Idlewild C.C., Chicago, IL (1912); Memphis C.C., Memphis, TN (1913); Interlachen C.C., Minneapolis, MN (1914); Glen Oak C.C., Chicago, IL (1915); Blue Mound C.C., Chicago, IL (1916); Westmoreland C.C., Chicago, IL (1917); Mayfield C.C., Cleveland, OH (1919); Olympia Fields C.C., Chicago, IL (1920, 1927, 1933, 1968, 1971); Oakwood Club, Cleveland, OH (1921); Oakland Hills, Detroit, MI (1922); Colonial C.C., Memphis, TN (1923); Calumet C.C., Chicago, IL (1924); Youngstown C.C., Youngstown, OH (1925); Highland G. & C.C., Indianapolis, IN (1926); North Shore G.C., Chicago, IL (1928); Ozaukee C.C., Milwaukee, WI (1929); Indianwood G. & C.C., Detroit, MI (1930); Miami Valley G.C., Dayton, OH (1931); Canterbury C.C., Cleveland, OH (1932, 1937); C.C. of Peoria, Peoria, IL (1934); South Bend C.C., South Bend, IN (1935); Davenport C.C., Davenport, IA (1936, 1951); Westwood C.C., St. Louis, MO (1938, 1952); Medinah C.C., Chicago, IL (1939, 1962, 1966); River Oaks C.C., Houston, TX (1940); Phoenix G.C., Phoenix, AZ (1941-42); Sunset C.C., St. Louis, MO (1946); Salt Lake City C.C., Salt Lake City, UT (1947); Brookfield C.C., Buffalo, NY (1948); Keller G.C., St. Paul, MN (1949); Brentwood C.C., Los Angeles, CA (1950); Bellrive C.C., St. Louis, MO (1953); Kenwood C.C., Cincinatti, OH (1954); Portland G.C., Portland, OR (1955); Presidio G.C., San Francisco, CA (1956); Plum Hollow G.C., Detroit, MI (1957); Red Run G.C., Royal Oak, MI (1958); Pittsburgh Field Club, Pittsburgh, PA (1959); Western G. & C.C., Detroit, MI (1960); Blythefield C.C., Grand Rapids, MI (1961); Tam O'Shanter C.C., Niles, IL (1964-65); Sunset Ridge, Winnetka, IL (1972); Butler National G.C., Oak Brook, IL (1974-1990), Oak Brook Village G.C., Oak Brook, IL (1987); Cog Hill C.C. (Dubsdread), Lemont, IL (1991-present).

Year	Player	Score
1899	*Willie Smith	156
1900	No Tournament	
1901	Laurie Auchterlonie	160
1902	Willie Anderson	299
1903	Alex Smith	318
1904	Willie Anderson	304
1905	Arthur Smith	278
1906	Alex Smith	306
1907	Robert Simpson	307

Motorola Open continued

1908	Willie Anderson	299
1909	Willie Anderson	288
1910	Chick Evans, Jr.	6&5
1911	Robert Simpson	2&1
1912	Mac Smith	299
1913	John McDermott	295
1914	Jim Barnes	293
1915	Tom McNamara	304
1916	Walter Hagen	286
1917	Jim Barnes	283
1918	No Tournament	
1919	Jim Barnes	283
1920	Jock Hutchinson	296
1921	Walter Hagen	287
1922	Mike Brady	291
1923	Jock Hutchinson	281
1924	Bill Mehlhorn	293
1925	Mac Smith	281
1926	Walter Hagen	279
1927	Walter Hagen	281
1928	Abe Espinosa	291
1929	Tommy Armour	273
1930	Gene Sarazen	278
1931	Ed Dudley	280
1932	Walter Hagen	287
1933	Mac Smith	282
1934	*Harry Cooper	274
1935	John Revolta	290
1936	Ralph Guldahl	274
1937	*Ralph Guldahl	288
1938	Ralph Guldahl	279
1939	Byron Nelson	281
1940	*Jimmy Demaret	293
1941	Ed Oliver	275
1942	Herman Barron	276
1943-45	No Tournament	
1946	Ben Hogan	271
1947	Johnny Palmer	270
1948	*Ben Hogan	281
1949	Sam Snead	268
1950	Sam Snead	282
1951	Marty Furgol	270
1952	Lloyd Mangrum	274
1953	Dutch Harrison	278
1954	*Lloyd Mangrum	277
1955	Cary Middlecoff	272
1956	*Mike Fetchick	284
1957	*Doug Ford	279
1958	Doug Sanders	275
1959	Mike Souchak	272
1960	*Stan Leonard	278
1961	Arnold Palmer	271
1962	Jacky Cupit	281
1963	*Arnold Palmer	280
1964	Chi Chi Rodriguez	268
1965	Billy Casper	270
1966	Billy Casper	283
1967	Jack Nicklaus	274
1968	Jack Nicklaus	273
1969	Billy Casper	276
1970	Hugh Royer	273
1971	Bruce Crampton	279
1972	Jim Jamieson	271
1973	Billy Casper	272
1974	Tom Watson	287
1975	Hale Irwin	283
1976	Al Geiberger	288
1977	Tom Watson	283
1978	*Andy Bean	282
1979	*Larry Nelson	286
1980	Scott Simpson	281
1981	Ed Fiori	277
1982	Tom Weiskopf	276
1983	Mark McCumber	284
1984	*Tom Watson	280
1985	Scott Verplank	279
1986	*Tom Kite	286
1987	D. A. Weibring	207
1988	Jim Benepe	278
1989	*Mark McCumber	275
1990	Wayne Levi	275
1991	Russ Cochran	275
1992	Ben Crenshaw	276
1993	Nick Price	269
1994	Nick Price	277
1995	Billy Mayfair	279

ANHEUSER-BUSCH GOLF CLASSIC

Silverado C.C., Napa, CA (1968-80); Kingsmill G.C., Kingsmill, VA (1981-present).

1968	Kermit Zarley	273
1969	Miller Barber	135
1969A	*Jack Nicklaus	273
1970	*Ken Still	278

Anheuser-Busch Classic continued

1971	Billy Casper	269
1972	George Knudson	271
1973	*Ed Sneed	275
1974	Johnny Miller	271
1975	Johnny Miller	272
1976	J. C. Snead	274
1977	Miller Barber	272
1978	Tom Watson	270
1979	John Fought	277
1980	Ben Crenshaw	272
1981	John Mahaffey	276
1982	Calvin Peete	203
1983	Calvin Peete	276
1984	Ronnie Black	267
1985	*Mark Wiebe	273
1986	Fuzzy Zoeller	274
1987	Mark McCumber	267
1988	*Tom Sieckmann	270
1989	*Mike Donald	268
1990	Lanny Wadkins	266
1991	Mike Hulbert	266
1992	David Peoples	271
1993	Jim Gallagher	269
1994	Mark McCumber	267
1995	Ted Tryba	272

DEPOSIT GUARANTY GOLF CLASSIC

Formerly known as the Magnolia Classic
Hattiesburg C.C., Hattiesburg, MS (1968-93);
Annandale G.C., Jackson, MS (1994-presnt).
Note: The Deposit Guaranty Classic was an unofficial event prior to 1995.

1968	*B.R. McLendon	269
1969	Larry Mowry	272
1970	Chris Blocker	271
1971	Roy Pace	270
1972	Mike Morey	269
1973	Dwight Nevil	268
1974	Dwight Nevil	133
1975	Bob Wynn	270
1976	Dennis Meyer	271
1977	Mike McCullough	269
1978	Craig Stadler	268
1979	Bobby Walzel	272
1980	*Roger Maltbie	65
1981	*Tom Jones	268
1982	Payne Stewart	270
1983	Russ Cochran	203
1984	*Lance Ten Broeck	201
1985	*Jim Gallagher, Jr.	131
1986	Dan Halldorson	263
1987	David Ogrin	267
1988	Frank Conner	267
1989	*Jim Booros	199
1990	Gene Sauers	268
1991	*Larry Silveira	266
1992	Richard Zokol	267
1993	Greg Kraft	267
1994	Brian Henninger	135
1995	Ed Dougherty	272

NEW ENGLAND CLASSIC

Formerly known as the Ideon Classic
Pleasant Valley C.C.,
Sutton, MA (1965-present).

1965	Tony Lema	279
1968	Arnold Palmer	276
1969	Tom Shaw	280
1970	Billy Casper	277
1971	Dave Stockton	275
1972	Bruce Devlin	275
1973	Lanny Wadkins	279
1974	Victor Regalado	278
1975	Roger Maltbie	276
1976	Bud Allin	277
1977	Raymond Floyd	271
1978	John Mahaffey	270
1979	Lou Graham	275
1980	*Wayne Levi	273
1981	Jack Renner	273
1982	Bob Gilder	271
1983	Mark Lye	273
1984	George Archer	270
1985	George Burns	267
1986	*Gene Sauers	274
1987	Sam Randolph	199
1988	Mark Calcavecchia	274
1989	Blaine McCallister	271
1990	Morris Hatalsky	275
1991	*Bruce Fleisher	268
1992	Brad Faxon	268
1993	Paul Azinger	268
1994	Kenny Perry	268
1995	Fred Funk	268

BUICK OPEN

Flint Elks C.C., Flint, MI (1972, 1974-77); Benton Harbor Elks C.C., Benton Harbor, MI (1973); Warwick Hills C.C., Grand Blanc, MI (1958-69, 1978-present).

Year	Winner	Score
1958	Billy Casper	285
1959	Art Wall	282
1960	Mike Souchak	282
1961	Jack Burke, Jr.	284
1962	Bill Collins	284
1963	Julius Boros	274
1964	Tony Lema	277
1965	Tony Lema	280
1966	Phil Rodgers	284
1967	Julius Boros	283
1968	Tom Weiskopf	280
1969	Dave Hill	277
1970-71	No Tournament	
1972	Gary Groh	273
1973	Wilf Homenuik	215
1974	Bryan Abbott	135
1975	Spike Kelley	208
1976	Ed Sabo	279
1977	Bobby Cole	271
1978	*Jack Newton	280
1979	*John Fought	280
1980	Peter Jacobsen	276
1981	*Hale Irwin	277
1982	Lanny Wadkins	273
1983	Wayne Levi	272
1984	Denis Watson	271
1985	Ken Green	268
1986	Ben Crenshaw	270
1987	Robert Wrenn	262
1988	Scott Verplank	268
1989	Leonard Thompson	273
1990	Chip Beck	272
1991	*Brad Faxon	271
1992	*Dan Forsman	276
1993	Larry Mize	272
1994	Fred Couples	270
1995	Woody Austin	270

THE SPRINT INTERNATIONAL

Castle Pines G.C., Castle Rock, CO (1986-present).

Year	Winner	Score
1986	Ken Green	Plus 12
1987	John Cook	Plus 11
1988	Joey Sindelar	Plus 17
1989	Greg Norman	Plus 13
1990	Davis Love III	Plus 14
1991	Jose M. Olazabal	Plus 10
1992	Brad Faxon	Plus 14
1993	Phil Mickelson	Plus 45
1994	Steve Lowery	Plus 35
1995	Lee Janzen	Plus 34

NEC WORLD SERIES OF GOLF

Firestone Country Club, South Course, Akron, OH (1962-present).

(Note: The World Series of Golf was played as a four-man exhibition only, 1962-75)

Year	Winner	Score
1962	Jack Nicklaus	(135)
1963	Jack Nicklaus	(140)
1964	Tony Lema	(138)
1965	Gary Player	(139)
1966	Gene Littler	(143)
1967	Jack Nicklaus	(144)
1968	Gary Player	(143)
1969	Orville Moody	(141)
1970	Jack Nicklaus	(136)
1971	Charles Coody	(141)
1972	Gary Player	(142)
1973	Tom Weiskopf	(137)
1974	Lee Trevino	(139)
1975	Tom Watson	(140)
1976	Jack Nicklaus	275
1977	Lanny Wadkins	267
1978	*Gil Morgan	278
1979	Lon Hinkle	272
1980	Tom Watson	270
1981	Bill Rogers	275
1982	*Craig Stadler	278
1983	Nick Price	270
1984	Denis Watson	271
1985	Roger Maltbie	268
1986	Dan Pohl	277
1987	Curtis Strange	275
1988	*Mike Reid	275
1989	*David Frost	276
1990	Jose-Maria Olazabal	262
1991	*Tom Purtzer	279
1992	Craig Stadler	273
1993	Fulton Allem	270
1994	Jose-Maria Olazabal	269
1995	Greg Norman	278

GREATER MILWAUKEE OPEN

Northshore C.C., Mequon, WI (1968-70); Tripoli G.C., Milwaukee, WI (1971-72); Tuckaway C.C., Franklin, WS (1973-1993); Brown Deer Park G.C., Milwaukee, WI (1994-present).

Year	Winner	Score
1968	Dave Stockton	275
1969	Ken Still	277
1970	Deane Beman	276
1971	Dave Eichelberger	270
1972	Jim Colbert	271
1973	Dave Stockton	276
1974	Ed Sneed	276
1975	Art Wall	271
1976	Dave Hill	270
1977	Dave Eichelberger	278
1978	*Lee Elder	275
1979	Calvin Peete	269
1980	Bill Kratzert	266
1981	Jay Haas	274
1982	Calvin Peete	274
1983	*Morris Hatalsky	275
1984	Mark O'Meara	272
1985	Jim Thorpe	274
1986	*Corey Pavin	272
1987	Gary Hallberg	269
1988	Ken Green	268
1989	Greg Norman	269
1990	*Jim Gallagher, Jr.	271
1991	Mark Brooks	270
1992	Richard Zokol	269
1993	Billy Mayfair	270
1994	Mike Springer	268
1995	Scott Hoch	269

CANADIAN OPEN

Rotated annually 1904-76; Royal Montreal G.C., Ile Bizard, Quebec (1980); Glen Abbey G.C., Oakville, Ontario (1977-79, 1981-present).

Year	Winner	Score
1904	J. H. Oke	156
1905	George Cumming	148
1906	Charles Murray	170
1907	Percy Barrett	306
1908	Albert Murray	300
1909	Karl Keller	309
1910	Daniel Kenny	303
1911	Charles Murray	314
1912	George Sargent	299
1913	Albert Murray	295
1914	Karl Keller	300
1915	No Tournament	
1916	No Tournament	
1917	No Tournament	
1918	No Tournament	
1919	J. Douglas Edgar	278
1920	*J. Douglas Edgar	298
1921	W. H. Trovinger	293
1922	Al Watrous	303
1923	C. W. Hackney	295
1924	Leo Diegel	285
1925	Leo Diegel	295
1926	Mac Smith	283
1927	Tommy Armour	288
1928	Leo Diegel	282
1929	Leo Diegel	274
1930	*Tommy Armour	273
1931	*Walter Hagen	292
1932	Harry Cooper	290
1933	Joe Kirkwood	282
1934	Tommy Armour	287
1935	Gene Kanes	280
1936	Lawson Little	271
1937	Harry Cooper	285
1938	*Sam Snead	277
1939	Harold McSpaden	282
1940	*Sam Snead	281
1941	Sam Snead	274
1942	Craig Wood	275
1943	No Tournament	
1944	No Tournament	
1945	Byron Nelson	280
1946	*George Fazio	278
1947	Bobby Locke	268
1948	C. W. Congdon	280
1949	Dutch Harrison	271
1950	Jim Ferrier	271
1951	Jim Ferrier	273
1952	John Palmer	263
1953	Dave Douglas	273
1954	Pat Fletcher	280
1955	Arnold Palmer	265
1956	Doug Sanders	273
1957	George Bayer	271
1958	Wesley Ellis, Jr.	267
1959	Doug Ford	276
1960	Art Wall, Jr.	269
1961	Jacky Cupit	270

Canadian Open continued

1962	Ted Kroll	278
1963	Doug Ford	280
1964	Kel Nagle	277
1965	Gene Littler	273
1966	Don Massengale	280
1967	*Billy Casper	279
1968	Bob Charles	274
1969	*Tommy Aaron	275
1970	Kermit Zarley	279
1971	*Lee Trevino	275
1972	Gay Brewer	275
1973	Tom Weiskopf	278
1974	Bobby Nichols	270
1975	*Tom Weiskopf	274
1976	Jerry Pate	267
1977	Lee Trevino	280
1978	Bruce Lietzke	283
1979	Lee Trevino	281
1980	Bob Gilder	274
1981	Peter Oosterhuis	280
1982	Bruce Lietzke	277
1983	*John Cook	277
1984	Greg Norman	278
1985	Curtis Strange	279
1986	Bob Murphy	280
1987	Curtis Strange	276
1988	Ken Green	275
1989	Steve Jones	271
1990	Wayne Levi	278
1991	Nick Price	273
1992	*Greg Norman	280
1993	David Frost	279
1994	Nick Price	275
1995	Mark O'Meara	274

B. C. OPEN
En Joie G.C., Endicott, NY (1971- present).

1971	*Claude Harmon, Jr.	69
1972	Bob Payne	136
1973	Hubert Green	266
1974	*Richie Karl	273
1975	Don Iverson	274
1976	Bob Wynn	271
1977	Gil Morgan	270
1978	Tom Kite	267
1979	Howard Twitty	270
1980	Don Pooley	271

1981	Jay Haas	270
1982	Calvin Peete	265
1983	Pat Lindsey	268
1984	Wayne Levi	275
1985	Joey Sindelar	274
1986	Rick Fehr	267
1987	Joey Sindelar	266
1988	Bill Glasson	268
1989	*Mike Hulbert	268
1990	Nolan Henke	268
1991	Fred Couples	269
1992	John Daly	266
1993	Blaine McCallister	271
1994	Mike Sullivan	266
1995	Hal Sutton	269

QUAD CITY CLASSIC
Formerly known as the Quad Cities Open
Crow Valley C.C., Bettendorf, IA (1972-74);
Oakwood C.C., Coal Valley, IL (1975-present).

1972	Deane Beman	279
1973	Sam Adams	268
1974	Dave Stockton	271
1975	Roger Maltbie	275
1976	John Lister	268
1977	Mike Morley	267
1978	Victor Regalado	269
1979	D. A. Weibring	266
1980	Scott Hoch	266
1981	*Dave Barr	270
1982	Payne Stewart	268
1983	*Danny Edwards	266
1984	Scoff Hoch	266
1985	Dan Forsman	267
1986	Mark Wiebe	268
1987	Kenny Knox	265
1988	Blaine McCallister	261
1989	Curt Byrum	268
1990	*Joey Sindelar	268
1991	D. A. Weibring	267
1992	David Frost	266
1993	David Frost	259
1994	Mark McCumber	265
1995	D.A. Weibring	197

BUICK CHALLENGE
Formerly known as the Southern Open.
Green Island C.C., Columbus, GA (1970-90);

Buick Challenge continued
Callaway Gardens Resort, Pine Mountain, GA
(1991-present).

1970	Mason Rudolph	274
1971	Johnny Miller	267
1972	*DeWitt Weaver	276
1973	Gary Player	270
1974	Forrest Fezler	271
1975	Hubert Green	264
1976	Mac McClendon	274
1977	Jerry Pate	266
1978	Jerry Pate	269
1979	*Ed Fiori	274
1980	Mike Sullivan	269
1981	*J. C. Snead	271
1982	Bobby Clampett	266
1983	*Ronnie Black	271
1984	Hubert Green	265
1985	Tim Simpson	264
1986	Fred Wadsworth	269
1987	Ken Brown	266
1988	*David Frost	270
1989	Ted Schulz	266
1990	*Kenny Knox	265
1991	David Peoples	276
1992	Gary Hallberg	206
1993	*John Inman	278
1994	Steve Elkington	200
1995	Fred Funk	272

WALT DISNEY WORLD/ OLDSMOBILE CLASSIC

Rotates among Palm, Magnolia, Lake Buena Vista C.C., Lake Buena Vista, FL (1971-present).

1971	Jack Nicklaus	273
1972	Jack Nicklaus	267
1973	Jack Nicklaus	275
1974	Hubert Green/ Mac McClendon	255
1975	Jim Colbert/ Dean Refram	252
1976	*Woody Blackburn/ Bill Kratzert	260
1977	Gibby Gilbert/ Grier Jones	253
1978	Wayne Levi/ Bob Mann	254
1979	George Burns/	255

	Ben Crenshaw	
1980	Danny Edwards/ David Edwards	253
1981	Vance Heafner/ Mike Holland	275
1982	*Hal Sutton	269
1983	Payne Stewart	269
1984	Larry Nelson	266
1985	Lanny Wadkins	267
1986	*Ray Floyd	275
1987	Larry Nelson	268
1988	*Bob Lohr	263
1989	Tim Simpson	272
1990	Tim Simpson	264
1991	Mark O'Meara	267
1992	John Huston	262
1993	Jeff Maggert	265
1994	Rick Fehr	269
1995	Brad Bryant	198

LAS VEGAS INVITATIONAL

Rotates among Las Vegas C.C., Las Vegas; Sahara C.C., Las Vegas; and TPC at Summerlin, Las Vegas (1992-present); also played at Desert Inn C.C. (1983-93); Dunes C.C., Las Vegas, NV (1983); Showboat C.C. (1983-84); Tropicana C.C., Las Vegas, NV (1984-85); Spanish Trail G. & C.C. (1986-90) and Sunrise G.C., Las Vegas, NV (1991).

1983	Fuzzy Zoeller	340
1984	Denis Watson	341
1985	Curtis Strange	338
1986	Greg Norman	333
1987	Paul Azinger	271
1988	Gary Koch	274
1989	*Scott Hoch	336
1990	*Bob Tway	334
1991	*Andrew Magee	329
1992	John Cook	334
1993	John Inman	331
1994	Bruce Leitzke	332
1995	Jim Furyk	331

LA CANTERA TEXAS OPEN

Brackenridge Park G.C., San Antonio, TX (1922-26, 1929-34, 1939-40, 1950-55, 1957-59); Willow Springs G.C., San Antonio, TX (1927-28, 1941-42, 1944-49); Ft. Sam Houston G.C., San Antonio, TX (1950-51, 1956, 1960); Pecan Valley C.C., San

La Cantera Texas Open continued
Antonio, TX (1967, 1969-70); Woodlake G.C., San Antonio, TX (1972-76); Oak Hills C.C., San Antonio, TX (1961-66, 1977-1994; La Cantera C.C., San Antonio, TX (1995).

Year	Player	Score
1922	Bob MacDonald	281
1923	Walter Hagen	279
1924	Joe Kirkwood	279
1925	Joe Turnesa	284
1926	Mac Smith	288
1927	Bobby Cruikshank	272
1928	Bill Mehlhorn	297
1929	Bill Mehlhorn	277
1930	Denny Shute	277
1931	Abe Espinosa	281
1932	Clarence Clark	287
1933	No Tournament	
1934	Witty Cox	283
1935-38	No Tournaments	
1939	Dutch Harrison	271
1940	Byron Nelson	271
1941	Lawson Little	273
1942	*Chick Harbert	272
1943	No Tournament	
1944	Johnny Revolta	273
1945	Sam Byrd	268
1946	Ben Hogan	264
1947	Ed Oliver	265
1948	Sam Snead	264
1949	Dave Douglas	268
1950	Sam Snead	265
1951	*Dutch Harrison	265
1952	Jack Burke, Jr.	260
1953	Tony Holguin	264
1954	Chandler Harper	259
1955	Mike Souchak	257
1956	Gene Littler	276
1957	Jay Hebert	271
1958	Bill Johnston	274
1959	Wes Ellis	276
1960	Arnold Palmer	276
1961	Arnold Palmer	270
1962	Arnold Palmer	273
1963	Phil Rodgers	268
1964	Bruce Crampton	273
1965	Frank Beard	270
1966	Harold Henning	272
1967	Chi Chi Rodriguez	277
1968	No Tournament	
1969	*Deane Beman	274
1970	Ron Cerrudo	273
1971	No Tournament	
1972	Mike Hill	273
1973	Ben Crenshaw	270
1974	Terry Diehl	269
1975	*Don January	275
1976	*Hutch Baird	273
1977	Hale Irwin	266
1978	Ron Streck	265
1979	Lou Graham	268
1980	Lee Trevino	265
1981	*Bill Rogers	266
1982	Jay Haas	262
1983	Jim Colbert	261
1984	Calvin Peete	266
1985	*John Mahaffey	268
1986	Ben Crenshaw	196
1987	Tom Watson	268
1988	Corey Pavin	259
1989	Donnie Hammond	258
1990	Mark O'Meara	261
1991	*Blaine McCallister	269
1992	*Nick Price	263
1993	Jay Haas	269
1994	Bob Estes	265
1995	Duffy Waldorf	268

THE TOUR CHAMPIONSHIP

Formerly known as the Nabisco Championships
Oak Hills C.C., San Antonio, TX (1987); Pebble Beach G.L., Pebble Beach, Ca (1988); Harbour Town G.L., Hilton Head Island, SC (1989); Champions G.C., Houston, TX (1990); Pinehurst No. 2, Pinehurst, NC (1991-92); The Olympic Club, San Francisco, CA (1993-94); Southern Hills G.C., Tulsa, OK (1995).

Year	Player	Score
1986	Ben Crenshaw	196
1987	Tom Watson	268
1988	*Curtis Strange	279
1989	*Tom Kite	276
1990	*Jodie Mudd	273
1991	*Craig Stadler	279
1992	Paul Azinger	276
1993	Jim Gallagher	277
1994	Mark McCumber	274
1995	Billy Mayfair	280

LINCOLN-MERCURY KAPALUA INTERNATIONAL

Kapalua G.C., Maui, HI (1983-present).

1983	Greg Norman	268
1984	Sandy Lyle	266
1985	Mark O'Meara	275
1986	Andy Bean	278
1987	Andy Bean	267
1988	Bob Gilder	266
1989	*Peter Jacobsen	270
1990	David Peoples	264
1991	*Mike Hulbert	276
1992	Davis Love III	275
1993	Fred Couples	274
1994	Fred Couples	279
1995	Jim Furyk	277

FRANKLIN FUNDS SHARK SHOOTOUT

Sherwood C.C., Thousand Oaks, CA (1989-present)

1989	Curtis Strange/ Mark O'Meara	190
1990	Ray Floyd/ Fred Couples	182
1991	Tom Purtzer/ Lanny Wadkins	189
1992	Davis Love III/ Tom Kite	191
1993	Steve Elkington/ Ray Floyd	188
1994	Fred Couples/ Brad Faxon	190

SKINS GAME

Desert Highlands C.C., Scottsdale, AZ (1983-84); Bear Creek C.C., Murieta, CA, (1985); TPC at PGA West (1986-1991); Bighom G.C., Palm Desert, CA(1992-present).

1983	Gary Player	$170,000
1984	Jack Nicklaus	$240,000
1985	Fuzzy Zoeller	$255,000
1986	Fuzzy Zoeller	$370,000
1987	Lee Trevino	$310,000
1988	Ray Floyd	$290,000
1989	Curtis Strange	$265,000
1990	Curtis Strange	$225,000
1991	Payne Stewart	$260,000
1992	Payne Stewart	$220,000
1993	Payne Stewart	$280,000
1994	Tom Watson	$210,000
1995	Fred Couples	$260,000

JCPENNEY CLASSIC

Formerly the Haig & Haig Scotch Foursome

Pinecrest Lake Club, Avon Park, FL (1960-64); Harder Hall, Sebring, FL (1960-64); La Costa C.C., La Costa, CA (1965-66); Doral C.C., Miami, FL (1976); Bardmoor C.C., Largo, FL (1977-89); Innisbrook Resort, Tarpon Springs, FL (1990-present).

1960	*Jim Turnesa/ Gloria Armstrong	139
1961	Dave Ragan/ Mickey Wright	272
1962	Mason Rudolph/ Kathy Whitworth	272
1963	Dave Ragan/ Mickey Wright	273
1964	Sam Snead/ Shirley Englehorn	272
1965	Gardner Dickinson/ Ruth Jessen	281
1966	Jack Rule/ Sandra Spuzich	276
1976	Chi Chi Rodriguez/ JoAnn Washam	275
1977	Jerry Pate/ Hollis Stacy	270
1978	*Lon Hinkle/ Pat Bradley	267
1979	Dave Eichelberger/ Murle Breer	268
1980	Curtis Strange/ Nancy Lopez	268
1981	Tom Kite/ Beth Daniel	270
1982	John Mahaffey/ JoAnne Carner	268
1983	Fred Couples/ Jan Stephenson	264
1984	Mike Donald/ Vicki Alvarez	270
1985	Larry Rinker/ Laurie Rinker	267
1986	Tom Purtzer/ Juli Inkster/	267

JCPenney Classic continued

Year	Winner	Score
1987	Steve Jones/ Jane Crafter	268
1988	John Huston/ Amy Benz	269
1989	*Bill Glasson/ Pat Bradley	267
1990	Davis Love III/ Beth Daniel	266
1991	*Billy Andrade/ Kris Tschetter	266
1992	Dan Forsman/ Dottie Mochrie	264
1993	Mike Spring/ Melissa McNamara	265
1994	*Brad Bryant/ Marta Figueras-Dotti	262
1995	Davis Love III/ Beth Daniel	257

LPGA TOUR

HEALTHSOUTH PALM BEACH CLASSIC

Dear Creek C.C. (1980-85); Stonebridge G. & C.C. (1986-89); Wycliffe G&C.C., Lake Worth, Fla. (1990-present).

Year	Winner	Score
1980	JoAnne Carner	282
1981	Sandra Palmer	284
1982	*Hollis Stacy	282
1983	Pat Bradley	272
1984	Silvia Bertolaccini	280
1985	Hollis Stacy	280
1986	Val Skinner	280
1987	*Kathy Postlewait	286
1988	Nancy Lopez	283
1989	*Dottie Mochrie	279
1990	*Pat Bradley	281
1991	Meg Mallon	276
1992	*Colleen Walker	279
1993	*Tammie Green	208
1994	Dawn Coe-Jones	201
1995	Pat Bradley	211

CUP NOODLES HAWAIIAN LADIES OPEN

Turtle Bay Resort (1987-89); Ko Olina G.C., Ewa Beach, Oahu, HI (1990-present).

Year	Winner	Score
1987	Cindy Rarick	207
1988	Ayako Okamoto	213
1989	Sherri Turner	205
1990	Beth Daniel	210
1991	Patty Sheehan	207
1992	Lisa Walters	208
1993	Lisa Walters	210
1994	Marta Figueras-Dotti	209
1995	Barb Thomas	204

CHRYSLER-PLYMOUTH TOURNAMENT OF CHAMPIONS

Grand Cypress Resort, Orlando, FL (1994).

Year	Winner	Score
1994	Dottie Mochrie	287
1995	No Tournament	

PING/WELCH'S CHAMPIONSHIP

Randolph Park North, Tucson, AZ (1981-present).

Year	Winner	Score
1981	Nancy Lopez	278
1982	*Ayako Okamoto	281
1983	Jan Stephenson	207
1984	Chris Johnson	272
1985	Amy Alcott	279
1986	Penny Pulz	276
1987	Betsy King	281
1988	Laura Davies	278
1989	Lori Garbacz	274
1990	Colleen Walker	276
1991	Chris Johnson	273
1992	Brandie Burton	277
1993	Meg Mallon	272
1994	Donna Andrews	276
1995	Dottie Mochrie	278

STANDARD REGISTER PING

Hillcrest G.C. (1980-82); Arizona Biltmore C.C. (1983-86); Moon Valley C.C., Phoenix, AZ (1987-present).

Year	Winner	Score
1980	Jan Stephenson	275
1981	Patty Hayes	277
1982	*Beth Daniel	278
1983	Anne-Marie Palli	205
1984	Chris Johnson	276
1985	*Betsy King	280
1986	M. B. Zimmerman	278
1987	Pat Bradley	286
1988	Ok-Hee Ku	281
1989	Allison Finney	282

Standard Register Ping continued

1990	Pat Bradley	280
1991	Danielle Ammaccapane	283
1992	Danielle Ammaccapane	279
1993	Patty Sheehan	275
1994	Laura Davies	277
1995	Laura Davies	280

CHICK-FIL-A CHAMPIONSHIP
Formerly the Atlanta Women's Championship
Eagle's Landing C.C., Stockbridge, GA (1992-present).

1992	Dottie Mochrie	277
1993	Trish Johnson	282
1994	Val Skinner	206
1995	Laura Davies	201

PINEWILD WOMEN'S CHAMPIONSHIP
Pinewild C.C., Pinehurst, NC (1995).

1995	Rosie Jones	211

SPRINT CHALLENGE
Killeam C.C. & Inn, Tallahassee, FL (1990-1994); Indigo Lakes G. & T. Resort, Daytona Beach, FL (1995).

1990	Beth Daniel	271
1991	Pat Bradley	278
1992	Danielle Ammaccapane	208
1993	Kristi Albers	279
1994	Sherri Steinhauer	273
1995	Val Skinner	273

SARA LEE CLASSIC
Hermitage G.C., Old Hickory, TN (1988-present).

1988	*Patti Rizzo	207
1989	Kathy Postlewait	203
1990	Ayako Okamoto	210
1991	Nancy Lopez	206
1992	*Maggie Will	207
1993	*Meg Mallon	205
1994	Laura Davies	203
1995	Michelle McGann	202

McDONALD'S CHAMPIONSHIP
White Manor C.C. (1981-86); Du Pont C.C., Wilmington, DE (1987-present).

1981	Sandra Post	282
1982	JoAnne Carner	276
1983	*Beth Daniel	286
1984	Patty Sheehan	281
1985	Alice Miller	272
1986	Juli Inkster	281
1987	Betsy King	278
1988	Kathy Postlewait	276
1989	Betsy King	272
1990	Patty Sheehan	275
1991	Beth Daniel	273
1992	Ayako Okamoto	205
1993	Laura Davies	277
1994	Laura Davies	279
1995	No Tournament	

LADY KEYSTONE OPEN
Sportsman's G.C. (1975-76); Armitage G.C. (1977); Hershey C.C., Hershey, PA (1978-1994).

1975	Susie Berning	142
1976	Susie Berning	215
1977	Sandra Spuzich	201
1978	Pat Bradley	206
1979	Nancy Lopez	212
1980	JoAnne Carner	207
1981	JoAnne Carner	203
1982	Jan Stephenson	211
1983	Jan Stephenson	205
1984	Amy Alcott	208
1985	Juli Inkster	209
1986	*Juli Inkster	210
1987	Ayako Okamoto	208
1988	*Shirley Furlong	205
1989	Laura Davies	207
1990	Cathy Gerring	208
1991	Colleen Walker	207
1992	Danielle Ammaccapane	208
1993	Val Skinner	210
1994	Elaine Crosby	211
1995	No Tournament	

LPGA CORNING CLASSIC
Corning C.C., Corning, NY (1979-present).

1979	Penny Pulz	284
1980	Donna Caponi	281
1981	Kathy Hite	282
1982	Sandra Spuzich	280
1983	Patty Sheehan	272
1984	JoAnne Carner	281

LPGA Corning Classic continued

1985	Patti Rizzo	272
1986	Laurie Rinker	278
1987	Cindy Rarick	275
1988	Sherri Turner	273
1989	Ayako Okamoto	272
1990	Pat Bradley	274
1991	Betsy King	273
1992	Colleen Walker	276
1993	*Kelly Robbins	277
1994	Beth Daniel	278
1995	Alison Nicholas	275

STAR BANK LPGA CHAMPIONSHIP

C.C. of the North, Beaver Creek, OH (1995)

1995	Chris Johnson	210

JCPENNEY LPGA SKINS GAME

Stonebriar C.C., Frisco, TX (1990-1994).

1990	Jan Stephenson	6 skins
1991	No Tournament	
1992	Pat Bradley	8 skins
1993	Betsy King	7 skins
1994	Patty Sheehan	13 skins
1995	No Tournament	

OLDSMOBILE CLASSIC

Walnut Hills C.C., East Lansing, MI (1992-present).

1992	Barb Mucha	276
1993	Jane Geddes	277
1994	Beth Daniel	268
1995	Dale Eggeling	274

EDINA REALTY LPGA CLASSIC

Formerly the Minnesota LPGA Classic
Edinburgh USA G.C., Brooklyn Park, MN (1990-present).

1990	Beth Daniel	203
1991	*Cindy Rarick	211
1992	Kris Tschetter	211
1993	Hiromi Kobayashi	205
1994	Liselotte Neumann	205
1995	Julie Larsen	205

ROCHESTER INTERNATIONAL

Locust Hill C.C., Pittsford, NY (1977-present).

1977	Pat Bradley	213
1978	Nancy Lopez	214
1979	Jane Blalock	280
1980	Nancy Lopez	283
1981	Nancy Lopez	285
1982	*Sandra Haynie	276
1983	Ayako Okamoto	282
1984	*Kathy Whitworth	281
1985	Pat Bradley	280
1986	Judy Dickinson	281
1987	Deb Richard	280
1988	*Mei-Chi Cheng	287
1989	*Patty Sheehan	278
1990	Patty Sheehan	271
1991	Rosie Jones	276
1992	Patty Sheehan	269
1993	Tammie Green	276
1994	Lisa Kiggens	273
1995	Patty Sheehan	278

SHOPRITE LPGA CLASSIC

Marriott Seaview C.C. & Resort (1986-87); Sands C.C. (1988-90); Greate Bay Resort & C.C., Somers Point, NJ (1991-present).

1986	Juli Inkster	209
1987	Betsy King	207
1988	*Juli Inkster	206
1989	Nancy Lopez	206
1990	Chris Johnson	275
1991	Jane Geddes	208
1992	Anne-Marie Palli	207
1993	Shelley Hamlin	204
1994	Donna Andrews	207
1995	Betsy King	204

YOUNGSTOWN-WARREN LPGA CLASSIC

Squaw Creek C.C., Warren, OH (1990-present).

1990	*Beth Daniel	207
1991	*Deb Richard	207
1992	*Betsy King	209
1993	Nancy Lopez	203
1994	Tammie Green	206
1995	Michelle McGann	205

JAMIE FARR TOLEDO CLASSIC

Glengarry C.C. (1984-88); Highland Meadows G.C., Sylvania, OH (1989-present).

1984	Lauri Peterson	278

Jamie Farr Toledo Classic continued

1985	Penny Hammel	278
1986	No Tournament	
1987	Jane Geddes	280
1988	Laura Davies	277
1989	Penny Hammel	206
1990	Tina Purizer	205
1991	*Alice Miller	205
1992	Patty Sheehan	209
1993	Brandie Burton	201
1994	*Kelly Robbins	204
1995	Kathryn Marshall	205

JAL BIG APPLE CLASSIC
Wykagyl C.C., New Rochelle, NY (1990-present).

1990	Betsy King	273
1991	Betsy King	279
1992	Juli Inkster	273
1993	Hiromi Kobayashi	278
1994	*Beth Daniel	276
1995	Tracy Kerdyk	273

PING/WELCH'S CHAMPIONSHIP
Radisson-Ferncroft C.C. (1980-84); Sheraton Tara Hotel (1985-89); Resort at Ferncroft (1985-89); Tara Ferncroft C.C. (1990); Blue Hill C.C., Canton, MA (1992-present).

1980	Dale Eggering	276
1981	Donna Caponi	276
1982	Sandra Palmer	281
1983	Patti Rizzo	277
1984	Laurie Rinker	286
1985	Judy Dickinson	280
1986	Jane Geddes	281
1987	Jane Geddes	277
1988	Colleen Walker	274
1989	Amy Alcott	272
1990	*Barb Mucha	277
1991	Juli Inkster	275
1992	Dottie Mochrie	278
1993	*Missie Berteotti	276
1994	Helen Alfredsson	274
1995	Beth Daniel	271

MCCALL'S LPGA CLASSIC AT STRATTON MOUNTAIN
Stratton Mountain C.C., Stratton Mountain, VT (1990-present).

1990	*Cathy Gerring	281
1991	M. McNamara	278
1992	F. Descampe	278
1993	D. Lofland-Dormann	275
1994	Carolyn Hill	275
1995	Dottie Mochrie	204

CHICAGO CHALLENGE
Oak Brook G.C. (1991); Eagle C.C., Naperville, IL (1992-1994).

1991	Martha Nause	275
1992	*Dottie Mochrie	216
1993	Cindy Schreyer	272
1994	Jane Geddes	272
1995	No Torunament	

STATE FARM RAIL CHARITY GOLF CLASSIC
Rail G.C., Springfield, IL (1976-present).

1976	*Sandra Palmer	213
1977	Hollis Stacy	271
1978	Pat Bradley	276
1979	Jo Ann Washam	275
1980	Nancy Lopez	275
1981	JoAnne Carner	205
1982	JoAnne Carner	202
1983	Lauri Peterson	210
1984	Cindy Hill	207
1985	Betsy King	205
1986	*Betsy King	205
1987	Rosie Jones	208
1988	Betsy King	207
1989	Beth Daniel	203
1990	Beth Daniel	203
1991	Pat Bradley	197
1992	*Nancy Lopez	199
1993	*Helen Dobson	203
1994	Barb Mucha	203
1995	M.B. Zimmerman	206

WEETABIX WOMEN'S BRITISH OPEN
Woburn G. & C.C., Milton Keynes, England (1995).

1995	Karrie Webb	278

PING-CELLULAR ONE GOLF CHAMPIONSHIP
Rotated among Portland G.C., Columbia Edgewater

Ping Cellular One Golf Championship continued
C.C., and Riverside G & C.C., Portland, OR (1972-present).

1972	Kathy Whitworth	212
1973	Kathy Whitworth	144
1974	JoAnne Carner	211
1975	JoAnn Washam	215
1976	Donna Caponi	217
1977	*JoAnne Carner/ Judy Rankin	202
1978	*Donna Caponi/ Kathy Whitworth	203
1979	Nancy Lopez/ JoAnn Washam	198
1980	Donna Caponi/ Kathy Whitworth	195
1981	*Donna Caponi/ Kathy Whitworth	203
1982	*Sandra Haynie/ Kathy McMullen	196
1983	*JoAnne Carner	212
1984	Amy Alcott	212
1985	Nancy Lopez	215
1986	Ayako Okamoto	207
1987	Nancy Lopez	210
1988	Betsy King	213
1989	M. Spencer-Devlin	214
1990	Patty Sheehan	208
1991	Michelle Estill	208
1992	*Nancy Lopez	209
1993	Donna Andrews	208
1994	Missie McGeorge	207
1995	Alison Nicholas	207

SAFECO CLASSIC
Meridian Valley C.C., Kent, WA (1982-present).

1982	Patty Sheehan	276
1983	Juli Inkster	283
1984	Kathy Whitworth	279
1985	JoAnne Carner	279
1986	Judy Dickinson	274
1987	Jan Stephenson	277
1988	Juli Inkster	278
1989	Beth Daniel	273
1990	Patty Sheehan	270
1991	*Pat Bradley	280
1992	Colleen Walker	277
1993	Brandie Burton	274
1994	Deb Richard	276
1995	Patty Sheehan	274

WORLD CHAMPIONSHIP OF WOMEN'S GOLF
The Country Club, (1980); Shaker Heights C.C. (1981-84); Stouffer PineIsle Resort (1985-89); Cely G.C. (1990); Paradise Palms G.C. (1991); Naples National G.C. (1993); Paradise G.C., Cheju Island, South Korea (1994-95).

1980	Beth Daniel	282
1981	Beth Daniel	284
1982	JoAnne Carner	284
1983	JoAnne Carner	282
1984	Nancy Lopez	281
1985	Amy Alcott	274
1986	Pat Bradley	279
1987	Ayako Okamoto	282
1988	Rosie Jones	279
1989	Betsy King	275
1990	Cathy Gerring	278
1991	Meg Mallon	216
1992	No Tournament	
1993	Dottie Mochrie	283
1994	Beth Daniel	274
1995	Annika Sorenstam	282

HEARTLAND CLASSIC
Forest Hills C.C., St. Louis, MO (1995)

1995	Annika Sorenstam	278

FIELDCREST CANNON CLASSIC
Peninsula C.C., Charlotte, NC

1995	Gail Graham	273

NICHIREI INTERNATIONAL
Moved annually.

	Individual	Team
1979	Yuko Moriguchi	USA
1980	Amy Alcott	USA
1981	Chako Higuchi	Japan
1982	Nayako Yoshikawa	USA
1983	Chako Higuchi	USA
1984	Hollis Stacy	Japan
1985	Jan Stephenson	USA
1986	Ayako Okamoto	USA
1987	Fukumi Tani	USA
1988	Beth Daniel	USA

Nichirei International continued

1989	Colleen Walker	USA
1990	-------	USA
1991	-------	USA
1992	-------	USA
1993	-------	USA
1994	-------	USA
1995	----	USA

TORAY QUEENS CUP
Moved annually (1973-present)

1973	Jan Ferraris	216
1974	Chako Higuchi	218
1975	Shelley Hamlin	218
1976	Donna Caponi	217
1977	Debbie Massey	220
1978	*Michiko Okada	216
1979	Amy Alcott	211
1980	Tatsuko Ohsako	213
1981	Patty Sheehan	213
1982	Nancy Lopez	207
1983	Pat Bradley	206
1984	Nayoko Yoshikawa	210
1985	Jane Blalock	206
1986	*Ai-Yu Tu	213
1987	Yuko Moriguchi	206
1988	*Patty Sheehan	206
1989	Elaine Crosby	205
1990	Debbie Massey	133
1991	Liselotte Neumann	211
1992	*Betsy King	205
1993	Betsy King	205
1993	Betsy King	205

JCPENNEY CLASSIC
Formerly the Haig & Haig Scotch Foursome
Pinecrest Lake Club, Avon Park, FL (1960-64); Harder Hall, Sebring, FL (1960-64); La Costa C.C., La Costa, CA (1965-66); Doral C.C., Miami, FL (1976); Bardmoor C.C., Largo, FL (1977-89); Innisbrook Resort, Tarpon Springs, FL (1990-present).

1960	*Jim Turnesa/ Gloria Armstrong	139
1961	Dave Ragan/ Mickey Wright	272
1962	Mason Rudolph/ Kathy Whitworth	272
1963	Dave Ragan/ Mickey Wright	273
1964	Sam Snead/ Shirley Englehorn	272
1965	Gardner Dickinson/ Ruth Jessen	281
1966	Jack Rule/ Sandra Spuzich	276
1976	Chi Chi Rodriguez/ JoAnn Washam	275
1977	Jerry Pate/ Hollis Stacy	270
1978	*Lon Hinkle/ Pat Bradley	267
1979	Dave Eichelberger/ Murle Breer	268
1980	Curtis Strange/ Nancy Lopez	268
1981	Tom Kite/ Beth Daniel	270
1982	John Mahaffey/ JoAnne Carner	268
1983	Fred Couples/ Jan Stephenson	264
1984	Mike Donald/ Vicki Alvarez	270
1985	Larry Rinker/ Laurie Rinker	267
1986	Tom Purtzer/ Juli Inkster	267
1987	Steve Jones/ Jane Crafter	268
1988	John Huston/ Amy Benz	269
1989	*Bill Glasson/ Pat Bradley	267
1990	Davis Love III/ Beth Daniel	266
1991	*Billy Andrade/ Kris Tschetter	266
1992	Dan Forsman/ Dottie Mochrie	264
1993	Mike Spring/ Melissa McNamara	265
1994	*Brad Bryant/ Marta Figueras-Dotti	262
1995	Davis Love III/ Beth Daniel	257

Senior PGA TOUR

TOURNAMENT OF CHAMPIONS
Formerly the Mercedes Championships
LaCosta C.C., Carlsbad, CA (1984-present).

1984	Orville Moody	288
1985	Peter Thomson	284
1986	Miller Barber	282
1987	*Don January	287
1988	Dave Hill	211
1989	Miller Barber	280
1990	George Archer	283
1991	Bruce Crampton	279
1992	Al Geiberger	282
1993	Al Geiberger	280
1994	Jack Nicklaus	279
1995	Jim Colbert	209

SENIOR SLAM
Cabo del Sol, Los Cabos, Mexico (1995).

1995	Raymond Floyd	139

ROYAL CARIBBEAN CLASSIC
Links at Key Biscayne,
Key Biscayne, FL (1987-1994).

1987	Gene Littler	207
1988	Lee Elder	202
1989	No Tournament	
1990	Lee Trevino	206
1991	Gary Player	200
1992	Don Massengale	205
1993	Jim Colbert	199
1994	Lee Trevino	205
1995	J.C. Snead	209

GTE SUNCOAST CLASSIC
TPC of Tampa Bay at Cheval,
Tampa, FL (1992-present).

1988	Dale Douglass	210
1989	*Bob Charles	207
1990	Mike Hill	207
1991	Bob Charles	210
1992	*Jim Colbert	200
1993	Jim Albus	206
1994	Rocky Thompson	201
1995	Dave Stockton	204

THE INTELLINET CHALLENGE
The Vineyards G. & C.C. (South),
Naples, FL (1991-present).

1988	Gary Player	207
1989	Gene Littler	209
1990	Lee Trevino	200
1991	Lee Trevino	205
1992	Jimmy Powell	197
1993	Mike Hill	202
1994	Mike Hill	201
1995	Bob Murphy	137

CHRYSLER CUP
TPC at Prestancia, Sarasota, FL (1987-present).

1986	United States	68.5
1987	International	59.9
1988	United States	55.0
1989	United States	71.0
1990	United States	53.5
1991	United States	58.5
1992	United States	54.0
1993	United States	-44
1994	International	-58
1995	United States	11-5

FHP HEALTHCARE CLASSIC
Ojai Valley Inn & C.C., Ojai, CA (1989-present).

1985	Peter Thomson	205
1986	Dale Douglass	202
1987	Bob Charles	208
1988	Harold Henning	214
1989	Walter Zembriski	197
1990	No Tournament	
1991	Chi Chi Rodriguez	132
1992	Bruce Crampton	195
1993	Al Geiberger	198
1994	Jay Sigel	198
1995	Bruce Devlin	130

VANTAGE AT THE DOMINION
Dominion C.C., San Antonio, TX (1985-present).

1985	Don January	206
1986	Bruce Crampton	202
1987	Chi Chi Rodriguez	203
1988	Billy Casper	205
1989	Larry Mowry	201
1990	Jim Dent	205

Vantage at the Dominion continued

1991	Lee Trevino	137
1992	Lee Trevino	201
1993	J.C. Snead	214
1994	Jim Albus	208
1995	Jim Albus	205

DOUG SANDERS KINGWOOD CELEBRITY CLASSIC

Deerwood Club, Houston, TX (1988-1994).

1988	Chi Chi Rodriguez	208
1989	Homero Blancas	208
1990	Lee Trevino	203
1991	Mike Hill	203
1992	Mike Hill	134
1993	Bob Charles	208
1994	Tom Wargo	209
1995	No Tournament	

DALLAS REUNION PRO-AM

Formerly the Muratec Reunion Pro-Am
Stonebriar C.C., Frisco, TX (1989-1994);
Oak Cliff C.C., Dallas, TX (1995).

1985	Peter Thomson	202
1986	Don January	203
1987	Chi Chi Rodriguez	201
1988	*Orville Moody	206
1989	Don Bies	208
1990	Frank Beard	207
1991	*Chi Chi Rodriguez	208
1992	*George Archer	211
1993	Dave Stockton	211
1994	Larry Gilbert	202
1995	Tom Wargo	197

TOSHIBA SENIOR CLASSIC

Mesa Verde C.C., Costa Mesa, CA (1995).

1985	George Archer	199

LAS VEGAS SENIOR CLASSIC

Desert Inn C.C., Las Vegas, NV (1986-present).

1986	Bruce Crampton	206
1987	Al Geiberger	203
1988	Larry Mowry	204
1989	*Charles Coody	205
1990	Chi Chi Rodriguez	204
1991	Chi Chi Rodriguez	204
1992	Lee Trevino	206
1993	Gibby Gilbert	204
1994	Ray Floyd	203
1995	Jim Colbert	205

LIBERTY MUTUAL LEGENDS OF GOLF

Barton Creek C.C., Austin, TX (1990-present).

1978	Sam Snead/ Gardner Dickinson	193
1979	Julius Boros/ Roberto De Vicenzo	195
1980	Tommy Bolt/ Art Wall	187
1981	Gene Littler/ Bob Rosburg	257
1982	Sam Snead/ Don January	183
1983	Rod Funseth/ Roberto DeVicenzo	258
1984	Billy Casper/ Gay Brewer	258
1985	Don January/ Gene Littler	257
1986	Don January/ Gene Littler	255
1987	Bruce Crampton/ Orville Moody	251
1988	*Bruce Crampton/ Orville Moody	254
1989	Harold Henning/ Al Geiberger	251
1990	Dale Douglass/ Charles Coody	249
1991	Lee Trevino/ Mike Hill	252
1992	Lee Trevino/ Mike Hill	251
1993	*Harold Henning	204
1994	Dale Douglass/ Charles Coody	188
1995	Lee Trevino/ Mike Hill	195

PAINEWEBBER INVITATIONAL

TPC at Piper Glen, Charlotte, NC (1989-present).

1980	*Gene Littler	211
1981	Miller Barber	282
1982	Gene Littler	280

PaineWebber Invitattional continued

1983	Doug Sanders	283
1984	Peter Thomson	281
1985	Miller Barber	277
1986	Bruce Crampton	279
1987	*Gary Player	207
1988	Dave Hill	206
1989	No Tournament	
1990	Bruce Crampton	205
1991	Orville Moody	207
1992	Don Bies	203
1993	Mike Hill	204
1994	Lee Trevino	203
1995	Bob Murphy	203

CADILLAC/NFL GOLF CLASSIC
Upper Montclair C.C., Clinton, NJ (1993-present).

1993	Lee Trevino	209
1994	Ray Floyd	206
1995	George Archer	205

BELL ATLANTIC CLASSIC
Chester Valley G.C., Malvem, PA (1985-present).

1985	Don January	135
1986	Gary Player	206
1987	Chi Chi Rodriguez	202
1988	*Bruce Crampton	205
1989	*Dave Hill	206
1990	*Dale Douglass	204
1991	Jim Ferree	208
1992	Lee Trevino	205
1993	Bob Charles	204
1994	Lee Trevino	206
1995	Jim Colbert	207

BRUNO'S MEMORIAL CLASSIC
Greystone G.C., Birmingham, AL (1992-present).

1992	George Archer	208
1993	Bob Murphy	203
1994	Jim Dent	201
1995	Graham Marsh	201

NATIONWIDE CHAMPIONSHIP
C.C. of the South, Alpharetta, GA (1991-present).

1991	Mike Hill	212
1992	Isao Aoki	208
1993	Lee Trevino	205
1994	Dave Stockton	198
1995	Bob Murphy	203

KROGER SENIOR CLASSIC
Jack Nicklaus Sports Center (Grizzly),
Kings Island, OH (1990-present).

1990	Jim Dent	133
1991	Al Geiberger	203
1992	*Gibby Gilbert	203
1993	Simon Hobday	202
1994	Jim Colbert	199
1995	Mike Hill	196

AMERITECH SENIOR OPEN
Stonebridge C.C., Aurora, IL (1991-present).

1989	Bruce Crampton	205
1990	Chi Chi Rodriguez	203
1991	Mike Hill	200
1992	Dale Douglass	201
1993	George Archer	133
1994	John Paul Cain	202
1995	Hale Irwin	195

BELLSOUTH SENIOR CLASSIC
Springhouse G.C., Nashville, TN (1995)

1995	Jim Dent	203

SOUTHWESTERN BELL CLASSIC
Loch Lloyd C.C.,
Belton, MO (1991-1994).

1987	Chi Chi Rodriguez	200
1988	*Gary Player	203
1989	*Bobby Nichols	209
1990	Jimmy Powell	208
1991	Jim Colbert	201
1992	Gibby Gilbert	193
1993	Dave Stockton	204
1994	Jim Colbert	196
1995	No Tournament	

NORTHVILLE LONG ISLAND CLASSIC
Meadow Brook Club, Jericho, NY (1988-present).

1988	Don Bies	202
1989	*Butch Baird	183
1990	George Archer	208
1991	George Archer	204
1992	George Archer	205
1993	Ray Floyd	208
1994	Lee Trevino	200
1995	Lee Trevino	202

BANK OF BOSTON CLASSIC
Nashawtuc C.C., Concord, MA (1984-present).

1981	Bob Goalby	208
1982	Arnold Palmer	276
1983	Don January	273
1984	Don January	209
1985	*Lee Elder	208
1986	Chi Chi Rodriguez	203
1987	Chi Chi Rodriguez	198
1988	Chi Chi Rodriguez	202
1989	Bob Charles	200
1990	Bob Charles	203
1991	Rocky Thompson	205
1992	*Mike Hill	136
1993	Bob Betley	204
1994	Jim Albus	203
1995	Isao Aoki	204

FIRST OF AMERICA CLASSIC
The Highlands, Grand Rapids, MI (1990-present).

1986	*Jim Ferree	204
1987	Billy Casper	200
1988	Orville Moody	203
1989	John Paul Cain	203
1990	Don Massengale	134
1991	*Harold Henning	202
1992	Gibby Gilbert	202
1993	*George Archer	199
1994	Tony Jacklin	136
1995	Jimmy Powell	201

BURNET SENIOR CLASSIC
Bunker Hills G.C., Coon Rapids, MN (1993-1995)

1993	Chi Chi Rodriguez	201
1994	Dave Stockton	203
1995	Ray Floyd	201

FRANKLIN QUEST CHAMPIONSHIP
Jeremy Ranch G.C., Park City, UT (1982-present).

1982	Billy Casper	279
1983	Bob Goalby/ Mike Reid	256
1984	Don January/ Mike Sullivan	250
1985	Miller Barber/ Ben Crenshaw	257
1986	Bobby Nichols/ Curt Byrum	249

1987	Miller Barber	210
1988	Miller Barber	207
1989	Tom Shaw	207
1990	Rives McBee	202
1991	Dale Douglass	209
1992	*Orville Moody	137
1993	Dave Stockton	197
1994	Tom Weiskopf	204
1995	Tony Jacklin	206

GTE NORTHWEST CLASSIC
Inglewood C.C., Kenmore, WA (1987-present).

1986	Bruce Crampton	210
1987	Chi Chi Rodriguez	206
1988	Bruce Crampton	207
1989	Al Geiberger	204
1990	George Archer	205
1991	Mike Hill	198
1992	Mike Joyce	204
1993	Dave Stockton	200
1994	Simon Hobday	209
1995	Walt Morgan	203

GTE NORTH CLASSIC
Broadmoor C.C., Indianapolis, IN (1988-1993).

1988	Gary Player	201
1989	Gary Player	135
1990	*Mike Hill	201
1991	George Archer	199
1992	Ray Floyd	199
1993	Bob Murphy	134
1994	No Tournament	
1995	No Tournament	

QUICKSILVER CLASSIC
Quicksilver C.C., Midway, PA (1993-present).

1993	Bob Charles	207
1994	Dave Eichelberger	209
1995	Dave Stockton	208

BRICKYARD CROSSING CHAMPIONSHIP
Brickyard Crossing G.C., Indianapolis, IN (1995)

1995	Simon Hobday	204

BANK ONE SENIOR CLASSIC
Kearney Hill Links, Lexington, KY (1990-present).

1983	Don January	269

Bank One Senior Classic continued

1984	Gay Brewer	204
1985	Lee Elder	135
1986	*Gene Littler	201
1987	Bruce Crampton	197
1988	Bob Charles	200
1989	Rives McBee	202
1990	Rives McBee	201
1991	*DeWitt Weaver	207
1992	Terry Dill	203
1993	Gary Player	202
1994	Isao Aoki	202
1995	Gary Player	211

VANTAGE CHAMPIONSHIP
Tanglewood Park, Clemmons, NC (1987-present).

1987	Al Geiberger	206
1988	Walt Zembriski	278
1989	Gary Player	207
1990	Charles Coody	202
1991	Jim Colbert	205
1992	Jim Colbert	132
1993	Lee Trevino	198
1994	Larry Gilbert	198
1995	Hale Irwin	199

THE TRANSAMERICA
Silverado C.C. (South), Napa, CA (1989-present).

1989	Billy Casper	207
1990	Lee Trevino	205
1991	Charles Coody	204
1992	Bob Charles	200
1993	Dave Stockton	203
1994	Kermit Zarley	204
1995	Lee Trevino	201

RALEY'S SENIOR GOLD RUSH
Rancho Murieta C.C.,
Rancho Murieta, CA (1987-present).

1987	Orville Moody	205
1988	Bob Charles	207
1989	Dave Hill	207
1990	George Archer	204
1991	George Archer	206
1992	Bob Charles	201
1993	George Archer	202
1994	Bob Murphy	208
1995	Don Bies	205

RALPH'S SENIOR CLASSIC
Rancho Park G.C.,
Los Angeles, CA (1990-present).

1990	Mike Hill	201
1991	*John Brodie	200
1992	Ray Floyd	195
1993	*Dale Douglas	196
1994	Jack Kiefer	197
1995	John Bland	201

KAANAPALI CLASSIC
Royal Kaanapali G.C. (North),
Maui, HI (1987-present).

1987	Orville Moody	132
1988	Don Bies	204
1989	Don Bies	132
1990	Bob Charles	206
1991	Jim Colbert	195
1992	Tommy Aaron	198
1993	George Archer	199
1994	Bob Murphy	195
1995	Bob Charles	204

DINERS CLUB MATCHES
PGA West, La Quinta, CA (1994-present).

1994	Ray Floyd/ Dave Eichelberger	1-up
1995	J. Colbert/B. Murphy	1-up

SENIOR TOUR CHAMPIONSHIP
Hyatt Dorado Beach (East), Dorado, Puerto Rico (1988-1993); The Dunes Club, Myrtle Beach, SC (1994-present).

1985	Don January/ Alice Miller	127
1986	Bob Charles/ Amy Alcott	193
1987	Miller Barber/ Nancy Lopez	191
1988	Dave Hill/ Colleen Walker	186
1989	Mike Hill/Patti Rizzo	191
1990	*Mike Hill	201
1991	Mike Hill	202
1992	Ray Floyd	197
1993	Simon Hobday	199
1994	Ray Floyd	273
1995	Jim Colbert	282

1995 COLLEGIATE GOLF

OVERVIEW: *Significant 1995 tournament results, plus All-American team selections since 1965, Men's Division I, II and III individual and team champions plus Women's individual and team champions, since the start of competition.*

1995 Collegiate Results

MEN

NCAA East Regional
Team: *Clemson*
Indiv: Christian Raynor, Florida State

NCAA West Regional
Team: *Arizona State*
Indiv: Mike Sauer, Univ. of New Mexico

NCAA Central Regional
Team: *Oklahoma*
Indiv: Alan Bratton, Oklahoma State

NJCAA
Team: *Midland*
Indiv: Robert Russell, Kansas City

NAIA
Team: *Texas Western*
Indiv: Steve Armstrong, Pfeiffer

Minority Championship
Team: *Jackson State*
Indiv: Robert Ames, Florida A&M

GOLFWEEK/Taylor Made National Rankings

1. Oklahoma State
2. Stanford
3. Texas
4. Arizona State
5. Georgia Tech
6. Oklahoma
7. Nevada-Las Vegas
8. North Carolina
9T. Florida
9T. Arizona
11. Texas Christian
12. Auburn
13. California
14. Arkansas
15T. Houston
15T. New Mexico
17. Tulsa
18. Ohio State
19. Florida State
20. Virginia
21T. North Carolina State
21T. Kent State
23. Southern California
24. Texas A&M
25. Clemson
26. Tennessee
27. Louisiana State
28. Wake Forest
29. Minnesota

WOMEN

NCAA West Regional
Team: *San Jose State Univ.*
Indiv: Wendy Ward, Arizona State Univ.

NCAA East Regional
Team: *Wake Forest*
Indiv: Siew Ai Lim, U. of South Carolina

NGCA Division II
Team: *Longwood*
Indiv: Charlaine Goetzee

NGCA Division III
Team: *Methodist*
Indiv: Elizabeth Horton

GOLFWEEK/Taylor Made National Rankings

1.   Arizona State
2.   San Jose State
3.   Stanford
4.   Wake Forest
5.   UCLA
6.   South Carolina
6.   Texas
8.   Indiana
9.   Furman
10. Florida
11. Tulsa
12. Duke
13. Oklahoma
13. North Carolina
13. Arizona
16. Georgia
17. Southern California
18. Louisiana State
18. Oregon
20. Oklahoma State
21. Florida State
22. New Mexico State
23. New Mexico
24. Tennessee
25. South Florida
25. Texas A&M
27. Ohio State
28. Miami
29. Washington

NCAA DIVISION I CHAMPIONS -MEN

Team (Italics), Individual

1897 *Yale Univ.*
     Louis Bayard Jr., Princeton
1898 *Harvard Univ., Yale Univ.*
     John Reid Jr., Yale
     James Curtis, Harvard
1899 *Harvard*
     Percy Pyne, Princeton

1900 No Meeting
1901 *Harvard Univ.*
     H. Lindsley, Harvard
1902 *Yale Univ., Harvard Univ.*
     Charles Hitchcock Jr., Yale
     Chandler Egan, Harvard
1903 *Harvard Univ.*
     F.O. Reinhart, Princeton
1904 *Harvard Univ.*
     A.L. White, Harvard
1905 *Yale Univ.*
     Robert Abbott, Yale
1906 *Yale Univ.*
     W.E. Clow Jr., Yale
1907 *Yale Univ.*
     Ellis Knowles, Yale
1908 *Yale Univ.*
     H.H. Wilder, Harvard
1909 *Yale Univ.*
     Albert Seckel, Princeton
1910 *Yale Univ.*
     Robert Hunter, Yale
1911 *Yale Univ.*
     George Stanley, Yale
1912 *Yale Univ.*
     F.C. Davison, Harvard
1913 *Yale Univ.*
     Nathaniel Wheeler, Yale
1914 *Princeton Univ.*
     Edward Allis, Harvard
1915 *Yale Univ.*
     Francis Blossom, Yale
1916 *Harvard Univ.*
     J.W. Hubbell, Harvard
1917 No Meeting
1918 No Meeting
1919 *Princeton Univ.*
     A.L. Walker Jr., Columbia
1920 *Princeton Univ.*
     Jess Sweetser, Yale
1921 *Dartmouth Univ.*
     Simpson Dean, Princeton
1922 *Princeton Univ.*
     Pollack Boyd, Dartmouth
1923 *Princeton Univ.*

Dexter Cummings, Yale
1924 *Yale Univ.*
Dexter Cummings, Yale
1925 *Yale Univ.*
Fred Laprecht, Yale
1926 *Yale Univ.*
Fred Laprecht, Yale
1927 *Princeton Univ.*
Watts Gunn, Georgia Tech.
1928 *Princeton Univ.*
Maurice McCarthy, Georgetown
1929 *Princeton Univ.*
Tom Aycock, Yale
1930 *Princeton Univ.*
G.T. Dunlap Jr., Princeton
1931 *Yale Univ.*
G.T. Dunlap Jr., Princeton
1932 *Yale Univ.*
J.W. Fisher, Michigan
1933 *Yale Univ.*
Walter Emery, Oklahoma
1934 *Michigan Univ.*
Charles Yates, Georgia Tech
1935 *Michigan Univ.*
Ed White, Texas
1936 *Yale Univ.*
Charles Kocsis, Michigan
1937 *Princeton Univ.*
Fred Haas Jr., LSU
1938 *Stanford Univ.*
John Burke, Georgetown
1939 *Stanford Univ.*
Vincent D'Antoni, Tulane
1940 *Princeton Univ., LSU*
Dixon Brooke, Virginia
1941 *Stanford Univ.*
Earl Stewart, LSU
1942 *Stanford Univ., LSU*
Frank Tatum, Stanford
1943 *Yale Univ.*
Wallace Ulrich, Carleton
1944 *Notre Dame Univ.*
Louis Lick, Minnesota
1945 *Ohio State Univ.*

John Lorms, Ohio State
1946 *Stanford Univ.*
George Hamer, Georgia
1947 *Louisiana State Univ.*
Dave Barclay, Michigan
1948 *San Jose State Univ.*
Bob Harris, San Jose St.
1949 *North Texas State Univ.*
Harvie Ward, N. Carolina
1950 *North Texas State Univ.*
Fred Wampler, Purdue
1951 *North Texas State Univ.*
Tom Nieporte, Ohio State
1952 *North Texas State Univ.*
Jim Vickers, Oklahoma
1953 *Stanford Univ.*
Earl Moeller, Oklahoma St.
1954 *Southern Methodist Univ.*
Hillman Robbins, Memphis St.
1955 *Louisiana State Univ.*
Joe Campbell, Purdue
1956 *Univ. of Houston*
Rick Jones, Ohio State
1957 *Univ. of Houston*
Rex Baxter Jr., Houston
1958 *Univ. of Houston*
Phil Rodgers, Houston
1959 *Univ. of Houston*
Dick Crawford, Houston
1960 *Univ. of Houston*
Dick Crawford, Houston
1961 *Purdue Univ.*
Jack Nicklaus, Ohio State
1962 *Univ. of Houston*
Kermit Zarley, Houston
1963 *Oklahoma State Univ.*
R. H. Sikes, Arkansas
1964 *Univ. of Houston*
Terry Small, San Jose St.
1965 *Univ. of Houston*
Marty Fleckman, Houston
1966 *Univ. of Houston*
Bob Murphy, Florida
1967 *Univ. of Houston*
Hale Irwin, Colorado

1968 *Univ. of Florida*
    Grier Jones, Oklahoma St.
1969 *Univ. of Houston*
    Bob Clark, Los Angeles St.
1970 *Univ. of Houston*
    John Mahaffey, Houston
1971 *Univ. of Texas*
    Ben Crenshaw, Texas
    Tom Kite, Texas
1972 *Univ. of Texas*
    Ben Crenshaw, Texas
1973 *Univ. of Florida*
    Ben Crenshaw, Texas
1974 *Wake Forest Univ.*
    Curtis Strange, Wake Forest
1975 *Wake Forest Univ.*
    Jay Haas, Wake Forest
1976 *Oklahoma State Univ.*
    Scott Simpson, So. Cal.
1977 *Univ. of Houston*
    Scott Simpson, So. Cal.
1978 *Oklahoma State Univ.*
    David Edwards, Okla. St.
1979 *Ohio State Univ.*
    Gary Hallberg, Wake Forest
1980 *Oklahoma State Univ.*
    Jay Don Blake, Utah State
1981 *Brigham Young Univ.*
    Ron Commans, So. Cal.
1982 *Univ. of Houston*
    Billy Ray Brown, Houston
1983 *Oklahoma State Univ.*
    Jim Carter, Arizona St.
1984 *Univ. of Houston*
    John Inman, N. Carolina
1985 *Univ. of Houston*
    Clark Burroughs, Ohio St.
1986 *Wake Forest Univ.*
    Scott Verplank, Oklahoma St.
1987 *Oklahoma State Univ.*
    Brian Watts, Oklahoma St.
1988 *UCLA*
    E.J. Pfister, Oklahoma St.
1989 *Univ. of Oklahoma*
    Phil Mickelson, Ariz St.

1990 *Arizona State Univ.*
    Phil Mickelson, Ariz. St.
1991 *Oklahoma State Univ.*
    Warren Schutte, Nevada-LV
1992 *Univ. of Arizona*
    Phil Mickelson, Ariz. St.
1993 *Univ. of Florida*
    Todd Demsey, Ariz. St.
1994 *Stanford*
    Justin Leonard, Texas
1995 *Oklahoma State Univ.*
    Chris Spratlin, Auburn

NCAA DIVISION II
MEN'S CHAMPIONS

1963 *Southwest Missouri State*
    Gary Head, Middle Tenn. St.
1964 *Southern Illinois Univ.*
    John Kurzynowski, Aquinas
1965 *Middle Tennessee State*
    Larry Gilbert, Mid. Tenn. St.
1966 *Chico State Univ.*
    Bob Smith, Sacramento St.
1967 *Lamar Univ.*
    Larry Hinson, E. Tenn. St.
1968 *Lamar Univ.*
    Mike Nugent, Lamar
1969 *Northridge State Univ.*
    Mike Spang, Portland St.
    Corky Bassler, Northridge St.
1970 *Rollins Univ.*
    Gary McCord, Cal-Riverside
1971 *New Orleans Univ.*
    Stan Stopa, New Orleans
1972 *New Orleans Univ.*
    Jim Hilderbrand, Ashland
1973 *Northridge State Univ.*
    Paul Wise, Fullerton St.
1974 *Northride State Univ.*
    Matt Bloom, Cal-Riverside
1975 *California-Irvine*
    Jerry Wisz, Cal-Irvine
1976 *Troy State Univ.*
    Mike Nicolette, Rollins

1977 *Troy State Univ.*
   David Thornally, Ark.-L. Rock
1978 *Columbus*
   Thomas Brannen, Columbus
1979 *California-Davis*
   Tom Gleeton, Fla. South.
1980 *Columbus*
   Paul Perini, Troy State
1981 *Florida Southern Univ.*
   Tom Patri, Fla. Southern
1982 *Fla. Southern Univ.*
   Vic Wilk, Northridge State
1983 *S.W. Texas State Univ.*
   Greg Chapman, Stephen Austin
1984 *Troy State Univ.*
   Greg Cate, C. Connecticut
1985 *Florida Southern Univ.*
   Hugh Royer, Columbus
1986 *Florida Southern Univ.*
   Lee Janzen, Fla. South.
1987 *Univ. of Tampa*
   Jeff Leonard, Univ. of Tampa
1988 *Univ. of Tampa*
   Jeff Leonard, Univ. of Tampa
1989 *Columbus*
   Brian Dixon, Columbus
1990 *Florida Southern Univ.*
   Bob Burns, Cal. State-Northridge
1991 *Florida Southern Univ.*
   Clete Cole, Columbus
1992 *Columbus*
   Diego Ventureire, Columbus
1993 *Abilene Christian*
   Jeev Singh, Abilene Christian
1994 *Columbus*
   Briny Baird, Valdosta St.
1995 *Florida Southern*
   Briny Baird, Valdosta

NCAA DIVISION III MEN'S CHAMPIONS

1975 *Wooster College*
   Charles Baskervill, Hampden
1976 *Stanislaus State*
   Dan Lisle, Stanislaus St.

1977 *Stanislaus State*
   David Downing, S.E. Mass.
1978 *Stanislaus State*
   Jim Quinn, Oswego State
1979 *Stanislaus State*
   Mike Bender, Stanislaus St.
1980 *Stanislaus State*
   Mike Bender, Stanislaus St.
1981 *Stanislaus State*
   Ryan Fox, N.C.-Greensboro
1982 *Ramapo College*
   Cliff Smith, Stanislaus St.
1983 *Allegheny College*
   Matt Clarke, Allegheny St.
1984 *Stanislaus State*
   Bob Osborn, Redlands
1985 *Stanislaus State*
   Brian Goldsworthy, Central
1986 *Stanislaus State*
   Eric Meerbach, Worcester Poly
1987 *Stanislaus State*
   Pat Weishan, Cal-San Diego
1988 *Stanislaus State*
   Glenn Andrade, Stanislaus St.
1989 *Stanislaus State*
   John McCullough, Methodist
1990 *Methodist*
   Rob Pilewski, Methodist
1991 *Methodist*
   Lee Palms, Emory
1992 *Methodist*
   Jon Lindquist, Gust. Adolphus
1993 *Univ. of California-San Diego*
   Ryan Jenkins, Methodist
1994 *Methodist*
   Scott Scovil, CNC
1995 *Methodist*
   Ryan Jenkins, Methodist

NCAA DIVISION I WOMEN'S CHAMPIONS

1941 Eleanor Dudley, Alabama
1942 *No Meeting*
1943 *No Meeting*
1944 *No Meeting*

1945 *No Meeting*
1946 Phillis Otto, Northwestern
1947 Shirley Spork, Mich. St.
1948 Grace Lenczyk, Stetson
1949 Marilynn Smith, Kansas
1950 Betty Rowland, Rollins
1951 Barbara Bruning, Wellesley
1952 Mary Ann Villega, Ohio St.
1953 Patricia Lesser, Seattle
1954 Nancy Reed, Ga.-Peabody
1955 Jackie Yates, Redlands
1956 Marlene Stewart, Rollins
1957 Miriam Bailey, Northwestern
1958 Carole Pushing, Carleton
1959 Judy Eller, Miami-Fla.
1960 JoAnne Gunderson, Ariz. St.
1961 Judy Hoetmer, Washington
1962 Carol Sorenson, Ariz. St.
1963 Claudia Lindor, West. Wash.
1964 Patti Shook, Valparaiso
1965 Roberta Albers, Miami-Fla.
1966 Joyce Kazmierski, Mich. St.
1967 Martha Wilkinson, Cal-Fullerton
1968 Gail Sykes, Odessa
1969 Jane Bastanchury, Ariz. St.
1970 *Miami-Fla.*
    Cathy Gaughan, Ariz. St.
1971 *UCLA*
    Shelley Hamlin, Stanford
1972 *Miami-Fla.*
    Ann Laughlin, Miami-Fla.
1973 *N.C. State-Greensboro*
    Bonnie Lauer, Mich. St.
1974 *Rollins*
    Mary Budke, Oregon St.
1975 *Arizona State Univ.*
    Barbara Barrow, San Diego St.
1976 *Furman Univ.*
    Nancy Lopez, Tulsa

1977 *Miami-Fla.*
    Cathy Morse, Miami-Fla.
1978 *Miami-Fla.*
    Deborah Petrizzi, U. of Texas
1979 *Southern Methodist Univ.*
    Kyle O'Brien, SMU
1980 *Tulsa Univ.*
    Patty Sheehan, San Jose St.
1981 *Florida State Univ.*
    Terri Moody, Georgia
1982 *Tulsa Univ.*
    Kathy Baker, Tulsa
1983 *Tulsa Univ.*
    Penny Hammel, Miami-Fla.
1984 *Miami-Fla.*
    Cindy Schrayer, Georgia
1985 *Univ. of Florida*
    Danielle Ammacapane, Ariz. St.
1986 *Univ. of Florida*
    Page Dunlap, Univ. of Fla.
1987 *San Jose State Univ.*
    Caroline Keggi, U. New Mex.
1988 *Vacated*
    Vacated
1989 *San Jose State Univ.*
    Pat Hurst, San Jose St.
1990 *Arizona State Univ.*
    Susan Slaughter, Arizona
1991 *UCLA*
    Annika Sorenstam, Arizona
1992 *San Jose State Univ.*
    Vicki Goetze, Georgia
1993 *Arizona State Univ.*
    Charlotta Sorenstam, Texas
1994 *Arizona State Univ.*
    Emilee Klein, Arizona State
1995 *Arizona State Univ.*
    Kristel Mourgue d'Algue

JUNIOR GOLF

OVERVIEW: *Winners and runners-up of all national junior amateur tournaments since inception, plus Junior amateur results for 1995 and Junior rankings since 1978. Winners for the American Junior Golf Association are through Oct. 31, 1995. Junior rankings are as reported by Golfweek magazine.*

U.S. Junior Boys' Amateur

Year	Winner
1948	Dean Lind
1949	Gay Brewer
1950	Mason Rudolph
1951	K. Thomas Jacobs
1952	Donald Bisplinghoff
1953	Rex Baxter, Jr.
1954	Foster Bradley, Jr.
1955	Billy J. Dunn
1956	Harlan Stevenson
1957	Larry Beck
1958	Gordon Baker
1959	Larry J. Lee
1960	William J. Tindall
1961	Charles S. McDowell
1962	James L. Wiechers
1963	Gregg McHatton
1964	John Miller
1965	James Masserio
1966	Gary Sanders
1967	John T. Crooks
1968	Eddie Pearce
1969	Aly Trompas
1970	Gary Koch
1971	Mike Brannan
1972	Robert T. Byman
1973	Jack Renner
1974	David Nevatt
1975	Brett Mullin
1976	Madden Hatcher III
1977	Willie Wood
1978	Donald Hunter
1979	Jack Larkin
1980	Eric Johnson
1981	Scott Erickson
1982	Rick Marik
1983	Tim Straub
1984	Doug Martin
1985	Charles Rymer
1986	Brian Montgomery
1987	Brett Quigley
1988	Jason Widener
1989	David Duval
1990	Mathew Todd
1991	Eldrick (Tiger) Woods
1992	Eldrick (Tiger) Woods
1993	Eldrick (Tiger) Woods
1994	Terry Noe
1995	Chris Wollman

U.S. Junior Girls' Amateur

Year	Winner
1949	Marlene Bauer
1950	Patricia A. Lesser
1951	Arlene Brooks
1952	Mickey Wright
1953	Mildred Meyerson
1954	Margaret Smith
1955	Carole Jo Kabler
1956	JoAnne Gunderson
1957	Judy Eller
1958	Judy Eller
1959	Judy Rand
1960	Carol Sorenson
1961	Mary Lowell
1962	Mary Lou Daniel
1963	Janis Ferraris
1964	Peggy Conley
1965	Gail Sykes
1966	Claudia Mayhew
1967	Elizabeth Story
1968	Margaret Harmon
1969	Hollis Stacy
1970	Hollis Stacy
1971	Hollis Stacy
1972	Nancy Lopez
1973	Amy Alcott
1974	Nancy Lopez
1975	Dayna Benson
1976	Pilar Dorado
1977	Althea Tome
1978	Lori Castillo
1979	Penny Hammel
1980	Laurie Rinker
1981	Kay Cornelius
1982	Heather Farr
1983	Kim Saiki
1984	Cathy Mockett
1985	Dana Lofland
1986	Pat Hurst
1987	Michelle McGann
1988	Jamille Jose
1989	Brandie Burton
1990	Sandrine Mendiburu
1991	Emilee Klein
1992	Jaime Koisumi
1993	Kellee Booth
1994	Kelli Kuehne
1995	Marcy Newton

American Junior Golf Association:
1995 winners: BOYS DIVISION

Tournament	Winner
Taylor Made Pinelsle Jr. Classic	Ryuji Imada
Taylor Made Woodlands Jr. Classic	Steve Scott
Hargray Junior Classic at Indigo Run	Brent Roof
Ping Phoenix Junior Championship	Greg Padilla
ClubCorp Junior Championship	Joel Kribel
Freeport-McMoRan Junior Classic	Edward Loar
Bluegrass Junior Invitational	Scott Moore
Aspen Junior Classic	Ty Cox
Northern Telecom Jr. Team Challenge	Joel Kribel
Ping Myrtle Beach Junior Classic	Charles Howell
Nabisco Mission Hills Desert Junior	Joel Kribel
Buick Junior Open	Phillip Caravia
Texace San Antonio Shootout	Billy Bennett
Wilson Grand Geneva Nat'l Junior Champ.	Ty Cox
Las Vegas Founders' Legacy Junior	Todd Rose
Rolex Tournament of Champions	Ryuji Imada
Todd Moore Memorial	Aaron Hickman
Shangri-La Junior Players Invitational	Chris Imanuel
Oklahoma Junior Classic	Ty Cox
ClubCorp Junior Players Championship	Nick Cassini
AJGA Boys Junior Championship	Mark Northey
Canon Cup	East Team
Kmart Greater Greensboro Junior	Jeremy Wilkinson
Ray Floyd Turnberry Isle Junior	Sal Spallone
Polo/Ralph Lauren Junior Golf Classic	Lucas Glover
Ashworth/Golfweek Aviara Junior	Terry Noe
AJGA Tucker Anthony Junior	Derek Gillespie
Marsh & McLennan Westchester Junior	Sal Spallone
Izzo Colorado Junior Roundup	Andy Doeden
Robert Trent Jones Golf Trail Junior Classic	Charlie Howell
Polo/Ralph Lauren Junior at Langdon Farms	Dustin Brett
Lake Tahoe Classic at Genoa Lakes	Andy Miller

1995 winners: GIRLS DIVISION

Tournament	Winner
Taylor Made Pinelsle Jr. Classic	Beth Bauer
Taylor Made Woodlands Jr. Classic	Cristie Kerr
Hargray Junior Classic at Indigo Run	Beth Bauer
Ping Phoenix Junior Championship	Jenny Lee
Golf for Women Girls Championship	Kristen Register
Freeport-McMoRan Junior Classic	Grace Park
Bluegrass Junior Invitational	Sharon Park
Aspen Junior Classic	Jody Niemann
Ping Myrtle Beach Junior Classic	Beth Bauer
Nabisco Mission Hills Desert Junior	Grace Park

Buick Junior Open	Jill Gomric
Texace San Antonio Shootout	Kelli Kuehne
Wilson Grand Geneva Nat'l Junior Champ.	Candy Hennemann
Las Vegas Founders' Legacy Junior	Cristie Kerr
Rolex Tournament of Champions	Beth Bauer
Todd Moore Memorial	Stacy Sewell
Shangri-La Junior Players Invitational	Sarah Maurer
Oklahoma Junior Classic	Wendy Martin
McDonald's Betsy Rawls Girls Nat. Champ.	Cristie Kerr
Kmart Greater Greensboro Junior	Sharon Park
Ray Floyd Turnberry Isle Junior	Lisette Lee
Polo/Ralph Lauren Junior Golf Classic	Amy Spooner
Ashworth/Golfweek Aviara Junior	Jenna Daniels
AJGA Tucker Anthony Junior	Rebecca Halpern
Marsh & McLennan Westchester Junior	Katy Loy
Izzo Colorado Junior Roundup	Rheba Mabie
Robert Trent Jones Golf Trail Junior Classic	Beth Bauer
Polo/Ralph Lauren Junior at Langdon Farms	Rachel Borcherts
Lake Tahoe Classic at Genoa Lakes	Grace Park

U.S. Junior Boys' Amateur Rankings

1978
1. Willie Wood
2. Don Hurter
3. Larry Gosewehr
4. Monty Leong
5. Tracy Phillips

1979
1. Tracy Phillips
2. Jack Larkin
3. Rick Fehr
4. Andy Dilllard
5. Willie Wood

1980
1. Tommy Moore
2. Tracy Phillips
3. Eric Johnson
4. Adam Armagost
5. Bill Andrade

1981
1. Sam Randolph
2. Bill Andrade
3. Tommy Moore
4. Scott Erickson
5. Jerry Haas

1982
1. Stuart Hendley
2. Scott Verplank
3. Rich Marik
4. Bill Mayfair
5. Peter Jordan

1983
1. Michael Bradley
2. Brian Nelson
3. Tim Straub
4. Hank Pfister
5. Bill McDonald

1984
1. Doug Martin
2. Brian Watts
3. David Toms
4. Bob May
5. Blair Manasse

1985
1. Len Mattiace
2. Steve Termeer
3. Charles Rymer
4. Dudley Hart
5. Kevin Wentworth

1986
1. Brian Montgomery
2. Phil Mickelson
3. Chris Cain
4. Bryan Pemberton
5. Nicky Goetze

1987
1. Jeff Manson
2. Phil Mickelson
3. Brett Quigley
4. Jim Furyk
5. Brian Craig

1988
1. Jason Widener
2. Phil Mickelson
3. Nicky Goetze
4. Jason Brigman
5. Jean-Paul Hebert

1989
Not available

1990
1. Eldrick (Tiger) Woods
2. Notah Bogayr

3. Lee McEntee
4. Stewart Cink
5. Matthew Todd

1991
1. Eldrick (Tiger) Woods
2. Scott Johnson
3. Brad Zwelschke
4. Justin Roof
5. Marcus Jones

1992
1. Eldrick (Tiger) Woods
2. Justin Roof
3. Mark Wilson
4. Michael Jones
5. Todd Lynch

1993
1. Ted Oh
2. Michael Henderson
3. Robert Floyd
4. Jeff Fahrenbruch
5. Grady Girard

1994
1. Ryuji Imada
2. Joel Kribel
3. Landry Mahan
4. Ted Oh
5. Jeremy Anderson

1995
1. Charles Howell
2. Ryuji Imada
3. Joel Kribel
4. James Driscoll
4. Steven Scott

U.S. Girls' Amateur Rankings

1979
1. Penny Hammel
2. Sharon Barrett
3. Amy Benz
4. Heather Farr
5. Viveca Vandergriff

1980
1. Laurie Rinker
2. Heather Farr

3. Kim Shipman
4. Jody Rosenthal
5. Joanne Pacillo

1981
1. Jenny Lidback
2. Cathy Johnston
3. Kay Cornelius
4. Flori Prono
5. Kathy Kostas

1982
1. Heather Farr
2. Tracy Kerdyk
3. Carey Ruffer
4. Robin Garnester
5. Melissa McNamara

1983
1. Kim Saiki
2. Page Dunlap
3. Melissa McNamara
4. Kris Tschetter
5. Tracy Kerdyk

1984
1. Susan Pager
2. Lisa Neodoba
3. Cheryl Morley
4. Cathy Mockett
5. Carey Ruffer

1985
1. Michiko Hattori
2. Dana Lofland
3. Pearl Sinn
4. Jean Zeditz
5. Kristen Parker

1986
1. Adele Moore
2. Pat Hurst
3. Michelle Lyford
4. Amy Fruhwith
5. Michelle McGann

1987
1. Michelle McGann
2. Adele Moore
3. Vicki Goetze
4. Christy Erb
5. Brandie Burton

1988
1. Vicki Goetze
2. Brandie Burton
3, Jamille Jose
4. Deborah Parks
5. Dana Arnold

1989
Not available

1990
1. Vicki Goetze
2. Emilee Kleinr
3. Maria Castelucci
4. Heather Bowie
5. Kellee Booth

1991
1. Emilee Klein
2. Kellee Booth
3. Heather Brown
4. Jeong Min Park
5. Kim Marshall

1992
1. Kellee Booth
2. Wendi Patterson
3. Betty Chen
4. Heather Bowie
5. Erika Hayashida

1993
1. Kellee Booth
2. Grace Ji-eun Park
3. Cristie Kerr
4. Kelli Kuehne
5. Betty Chen

1994
1. Grace Ji-eun Park
2. Cristie Kerr
3. Kelli Kuehne
4. Elizabeth Bauer
5. Jenny Lee

1995
1. Cristie Kerr
2. Beth Bauer
3. Grace Park
4. Candy Hannemann
5. Stephanie Keever

Winners of leading AJGA Tournaments of the Past

Taylor Made Woodlands Junior Classic

Year	Boys Champion
1985	Bob May
1986	Scott Frisch
1987	John Sosa
1988	John Sosa
1989	Kevin Hammer
1990	Steve White
1991	Brian Bateman
1992	Robert Dean
1993	Marcus Jones
1994	Landry Mahan

Year	Girls Champion
1985	Lisa Nedoba
1986	Amy Fruhwirth
1987	Christy Erb
1988	Dana Amold
1989	Maria Castellucci
1990	Maria Castellucci
1991	Emilee Klein
1992	Kellee Booth
1993	Kellee Booth
1994	Jenny Lee

Freeport-McMoRan Junior Classic

Year	Boys Champion
1977	Tommy Moore
1978	Tommy Moore
1979	Tommy Moore
1980	Tommy Moore
1981	Scott Verplank
1982	Kevin Whipple
1983	Brian Watts
1984	Brian Nelson
1985	Nicky Goetze
1986	Steve Runge
1987	Michael Suckling
1988	Keith Rick
1989	Brian Bateman
1990	Alan Bratton
1991	Grant Masson
1992	Marcus Jones
1993	Michael Henderson
1994	Jeff Fahrenbruch

Year	Girls Champion
1980	Jenny Lidback
1981	Jenny Lidback
1982	Rita Moore
1983	Melissa McNamara
1984	Kristin Parker
1985	Terri Thompson
1986	Tina Triable
1987	Michelle McGann
1988	Barbara Blackwell
1989	Sandy Hamby
1990	Maria Castellucci
1991	Julie Brand
1992	Heather Bowie
1993	Betty Chen
1994	Grace Park

Bluegrass Junior Invitational

Year	Boys 15-18
1981	Jay Wainesscott
1982	Tom Belobraydic
1984	Chris Tolson
1985	Steve Flesch
1986	Jerry Hounchell
1987	Nicky Goetze
1988	Matt McIntire
1989	Billy Faeth
1990	J.J. West
1991	David Mathis
1992	Matt Trevino
1993	Brian McCann
1994	Ben Curtis

Year	Girls Champion
1981	Wendy Lawson
1982	Robin Hood
1984	Vicki Goetze
1985	Adele Moore
1986	Vicki Goetze
1987	Terri Thompson
1988	Vicki Goetze
1989	Vicki Goetze
1990	Mandy Kuhn
1991	Heather Bowie
1992	Betty Chen
1993	Wendi Patterson
1994	Ashley Winn

Buick Junior Open

Year	Boys 15-18
1985	J.D. Meyer
1986	Duke Donahue
1987	Phil Mickelson
1988	Phil Mickelson
1989	Nick Clinard
1990	Jamie Fairbanks
1991	Alex Buecking
1992	Joe Ogilvie
1993	Ryan Armour
1994	Matthew McDougall

Year	Girls Champion
1985	Susan Wineinger
1986	Kelly Robbins
1987	Jodi Figley
1988	Kim Cayce
1989	Renee Heiken
1990	Stephanie Sparks
1991	Stephanie Sparks
1992	Lisa Penske
1993	Wendi Patterson
1994	Jenny Chuasiriporn

Wilson Grand Geneva Junior Championship

Year	Boys 15-18
1988	Jean-Paul Hebert
1989	David Duval
1990	Todd Ormsby
1991	Dan Dalton
1992	Jason Buha
1993	Jason Buha
1994	Alberto Ochoa

Year	Girls Champion
1988	Vicki Goetze
1989	Kim Tyrer
1990	Annie Deets
1991	Dana Mackey
1992	Kellee Booth
1993	Kellee Booth
1994	Heather Graff

Rolex Tournament of Champions

Year	Boys Champion
1978	Willie Wood
1979	Andy Dillard
1980	Tommy Moore
1981	Tommy Moore
1982	Louis Brown
1983	Brian Nelson
1984	Bobby May
1985	Dudley Hart
1986	Phil Mickelson
1987	Phil Mickelson
1988	Phil Mickelson
1989	David Duval
1990	Harrison Frazar
1991	Chris Edgmon

1992	Patrick Vadden	
1993	Gilberto Morales	
1994	Robert Floyd	

Year	Girls Champion
1978	Denise Hermida
1979	Amy Benz
1980	Jody Rosenthal
1981	Jenny Lidback
1982	Heather Farr
1983	Kris Tschetter
1984	Page Dunlap
1985	Katie Peterson
1986	Amy Fruhwirth
1987	Christy Erb
1988	Stefania Croce
1989	Leta Lindley
1990	Kellee Booth
1991	Heather Bowie
1992	Emilee Klein
1993	Kellee Booth
1994	Beth Bauer

Todd Moore Memorial Junior

Year	Boys 15-18
1981	Scott Verplank
1982	Scott Verplank
1983	Ed Pfister
1984	Blair Manasse
1985	Craig Kanada
1986	Graig Reed
1987	Phil Mickelson
1988	John-Paul Hebert
1989	Jason Hill
1990	Chris Edgmon
1991	Dirk Mitchell
1992	Patrick Barley
1993	John Gaddy
1994	Alberto Ochoa

Year	Girls Champion
1981	Donna Linder
1982	Melissa McNama

1983	Kathy McCarthy
1984	Cheryl Morley
1985	Cathy Mockett
1986	Kathy Highfill
1987	Debbie Koyama
1988	Stephanie Davis
1989	Jennifer Holt
1990	Emilee Klein
1991	Heather Bowie
1992	Kelli Kuehne
1993	Kelli Kuehne
1994	Stacy Rambin

Lake Tahoe Classic at Genoa Lakes

Year	Boys Champion
1980	Doug Thompson
1981	Randy Cross
1982	Mike Barnett
1983	Rick Marik
1984	Bob May
1985	Brady Riggs
1986	Bob May
1987	Bob May
1988	Phil Mickelson
1989	Matt Masluk
1990	Scott Johnson
1991	Tiger Woods
1992	Michael Walton
1993	Joel Kribel
1994	Joel Kribel

Year	Girls Champion
1980	Kathy Kostas
1981	Nancy Mockett
1982	Kathy Kostas
1983	Melissa McNamar
1984	Kim Saiki
1985	Pearl Sinn
1986	Amy Fruhwirth
1987	Christy Erb
1988	Brandie Burton
1989	Sheri Vincent
1990	Kathryn Weber
1991	Jeong Min Park

1992	Kellee Booth
1993	Kellee Booth
1994	Jenny Lee

Rolex Junior Classic

Year	Boys Champion
1978	Tracy Phillips
1979	Tracy Phillips
1980	Adam Armagost
1981	Peter Jordan
1982	Sam Randolph
1983	Michael Bradley
1984	Brian Watts
1985	Steve Termeer
1986	Bryan Pemberton
1987	Jeff Manson
1988	Jaxon Brigman
1989	Stewart Cink
1990	Chris Stutts
1991	Tiger Woods
1992	Eddy Lee
1993	Michael Boyd
1994	Mark Northey

Year	Girls Champion
1978	Jenny Lidback
1979	Heather Farr
1980	Amy Benz
1981	Tracy Kerdyk
1982	Jenny Lidback
1983	Page Dunlap
1984	Cheryl Morley
1985	Kristin Parker
1986	Stefania Croce
1987	Adele Moore
1988	Vicki Goetze
1989	Vicki Goetze
1990	Emilee Klein
1991	Emilee Klein
1992	Wendi Patterson
1993	Kellee Booth
1994	Grace Park

AWARDS

OVERVIEW: *Player, administrator, public and/or humanitarian service, and media awards from major organizations such as the PGA TOUR, LPGA Tour, National Golf Foundation, and the PGA of America.*

PGA TOUR Player of the Year
Awarded by:
PGA TOUR

Year	Player
1990	Wayne Levi
1991	Fred Couples
1992	Fred Couples
1993	Nick Price
1994	Nick Price
1995	Greg Norman

Vardon Trophy
Awarded by:
PGA TOUR
Criteria:
Lowest stroke average, based on scaled PGA TOUR formula (minimum 60 rounds).

Year	Player
1937	Harry Cooper
1938	Sam Snead
1939	Byron Nelson
1940	Ben Hogan
1941	Ben Hogan
1942-46	No awards
1947	Jimmy Demaret
1948	Ben Hogan
1949	Sam Snead
1950	Sam Snead
1951	Lloyd Mangrum
1952	Jack Burke
1953	Lloyd Mangrum
1954	E.J. Harrison
1955	Sam Snead
1956	Cary Middlecoff
1957	Dow Finsterwald
1958	Bob Rosburg
1959	Art Wall
1960	Billy Casper
1961	Arnold Palmer
1962	Arnold Palmer
1963	Billy Casper
1964	Arnold Palmer
1965	Billy Casper
1966	Billy Casper
1967	Arnold Palmer
1968	Billy Casper
1969	Dave Hill
1970	Lee Trevino
1971	Lee Trevino
1972	Lee Trevino
1973	Bruce Crampton
1974	Lee Trevino
1975	Bruce Crampton
1976	Don January
1977	Tom Watson
1978	Tom Watson
1979	Tom Watson
1980	Lee Trevino
1981	Tom Kite
1982	Tom Kite
1983	Raymond Floyd
1984	Calvin Peete
1985	Don Pooley
1986	Scott Hoch
1987	Dan Pohl
1988	Chip Beck
1989	Greg Norman
1990	Greg Norman
1991	Fred Couples
1992	Fred Couples
1993	Nick Price
1994	Greg Norman
1995	Steve Elkington

PGA Player of the Year
Awarded by:
PGA of America

Year	Player
1948	Ben Hogan
1949	Sam Snead
1950	Ben Hogan
1951	Ben Hogan
1952	Julius Boros
1953	Ben Hogan
1954	Ed Furgol
1955	Doug Ford
1956	Jack Burke
1957	Dick Mayer
1958	Dow Finsterwald
1959	Art Wall
1960	Arnold Palmer
1961	Jerry Barber
1962	Arnold Palmer
1963	Julius Boros
1964	Ken Venturi
1965	Dave Marr
1966	Billy Casper
1967	Jack Nicklaus
1968	Not Awarded
1969	Orville Moody
1970	Billy Casper
1971	Lee Trevino
1972	Jack Nicklaus
1973	Jack Nicklaus
1974	Johnny Miller
1975	Jack Nicklaus
1976	Jack Nicklaus
1977	Tom Watson
1978	Tom Watson
1979	Tom Watson
1980	Tom Watson
1981	Bill Rogers
1982	Tom Watson
1983	Hal Sutton
1984	Tom Watson
1985	Lanny Wadkins
1986	Bob Tway
1987	Paul Azinger
1988	Curtis Strange

Awards

1989	Tom Kite
1990	Nick Faldo
1991	Corey Pavin
1992	Fred Couples
1993	Nick Price
1994	Nick Price
1995	Greg Norman

LPGA Player of the Year
Awarded by:
LPGA Tour

1966	Kathy Whitworth
1967	Kathy Whitworth
1968	Kathy Whitworth
1969	Kathy Whitworth
1970	Sandra Haynie
1971	Kathy Whitworth
1972	Kathy Whitworth
1973	Kathy Whitworth
1974	JoAnne Carner
1975	Sandra Palmer
1976	Judy Rankin
1977	Judy Rankin
1978	Nancy Lopez
1979	Nancy Lopez
1980	Beth Daniel
1981	JoAnne Carner
1982	JoAnne Carner
1983	Patty Sheehan
1984	Betsy King
1985	Nancy Lopez
1986	Pat Bradley
1987	Ayako Okamoto
1988	Nancy Lopez
1989	Betsy King
1990	Beth Daniel
1991	Pat Bradley
1992	Dottie Mochrie
1993	Betsy King
1994	Beth Daniel

Vare Trophy
Awarded by:
LPGA Tour
Criteria:
Lowest stroke average (minimum 70 rounds).

1953	Patty Berg
1954	Babe Zaharias
1955	Patty Berg
1956	Patty Berg
1957	Louise Suggs
1958	Beverly Hanson
1959	Betsy Rawls
1960	Mickey Wright
1961	Mickey Wright
1962	Mickey Wright
1963	Mickey Wright
1964	Mickey Wright
1965	Kathy Whitworth
1966	Kathy Whitworth
1967	Kathy Whitworth
1968	Carol Mann
1969	Kathy Whitworth
1970	Kathy Whitworth
1971	Kathy Whitworth
1972	Kathy Whitworth
1973	Judy Rankin
1974	JoAnne Carner
1975	JoAnne Carner
1976	Judy Rankin
1977	Judy Rankin
1978	Nancy Lopez
1979	Nancy Lopez
1980	Amy Alcott
1981	JoAnne Carner
1982	JoAnne Carner
1983	JoAnne Carner
1984	Patty Sheehan
1985	Nancy Lopez
1986	Pat Bradley
1987	Betsy King
1988	Colleen Walker
1989	Beth Daniel
1990	Beth Daniel
1991	Pat Bradley
1992	Dottie Mochrie
1993	Betsy King
1994	Beth Daniel

Richardson Award
Awarded by:
Golf Writers Association of America

Criteria:
Lifetime contribution to the game.

1948	Robert A. Hudson
1949	Scotty Fessenden
1950	Bing Crosby
1951	Richard Tufts
1952	Chick Evans
1953	Bob Hope
1954	Babe Zaharias
1955	Dwight Eisenhower
1956	George S. May
1957	Francis Ouimet
1958	Bob Jones
1959	Patty Berg
1960	Fred Corcoran
1961	Joseph C. Dey
1962	Walter Hagen
1963	Joe & Herb Graffis
1964	Cliff Roberts
1965	Gene Sarazen
1966	Robert E. Harlow
1967	Max Elbin
1968	Charles Bartlett
1969	Arnold Palmer
1970	Roberto De Vicenzo
1971	Lincoln Werden
1972	Leo Fraser
1973	Ben Hogan
1974	Byron Nelson
1975	Gary Player
1976	Herbert W. Wind
1977	Mark Cox
1978	Jack Nicklaus
1979	Jim Gaquin
1980	Jack Tuthill
1981	Robert Trent Jones
1982	Chi Chi Rodriguez
1983	William C. Campbell
1984	Sam Snead
1985	Lee Trevino
1986	Kathy Whitworth
1987	Frank Hannigan
1988	Roger Barry
1989	Ben Crenshaw
1990	P.J. Boatwright
1991	Tom Watson
1992	Deane R. Beman

1993	Harvey Penick	
1994	Peggy Kirk Bell	

Ben Hogan Award
Awarded by:
Golf Writers Association of America
Criteria:
Overcoming injury.

1954	Babe Zaharias
1955	Ed Furgol
1956	Dwight Eisenhower
1957	Clint Russell
1958	Dale Bourisseau
1959	Charlie Boswell
1960	Skip Alexander
1961	Horton Smith
1962	Jimmy Nichols
1963	Bobby Nichols
1964	Bob Morgan
1965	Ernest Jones
1966	Ken Venturi
1967	Warren Pease
1968	Shirley Englehorn
1969	Curtis Person
1970	Joe Lazaro
1971	Larry Hinson
1972	Ruth Jessen
1973	Gene Littler
1974	Gay Brewer
1975	Patty Berg
1976	Paul Hahn
1977	Des Sullivan
1978	Dennis Walters
1979	John Mahaffey
1980	Lee Trevino
1981	Kathy Linney
1982	Al Geiberger
1983	Calvin Peete
1984	Jay Sigel
1985	Rod Funseth
1986	Fuzzy Zoeller
1987	Charles Owens
1988	Pat Browne
1989	Sally Little
1990	Linda Craft
1991	Pat Bradley
1992	Jim Nelford

1993	Shelley Hamlin
1994	Jim Ferree

Charlie Bartlett Award
Awarded by:
Golf Writers Association of America
Criteria:
Unselfish contributions to the betterment of society.

1971	Billy Casper
1972	Lee Trevino
1973	Gary Player
1974	Chi Chi Rodriguez
1975	Gene Littler
1976	Arnold Palmer
1977	Lee Elder
1978	Bert Yancey
1979	No award
1980	No award
1981	No award
1982	Patty Berg
1983	No award
1984	Gene Sarazen
1985	No award
1986	No award
1987	No award
1988	Patty Sheehan
1989	Mary Bea Porter
1990	No award
1991	No award
1992	John Daly
1993	No award
1994	Betsy King

Joe Graffis Award
Awarded by:
National Golf Foundation
Criteria:
Contribution to education and junior golf.

1970	Ellen Griffin
1971	Barbara Rotvig
1972	Les Bolstad
1973	No award
1974	Opal Hill
1975	Patty Berg
1976	Shirley Spork
1977	Bill Strausbaugh

1978	Gary Wiren
1979	Conrad Rehling
1980	Bob Toski
1981	Peggy Kirk Bell
1982	Jim Flick
1983	Carol Johnson
1984	Paul Runyan
1985	No award
1986	DeDe Owens
1987	Edwin Cottrell
1988	Thomas Addis III
1989	Kathy Corbin
1990	Davis Love, Jr.
1991	Kerry Graham
1992	Robert F. MacNelly
1993	Chi Chi Rodriguez
1994	Dennis Walters

Herb Graffis Award
Awarded by:
National Golf Foundation
Criteria: *Contribution to golf as recreation, good fellowship, and as a happy pastime.*

1977	Joe Jemsek
1978	Arnold Palmer
1979	Carol McCue
1980	Bob Hope
1981	Patty Berg
1982	Jack Nicklaus
1983	Herb Graffis
1984	William Davis and Howard Gill
1985	Howard Clark
1986	Joe Dey
1987	Deane Beman
1988	John Laupheimer
1989	William Campbell
1990	Don Rossi
1991	P.J. Boatwright

NGF/Jack Nicklaus Golf Family of the Year Award
Awarded by:
National Golf Foundation
Criteria:
Families who have made significant contributions to the game.

1986	Nicklaus Family

Awards 251

1987	Lopez/Knight Family	1986	David Ogilvie	1979	Howard Smith
1988	Cook Family	1987	Bob Ford	1980	Dale Mead
1989	Bradley Family	1988	Hank Majewski	1981	Tom Addis III
1990	Gallagher Family	1989	Tom Addis III	1982	Kent Cayce
1991	Jemsek Family	1990	Jim Albus	1983	Bill Strausbaugh
1992	Powell Family	1991	Joe Jemsek	1984	Don Essig
1993	Eller Family	1992	Martin Kavanaugh II	1985	Larry Startzel
1994	Solheim Family	1993	Don Kotnik	1986	Mark Darnell
		1994	Dick Murphy	1987	Ken Lindsay
				1988	Guy Wimberly

PGA Golf Professional of the Year

Awarded by:
PGA of America
Criteria:
Distinguished service as a working club professional.

PGA Club Pro of the Year

Awarded by:
PGA of America
Criteria:
Leading club pro player.

				1989	Verne D. Perry
				1990	Mike Hebron
				1991	Joe Terry
				1992	Conrad Rehling
				1993	Rick Burton
				1994	Bill Eschenbrenner

Bob Jones Award

Awarded by:
United States Golf Association
Criteria:
Distinguished sportsmanship in golf.

1955	Bill Gordon	1984	Bill Schumaker	1955	Francis Ouimet
1956	Harry Shepard	1985	Ed Dougherty	1956	Bill Campbell
1957	Dugan Aycock	1986	Lonnie Lielsen	1957	Babe Zaharias
1958	Harry Pezzullo	1987	Lonnie Nielsen	1958	Margaret Curtis
1959	Eddie Duino	1988	Bob Ford	1959	Findley S. Douglas
1960	Warren Orlick	1989	Lonnie Nielsen	1960	Charles Evans, Jr.
1961	Don Padgett	1990	Brett Upper	1961	Joe Carr
1962	Tom LoPresti	1991	Bruce Zabriski	1962	Horton Smith
1963	Bruce Herd	1992	Tom Wargo	1963	Patty Berg
1964	Lyle Wherman	1993	Mike San Fillipo	1964	Charles Coe
1965	Hubby Habjan	1994	Bruce Zabriski	1965	Glenna Collett Vare
1966	Bill Strausbaugh			1966	Gary Player
1967	Ernie Vossler			1967	Richard S. Tufts
1968	Hardy Loudermilk	## Horton Smith Trophy		1968	Robert Dickson
1969	Wally Mund and Hubert Smith	Awarded by: *PGA of America* Criteria: *Outstanding contribution by PGA Professionals to education.*		1969	Gerald Micklem
1970	Grady Shumate			1970	Roberto De Vicenzo
1971	Ross Collins			1971	Arnold Palmer
1972	Howard Morrette			1972	Michael Bonallack
1973	Warren Smith	1965	Emil Beck	1973	Gene Littler
1974	Paul Harney	1966	Gene C. Mason	1974	Byron Nelson
1975	Walker Inman	1967	Donald Fischesser	1975	Jack Nicklaus
1976	Ron Letellier	1968	R. William Clarke	1976	Ben Hogan
1977	Don Soper	1969	Paul Hahn	1977	Joe Dey
1978	Walter Lowell	1970	Joe Walser	1978	Bob Hope and Bing Crosby
1979	Gary Ellis	1971	Irv Schloss		
1980	Stan Thirsk	1972	John Budd		
1981	John Gerring	1973	George Aulbach		
1982	Bob Popp	1974	Bill Hardy		
1983	Ken Lindsay	1975	John Henrich		
1984	Jerry Mowlds	1976	Jim Bailey		
1985	Jerry Cozby	1977	Paul Runyan		
		1978	Andy Nusbaum		

1979	Tom Kite	1964	Sally Doyle	1990	Chris Burkhart
1980	Charles R. Yates	1965	Goldie Bateson	1991	Paula Wagasky
1981	JoAnne Carner	1966	Ann C. Johnstone	1992	Lorraine Kippel
1982	Billy Joe Patton	1967	Jackie Pung	1993	Sue Fiscoe
1983	Maureen Garrett	1968	Gloria Fecht	1994	Nancy Bunton
1984	Jay Sigel	1969	JoAnne Winter		
1985	Fuzzy Zoeller	1970	Gloria Armstrong		

Patty Berg Award
Awarded by:
LPGA
Criteria: *Unselfish contribution to the game.*

1979	Marilynn Smith
1980	Betsy Rawls
1981	No award
1982	No award
1983	No award
1984	Ray Volpe
1985	Dinah Shore
1986	David Foster
1987	Kathy Whitworth
1988	No award
1989	John D. Laupheimer
1990	Patty Berg
1991	Karsten Solheim
1992	Judy Dickinson
1993	Kerry Graham
1995	Charles Mecham

1986	Jess Sweetser	1971	Jeanette Rector
1987	Tom Watson	1972	Lee Spencer
1988	Isaac Grainger	1973	Penny Zavichas
1989	Chi Chi Rodriguez	1974	Mary Dagraedt
1990	Peggy Kirk Bell	1975	Carol Johnson
1991	Ben Crenshaw	1976	Marge Burns
1992	Gene Sarazen	1977	DeDe Owens
1993	P.J. Boatwright	1978	Shirley Englehorn
1994	Lewis Oehmig	1979	Bobbie Ripley
		1980	Betty Dodd
		1981	Jane Read

Card Walker Award
Awarded by:
PGA TOUR
Criteria:
Contribution to junior golf.

1981	Mrs. Lou Smith
1982	Fran Emmett
1983	Jack Nicklaus
1984	Sally Carroll
1985	Don Padgett, Sr.
1986	Chi Chi Rodriguez
1987	James S. Kemper
1988	William V. Powers
1989	Selina Johnson
1990	Tucson Conquistadores
1991	AJGA
1992	Bill Dickey
1993	Western Golf Assoc.
1994	Fred Engh
1995	Ryder System, Inc.

1982	Barbara Romack
1983	Rina Ritson
1984	Shirley Spork
1985	Annette Thompson
1986	B. Crawford-O'Brien
1987	Linda Craft
1988	Judy Whitehouse
1989	Sharon Miller
1990	Dana Rader
1991	Dr. Betsy Clark
1992	Lynn Marriott
1993	Dr. DeDe Owens
1994	Jane Frost

LPGA Golf Pro of the Year
Awarded by:
LPGA
Criteria: *Achievement by a woman managing a total golf program.*

1980	Nancy Gammon
1981	Peggy Kirk Bell
1982	Nell Frewin
1983	Lorraine Klippel
1984	Mary Dagraedt
1985	Bobbie Stewart
1986	Margo Walden
1987	Becky Sauers
1988	Kathy Murphy
1989	Pat Lange

Old Tom Morris Award
Awarded by:
GSCA of America.
Criteria:
Contribution to the game

1983	Arnold Palmer
1984	Bob Hope
1985	Gerald Ford
1986	Patty Berg
1987	Robert Trent Jones
1988	Gene Sarazen
1989	Chi Chi Rodriguez
1990	Sherwood Moore
1991	William C. Campbell
1992	Tom Watson
1993	Dinah Shore
1994	Byron Nelson
1995	Dr. James Watson

LPGA Teacher of the Year
Awarded by:
LPGA

1958	Helen Dettweiler
1959	Shirley Spork
1960	Barbara Rotvig
1961	Peggy Kirk Bell
1962	Ellen Griffin
1963	Vonnie Colby

MEMORABLE DATES IN GOLF HISTORY

OVERVIEW: *A selection of the major events in professional golf, the development of the rules, opening of prominent courses and changes in their structure, plus the publishing of famous golf books, the passing of great players, and the sometimes harried world of golf legalities (from the banning of golf several times in its early history to the modern-day lawsuits between companies and the governing bodies of the game).*

Pre-1353

No one knows for sure how or when golf reached a recognizably modern form, but there were several variations on field hockey played in Holland, Belgium, France, England and Scotland during the 14th century, a product of the increased leisure time which came with the relative prosperity of the age and the rise of a merchant class which provided the bulk of golf's original constituency. The increased trade between Scotland and the Low Countries in the 14th century as well as the constant wars with the English may have provided the conduit for spreading the game to new shores. The most probable origin of golf is that it spread to Scotland in the 14th century from the Low Countries as a by-product of increased trade. The development of a hole in the ground as the goal and the carrying of several clubs are significant developments that were completely Scottish in their origin.

1353

The first recorded reference to chole, a probable antecedent of golf. It is a derivative of hockey played in Flanders (Belgium).

1421

A Scottish regiment aiding the French against the English at the Siege of Bauge is introduced to the game of chole. Hugh Kennedy, Robert Stewart and John Smale, three of the identified players, are credited with introducing the game in Scotland.

1457

Golf, along with football, is banned by the Scots Parliament of James II because it has interfered with military training for the wars against the English.

1470

The ban on golf is reaffirmed by the Parliament of James III.

1491

The golf ban is affirmed again by Parliament, this time under King James IV.

1502

With the signing of the Treaty of Glasgow between England and Scotland, the ban on golf is lifted.

James IV makes the first recorded purchase of golf equipment, a set of clubs from a bow-maker in Perth, Scotland.

1513

Queen Catherine of England, in a letter to Cardinal Wolsey, refers to the growing popularity of golf in England.

1527

The first commoner recorded as a golfer is Sir Robert Maule, described as playing on Barry Links (near the modern-day Carnoustie).

1552
The first recorded evidence of golf at St. Andrews.

1553
The Archbishop of St. Andrews issues a decree giving the local populace the right to play golf on the links at St. Andrews.

1567
Mary, Queen of Scots, seen playing golf shortly after the death of her husband Lord Darnley, is the first known female golfer.

1589
Golf is banned in the Blackfriars Yard, Glasgow. This is the earliest reference to golf in the west of Scotland.

1592
The City of Edinburgh bans golfing at Leith on Sunday "in tyme of sermonis."

1618
Invention of the feathery ball.

King James VI and I confirms the right of the populace to play golf on Sundays.

1621
First recorded reference to golf on the links of Dornoch (later Royal Dornoch), in the far north of Scotland.

1641
Charles I is playing golf at Leith when he learns of the Irish rebellion, marking the beginning of the English Civil War. He finishes his round.

1642
John Dickson receives a license as ball-maker for Aberdeen, Scotland.

1659
Golf is banned from the streets of Albany, New York—the first reference to golf in America.

1682
In the first recorded international golf match, the Duke of York and John Paterstone of Scotland defeat two English noblemen in a match played on the links of Leith.

Andrew Dickson, carrying clubs for the Duke of York, is the first recorded caddy.

1687
A book by Thomas Kincaid, "Thoughts on Golve," contains the first references to how golf clubs are constructed.

1721
Earliest reference to golf at Glasgow Green, the first course of which we have record in the west of Scotland.

1724
"A solemn match of golf" between Alexander Elphinstone and Captain John Porteous becomes the first match reported in a newspaper. Elphinston fights and wins a duel on the same ground in 1729.

1743
Thomas Mathison's epic *The Goff* is the first literary effort devoted to golf.

1744
The Honourable Company of Edinburgh Golfers is formed, playing at Leith links. It is the first organized golf club.

The City of Edinburgh pays for a Silver Cup to be awarded to the annual champion in an open competition played at Leith Links. John Rattray is the first champion.

1754
Eager to match the Silver Cup competition in Edinurgh, golfers at St. Andrews purchase a Silver Cup for an open championship played on the Old Course. Bailie William Landale is the first champion.

1754 (continued)

The first codified Rules of Golf published by the St. Andrews Golfers (later the Royal & Ancient Golf Club).

1759

Earliest reference to stroke-play, at St. Andrews. Previously, all play was match.

1764

The competition for the Silver Club at Leith is restricted to members of the Honourable Company of Edinburgh Golfers.

The first four holes at St. Andrews are combined into two, reducing the round from twenty-two holes (11 out and in) to 18 (nine out and in). St. Andrews is the first 18-hole golf course, and sets the standard for future courses.

1766

The Blackheath Club becomes the first golf club formed outside of Scotland.

1767

The score of 94 returned by James Durham at St. Andrews in the Silver Cup competition sets a record unbroken for 86 years.

1768

The Golf House at Leith is erected. It is the first golf clubhouse.

1773

Competition at St. Andrews is restricted to members of the Leith and St. Andrews societies.

The Royal Burgess Golfing Society of Edinburgh is formed.

1774

Thomas McMillan offers a Silver Cup for competition at Musselburgh. He wins the first championship.

The first part-time golf course professional (at the time also the greenkeeper) is hired, by the Edinburgh Burgess Society.

1780

The Aberdeen Golf Club (later Royal Aberdeen) is formed.

1783

A Silver Club is offered for competition at Glasgow.

1786

The South Carolina Golf Club is formed in Charleston, the first golf club outside of the United Kingdom.

The Crail Golfing Society is formed.

1787

The Bruntsfield Club is formed.

1788

The Honourable Company of Edinburgh Golfers requires members to wear club uniform when playing on the links.

1797

The Burntisland Golf Club is formed.

The town of St. Andrews sells the land containing the Old Course (known then as Pilmor Links), to Thomas Erskine for £805. Erskine was required to preserve the course for golf.

1806

The St. Andrews Club chooses to elect its captains rather than award captaincy to the winner of the Silver Cup. Thus begins the tradition of the Captain "playing himself into office," by hitting a single shot before the start of the annual competition.

1810

Earliest recorded reference to a women's competition at Musselburgh.

1820

The Bangalore Club is formed, the first club outside of the British Isles.

1824

The Perth Golfing Society is formed, later Royal Perth (the first club so honored).

1826

Hickory imported from America is used to make golf shafts.

1829

Calcutta Golf Club (later Royal Calcutta) is formed.

1832

The North Berwick Club is founded, the first to include women in its activities, although they are not permitted to play in competitions.

1833

King William IV confers the distinction of "Royal" on the Perth Golfing Society; as Royal Perth it is the first Club to hold the distinction.

The St. Andrews Golfers ban the stymie, but rescind the ban one year later.

1834

William IV confers the title "Royal and Ancient" on the Golf Club at St. Andrews.

1836

The Honourable Company of Edinburgh Golfers abandons the deteriorating Leith Links, moving to Musselburgh.

The longest driver recorded with a feathery, 361 yds., is achieved by Samuel Messieux at Elysian Fields.

1842

The Bombay Golfing Society (later Royal Bombay) is founded.

1844

Blackheath follows Leith in expanding its course from five to seven holes. North Berwick also had seven holes at the time, although the trend toward a standard eighteen had begun.

1848

Invention of the "guttie," the gutta-percha ball. It travels farther than the feathery and is much less expensive. It contributes greatly to the expansion of the game, despite the initial reluctance of Allan Robertson to accept it.

1851

The Prestwick Golf Club is founded.

1856

The Royal Curragh Golf Club is founded at Kildare, the first golf club in Ireland.

Pau Golf Club is founded, the first on the Continent.

A rule change is enacted that, in match play, the ball must be played as it lies or the hole be conceded. It is the last recorded toughening of the rules structure.

1857

The Golfer's Manual, by "A Keen Hand" (H.B. Farnie), is published, the first book of instruction.

The Prestwick Club institutes the first Championship Meeting, a foursomes competition at St. Andrews attended by eleven golf clubs. George Glennie and J.C. Stewart win for Blackheath.

1858

The format of the Championship Meeting is changed to individual match play and is won by Robert Chambers of Bruntsfield.

Allan Robertson becomes the first golfer to break 80 at the Old Course, recording a 79.

1859

The first Amateur Championship is won by George Condie of Perth.

Death of Allan Robertson, the first great professional golfer.

1860

The Prestwick Club institutes a Professional Championship played at Prestwick—the first Championship Belt is won by Willie Park.

1861

The Professionals Championship is opened to amateurs, and the British Open is born. The first competition is won by Old Tom Morris.

1864

The North Devon Golf Club is founded at Westward Ho!

1867

The Ladies' Golf Club at St. Andrews is founded, the first golf club for women.

1869

The Liverpool Golf Club is founded at Hoylake, later Royal Liverpool.

Young Tom Morris, age 17, wins the first of four successive British Open championships. His streak would include an 11-stroke victory in 1869 and a 12-stroke victory in 1870 (in a 36-hole format). His 149 in the 1870 British Open over 36 holes is a stroke average that would not be equalled until the invention of the rubber-cored ball.

1870

Young Tom Morris wins his third consecutive British Open Championship, thus winning permanent possession of the Belt.

The Royal Adelaide Golf Club is founded, the first golf club in Australia.

1872

The British Open Championship is reinstituted when Prestwick, St. Andrews and the Honourable Company offer a new trophy, with the Open Championship to be hosted in rotation by the three clubs.

Young Tom Morris wins his fourth consecutive British Open Championship.

1873

The Royal Montreal Golf Club is formed, the first club in Canada.

The British Open is held for the first time at the Old Course.

1875

The Oxford and Cambridge University Golf Clubs are founded.

1878

The first University Match is played at Wimbledon, won by Oxford.

1880

Royal Belfast is founded.

The use of moulds is instituted to dimple the gutta-percha ball. Golfers had long noticed that the guttie worked in the air much better after it had been hit several times and scuffed up.

1883

Bob Ferguson of Musselburgh, losing the British Open in extra holes, comes one victory shy of equalling Young Tom Morris' record of four consecutive titles. Ferguson ends up later in life penniless, working out of the Musselburgh caddy-shack.

1884

The Oakhurst Golf Club is founded at White Sulphur Springs in the United States, the first full course in America.

1885

The Royal Cape Golf Club is founded at Wynberg, South Africa, the first club in Africa.

1886

A.J. Balfour is appointed Chief Secretary (Cabinet Minister) for Ireland—his rise to political and social prominence has an incalculable effect on the popularity of golf, as he is an indefatigable player and catalyzes great interest in the game through his writing and public speaking.

1887

The Art of Golf by Sir Walter Simpson is published.

1888

The St. Andrews Golf Club is founded in Yonkers, N.Y., the oldest surviving golf club in America.

1890

John Ball, an English amateur, becomes the first non-Scotsman and first amateur to win the British Open.

Bogey is invented by Hugh Rotherham, as the score of the hypothetical golfer playing perfect golf at every hole. Rotherham calls this a "Ground Score," but Dr. Thomas Brown, honorary Secretary of the Great Yarmouth Club, christens this hypothetical man a "Bogey Man," after a popular song of the day, and christens his score a "Bogey." With the invention of the rubber-cored ball golfers are able to reach the greens in fewer strokes, and so bogey has come to represent one over the par score for the hole.

1891

Shinnecock Hills Golf Club is founded.

1892

Gate money is charged for the first time, at a match between Douglas Rollard and Jack White at Cambridge. The practice of paying for matches through private betting, rather than gate receipts and sponsorships, survives well into the 20th Century as a "Calcutta," but increasingly gate receipts are the source of legitimate prize-purses.

The Amateur Golf Championship of India and the East is instituted, the first international championship event.

1893

The [British] Ladies' Golf Union is founded and the first Open Championship won by Lady Margaret Scott, at St. Anne's.

1894

The Open is played on an English course for the first time (Royal St. George's) and is won for the first time by an English professional, John H. Taylor.

The United States Golf Association is founded as the Amateur Golf Association of the United States. Charter members are the Chicago Golf Club, The Country Club, Newport Golf Club, St. Andrews Golf Club, and Shinnecock Hills Golf Club.

Tacoma Golf Club is founded, the first golf club on the Pacific Coast.

1895

The United States Open is instituted. Willie Anderson is the first winner.

Chicago Golf Club opens the United States' first 18-hole golf course.

The pool cue is banned as a putter by the USGA.

The U.S. Women's Amateur is instituted. Mrs. Charles S. Brown is the first winner.

1896

Harry Vardon wins his first British Open.

1897

The first NCAA championship is held. Louis Bayard Jr. is the champion.

1897 (continued)

Golf, America's first golfing magazine, is published for the first time.

1898

Freddie Tait, betting he could reach the Royal Cinque Ports G.C. clubhouse from the clubhouse at Royal St. George's—a three mile distance— in forty shots or less, puts his 32nd stroke through a window at the Cinque Ports club.

The Haskell ball is designed and patented by Coburn Haskell. It is the first rubber-cored ball. The term "birdie" is coined at Atlantic C.C.—from "a bird of a hole."

1899

The Western Open is first played at Glenview G.C.—the first tournament in what would evolve into the PGA TOUR.

1900

Harry Vardon wins the U.S. Open, the first golfer to win both the British and U.S. Opens.

Golf is placed on the Olympic calendar for the 2nd Games at Paris.

1901

Walter Travis becomes the first golfer, in the U.S. Amateur, to win a major title with the Haskell ball. When Sandy Herd wins the British Open and Laurie Auchterlonie the U.S. Open the next year with the Haskell, virtually all competitors switch to the new ball.

Sunningdale, a course built amidst a cleared forest, opens for play. It is the first course with grass grown completely from seed. Previously, golf courses were routed through meadows, which frequently created drainage problems as the meadows were typically atop clay soil.

The first course at the Carolina Hotel (later the Pinehurst Resort & C.C.) in Pinehurst, NC, is completed by Donald Ross. Ross will go on to design 600 courses in his storied career as a golf course architect.

1902

England and Scotland inaugurate an Amateur Team competition, with Scotland winning at Hoylake.

The first grooved-faced irons are invented.

1903

Oakmont C.C. is founded in Oakmont, Pennsylvania, designed by Henry Fownes. It is widely regarded as one of the finest examples of penal-style golf architecture.

1904

Walter J. Travis becomes the first American to win the British Amateur.

1905

Women golfers from Great Britain and the United States play an international match, with the British winning 6 matches to 1.

The first dimple-pattern for golf balls is patented by William Taylor in England.

The Complete Golfer by Harry Vardon is published. It promotes and demonstrates the Vardon or overlapping grip.

1906

Goodrich introduces a golf ball with a rubber core filled with compressed air. The "Pneumatic" proves quite lively, but also prone to explode in warm weather, often in a golfer's pocket. The ball is eventually discontinued; at this time the Haskell ball achieves a dominance of the golf ball market.

1907

Arnaud Massey becomes the first golfer from the Continent to win the British Open.

1908

Mrs. Gordon Robertson, at Princes Ladies G.C., becomes the first female professional.

The Mystery of Golf by Arnold Haultain is published.

1909

The USGA rules that caddies, caddymasters and greenkeepers over the age of sixteen are professional golfers. The ruling is later modified and eventually reversed in 1963.

1910

The R&A bans the center-shafted putter while the USGA keeps it legal—marking the beginning of a 42-year period with two official versions of *The Rules of Golf*.

Steel shafts are patented by Arthur F. Knight.

1911

J.J. McDermott becomes the first native-born American to win the U.S. Open. At 17 years of age, he is also the youngest winner to date.

1912

John Ball wins his eighth British Amateur championship—a record not yet equalled.

1913

Francis Ouimet, age 20, becomes the first amateur to win the U.S. Open, defeating favorites Harry Vardon and Ted Ray in a play-off.

The first professional international match is played between France and the United States at La Boulie, France.

1914

Formation of The Tokyo Club at Komozawa kicks off the Japanese golf boom.

Walter Hagen wins his first major championship, the U.S. Open.

Harry Vardon wins his sixth British Open—a record to this day (Peter Thomson and Tom Watson have since won five Opens each).

1915

The British Open is discontinued for the duration of the First World War.

1916

The PGA of America is founded by 82 charter members and the PGA Championship is inaugurated. James Barnes is the first champion.

The first miniature golf course opens in Pinehurst, North Carolina.

Francis Ouimet is banned from amateur play for his involvement with a Spalding, sporting goods business. The ruling creates a stir of protest and is reversed in 1918.

1917

The PGA Championship and the U.S. Open are discontinued for the duration of the First World War.

1919

The Royal & Ancient Golf Club of St. Andrews assumes control over the British Open and the British Amateur.

Pebble Beach Golf Links opens as the Del Monte G.L. in Pebble Beach, California.

1920

The USGA founds its famed Green Section to conduct research on turfgrass.

The first practice range is opened in Pinehurst, North Carolina.

The *Professional Golfer of America* is first published which, today known as *PGA Magazine*, is the oldest continually-published golf magazine in the United States.

1921
The R&A limits the size and weight of the ball.

1922
Walter Hagen becomes the first native American to win the British Open. He subsequently becomes the first professional golfer to open a golf equipment company under his own name.

The Walker Cup Matches are instituted. The grandson of Walker Cup founder George Herbert Walker is George H.W. Bush, the 41st President of the United States.

The Prince of Wales is elected Captain of the R&A.

The Texas Open is inaugurated, the second-oldest surviving PGA TOUR event.

Pine Valley Golf Club opens.

1923
The West and East courses at Winged Foot Golf Club open for play, designed by A.W. Tillinghast.

1924
Joyce Wethered wins her record fifth consecutive English Ladies' Championship.
The Olympic Club in San Francisco opens for play.

The USGA legalizes steel shafted golf clubs. The R&A does not follow suit until 1929, widening the breach in *The Rules of Golf*.

1925
The first fairway irrigation system is developed in Dallas, Texas.

Deep-grooved irons are banned by both the USGA and the R&A.

1926
Jesse Sweetser becomes the first native-born American to win the British Amateur.

Bobby Jones wins the British Open.

Gate money is instituted at the British Open.

Walter Hagen defeats Bobby Jones 12 and 11 in a privately sponsored 72-hole match in Florida.

The Los Angeles Open is inaugurated, the third-oldest surviving PGA TOUR event. The L.A. Open is also the first tournament to offer a $10,000 purse.

1927
The inaugural Ryder Cup Matches are played between Britain and the United States.

Creeping bentgrass is developed for putting greens by the U.S. Department of Agriculture.

1928
Cypress Point Club opens, designed by Alister Mackenzie.

1929
Walter Hagen wins the British Open for the fourth time.

Seminole Golf Club opens in Palm Beach, Fla., from a design by Donald Ross.

1930
Bobby Jones completes the original Grand Slam, winning the U.S. and British Amateurs and the U.S. and British Opens in the same year. Since Jones is an amateur, however, the financial windfall belongs to professional Bobby Cruickshank, who bets on Jones to complete the Slam, at 120-1 odds, and pockets $60,000.

The Minehead Club makes Captaincy elective. They had been the last club to award the Captaincy to the winner of the annual competition.

The Duke of York (later King George VI) is elected Captain of the R&A.

1930 (continued)

Shinnecock Hill Golf Club opens its modern course on Long Island, NY.

Bob Harlow is hired as manager of the PGA's Tournament Bureau, and he first proposes the idea of expanding "The Circuit," as the TOUR is then known, from a series of winter events leading up to the season ending North & South Open in spring, into a year-round TOUR.

1931

Billy Burke defeats George Von Elm in a 72-hole playoff at Inverness to win the 1931 U.S. Open, in the longest playoff ever played. They were tied at 292 after regulation play, and both scored 149 in the first 36-hole playoff. Burke is the first golfer to win a major championship using steel-shafted golf clubs.

The USGA increases the minimum size of the golf ball from 1.62 inches to 1.68 inches, and decreases the maximum weight from 1.62 ounces to 1.55. The R&A does not follow suit. The lighter, larger "balloon ball" is universally despised and eventually the USGA raises the weight back to 1.62 ounces.

1932

The first Curtis Cup Matches are held at Wentworth in England.

The concave-faced wedge is banned.

Gene Sarazen introduces the modern sand-wedge, improving on several competing designs.

1933

The Prince of Wales reaches the final of the Parliamentary Handicap Tournament.

Augusta National Golf Club, designed by Alister Mackenzie with advice from Bobby Jones, opens for play.

Craig Wood hits a 430-yard drive at the Old Course's fifth hole in the British Open—this is still the longest drive in a major championship.

Hershey Chocolate Company, in sponsoring the Hershey Open, becomes the first corporate title sponsor of a professional tournament.

1934

The first Masters is played. Horton Smith is the first champion. In this inaugural event, the present-day back and front nines were reversed.

1935

Glynna Collett Vare wins the U.S. Women's Amateur a record sixth time.

Pinehurst #2 is completed by Donald Ross, generally described as his masterpiece.

Gene Sarazen double-eagles the par-5 15th hole to catch the leaders at the Masters. His "Shot Heard Round the World" propels him to victory, and due to the coverage of his feat by sportswriters visiting Augusta while returning from baseball spring training, propels both the game of golf and Augusta National to new heights of popularity.

1936

Henry Cotton wins his third consecutive British Open.

Johnny Fisher becomes the last golfer to win a major championship (the U.S. Amateur) with hickory-shafted clubs.

1937

The Bing Crosby Pro-Am is inaugurated in San Diego. A few years later it moves to the Monterey Peninsula.

1938

The British amateurs score their first victory over the United States in the Walker Cup Matches at the Old Course.

1938 (continued)

The Palm Beach Invitational becomes the first tournament to make a contribution to charity—$10,000.

The 14-club rule is instituted by the USGA, in response to the proliferation of specialty clubs.

1940

The British Open and Amateur are discontinued for the duration of the Second World War.

1942

The U.S. Open is discontinued for the duration of the war. A world-wide shortage of rubber, a vital military supply, creates a shortage and huge price increase in golf balls. Sam Snead manages to complete an entire four-day tournament playing one ball, but the professional circuit is severely curtailed.

The U.S. government halts the manufacture of golf equipment for the duration of the war.

1943

The PGA Championship is cancelled for the year, and the Masters is discontinued for the duration of the war.

1944

The PGA expands the TOUR to 22 events despite the absence of many of its star players due to military service.

1945

Byron Nelson wins 18 tournaments in a calendar year to set an all-time PGA TOUR record—including a record 11 in a row and a record 19 consecutive rounds under 70. His total prize earnings during his 11-win streak, $30,000, is less than last place money for the PGA TOUR Championship by 1992.

The Tam O'Shanter Open offers a then-record purse of $60,000.

1946

The U.S. Women's Open is instituted. Patty Berg is the first winner.

1947

Mildred "Babe" Zaharias becomes the first American to win the British Women's Open, at Gullane.

Golf is televised for the first time, in a local St. Louis telecast of the U.S. Open.

Golf World magazine is founded.

1948

Bobby Locke becomes the first South African to win the British Open.

Bobby Locke sets a PGA TOUR record with a 16-stroke winning margin in the Chicago Victory National Championship.

Herbert Warren Wind's authoritative *The Story of American Golf* is published.

The U.S. Junior Amateur is instituted. Ken Venturi loses to Dean Lind in the first final.

The *USGA Golf Journal* is founded.

1949

Louise Suggs wins the U.S. Women's Open by a record margin of 14 strokes.

Marie Roke of Wollaston, Massachusetts aces a 393-yard hole—the longest ace ever recorded by a woman.

1950

The LPGA is founded, replacing the ailing Women's Professional Golf Association.

Ben Hogan, only weeks after returning to the PGA TOUR following a near-fatal auto accident, wins the U.S. Open at Oakland Hills.

1951

Francis Ouimet becomes the first American Captain of the R&A.

The USGA and the R&A, in a conference, complete a newly revised *Rules of Golf.* Although the R&A and the USGA continue to differ over the size of the golf ball, all other conflicts are resolved in this momentous conference. The center-shafted putter is legalized world-wide. The out-of-bounds penalty is standardized at stroke-and-distance, and the stymie is finally and forever abolished.

Golf Digest is founded, with Bill Davis as editor.

Al Brosch shoots 60 in the Texas Open to set an 18-hole PGA TOUR record.

1952

Marlene Hagge wins the Sarasota Open when she is 18 years 14 days old—an LPGA record.

Patty Berg shoots an LPGA-record of 64 for an 18-hole round.

The National Hole-in-One Clearing House is established by *Golf Digest.*

1953

Tommy Armour's *How to Play Your Best Golf All the Time* is published and becomes the first golf book ever to hit the best-seller lists.

Ben Hogan wins the first three legs of the modern "Grand Slam" (The Masters, U.S. Open, and British Open), but fails to win the final leg, the PGA Championship.

The Tam O'Shanter World Championship becomes the first tournament to be nationally televised. Lew Worsham holes a 104-yard wedge shot on the final hole for eagle and victory in one of the most dramatic finishes ever.

The Canada Cup is instituted, the first event that brings together teams from all over the world. After 1966 the tournament is known as the World Cup.

1954

Peter Thomson becomes the first Australian to win a major tournament with a victory in the British Open.

Architect Robert Trent Jones, upon receiving complaints that he has made the par-3 fourth hole at Baltusrol too hard for the upcoming U.S. Open, plays the hole to see for himself—and records a hole-in-one.

The U.S. Open is nationally televised for the first time.

The Tam O'Shanter World Championship offers the first $100,000 purse for a golf tournament.

"All-Star Golf," a filmed series of matches, debuts on network television.

Babe Zaharias returns to the LPGA Tour following cancer surgery and wins the U.S. Women's Open.

The first PGA Merchandise Show is held in a parking lot in Dunedin, Florida, outside the PGA National Golf Club. Salesmen work the show out of the trunks of their cars. The Show goes on to become one of the main events on the golfing calendar—by 1994 it grows to over 30,000 attendees, four days, and has become the single-largest tenant of the Orange County Convention Center in Orlando, spilling over 220,000 square feet of exhibit space.

1955

Mike Souchak shoots 60-68-64-65 for a PGA TOUR record 27-under-par 257 for 72 holes, at Brackenridge Park G.C. in the Texas Open. The record still stands today.

1956

The current yardage guides for par are adopted by the USGA.

1957

Great Britain wins the Ryder Cup matches at Lindrick—ending a drought that dates back to 1935. They would not win again until, in the 1980s, eligibility was expanded to include all European players.

E. Harvie Ward loses his amateur status for accepting expenses from sponsors for golf tournaments. The ruling is reversed in 1958.

Ben Hogan's *Five Lessons* is published.

1958

Arnold Palmer is allowed a controversial free drop to save par in the final round of the Masters, and he goes on to defeat Ken Venturi.

1959

Bill Wright, in winning the U.S. Amateur Public Links, becomes the first African-American to win a national championship.

Golf Magazine is founded, with Charles Price as the first editor.

1960

Arnold Palmer comes back from six shots down in the final round to win the US Open. With his victory, he completes the first two legs of the modern Grand Slam after winning the Masters in April, the first to do so since Ben Hogan in 1953. He finishes second to Kel Nagle in the British Open to end his bid. Palmer's entry in the British Open is credited with reviving world-wide interest in the championship. Palmer went on to win the British Open in both 1961 and 1962.

Lifting, cleaning, and repairing ball marks is allowed on the putting green for the first time.

1961

Gary Player becomes the first foreign player to win the Masters.

Caucasians-only clause stricken from the PGA constitution, and at the Greater Greensboro Open Charlie Sifford becomes the first black golfer to play in a PGA co-sponsored tournament in the South.

1962

Dr. Joseph Boydstone records 11 aces in one calendar year. Three were recorded in one round, at Bakersfield C.C., Calif.

Jack Nicklaus wins his first professional tournament—the U.S. Open, the last player to win the U.S. Open as his first pro victory.

Painted lines are first utilized to mark water hazards at the U.S. Open.

1963

Arnold Palmer becomes the first professional to earn over $100,000 in official prize money in one calendar year.

Mickey Wright wins a record 13 events on the LPGA Tour in one year.

The casting method for irons is first employed.

1964

PGA National opens, in Palm Beach, Fla.

Mickey Wright sets the LPGA 18-hole record with a 62 at Hogan Park GC in the Tall City Open.

Norman Manley, an amateur from Long Beach, Calif., scores holes-in-one on two successive par-4s at Del Valley CC, Calif. It is the first and only time this feat has been accomplished.

1965

Sam Snead wins the Greater Greensboro Open—his

1965 (continued)

81st TOUR victory, a record. His victory is the eighth in the Greensboro event, also a record. Finally, he wins at the age of 52, also a PGA TOUR record to this day.

Jack Nicklaus sets a tournament record of 271 in winning the Masters.

Mrs. William Jenkins Sr. of Baltimore, Md., double-eagles the par-five 12th hole at Longview G.C., the longest ever recorded by a woman.

PGA TOUR Qualifying School is inaugurated at PGA National, with 17 golfers of the 49 applicants winning their playing cards.

1966

Arnold Palmer blows a six-shot lead in the final round of the US Open, losing to a surging Billy Casper at Olympic.

1967

Charlie Sifford, by winning the Greater Hartford Open, becomes the first African-American to win a PGA TOUR event.

Catherine Lacoste becomes the first amateur to win the U.S. Women's Open.

The Canada Cup changes its name to the World Cup.

1968

Arnold Palmer passes the $1 million mark in career PGA earnings.

The PGA of America and the PGA TOUR officially split, with the professionals forming a breakaway group known as the Association of Professional Golfers. The breach is eventually healed, and a Tournament Players Division of the PGA is formed. Joe Dey is elected the next year as the first PGA TOUR commissioner.

Tommy Moore, age 6 years 1 month, 1 week, becomes the youngest player to score a hole-in-one. Moore also becomes, in 1975, the youngest player ever to score a double-eagle.

Roberto DeVicenzo ties Bob Goalby after regulation play in the Masters, but signs an incorrect scorecard and loses the event.

1969

Ollie Bowers of Gaffney, SC completes a record 542 rounds (9,756 holes) in one calendar year.

Jack Nicklaus concedes Tony Jacklin's final putt and England ties the U.S. in the Ryder Cup matches, after five consecutive defeats. The gesture is often hailed as "the greatest single act of sportsmanship in history."

The trendsetting Harbour Town Golf Links opens on Hilton Head Island, S.C., designed by Pete Dye with assistance from Jack Nicklaus.

1970

Bill Burke, with a 57 at Normandie C.C., sets the all-time official record for low 18-hole score.

Thad Doker of Durham, N.C., records a record two-under par 70 in the World One Club Championship at Lochmere C.C.

1971

Laura Baugh wins the US Amateur at 16 years 2 months of age.

Alan Shepard hits a six-iron at "Fra Mauro Country Club" on the moon.

1972

Carolyn Gidone wins the US Senior Women's Amateur for a record fifth consecutive time.

Dick Kimbrough completes 364 holes in 24 hours at the 6,068 North Platte C.C. in Nebraska.

1972 (continued)

Tom Doty records 10-under-par in four holes at Brookwood C.C., Illinois. His streak includes a double-eagle, two holes-in-one, and an eagle.

Spalding introduces the first two-piece ball, the Top-Flite.

Jack Nicklaus completes the first two legs of the modern Grand Slam, winning the Masters and the US Open (at Pebble Beach), but like Arnold Palmer in 1960, falters in the British Open by finishing second (to Lee Trevino).

1973

Ben Crenshaw wins the NCAA title for a record 3rd consecutive time. Later in the year, after earning his PGA TOUR card, he wins the first event he plays as a PGA TOUR member, the San Antonio Open.

Johnny Miller fires a record 63 in the final round to win the US Open at Oakmont.

The graphite shaft is invented.

The classic golf book *Golf in the Kingdom*, by Michael Murphy, is published.

Jack Nicklaus wins the PGA Championship and breaks Bobby Jones' record for most major victories with his 14th.

1974

Deane Beman is elected as the second PGA TOUR commissioner.

Roberto DeVicenzo scores six birdies, an eagle, and three more birdies for a record 11-under par for ten holes, at Valla Allende G.C., Argentina.

The World Golf Hall of Fame is opened in Pinehurst, North Carolina.

Mike Austin hits a 515-yard drive at the 1974 National Seniors Open in Las Vegas, Nev., the longest drive ever recorded in competition.

Jack Nicklaus' *Golf My Way* is published.

Tom Weiskopf strikes a 420-yard drive to the greenside bunker on the 10th hole at Augusta National—the longest drive in Masters history.

Muirfield Village Golf Club opens from a Desmond Muirhead/Jack Nicklaus design.

The Tournament Players Championship is inaugurated.

1975

Lee Elder becomes the first black golfer to play in the Masters.

Lee Trevino, Jerry Heard and Bobby Nichols are struck by lightning during the 1975 Western Open. The incident prompts new safety standards in weather preparedness at PGA events, but four spectators are killed when struck by lightning during the 1991 U.S. Open at Hazeltine National.

1976

Judy Rankin becomes the first LPGA professional to earn more than $100,000 in a season.

Richard Stanwood sets the record for fewest putts in one round-15- at Riverside G.C. in Pocatello, ID.

The USGA institutes the Overall Distance Standard—golf balls that fly more than 280 yards during a standard test are banned.

1977

Al Geiberger shoots 59 at Colonial CC in the second round of the Memphis Classic, to set a new PGA TOUR 18-hole record.

Bing Crosby dies after completing a round of golf in Spain. His Bing Crosby National Pro-Am continues

1977 (continued)

for several years, but after relations sour between the PGA TOUR and the Crosby family, AT&T takes over sponsorship of the event.

The "sudden-death" playoff is used for the first time in a major championship, when Lanny Wadkins defeats Gene Littler for the PGA Championship played at Pebble Beach G.L.

In what has been described as the most exciting tournament in history, Tom Watson defeats Jack Nicklaus by one stroke in the British Open, at Turnberry. They were tied after the second and third rounds, and were paired with each other during the final 36 holes.

1978

The Legends of Golf is inaugurated at Onion Creek C.C. in Austin, Texas. Its popularity leads to the formation of the Senior TOUR two years later.

1979

The Ryder Cup is reformatted to add European continent players to the British-Scottish-Irish side, making the event far more competitive.

Taylor Made introduces the first metal woods.

1980

Tom Watson is the first golfer to earn $500,000 in prize money in a single season.

The PGA Senior TOUR is born, with four official events.

The U.S. Senior Open is instituted. Roberto De Vicenzo is the first winner.

Jack Nicklaus sets a record of 272 in the U.S. Open at Baltusrol. His mark is equalled in the 1993 U.S. Open by Lee Janzen, also at Baltusrol.

The USGA introduces the Symmetry Standard, banning balls such as the Polaris which correct themselves in flight.

Gary Wright completes 18 holes in a record 28 minutes 9 seconds at Twantin Noosa G.C., Australia (6,039 yards).

1981

The Tournament Players Club at Sawgrass opens, with its controversial island green 17th hole, and immediately becomes the permanent host of the Tournament Players Championship. The TPC at Sawgrass becomes the prototype for a dozen "stadium" TPC courses around the United States, built specifically to host PGA TOUR co-sponsored events and affording better viewing for spectators.

The USGA institutes the Mid-Amateur. The Women's Mid-Amateur would follow in 1987.

Kathy Whitworth becomes the first woman to earn $1 million in career prize money.

1982

Kevin Murray double-eagles the 647-yard second hole at the Guam Navy G.C., the longest double-eagle ever recorded.

1983

The PGA TOUR introduces the all-exempt Tour, with the top 125 players exempt from Monday qualifying for its tournaments.

1984

Desert Highlands opens in Phoenix from a design by Jack Nicklaus utilizing only 80 irrigated acres for 18 holes, instead of the typical 100-150 for a major course. The success of Nicklaus' concept of "target golf" ushers in the era of environmentally-sensitive desert design.

1985

Nancy Lopez sets the LPGA 72-hole record with 268 in the Henredon Classic.

1985 (continued)

The United States loses the Ryder Cup matches for the first time since 1957, to the expanded European team.

The USGA introduces the Slope System to allow golfers to adjust their handicaps to allow for the relative difficulty of a golf course compared to players of their own ability.

1986

Bob Tway sinks a miracle bunker shot to beat a stunned Greg Norman in the PGA Championship. Norman had held the lead on Sunday morning in each of the four major championships of 1986, but was able to win only in the British Open. Only Bobby Jones had previously held the Sunday morning lead in each Grand Slam event. Tway's stroke inaugurated a celebrated series of miracle shots holed by golfers such as Larry Mize and Robert Gamez to defeat Norman.

The Pete Dye-designed PGA West opens amid great controversy concerning the difficulty of the course.

The Panasonic Las Vegas Invitational offers the first $1 million purse.

The PGA TOUR Team Charity Competition debuts. By 1987, TOUR-related contributions to charity exceed $100,000,000, and by 1992 they reach a total of $200,000,000.

1987

The Links at Spanish Bay opens, the first true links course in the Western United States. It is a co-design by Robert Trent Jones, Jr., Tom Watson, and former USGA President Frank "Sandy" Tatum.

Judy Bell becomes the first woman elected to the USGA Executive Committee.

The Nabisco Championships (later the TOUR Championship) debuts as a season-ending event for the top 30 money winners. The first winner is Tom Watson, breaking a three year victory drought.

Walter Dietz, a blind golfer, aces the 155-yard seventh hole at Manakiki G.C., California.

1988

Links Magazine is founded (originally *Southern Links*), with Mark Brown as editor-in-chief.

Lori Garbacz orders a pizza between holes at the U.S. Women's Open to protest slow play.

Square-grooved clubs such as the PING Eye2 irons are banned by the USGA, which claims that tests show the clubs give an unfair competitive advantage to PING customers. The PGA TOUR also bans the clubs in 1989. Karsten Manufacturing, maker of the clubs, fights a costly two-year battle with both the USGA and the PGA TOUR to have the ban rescinded after winning a temporary injunction. Eventually both organizations drop the ban, while Karsten acknowledges the right of the organizations to regulate equipment and pledges to make modifications to future designs.

Curtis Strange wins the season-ending Nabisco Championships at Pebble Beach, and his $360,000 paycheck lifts his official 1988 TOUR earnings to $1,147,644—and thus he becomes the first player to win over $1,000,000 in a single season.

1989

Four golfers, Doug Weaver, Mark Wiebe, Jerry Pate and Nick Price, hit aces on the par-three sixth hole on the same day in the U.S. Open at Oak Hill.

Nick Faldo sinks a 100-foot birdie putt on the second hole at Augusta National in the Masters—the longest putt holed to date in a major tournament. Faldo goes on to win the Masters.

1990

Hall Thompson of Shoal Creek GC, on the eve of

1990 (continued)

the PGA Championship at Shoal Creek, defends his club's policy of not admitting black members. Amidst a public outcry, Shoal Creek is forced to change its policy and the PGA TOUR and the USGA insist that in future all clubs submit to a standard set of guidelines on membership policies. Cypress Point Club and Aronimink, among others, decide they are unable to comply and withdraw from the professional tournament arena.

Bill Blue resigns after a short reign as LPGA Commissioner. Charles Mecham is selected as his successor.

Construction begins on Shadow Creek Golf Club, the most expensive golf course ever built, with cost estimates ranging from $35 to $60 million as Tom Fazio creates an oasis in the Las Vegas desert . The club in 1994 vaults into eighth place on the *Golf Digest* top-100 course rankings, sparking controversy.

The R&A, after 38 years, adopts the 1.68 inch diameter ball, and for the first time since 1910 *The Rules of Golf* are standardized throughout the world.

The initial Solheim Cup is played at Lake Nona G.C., Orlando, commencing a biennial USA vs. Europe competition for women, a recognition of the growing strength of women's golf on both sides of the Atlantic.

The Ben Hogan Tour is launched as a minor league for the PGA TOUR, following the increased success of mini-tours such as the U.S. Golf Tour in 1989.

1991

The Ocean Course at Kiawah Island, S.C., the first course to be awarded the Ryder Cup Matches before the course has been completed, is the scene of the United States' first victory in the event since 1983. The competition comes down to a twisting seven-footer on the 18th hole missed by Bernhard Langer in the final match (against Hale Irwin).

John Daly wins the PGA Championship at Crooked Stick when, as ninth alternate, a slot in the tournament opens up for him on the night before the Championship began. The golfer who withdrew and gave Daly his place, Nick Price, wins the PGA Championship in 1992 at Bellerive.

Oversized metal woods are introduced, with Callaway Golf's Big Bertha quickly establishing itself as the dominant brand—the Big Bertha driver becomes one of the biggest-selling clubs of all time.

Harvey Penick's Little Red Book becomes the all-time best selling golf book.

1992

Simon Clough and Boris Janic complete 18-hole rounds in five countries in one day, walking each course. They played rounds in France, Luxembourg, Belgium, Holland, and Germany, and completed their journey in 16 hours, 35 minutes.

Brittany Andres, age 6 years 19 days, scores an ace at the 85-yard second hole at the Jimmy Clay G.C. in Austin, Texas.

1993

An ownership group led by Joe Gibbs and Arnold Palmer announces plans for The Golf Channel, a 24-hour, 365-day cable service.

The European PGA Tour announces a reduction in the Ryder Cup captain's wild-card selections from three to two.

1994

Deane Beman announces his retirement as Commissioner of the PGA TOUR. Deputy Commissioner Tim Finchem succeeds him.

The PGA TOUR announces that none of its member pros would be allowed to play in a World Tour proposed by an American-based group of entrepreneurs.

THE TOP 250 COURSES

OVERVIEW: *Courses included are those which met any of the following criteria: Listed in the 1993 or 1995 Golf Digest ranking of the top 100 courses in the United States; listed in the 1993 Golf Magazine Top 100 Courses in the United States and the World; host courses for the Major championships for men, women and seniors since 1990 if not otherwise selected; listed in the Golf World (U.K.) ranking of the Top 40 courses in the United Kingdom and Ireland; listed in the Golf World (U.K.) Top 20 Courses in Continental Europe; listed in Golf Digest's Top 25 Courses in Canada.*

In total, 226 courses qualified within these criteria. An additional 24 courses have been added in a special section following the regular listings. These selections were made by a **Golfer's Almanac** *committee in order to recognize hidden gems, newer courses, and courses which have made an outstanding contribution to the history and traditions of the game. In total, 147 courses were selected from the United States, and 113 from the rest of the world.*

No ranking of courses should be considered as authoritative; rather, they represent the attempt of the rating boards to balance the aesthetic, strategic, and historical appeal of a small percentage of the world's golf courses. There is room for disagreement.

Tom Fazio recently made the apt observation that with modern rankings it is not a question of which courses should "get in," but which will have to be left out to make room. Each course, however, is able to qualify for this list through the hosting of championships or the voting of experienced critics. If the results are sometimes controversial, the process is one that is fair and for the vast majority of courses provides well-deserved recognition.

UNITED STATES

ARONIMINK
LOCATION: Newtown Square, Penn.
FOUNDED: 1928 PAR: 70 YARDAGE: 6974
SELECTION CRITERIA: #77, Golf Digest, 1995.
NOTES: Donald Ross's great Philadelphia course; hosted the 1977 U.S. Amateur where John Fought recorded the most lopsided victory (9&8 over Doug Fischesser) since 1949. Also the site of Gary Player's 1962 PGA Championship.

ATLANTA ATHLETIC CLUB (HIGHLANDS)
LOCATION: Atlanta, Ga.
FOUNDED: 1967 PAR: 72 YARDAGE: 6976
CRITERIA: Host, 1990 U.S. Women's Open.
NOTES: Hosted 1976 U.S. Open, a rare foray into the South by the USGA and a championship won with a rare birdie on the final hole by Jerry Pate. Atlanta A.C. recently tumbled out of the Golf Digest top-100 rankings but continues to be part of the USGA rotation, hosting the 1990 U.S. Women's Open.

ATLANTA
LOCATION: Atlanta, Ga.
FOUNDED: 1965 PAR: 72 YARDAGE: 7015
CRITERIA: #96, Golf Digest, 1995.
NOTES: Outstanding Willard Byrd course remodeled by Bob Cupp in 1990, which reentered the Golf Digest rankings in 1995. Hosted the 1968 Senior Amateur and the 1971 Women's Amateur.

AUGUSTA NATIONAL
LOCATION: Augusta, Ga.
FOUNDED: 1933 PAR: 72 YARDAGE: 6905
CRITERIA: #2, Golf Digest, 1995
NOTES: Hosted The Masters each April since 1934; Alister Mackenzie designed with advice from Bobby Jones, with Perry Maxwell, Robert Trent Jones, George Cobb, Jack Nicklaus, and Tom Fazio credited with remodeling over the years; ranked #4 in the world by Golf Magazine, 1993.

BALTIMORE (EAST)
LOCATION: Timonium, Md.
FOUNDED: 1926 PAR: 70 YARDAGE: 6662

CRITERIA: #42, Golf Digest, 1995.
NOTES AND AWARDS: Hosted the 1899 U.S. Open; 1928 PGA, 1932 Amateur; 1965 Walker Cup; and site of Liselotte Neumann's record 277 in the 1988 U.S. Women's Open.

BALTUSROL G.C. (LOWER)

LOCATION: Springfield, N.J.
FOUNDED: 1922 PAR: 72 YARDAGE: 7138
CRITERIA: #20, Golf Digest, 1995.
NOTES: Site of 14 different USGA Championships, including seven U.S. Opens; Lee Janzen and Jack Nicklaus' low U.S. Open scores set here in 1993. Ranked #30 in the world by Golf Magazine.

BALTUSROL (UPPER)

LOCATION: Philadelphia, PA.
FOUNDED: 1916 PAR: 72 YARDAGE: 6807
CRITERIA: #99, Golf Magazine, 1995.
NOTES: Snuck onto the tail-end of the rankings; Baltusrol joins Winged Foot and Sunningdale (England) among the few clubs with two ranked courses.

BARTON CREEK C.C. (FAZIO)

LOCATION: Austin, Tex.
FOUNDED: 1986 PAR: 72 YARDAGE: 6956
CRITERIA: #94, Golf Digest, 1995.
NOTES: Acclaimed Tom Fazio design from his "golden" period in the mid-80s once overshadowed by Lake Nona, Wade Hampton, and Black Diamond; now recognized as one of his best.

BAY HILL CLUB

LOCATION: Orlando, Fla.
FOUNDED: 1961 PAR: 72 YARDAGE: 7114
CRITERIA: #89, Golf Digest, 1995.
NOTES: Site of the Nestle Classic; hosted the 1991 Junior Amateur where winner Tiger Woods, age 15, first leapt into the public eye. Course redesigned by and at one time the Florida base for Arnold Palmer.

BELLERIVE C.C.

LOCATION: St. Louis, Mo.
FOUNDED: 1960 PAR: 71 YARDAGE: 7,302
CRITERIA: #53, Golf Digest, 1995.
NOTES: Site of several national championships including Nick Price's 1992 PGA Championship, and Gary Player's completion of the career Grand Slam in the 1965 U.S. Open. One of the longest courses in the country when it first opened from a design by Robert Trent Jones, curiously it has favored the shorter hitters.

BETHPAGE (BLACK)

LOCATION: Farmingdale, N.Y.
FOUNDED: 1936 PAR: 71 YARDAGE: 7065
CRITERIA: #92, Golf Magazine, 1995.
NOTES: A late design by A.W. Tillinghast (of Winged Foot fame, &c.), this course has become increasingly popular as a Hidden Gem. One of the few ranked U.S. courses open to the public; hosted the Publinx in its first year and virtually nothing since.

BLACK DIAMOND (QUARRY)

LOCATION: Lecanto, Fla.
FOUNDED: 1988 PAR: 72 YARDAGE: 7159
CRITERIA: #55, Golf Digest, 1995.
NOTES: Tom Fazio's masterpiece? The quarry holes are perhaps his most-admired work. Black Diamond has yet to host a significant tournament due to its tender years and middle-of-nowhere location. But a classic, nonetheless.

BLACKWOLF RUN (RIVER)

LOCATION: Kohler, Wisc.
FOUNDED: 1989 PAR: 72 YARDAGE: 6991
CRITERIA: #62, Golf Digest, 1995.
NOTES: In 1993 the Golf Digest rankings placed Blackwolf Run at #31, but despite the drop, Blackwolf Run remains one of the newest courses on the list.

BROOKLAWN

LOCATION: Fairfield, Conn.
FOUNDED: N/A PAR: 71 YARDAGE: 6599
CRITERIA: 1987 U.S. Senior Open.
NOTES: A short course, Brooklawn was the site of Gary Player's 1987 Senior Open victory (his record 14-under par score is still the Senior Open record); however, even par won for Jerilyn Britz in the 1979 U.S. Women's Open.

BUTLER NATIONAL

LOCATION: Oak Brook, Ill.
FOUNDED: 1974 PAR: 72 YARDAGE: 7309
CRITERIA: #49, Golf Digest, 1995.
NOTES: Longtime host of the Western Open, the members opted out of the PGA TOUR after the Shoal Creek-inspired focus on minority membership policies.

CAMARGO

LOCATION: Indian Hill, Ohio
FOUNDED: 1921 PAR: 70 YARDAGE: 6559

CRITERIA: #84, Golf Digest, 1995.
NOTES: Never the site of a major championship of golf, nevertheless this Seth Raynor design has ridden the crest of Raynor's increasing reputation.

CANTERBURY
LOCATION: Shaker Heights, Ohio
FOUNDED: 1922 PAR: 72 YARDAGE: 6911
CRITERIA: #56, Golf Digest, 1995.
NOTES: Considered just a notch or two behind the likes of Scioto, Inverness, and Muirfield Village as one of Ohio's premier courses, Canterbury has hosted the 1940 and 1948 U.S. Opens, the 1946 Open featuring a three-way, 36-hole playoff resulting in Lloyd Mangrum's one-stroke victory.

CASCADES
LOCATION: Hot Springs, Va.
FOUNDED: 1923 PAR: 70 YARDAGE: 6566
CRITERIA: #39, Golf Digest, 1995.
NOTES: Long-renowned as one of the finest mountain courses, Cascades has hosted five national championships, including Glenna Collett Vare's record 13 & 12 win in the U.S. Amateur files.

CASTLE PINES
LOCATION: Castle Rock, Colo.
FOUNDED: 1981 PAR: 72 YARDAGE: 7559
CRITERIA: #42, Golf Digest, 1995.
NOTES: Host of popular PGA TOUR tournament The International, featuring a modified Stableford scoring system which makes the reachable par-fives the key holes. Designed by Jack Nicklaus.

CHAMPIONS (CYPRESS CREEK)
LOCATION: Houston, Tex.
FOUNDED: 1959 PAR: 71 YARDAGE: 7147
CRITERIA: #83, Golf Magazine, 1995.
NOTES: Hosted 1969 U.S. Open (won by Orville Moody), and the 1967 Ryder Cup matches; also was the stage of the 1990 Nabisco Championships (now the TOUR Championship) won by Jodie Mudd.

CHERRY HILLS
LOCATION: Englewood, Colo.
FOUNDED: 1923 PAR: 72 YARDAGE: 7160
CRITERIA: #31, Golf Digest, 1995.
NOTES: Immortalized as the site of Arnold Palmer's famous charge to victory in the 1960 U.S. Open; also hosted the 1978 Open won by unknown Andy North; designed by William Flynn and remodeled by Arnold Palmer and Ed Seay in 1978, and by Geoffrey Cornish in 1992.

CHICAGO
LOCATION: Wheaton, Ill.
FOUNDED: 1894 PAR: 70 YARDAGE: 6574
CRITERIA: #18, Golf Digest, 1995.
NOTES: The oldest ranked American course, a classic designed by U.S. golf pioneer Charles Blair Macdonald and remodeled in 1923 by Seth Raynor; ranked #45 in the world by Golf Magazine (1993). Bobby Jones still holds the course record of 66.

COG HILL (NO. 4)
LOCATION: Lemont, Ill.
FOUNDED: 1964 PAR: 72 YARDAGE: 6992
CRITERIA: #59, Golf Digest, 1995.
NOTES: No. 4, also known as Dubsdread, has hosted the Western Open since 1991. One of the most highly regarded public courses in the country, the design is by Dick Wilson and Joe Lee.

COLONIAL
LOCATION: Fort Worth, Tex.
FOUNDED: 1935 PAR: 70 YARDAGE: 7010
CRITERIA: #41, Golf Digest, 1995.
NOTES: The best-known Texan course and host to the Colonial Invitational, in addition to the 1941 U.S. Open and the 1975 Players Championship won by Al Geiberger (back when that tournament rotated between great courses).

CONGRESSIONAL (BLUE)
LOCATION: Bethesda, Md.
FOUNDED: 1961 PAR: 72 YARDAGE: 7270
CRITERIA: #68, Golf Digest, 1995.
NOTES: Hosted the 1964 U.S. Open famed for extremely high temperatures and the heroic persistence of winner Ken Venturi. Designed by Robert Trent Jones and later remodeled by Rees Jones. Hosted the 1995 U.S. Senior Open.

C.C. OF DETROIT
LOCATION: Grosse Pointe Farms, Mich.
FOUNDED: 1914 PAR: 72 YARDAGE: 6800
CRITERIA: #86, Golf Magazine, 1995.
NOTES: Hosted the 1915 and 1954 Amateurs, the latter won by a young Arnold Palmer in his first major victory. Designed by Colt & Alison, later remodeled by Robert Trent Jones.

C.C. OF NORTH CAROLINA (DOGWOOD)
LOCATION: Pinehurst, N.C.
FOUNDED: 1963 PAR: 72 YARDAGE: 7154
CRITERIA: #78, Golf Digest, 1995.

NOTES: Host of 1980 Amateur won by Hal Sutton in a stunning 9&8 victory. Designed by Willard Byrd and Ellis Maples in the early 1960s, it has remained a prestigious course even among Pinehurst's riches.

THE COUNTRY CLUB

LOCATION: Brookline, Mass.
FOUNDED: 1895 PAR: 71 YARDAGE: 7010
CRITERIA: #10, Golf Digest, 1995.
NOTES: Host of three U.S. Opens, the latest in 1988, won by Curtis Strange after a widely praised remodeling by Rees Jones; also the site of the famed 1913 U.S. Open won by underdog Francis Ouimet over heavy favorites Harry Vardon and Ted Ray. Hosted five U.S. Amateurs; one of the oldest courses in the United States; ranked #34 in the world by Golf Magazine.

THE COUNTRY CLUB

LOCATION: Pepper Pike, Ohio
FOUNDED: 1931
CRITERIA: #56, Golf Magazine, 1993.
NOTES: Hosted 1935 U.S. Amateur won by Lawson Little; ranked #93 in the world by Golf Magazine.

CROOKED STICK

LOCATION: Carmel, Ind.
FOUNDED: 1964 PAR: 72 YARDAGE: 7516
CRITERIA: #66, Golf Digest, 1995.
NOTES: The course which put Pete Dye on the golfing map, it also was the site of John Daly's miraculous win in the 1991 PGA Championship after receiving the final spot in the field. Also hosted the 1993 U.S. Women's Open won by Laurie Merten.

CRYSTAL DOWNS

LOCATION: Frankfort, Mich.
FOUNDED: 1931 PAR: 70 YARDAGE: 6518
CRITERIA: #13, Golf Digest, 1995.
NOTES: Perhaps the definitive "hidden gem," Crystal Downs had never hosted a national tournament until the 1991 U.S. Senior Amateur; designed by Alister Mackenzie and Perry Maxwell; ranked #15 in the world by Golf Magazine, 1993.

CYPRESS POINT

LOCATION: Pebble Beach, Calif.
FOUNDED: 1928 PAR: 72 YARDAGE: 6536
CRITERIA: #4, Golf Digest, 1995.
NOTES: Long-time host of the Crosby (later the AT&T National Pro-Am); also hosted the 1981 Walker Cup Matches. Designed by Alister MacKenzie; ranked #2 in the world by Golf Magazine; frequently cited as the greatest 17-hole course in the world, due to its weak 18th.

DEL PASO

LOCATION: Sacramento, Calif.
FOUNDED: 1982 PAR: 72 YARDAGE: 6300
CRITERIA: Host, 1982 U.S. Women's Open.
NOTES: In addition to Janet Alex's six-stroke victory in the 1982 Women's Open, Del Paso has hosted two U.S. Women's Amateurs (1957, 1976) and the 1964 Senior Women's Amateur.

DESERT FOREST

LOCATION: Carefree, Ariz.
FOUNDED: 1962 PAR: 72 YARDAGE: 6981
CRITERIA: #67, Golf Digest, 1995.
NOTES: The first Arizona course to crack the rankings, the Red Lawrence design is still one of the top-ranked Southwestern tracks, hosting the 1990 Senior Amateur. Ranked #91 by Golf Magazine, 1993.

DESERT HIGHLANDS

LOCATION: Scottsdale, Ariz.
FOUNDED: 1984 PAR: 72 YARDAGE: 7099
CRITERIA: #98, Golf Digest, 1995.
NOTES: Host of 1983-1984 Skins Game. One of the few genuine trendsetters in golf course design, Jack Nicklaus' revolutionary "target golf" concept, with only 80 acres of grass surrounded by virgin desert, has led to a host of imitators in the American Southwest.

DESERT MOUNTAIN (RENEGADE)

LOCATION: Scottsdale, Ariz.
FOUNDED: 1986 PAR: 72 YARDAGE: 7515
CRITERIA: #100, Golf Digest, 1995.
NOTES: One of the few clubs to have two courses in the top 100 (Winged Foot and Sunningdale are among the others).

DESERT MOUNTAIN (COCHISE)

LOCATION: Scottsdale, Ariz.
FOUNDED: 1987 PAR: 72 YARDAGE: 7045
HOST: The Tradition.
NOTES: Host of The Tradition since 1989; designed by Jack Nicklaus.

DORAL (BLUE MONSTER)

LOCATION: Miami, Fla.
FOUNDED: 1916 PAR: 72 YARDAGE: 6939

CRITERIA: #71, Golf Magazine, 1993.
NOTES: Host of Doral Ryder Open since 1962; designed by Dick Wilson and Joe Lee.

DOUBLE EAGLE
LOCATION: Galena, Ohio
FOUNDED: 1991
CRITERIA: #62, Golf Magazine, 1993.
NOTES: One of the first 1990s designs to make it into the rankings; designed by Jay Morrish and Tom Weiskopf; just missed Golf Magazine's top-100 courses in the world.

DUNES CLUB
LOCATION: Myrtle Beach, S.C.
FOUNDED: 1949 PAR: 72 YARDAGE: 7165
CRITERIA: #93, Golf Magazine, 1993.
NOTES: Will host the Senior TOUR Championship several times in the 1990s; hosted the 1962 U.S. Women's Open won by Murle Lindstrom; one of the definitive heroic designs of Robert Trent Jones.

DUPONT C.C.
LOCATION: Wilmington, Md.
FOUNDED: N/A PAR: 71 YARDAGE: 6398
CRITERIA: Host, McDonalds LPGA Championship.
NOTES: The home of the McDonalds LPGA Championship, since 1992.

EUGENE
LOCATION: Eugene, Ore.
FOUNDED: 1967 PAR: 72 YARDAGE: 6847
CRITERIA: #74, Golf Digest, 1993.
NOTES: Hosted the 1993 Mid-Amateur; designed by Robert Trent Jones. Ranked #78 by Golf Magazine.

FIRESTONE (SOUTH)
LOCATION: Akron, Ohio
FOUNDED: 1960 PAR: 70 YARDAGE: 7139
CRITERIA: #47, Golf Magazine, 1995.
NOTES: Longtime host of the NEC World Series of Golf; 3-time host of the PGA Championship (1960, 1966 and 1975); designed by Robert Trent Jones; ranked #79 in the world by Golf Magazine.

FISHERS ISLAND
LOCATION: Fishers Island, N.Y.
FOUNDED: 1917 PAR: 72 YARDAGE: 6544
CRITERIA: #25, Golf Magazine, 1995.
NOTES: A hidden gem designed by cult-figure Seth Raynor; ranked #47 in the world by Golf Magazine; ultra-private, bordering on reclusive.

FOREST HIGHLANDS
LOCATION: Scottsdale, Ariz.
FOUNDED: 1988 PAR: 71 YARDAGE: 7051
CRITERIA: #44, Golf Digest, 1995.
NOTES: One of several Morrish/Weiskopf courses leaping into the rankings in the 1990s.

GARDEN CITY
LOCATION: Garden City, N.Y.
FOUNDED: 1899 PAR: 72 YARDAGE: 7064
CRITERIA: #30, Golf Digest, 1995.
NOTES: Hosted the 1902 U.S. Open, four U.S. Amateurs, and the 1924 Walker Cup matches; designed by Devereux Emmet and remodeled by Walter Travis in 1926; ranked #58 in the world by Golf Magazine, 1993.

THE GOLF CLUB
LOCATION: New Albany, Ohio
FOUNDED: 1967 PAR: 72 YARDAGE: 7268
CRITERIA: #28, Golf Digest, 1995
NOTES: An early milestone for designer Pete Dye; forbids tournaments not open to the membership; ranked #32 in the world by Golf Magazine, 1993.

GRANDFATHER
LOCATION: Linville, N.C.
FOUNDED: 1968 PAR: 72 YARDAGE: 7010
CRITERIA: #92, Golf Digest, 1993.
NOTES: A hidden gem from Ellis Maples that snuck into the rankings this year.

GREENVILLE (CHANTICLEER)
LOCATION: Greenville, S.C.
FOUNDED: 1966 PAR: 72 YARDAGE: 6668
CRITERIA: #81, Golf Digest, 1995.
NOTES: Shorter design from Robert Trent Jones that rarely hosts national tournaments.

HAIG POINT (CALIBOGUE)
LOCATION: Daufuskie Island, S.C.
FOUNDED: 1986 PAR: 72 YARDAGE: 7114
CRITERIA: #71, Golf Digest, 1995.
NOTES: A hard-to-find Rees Jones design tucked on a South Carolina barrier island; not accessible for national tournaments; ranked #87 by Golf Magazine, 1993.

HARBOUR TOWN
LOCATION: Hilton Head Island, S.C.
FOUNDED: 1969 PAR: 71 YARDAGE: 6912
CRITERIA: #57, Golf Digest, 1995.
NOTES: The prototypical Southern coastal course

designed by Pete Dye with Jack Nicklaus; hosted the Nabisco Championships (now the TOUR Championship) in 1989; hosted the 1974 Senior Amateur; site of the MCI Heritage Classic; ranked #42 in the world by Golf Magazine.

HAZELTINE NATIONAL
LOCATION: Chaska, Minn.
FOUNDED: 1962 PAR: 72 YARDAGE: 7237
CRITERIA: #50, Golf Digest, 1995.
NOTES: Hosted the 1970 and 1991 U.S. Opens, the 1966 and 1977 U.S. Women's Opens, and the 1983 Senior Open; designed by Robert Trent Jones and remodeled in 1990 by son Rees; ranked #72 by Golf Magazine.

HIGH POINTE
LOCATION: Williamsburg, Mich.
FOUNDED: 1989 PAR: 71 YARDAGE: 6819
CRITERIA: #97, Golf Magazine, 1993.
NOTES: Acclaimed new design by Tom Doak, Golf Magazine's architectural critic.

THE HONORS COURSE
LOCATION: Chattanooga, Tenn.
FOUNDED: 1983 PAR: 72 YARDAGE: 7064
CRITERIA: #37, Golf Digest, 1995.
NOTES: Host of the 1991 U.S. Amateur; regarded by many experts as Pete Dye's finest creation in the U.S. (Pete was aided by son P.B. in the design); ranked #60 in the world by Golf Magazine, 1993.

INDIANWOOD (OLD)
LOCATION: Lake Orion, Mich.
FOUNDED: 1928 PAR: 71 YARDAGE: 6814
CRITERIA: #74, Golf Magazine, 1993.
NOTES: Hosted the 1989 U.S. Women's Open won by Betsy King, as well as last year's 1994 U.S. Women's Open won by Patty Sheehan.

INTERLACHEN
LOCATION: Edina, Minn.
FOUNDED: 1911 PAR: 73 YARDAGE: 6733
CRITERIA: #54, Golf Digest, 1995.
NOTES: Hosted the 1930 U.S. Open where Bobby Jones won the first leg of the Grand Slam; hosted the 1993 Walker Cup matches; designed by Willie Watson and remodeled by Donald Ross in 1919.

INVERNESS
LOCATION: Toledo, Ohio
FOUNDED: 1919 PAR: 71 YARDAGE: 6952
CRITERIA: #35, Golf Digest, 1995.

NOTES: Host of four U.S. Opens (the last in 1979) and the 1973 U.S. Amateur; the first major club to allow professionals into the clubhouse; designed by Donald Ross, remodeled by Tom Fazio in 1977; rated #51 in the world by Golf Magazine.

JUPITER HILLS CLUB (HILLS)
LOCATION: Tequesta, Fla.
FOUNDED: 1970 PAR: 72 YARDAGE: 6911
CRITERIA: #64, Golf Digest, 1995.
NOTES: Host of the 1987 U.S. Amateur; ranked #91 in the world by Golf Magazine.

KAUAI LAGOONS (KIELE)
LOCATION: Lihue, Ha.
FOUNDED: 1989 PAR: 72 YARDAGE: 7070
CRITERIA: #88, Golf Digest, 1993.
NOTES: Designed by Jack Nicklaus.

KIAWAH (OCEAN)
LOCATION: Kiawah Island, S.C.
FOUNDED: 1991 PAR: 72 YARDAGE: 7371
CRITERIA: #77, Golf Magazine, 1993.
NOTES: Host of the 1991 Ryder Cup Matches won by the United States.

KITTANSETT CLUB
LOCATION: Marion, Mass.
FOUNDED: 1922 PAR: 71 YARDAGE: 6640
CRITERIA: #58, Golf Digest, 1995
NOTES: Hosted the 1953 Walker Cup matches; designed by Frederic Hood.

LA GRANGE
LOCATION: LaGrange, Ill.
PAR: 72 YARDAGE: 6685
CRITERIA: Host, 1974 U.S. Women's Open.
NOTES: Hosted 1974 U.S. Women's Open won by Sandra Haynie.

LAKE NONA
LOCATION: Orlando, Fla.
FOUNDED: 1986 PAR: 72 YARDAGE: 7011
CRITERIA: #44, Golf Magazine, 1993.
NOTES: Hosted 1990 Solheim Cup matches and 1993 World Cup; designed by Tom Fazio; ranked #71 in the world by Golf Magazine.

LA QUINTA (MOUNTAIN)
LOCATION: La Quinta, Calif.
FOUNDED: 1981 PAR: 72 YARDAGE: 6402
CRITERIA: #98, Golf Magazine, 1993.
NOTES: Designed by Pete and Alice Dye.

LAUREL VALLEY
LOCATION: Ligonier, Penn.
FOUNDED: 1960 PAR: 72 YARDAGE: 7060
CRITERIA: #45, Golf Digest, 1995.
NOTES: Hosted the 1989 U.S. Senior Open (won by Orville Moody), the 1975 Ryder Cup matches, and the 1965 PGA Championship (won by Dave Marr); designed by Dick Wilson, remodeled by Arnold Palmer and Ed Seay in 1988.

LONG COVE
LOCATION: Hilton Head Island, S.C.
FOUNDED: 1981 PAR: 71 YARDAGE: 6900
CRITERIA: #46, Golf Digest, 1995.
NOTES: Hosted the 1991 U.S. Men's Mid-Amateur; designed by Pete Dye; ranked #63 in the world by Golf Magazine, 1993.

LOS ANGELES (NORTH)
LOCATION: Los Angeles, Calif.
FOUNDED: 1921 PAR: 71 YARDAGE: 6895
CRITERIA: #33, Golf Digest, 1995.
NOTES: Hosted the 1930 U.S. Women's Amateur and the 1954 Junior Amateur; designed by George Thomas, Jr.; ranked #49 in the world by Golf Magazine, 1993.

MAIDSTONE
LOCATION: East Hampton, N.Y.
FOUNDED: 1899 PAR: 72 YARDAGE: 6390
CRITERIA: #38, Golf Digest, 1995.
NOTES: Designed by W.H. Tucker, remodeled by Willie Park, Jr. in 1925.

MAUNA KEA
LOCATION: Kohala Coast, Ha.
FOUNDED: 1965 PAR: 72 YARDAGE: 7114
CRITERIA: #69, Golf Digest, 1993.
NOTES: Designed by Robert Trent Jones; a landmark Hawaiian design, as it was the first built on a bed of lava rock.

MEDINAH C.C. (NO. 3)
LOCATION: Medinah, Ill.
FOUNDED: 1928 PAR: 72 YARDAGE: 7366
CRITERIA: #14, Golf Digest, 1995
NOTES: Hosted three U.S. Opens, the latest in 1990 (won by Hale Irwin), and the 1988 U.S. Senior Open; designed by Tom Bendelow, remodeled in 1986 by Roger Packard; ranked #47 in the world by Golf Magazine.

MERION (EAST)
LOCATION: Ardmore, PA.
FOUNDED: 1912 PAR: 70 YARDAGE: 6482
CRITERIA: #5, Golf Digest, 1995.
NOTES: Hosted four U.S. Opens, the latest in 1981 (won by David Graham of Australia), and five U.S. Amateurs; designed by Hugh Wilson, remodeled in 1925 by William Flynn; ranked #10 in the world by Golf Magazine.

MILWAUKEE
LOCATION: Milwaukee, Wisc.
FOUNDED: 1929 PAR: 72 YARDAGE: 6868
CRITERIA: #85, Golf Digest, 1995.
NOTES: Hosted the 1969 Walker Cup matches, and the 1988 Men's Senior Amateur; designed by Colt and Alison.

MISSION HILLS C.C.
LOCATION: Rancho Mirage, Calif.
FOUNDED: 1967 PAR: 72 YARDAGE: 6437
CRITERIA: Host, Nabisco Dinah Shore.
NOTES: Longtime host of the Dinah Shore and the course which perhaps more than any other put the LPGA on the map. Also hosted the 1976 World Cup won by Spain, which marked Seve Ballesteros's first breakthrough in the United States.

MUIRFIELD VILLAGE
LOCATION: Dublin, Ohio
FOUNDED: 1974 PAR: 72 YARDAGE: 7104
CRITERIA: #16, Golf Digest, 1995.
NOTES: Annual site of The Memorial; hosted the 1987 Ryder Cup matches and the 1992 Amateur; designed by Jack Nicklaus and Desmond Muirhead; ranked #24 in the world by Golf Magazine.

NCR (SOUTH)
LOCATION: Kettering, Ohio
FOUNDED: 1954 PAR: 71 YARDAGE: 6824
CRITERIA: #73, Golf Digest, 1995.
NOTES: Hosted the 1986 U.S. Women's Open (won by Jane Geddes), and the 1969 PGA Championship (won by Ray Floyd); designed by Dick Wilson.

NATIONAL GOLF LINKS OF AMERICA
LOCATION: Southampton, N.Y.
FOUNDED: 1911 PAR: 73 YARDAGE: 6779
CRITERIA: #19, Golf Digest, 1995.
NOTES: Hosted the 1922 Walker Cup matches;

designed by Charles Blair Macdonald; ranked #44 in the world by Golf Magazine.

OAK HILL (EAST)
LOCATION: Rochester, N.Y.
FOUNDED: 1925 PAR: 71 YARDAGE: 6902
CRITERIA: #20, Golf Digest, 1995.
NOTES: Hosted three U.S. Opens (the latest in 1989, won by Curtis Strange), plus the 1980 PGA Championship, the 1949 U.S. Amateur, and the 1984 Senior Open; hosted the 1995 Ryder Cup matches; designed by Donald Ross, remodeled by Tom Fazio in 1979; ranked #37 in the world by Golf Magazine.

OAKLAND HILLS (SOUTH)
LOCATION: Bloomfield Hills, Mich.
FOUNDED: 1918 PAR: 72 YARDAGE: 7105
CRITERIA: #12, Golf Digest, 1995.
NOTES: Hosted five U.S. Opens, the latest in 1985 (won by Andy North), the 1972 and 1979 PGA Championships, the 1981 and 1991 U.S. Senior Opens (the latest won by Jack Nicklaus in a playoff), and the 1929 U.S. Women's Amateur; designed by Donald Ross, remodeled by Robert Trent Jones in 1950; ranked #22 in the world by Golf Magazine.

OAKMONT
LOCATION: Oakmont, Penna.
FOUNDED: 1903 PAR: 71 YARDAGE: 7018
CRITERIA: #6, Golf Digest, 1993.
NOTES: Hosted seven U.S. Opens (the latest in 1994, won by South African Ernie Els), four U.S. Amateurs, the 1992 U.S. Women's Open, and the 1922 and 1951 PGA Championships; designed by Henry Fownes; ranked #14 in the world by Golf Magazine.

OAK TREE
LOCATION: Edmond, Okla.
FOUNDED: 1976 PAR: 71 YARDAGE: 7015
CRITERIA: #69, Golf Digest, 1995.
NOTES: Hosted the 1988 U.S. Amateur (won by Jeff Sluman) and the 1984 U.S. Amateur; designed by Pete Dye; ranked #92 in the world by Golf Magazine.

OHIO STATE (SCARLET)
LOCATION: Columbus, Ohio
FOUNDED: N/A PAR: 72 YARDAGE: 7140
CRITERIA: #94, Golf Magazine, 1993.
NOTES: Hosted the 1977 Junior Amateur; designed by Alister Mackenzie and Perry Maxwell.

OLD MARSH
LOCATION: Palm Beach Gardens, Fla.
FOUNDED: 1987 PAR: 72 YARDAGE: 6914
CRITERIA: #78, Golf Digest, 1993.
NOTES: Hosted the 1992 Women's Mid-Amateur; designed by Pete Dye.

OLD WARSON
LOCATION: Ladue, Mo.
FOUNDED: 1955 PAR: 71 YARDAGE: 6926
CRITERIA: #93, Golf Digest 1995.
NOTES: Host of 1971 Ryder Cup matches; designed by Robert Trent Jones.

OLD WAVERLY
LOCATION: West Point, Miss.
FOUNDED: 1988 PAR: 72 YARDAGE: 7000
CRITERIA: #88, Golf Digest 1995.
NOTES: One of the few new entries in the 1995 Golf Digest rankings, the outstanding Jerry Pate/Bob Cupp design is one of the most highly-admired new courses of the 1980s.

OLYMPIA FIELDS (NORTH)
LOCATION: Olympia Fields, Ill.
FOUNDED: 1922 PAR: 70 YARDAGE: 6857
CRITERIA: #63, Golf Digest, 1995.
NOTES: Host of 1928 U.S. Open (won by Johnny Farrell); designed by Willie Park, Jr.; ranked #96 by Golf Magazine.

THE OLYMPIC CLUB (LAKE)
LOCATION: San Francisco, Calif.
FOUNDED: 1967 PAR: 72 YARDAGE: 6976
CRITERIA: #11, Golf Digest 1995.
NOTES: Has hosted many major events, including three U.S. Opens (1955, 1966 and 1987), two U.S. Amateurs (1958 and 1981) and the TOUR Championship in 1993-4. Site of Arnold Palmer's fabled collapse in the final round of the 1966 Open, Greg Norman's final hole woes in the 1994 TOUR Championship, as well as Jack Fleck's dramatic play-off upset of Ben Hogan in 1955.

PGA NATIONAL (GENERAL)
LOCATION: Palm Beach Gardens, Fla.
FOUNDED: 1983 PAR: 72 YARDAGE: 6768
CRITERIA: Host, PGA Seniors Championship.
NOTES: Hosted the 1983 Ryder Cup matches as well as the 1971 PGA Championship; annual host of the PGA Seniors' Championship; designed by Tom Fazio. The original PGA National is now known as JDM C.C.

PGA WEST (STADIUM)
LOCATION: La Quinta
FOUNDED: 1986 PAR: 72 YARDAGE: 7261
CRITERIA: #93, Golf Digest, 1993.
NOTES: Host of Skins Game, 1986-91; designed by Pete and Alice Dye; ranked #75 by Golf Magazine.

PASATIEMPO
LOCATION: Santa Cruz, Calif.
FOUNDED: 1929 PAR: 71 YARDAGE: 6483
CRITERIA: #99, Golf Digest, 1995.
NOTES: Host of 1986 Women's Amateur; designed by Alister Mackenzie, one of his few public courses; ranked #100 in the world by Golf Magazine.

PEACHTREE
LOCATION: Atlanta, Ga.
FOUNDED: 1947 PAR: 72 YARDAGE: 7043
CRITERIA: #26, Golf Digest, 1995.
NOTES: Host of 1989 Walker Cup matches; designed by Robert Trent Jones with Bobby Jones; ranked #87 in the world by Golf Magazine, 1993.

PEBBLE BEACH
LOCATION: Pebble Beach, Calif.
FOUNDED: 1919 PAR: 72 YARDAGE: 6799
CRITERIA: #3, Golf Digest, 1995.
NOTES: Host of three U.S. Opens, the latest in 1992 (won by Tom Kite), three U.S. Amateurs, two U.S. Women's Amateurs, the 1988 Nabisco Championships (now the TOUR Championship); annual site of the AT&T National Pro-Am; designed by Jack Neville and Douglas Grant; ranked #3 in the world by Golf Magazine, 1993.

PINEHURST (NO. 2)
LOCATION: Pinehurst, N.C.
FOUNDED: 1935 PAR: 72 YARDAGE: 7020
CRITERIA: #9, Golf Digest, 1993.
NOTES: Host of the 1994 U.S. Senior Open, the 1962 U.S. Amateur, the 1989 U.S. Women's Amateur, the 1992-93 TOUR Championships, the 1936 PGA Championship, and the 1951 Ryder Cup Matches; selected to host the 1999 U.S. Open; the masterpiece and home course of architect Donald Ross; ranked #11 in the world by Golf Magazine, 1993.

PINE TREE
LOCATION: Boynton Beach, Fla.
FOUNDED: 1962 PAR: 72 YARDAGE: 7201
CRITERIA: #86, Golf Digest, 1995.
NOTES: Host of the 1978 Senior Amateur; designed by Dick Wilson; just missed the top-100 world rankings by Golf Magazine for 1993.

PINE VALLEY
LOCATION: Pine Valley, N.J.
FOUNDED: 1922 PAR: 70 YARDAGE: 6667
CRITERIA: #1, Golf Digest, 1995.
NOTES: Hosted the 1936 and 1985 Walker Cup matches; designed by George Crump and H.S. Colt; ranked #1 in the world by Golf Magazine, 1993.

PLAINFIELD
LOCATION: Plainfield, N.J.
FOUNDED: 1920 PAR: 72 YARDAGE: 6865
CRITERIA: #43, Golf Digest, 1995.
NOTES: Hosted the 1987 U.S. Women's Open (won by Laura Davies) and the 1978 U.S. Amateur; designed by Donald Ross; ranked #97 in the world by Golf Magazine, 1993.

POINT O'WOODS
LOCATION: Benton Harbor, Mich.
FOUNDED: 1958 PAR: 72 YARDAGE: 7050
CRITERIA: #65, Golf Digest, 1995.
NOTES: Designed by Robert Trent Jones.

PRAIRIE DUNES
LOCATION: Hutchinson, Kan.
FOUNDED: 1937 PAR: 70 YARDAGE: 6593
CRITERIA: #21, Golf Digest, 1995.
NOTES: Host of three U.S. Women's Amateurs, the 1986 Curtis Cup matches, and the 1988 U.S. Mid-Amateur; designed by Perry Maxwell, remodeled by Press Maxwell in 1957; ranked #20 in the world by Golf Magazine.

PRINCEVILLE (THE PRINCE)
LOCATION: Princeville, Ha.
FOUNDED: 1990 PAR: 72 YARDAGE: 7309
CRITERIA: #72, Golf Digest, 1995.
NOTES: One of the first 1990s designs to be ranked; designed by Robert Trent Jones, Jr.

QUAKER RIDGE
LOCATION: Scarsdale, N.Y.
FOUNDED: 1926 PAR: 70 YARDAGE: 6819
CRITERIA: #22, Golf Digest, 1995.
NOTES: Designed by A.W. Tillinghast, remodeled by Robert Trent Jones in 1960; ranked #41 in the world by Golf Magazine.

RICHLAND
LOCATION: Nashville, Tenn.

PAR: 71 YARDAGE: 6825
CRITERIA: Host, 1980 U.S. Women's Open.
NOTES: Host of 1975 Junior Amateur and 1980 U.S. Women's Open.

RIDGEWOOD (EAST-WEST)
LOCATION: Paramus, N.J.
FOUNDED: 1927 PAR: 71 YARDAGE: 6938
CRITERIA: #97, Golf Digest, 1995.
NOTES: Host of 1990 U.S. Senior Open, 1974 U.S. Amateur, the 1957 U.S. Senior Amateur, and the 1935 Ryder Cup matches; designed by A.W. Tillinghast.

RIVIERA
LOCATION: Pacific Palisades, Calif.
FOUNDED: 1926 PAR: 72 YARDAGE: 7016
CRITERIA: #29, Golf Digest, 1995.
NOTES: Host of 1983 and 1995 PGA Championships and 1948 U.S. Open, the first won by Ben Hogan; designed by George Thomas, Jr.; ranked #49 in the world by Golf Magazine.

SAHALEE (SOUTH/NORTH)
LOCATION: Redmond, Wash.
FOUNDED: 1969 PAR: 72 YARDAGE: 6955
CRITERIA: #87, Golf Digest, 1995.
NOTES: Designed by Ted Robinson; scheduled to host the 1998 PGA Championship.

SALEM
LOCATION: Peabody, Mass.
FOUNDED: 1963 PAR: 72 YARDAGE: 6807
CRITERIA: #52, Golf Digest, 1995.
NOTES: Host of the 1954 and 1984 U.S. Women's Open, the 1932 U.S. Women's Amateur, and the 1977 U.S. Senior Amateur; designed by Donald Ross.

SAN FRANCISCO
LOCATION: San Francisco, Calif.
FOUNDED: 1914 PAR: 71 YARDAGE: 6627
CRITERIA: #23, Golf Digest, 1995.
NOTES: Designed by A.W. Tillinghast and one of his earliest courses; in contrast to Olympic Club, San Francisco G.C. generally frowns on big tournaments, although it hosted the 1974 Curtis Cup.

SAUCON VALLEY (GRACE)
LOCATION: Philadelphia, PA.
FOUNDED: 1957 PAR: 72 YARDAGE: 7051
CRITERIA: #83, Golf Digest, 1995
NOTES: Designed by William and David Gordon, the Grace course is more highly rated than Saucon Valley's Old Course despite hosting fewer national championships.

SCIOTO
LOCATION: Columbus, Ohio
FOUNDED: 1916 PAR: 71 YARDAGE: 6901
CRITERIA: #36, Golf Digest, 1995.
NOTES: Host of 1926 U.S. Open (won by Bobby Jones), the 1986 U.S. Senior Open (won by Dale Douglass), and the 1968 U.S. Amateur; designed by Donald Ross, remodeled by Dick Wilson in 1963; ranked 52nd in the world by Golf Magazine.

SEMINOLE G.C.
LOCATION: North Palm Beach, Fla.
FOUNDED: 1929 PAR: 72 YARDAGE: 6752
CRITERIA: #16, Golf Digest 1995.
NOTES: Perhaps the definitive Palm Beach course, designed by Donald Ross. Was home to the prestigious Seminole Pro-Am which attracted the top players in the country in the 50s and 60s. Ben Hogan used the course to 'tune up' for The Masters. Ultra-private; does not host national championships or professional tournaments.

SHADOW CREEK
LOCATION: Las Vegas, Nev.
FOUNDED: 1990 PAR: 72 YARDAGE: 7194
CRITERIA: #17, Golf Digest, 1995.
NOTES: One of the fastest appearances in Golf Digest's top-10 rankings ever; designed by Tom Fazio; ultra-private; ranked #70 in the world by Golf Magazine.

SHADOW GLEN G.C.
LOCATION: Olathe, Kan.
FOUNDED: 1989 PAR: 72 YARDAGE: 7051
CRITERIA: #82, Golf Digest, 1995.
NOTES: One of the new arrivals in the Golf Digest rankings for 1995, and one of the ten newest courses in the top 250. Designed by Jay Morrish and Tom Weiskopf.

SHERWOOD
LOCATION: Thousand Oaks, Calif.
FOUNDED: 1989 PAR: 72 YARDAGE: 7025
CRITERIA: #95, Golf Digest, 1995.
NOTES: Hosts annual Shark Shootout; designed by Jack Nicklaus.

SHINNECOCK HILLS
LOCATION: Southampton, N.Y.

FOUNDED: 1931 PAR: 70 YARDAGE: 6813
CRITERIA: #6, Golf Digest, 1995.
NOTES: Host of 1986 and 1995 U.S. Opens, 1967 Senior Amateur, and the 1977 Walker Cup matches; original course hosted 1896 U.S. Open and Amateur, and 1900 U.S. Women's Amateur; designed by William Flynn; ranked #9 in the world by Golf Magazine.

SHOAL CREEK
LOCATION: Shoal Creek, Ala.
FOUNDED: 1977 PAR: 72 YARDAGE: 7145
CRITERIA: #61, Golf Digest, 1995.
NOTES: Hosted 1984 and 1990 PGA Championships; designed by Jack Nicklaus; ranked #57 in the world by Golf Magazine.

SKOKIE
LOCATION: Glencoe, Ill.
FOUNDED: 1915 PAR: 72 YARDAGE: 6913
CRITERIA: #97, Golf Digest, 1993.
NOTES: Hosted 1922 U.S. Open (won by Gene Sarazen); designed by Donald Ross, remodeled by W.B. Langford in 1938.

SOMERSET HILLS
LOCATION: Bernardsville, N.J.
FOUNDED: 1917 PAR: 71 YARDAGE: 6512
CRITERIA: #60, Golf Digest, 1995.
NOTES: Hosted 1990 Curtis Cup matches, 1973 and 1983 U.S. Girls' Junior Amateur; designed by A.W. Tillinghast; ranked #84 in the world by Golf Magazine, 1993.

SOUTHERN HILLS
LOCATION: Tulsa, Okla.
FOUNDED: 1936 PAR: 71 YARDAGE: 6931
CRITERIA: #25, Golf Digest, 1995.
NOTES: Host of two U.S. Opens (the latest in 1977 won by Hubert Green), the 1965 U.S. Amateur, the 1946 U.S. Women's Amateur, and the 1982 PGA Championship (won by Ray Floyd); designed by Perry Maxwell; ranked #38 in the world by Golf Magazine.

SPYGLASS HILL
LOCATION: Pebble Beach, Calif.
FOUNDED: 1966 PAR: 71 YARDAGE: 6627
CRITERIA: #34, Golf Digest, 1995.
NOTES: Annual host of AT&T National Pro-Am; designed by Robert Trent Jones; ranked #68 by Golf Magazine, 1993.

STANWICH CLUB
LOCATION: Greenwich, Conn.
FOUNDED: 1964 PAR: 72 YARDAGE: 7133
CRITERIA: #76, Golf Digest, 1995.
NOTES: Designed by William and David Gordon.

SYCAMORE HILLS
LOCATION: Fort Wayne, Ind.
FOUNDED: 1989 PAR: 72 YARDAGE: 7240
CRITERIA: #75, Golf Digest, 1995.
NOTES: Designed by Jack Nicklaus.

TPC AT SAWGRASS
LOCATION: Ponte Vedra, Fla.
FOUNDED: 1981 PAR: 72 YARDAGE: 6857
CRITERIA: #40, Golf Digest, 1995.
NOTES: Annual site of The Players' Championship; hosted the 1994 U.S. Amateur; designed by Pete Dye; ranked #74 in the world by Golf Magazine.

TPC OF MICHIGAN
LOCATION: Dearborn, Mich.
FOUNDED: 1990 PAR: 72 YARDAGE: 6876
CRITERIA: Host, Senior TPC.
NOTES: Became the annual host of the FORD Senior Players Championship in 1991. Designed by Jack Nicklaus (ironically Nicklaus did not win his Senior TPC title here, but at Dearborn C.C., the previous host).

TROON
LOCATION: Scottsdale, Ariz.
FOUNDED: 1985 PAR: 72 YARDAGE: 7041
CRITERIA: #80, Golf Digest, 1995.
NOTES: Hosted the 1990 Men's Mid-Amateur; designed by Jay Morrish and Tom Weiskopf; ranked #81 in the world by Golf Magazine, 1993.

TROON NORTH
LOCATION: Scottsdale, Ariz.
FOUNDED: 1990 PAR: 72 YARDAGE: 7008
CRITERIA: #90, Golf Digest, 1995.
NOTES: One of the few courses to have two ranked courses; designed by Jay Morrish and Tom Weiskopf; ranked #70 by Golf Magazine, 1993.

VALHALLA
LOCATION: Louisville, Ky.
FOUNDED: 1986 PAR: 72 YARDAGE: 7115
CRITERIA: #51, Golf Digest, 1995.
NOTES: Designed by Jack Nicklaus. Will host the 1996 PGA Championship.

VALLEY CLUB OF MONTECITO
LOCATION: Santa Barbara, Calif.
FOUNDED: 1926 PAR: 72 YARDAGE: 6623
CRITERIA: #79, Golf Digest, 1995.
NOTES: Designed by Alister Mackenzie.

WADE HAMPTON
LOCATION: Cashiers, N.C.
FOUNDED: 1987 PAR: 72 YARDAGE: 7154
CRITERIA: #32, Golf Digest, 1995.
NOTES: Designed by Tom Fazio; ranked #66 in the world by Golf Magazine, 1993.

WANNAMOISETT
LOCATION: Rumford, R.I.
FOUNDED: 1916 PAR: 69 YARDAGE: 6631
CRITERIA: #47, Golf Digest, 1995.
NOTES: Hosted the 1931 PGA Championship (won by Tom Creavy); designed by Donald Ross; ranked #65 by Golf Magazine, 1993.

WILD DUNES (LINKS)
LOCATION: Isle of Palms, S.C.
FOUNDED: 1980 PAR: 72 YARDAGE: 6722
CRITERIA: #91, Golf Digest, 1995.
NOTES: Hosted the 1985 U.S. Senior Amateur; designed by Tom Fazio.

WILMINGTON (SOUTH)
LOCATION: Wilmington, Del.
CRITERIA: #92, Golf Digest, 1995.
NOTES: Hosted 1913 U.S. Women's Amateur, 1971 U.S. Amateur, 1965, 1978 U.S. Junior Amateur, and the 1978 U.S. Girls' Junior Amateur.

WINGED FOOT (EAST)
LOCATION: Mamaroneck, N.Y.
FOUNDED: 1923 PAR: 72 YARDAGE: 6664
CRITERIA: #27, Golf Digest, 1995.
NOTES: One of the few clubs to have two ranked courses; designed by A.W. Tillinghast; ranked #83 in the world by Golf Magazine, 1993.

WINGED FOOT (WEST)
LOCATION: Mamaroneck, N.Y.
FOUNDED: 1923 PAR: 72 YARDAGE: 6956
CRITERIA: #8, Golf Digest, 1995.
NOTES: Hosted four U.S. Opens (the latest in 1984 won by Fuzzy Zoeller), two U.S. Women's Opens (the latest in 1972 won by Susie Berning), the 1940 U.S. Amateur, the 1980 U.S. Senior Open, and the 1949 Walker Cup matches; designed by A.W. Tillinghast; ranked #17 in the world by Golf Magazine, 1993.

WYNSTONE
LOCATION: North Barrington, Ill.
FOUNDED: 1989 PAR: 72 YARDAGE: 7003
CRITERIA: #85, Golf Digest, 1993.
NOTES: Designed by Jack Nicklaus.

AUSTRALIA

THE AUSTRALIAN
LOCATION: Sydney, New South Wales
FOUNDED: 1978 PAR: 72 YARDAGE: 7148
CRITERIA: Golf Magazine Top 100 ranking, 1991.
NOTES: Occasional site of the Australian Open; designed by Jack Nicklaus.

COMMONWEALTH
LOCATION: South Oakleigh, Victoria
FOUNDED: 1919 PAR: 73 YARDAGE: 6777
CRITERIA: #88 (World), Golf Magazine, 1993.
NOTES: Designed by S. Bennett, Charles Lane and Sloan Morpeth.

KINGSTON HEATH
LOCATION: Cheltenham, Victoria
FOUNDED: 1925 PAR: 72 YARDAGE: 6814
CRITERIA: #35 (World), Golf Magazine, 1993.
NOTES: Hosts the annual Mercedes-Benz Australian Match Play Championship. Remodeled in 1928 by Alister Mackenzie.

NEW SOUTH WALES
LOCATION: La Perouse, New South Wales
FOUNDED: 1928 PAR: 72 YARDAGE: 6768
CRITERIA: #59 (World), Golf Magazine, 1993.
NOTES: Designed by Alister Mackenzie.

ROYAL ADELAIDE
LOCATION: Seaton, South Australia
FOUNDED: 1904 PAR: 73 YARDAGE: 7000
CRITERIA: #53 (World), Golf Magazine, 1993.
NOTES: Hosts the annual South Australian Open, and is in the Australian Open rotation; remodeled by Alister Mackenzie, 1926.

ROYAL MELBOURNE (COMPOSITE)
LOCATION: Black Rock, Victoria
FOUNDED: 1926 PAR: 72 YARDAGE: 6586
CRITERIA: #5 (World), Golf Magazine, 1993.
NOTES: Is in the Australian Open rotation; designed

by Alister Mackenzie. Generally regarded as the finest course outside of the United States and the British Isles.

VICTORIA
LOCATION: Cheltenham
FOUNDED: 1927 PAR: 72 YARDAGE: 6801
CRITERIA: #77 (World), Golf Magazine, 1993.
NOTES: In the Australian Open and Australian Masters rotations; designed by Alister Mackenzie.

CANADA

ASHBURN G.C.
LOCATION: Kinsac Lake, Nova Scotia
FOUNDED: N/A PAR: 72 YARDAGE: 7121
CRITERIA: Canadian Top 25, Golf Digest, 1982.

BANFF SPRINGS G.C.
LOCATION: Banff, Alberta
FOUNDED: 1911 PAR: 71 YARDAGE: 6729
CRITERIA: Canadian Top 25, Golf Digest, 1982.
NOTES: Designed by Stanley Thompson

BRANTFORD G. & C.C.
LOCATION: Brantford, Ontario
FOUNDED: N/A PAR: 72 YARDAGE: 6612
CRITERIA: Canadian Top 25, Golf Digest, 1982.

CAPILANO
LOCATION: Vancouver, British Columbia
FOUNDED: 1937 PAR: 72 YARDAGE: 6562
CRITERIA: Canadian Top 25, Golf Digest, 1982.
NOTES: Designed by Stanley Thompson.

CHERRY HILL
LOCATION: Ridgeway, Ontario
FOUNDED: N/A PAR: 72 YARDAGE: 6755
CRITERIA: Canadian Top 25, Golf Digest, 1982.

GLEN ABBEY
LOCATION: Oakville, Ontario
FOUNDED: 1976 PAR: 72 YARDAGE: 7133
CRITERIA: Canadian Top 25, Golf Digest, 1982.
NOTES: Annual host of the Canadian Open; designed by Jack Nicklaus.

THE HAMILTON
LOCATION: Ancaster, Ontario
FOUNDED: N/A PAR: 70 YARDAGE: 6750
CRITERIA: Canadian Top 25, Golf Digest, 1982.

LONDON HUNT
LOCATION: London, Ontario
FOUNDED: N/A PAR: 72 YARDAGE: 7168
CRITERIA: Canadian Top 25, Golf Digest, 1982.

MAYFAIR
LOCATION: Edmonton, Alberta
FOUNDED: N/A PAR: 70 YARDAGE: 6632
CRITERIA: Canadian Top 25, Golf Digest, 1982.

MISSISSAUGUA
LOCATION: Mississaugua, Ontario
FOUNDED: N/A PAR: 72 YARDAGE: 6860
CRITERIA: Canadian Top 25, Golf Digest, 1982.

THE NATIONAL
LOCATION: Woodbridge, Ontario
FOUNDED: 1974 PAR: 71 YARDAGE: 6975
CRITERIA: Canadian Top 25, Golf Digest, 1982.
NOTES: Designed by George and Tom Fazio; rated #1 in Canada by SCORE Magazine.

THE ROYAL COLWOOD
LOCATION: Victoria, British Columbia
FOUNDED: N/A PAR: 70 YARDAGE: 6425
CRITERIA: Canadian Top 25, Golf Digest, 1982.

THE ROYAL MONTREAL (BLUE)
LOCATION: Ile Bizard, Quebec
FOUNDED: 1873 PAR: 70 YARDAGE: 6433
CRITERIA: Canadian Top 25, Golf Digest, 1982.
NOTES: Hosted the 1975 and 1980 Canadian Opens; present facility designed by Dick Wilson in 1959.

ST. GEORGE'S
LOCATION: Islington, Ontario
FOUNDED: N/A PAR: 71 YARDAGE: 6797
CRITERIA: Canadian Top 25, Golf Digest, 1982.

COLOMBIA

EL RINCON
LOCATION: Bogota
FOUNDED: 1960 PAR: 72 YARDAGE: 7516
CRITERIA: Golf Magazine Top 100 (World), 1991.
NOTES: Along with Lagunita, considered the finest of the South American courses; designed by Robert Trent Jones.

DOMINICAN REPUBLIC

CASA DE CAMPO
LOCATION: La Romana
FOUNDED: 1972 PAR: 72 YARDAGE: 6888
CRITERIA: #29 Golf Magazine (World), 1993.
NOTES: The course is known as Teeth of the Dog. One of the earliest gems from the design portfolio of Pete Dye. Considered the finest Caribbean course.

ENGLAND

ALWOODLEY
LOCATION: Leeds, Yorkshire
FOUNDED: 1908 PAR: 70 YARDAGE: 6686
CRITERIA: #33, Golf World (U.K.), 1988.
NOTES: Designed by Colt and Alison.

THE BELFRY
LOCATION: Sutton Coldfield, West Midlands
FOUNDED: 1977 PAR: 73 YARDAGE: 6975
CRITERIA: #35 Golf World (U.K.), 1988.
NOTES: Hosted the 1985, 1987, and 1993 Ryder Cup matches; designed by Peter Alliss.

BERKSHIRE (RED)
LOCATION: Ascot, Berkshire
FOUNDED: 1928 PAR: 72 YARDAGE: 6356
CRITERIA: #20, Golf World (U.K.), 1988.
NOTES: Designed by Herbert Fowler, H.S. Colt and Tom Simpson.

FORMBY
LOCATION: Formby, Merseyside
FOUNDED: 1884 PAR: 72 YARDAGE: 6781
CRITERIA: #23, Golf World (U.K.), 1988.

GANTON
LOCATION: Ganton, Yorkshire
FOUNDED: 1891 PAR: 72 YARDAGE: 6693
CRITERIA: #14, Golf World (U.K.), 1988.
NOTES: Hosted the 1949 Ryder Cup; ranked #68 in the world by Golf Magazine, 1993; designed by Tom Dunn and Harry Vardon.

HILLSIDE
LOCATION: Southport, Merseyside
FOUNDED: 1909 PAR: 72 YARDAGE: 6850
CRITERIA: #19, Golf World (U.K.), 1988.
NOTES: Designed by Fred Hawtree.

LINDRICK
LOCATION: Worksop, Yorkshire
FOUNDED: 1891 PAR: 71 YARDAGE: 6615
CRITERIA: #31, Golf World (U.K.), 1988.
NOTES: Hosted 1957 Ryder Cup matches; designed by Tom Dunn.

LITTLE ASTON
LOCATION: Streetly, West Midlands
FOUNDED: 1908 PAR: 72 YARDAGE: 6724
CRITERIA: #27, Golf World (U.K.), 1988.
NOTES: Designed by Harry Vardon.

NOTTS
LOCATION: Hollinwell, Nottinghamshire
FOUNDED: 1887 PAR: 72 YARDAGE: 7020
CRITERIA: #24, Golf World (U.K.), 1988.
NOTES: Designed by Willie Park, Jr.

ROYAL BIRKDALE
LOCATION: Southport, Merseyside
FOUNDED: 1889 PAR: 71 YARDAGE: 6968
CRITERIA: #2, Golf World (U.K.), 1988.
NOTES: Hosted six British Opens (the latest in 1991 won by Ian Baker-Finch), and the 1965 and 1969 Ryder Cup matches; designed by George Lowe, remodeled in 1931 by Fred Hawtree; ranked #21 in the world by Golf Magazine, 1993.

ROYAL LIVERPOOL (HOYLAKE)
LOCATION: Hoylake, Merseyside
FOUNDED: 1869 PAR: 72 YARDAGE: 7110
CRITERIA: #26, Golf World (U.K.), 1988.
NOTES: Hosted ten British Opens (the latest in 1967, won by Roberto De Vicenzo); designed by R. Chambers, G. Morris, and John Braid; ranked #78 in the world by Golf Magazine, 1993.

ROYAL LYTHAM & ST. ANNE'S
LOCATION: Lytham St. Anne's, Lancashire
FOUNDED: 1886 PAR: 71 YARDAGE: 6673
CRITERIA: #13, Golf World (U.K.), 1988.
NOTES: Hosted eight British Opens (the latest in 1988, won by Seve Ballesteros), plus the 1961 and 1977 Ryder Cup matches; designed by George Lowe; ranked #67 in the world by Golf Magazine, 1993.

ROYAL ST. GEORGE'S
LOCATION: Sandwich, Kent
FOUNDED: 1887 PAR: 70 YARDAGE: 6891
CRITERIA: #18, Golf World (U.K.), 1988.

NOTES: Hosted twelve British Opens (the latest in 1993 won by Greg Norman); designed by Laidlaw Purves; ranked #26 in the world by Golf Magazine, 1993.

ROYAL WEST NORFOLK
LOCATION: Brancaster, Norfolk
FOUNDED: 1892 PAR: 71 YARDAGE: 6428
CRITERIA: #39, Golf World (U.K.), 1988.
NOTES: Designed by Horace Hutchinson.

SAUNTON (EAST)
LOCATION: Braunton, Devon
FOUNDED: 1897 PAR: 71 YARDAGE: 6703
CRITERIA: #29, Golf World (U.K.), 1988.
NOTES: Designed by Herbert Fowler.

SUNNINGDALE (NEW)
LOCATION: Sunningdale, Surrey
FOUNDED: N/A PAR: 70 YARDAGE: 6676
CRITERIA: #25, Golf World (U.K.), 1988.
NOTES: One of the few clubs to have two ranked courses; designed by Harry Colt.

SUNNINGDALE (OLD)
LOCATION: Sunningdale, Surrey
FOUNDED: 1901 PAR: 70 YARDAGE: 6580
CRITERIA: #8, Golf World (U.K.), 1988.
NOTES: Designed by Willie Park, Jr.; ranked #40 in the world by Golf Magazine, 1993. Hosted 1903 British Match Play and remains on the European Tour rotation.

SWINLEY FOREST
LOCATION: Ascot, Berkshire
FOUNDED: 1909 PAR: 68 YARDAGE: 6001
CRITERIA: #36, Golf World (U.K.), 1988.
NOTES: designed by Harry Colt.

WALTON HEATH (OLD)
LOCATION: Tadworth, Surrey
FOUNDED: 1904 PAR: 73 YARDAGE: 6813
CRITERIA: #38, Golf World (U.K.), 1988.
NOTES: Hosted 1981 Ryder Cup matches, and two European Opens; designed by Herbert Fowler; ranked #76 in the world by Golf Magazine, 1993.

WENTWORTH (WEST)
LOCATION: Virginia Water, Surrey
FOUNDED: 1924 PAR: 72 YARDAGE: 6945
CRITERIA: #12, Golf World (U.K.), 1988.
NOTES: Hosted the 1953 Ryder Cup; designed by Colt, Alison, and Morrison; ranked #61 in the world by Golf Magazine, 1993.

WOODHALL SPA
LOCATION: Woodhall Spa, Lincolnshire
FOUNDED: 1905 PAR: 73 YARDAGE: 6866
CRITERIA: #10, Golf World (U.K.), 1988.
NOTES: Designed by S.V. Hotchkin and Harry Vardon; ranked #27 in the world by Golf Magazine, 1993.

FRANCE

CHANTILLY (OLD)
LOCATION: Chantilly
FOUNDED: N/A PAR: 71 YARDAGE: 7214
CRITERIA: European Top 20 Courses, Golf World (U.K.), 1988.
NOTES: Hosted many French Opens, beginning in 1913; designed by Tom Simpson.

LE TOQUET (MER)
LOCATION: Le Toquet
FOUNDED: 1916 PAR: 72 YARDAGE: 6807
CRITERIA: European Top 20 Courses, Golf World (U.K.), 1988.
NOTES: Designed by Harry Holt.

MORFONTAINE
LOCATION: Senlis
FOUNDED: 1927 PAR: 70 YARDAGE: 6630
CRITERIA: European Top 20 Courses, Golf World (U.K.), 1988.
NOTES: Designed by Tom Simpson; ranked #85 in the world by Golf Magazine, 1993.

SEIGNOSSE
LOCATION: Seignosse
FOUNDED: 1990 PAR: N/A YARDAGE: N/A
CRITERIA: Golf Magazine Hidden Gem, 1993.
NOTES: Designed by Robert von Hagge.

GERMANY

CLUB ZUR VAHR
LOCATION: Bremen
FOUNDED: N/A PAR: 74 YARDAGE: 7037
CRITERIA: European Top 20 Courses, Golf World (U.K.), 1988.
NOTES: Designed by Bernard von Limburger.

HAMBURGER (FALKENSTEIN)
LOCATION: Hamburg
FOUNDED: N/A PAR: 71 YARDAGE: 6480
CRITERIA: European Top 20 Courses, Golf World (U.K.), 1988.
NOTES: Designed by Colt, Alison, and Morrison.

HOLLAND

KENNEMER
LOCATION: Kennemerweg, Zandvoort
FOUNDED: N/A PAR: 72 YARDAGE: 6408
CRITERIA: European Top 20 Courses, Golf World (U.K.), 1988.
NOTES: Designed by Colt and Morrison.

NOORDWIJK
LOCATION: Noordwijk
FOUNDED: N/A PAR: 72 YARDAGE: 6463
NOTES: Designed by Frank Pennink.

INDONESIA

JAGORAWL
FOUNDED: 1978 PAR: N/A YARDAGE: N/A
CRITERIA: Golf Magazine Hidden Gem, 1993.
NOTES: A magnet for national and Asian tournaments.

IRELAND

BALLYBUNION (NEW)
LOCATION: Ballybunion, Kerry
FOUNDED: N/A PAR: 72 YARDAGE: 6477
CRITERIA: #28, Golf World (U.K.), 1988.
NOTES: One of the few clubs to have two ranked courses; designed by Robert Trent Jones.

BALLYBUNION (OLD)
LOCATION: Ballybunion, Kerry
FOUNDED: 1896 PAR: 71 YARDAGE: 6542
CRITERIA: #3, Golf World (U.K.), 1988.
NOTES: Designed by P. Murphy and M. Smyth; ranked #12 in the world by Golf Magazine, 1993.

COUNTY LOUTH
LOCATION: Baltray, Drogoheda, Louth
FOUNDED: 1892 PAR: 73 YARDAGE: 6978
CRITERIA: #37, Golf World (U.K.), 1988.
NOTES: Designed by Tom Simpson.

COUNTY SLIGO
LOCATION: Rosses Point, Sligo
FOUNDED: 1894 PAR: 72 YARDAGE: 6600
CRITERIA: #34, Golf World (U.K.), 1988.
NOTES: Designed by Colt & Alison.

LAHINCH
LOCATION: Lahinch, Clare
FOUNDED: 1892 PAR: 72 YARDAGE: 6699
CRITERIA: #30, Golf World (U.K.), 1988.
NOTES: Designed by Old Tom Morris; ranked #89 in the world by Golf Magazine, 1993.

PORTMARNOCK
LOCATION: Portmarnock, Dublin
FOUNDED: 1894 PAR: 72 YARDAGE: 7097
CRITERIA: #6, Golf World (U.K.), 1988.
NOTES: Designed by G. Ross and W.L. Pickeman; ranked #31 in the world by Golf Magazine, 1993.

ROYAL COUNTY DOWN
LOCATION: Newcaster, Down
FOUNDED: 1889 PAR: 71 YARDAGE: 6968
CRITERIA: #9, Golf World (U.K.), 1988.
NOTES: Designed by Old Tom Morris; ranked #7 in the world by Golf Magazine, 1993.

ROYAL PORTRUSH (DUNLUCE)
LOCATION: Portrush, Antrim
FOUNDED: 1888 PAR: 72 YARDAGE: 6772
CRITERIA: #15, Golf World (U.K.), 1988.
NOTES: Hosted 1951 British Open (the only course outside of England and Scotland to have the honor) and 1993 British Amateur; designed by Harry Colt; ranked #18 in the world by Golf Magazine, 1993.

ITALY

MILANO
LOCATION: Monza
FOUNDED: N/A PAR: 72 YARDAGE: 6799
CRITERIA: European Top 20 Courses, Golf World (U.K.), 1988.
NOTES: Designed by John Blenford.

PEVERO
LOCATION: Porto Cervo, Sardinia
FOUNDED: N/A PAR: 72 YARDAGE: 6386
CRITERIA: European Top 20 Courses, Golf World (U.K.), 1988.
NOTES: Designed by Robert Trent Jones.

JAPAN

HIRONO
LOCATION: Kobe
FOUNDED: 1932 PAR: 72 YARDAGE: 6950
CRITERIA: #40 (World), Golf Magazine, 1993.
NOTES: Designed by Charles Alison; ultra-private membership, no major tournaments.

KASUMIGASEKI (EAST)
LOCATION: Kawagoe
FOUNDED: 1929 PAR: N/A YARDAGE: N/A
CRITERIA: #54 (World), Golf Magazine, 1993.
NOTES: Hosted the 1957 Canada Cup; designed by Kinya Fujita, remodeled by Charles Alison in 1931

KAWANA (FUJI)
LOCATION: Shizuoka
FOUNDED: 1936 PAR: 70 YARDAGE: 6970
CRITERIA: #50 (World,) Golf Magazine, 1993.
NOTES: Designed by Alison and Fuijita.

TOKYO
LOCATION: Tokyo
FOUNDED: 1940 PAR: N/A YARDAGE: N/A
CRITERIA: Golf Magazine Hidden Gem, 1993.
NOTES: Designed by Komei Ohtani.

MOROCCO

ROYAL DAR-ES-SALAAM
LOCATION: Rabat
FOUNDED: 1971 PAR: 73 YARDAGE: 7329
CRITERIA: #99 (World), Golf Magazine, 1993.
NOTES: Annual host of Morocco Open; designed by Robert Trent Jones.

NEW ZEALAND

PARAPARAUMU BEACH
LOCATION: Paraparaumu Beach
FOUNDED: 1949 PAR: 71 YARDAGE: 6510
CRITERIA: #72 (World), Golf Magazine, 1993.
NOTES: Designed by Alex Russell and Douglas Whyte.

PORTUGAL

QUINTO DO LAGO (B&C)
LOCATION: Quinto do Lago
FOUNDED: N/A PAR: 72 YARDAGE: 7032
CRITERIA: European Top 20 Courses, Golf World (U.K.), 1988.
NOTES: Designed by William Mitchell.

SAN LORENZO
LOCATION: Quinto do Lago
FOUNDED: 1987 PAR: N/A YARDAGE: N/A
CRITERIA: Golf Magazine Hidden Gem, 1993.
NOTES: Designed by Joe Lee.

VILAMOURA (NO. 1)
LOCATION: Quarteria, Algarve
FOUNDED: 1969 PAR: 73 YARDAGE: 6924
CRITERIA: European Top 20 Courses, Golf World (U.K.), 1988.
NOTES: Designed by Frank Pennick.

SCOTLAND

BLAIRGOWRIE (ROSEMOUNT)
LOCATION: Blairgowrie, Perthshire
FOUNDED: 1889 PAR: 72 YARDAGE: 6588
CRITERIA: #38, Golf World (U.K.), 1988.
NOTES: Designed by James Braid.

CARNOUSTIE (CHAMPIONSHIP)
LOCATION: Carnoustie, Angus
FOUNDED: 1842 PAR: 72 YARDAGE: 6931
CRITERIA: #7, Golf World (U.K.), 1988.
NOTES: Hosted five British Opens (the latest, in 1975, won by Tom Watson); designed by Allan Robertson, Tom Morris, and Willie Park, Jr.; ranked #25 in the world by Golf Magazine, 1993.

CRUDEN BAY
LOCATION: Cruden Bay, Aberdeenshire
FOUNDED: 1791 PAR: 70 YARDAGE: 6370
CRITERIA: #40, Golf World (U.K.), 1988.
NOTES: Designed by Herbert Fowler and Tom Simpson.

GLENEAGLES (KINGS)
LOCATION: Auchterarder, Perthshire
FOUNDED: 1919 PAR: 72 YARDAGE: 6826
CRITERIA: #22, Golf World (U.K.), 1988.
NOTES: Designed by James Braid; has played host to the Scottish Open.

MUIRFIELD
LOCATION: Gullane, East Lothian
FOUNDED: 1891 PAR: 71 YARDAGE: 6963
CRITERIA: #1, Golf World (U.K.), 1988.
NOTES: Hosted fourteen British Opens (the latest, in

1992, won by Nick Faldo), and the 1973 Ryder Cup matches; designed by Old Tom Morris; home club of the Honourable Company of Edinburgh Golfers, the oldest golf club in existence; ranked #6 in the world by Golf Magazine, 1993.

ROYAL DORNOCH
LOCATION: Dornoch, Sutherland
FOUNDED: Unknown PAR: 70 YARDAGE: 6751
CRITERIA: #11, Golf World (U.K.), 1988.
NOTES: Designed by Old Tom Morris; ranked #13 in the world by Golf Magazine, 1993; the third oldest golf course, and the second oldest still surviving (after the Old Course).

ROYAL TROON (OLD)
LOCATION: Troon, Ayrshire
FOUNDED: 1878 PAR: 72 YARDAGE: 7067
CRITERIA: #16, Golf World (U.K.), 1988.
NOTES: Hosted six British Opens (the latest, in 1989, won by Mark Calcavecchia); designed by C. Hunter and Willie Fernie; the last course to date to receive the honorific "Royal" (1978); ranked #28 in the world by Golf Magazine, 1993.

ST. ANDREWS (OLD)
LOCATION: St. Andrews, Fife
FOUNDED: Unknown PAR: 72 YARDAGE: 6933
CRITERIA: #5, Golf World (U.K.), 1988.
NOTES: Host of 24 British Opens (the latest, in 1990, won by Nick Faldo), and the annual Alfred Dunhill Cup matches; the home of golf; the home of the Royal & Ancient Golf Club of St. Andrews, golf's original governing body; ranked #8 in the world by Golf Magazine, 1993.

TURNBERRY (AILSA)
LOCATION: Turnberry, Ayrshire
FOUNDED: 1909 PAR: 70 YARDAGE: 6950
CRITERIA: #4, Golf World (U.K.), 1988.
NOTES: Host of four British Opens (the latest, in 1994, won by Nick Price); course reconstructed in 1947 by C.K. Hutchinson and P. Mackenzie Ross; ranked #16 in the world by Golf Magazine, 1993.

SOUTH AFRICA

DURBAN
LOCATION: Durban
FOUNDED: 1922 PAR: 72 YARDAGE: 6576
CRITERIA: #6 (World), Golf Magazine, 1993.
NOTES: Designed by Waters & Waterman, remodeled by Hotchkin, 1928; ranked #56 in the world, Golf Magazine, 1993; hosted many South African Opens, beginning in 1924.

SPAIN

CLUB DE CAMPO
LOCATION: Carretera Castilla, Madrid
FOUNDED: N/A PAR: 72 YARDAGE: 6691
CRITERIA: European Top 20, Golf World (U.K.), 1988.
NOTES: Designed by Javier Arana.

EL PRAT
LOCATION: Prat de Llobregat, Barcelona
FOUNDED: N/A PAR: 72 YARDAGE: 6452
CRITERIA: European Top 20, Golf World (U.K.), 1988.
NOTES: Designed by Javier Arana.

EL SALER
LOCATION: Valencia
FOUNDED: 1967 PAR: 72 YARDAGE: 7092
CRITERIA: European Top 20, Golf World (U.K.), 1988.
NOTES: Designed by Javier Arana; ranked #55 in the world by Golf Magazine, 1993.

LAS BRISAS
LOCATION: Nueva Andalusia, Costa del Sol
FOUNDED: N/A PAR: 72 YARDAGE: 6778
CRITERIA: European Top 20, Golf World (U.K.), 1988.
NOTES: Designed by Robert Trent Jones.

PUERTO DE HIERRO
LOCATION: Madrid
FOUNDED: N/A PAR: 72 YARDAGE: 6941
CRITERIA: European Top 20, Golf World (U.K.), 1988.
NOTES: Designed by Colt and Alison.

SOTOGRANDE (OLD)
LOCATION: Sotogrande, Costa del Sol
FOUNDED: 1965 PAR: 72 YARDAGE: 6849
CRITERIA: European Top 20, Golf World (U.K.), 1988.
NOTES: Designed by Robert Trent Jones; ranked #98 in the world by Golf Magazine, 1993; will host the 1997 Ryder Cup matches.

VALDERRAMA
LOCATION: Sotogrande, Cadiz
FOUNDED: 1975 PAR: 72 YARDAGE: 6691
CRITERIA: #86 (World), Golf Magazine, 1993.
NOTES: Designed by Robert Trent Jones and Cabell Robinson.

SWEDEN

FALSTERBO
LOCATION: Falsterbo
FOUNDED: N/A PAR: 71 YARDAGE: 6671
CRITERIA: European Top 20, Golf World (U.K.), 1988.
NOTES: Designed by Gunnar Bauer.

HALMSTAD
LOCATION: Halmstad
FOUNDED: N/A PAR: 72 YARDAGE: 6540
CRITERIA: European Top 20, Golf World (U.K.), 1988.
NOTES: Designed by Frank Pennick.

SWITZERLAND

LAUSANNE
LOCATION: Lausanne
FOUNDED: N/A PAR: 72 YARDAGE: 6742
CRITERIA: European Top 20, Golf World (U.K.), 1988.
NOTES: Designed by Oscar Dollfus.

WALES

ROYAL PORTHCAWL
LOCATION: Porthcawl, Mid Glamorgan
FOUNDED: 1891 PAR: 72 YARDAGE: 6643
CRITERIA: #21, Golf World (U.K.), 1988.
NOTES: Designed by Charles Gibson, with James Braid, Harry Colt, John H. Taylor, Fred Hawtree, Tom Simpson, and C.K. Cotton credited in remodeling; the only course in Wales given the honorific "Royal." Hosted the 1995 Walker Cup matches.

HIDDEN GEMS

CHIBERTA
(Designed 1926) Biarritz, France

COLLETON RIVER
(1993) South Carolina, USA

DEVIL'S PULPIT
(1991) Ontario, Canada

ESTORIL
(1945) Estoril, Portugal

GRAND NATIONAL (LINKS)
(1993) Alabama, USA

GOLF CLUB OF GEORGIA
(1993) Georgia, USA

GOLF DE PAU
(1856) Pau, France

LAGUNITA
(1956) Caracas, Venezuela

LINKS AT KUILIMA
(1994) Hawaii, USA

NAIRN
(1887) Nairn, Scotland

OLD TABBY LINKS
(1993) South Carolina, USA

PGA WEST (NICKLAUS PRIVATE)
(1986) California, USA

PALMILLA
(1993) Baja California, Mexico

PRESTWICK
(1851) Prestwick, Scotland

PRINCE'S
(1904) Sandwich, England

ROYAL BURGESS
(1735) Edinburgh, Scotland

ROYAL CALCUTTA
(1829) Calcutta, India

ROYAL CINQUE PORTS
(1892) Deal, England

ROYAL MUSSELBURGH
(1774) Edinburgh, Scotland

ROYAL NORTH DEVON
(1864) Devon, England

SAND HILLS
(1994) Nebraska, USA

SANDPINES
(1994) Oregon, USA

TIDEWATER
(1991) South Carolina, USA

WORLD WOODS (PINE BARRENS)
(1993) Florida, USA

GOLF SCHOOLS

OVERVIEW: *Locations, rates, teacher/student ratios, and head instructors at every major golf school in the United States. Brief descriptions are included which discuss the program, and the staff in detail, including the names of prominent students and national awards and recognition. The Almanac does not endorse any particular instruction methodology or school.*

THE ACADEMY OF GOLF
PGA National Resort
1000 Avenue of Champions
Palm Beach Gardens, FL 32444
(800) 555-1212
In Florida: (305) 555-1212
Costs: From $895 for the three-day program.
Student/Teacher Ratio: 3/1.
Head Instructor: Mike Adams.
About the Program: If there's a "hot seat" in golf instruction, the head instructor at PGA National, the home of the PGA of America, has to be the one sitting on it. Mike Adams is the pro in question, and his program has not only passed muster for the PGA—it's become one of the best-known programs in the country, with a summer program at The Broadmoor in Colorado in addition to the main campus at PGA National Resort & Spa.

The Academy of Golf is a three-day program with a price tag of $895 (four days for juniors). The programs run Tuesday through Thursday and Friday through Sunday throughout the year at PGA National (Monday through Thursday for juniors). The satellite school at The Broadmoor runs from June through mid-September.

The PGA National experience is high-tech by golf instruction standards—biomechanical golf analysis, high speed split-screen video, quadscreen video analysis, laser analysis for putting, a full-time sports psychologist and personal physiologist for muscle development and exercise design.

It all sounds pretty forbidding—something like Dr. Frankenstein would think up. But Mike Adams actually puts his emphasis on the individual, on working with what the golfer brings to the school. The idea is to have the technology serve the student, not the other way around.

Each student is videotaped daily on the full swing and once on putting and pitching (putting and pitching techniques tend to be more individualistic—most reputable schools focus on teaching the repeatable full swing). The videotapes are recorded for personal take-home videos with graphics and computer swing analysis included. Each student receives a personal fitness analysis with a recommended program from the staff physiologist—as well as instruction on mental toughness and course management skills.

In short PGA National offers a range of instruction activities which, in its embracing of technology yet insistence on individualized instruction, offers a model for any aspiring golf school guru.

The Robb Report recently rated The Academy of Golf the finest program in the nation.

ACADEMY OF GOLF DYNAMICS
Colorado Springs, Colorado; Austin, Texas.
Programs: Three-day schools, February-November. Midweek and long weekend options available.
Costs: Colorado Springs, $695 to $995 per person. Austin, $600 to $825 per person.
Head Instructor: Bill Moretti, 1993 South Texas PGA Teacher of the Year and GOLF Magazine contributor.
Student/Teacher Ratio: 3/1.
About the Program: A number of fairly authoritative sources have rated this program one of the finest in the country, including Money Magazine, and Tom Kite went so far in GOLF Magazine as to rate this number-one! Both President Bill Moretti and Head Instructor Jay Bowden subscribe to the "Learning Styles" method of teaching, which acknowledges that different students learn in different ways. The trick

is, of course, to design a program that caters to individual learning styles without tumbling into chaos. Hence the low student/teacher ratios and an emphasis on the student and teacher as a team. Mental aspects of the game including course management skills are also taught. High-speed, stop-action videotaped analysis is employed, as well as specialized swing training aids. The program includes a Welcome breakfast and a Graduation lunch. The school offers assistance for area accommodations, but just in case we recommend Texas Timeshares in Lakeway (800-826-1841) offering two-bedroom villas, swimming, tennis, hot tub and a marina on Lake Travis for boaters.

AL FRAZZINI'S SCHOOL OF GOLF
Wesley Chapel, Florida; Lake Geneva, Wisconsin.
Quail Hollow Country Club
6225 Old Pasco Road
Wesley Chapel, FL 33544
(800) 598-8127 or (414) 248-8811
Programs: Five-day golf schools: October-May, Tampa; May-September, Lake Geneva.
Costs: $175 per person per day.
Accommodations: Included in package price.
Student/Teacher Ratio: 4/1.
Head Instructor: Robert Macmillan.
About the Program: Al Frazzini has been in the instruction business for over thirty years now, dividing his time almost equally between Wisconsin and Florida. His style is a hybrid of the range-oriented teachers and the on-course instruction pioneered by Ben Sutton—on-course instruction is part of the program, but so is long hours of work on the range along with high-speed, stop-action video analysis. New head instructor Robert Macmillan, a former European Tour player, carries on the tradition with extra focus on the mental side of the game and takes on anyone from the rankest beginner to the most ancient of veterans. Classes are quite small, and include forty hours instruction (a hefty bonus over typical five-day programs), 9-hole playing lesson, golf cart and green fees, club cleaning and storage, daily breakfast and lunch plus a cocktail party.

AMERICA'S FAVORITE GOLF SCHOOLS
P.O Box 3325
Ft. Pierce, FL 34948
(800) 365-6640
In Florida (407) 464-3706
Headquarters in Ft. Pierce, Fla; 20 locations nationwide including California, Nevada, Colorado, Arizona, Oklahoma, Illinois, Ontario, Connecticut, Pennsylvania, South Carolina, Florida, and The Bahamas.
Costs: From $535, rates vary tremendously depending upon location and length of program.
Student/Teacher Ratio: 4/1.
About the Program: America's Favorite represents one of the most successful national instruction programs in the country, and their success is all the more remarkable because they have de-emphasized the role of the celebrity instructor. Instead, like John Jacobs' program, America's Favorite is centered around fundamental, practical instruction from highly-trained yet low-profile instructors, with low student/teacher ratios and the aid of straightforward devices such as videotape replays.

Each of the staff instructors teaches golf full-time on a year-round basis—no moonlighting club pros picking up a few quick bucks—and they are all certified by the PGA or the United States Golf Teachers' Association. The programs are run at a variety of lengths in attractive locations throughout the country.

The typical program at America's Favorite includes five hours of lessons both on the range and in the form of playing lessons. Video analysis for analyzing swing faults and monitoring of progress is used. There are classroom sessions on theory and course management skills, and on-course play with the instructing professional. All golfers are grouped by ability and class size is limited to four golfers per professional.

Frankly, one of the prime advantages of the America's Favorite approach to golf schooling is the affordability. Considering the locations (which include Hilton Head, Palm Springs, Las Vegas, Tempe, Orlando and The Bahamas), the costs are excellent. One note, however—costs do not include meals, so make allowances.

In addition to the regular programs, America's Favorite Golf Schools acts as a clearinghouse for the International Junior Golf Association (IJGA), a division of the USGTA which offers a series of one week summer golf camps in four locations including Ft. Myers in southwest Florida and Hilton Head Island, plus a spring break camp in Orlando. Both options are definitely worth a look, as junior golf instruction has been somewhat overlooked by the major national golf schools.

The philosophy of America's Favorite Golf Schools is extremely low-key—there isn't much advanced swing theory here. Analysis, instruction and plenty of practice under close supervision is the whole program. The locations are excellent, the costs very favorable, and as a basic golf instruction and vacation package this one is a winner.

All schools regardless of location offer three or five nights accommodation, five hours of daily instruction including on-course play, daily videotape and critique, green fees and carts both during and after class, unlimited range balls, all taxes and full use of resort facilities.

ARNOLD PALMER GOLF ACADEMY
9000 Bay Hill Blvd.
Orlando, FL 32819-4899
(800) 523-5999
In Florida (407) 876-2429
Costs: Three-day (three night) single occupancy $1,150; commuter $750. Five-day (five night) single occupancy $1,850; commuter $1,250.
Student/Teacher Ratio: 5/1.
Head Instructor: Brad Brewer.
About the Program: The Palmer philosophy is to work with the individual's skills rather than forcing a new technique, and to stress fundamentals, the scoring zone, practicing like a pro, course strategy and attitude over complex mechanics. Academies are available at three ability levels—Beginners (20 handicap and above), Intermediates (10-19 handicap) and Advanced (9 handicap and below). Special programs are also available for executive men and women, seniors, parents/children and disabled golfers. All Academies include daily instruction from 9am-5pm, drills, exercises, video analysis, the Arnold Palmer golf instruction book and tape, daily playing lessons, gifts and awards. All prices include accommodations, cocktail party and farewell dinner, club cleaning and storage, unlimited use of resort facilities, and a special rate for extended resort vacation packages. Please note that Arnold Palmer does not personally instruct at or attend his Academies. His role is in the development of the program and techniques as well as in the selection of his instructors. Arnold does give frequent clinics and exhibitions to coincide with grand openings and anniversaries at Arnold Palmer-designed golf courses. To see Palmer at work personally, follow his playing schedule (selected Senior events, the Senior Skins, and the Masters) and look for announcements by Palmer courses in the area for a Monday or Tuesday clinic. He gives a good clinic and is worth seeing, especially for his analysis of the golf grip.

APGA also maintains an Alumni Progress Program. Alumni submit a videotape 30 days after leaving the school, and the instructor prepares a Progress Analysis Report free of charge with a detailed practice plan and suggestion list for continued improvement.

At the Saddlebook Academy for Young Golfers, Students in grades 9-12 combine a full-time accredited college prep education program with instruction from APGA. Each student receives five hours of classroom study and 4-1/2 hours of golf and fitness practice daily. On-premises housing matches five students with a qualified live-in house parent, comfortable lodgings and a full meal plan seven days a week.

AVIARA GOLF ACADEMY
7447 Batiquitos Drive
Carlsbad, CA 92009
(800) 433-7468
In California (619) 438-4539
Costs: Half-day schools: (alumni) $125. Weekend school: (1-1/2 days) $595, (1-1/2 days plus 18 holes) $695, (two full days) $695. Three-day school: $995. Four-day school: $1295.
Student/Teacher Ratio: 5/1.
Head Instructor: Kip Puterbaugh.
About the Program: The Aviara Golf Academy philosophy is to work with the golfer's current swing and to give practical instruction for correcting both minor and major swing flaws as well as tips for stance, alignment and execution in the short game. Playing lessons are video-taped and analyzed in the Learning Center to pin-point specific areas for additional work in practice sessions. While the instructors view tapes and make notes, the students are free to play extra holes at Aviara, a finalist for Resort Course of the Year honors from both Golf Digest and GOLF Magazine when it opened four years ago.

The practice range was designed by course designers Arnold Palmer and Ed Seay to incorporate fairway-quality tee areas, pitching greens, practice bunkers, specifically designed slopes for practice in uphill, downhill and sidehill lies.

The Half-day school begins with an opening clinic on the fundamentals of the golf swing, followed by full swing work moving from irons to driver, high-speed, stop-action video-tape sessions with playback and analysis including graphics, audio overlays and side-by-side comparisons with the world's best players.

The Junior clinics include swing work, video-analysis, side-by-side comparisons of the student's swing with the world's top players (emphasized here especially because of a junior golfer's ability to mimic physical motion), teaching how to construct a productive practice session, plus drills on putting, chipping, pitching and sand play.

The Weekend schools come in two styles—1-1/2 days or two full days (the student may elect to use the second afternoon for play on the Aviara course). Instruction begins with a clinic on the fundamentals of the golf swing, video analysis of past and current tour players' swings, demonstration of alignment and preshot routine, plus videotaping and analysis of each student's swing. Following lunch, students take on full swing work plus a session with pitch shots involving video-taping and working on pitch shot corrections. The second morning begins with full swing work and video analysis before moving into a session on putting and chipping before lunch. Students who return for the afternoon session receive special instruction in handling poor lies, plus a final long game and short game wrap-up session with the instructor, identifying specifics to continue to work on at home.

The full three- and four- day schools divide into two types: Beginners and Experienced players. The Three-day beginners school covers the fundamentals of putting, chipping and pitching on the first day, rules, full swing, exercises and instruction on creating a practice plan, followed by a third day with on-course instruction on rules and etiquette, video analysis of the full swing, bunker-play and a review.

The regular four-day school begins on the first day with a clinic on the fundamentals of the golf swing, video analysis of past and current tour players' swings, and videotaping and analysis of each student's swing. Following lunch, full swing work and instruction and video analysis of pitch shots is undertaken. The second day begins with instruction on the mental side of the game including visualization of the shot, followed by full swing work and putting and chipping sessions until lunch. After lunch there is a clinic in handling poor lies followed by full swing and short game instruction. The third morning is absorbed by a playing lesson on the Aviara course, with a playing lesson review, full swing work, bunker play and pitching instruction, a personal equipment evaluation and a closing session for the three-day school attendees. The optional fourth day is spent with a morning playing lesson and after lunch a playing lesson review, Q&A session on trouble shots and individual practice in areas of the game that require extra work.

All three- and four-day programs include take-home video, lunch daily in the Argyle Restaurant, unlimited range balls, private locker, cart rental, bag tag and notebook, the Aviara Golf Academy instruction manual and videotape and optional golf course play after school hours for a reduced fee.

BEN SUTTON GOLF SCHOOLS
2920 Market Avenue South
Canton, OH 44711
(800) 225-6923 or (216) 453-4350
Costs: From $450-$2225.
Student/Teacher Ratio: 7/1.

Head Instructor: Dick Sutton.
About the Program: Ben Sutton Golf Schools is the "Grandaddy of 'em All," having pioneered the concept of the national golf school back in 1968. Experience has its advantages, as shown when a recent survey revealed that 98% of former Sutton students said their game would improve as a result of Sutton instruction, 99% said it was worth their investment of time and money, 97% said they would recommend Sutton to their friends and 93% said that they would return for more instruction.

The 42-acre Ben Sutton learning facility is the largest I'm aware of except for the World Woods facility in western Florida (which does not have a golf school at this time). The facility has more than the usual driving range, practice bunkers, chipping and putting greens. It has entire holes constructed with real situations ripe for instruction—the uneven lies, guarded greens, pesky bunkers, impenetrable rough, sprawling forced carries over water and an assortment of trees to learn to hit through, over or around with confidence.

Primarily Ben Sutton shys away from quick fixes and emphasizes repetition and building muscle memory under real course conditions. The full-swing instruction puts a premium on development of a consistent pre-shot routine for proper set-up and alignment, shoulder turn, weight-shift and wrist-cock for maximum distance and control. Short game instruction emphasizes practice not only in familiar putting, chipping and sand situations but also on the pitching game from the odd distances—73, 98 or 129 yards—typical of game conditions.

The three-day school includes 16 hours of instruction, high-speed, stop-action video-analysis and instant replay, graph-check sequence photographs of the student's swing, instructional films, free golf after classes, club cleaning and storage and green fees and cart for non-school spouse. The five-day school is much the same except for instruction bumps up to 26 hours, while the eight-day school (the longest duration for any golf school in the country) features 31 hours of instruction plus two tournaments including a pro-am with instructors. Several "Beat-the-Pro" putting and chipping clinics help to break up the routine throughout the week.

BERTHOLY-METHOD GOLF SCHOOL
Edgewood Drive I
Foxfire Village, NC 27281
(910)281-3093
Costs: Three-day schools every Monday-Wednesday, March-November. $950 for regular school; $1500 for personal private instruction. Bertholy also gives

personal private instruction only during December and January. Note: 30-handicappers and higher and left-handers, personal private instruction only. "We love beginners and left-handers," explains Bertholy, "but the other students become confused."
Student/Teacher Ratio: 1/2 to 4/1.
Head Instructor: Paul Bertholy.
About the Program: The irrepressible Paul Bertholy, once described as "the best [instructor] in golf history," holds court adjacent to Foxfire G.C. in Jackson Springs, in the Pinehurst area. It's one of the most interesting programs around, where the instructors will sometimes outnumber the students, and where students will experience the Bertholy-Method Isotonic Swing Trainer, one of the earliest swing trainers developed and still one of the best.

Bertholy is a PGA master teacher and a former instruction editor of Golf Magazine, and works with one full-time assistant.

The Bertholy-Method refers to the swing that Paul Bertholy "cloned" from observation of Ben Hogan during the early and mid-1940s, and his efforts to teach that swing to golfers. (An interesting note: Bertholy's own swing is, in still photography, an almost perfect reproduction of the great Hogan's.) The program begins with Progressive Precise Intensified Conditioning, or sensitizing and training the muscles for the golf swing. A swing pipe developed by Bertholy is utilized to produce a sense memory of a correct swing. The program's aim is to reduce and contain the instinctive right hand cast, right arm thrust and right shoulder roll we all naturally manifest.

Bertholy also teaches the short game and putting techniques—the distinctive putting jab stroke used most famously by Arnold Palmer is the type taught here. Also, command and control of emotion on the course is addressed during the sessions.

In short, as the school's name implies, Bertholy teaches a system of golf, not modest improvement.

BILL SKELLEY SCHOOL OF GOLF
Main Street
Miami Lakes, FL 33014
(305) 828-9740
Gold Canyon, Arizona; Copper Mountain, Colorado; Miami Lakes, Florida; Niceville, Florida; Fairfield Glade, Tennessee.
Programs: Three- and five-day schools at Gold Canyon Ranch, Arizona, January-March; Three- and five-day schools at Copper Mountain Resort, Colorado, June-September; Three-, four- and five-day schools at Miami Lakes, Florida, November-May; Three- and five-day schools at Bluewater Bay Resort (Niceville), Florida, March-July, September-November; Three- and five-day schools at Fairfield Glade, Tennessee, June-September.
Costs: From $1500.
Student/Teacher Ratio: 4/1.
Head Instructor: Bill Skelley.
About the Program: The Bill Skelley method is a fairly regimented program taught by staff professionals who have gone through a two-year training program themselves. It's a program that has its focus on the mechanics of the swing rather than mental aspects of the game. High-speed, stop-action video analysis is utilized in conjunction with a Bill Skelley instruction handbook and swing training aids to communicate a correct swing sequence for the upper body, leg and arm muscles. A special bonus for corporate clients: TOUR veteran Bruce Fleischer is associated with the school and makes appearances at corporate schools and clinics by special arrangement.

The three-day program includes fifteen hours of on-course and range-based instruction, green fees and cart, two breakfasts and lunches, farewell dinner and welcome reception. The four-day program adds an additional breakfast, lunch and five hours of instruction including on-course work. The five-day program adds an additional breakfast and lunch, a second dinner and reception, and five hours of instruction.

CHUCK HOGAN GOLF SCHOOLS
Chuck Hogan Golf Schools
4880 Valleydale Road
Birmingham, AL 35242-9981
Reservations: (800) 345-4245;
In Alabama (205) 991-FORE
Costs: $695-$1795.
Student/Teacher Ratio: 3/1.
Head Instructor: Chuck Hogan.
About the Program: This is the school where Chuck Hogan hangs his hat, perhaps the best known of the coaches who focus on the mental side of instruction. Peter Jacobsen recalled a session with Hogan in which the coach pretended to toss five golf balls on the putting surface, telling Jacobsen, "Here, putt these first for me," and only accepted Jacobsen as a student after Jake reported making every one of the five imaginary putts.

Chuck Hogan schools offer three distinct curriculums. The Expert Schools are designed for the low handicap golfer who is interested in exploring the mental side of the game as the primary emphasis of study. The Golfers Schools provide a well-rounded approach to the game encompassing mental, mechanical, physical fitness, and club fitting instruction. In the Players School, students are paired with an instructor who actually takes the group on the course for "playing" instruction.

CRAFT-ZAVICHAS GOLF SCHOOLS
600 Dittmer
Pueblo, CO 81005
(800) 858-9633
In Colorado (719) 564-4449
Costs: $605-$2205.
Student/Teacher Ratio: 4/1.
Head Instructor: Penny Zavichas.
About the Program: A pioneer among golf schools, operating continuously since 1968. The instruction concentrates on building leverage with the body for a powerful swing, maximizing the release of that energy for power and proper rotation of the club face through the swing for a squared clubface at impact and straight shots. A special emphasis is placed on instruction for women, with women-only schools featuring female instructors. Personalized attention and care is the rule, not the exception, here—Craft-Zavichas prides itself as a "Non-factory-assembly golf school" and a good starting place for beginners, lefties and women.

The 2-1/2 day program includes four days/three nights accommodation, daily lunches and one dinner, 15 hours of instruction, green fees/cart for after class play, practice facilities and unlimited range balls, club cleaning and storage, the Craft-Zavichas Instruction Manual, video analysis (two camera, strobe effect, split screen system for simultaneous viewing from two angles) and a take home tape. Instructors add personalized comments and optics to the student's tape for follow up study. Bunker play and other trouble shots are covered in depth. Short game and long game instruction alternate every 75 minutes to keep energy at a high level throughout the day.

The four day program expands to 20 hours of instruction and six days/five nights accommodations, plus Welcome and Farewell banquets. The five-day school expands to 25 hours of instruction with seven days/six nights accommodations, plus a third dinner and two receptions.

DAVE PELZ SHORT GAME SCHOOL
1200 Lakeway Drive, Suite 21
Austin, TX 78734
(800) 833-7370
In Texas (512) 261-6493
Costs: $1310-$2975.
Student/Teacher Ratio: 4/1.
Head Instructor: Dave Pelz.
About the Program: Dave Pelz is on most short lists of the top golf instructors, as his costs reflect, and this school is concentrated on the short game, where three strokes can be turned into two and where improvement has the most direct impact on scoring. Noting that the short game accounts for 65% of the total shots per round, Pelz combines theory and outdoor execution sessions for wedge play, pitching, chipping, sand play and putting. Pelz structures his teaching to players of all ability levels, and thus on occasion amateurs are learning side-by-side with PGA and LPGA tour pros! Pelz has a Putting Robot on-site, plus Wedgy the mechanical wedge robot, video analysis, laser alignment and practice aids, all grouped into a Short Game Center designed to house the Short Game School.

There are three programs at the Pelz school. The Premier sessions are conducted by the highly skilled professional instruction team trained by Dave Pelz. The Executive sessions are priced approximately $500 higher—they follow the same format as the Premier sessions but include personal instruction from Dave Pelz (or in a few cases PGA TOUR professional Tom Jenkins). In addition there are four Alumni sessions per year which are priced at a slight discount off the Premier rate and which are restricted to graduates of the Dave Pelz Short Game School.

One of the most striking success stories for Pelz in the 1990s has been the resurgence of Peter Jacobsen's career. The clown prince of the PGA TOUR put himself under Pelz's tutelage and went on to record one of the most impressive spring campaigns ever seen on TOUR, with over $1,000,000 in prize money in 1995.

DAVID LEADBETTER ACADEMY OF GOLF
Lake Nona Golf Club
9100 Chiltern Drive
Orlando, FL 32827
(407) 857-8276
Costs: Two-day retreats from $1200-$2000.
Student/Teacher Ratio: 2/1.
Head Instructor: David Leadbetter.
About the Program: Just about as highly-priced as instruction gets, but Leadbetter is after all perhaps the most prominent golf guru in the world and has had phenomenal success with players such as Nick Price, David Frost, Ernie Els and Nick Faldo who have been extravagant in their praise of his observations and advice. His success with some players has been mixed—such as Ian Baker-Finch. Leadbetter is known not only as a celebrity instructor but as one of the top theoretical teachers—his swing theories focus on movement of the big muscles of the torso and taking the hands out of the action. Video swing analysis, the David Leadbetter Putting System, The Right Angle, Swing Mirror, Swing Links, and the Powerball are employed as devices to aid students. Students are encouraged not only to improve their

game but to come to understand it better and to become their own best teachers.

Leadbetter has, like most major teachers, a stable of staff instructors who handle the bulk of the instruction, but Leadbetter himself is available at super-premium costs for those who want advice from the Great Guru himself.

DORAL GOLF LEARNING CENTER
4400 N.W. 87th Avenue
Miami, FL 33178
(800) 723-6725
Costs: $300-$1275.
Student/Teacher Ratio: 2/1 to 4/1.
Head Instructor: Jim McLean.
About the Program: The basic program includes full swing instruction, video analysis, breakfast, range balls, gift package, instructional videotape and workbook. The Jim McLean schools have a 2/1 student/teacher ratio and a maximum of six students (Jim works with two additional instructors), while the Master Instructor schools feature up to 20 students and a 4/1 student/teacher ratio. Each program option includes approximately five hours of instruction in the Learning Center per day—but with the three and five day schools the program includes personalized on-course instruction (carts and green fees included in the package).

The Five-Day Players School is the most expensive format—for a good reason. This premium offering is for accomplished players only—men with handicaps of 12 or under; women with handicaps of 18 or under. The five-day program includes 35 hours of golf instruction at The Learning Center, video analysis and extensive on-course work. Students play 18 holes per day for four days with Jim and Master Instructors, and there is a 3/1 student/teacher ratio and a limit of 12 students. This option is offered typically only twice a year and fills up quickly.

In addition to the regular schools, Doral offers several special schools worth a mention. There are two Junior Clinics offered at Thanksgiving (two-day) and Christmas (three-day) which includes six hours of instruction, video analysis and a workbook. Yankee great Bobby Murcer and NFL coach Bruce Coslet attend one three-day school each per year and answer questions and socialize with the students. Finally, Doral offers a two-day pro-only school once a year, offering expert diagnosis and individual improvement suggestions; the program features Jim McLean and two Master Instructors and a maximum of nine students.

GALVANO INTERNATIONAL GOLF ACADEMY
P.O. Box 119
Wisconsin Dells, WI 52965
(800) 234-6121
(608) 254-6361
Ft. Myers, Florida; Green Lake, Wisconsin; Sturgeon Bay, Wisconsin; Wisconsin Dells, Wisconsin.
Costs: $135-$435.
Student/Teacher Ratio: 4/1.
Head Instructor: Phil Galvano.
About the Program: The longest running golf school in the nation, founded in 1941. Notable students have included Bob Hope, Johnny Carson, Carol Burnett, Morey Amsterdam, Milton Berle, Willie Mosconi and Dwight Eisenhower. The school doesn't attract quite such a high-octane crowd now that Phil Galvano Sr. is getting on in years, but the school has kept up with the latest technology, adding high-speed, stop-action video analysis to its usual techniques. Mental conditioning and course strategy are given strong emphasis in the program, which alternates morning instruction on the range with afternoon playing lessons.

THE GOLF CLINIC
P.O. Box 1129
Pebble Beach, CA 93953
(800) 321-9401
In California (408) 624-5421
Pebble Beach, California; Waikoloa, Hawaii.
Student/Teacher Ratio: 4/1.
Head Instructors: John Geersten, Ben Alexander.
About the Program: Small classes and personalized, fundamental instruction are the hallmarks of the program. The methods of instruction are outlined by John Geertsen in his book "Your Turn For Success!" and roughly speaking offer a balance of basic mechanics along with a positive mental approach which brings consistency to sound technique.

The basic three-day program is based at Poppy Hills, one of the sites of the AT&T National Pro-Am, and offers daily instruction, video analysis, video instruction tape, on-course instruction in the full-swing and short-game, a copy of Geertsen's book, and daily lunches. Daily rounds at the resort courses are offered, which is a decided advantage at Waikoloa with three outstanding Hawaii courses offered—and a positive boon at Pebble Beach, with Poppy Hills, Spyglass Hill and Pebble Beach rounds thrown into the package.

GOLF DIGEST SCHOOLS

Golf Digest Schools
5520 Park Ave., Box 395
Trumbull, CT 06111-0395
(800) 243-6121 (203) 373-7130
North Scottsdale, Arizona; Carmel, California; Fallbrook, California; La Quinta, California; Vail, Colorado; Tarpon Springs, Florida; Braselton, Georgia; Sea Island, Georgia; Sun Valley, Idaho; Chicago, Illinois; Bend, Oregon; Williamsburg, Virginia.

Costs: $500-$4500.
Student/Teacher Ratio: 3/1.
About the Program: Along with John Jacobs this is the biggest and best-known of the golf schools world-wide ... although far from the first. In 1971 Bob Toski and Dick Aultman started instruction under the Golf Digest banner, with one school that year. Golf Digest really hit its stride in the mid-1970s when future top instructors such as Jim Flick and Jack Lumpkin joined the staff. Legendary coach and two-time PGA champion Paul Runyan joined the staff in 1976. Jim McLean became associated with the schools in the 1980s, by which time annual attendance had passed 2,000 students.

So what is a Golf Digest School?

Well, firstly it is a school about fundamentals: posture, grip and alignment. But more than basic fundamentals and drills, Golf Digest succeeded in the golf instruction market for the same reason that IBM succeeded in the computer market: While everyone else sold gizmos and miracle-cures, Golf Digest sold service. As in individual solutions for individual golfers. As in credibility and a proven, reliable training philosophy. As in listening.

As golf schools proliferate, Golf Digest has lost some of the celebrity aura that surrounded the instruction staff—and at times the teaching breakthroughs seem to come from other schools a tad faster, but these schools still have the corner on name-brand recognition and the personal, student-driven style that built the empire.

Like all the major golf schools, Golf Digest is heavily into video-taping golf swings for analysis. An innovative feature is the fact that they store the images on computer to compare on a student's return engagement—a tactic pioneered for touring pros which Digest has expanded to the ordinary amateur golfer. Students also receive a take-home tape with voice-over analysis from their personal instructor.

The basic program includes full-swing, chipping, putting, pitching and bunker instruction, plus mental conditioning and course strategy. Students are skills-tested in each of these areas and an assessment is made for potential improvement. Each student also receives on-course instruction (except in mini- and two-day school formats), daily lunches, gift packages, a notebook, and unlimited range balls.

Program length runs the full gamut from two half-days to five days. There are five specialty schools in addition to the basic program: Low-Handicap (with an emphasis on shotmaking and scoring strategies); Ladies; Short Game; Couples and Parent/Child (a five-day program designed for learning and interaction between parent and child).

THE GOLF INSTITUTE

Innisbrook Hilton Resort
P.O. Drawer 1088
Tarpon Spring, FL 34286
(813) 942-2000
Costs: $575-$2000.
Student/Teacher Ratio: 4/1.
Head Instructors: Jay Overton, Lew Smither III.
About the Program: Founded by legendary instructor and PGA TOUR veteran Jay Overton, this has been one of the top-ranked programs in the country for fifteen years. The unique teaching methods feature intensive on-line sessions and on-course instruction, providing golfers with both confidence and consistency in their games. The philosophy is summed up by Jay Overton as "P.G.A.—Posture, Grip, and Alignment." Awarded a "Best of the South" award by LINKS Magazine in 1992, and well-deserving the honor. This program is really among the elite, and is one of the best managed as well.

The basic program is the four-day, three-night program, which includes breakfast and lunch daily, 16 hours of instruction with drills and exercises, on-course play and instruction, videotape analysis, green fees, golf club and locker room service, social functions, gifts and transfers.

The five-day school is the same except for three full rounds of golf and an additional four hours of instruction.

The Playing School ofers on-course instruction with Host professional Jay Overton, plus three afternoon sessions of on-line instruction and all the other amenities offered in the Golf Institute. Dinners are also included with The Players School.

The Junior School is restricted to golfers ages 10-17 of all skill levels. The program covers fundamentals, rules and etiquette and team competitions. Each student receives one-on-one instruction and play on-course with the professional staff. Schools are limited to 16 students, and include 30 hours of individual instruction, videotape analysis, all meals, and one resident counselor per two-bedroom suite.

The condensed Summer program covers all the

fundamentals of the game in 12 hours of instruction and two hours of on-course instruction. The Summer Institute includes breakfast and lunch daily and videotaped swing analysis, as well as gifts and transfers.

THE GOLF SCHOOL
The Golf School
9301 West Fort Island Trail
Crystal River, FL 34423
(800) 632-6262
In Florida (904) 795-4211
Ocean City, Maryland; Mt. Snow, Vermont.
Costs: $393-$1143.
Student/Teacher Ratio: 4/1.
Head Instructor: Jay Morelli.
About the Program: Jay Morelli has polished his method to the point that it's now trademarked—The Accelerated Method. It's a process of speeding up the process of golf instruction to the point that swing fundamentals and finesse tactics can be effectively covered in the one school. It's an interesting idea—one which makes one wonder why other pros haven't given so much thought as to how their techniques will stay with the student after school.

Posture, grip and alignment are the foundation of the instruction. High-speed, stop-action video is then brought in to address timing, balance and rhythm. On-course instruction is then added to the mix. The final goal is the elusive repeating swing—that same effortless flow first developed by Harry Vardon at the turn of the century and exemplified by Fred Couples today.

The basic program package includes five hours of instruction daily, video analysis, green fees with cart for after-school play, club fitting, welcome reception, farewell banquet, and lunch daily (daily breakfast included at Ocean City).

THE GOLF UNIVERSITY OF SAN DIEGO
17550 Bernardo Oaks Drive
San Diego, CA 92128
(800) 426-0966
In California (619) 485-8880
Costs: $895-$1535.
Student/Teacher Ratio: 3/1.
Head Instructor: Tom Wischmeyer.
About the Program: The Golf University was founded in 1988 by Ken Blanchard to reach out to golfers and bring them an easy-to-learn, individualized golf curriculum. Blanchard's innovative management ideas are applied to golf in a way that enhances performance and enjoyment of the game. Over 3500 students have graduated to date from the schools, which begin with goal-setting and working out a curriculum with the professional. The Golf University adapts itself to the student's needs, rather than imposing a training and swing regimen.

The typical four-day program includes an opening night dinner, four days of classroom and swing instruction work, on-course playing lessons, videotape swing evaluation with voice-over analysis, personal practice programs, personal club evaluation and fitting, physical evaluation and exercise program, instruction manual and notebook, take home video cassette, unlimited green fees and carts, range balls, club storage and shoe service, and deluxe accommodations on-site at the Rancho Bernardo Inn. The club-fitting service and continuous video analysis receive special emphasis, as well as transferring the teaching role gradually from the instructor to the student. The goal of the program is to have the students correcting their own mistakes, noticing what went well and where improvement can be made. Instruction ranges from the full swing right through the short game to putting. In addition, the Golf University provides a back-home practice program to continue the learning process beyond graduation.

GRAND CYPRESS ACADEMY OF GOLF
One North Jacaranda
Orlando, FL 32836
(800) 835-7377
Costs: $1125-$2675.
Student/Teacher Ratio: 3/1.
Head Instructor: Fred Griffin. Phil Rodgers is an advisor and instructor to the Academy of Golf.
About the Program: One of the most highly-regarded programs in the country, situated at the elegant Grand Cypress Resort southwest of downtown Orlando. The Academy offers a private and natural setting alongside the highly regarded Grand Cypress courses designed by Jack Nicklaus.

The Academy is based in an unusual technology developed by Dr. Ralph Mann called CompuSport. Mann studied and recorded the swings of 50 top PGA Tour pros (such as Nicklaus, Palmer and Norman) to create a computer model of a perfect golf swing, which is then adjusted by the computer to allow for the student's size and body type. By comparing the computer model with a high-resolution, slow-motion video of the student's swing, the instructors perform swing analysis and design a program to accent the student's strengths while correcting weaknesses. CompuSport also performs in-depth analysis of the putting stroke.

The Academy has its own 21-acre practice course, one of the only such facilities in the world, with par-three, four and five holes designed specifically by Jack Nicklaus to offer every challenge of the game for learning purposes. Uneven lies, fairway bunkers and rough shots pose realistic tests for the learning process. Club-fitting is also offered to analyze the ideal length, lie of club, swing weight and shaft flex for each student.

The standard school, the Grand Cypress series, offers three full days of instruction, plus accommodations at the Villas at Grand Cypress or the Hyatt regency Grand Cypress, unlimited golf on the 45-hole Jack Nicklaus-designed courses, lunch and beverages, welcome reception, comprehensive full swing and short game instruction, on-course playing instruction, CompuSport computer video analysis to take home with model overlay and instructor comments recorded live, club fitting, unlimited use of the practice range, three practice holes, club cleaning and storage, gifts, books and locker. The mini-schools offer most of the above, with the prominent exception of on-course instruction. Students attending the premium-rate Phil Rodgers series also receive a copy of Phil Rodgers' book Play Lower Handicap Golf.

Only the best teach at Grand Cypress, including longtime director Fred Griffin, PGA Senior TOUR player Phil Rodgers, and biomechanics expert Dr. Ralph Munn.

JIMMY BALLARD GOLF WORKSHOP
(800) 327-4202
Costs: $250-$795
Student/Teacher Ratio: 5/1.
Head Instructor: Jimmy Ballard.
About the Program: Despite the fact that Jimmy is still only in his early fifties, this is one of the pioneering golf school programs in the country and only the fact that so many teachers and schools now accept Jimmy's theories and emulate his methods disguise exactly how revolutionary a teacher Jimmy was and is. This is not for the faint at heart!

The seminar begins with a videotape of your golf swing, which is used as a reference point throughout the program. Ballard then launches into a seminar demolishing most of what you knew or thought you knew about golf instruction terminology. From there Ballard introduces his theory of swing connection, and then students go to work on establishing connection throughout their swings via one-on-one instruction on the practice range. At the end of the Workshop, each student is given a videotape record of his or her original swing, a five-six minute segment of personal instruction from Jimmy Ballard on areas of potential improvement, and finally the students' reconstructed golf swing taped at the end of the Workshop.

Sounds simple? Let's go back to the Theory of Connection for a minute. "Connection" is based on two statements. First: Ben Hogan's contention that the golf swing is as simple as making an underhanded tossing motion. Second: Ballard mentor Sam Byrd's contention that the golf swing that brought him 15 PGA TOUR victories wasn't any different than the baseball swing which won him, earlier in his career, a slot with the New York Yankees—the plane changed, but not the swing. Ballard formulated the theory that there is a strong position which every athlete, regardless of the sport, gets into in order to propel a ball forward—golf, baseball, tennis or football. Athletes, goes the theory, use the large muscles of the legs, torso and shoulders to deliver the powerful blow. This motion, this fundamental action common to athletes in many sports, is what Jimmy Ballard calls Connection, and Connection is what the Jimmy Ballard Golf Workshop is all about.

In addition to video analysis, the Workshop is the home of the Jimmy Ballard Swing Connector, a patented contraption which Jimmy uses to teach the connected swing. The Swing Connector "connects" the left arm to the left breast in a soft but restrictive manner. It prevents the left arm from running out of the left shoulder socket which, according to Jimmy, causes over 95% of all inconsistencies in hitting the golf ball. It's an unusual and highly effective device, and makes the Jimmy Ballard Golf Workshop certainly one of the most interesting programs in the country and one of the best.

JOHN JACOBS' PRACTICAL SCHOOL OF GOLF
7825 East Redfield Road
Scottsdale, AZ 85260-6977
(800) 472-5007
In Arizona (602) 991-8587
Costs: $275-$2695.
Student/Teacher Ratio: 5/1.
Head Instructors: John Jacobs, Shelby Futch.
About the Program: This is the big enchilada of golf schools—the largest of all golf schools worldwide and over three times as large as the second largest company (Golf Digest), with over 10,000 students graduating annually from Jacobs schools. Founded in 1971 by former British Ryder Cup captain and PGA professional Shelby Futch, the basis of the program has always been practical, results-oriented instruction, primarily in correcting the swing plane and in developing consistency.

Since 1971 the schools have grown to 30 sites stretching from the United States to Austria, Spain,

Germany and mainland China. The schools today are the official golf schools of Marriott Resorts and GOLF Magazine (where Futch doubles as a teaching editor). The schools boast that 40% of their schools today are comprised of repeat students. Jacobs offers corporate group schools, custom-designed incentive programs and convention clinics, a club making and club fitting subsidiary, a travel & tour company devoted to golfing getaways and a golf course ownership and management subsidiary.

The school offers instruction via International, Junior, Low Handicap, Short Game and Playing Schools options. A typical program will focus on teaching straight driving, a balanced and fluid swing, accuracy in the short game, playing trouble shots with confidence, approaching and reading greens like a pro, aligning and stroking putts with greater accuracy and developing a winning course strategy.

The standard school runs for two to five days and includes six hours of daily golf instruction, the Jacobs' Golf Manual, High-Tech Visual Analysis with high-speed, stop-action video, equipment analysis, gift package, accommodations, breakfast and lunch daily, opening and closing dinners, nightly cocktail parties, plus green fees and carts for after-hours golfing. Non-resort programs do not typically include cocktail parties or dinners, and breakfast may be continental style. Golf course privileges typically begin at 1:00 PM.

The short game school makes its focus the putting, chipping, pitching and sand play aspects of the game. Two five-day sessions are also available for Juniors, offered in conjunction with Texas A&M University, with five days of instruction, accommodations at the Texas A&M dorms, all meals and an 18-hole tournament. The junior schools are limited to boys and girls 13-16.

All classes are led by PGA and LPGA professionals—and John Jacobs' is one of the handful of schools with two of the Best 50 Teachers in America (as selected by GOLF Magazine) on staff, in Shelby Futch and Co-Director of Instruction Craig Bunker.

KEN VENTURI GOLF LEARNING CENTERS
The Market Place
7600 Dr. Phillips Blvd., Suite 72
Orlando, FL 32819
(800) 735-3357
In Florida (407) 352-9669
Costs: $25-$299.
Student/Teacher Ratio: 4/1.
Head Instructor: Ken Venturi.
About the Program: Who could resist a lesson from the original "Stroke Saver" himself, Ken Venturi, who has graced the CBS golf telecasts for years with his insights and instructional tips? Venturi appears at both schools on selected dates, but throughout the year his hand-picked staff of instructors teach the "Venturi System"—a proven program of basic fundamentals designed to meet the individual needs and goals of each student.

The Stroke Saver Clinics are conducted by the Center's staff, focussing on chipping, pitching, putting and bunker shots, just as in the CBS Sports "Stroke Saver" segments.

The half-day schools include 3-1/2 hours of instruction, take-home video analysis, and a special focus on the "Stroke Savers" short game techniques.

The full-day schools offer the best value, as they stretch to a full eight hours of instruction complete with a nine-hole playing lesson. Comprehensive full swing and short game instruction is provided, as well as the take-home videotaped swing analysis, a take-home audio cassette, lunch and refreshments. Students are paired with others of similar abilities. The Venturi School is well-grounded in the Venturi philosophy, and so one needn't wait for the maestro to make an appearance.

But Kenny's worth waiting for if your calendar is flexible. He makes his appearance at Hilton Head to coincide with the MCI Classic (April 10-16 in 1995), typically between Tuesday and Thursday.

LA COSTA SCHOOL OF GOLF
La Costa Resort
Costa del Mar Road
Carlsbad, CA 92009
(800) 653-7888
In California (619) 438-9111
Costs: $85 per hour.
Student/Teacher Ratio: 1/1.
Head Instructor: Carl Welty.
About the Program: A "must-consider" golf school, under the direction of Carl Welty, who teaches Tom Kite, Curtis Strange, Davis Love III, and Sandy Lyle, and who also was Jim McLean's teacher (see DORAL). His specialty is videotape swing analysis, and La Costa is considered by most authorities to offer the best video facilities in the world. Tom Kite once came in during the Tournament of Champions to check on his putting stroke by comparing putts from 1988 to those in 1993, and fired a record-tying 64 the next day including four ten-foot or longer birdie putts. Welty is a featured instructor in the Tommy Armour PGA Teaching & Coaching Summit. Welty ignores most of the truisms of golf instruction for a simple "First we determine where the ball went. Second, we figure out where the club went. Then we can start to fix the problem." Fix it he will. At fairly low costs.

Welty-World is high-tech, to say the least, and if you think at some stage that you've dropped into the 24th century, don't worry. You're not the first to have these thoughts.

The program offers Lebelon tape for sweet spot analysis, cybernetic repetition, laser beam alignment, swing analyzers to measure swing and accuracy, high-speed video cameras with super slow motion VCR playback, indoor driving in the indoor studio, and large full-length mirrors for swing analysis. Among the many unique teaching techniques Welty employs is to have students describe their feelings and the ball's action during the video recording, after Welty realized that golfers forget which ball felt good when they review video playbacks of their swings. Almost all instruction and certainly all video-taping is conducted on-source rather than on a range.

MARLENE FLOYD'S FOR WOMEN ONLY GOLF SCHOOL
5350 Club House Lane
Hope Mills, NC 28348
(800) 637-2694
In North Carolina (919) 323-9606
Costs: $399.
Student/Teacher Ratio: 3/1.
Head Instructor: Marlene Floyd.
About the Program: The Marlene Floyd program is taught by women and is for women—even the program assistants are female. It all stems from Floyd's observation that women, particularly those new to the game of golf, become intimidated less easily if instruction is given by other women.

The program begins with Basic Fundamentals, concentrating on grip, alignment, stance and posture. Floyd's instruction even can go all the way back to as simple a device as teaching students how to toss a ball and how to achieve the power positions for throwing or swinging. The school progresses to the full swing with irons and woods, emphasizing increased distance which, of course, is a particularly important subject in women's golf. The final phase of the two-day program concentrates on chipping, pitching, sand play and putting. The emphasis throughout the program is on a relaxed, natural swinging of the club like that taught by Floyd's renowned father, golf instructor L.B. Floyd and by legendary instructor Johnny Revolta. All instructors are PGA and LPGA certified, and Marlene leads each school in person.

NICKLAUS/FLICK GOLF SCHOOLS
11780 U.S. Highway 1
North Palm Beach, FL 33408
(800) 642-5528
In Florida (407) 626-3900
Costs: $1795-$4995.
Student/Teacher Ratio: 1/1.
Head Instructor: Jim Flick.
About the Program: All Nicklaus/Flick instructors are handpicked by Jack Nicklaus and Jim Flick and are under the direct supervision of Flick who is based at Nicklaus/Flick headquarters in Palm Beach. Their operation is part of the Golden Bear colossus in West Palm Beach, but they fan out to several sites throughout the country.

The program includes a seminar by a sports psychologist, one-on-one instruction on the full swing, short game and course management, video swing analysis, take-home video with computer graphic enhancement, golf equipment fitting and evaluation, a nine-hole daily round, and the popular 18-hole Tournament with prizes.

PARADISE GOLF SCHOOLS
Paradise Golf Schools
975 Imperial Golf Course Blvd.
Naples, FL 33942
(800) 624-3543
In Florida (813) 592-0204
Marco Island, Florida; Naples, Florida.
Costs: $100-$2275.
Head Instructor: Bill Beyer.
Student/Teacher Ratio: 3/1.
About the Program: This is a "Work with what you have" school, using videotape analysis at the commencement of the school to identify the golfer's natural abilities and plan out a program for the school and for after-school review. Following in the Ben Sutton tradition of on-course instruction, classes are limited to around twenty students and cover the entire range of instruction from rules and etiquette to full-swing instruction.

A masters program is available with instructor Jim Wright at the Apache Junction and Carmel locations. The format is essentially the same but the instruction with Wright is one-on-one.

The three-day program features 18 hours instruction, two playing lessons, tapes, instruction handbook, club cleaning and storage, green and cart fees, and club fitting. The five-day program adds nine more hours of instruction, an extra playing lesson and two cocktail receptions.

THE PHIL RITSON GOLF SCHOOL
2710 Butler Bay Drive North
Windermere, FL 34786
(407) 876-6487
Overland Park, Kansas; Myrtle Beach, South

Carolina; Pawley's Island, South Carolina
Costs: $530-$1410.
Student/Teacher Ratio: 3/1.
Head Instructor: Phil Ritson, Andy O'Brien.
About the Program: One of the most respected programs in the country, Phil Ritson doesn't have the name recognition of, say, David Leadbetter or Jimmy Ballard, but he packs 'em in, the professionals that is, at his schools. It's hard to say if a heavy turnout by professionals is a sign of a good school for amateurs—but if it is, then this is a fine one.

What's the school about? Fundamentals, mostly. There is a smattering of fashionable sports psychology instruction, and Phil is perhaps the only major instructor with a major associate who is left-handed and teaches from the other side. It's great news for southpaws, but not bad for righties, either. Watching O'Brien is like studying the golf swing in a mirror.

The basic three-day course involves 3-1/2 hours of instruction per day, and includes high-speed, stop-action video analysis, and a take-home video with audio comments from the instructors, a Phil Ritson video and unlimited range balls.

Ritson achieved a small amount of fame through his "Encyclopedia of Golf" video series. It established for a lot of people who hadn't heard much of Ritson that he really knows his golf. One of his professional students is one of my own golf teachers, and I can tell you that the instruction is precise and fruitful.

PINE NEEDLES/GOLFARI
600 Midland Road
Southern Pines, NC 28388
(910) 692-7111
Costs: $925-$1495.
Student/Teacher Ratio: 4/1.
Head Instructor: Peggy Kirk Bell.
About the Program: Pinehurst is loaded with top-flight instructors, but Peg Bell still shines head and shoulders above the rest—a legendary instructor for decades now, she still barks out her advice along with fellow instructors Dr. Jim Suttie and PGA TOUR professional Pat McGowan. Peggy Kirk Bell also offers highly-regarded youth camps and the famed Golfari, the women-only five-day program that did much to land Ms. Bell the Richardson Award for Lifetime Achievement from the Golf Writers' Association of America last year.

The Learning Center programs employ a combination of sight-sound-feel "cues" and concentrate on high-speed video to film the swing from different angles, using a computer overlay to turn the taped swing into a three-dimensional model.

From there, basics of the short game and full swing are addressed, as well as the psychology of the game, course management, physical preparedness and equipment evaluation. In addition to range work there is on-course instruction utilizing the Donald Ross-designed course. The combination of Peggy Bell, her staff of instructors and a Ross course is bound to excite the golf traditionalist—and the opportunity to study the short game on a Ross course should put this school on the short list especially if the short game improvement is on your list.

PINEHURST ADVANTAGE GOLF SCHOOL
Pinehurst Resort & Country Club
P.O. Box 4000
Pinehurst, NC 28374
(800) 795-GOLF
Costs: $850-$2195.
Student/Teacher Ratio: 5/1.
Head Instructor: Don Padgett.
About the Program: The Pinehurst Advantage Golf School has become one of the most respected programs in the country and is based in state-of-the-art video analysis, on-course and in-classroom instruction. The classroom area is a 4500 sq. ft. facility with a covered hitting area, video room and classrooms.

The basic program includes lodging at the Pinehurst Hotel, three meals daily, daily green fees on the Pinehurst resort courses, cart rental, club storage and cleaning, unlimited range balls, personalized video analysis and a taped record of schoolwork, personalized club fitting, access to all Pinehurst amenities and a graduation cocktail party and awards ceremony.

The daily schedule includes a morning clinic, full swing practice and videotaping, followed by short game around the lunch hour and the all clear to play golf after 2:30 pm on the Pinehurst courses.

The Junior program accepts boys and girls ages 11-17 with no handicap restrictions. These are week-long schools held in the summer and include adult supervision. Rules, etiquette and fundamentals are stressed, the last via supervised instruction, drills, exercises and playing lessons. There is also an Advanced Junior Golf Advantage School restricted to golfers with 15 handicaps or less.

Juniors and adults take weekends or week-long programs of instruction, and one would be hard pressed to name any better course for learning than the famed Pinehurst No. 2—which is a golf school all in itself.

PROFESSIONAL GOLF SCHOOLS OF AMERICA
4105 Luff Street #1, Panama City Beach, FL 32408

(800) 447-2744
In North Carolina (904) 233-9200
Summers P.O. Box 1543, Maggie Valley, NC 28751
(800) 447-2744 (704) 926-0132Mesa, Arizona; Hollywood, Florida; Maggie Valley, North Carolina; Mt. Pocono, Pennsylvania.
Costs: $425-$1490.
Student/Teacher Ratio: 4/1.
Head Instructor: Mike Lucas.
About the Program: One of the oldest acronyms around has to be KISS, for Keep it Simple, Stupid. It's indicative of this gentlemanly group that they've subtracted the Stupid from the equation—and present their teaching philosophy simply as Keep it Simple, or K.I.S.—no student is stupid in their eyes.

The K.I.S. program aims to expose misconceptions and teach clarity with respect to the golf swing. Mike Lucas says, "I'd venture that every golfer can get a lot better by grasping the simplicity of the swing rather than the complexities."

The five-day program features 25 hours of course or range instruction broken into one hour intervals, with sessions on video analysis and mental conditioning in between. In a departure from typical golf school protocol, on-course instruction is included in each day's teaching routine. But the most unique aspect of the school is the emphasis on teaching swing mechanics through extensive short game and short-iron instruction before moving on to long irons and woods. It isn't until the afternoon of the third day that students work with the driver, and repeated emphasis is given throughout the program to drilling in up-and-down situations—and this is the only school with a scheduled session on the crucial area of lag putting....and PGSA adds another session on reading greens. Bravo!

Video analysis is given perhaps less emphasis here than high-tech oriented schools—the key here is personal instruction and a well-structured program. Mike Lucas abhors 'Paralysis through Analysis' so students should expect to spend more time grooving their swings than looking at them and discussing the latest in kinaesthetic philosophy.

Each school includes all range balls, daily green fees, video analysis, bag storage and club cleaning, and the PGSA instruction manual.

RICK SMITH GOLF ACADEMY
3962 Wilkinson Road
Gaylord, MI 49735
(800) 444-6711
In Michigan (517) 732-6711
Costs: $300-$1848.
Student/Teacher Ratio: 4/1.
Head Instructor: Rick Smith.

About the Program: "Rick's not a method teacher, and that's what I like about him." So goes one of the recent testimonials to Rick Smith and his Academy. From a fellow by the name of Jack Nicklaus.

For several years now the Rick Smith Academy has been one of the hottest around, attracting pilgrims from both the amateur and professional ranks, including several stars of the PGA TOUR, to the Treetops Sylvan Resort in Northern Michigan or to Smith's winter headquarters at The Breakers.

The Rick Smith Golf Academy has three separate programs: the Rick Smith Signature Session, which is a three-day-a-week half-day workshop for four students. His Director of Instruction, Henry Young, conducts a half-day workshop four times a week, and an occasional weekend school.

The Rick Smith Signature Session includes two video tapes, unlimited range balls and a personally autographed photo of Rick Smith. The Henry Young Masters Session is broken into a full-swing session three times a week and a session on the short game each Tuesday. The session includes unlimited range balls and a personal video tape with audio analysis. The weekend session includes both full-swing and short-game instruction, unlimited range balls and a personal take-home video with audio analysis.

RILEY SCHOOL OF GOLF
P.O. Box 3695
Palm Desert, CA 92261
(800) 847-4539
Costs: $494-$1666.
Student/Teacher Ratio: 3/1.
Head Instructor: Mike Schroeder.
About the Program: Riley emphasizes personally fitted clubs and instruction in groups based on similar levels of ability. Technical instruction is balanced with physical training regimens, while leaving plenty of free time to apply lessons in unsupervised play or in enjoying the other resort amenities. A low student/instructor ratio is a decided bonus.

The overriding philosophy of the school is to "Simplify Your Circle" in the full-swing—to eliminate swing movements which golfers believe are essential and are actually superfluous or even harmful.

The program begins with morning clinics spent with the instructor working on improvements in mechanics and technique. After lunch, students opt for either continued technical work on the range or on-course playing instruction with the Riley instructors.

Personal evaluation is accomplished both through observation and high-speed, stop-action video. Students also receive an instructional video that can help in review of fundamental swing concepts.

Classroom instruction covers golf fitness, course management, rules and equipment selection.

The basic package includes daily instruction, accommodations, lunch, green fees and cart, club cleaning and storage and a follow-up with the teacher after the completion of the school.

ROLAND STAFFORD GOLF SCHOOLS
P.O. Box 81
Arkville, NY 12406
(800) 447-8894
In New York (914) 386-3187
Costs: $332-$1232.
Student/Teacher Ratio: 6/1.
Head Instructor: Roland Stafford.
About the Program: Roland Stafford Golf Schools are one of the most successful golf school operators in the country, and they attribute their success to their PGA-trained staff, the custom club-fitting program, the instructional tapes and books that are available of the Stafford method, the large student practice areas, small classes, and video analysis.

The Stafford Method avoids over-analysis of the swing—he emphasizes a good grip, understanding how connection between the arms and the body generates power, keeping a level swing plane, and maintaining a steady tempo for a smooth, rhythmic swing.

School begins with a presentation of the Roland Stafford Golf School Method and continues for morning work each day on assigned practice areas such as full swing, pitching, chipping and putting. Groups rotate through the various practice areas and participate in video analysis. School is complete by the mid-afternoon allowing for time to play on-course, practicing or enjoying resort amenities. In addition, golf etiquette and rules clinics are conducted, along with golf equipment presentations and demonstrations.

One unique feature of the Stafford program is the Frequent Golfer Reward Program. Second-time attendees receive a $15 per day discount, and the discount grows by $5 per day per visit (e.g. $20 discount for 3-time attendees, $25 for four-time attendees, etc.).

THE SCHOOL OF GOLF (EXCLUSIVELY FOR WOMEN)
2252 Caminito Preciosa Sur
La Jolla, CA 92037
(619) 270-6230
Costs: $850-$1875.
Student/Teacher Ratio: 5/1.
Head Instructor: Shirley Spork.
About the Program: While THE School of Golf is not for the rank beginner, it is one of the few programs available which cater exclusively to the needs of the female golfer. High-handicappers to scratch players are welcomed to study golf at the school and develop the confidence in a consistent swing which leads to a positive mental attitude and success on the course. All instructors are women, and the crew is led by the indefatigable Master professional Shirley Spork, one of the founders of the LPGA (along with Peggy Kirk Bell), and a pioneer in instruction for women.

The program begins with morning range instruction including full swing and pitching, chipping, putting and bunker practice in specially designated practice areas. Afternoons are devoted to playing lessons and one pro-am scramble tournament. Evenings are taken up with a number of social events. High-speed, stop-action video analysis is provided plus a take-home tape for after-school follow-through.

The program fee covers all expenses including instruction, books, tapes, range balls, seminars, green and cart fees, social events, accommodations, and airport transfers.

SEA PINES ACADEMY OF GOLF
P.O. Box 7000
Hilton Head Island, SC 29938
(800) 925-GOLF
Costs: From $500.
Student/Teacher Ratio: 4/1.
Head Instructor: Don Trahan.
About the Program: This is the school that camps out in the shadow of the famed Harbour Town lighthouse at Harbour Town Golf Links. Don Trahan, "The Swing Surgeon," heads the school, which is based on the Trahan method as explained in his book "Golf Plain and Simple" and its successors "Golf Tips Plain and Simple" and "Golf, Plain and Simple: Straight Golf."

There are three schools offered in th Sea Pines program. The half-day school/half-day golf includes four hours of morning instruction including full swing instruction, drills and exercises, written analysis and video analysis. Following the lesson players have the option of playing a complementary 18 holes of golf (alas, Harbour Town is excluded from the offer).

The Sea Pines Academy of Beginner Golf is a four-day program offering ten hours of instruction including a complete introduction to rules, set-up fundamentals, full swing, pitching, bunker play, chipping, putting, equipment recommendations and club fitting.

The Sea Pines Academy of Golf is taught by Don Trahan and Director of Instruction Rick Barry, and is a one-day school offering seven hours of instruction including full swing, short game, drills and exercises, video analysis, supervised practice, continental breakfast and lunch.

Individual lessons, private group clinics, and playing lessons are also offered by the Sea Pines instructional staff.

Trahan has developed a number of unique training tools to amplify the instruction offered in his books and video including The Plane-Trainer, Alignment-Arrows and Compu-Golf. Compu-Golf, a PC-and Windows-based computer program which gives a personalized diagnosis of swing problems and prescriptions for cures and keeps track of the student's progress each time the program is used. The program contains color graphics and analyzes over 30,000 combinations of grip, stance, posture, alignment, weight distribution and ball flight patterns.

STRATTON GOLF SCHOOL
Stratton Mountain Resort
Stratton Mountain, VT 05155
(800) 843-6867
In Vermont (802) 297-2200
Costs: $356-$880.
Student/Teacher Ratio: 5/1.
Head Instructor: Keith Lyford.
About the Program: To begin with, Stratton has each golfer fill out a questionnaire prior to attending the school to allow for complete tailoring of the school to each student's abilities. The objective is to work with students' strengths and weaknesses and suggesting one or two areas of improvement rather than rebuilding the entire swing.

The school features extensive high-speed, stop-action video analysis, teaching aids and drills, exclusive practice areas with target greens, putting and chipping greens, wide fairways, practice bunkers and teaching classrooms.

Two-day and five day programs are offered in both locations. Each program includes an instruction booklet, welcome party, graduation banquet, greens fees, and continental breakfast and lunch daily. The five-day program includes four days on instruction and a fifth free day for golf. The Instruction program includes 1-1/2 days of on-course instruction and a pro-am tournament.

SWING'S THE THING GOLF SCHOOLS
Box 200 River Road
Shawnee-on-Delaware, PA 18356
(800) 221-6661
In Pennsylvania (717) 421-6666
Costs: $645-$875.
Student/Teacher Ratio: 4/1.
Head Instructors: Rick McCord and Dick Farley.
About the Program: The Swing's The Thing teachers emphasize "Learning for a Lifetime" and the "Swing's The Thing Consistency System" in this low-cost, low-key instructional program. Swing's The Thing is a school that works with the student's individual swing rather than reconstruction—the goal is to achieve understanding of the swing and to achieve consistency of results from it. Ken Venturi, former Masters Champion Art Wall, and two-time U.S. Open winner Julius Boros are among the golf greats who have endorsed the school's methods over the years.

The basic program is a three-day school including 18 hours of instruction, use of the school's patented swing training devices, high-speed, stop-motion video swing analysis, club cleaning and storage, textbook, and a Swing's The Thing videotape. Hotel accommodations are included in the price.

Swing's The Thing also offers a One-day refresher school eight times a year in three locations, featuring seven hours of instruction, special attention to personal profiles and individual area of improvement, a new video analysis, a review of swing basics and short game drills.

UNITED STATES GOLF SCHOOLS
1631 S.W. Angelico Lane
Port St. Lucie, FL 34984
(800) 354-7415
Clearwater, Florida; Palm City, Florida; Sebring, Florida; French Lick, Indiana; Biloxi, Mississippi.
Costs: $320-$1850.
Student/Teacher Ratio: 4/1.
Head Instructors: Mitchell Crum and Mike Mallon.
About the Program: In an unusually designed and pleasing approach to golf instruction, the United States Golf Schools devote half of the instruction program to the short game, which gets short shrift at times elsewhere—and place heavy emphasis also with on-course instruction. Te USGS offers a nicely-balanced curriculum of short and long-game emphasis with plenty of on-course work in addition to range drills. In addition, each student works with the same instructor throughout the program, another relatively unusual feature. High-speed, stop-action video tape analysis is utilized throughout the school.

The basic curriculum includes five hours of instruction each day, two hours of on-course instruction, unlimited golf, club cleaning and storage, daily breakfast and dinner and unlimited range balls.

GOLF, BY NATION

OVERVIEW: *Key statistics, history, prominent players, tournaments, and courses, plus a census of golfers.*

ANTIGUA and BARBUDA

No. of Players (Rank): 100 (69)
No. of Courses (Rank): 1 (66)
Players/Course (Rank): 100 (6)
World Cup results 1995: Did not compete.

History: Golf has had limited exposure in Antigua and Barbuda, two of the former British West Indies which have only 32 square miles of arable land for its 64,000 inhabitants. Nevertheless, Antigua has the Cedar Valley C.C. to service the small number of local golfers, and tourists who swing through the islands on cruise ship packages. The islands have yet to produce a golfer of world-class ability.

ARGENTINA

No. of Players (Rank): 30,000 (21)
No. of Courses (Rank): 160 (12)
Players/Course (Rank): 188 (24)
World Cup results 1995: 23rd. Eduardo Romero finished 16th in the individual competition.
Prominent Players: Ruben Alvarez, Roberto de Vicenzo, Miguel Guzman, Fabian Montovia, Antonio Ortiz, Eduardo Romero, Adan Sowa.
Prominent Courses: Jockey Club.
Golf Professionals: 350
Prominent Publications: Golf en la Argentina, Golf Digest Argentina, Notigolf, and Green Fields.
National Golf Association: Asociacion Argentina de Golf, Calle Corientes 538-piso 11, 1043 Buenos Aires, Tel. 54-1-325-7498

History: In 1885, a group of British subjects brought golf to Argentina. The first golf club was founded in 1890, and the Association of Golf Clubs of the River Plate was founded in 1897. The Argentine Golf Association was founded in 1926, but it wasn't until the 1950s that Argentina first played a role on the world golfing stage, when the emergence of the great Roberto de Vicenzo led to Argentina's victory in the inaugural Canada Cup in 1953. The Canada Cup was subsequently hosted by the Jockey Club in Buenos Aires in 1962 and again in 1970. Roberto de Vicenzo was the victim in the famed scorecard controversy in the 1968 Masters, when he was excluded from a playoff because he had signed an incorrect scorecard (de Vicenzo did win one major in his career, the 1967 British Open in which he bested Jack Nicklaus by two strokes at Hoylake.)

In recent years Eduardo Romero has emerged as a prominent international player, winning both the Spanish and French Opens in 1991 after dominating the South American circuit early in his career. After the initial success in the Canada Cup (now the World Cup), Argentina was the runner-up in 1954, 1962, 1964, and 1970.

AUSTRALIA

No. of Players (Rank): 1,750,000 (4)
No. of Courses (Rank): 1,495 (4)
Players/Course (Rank): 1,171 (68)
World Cup results 1995: 2nd. Robert Allenby placed 14th and Brett Ogle 11th in the individual competition.
Prominent Players: Greg Norman, Jack Newton, Ian Baker-Finch, Peter Thomson, Craig Parry, Brett Ogle, Kel Nagle, Graham Marsh, Mike Harwood, Peter Senior, Wayne Grady, Steve Elkington.
Prominent Courses: Royal Melbourne, Royal Sydney, Royal Adelaide, The Australian National G.C.
Golf Professionals: 1,400
Prominent Publications: Australian Golf Digest, Golf Australia.
Collegiate Golf Programs: Australian Institute of Sport.
Golf Schools: Kooralbyn International School.
National Golf Association: Australian Golf Union, 153-155 Cecil Street, South Melbourne, Victoria 3205.

History: Golf was first recorded in the colony of Victoria, in Melbourne, in 1847. By 1851 golf had been introduced to Sydney by a Scottish-born enthusiast named John Dunsmore. Royal Adelaide was the first permanent club (although it was in hiatus for sixteen years from 1876-1892). The Australian Golf Club and Royal Brisbane followed in the 1880s but it was not until 1891 and the founding of Royal Melbourne that a club was founded that has survived without interruption until today. In the 20th century golfers such as Norman Von Nida and Peter Thomson brought Australian professional golf into the international spotlight with Thomson winning the British Open in 1951 for the first major victory by an Australian.

During the 1950's golf in Australia bloomed (albeit with an image as an elitist sport) with Australia winning the Canada Cup in 1954 and 1959, and the World Cup in 1970 and 1989, and Brett Ogle in 1992 and Peter Fowler in 1989 taking the individual medal in the event. Peter Thomson won the British Open five times between 1953 and 1965, while Kel Nagle edged out Arnold Palmer at St. Andrews. Graham Marsh and Jack Newton kept Australia in the international spotlight through the 1970s.

Golf boomed in the 1980s in Australia, with the emergence of international stars such as Wayne Grady (U.S. PGA champion in 1990), Ian Baker-Finch (British Open victor in 1992), and the hugely popular Greg Norman, winner of the 1986 and 1993 British Opens as well as over sixty tournaments world-wide. Economic downturns forced a reduction in the tour in the early 1990s, resulting in an exodus of the nation's most prominent players for the European and American circuits, with Brett Ogle and Robert Allenby showing the most promise. Increasing cooperation with the European Tour and participation in the President's Cup series has kept Australia, however, very much at the forefront of contemporary golf.

AUSTRIA

No. of Players (Rank): 24,735 (21)
No. of Courses (Rank): 73 (20)
Players/Course (Rank): 339 (40)
World Cup results 1995: Did not compete.
Prominent courses: G.C. of Vienna, Murhof.
Prominent Players: Marcus Burger, Oswald Gartenmaier, Rudolph Hauser, Franz Laimer, Johannes Lamberg, Klaus Nierlich.
Golf Publications: Golf-Revue.
Golf Professionals: 80
National Golf Association: Orreicher Golf-Verband, Eugen-Strasse 12, Vienna

History: Golf has been a minor sport until recently in Austria, but the Golf Club of Vienna dates back to 1901. The Golf Association was founded in 1931, but the game was abandoned during the Second World War, and the G.C. of Vienna was not refounded until 1947.

Oswald Gartenmaier and Rudolph Hauser became a well-known pairing in the World Cup and, although in eleven consecutive appearances together they finished no higher than a tie for 17th in 1974, both Gartenmaier (T11th, 1978) and Hauser (T16th, 1974) found individual success in the event. Gartenmaier made 21 appearances in the World Cup between 1965 and 1991.

The golf boom reached Austria in the late 1980s and, after playing host to the European Amateur Team Championship in 1987, by 1990 an Austrian Open was held as a stop on the European PGA Tour, played intermittently throughout the decade..

THE BAHAMAS

No. of Players (Rank): (est.) 1,100 (51)
No. of Courses (Rank): (est.) 26 (37)
Players/Course (Rank): 42 (1)
World Cup results 1995: Did not compete.
Prominent Courses: Cotton Bay Club, Paradise Island G.C., Lucaya G. & C.C., Divi Bahamas C.C., Bahama Princess Resort.
National Golf Association: Bahamas Golf Federation, P.O. Box N 4568, Nassau, The Bahamas

History: Golf in the Bahamas dates back to the late 18th century, but an early course laid out by Alexander Campbell did not survive. The first modern course dates from the 1920s, and while The Bahamas have yet to compete successfully on an international basis since earning independence from Great Britain in 1973, they have certainly provided some of golf's most stunning Caribbean-style courses. With the plentiful supply of resort courses, in fact, The Bahamas have the lowest ratio of golfers-to-courses in the world.

The Duke of Windsor (an enthusiastic golfer and former captain of the R&A) served as Governor here during the Second World War, and construction of The Bahamas' legendary courses began shortly afterwards with the completion of Cotton Bay (designed by Robert Trent Jones) in the late 1950s. Jones' design rival Dick Wilson was also active as a designer in these parts during the early 1960s. In recent years new courses by Joe Lee have added to the allure of the islands.

BARBADOS

No. of Players (Rank): 120 (68)

No. of Courses (Rank): 2 (66)
Players/Course (Rank): 60 (2)
World Cup results 1995: Did not compete.
Prominent Courses: Sandy Lane G.C.
National Golf Association: None.

History: As with many of the Caribbean island-nations, Barbados has lacked the large base of active golfers necessary to compete internationally, and is best known as the home of the outstanding Sandy Lane course.

BELGIUM

No. of Players (Rank): 15,000 (26)
No. of Courses (Rank): 40 (29)
Players/Course (Rank): 375 (44)
World Cup results 1995: Did not compete.
Prominent Players: King Leopold of the Belgians, Arthur de Vulder, Donald Swaelens, Phillippe Toussaint, Flory Van Donck.
Prominent Courses: Royal Zoute.
National Golf Association: Federation Royale Belge de Golf Chemin de Baudemont, 23B-1400 Nivelles Belgium 32-67-220440

History: Belgium has an association with golf that, in its probable early form of chole, precedes even that of the Scots. Chole was a game that combined elements of hockey and modern golf, and was played in the fields of Flanders as early as 1353. The game, which survives in Belgium, is thought to have been imported by Scots mercenaries and modified for play in the linksland surrounding Scottish port-towns. The modern game of golf was introduced to continental Europe in the late-19th century, with the oldest course—Royal Antwerp—founded in 1888. The Belgians' interest in it was sparked primarily by that zeal and success of Leopold, King of the Belgians (a cousin to the English royal family) who played very successfully in a limited number of amateur events in the 1940s, including advancing to the final eight in the 1949 French Amateur.

In the 1950s Flory Van Donck became one of the leading golfers in the world, tying for individual medallist in the 1954 Canada Cup and taking the Individual title in 1960 at Portmarnock. He also finished runner-up in the British Open in 1956 (to Peter Thomson) and 1959 (to a young Gary Player) Van Donck and Donald Swaelens were formidable in team play.

In recent years Royal Zoute has been the site of the Belgian Open, an annual stop on the European PGA Tour, but no Belgians have recorded any major successes on the Tour itself. Phillippe Toussaint and Andre Van Damme have been the most prominent golfers in the past decade. Belgium has also hosted two European Ladies Amateur Championships and the 1961 European Amateur Team Championship.

BERMUDA

No. of Players (Rank): 3,000 (42)
No. of Courses (Rank): 8 (49)
Players/Course (Rank): 375 (44)
World Cup results 1995: Did not compete.
Prominent Players: Dwayne Pearman, Keith Smith, Kim Swan.
Prominent Courses: Castle Harbour G.C., Mid-Ocean C., Port Royal G.C., St. George's G.C.
National Golf Association: Bermuda Golf Association, Box HM BX-433, Hamilton

History: Golf first organized on Bermuda in 1950 with the formation of the Bermuda Golf Association and, since 1953, Bermuda has been the site of the club-oriented Bermuda Goodwill Tournament which attracts teams from the United States and Europe.

One of the chief attractions of Bermudan golf is the Mid-Ocean Club, revered as one of the finest tests of golf in the world since its opening in 1925. But Bermuda has an excellent assortment of public courses and has become a highly-regarded tourism destination for golf.

In the 1980s Bermuda began competing in the World Cup; the team's best finish was 25th in 1993.

BOTSWANA

No. of Players (Rank): 1,100 (51)
No. of Courses (Rank): 6 (54)
Players/Course (Rank): 142 (21)
World Cup results 1995: Did not compete.

History: Botswana is better known as the home of the Kalahari Desert than as a golfing nation, but several courses have been built as a result of the British colonial influence dating back to the late 1880s. The proximity of Southern Botswana to the South African metropolis of Johannesburg and the fabulous resort complex at Sun City may mean that more courses may be erected in the interesting mountain terrain to the south, but for the present Botswana has yet to make a mark in the international arena.

BRAZIL

No. of Players (Rank): 8,000 (35)

No. of Courses (Rank): 42 (28)
Players/Course (Rank): 190 (30)
World Cup results 1995: Did not compete.
Prominent Players: Antonio Barcellos, Joao Corteiz, Jaime Gonzalez, Jose Gonzalez, Merio Gonzalez, Rafael Navarro.
Prominent Courses: PL Golf Club.
Prominent Publications: Golf Sport.
Golf Professionals: 50
National Golf Association: Confederacao Braseleira de Golf, Rua 7 de Abril, 282-s/83 01044 Sao Paolo
History: Golf was introduced to Brazil by the English and Scots, and the first club founded was Sao Paolo G.C. in 1903. The second course to open was the Gavea Golf & Country Club in Rio de Janeiro, in 1924. The first competition was the Trophy Boies Harte, which featured two eight-man teams.

The first amateur championship was played in 1934 at Gavea, won by a Mr. Bill Wooley. Martin Pose of Argentina subsequently became the first winner of the Brazil Open.

Golf has become relatively well-established in Brazil despite the overwhelming popularity of football and the prohibitive cost of course construction. Brazil has competed successfully internationally since the 1950s. The high point in Brazilian golf to date has been the 4th place finish of the national team at the 1979 World Cup played in Athens, where Jaime Gonzalez also finished fourth in the individual competition after being tied for the lead through the third round.

CANADA

No. of Players (Rank): 2,200,000 (3)
No. of Courses (Rank): 1,796 (2)
Players/Course (Rank): 1,225 (71)
World Cup results 1995: 17th. Rick Gibson finished 14th in the individual competition.
Prominent Players: Dave Barr, Al Balding, Dan Halldorson, George Knudson, Stan Leonard, Jim Nelford, Moe Norman, Rick Gibson, Richard Zokol.
Prominent Courses: Banff Springs G.C., Capilano G. & C.C., Glen Abbey G.C., The Hamilton G. & C.C., The National G.C., The Royal Montreal G.C., St. George's G.C.
Prominent Publications: Score Magazine.
National Golf Association: Canadian Golf Foundation, 1333 Dorval Drive Oakville Ontario L6J 4Z3, Canada (905) 849-9700

History: There is evidence of golf arriving in Canada as early as 1824, but the game began to flourish in Canada after the organization of Royal Montreal in 1873, only a few years after Confederation and well before the game took root in the United States. A club was subsequently founded in Quebec in 1875 by a daughter of Old Tom Morris. The first inter-club match in the Americas was staged between the clubs in 1876 and, with the founding of the Toronto Club in 1976, the oldest trio of North American courses was complete. One of the great curiosities of the development of the modern game is that no Canadian golfers emerged early on to further the popularity of the game in the manner of Hagen, Jones, et al in the United States. So, although the Canadian Open has been played continuously throughout this century and still forms a cornerstone of the PGA TOUR, Canadian golf has continued to be quite popular among the Canadians but very much a step-child of the American game in terms of mass appeal and international success.

Nevertheless, Canada has produced some excellent golfers and from time to time golfers such as George Knudson and Dave Barr have been prominent on the PGA TOUR. The World Cup originated at Royal Montreal in 1953 as the Canada Cup and was known as such through 1966. The Canadians themselves have won the Cup three times (in 1968, 1980, and 1985), while Canadians have taken the individual competition five times (Stan Leonard in 1954 and 1959, George Knudson in 1966, Al Balding in 1968, and Dave Barr in 1983). Canada also won the Eisenhower Trophy (World Amateur Team Championship) in 1986 at Caracas.

In recent years a Canadian Tour has sprung up involving a dozen or so tournaments, but the Canadian Open is still considered an official PGA TOUR event and the Canadian circuit only occasionally is able to attract the top players.

Canada pulled a major upset in late 1994 in winning the Alfred Dunhill Cup with a 2-1 victory over the United States in the final. The victory was Canada's most significant to date in proving the quality of Canadian golf.

CAYMAN ISLANDS

No. of Players (Rank): 100 (69)
No. of Courses (Rank): 1 (67)
Players/Course (Rank): 100 (6)
World Cup results 1995: Did not compete.
Prominent Courses: Cayman G.C.

History: The Cayman Islands, one of the last vestiges of British colonial power in the West Indies, has had a rather interesting impact on the history of golf because of the (failed) Cayman course experiment carried out in constructing a course on Grand Cayman. The land was too small for a regulation course, so rather than put in a precision-length course the developers hired Jack Nicklaus and developed the Cayman ball, which travels a much shorter distance than the standard ball. The intention was to build a series of Cayman courses where land prices or availability stifled golf course development, but the concept did not prove a hit with golfers and the original Cayman course is now something of a curiosity.

CHILE

No. of Players (Rank): 4,000 (36)
No. of Courses (Rank): 36 (30)
Players/Course (Rank): 111 (11)
Prominent Players: Edwin Corrie, Jack Corrie, Guillermo Gomez, Ricardo Orellana, Arturo Pellermo, Carlos Puebla
Prominent Courses: Casa de Campo (Teeth of the Dog)
National Golf Association: Dominican Golf Association, P.O. Box 641, Santa Domingo, Dominican Republic

History: Golf arrived in Chile during the late 19th century, with the formation of the Valparaiso Golf Club in 1897 (the club and course still exist today, as Granadilla).

The Federation was founded in 1932 and beginning in 1954 Chile has made regular appearances in the World Cup, with the 1992 entry (finishing in a tie for 11th place) being the most successful to date. Chileans have not been able to crack the Sony World rankings for individual play, but Francisco Cerda in the 1970s put in quite credible showings at the World Cup, his high point in 1974 at Lagunita in Caracas when he finished in a tie for 11th place.

In recent years the Prince of Wales Open has been considered part of the fledgling South American PGA circuit, and the Chile Open has been a regular stop for the top South Americans, with Eduardo Romero winning in 1984 and 1986.

CHINA

No. of Players (Rank): 500 (60)
No. of Courses (Rank): 4 (58)
Players/Course (Rank): 250 (36)
World Cup results 1995: 27th.

History: A shortage of suitable land and a capitalistic image have prevented golf from establishing more than a toehold on the mainland of China. The mainland had several courses built during the last years of the Manchu dynasty and the Nationalist period, and shortly before the Second World War the golf course tally reached a high of 11 courses including clubs in Beijing, Shanghai, Tientsin, Xingdao and even a small 9-holer in Manchuria. From 1924 until the late 1930s a Chinese Amateur was played in the International District of Shanghai. The courses and competitions were abandoned by the time of the 1946-49 Civil War. Today, the Chinese have a limited number of golfers and only two courses to date in the fourth largest nation on earth. The construction of an Arnold Palmer course in Guandong province by Arnold Palmer and Ed Seay, however, was been seen by many as the harbinger of change, and the staging of the Asian Games in Beijing during 1990, including golf as a competitive sport, expanded local interest in the game. In 1995, the Beijing Golf Club hosted the World Cup, easily the most significant golfing event ever staged in Asia, and a huge boost to the hopes of Chinese golfers that a new era is dawning for golf in the People's Republic.

COLOMBIA

No. of Players (Rank): 8,300 (34)
No. of Courses (Rank): 35 (31)
Players/Course (Rank): 237 (33)
World Cup results 1995: 30th.
Prominent Players: Alfonso Bohorquez, Eduardo Herrera, Juan Pizon, Paul Posse, Alberto Rivadeneira, Miguel Sala.
Prominent Courses: El Rincon.
National Golf Association: Federacion Colombiana de Golf Carrera 7a N. 72-64, Of. Int. 26 Apartado Aereo 90985 Bogota, D.E.Columbia

History: Although golf in Columbia dates back to the establishment of the C.C. of Bogota in the 1910s, the game began to flourish in Colombia in the 1950s, when golfers such as Paul Posse and Pablo Molina found success in the Canada Cup (placing 10th in 1955 and 1958). Late in the 1950s Miguel Sala (who finished 4th in the individual competition in the 1958 Canada Cup) established himself as perhaps the greatest South American golfer after Roberto de Vicenzo. Sala continued to play a leading role in Colombian golf through the late 1960s.

In addition to international success, Colombia is home to one of the finest courses in the world in Bogota's El Rincon, which hosted the 1980 World Cup.

Since the 1970s Colombia has enjoyed less conspicuous success in international competition, but Alberto Rivadeneira placed fifth in the 1980 World Cup.

COSTA RICA

No. of Players (Rank): 400 (63)
No. of Courses (Rank): 4 (58)
Players/Course (Rank): 100 (6)
Prominent Players: Jose Chavez, Manfred Hachner, Mario Herrera, Francisco Jimenez, Hector Jimenez.
Golf Professionals: 8.
World Cup results 1995: Did not compete.
National Golf Association: Associacion Nacional de Golf, Apartdao 10969, 1000 San Jose

History: Golf has had a foothold in Costa Rica since the Second World War, but the relative prosperity of this Central American nation has not yet translated into significant golf development. Costa Rica did field teams in the World Cup during the 1970s and early 1980s, finishing no higher than 36th. In recent years Costa Ricans have won the Central America and Panama Opens, and golf is experiencing a modest boom with the construction of several courses in the past decade, with a new layout on the Pacific Coast by Robert Trent Jones ready to debut.

CZECH REPUBLIC

No. of Players (Rank): 1,371 (50)
No. of Courses (Rank): 7 (52)
Players/Course (Rank): 196 (25)
World Cup results 1994: Did not compete.
Prominent Players: Jari Dvorak, J. Janda, Jan Kunstra, Miroslav Plodek.
National Golf Association: Czech Golf Federation, Na Porici 12, CS-11530 Praha 1 Czech Republic 42(2) 2350065-84

History: Golf was played in the old Austria-Hungarian empire—with the first course, at Carlsbad, dating from 1904—but golf has developed slowly in the Czech Republic largely due to the effects of the Cold War. The highlight of the pre-war period was the staging of a Czechoslovakian Open in 1935-37 at Marienbad.

Beginning in 1965 Czech teams were permitted to compete in the World Cup: amateurs Jari Dvorak and Jan Kunstra played together in five consecutive events without much success, their best finish being 36th place in 1966.

Since 1971, Czechs have rarely competed internationally but have maintained a lively amateur championship for men and women. The Czech Republic has been mentioned frequently as a country well-suited to a rapid expansion of the game.

DENMARK

No. of Players (Rank): 34,000 (20)
No. of Courses (Rank): 55 (24)
Players/Course (Rank): 618 (58)
World Cup results 1994: 24th.
Prominent Players: Per Greve, Henning Kistensen, Hans Hendrik Larsen, Henrik Lund, Carl Poulsen, Jacob Rasmussen, Anders Sorenson, Steen Tinning.
National Golf Association: Danish Golf Union, Golfsvingt 22625 Vallensbaek, Denmark 45-4-264-0666

History: Danish golf began early in this century, but reached a new level of success when Carl Poulsen played on an all-Scandinavian team in the 1954 and 1955 Canada Cup competitions, placing 25th individually in 1955. From 1956 Denmark has fielded its own team, with Poulsen making eight more appearances along with players such as Henning Kristensen and Jorgen Korfitzen.

Denmark reached a new level of success in world competition in the 1980s when 25-year-old Anders Sorenson and Steen Tinning joined together in 1987 and finished in 12th place. Both Tinning and Sorenson have gone on to distinguished careers on the European Tour. Sorenson has distinguished himself as Denmark's greatest golfer, winning the Nescafe Cup and the Volva Albatross Open on the European Tour as well as finishing second in the 1989-90 World Cups in individual competition.

DOMINICAN REPUBLIC

No. of Players (Rank): 700 (55)
No. of Courses (Rank): 5 (55)
Players/Course (Rank): 140 (20)
World Cup results 1995: Did not compete.
Prominent Players: Edwin Corrie, Jack Corrie, Guillermo Gomez, Ricardo Orellana, Arturo Pellermo, Carlos Puebla
Prominent Courses: Casa de Campo (Teeth of the Dog)
National Golf Association: Dominican Golf Association, P.O. Box 641, Santa Domingo, Dominican Republic

History: The Dominican Republic is best known in the world of golf for Teeth of the Dog, the astonishing course built by Pete Dye which has been at the pinnacle of the world course rankings since it opened twenty years ago.

However, the tiny republic does have a small contingent of golfers and fielded several teams in the

World Cup during the 1970s, although without conspicuous success. Carlos Puebla was selected three times, as was Edwin Corrie. The team's best finish was 31st in 1971.

Robert Trent Jones is now completing a course called Palaya Garnde which, situated on the northern shores of the island, is said to be a classic in the making, and it may prove a catalyst for a golf renaissance.

EGYPT

No. of Players (Rank): 1,100 (51)
No. of Courses (Rank): 5 (55)
Players/Course (Rank): 220 (31)
World Cup results 1995: Did not compete.
Prominent Players: Naaman Aly, Farouk Badr, Mohamed Abdel Hanfi, Abdel Halim, Mohamed Said Moussa, Cherif Said.
National Golf Association: The Egyptian Golf Federation, Gezira Sporting Club, Gezira Cairo, Egypt

History: Golf in Egypt dates back to the First World War when a course was laid out by the Gezira Sporting Club, and golf proved quite popular in the country, with an Egyptian Amateur inaugurated as early as 1908 and an Open following in 1921. The country competed quite successfully on an international level in the years following the Second World War. The Egyptian Open and the Egyptian Match Play became prominent tournaments during the reign of King Farouk in the 1950s. Following the coup by Nasser, golf continued but its growth was minimal. The Egyptian national team during this period was led by Mohamed Said Moussa, who represented Egypt no less than 22 times between 1957 and 1980, finishing as high as 18th in the individual competition. Egypt managed to place 10th in 1977, but shortly after that the tightening of the field left the nation out, and Egypt hasn't returned since 1980.

ENGLAND

No. of Players (Rank): 596,000 (5)
No. of Courses (Rank): 1,300 (5)
Players/Course (Rank): 458 (48)
World Cup results 1995: 20th. Mark Roe finished 17th in the individual competition.
Prominent Players: Peter Alliss, John Ball, Peter Baker, Howard Clark, Sir Henry Cotton, Nick Faldo, David Gilford, Harold H. Hilton, Bernard Hunt, Tony Jacklin, Mark James, Barry Lane, Ted Ray, Mark Roe, Steven Richardson, John H. Taylor, Harry Vardon, Brian Waites, Harry Weetman.

Prominent Courses: Alwoodley, The Belfry, Berkshire, Formby, Ganton, Hillside, Lindrick, Little Aston, Notts, Royal Birkdale, Royal Cinque Ports (Deal), Royal Liverpool (Hoylake), Royal Lytham & St. Anne's, Royal North Devon (Westward Ho!), Royal St. George's, Sunningdale, Swinley Forest, Walton Heath, Wentworth, Woodhall Spa.
National Golf Association: The English Golf Union, 1-3 Upper King Street, Leicester LE1 6XF

History: The first reference we have for golf in England is a letter written in 1513 by Queen Catherine to Cardinal Wolsey referring to the growing popularity of the game. The first evidence of a golf course in England was the formation of The Blackheath Club in 1766; the Old Manchester Club was founded in 1818 and shortly after the invention of the gutta-percha ball in 1848 the (now Royal) North Devon Golf Club was formed and golf was well underway in England.

The cause of English golf was aided socially by the prominent backing and enthusiasm of Arthur Balfour, a darling of the social and aesthetic sets who went on to Parliament and eventually became Prime Minister. The game was advanced materially by the success of John Ball who, in 1890, became the first Englishman to win the British Open, and at the same time became the first to win the Amateur and the Open in the same year. Shortly afterwards Harry Vardon and John H. Taylor became two, along with Scotsman James Braid, of "The Great Triumvirate" which dominated open golfing competition for twenty years.

After the War the English began to pick up where they left off with Ted Ray coming to the fore and winning the Open in 1922, but a period of decline set in and the English became perpetual bridesmaids in the Ryder Cup matches with America and in their own British Open. The success of Sir Henry Cotton in the 1930s was one of the few bright lights.

Following the Second World War, economic exhaustion prostrated many golf clubs and English golf ceased to produce champions almost entirely. Only the fantastic upset victory at Lindrick in the 1957 Ryder Cup and a second place finish in the 1960 World Cup gave much encouragement to the English, who now faced international competition from Australians, South Africans, Canadians and Americans. The rise of Peter Alliss and Bernard Hunt in the late 1950s and early 1960s was encouraging, but they could do little to stop the foreign onslaught on the British Open crown by the likes of Palmer, Nicklaus, Trevino, and Player.

In 1969 young Tony Jacklin won the British Open and was a key player in the British halve with America in the Ryder Cup. Later on his captaincy of the

European side was to prove a decisive factor in swinging the balance of power back toward the Continent. In the 1970s players like Howard Clark, Mark James, Nick Faldo and Mark Roe began to achieve international prominence on the European and American tours and in international competitions. Howard Clark won the individual competition at the 1985 World Cup (in which the English team finished second); Nick Faldo was runner-up in the 1983 World Match Play Championship and won in 1987; England emerged victorious in the 1987 Alfred Dunhill Cup competition; Nick Faldo won the 1987, 1990 and 1992 British Opens and the 1989 and 1990 Masters. In short, England had regained a position in world golf by the late 1980s that it had not held since the late 1920s. Younger players such as Peter Baker are thought to be the best hopes for England in continuing their conspicuous success throughout the 1990s, although none made a particularly strong showing on either the European Tour or the Ryder Cup matches in 1995.

FIJI

No. of Players (Rank): 700 (55)
No. of Courses (Rank): 9 (48)
Players/Course (Rank): 78 (5)
World Cup results 1995: Did not compete.
Prominent Players: Arun Kumar, Bose Lutunatabua, Vilikese Kalou, Dharam Prakesh, Mamoa Rsigatale, Vijay Singh.
National Golf Association: Fiji Golf Association, P.O. Box 177, Suva, Fiji

History: Golf in Fiji has been in part based on the resort traffic, which boomed in the 1970s as jets travelling between Australia and America stopped in Fiji for refueling. A small but active band of Fiji golfers thus have one of the lowest golfer/course ratios in the world.

Fiji stepped into the international competitive arena in the mid-1970s, entering the World Cup competition. Six subsequent appearances have yielded little success, with the best finish to date a 26th place result in 1980. Fiji also hosted the 1978 Eisenhower Trophy matches won by the United States.

In recent years the most exciting Fijian development has been the rise of Vijay Singh, easily the greatest Fijian golfer of all time, who has made strong showings on both the American and European tours in the 1990s, even leading by four strokes after the second round of the 1992 PGA Championship (he finished fourth).

FINLAND

No. of Players (Rank): 12,200 (28)
No. of Courses (Rank): 33 (32)
Players/Course (Rank): 370 (42)
World Cup results 1995: 19th.
Prominent Players: Juhani Hamalainen, Anssi Kankkonnen, Markku Louhid, Sigurd Nystrom, Mikael Piltz, Timo Sipponen.
Prominent Publications: Suomen Golf.
National Golf Association: Finlands Golfforbund, Radiokatu 12, SF-00240, Helsinki, Finland

History: Of all the Scandinavian states Finland has had the slowest golf development, no doubt a product of its relative remoteness and harsh climate. The game was not introduced to Finland until 1930 and the Helsinki Golf Club, the first formal club, not opened until 1932. Golf remains an acquired taste here but golfers have a good selection of courses to choose from and have fielded four teams in the World Cup with increasing success, the best to date being the 22nd place finish in 1988. Excel, the golf equipment maker, has located a factory here in recent years, adding to the golf boomlet in the far north.

FRANCE

No. of Players (Rank): 220,000 (11)
No. of Courses (Rank): 480 (7)
Players/Course (Rank): 458 (48)
World Cup results 1995: 6th. Jean Van de Velde finished 11th and Jean Louis Guepy 19th in the individual competition.
Prominent Players: Michel Besanceney, Patrick Cotton, Emmanuel Dussart, Marc Farry, Jean Garaiade, Jean Louis Guepy, Jean Harismendy, Arnaud Massy, Bernard Pascassio, Francis Saubaber, Jean van de Velde, Gery Watine.
Prominent Courses: Chantilly, Golf de St-Nom-la-Breteche Le Tocquet, Morfontaine, Seignosse.
National Golf Association: Federation Francaise de Golf, 69 Victor Hugo, F-75783
Paris Cedex 16 France
Tel. 33-1-4-4176300 Fax 33-1-4-4176363

History: Pau was founded in 1856 as a nine-hole course with a clubhouse in a room in a wayside inn, and it specialized for years as a French resort geared to the needs of the British tourist who required golf. It wasn't until 1907 when French professional Arnaud Massy won the British Open that golf much exceeded this humble role in France. British professionals flocked to France to avenge the defeat, but this time they were held off by Massy and Jean Gassiat. Golf thus achieved a certain status and courses began to be established in the Riviera and around Biarritz to accommodate English tourists and the small legion of French enthusiasts.

By the 1920s French players were routinely competing at the championship level in golf. French women Maette le Blan and Simone Thion de la Chaume won the 1928-9 Ladies' Championship in Britain. Their success dwindled after the Second World War in the face of American competition, but Jean Garaiade led the national team to success in the World Cup during the 1950s. Garaiade finished ninth in the individual competition in 1954 and 1963 and improved to sixth in 1970. The French team placed 5th in 1962 behind the combined efforts of Garaiade and Roger Cotton, and in 1963 France hosted the World Cup. 1969 was a high point for France in these years when France won both the European Ladies Amateur Team Championship in Sweden, and hosted the Vagilano Trophy at Chantilly where Europe defeated the British Isles.

French golf fell into the second tier during the 1970s for the male professionals (although the women amateurs won the European Ladies' Amateur in 1975 and were runners-up in 1969, 1971 and 1973), but in the 80s one of the most astonishing revivals took place at the amateur level. France hosted the European Amateur Team Championship in 1983 at Chantilly, while in the 80s the number of courses doubled and France produced Jean van de Velde, who placed fifth in the individual competition in 1993.

French courses have also had increasing exposure as golfing tourism to the South of France has long ago exceeded just the number of British visitors. Cannes Mougins hosts the annual Cannes Open, while Monte Carlo hosts the Monte Carlo Open at Mont Agel. The Lancome Trophy and Peugeot French Open are still highly prized victories on the PGA European Tour, as well.

GERMANY

No. of Players (Rank): 95,863 (15)
No. of Courses (Rank): 239 (12)
Players/Course (Rank): 401 (47)
World Cup results 1995: 8th. Bernhard Langer finished in first place in the individual competition.
Prominent Players: Georg Bessner, Oliver Ekstein, Torsten Giedeon, Jurgen Harder, Tony Kugelmueller, Bernhard Langer, Friedal Schmaderer, Heinz-Peter Thuel.
Prominent Courses: Club Zur Vahr, Hamburger.
National Golf Association: Deutscher Golf Verband, eV. Postfach 2106, Wiesbaden D-6200
Germany 49 (6121) 526-041

History: A The enthusiastic golfers of England's Royal family were closely related to the German aristocracy, and close ties between the two countries that resulted led to golf arriving in the country as early as 1895 with the building of a course in Berlin. A German Open was played as early as 1912—but golf did not truly flower until after the Second World War, when the team of Georg Bessner and Hans Goermert represented Germany in the first Canada Cup. After some early success in international golf (a sixth-place finish in 1953 and 1955), the German national teams had little or no success in the international arena until the late 1970s and the emergence of the country's greatest golfer, Bernhard Langer.

Langer was successful on the European PGA TOUR since the mid-1970s, but two back-to-back second-place finishes in the 1979-80 World Cup matches and a spot on the 1981 Ryder Cup team sealed his place in the top-rank of European players. Germany's subsequent success in international team competition has largely rested on their success in finding a suitable partner for Langer.

In the 1980s a great wave of interest in golf was sparked by Langer's victory in the 1985 Masters, and the reunification of Germany made more land available for courses. By 1990 a new generation of German professionals were more competitive on the European PGA Tour and Germany won the 1990 World Cup when Langer and Torsten Giedeon tied for fifth in the individual competition. Golfers such as Heinz-Peter Thuel and Sven Struver have also recently found success on the European PGA Tour and the European Challenge Tour. Meanwhile golf continues to expand in Germany with the enthusiastic backing of German corporations such as BMW and Mercedes-Benz which have developed a close association with the game in the United States and other areas of operation. A new two-course complex outside of Berlin with courses by Nick Faldo and Arnold Palmer/Ed Seay is scheduled to in 1996 as the largest golf facility yet constructed in the country.

GREECE

No. of Players (Rank): 2,500 (45)
No. of Courses (Rank): 4 (58)
Players/Course (Rank): 625 (59)
World Cup results 1995: Did not compete.
Prominent Players: Basilli Anastassiou, Basilli Karatzias, Vassilios Karatzias, George Nikitaidis, Craigen Pappas, John Sotiropoulos, Stefano Vafiadis
Prominent Courses: Glyfada G.C.

Prominent Publications: Golf News.
Number of golf professionals: 8
National Golf Association: Hellenic Golf Federation, P.O. Box 70003, GR 166 10 Athens

History: Golf was played on a nine-hole course in Athens until 1962, when the 18-hole Glyfada G.C. was founded. Greece fielded its first international team in 1968 in the World Cup, finishing 41st. John Sotiropoulos was selected ten times to represent Greece in World Cup competition, but the best Greece could manage was a 20th place finish in 1976 behind George Vafiadis' 29th place finish in the individual competition.

In 1979 Greek golf took a major step forward when Glyfada played host to the World Cup, and in 1981 the Hellenic Golf Federation was founded. Greece has not yet had a high finish in international competition, but there are now additional courses in Corfu, on Rhodes, and in Khalkadiki near Thessalonica.

GUADALOUPE

No. of Players (Rank): 200 (66)
No. of Courses (Rank): 1 (67)
Players/Course (Rank): 200 (26)
World Cup results 1995: Did not compete.

HONG KONG

No. of Players (Rank): 20,000 (25)
No. of Courses (Rank): 7 (53)
Players/Course (Rank): 2,667 (71)
World Cup results 1995: Did not compete.
Prominent Players: Dominique Boulet, Joe Hardwick, Richard Kan, Lai Wau Che, Lee Parker, Alex Tang, Peter Tang, Yau Sui Ming, Yau Wah Tah
Prominent Courses: The Royal Hong Kong G.C., Iris G.C.
National Golf Association: The Hong Kong Golf Association, Ltd., 1420 Prince's Building, 10 Charter Road, Central Hong Kong

History: Hong Kong was the original home of Far East Asian golf, for The Royal Hong Kong Golf Club's history dates all the way back to 1889. The mountainous terrain and the need to build housing on every available space has greatly slowed golf's growth, but Iris has 63 holes. Green fees and memberships are among the highest in the world.

Hong Kong has distinguished itself, though, in the international arena with fourteen appearances in the World Cup between 1973 and 1993, with a 23rd place finish in 1985 behind Yau Sui Ming's 32nd place finish in the individual competition. Hong Kong was also in the news recently because Tom Watson, in winning the 1992 Hong Kong Open, broke his five-year winless streak. Hong Kong stages an annual PGA championship in addition to the Open, and has competed in the Eisenhower (World Amateur) Cup. The Hong Kong team managed a 20th place finish in the 1993 World Cup, its best-ever finish, with rookie Richard Kan placing 39th in the individual competition.

With the return of Hong Kong to Chinese control in 1997, many have speculated that Hong Kong's golfing future may be bright indeed, given the recent Chinese interest in the game.

ICELAND

No. of Players (Rank): 3,500 (40)
No. of Courses (Rank): 29 (34)
Players/Course (Rank): 121 (14)
World Cup results 1995: Did not compete.
Prominent Players: Ragnar Olasson, Sigurdur Petursson, Bjorgvin Thorsbeinsson.
National Golf Association: Golfsamband Islands P.O. Box 1076, Reykjavik IS-101 Iceland 354-168-6686

History: Golf arrived in the island kingdom in 1934, and Iceland emerged from relative obscurity to place two teams of amateurs in the World Cup in the late 1970s, with a best finish of 43rd in 1977. Another appearance with a 29th place finish in 1984 marked the high point in Icelandic golf to date.

INDIA

No. of Players (Rank): 15,000 (25)
No. of Courses (Rank): 150 (15)
Players/Course (Rank): 100 (6)
World Cup results 1995: Did not compete.
Prominent Players: Basad Ali, Brandon de Souza, Shadi Lal, Rohta Singh, Ruda Valjni.
Prominent Courses: Royal Calcutta, Royal Bombay, Tollyguge, Bangalore
National Golf Association: The Indian Golf Union, Tta Centre, 3rd. Floor, 43 Chowringhee Road, Calcutta 700-071 India

History: The Calcutta Golf Club was founded in 1829 and is the oldest surviving golf club outside of the British Isles (it became Royal Calcutta in 1912). Royal Bombay was founded in 1842—thus in the mid-19th century there were as many golf clubs in India as in England. Bangalore was founded in 1870.

The Amateur Championship was founded in 1892, open to club members from India, Burma, Ceylon, and the Straits Settlements. Prominent courses of the era were all nine-holes, and the first eighteen-hole course was the Tollygune Club's course which was completed in 1906. Golf in this era was exclusively for British colonists and a select band of the Indian elite.

With the arrival of the Second World War and the subsequent independence of India from Britain granted in 1947, the growth of golf slowed to a crawl through the 1950s and 1960s. Consequently India has one course today for every 100 golfers, an astonishingly good supply.

In the 1970s and 80s, India fielded a few teams in international tournaments with limited success. Their 24th place finish, however, in their last World Cup appearance in 1988 was the best yet, with Rohtas Singh finishing 41st in the individual competition.

As a golfing destination, the primary drawing card for India is still the India Open Championship, which has attracted some top-ranked international players over the years, and was won by Payne Stewart in 1981.

INDONESIA

No. of Players (Rank): 11,600 (31)
No. of Courses (Rank): 70 (21)
Players/Course (Rank): 166 (22)
World Cup results 1995: Did not compete.
Prominent Players: Salam Denin, Mamatkajal, Aziz Narwi, Sumarno, Suparman.
Prominent Courses: Gunung Geulis, Jagorawl, Pondok Indah
National Golf Association: Indonesian Golf Association J1. Rawamangun Muka Taya, Jakarta 13220, Indonesia

History: There are two distinct phases of golf in Indonesia, the first beginning with the founding of Royal Batavia Golf Club in 1872 and the construction of a nine-hole course—the first in Asia outside of India and twenty years before the building of the first course in Holland, whence the colonists came. The game never caught on strongly, perhaps due to climate, and with independence from the Netherlands the Indonesians did not encourage growth of the game.

Nevertheless, Indonesia fielded teams with success in the World Cup in late 1970s and in 1980 had its best season, with a 20th place finish in the World Cup which was played at Pondok Indah at home. Subsequently the Indonesians have been quiet in the arena of international golf, but course development has begun to take off in the 1990s and the nascent Asian PGA TOUR has stops planned for here.

IRELAND

No. of Players (Rank): 160,000 (12)
No. of Courses (Rank): 253 (10)
Players/Course (Rank): 632 (60)
Golf Professionals: 140
World Cup results 1995: 6th. Darren Clarke finished fifth in the individual competition.
Prominent Players: Hugh Boyle, Harry Bradshaw, Fred Daly, Eamonn Darcy, Norman Drew, David Feherty, Christy Greene, Hugh Jackson, Ernie Jones, Jimmy Kinsella, Jimmy Martin, Christy O'Connor, Sr., Christy O'Connor, Jr., John O'Leary, Eddie Pollard, Ronan Rafferty, Des Smyth.
Prominent Courses: Ballybunion, County Louth, County Sligo, Lahinch, Portmarnock, Royal County Down, Royal Portrush.
Prominent Golf Publications: Golfer's Companion, Golf Link Magazine.
National Golf Association: Golfing Union of Ireland, Glancar House 81, Elginton Road, Donnybrook Dublin 4

History: The roots of Irish golf go back as far as the 17th century, when Viscount Montgomery of the Ards made a gift of land for a school that included grounds for golf. But the story of Irish golf properly picks up in the 1850s with the Scots regiments quartered at Curragh who played golf there and laid the grounds for the Royal Curragh Club. The formal history opens with the founding of Royal Belfast Golf Club by George Baillie in 1881. The game expanded to Dublin by 1884 with a few short holes laid out in Phoenix Park. The Irish Secretary of the time was England's most socially prominent golfer, Arthur Balfour, whose enthusiasm for the game at Phoenix Park led to its destruction by Irish separatists. Subsequently Royal Dublin Golf Club was founded in 1887.

By 1899 Ireland had its first champions in May Hezlet and Rhona Adair who won the Ladies' Championship five times between 1899 and 1907, with the Championship taking place in Ireland in 1899.

Despite the excellent and plentiful supply of courses, Irish golf went into a coma during the mid-war years, but after the Second World War Irish golf came to the forefront with the victories of James Bruen in 1946, Max McCready in 1949 (at Portmarnock) and Joe Carr in 1953 in the Amateur. In addition, Fred Daly won the 1947 British Open, and was selected to the Ryder Cup team in 1947.

Highlights of Irish golf in the 1950s included a victory in the 1956 World Cup when Harry Bradshaw finished second and Christy O'Connor tenth, and the emergence of Christy O'Connor as a top-ranked international player. O'Connor was selected to four World Cup teams and three Ryder Cups in the 1950s, including a resounding 7&6 defeat of Dow Finsterwald in the 1957 Ryder Cup matches at Lindrick that marked the first American defeat since 1933.

The 1960s opened with the hosting of the World Cup at Portmarnock (the Irish team finishing fourth), and O'Connor continued to be a force in world golf, winning spots on all five Ryder Cup teams in the 60s as well as finishing third in the 1961 World Cup individual standings, but other Irish successes were primarily on the amateur side. The Great Britain & Ireland team won the Eisenhower Trophy (World Amateur Championship) in 1968, and Ireland took home the European Amateur Team Championship in 1965 and '67.

In the 1970s Irish golf expanded with the growth of the European PGA Tour, and the Carrolls Irish Open has proved to be a very successful tournament on the PGA European Tour at Royal Dublin and Portmarnock.

In the 1980s, Irish golf became stronger with the emergence of players such as Ronan Rafferty and David Feherty. Ronan Rafferty in particular has enjoyed great success, winning over fourteen tournaments and winning a spot on the victorious 1989 Ryder Cup. Ireland was victorious in the 1988 Alfred Dunhill Cup tournament.

By the early 1990s the late-80s golf boom had faded, but new courses such as The European Club were opening, and players such as Rafferty, Feherty, and Eamonn Darcy were finding regular success on the European Tour. The Irish team placed 2nd in the 1990 World Cup behind David Feherty's strong 3rd place finish. In 1995 the Irish team placed a strong sixth at the World Cup in Puerto Rico, as well as scoring a stunning upset over the United States in the 1995 Dunhill Cup. The staging of the Curtis Cup matches at Killarney G. & F.C. in 1996 marks another step forward in the story of Irish golf, with rumors surfacing of a return to Ireland for the British Open.

ISRAEL

No. of Players (Rank): 600 (58)
No. of Courses (Rank): 1 (67)
Players/Course (Rank): 600 (57)
Golf Professionals: 5
World Cup results 1995: Did not compete.
Prominent Players: Rami Assyag, Jacob Avnaim, Lauie Been, Brian Cooper, Barry Mandel, Neil Shochet.
Prominent Courses: Caesarea G.C.
National Golf Association: Israel Golf Federation, P.O. Box 1010, Caesarea

History: Golf began in Israel in 1961 when the Rothschild family founded the nation's first and only (to date) golf course amongst the ruins of the ancient city of Caesarea, where Roman relics are an integral part of the course. Israel began competing internationally in 1974 with a team in the World Cup which placed 44th. Subsequently the Israelis competed four more times in the World Cup during the 1970s with only limited success, their highest finish being 42nd place in 1979.

During the 1980s Israel had only a limited international golfing exposure, and development of the game was limited due to having only one course in the country. But an Israeli team qualified for the 1994 World Cup and finished 29th.

ITALY

No. of Players (Rank): 24,000 (22)
No. of Courses (Rank): 82 (19)
Players/Course (Rank): 293 (37)
World Cup results 1995: 12th. Constantino Rocca finished in fourth place in the individual competition.
Prominent Players: Alfonso Angelini, Roberto Bernardini, Alberto Binaghi, Olivio Bolognesi, Giuseppe Cali, Renato Campagnoli, Baldovino Dassu, Gerolamo Dellfino, Ettore Della Torre, Silvio Grappasonni, Ugo Grappasonni, Silvio Locatelli, Delio Lovato, Massimo Mannelli, Constantino Rocca
Prominent Courses: Castelgondolfo, Circolo Golf Olgiata, Le Querce, Monticello, Milano, Pevero
National Golf Association: Federazione Italiana Golf, Via Flaminia 388, Roma 1-00196 Italy 39(6) 394641

History: The archival record indicates that golf's Italian history dates from the life in exile spent here by James III and VIII and his son Charles III (Bonnie Prince Charlie) in the 17th century. Italy has had a prominent place in world golf since the Second World War, although the absence of top-ranked international players has until recent years kept Italian golf a secret internationally.

In the 1950s the Italian team first competed in the Canada Cup, finishing in a strong 9th place in 1955. Alfonso Angelini was a consistently strong international player throughout this decade, with a 12 place individual finish in the 1956 Canada Cup.

In the 1960s Italy began to host major international tournaments, with the 1968 World Cup played in

Rome, the 1964 Eisenhower (World Amateur) Trophy also played at Olgiata in Rome, and the 1967 European Amateur Team Championship played in Turin. The Italian team placed 3rd in the 1968 World Cup, with Roberto Bernardini placing second in the individual competition. Bernardini, Angelini, and Olivio Bolognesi were the best players during this time.

In the 1970s Italy continued to have success in the World Cup but not as consistently, with a 5th place finish in 1970 their best. Roberto Bernardini, who placed 7th individually in the 1970 World Cup, continued to be Italy's best player, although Baldovino Dassu had replaced him by the end of the decade. The 1975 European Amateur Championship team finished second at Killarney.

The 1980s marked a resurgence of Italian golf, with the 1984 World Cup returning to Rome and the women amateurs finishing runners-up in the 1985 European Ladies Amateur Team Championship. Italy placed third in the 1982 World Cup and seventh in 1984. Baldovino Dassa, who finished fourth individually at the 1982 World Cup, began the decade as Italy's best player, but by the end of the decade Constantino Rocca had emerged from the pack. With the surge in interest in the European PGA Tour, the Italian Open was attracting a strong international field throughout the 1980s with winners including Bernhard Langer, Sandy Lyle and Greg Norman.

Golf in Italy has continued to grow in the 1990s with the Roma Masters and the Italian Open drawing strong fields to Milano and Rome. Rome also hosted the 1991 World Cup, in which the Italian team finished 15th. Perhaps the highlight of the decade, though, came in 1993 when the Italian team finished ninth in the World Cup and its top player, Constantino Rocca, became the first Italian to qualify for the Ryder Cup team in 1993 and lost a heart-stopping playoff to John Daly in the 1995 British Open. Rocca also completed his season on the PGA European Tour by finishing fourth in the 1995 World Cup.

JAMAICA

No. of Players (Rank): 1,600 (52)
No. of Courses (Rank): 12 (44)
Players/Course (Rank): 133 (18)
World Cup results 1995: Did not compete.
Prominent Players: Christian Bernard, Basil Campbell, Alvin Cunningham, Jasper Markland, Norman Marsh, Peter Millhouse, Seymour Rose, Wesley Scott.
Prominent Courses: Half Moon Club, Tryall.
National Golf Association: Jamaica Golf Association, P.O. Box 743 Kingston 8, Jamaica

History: Golf on Jamaica dates back to the mid-19th century, with the Manchester Club founded in 1868, but golf has generally played a minor role on Jamaica, with the island generally having more of a reputation as home to great golf courses more than great golfers, but the Jamaicans have had some success at the international level, too.

Big time golf first beckoned in 1961 when Robert Trent Jones completed his course at Half Moon Club. Tryall followed afterwards, from a design by Ralph Plummer. The Jamaican national team first broke through into the World Cup field later in the decade, in 1967, when they placed 33rd at Mexico City. Seymour Rose, now 54, has managed to win a slot on each one of the eleven teams fielded by Jamaica in the Cup, a remarkable feat of longevity. It's only in recent years that he has been able to find a partner up to his caliber, and thus Jamaica has struggled in the World Cup, recording a best of 28th place in 1974, and in 1993 at Orlando.

Jamaica has perhaps become best known as the host of the Johnnie Walker World Championship at Tryall, played at the end of the golf season and generating solid television ratings.

JAPAN

No. of Players (Rank): 11,300,000 (2)
No. of Courses (Rank): 1,558 (3)
Players/Course (Rank): 7,253 (72)
World Cup results 1995: 4th. Hisayuki Sasahi finished in a tie for first in the individual competition.
Prominent Players: Isao Aoki, Michio Ishii, Tomoo Ishii, Tadashi Kitta, Misutaka Kono, Takaaki Kono, Takashi Murakami, Tommy Nakajima, Torokichi Nakamura, Koichi Ono, Mashashi Ozaki, Naomichi Ozaki, Hisayuki Sasahi, Kosaku Shimada, Hideyo Sugimoto, Norio Suzuki, Namio Takasu, Harou Yasuda.
Prominent Courses: Hirono, Kasumigaseki, Kawana, Tokyo, Yomiuri
National Golf Association: National Golf Foundation Japan, 3-3-4 Sebdagaya Shibuya-ku, Tokyo, Japan 81 (03) 478-4355

History: The story of Japanese golf began with the construction of a course by Arthur Groom, and the founding of a four-holer at Mt. Rokko, near Kobe, in 1903. The course was subsequently expanded to eighteen holes, but the golf boom in Japan truly dates from the opening of the Tokyo Klub in 1914.

Prior to the Second World War Japanese golfers appeared in European and American competitions; but the game became even more firmly established in

Japan after the Second World War.

Japan quickly became one of the leading international teams in the early Canada Cup competitions of the 1950s, finishing fourth in 1956 and winning in 1957 at Kasumagaseki in Tokyo. Torakichi Nakamura took an incredible nine-stroke lead into the final round and emerged with a seven shot victory in the individual competition.

In the 1960s success was not as conspicuous, but Japan secured six top-10 finishes in the World Cup in the decade including second place in 1969, while in 1966 at Yomiuri, Japan, Hideyo Sugimoto lost the individual medal in a play-off. In the amateur arena Japan hosted the 1962 Eisenhower Trophy.

The golf boom accelerated in Japan throughout the 1970s as prosperity increased rapidly, and many more courses were constructed, including many by celebrated international players such as Arnold Palmer, putting pressure on land availability. Japanese international success in golf also increased with players such as Takaaki Kono, Mashaski Ozaki, Seiichi Kanai and most importantly Isao Aoki emerging as first-class golfers. Aoki not only enjoyed success in Japan and in the World Cup, but was victorious in the 1978 World Match Play Championships at Wentworth, England in 1978 (and runner-up in 1979), as well as proving a tough competitor in US and European PGA Tour events. Japanese amateurs finished runners-up in the Eisenhower Trophy in both 1976 and 1978.

By the 1980s the quality of play in Japan was strong enough that the Nissan Cup was born, pitting touring pros from each of the four "major" tour circuits (US, European, Australian, and Japanese). Japan finished runner-ups, also, in the 1986 Dunhill Cup as well as winning in the 1986 Nissan Cup. Isao Aoki, in his defeat by Jack Nicklaus at Baltusrol in the 1980 U.S. Open, came the closest of any Japanese golfer to winning a major. Prominent new stars of the decade included Takaaki Ono and Koichi Suzuki.

Japanese expansion in golf, by the 1990s, included strategic properties in the United States, and by 1994 Japanese investors either held major positions in or owned outright such top-ranked American gems as Pebble Beach, Riviera, the GC of Georgia, and World Woods. Japanese equipment manufacturers also continued to expand international operations, with such companies as Yonex, Yamaha, Mizuno, Bridgestone and Maruman active throughout the world.

In competition, Japan hadfared less successfully in the 1990s until Hisayuki Sassahi won the individual World Cup competition in 1995, with Japan finishing in fourth place.

KENYA

No. of Players (Rank): 3,000 (42)
No. of Courses (Rank): 29 (33)
Players/Course (Rank): 103 (10)
World Cup results 1995: Did not compete.
Prominent Course: Muthaiga G.C.

History: Kenya has been a home to golf since the British colonial period, with seniority belonging to the Nairobi (now Royal Nairobi) Golf Club founded in 1906. The Kenya Open has been played for may years and has attracted a number of prominent international players, including past winners such as Jose Canizares, Ian Woosnam and Christy O'Connor, Jr. The Kenya Open is now a stop on the small but fertile African Tour and is played annually at Muthaiga in Nairobi. Kenya has yet to produce a player of world-class calibre.

KOREA

No. of Players (Rank): 260,000 (9)
No. of Courses (Rank): 30 (32)
Players/Course (Rank): 11,628 (73)
World Cup results 1995: Did not compete.
Prominent Players: Yoo Soo Choi, Sang Ho Choi, Chang Sang Hahn, Seung Hak Kim, Kang-Sun Lee, Nam-Sin Park
Prominent Course: Nam Seoul, New Korea.
National Golf Association: Korea Golf Association, Room 18 - 13 Floor Manhattan Building, 36-2 Yeo Eui Do-Dong, Yeong Deung Po-Ku, Seoul, Korea 82 (02)783-4748

History: Korea is making up for its short golf history with one of the most vigorous golf booms in the world, producing tremendous pressure on the limited number of courses in the country.

The first course, Seoul Country Club, dates to 1931, but it wasn't until the 1950s that the Republic of Korea teams first participated in world golf via the Canada Cup matches, with Hak Young Kim finishing 40th in the individual competition in 1959. After an absence of several years, the ROK team, featuring star player Chang Sang Hahn, became a strong contender in the Canada and World Cup event, finishing as high as 5th in 1971 at PGA National, with Hahn placing 13th.

Although Korean players have not played on the high-profile American and European tours, throughout the 1970s players such as Jung Ung Park, Chang, and Il Ahn Lee played world-class golf that kept Korea in the top ten at the World Cup in 1971,

1972, 1975, 1977 and 1978. By the 1980s new players such as Sang Ho Choi and Nam Sin Park were figuring prominently, each winning the Korea Open and appearing on several World Cup teams.

Golf course construction is at an all-time high in Korea at present, and the locals have continued to hold their own in the Korea Open despite the increasing presence of PGA TOUR veterans such as Guy Boros, Ray Stewart, and former U.S. Amateur Champion Eric Meeks.

MALAWI

No. of Players (Rank): 600 (58)
No. of Courses (Rank): 10 (46)
Players/Course (Rank): 60 (2)
World Cup results 1995: Did not compete.

History: Golf here dates back to the establishment of Blantyre in 1911.

MALAYSIA

No. of Players (Rank): 120,000 (14)
No. of Courses (Rank): 150 (15)
Players/Course (Rank): 800 (63)
World Cup results 1995: 29th.
Prominent Players: Zainal Abadin, Eshak Buluah, Jalal Deran, Lim Voot Fung, Marmuthe Ramayah, Nazaruddin Yusoff.
Prominent Courses: Bukit Jumbul, Kelab Rahman Putra G.C., Royal Selangor G.C.
Golf Professionals: 98
Prominent Publications: FORE, Golf Malaysia.
National Golf Association: Malaysian Golf Association, No. 12-A Persiaran Ampang, 55000 Kuala Lumpur

History: Malaysia has only recently entered into the international golf arena but golf dates back to 1890 with the founding of the New Taiping Club. The Malaysian Golf Association was founded in 1894 with a mission to organize the Malaysian Amateur and other amateur golf matters. Following the withdrawal of British colonial forces in the 1960s, Malaysians have been able to take advantage of courses built by the British colonists, and a relatively strong golf boom has been underway since then.

Malaysia has been fielding international golf teams since the late 1960s without notable success, although the team of Ramayah and Yusoff placed 11th in the 1979 World Cup at Athens. The Malysian Open has been a regular stop on the Asian Tour for many years and has attracted many prominent pros (including past winners Stewart Ginn, Glen Day and Jeff Maggert), while a Women's Open has been staged annually since 1987 and is now part of the Asian Women's Tour. The Malaysian Open continues to be one of the more lucrative stops on the Asian PGA Tour, and Vijay Singh has been particularly strong here.

MEXICO

No. of Players (Rank): 14,670 (28)
No. of Courses (Rank): 124 (17)
Players/Course (Rank): 118 (12)
World Cup results 1995: 10th. Esteban Toledo finished 11th in the individual competition.
Prominent Players: Ernesto Acosta, Rafael Alarcon, Antonio Cerda, Ramon Cruz, Carlos Espinoza, Jose Gonzalez, Augustin Martinez, Margaroto Martinez, Juan Neri, Victor Regaldo, Enrique Serna, Esteban Toledo.
Prominent Courses: Cabo del Sol, Club de Golf, La Hacienda, Palmilla, Pierre Margues.
National Golf Association: Federacion Mexicana de Golf, Cincinati No 40-104 Col Napoles, 03710, Mexico (5) 563-9194

History: Mexico has been overshadowed by Canada and the United States, but has achieved a measure of success in developing its own golf story. "South of the Border" development began in the 1890s with the establishment of Puebla in Mexico City in 1897. Mexico did not produce a world-class player until the team of Al Escalante and Juan Neri began competing in the Canada Cup in the 1950s (along with several "guest" appearances by Roberto de Vicenzo and Antonio Cerda). In 1958 Mexico cemented its place in world golf by successfully hosting the 1958 Canada Cup, the first Hispanic country so honored.

By the mid 1960s, Mexico had put a team as high as third in the World Cup (in 1967, when the competition returned to Club de Golf in Mexico City), and begun to establish the Mexican Open as an increasingly lucrative and challenging stop on the golf calendar.

In the 1970s Ernesto Acosta became the first Mexican player to take first place in the World Cup competition, and Mexico continued to place highly in the event throughout the late 1970s and 1980s. By the late 1980s Rafael Alarcon had replaced Acosta as Mexico's leading player, and led a spirited run at the 1993 Dunhill Cup in which the Mexicans nearly pulled off an upset over England and defeated South Africa in bitter cold at St. Andrews. Mexico went on to place a strong 10th in the 1995 World Cup.

MOROCCO

No. of Players (Rank): 2,000 (48)
No. of Courses (Rank): 4 (58)
Players/Course (Rank): 500 (49)
World Cup results 1995: Did not compete.
Prominent Courses: Golf Royal de Agadir, Royal Golf Dar-es-Salaam
National Golf Association: Federation Royale Marociane de Golf, Royal Golf Rabat dar es Salam, Route des Zaers, Rabat, Morocco

History: Golf has had the steady support of the royal family of Morocco for many years (hence the proliferation of "Royal" courses), and provides the arena for events on both the European PGA Tour (the Moroccan Open) and the African Tour (the Hassan II Trophy). Despite the enthusiasm of Morocco's royals, the game has not acquired massive popularity in the small northern African country and thus the country is yet to produce its first world-class player. After a fifteen-year hiatus, Morocco fielded an entry for the 1993 World Cup, but the lack of international experience showed and the team finished a disappointing 32nd.

NETHERLANDS

No. of Players (Rank): 23,975 (23)
No. of Courses (Rank): 44 (27)
Players/Course (Rank): 545 (54)
World Cup results 1995: 18th.
Prominent Players: Kees Borst, Ruud Bos, Kees Cramer, Jan Dorrestein, Gerry de Wit, Martin Roesink, Chris van der Velde, Bertus van Mook, Constant Smits van Waesberghe, Piet Witte.
Prominent Courses: Eindhovensche, Haagsche, Hattemse, Kennemer, Noordwik, Oosterhout, Utrechtse.
National Golf Association: Nederlandse Golf Federatie P.O. Box 2213454 PV De Meern Netherlands (31) 34-06-21888

History: The Netherlands has a connection with golf that stretches back to the turn of the century...or back into the 15th century, depending on which history of golf one consults. The Dutch game of kolven dates back in the records to the mid-1400s, and several pictures of Dutch town life include portraits of the people playing their game of kolven, with clubs called kolf, across the ice or in courtyards attached to inns. The Kolf or club looks something like a crude one-iron made with a brass head and the ball is the size of a baseball. Kolven is still played in Northern Holland, but efforts to link the game with the evolution of golf have lost favor in recent years. The most plausible connection may well be that, since there was active trading between Scotland and the Low Countries in the 14th and 15th centuries and Scotland did not have any organized metalworks in these years, The Netherlands may well have been the source of the early equipment, if not the game itself—and like the equally popular game of football the game eventually acquired the name of the equipment—hence golf.

Modern golf history in The Netherlands dates back to the last years of the 19th century—several courses, namely Haagsche (1893), Utrechtse (1894), and Rosendaelsche (1895) date from before the turn of the century. Fourteen of the present-day courses were established prior to the Second World War, making The Netherlands one of the earliest European countries to embrace modern golf.

After the war, teams from The Netherlands began competing in world competition, but the country has produced few golfers who have made a mark on the international scene, and only Gerry de Wit (in 1960) and Martin Roesink (in 1969) managed a top ten finish in the individual competition at the World Cup.

In the 1990s Chris van der Velde has been the most consistent Dutch player—playing the European Tour with some success. In addition, The Netherlands play host to the Dutch Open which attracts a top field of European PGA players, and the Leiden Open on the fledgling Women's European Tour.

NEW ZEALAND

No. of Players (Rank): 350,000 (8)
No. of Courses (Rank): 412 (9)
Players/Course (Rank): 850 (65)
World Cup results 1995: 5th. Michael Campbell finished fifth in the individual competition.
Prominent Players: Frank Buckler, Michael Campbell, Bob Charles, John Lister, Frank Nobilo, Peter Oosterhuis, Simon Owen, Ernie Southerden, Greg Turner.
Prominent Courses: The Grange, Paraparaumu, Rotorua.
National Golf Association: New Zealand Golf Association, Dominion Sports House, Mercer Street, P.O. Box 11842, Wellington, New Zealand

History: Formal golf history began in New Zealand with the founding of the Christchurch Golf Club in 1873, one of the first golf clubs formed within the Commonwealth of Nations and outside of the immediate British Isles (only Royal Adelaide, Bangalore,

Royal Calcutta and Royal Bombay have seniority). New Zealand is possessed of a climate and geology perfect for golf, and the strong Scottish immigrant element ensured the success of the game, so much so that New Zealand today has one of the highest per-capita participation rates in the world. Limited population, however, has prevented New Zealand from a place in the first rank of golfing nations until recent years.

The first great New Zealand golfer was left-handed Bob Charles, who emerged in the early 1960s as a first-class player and scored well at both the Canada Cup and in winning the British Open in 1963. Charles also won the World Match Play title in 1969. Indeed, Charles led New Zealand to a second place finish at the World Cup in 1967.

In the 1970s John Lister and Simon Owen were New Zealand's dominant players, with Frank Nobilo and Greg Turner succeeding them in the 1980s. Bob Charles, meanwhile, has become one of the leading all-time greats of the PGA Senior Tour. In recent years Frank Nobilo has made strong showings in major championships in the U.S. and Britain while making a mark on the European Tour. Michael Campbell also recorded an outstanding season in 1995, briefly holding the lead in the British Open before finishing in a tie for third, and placing fifth at the World Cup in the individual competition.

In addition to the individual play of great golfers, New Zealand has become a key stop on the Australian PGA Tour, with the Air New Zealand and the New Zealand Opens. In addition to regular World Cup appearances, New Zealand has had success in the Alfred Dunhill Cup with a third place finish in 1990.

In amateur golf New Zealand has fared well, with Marnie McGuire winning the 1986 British Amateur, while the New Zealand men finished runners up in the 1970 Eisenhower Trophy at Madrid, and again in 1990 when Christchurch was the venue. In 1992 the Kiwis finally brought home the Eisenhower Trophy, representing the pinnacle of world amateur golf.

NORWAY

No. of Players (Rank): 10,000 (33)
No. of Courses (Rank): 12 (49)
Players/Course (Rank): 833 (70)
World Cup results 1995: Did not compete.
Prominent Players: Per Haugsrud, Johan Horn, Gard Midtvage, Tore Sviland, Arne Werkel.
Prominent Courses: Onsoy, Oslo, Oustoen
National Golf Association: Norwegian Golf Association, Hauger Skolevie 11351 Rud Oslo Norway 47 (2) 518800

History: Norway is a relatively late entrant to the world golf scene, although the first courses were built well before the Second World War at Oslo (1924) and Borregaard (1927). The dozen courses and short golfing season have yet to produce an international champion, but Norwegian teams have competed internationally since 1954 with some success, with a 16th place finish at the 1991 World Cup.

PAKISTAN

No. of Players (Rank): 10,000 (23)
No. of Courses (Rank): 8 (49)
Players/Course (Rank): 1,125 (63)
World Cup results 1995: Did not compete.
Prominent Players: Muhammed Ejaz, Tamiur Hassan, Ghulam Nabi, Muhammed Shafique.
National Golf Association: Pakistan Golf Federation, P.O. Box No. 1295, Rawalpindi, Pakistan

History: Pakistan has had only a limited impact on world golf, but the British colonial influence has left Pakistan with a rich legacy of golf courses and an active amateur group.

In the 1970s Pakistan began to field teams in the World Cup with some success, placing 29th in their initial outing in 1975 and, by their final appearance in 1982, improving to a 24th place finish behind the play of Mohammed Shafique and Ghulam Nabi. Pakistan does not yet host a tournament on the Asian Tour, but the Pakistan Open, Amateur, and Ladies Amateur are fixtures on the local calendar. Nabi is a four-time winner of the Pakistan Open.

PANAMA

No. of Players (Rank): 3,000 (42)
No. of Courses (Rank): 8 (49)
Players/Course (Rank): 375 (43)
World Cup results 1995: Did not compete.
Prominent Players: Leo Dehlinger, Anaibel Galindo, Alberto Gonzalez, Ricardo Jurado, Juan Rivera.
National Golf Association: Panama Golf Association, P.O. Box 8613, Panama 5, Panama

History: Panama has a small but dedicated band of golfers who have managed some excellent results in international golf considering the small base of golfers.

Although the Panama Open and the first courses date back to the 1930s, Panama's first world-class player was Ricardo Jurado, who managed a 20th place finish in the 1962 Canada Cup. Panama has made five additional appearances in Canada/World

Cup competition, with three 30th place finishes (in '62, '71, and '74) their best results to date.

The military regime in Panama did not favor golf and the Panama Open, won in the past by luminaries such as Curtis Strange, Sam Snead, Roberto De Vicenzo, Art Wall, Arnold Palmer and Chi Chi Rodriguez will be revived in 1995. A senior tournament was inaugurated recently won by Orville Moody over Billy Casper.

PARAGUAY

No. of Players (Rank): 400 (63)
No. of Courses (Rank): 3 (65)
Players/Course (Rank): 133 (18)
World Cup results 1995: 20th.
Prominent Players: Luis Boschian, Genaro Espinola, Angel Franco, Eladio Franco, Ramon Franco, Sebastian Franco, Raul Fretes, Angel Gimenez.
Prominent Courses: Yacht y Golf Club.
National Golf Association: Asociacion Paraguaya de Golf Casilla de Correo 1795 Asuncion, Paraguay

History: Paraguay is not known as a great golfing nation but in recent years the country has produced some outstanding golf teams.

Paraguay's first appearances in international golf, in the Canada Cup competitions in the early 1960s, were not successful, with a best finish of 32nd in 1961. The teams did not break into the top thirty until the early 1980s, but in 1992 two rookies, Raul Fretes and Carlos Franco, managed to place 13th (with Fretes placing 14th in the individual competition). Two new players, Ramon Franco and Pedro Martinez, took the field in the 1993 World Cup and finished 15th. In addition, Paraguay scored huge upsets over Scotland and Wales in the 1993 Alfred Dunhill Cup behind Fretes and Carlos Franco's efforts, and narrowly missed the semi-finals. Paraguayans have dominated the South American Tour in recent years, winning four tournaments in 1993 alone with two runner-up finishes.

PERU

No. of Players (Rank): 2,500 (47)
No. of Courses (Rank): 13 (43)
Players/Course (Rank): 192 (14)
World Cup results 1995: 32nd.
Prominent Players: Eugenio Dunezat, Benarbe Fajardo, Hugo Nari, Sabino Quispe, Alex Tibbles, Wilfredo Uculmana.
Prominent Courses: Lima, Los Inkas
Prominent Publications: Golf Madera 3
Golf Professionals: 30

National Golf Association: Federacion Peruana de Golf, Estadio Nacional Puerto 4, Piso 4, Casilla 5637, Lima

History: The English introduced golf to Peru around the turn of the century, utilizing land near Callao for practice-fields. They moved to Santa Beatriz, a racetrack, by 1915. The first golf course, Lima Golf Club, was built in 1926.

Today, Lima and Los Inkas are the two best-known Peruvian courses: golf is established in most regions of the country, but the two most important events on the golf calendar, International de Nobles and the Peru Open, are played at Lima and Los Inkas. The Peru Open is now a part of the South American circuit and is played by all the leading South American pros.

In 1995, Peru made a rare appearance in the World Cup but finished in last place.

THE PHILIPPINES

No. of Players (Rank): 40,000 (17)
No. of Courses (Rank): 46 (26)
Players/Course (Rank): 870 (66)
World Cup results 1995: 20th
Prominent Players: Ben Arda, Antolin Fernando, Rudy Lavares, Ireneo Legaspi, Frankia Minoza, Eleuterio Nival, Robert Pactolerin, Mario Siodina, Celestino Tugot.
Prominent Courses: Manila Southwoods, Puerto Azul, Wack Wack.
National Golf Association: Republic of the Philippines Golf Association, Rm. 209 Administration Building, Rizal Memorial Sports Complex, Vito Cruz, Manila, The Philippines

History: Golf arrived in The Philippines during the 1900s, in the first years of American occupation. Among Asian nations, The Philippines were the first to compete successfully in world golfing competition after the Japanese, playing annually in the Canada Cup from the mid-1950s with conspicuous success. Celestine Tugot was the first great Philippine player, finishing 10th in the 1955 Canada Cup and anchoring the strong Philippine team throughout the 1960s. In the mid-1960s Ben Arda became the leading player, and with Eleuterio Nival formed a contending pair at the World Cup, with sixth place finishes in 1969, 1971 and 1975, with Arda finishing second to Johnny Miller in 1975 at Bangkok.

The World Cup came to The Philippines in 1977, at Wack Wack, and the team had its best ever finish, second place behind Spain, with Rudy Lavares' individual second place finish providing the impetus.

Since 1977, Philippine golfers have been hard pressed to duplicate this high level of achievement, and they have not managed a top-ten finish in the World Cup since 1978. The Philippine Open is one of the regular events on the Asian Tour, and continues to attract a top field. In 1996 the World Amateur Team Championships and the Women's World Amateur Team Championships will be staged in Manila.

PORTUGAL

No. of Players (Rank): 4,000 (36)
No. of Courses (Rank): 20 (39)
Players/Course (Rank): 200 (26)
World Cup results 1995: Did not compete.
Prominent Players: Henrique Paulino, Hernando Pina, Manuale Ribeiro, Joaquim Rodrigues, Daniel Silva, David Sulva, Fernando Silva, Rogerio Valente
Prominent Courses: Lisbon Sports Club, Quinta Do Lago, San Lorenzo, Vale Do Lobo, Vilamoura, Vila-Sol.
National Golf Association: Federacao Portuguesa de Golf Rua Almeida Brandao, 39P-1200 Lisboa, Portugal 351 (1) 661121

History: Portugal has not yet become the prominent golfing nation that Spain is, but the nation is home to some of Europe's most spectacular courses so hopes are high for a golf boom.

Golf in Portugal dates back to the founding of Oporto in 1890, making Portugal one of the oldest non-English speaking golf nations. After the founding of the Lisbon Sports Club in 1922, a few more courses were built before the war including the prestigious Estoril in 1929, but subsequently golf course construction halted.

Portugal began competing in the Canada Cup in the mid-1950s but has never enjoyed conspicuous success, with a best finish of 21st in 1966. Portugal has been host to an annual Open Championship which attracts a good field, and Portugal also hosted the 1976 Eisenhower Trophy (symbolic of the pinnacle of amateur golf achievement).

In the late 1960s and early 1970s, the opening of courses such as Quinta do Lago and Vilamoura signalled a new commitment to course quality, and since then Portugal has been promoted as a golf destination.

PUERTO RICO

No. of Players (Rank): 2,500 (45)
No. of Courses (Rank): 11 (45)
Players/Course (Rank): 227 (32)
World Cup results 1995: Did not compete.
Prominent Players: Rafael Castrillo, Juan Gonzalez, David Jimenez, Chi Chi Rodriguez, Jesus Rodriguez.
Prominent Courses: Dorado Beach, Palmas del Mar.
Golf Professionals: 21
Prominent Publications: Golf y Leisure, Puerto Rico Golf Magazine.
National Golf Association: Puerto Rico Golf Association, GPO Box 3862, San Juan, PR 00936

History: Golf was introduced to Puerto Rico in early 1920, through the military presence of the United States and through the growth of the large sugar plantations on the islands. Golf expanded after the Second World War and the Puerto Rico Golf Association was organized in 1954. About this time the first major resorts were built on the island, the best known of them the complex at Dorado Beach, including the famed Trent Jones-designed Dorado Beach G.C., which brought international exposure to the island.

The first world-class Puerto Rican golfer was Juan "Chi Chi" Rodriguez, who rose to prominence in the early 1960s and eventually became a multiple winner on the PGA TOUR. The 1961 World Cup was staged at Dorado, and Chi Chi Rodriguez teamed with his mentor Pete Cooper to finish in seventh place. The Puerto Rican team, usually featuring Chi Chi and David Jimenez, placed several times in the top ten during the 1960s in Canada/World Cup competition, although the team's fortunes faded in the 1970s.

In the 1980s Puerto Rico has become known mostly as a resort haven, with development of Palmas Del Mar complimenting the Dorado complex. The Johnnie Walker World Championship has been played here, as well as several Senior events. In addition to high-profile tournaments, the 1980s brought Chi Chi back to prominence, this time on the PGA Senior TOUR where he won many tournaments and lost in a heart-breaking playoff to Jack Nicklaus in the 1991 Senior Open.

After an absence of several years, the Puerto Rican team reappeared in the World Cup in 1992-93, managing a 26th place finish in '93.

ST. MAARTEN

No. of Players (Rank): 200 (66)
No. of Courses (Rank): 1 (68)
Players/Course (Rank): 200 (26)

History: St Maarten has a modest place in golf lore, but Joe Lee has designed the very playable Mullet Bay course which has attracted a certain following amongst aficionados of Caribbean golf.

SCOTLAND

No. of Players (Rank): 143,000 (13)
No. of Courses (Rank): 485 (6)
Players/Course (Rank): 295 (39)
World Cup results 1995: 3rd. Sam Torrance finished third in the individual competition.
Prominent Players: Laurie Auchterlonie, James Braid, Gordon Brand Jr., Eric Brown, Ken Brown, Bob Ferguson, Willie Fernie, Bernard Gallagher, Thomas Haliburton, Sandy Lyle, Colin Montgomerie, Old Tom Morris, Young Tom Morris, John Panton, Willie Park Jr., Willie Park Sr., Allan Robertson, Sam Torrance.
Prominent Courses: Blair Atholl, Blairgowrie, Bruntsfield, Burntisland, Carnoustie, Crail, Cruden Bay, Dumfries, Gleneagles, Gullane, Kilmarnock, Muirfield, Musselburgh, Nairn, North Berwick, North Inch, Prestwick, Royal Aberdeen, Royal Burgess Golfing Society of Edinburgh, Royal Dornoch, Royal Montrose, Royal Troon, St. Andrews, Turnberry, Wick.
National Golf Association: Scottish Golf Union, The Cottage 181A Whitehouse Road, Barnton, Edinburgh EH4 6BY   Scotland 44(31) 339-7546

History: Although the dispute about the actual origin of golf will likely never be solved to everyone's satisfaction, the plain truth is that, wherever golf was first played, it achieved its world-wide popularity due to its adoption by the Scottish people and by Scots royalty in particular (after 1503).

Golf almost certainly is a descendent of a rudimentary form of hockey, and the antiquity of the word Goff in the Scots dialect of English (which is in turn descended from the Northumbrian dialect of Anglo-Saxon) seems to suggest that golf was well-established in Scotland before it first appeared in written records in the mid-15th century. The term links is also derived from the Anglo-Saxon tongues. All the evidence thus points to golf developing from a form of hockey played by the English-speaking Lowland Scots. Its connection to the aristocracy and military training grounds (such as St. Andrews) also strongly suggests that it was particularly popular among feudal knights and the small private armies of Scottish nobles.

The Scottish economy was enjoying a particular boom in the early years of the 15th century and while it is ultimately unclear exactly what was the connection between golf and the European games of *chole* and *kolven* (the most plausible connection is that the Scottish game of golf was improved by the adaptation of some of the ideas of chole and the equipment of kolven), golf certainly acquired relatively massive popularity by 1457. In that year King James IV banned golf because its popularity had superceded archery and thus interfered with Scottish military preparations in the ongoing struggle with the English.

The ban on golf was renewed several times in the late 15th century, suggesting that its popularity continued to grow. But in 1502 a lasting peace between Scotland and England was announced, and the daughter of Henry VII was married to the heir to the Scottish throne. The ban on golf was rescinded and James IV himself took up the game. Golf thus has always been one of the key symbols of the peace (and eventual union) of Scotland and England. By 1513 we have evidence that the game had spread to England.

The first grounds for which we have evidence of golf in Scotland are Barrie Links (near what is now Carnoustie) in 1527—St. Andrews figures in the historical records from 1552 and Leith Links from 1592. Royal Dornoch is the fourth course we know of, dating back to at least 1621. Golf, due to the expense of equipment, was a wealthy man's game and particularly at this stage a royal one. Eight consecutive Stuart monarchs from James IV through Charles II were active golfers.

Although the game had spread to England by the early 16th century, golf was primarily a Lowland game in Scotland and is not known to have been played in the west of Scotland before 1721. By 1744 the first golf club was formed (the Honourable Company of Edinburgh Golfers, at Leith), and the St. Andrews golfers formed a club (which became the R&A) in 1754.

The Scots began to standardize the game in the mid-18th century, with the publication of an official rulebook and the standardization of courses at eighteen holes. Also in the late 18th century the first clubhouses were built and (in 1774) the first full-time greenkeeper and professional was hired. Golf continued to grow in popularity and clubs such as Burntisland, Aberdeen, Crail, and Bruntsfield were formed.

The early 19th century was a time of further expansion in Scotland, with Perth and Prestwick opening—professionals were in place at most clubs, and Allan Robertson was considered the greatest professional of his day. The expansion in the number of clubs (and in the professional ranks) led to calls for a national championship, and the Open Championship was established in 1861 (The Amateur dates back to 1859).

The popularity of golf began to soar in the second half of the 19th century as the introduction of the gutta-percha ball made the game much more affordable. At the same time the growth of modern mass-circulation newspapers (which emphasized sports coverage) and a drive for more open space and a more active lifestyle by English aristocrats led many to take up golf and bring a new popularity to the game. By 1872 the Open was no longer played exclusively at Prestwick but included a rotation of the courses (St. Andrews, Musselburgh, and Prestwick) in the Scottish Lowlands.

By the late 1890s the popularity of the game had increased so much that Scotland, with its smaller population, was superceded by England as the epicenter of golf. For the first time professionals such as J.H. Taylor (from England) and Harry Vardon (from the Channel Isles), as well as amateurs such as John Ball were considered the leading players. In 1894 the Open Championship course rotation was expanded to include Hoylake and Royal St. George in England.

In the early 1900s Scottish professional James A. Braid emerged as the leading Scottish player, and with Taylor and Vardon was part of the Great Triumvirate of leading players that dominated golf until the First World War. With the introduction of the Haskell (rubber-core) ball, golf found new popularity around the globe and Scotland lost its dominant position in the game, although its courses are still considered the traditional home of golf.

Muirfield was added to the Open rotation in 1892 (replacing Musselburgh), Troon in 1923, Carnoustie in 1931, and Turnberry in 1977 as championship golf was extended to the West of Scotland. The Royal & Ancient assumed direction of the Open in the early 1900s, ensuring that Scotland and Scottish golfers remained at the helm of championship golf even as the Open rotation of courses expanded to include English courses such as Birkdale, Deal and even Portrush in Ireland.

After a drought of great players between the 1920s and 1940s, Scotland's Eric Brown and John Panton combined in the 1950s and 1960s to restore a certain glamour to Scottish golf with several top-five finishes in the Canada Cup. In the late 1960s a new generation of Scottish players such as Bernard Gallacher, Brian Barnes and Sandy Lyle emerged to lead Scotland to four top-five finishes in five years in the 1975-79 World Cups.

With the founding of the Alfred Dunhill Cup matches at St. Andrews, a return to traditional principles of golf course design, and the ascendancy of Sandy Lyle in the late 1980s, Scotland achieved a prominence in modern golf that it had hitherto lacked. American golfers in particular have made pilgrimages to the great Scottish courses in large numbers, and such revered golf books such as *Golf in the Kingdom* have celebrated Scotland and golf. In 1985 Sandy Lyle became the first Scotsman to win the Open in generations (ironically, he won in England, at Royal St. George), a triumph he followed up with a victory in the 1988 Masters (previously the only major championship never won by a Scotsman). Scotland reached the finals of the 1987 and 1992 Dunhill Cups, losing each time to England.

In the late 1980s and early 1990s Scotland provided a number of key players to the European Ryder Cup teams, notably Sam Torrance and Colin Montgomerie. In addition, the amateur game continues to flourish with Scotland maintaining one of the highest per-capita participation rates in the world in addition to winning the European Amateur Team Championship in 1975, 1977 and 1985. Scotland had in 1995 perhaps its most distinguished year since the early 20th century, with a victory in the Dunhill Cup combined with the leading role Sam Torrance and Colin Montgomerie played on the winning Ryder Cup team.

Scotland also continues to host a large percentage of international golf championships over its classic links courses, and is revered internationally as the ancestral home of the game and, through the offices of the Royal & Ancient Golf Club, as its primary international authority.

SINGAPORE

No. of Players (Rank): 12,000 (30)
No. of Courses (Rank): 16 (41)
Players/Course (Rank): 750 (62)
World Cup results 1995: Did not compete.
Prominent Players: Phua Thiu Kiay, Kim Swee Chew, Samson Grimson, Bill Fung Hee Kwan, Alvin Liau, Lim Kian Kee, Lim Kian Tiong, Lim See Wah.
Prominent Courses: Singapore Island, Tanah-Marah.
National Golf Association: Singapore Golf Association, c/o C.L. Loong & Company, 4 Battery Road, #12000 Bank of China Building Singapore 0104, Singapore

History: Golf in Singapore dates back to 1891 when a nine-hole course, Singapore Golf Club, was built in the British fortress city. For most of its history Singapore was considered part of Malaysia, and so the city-state did not begin to field its own teams in international events until after independence in 1965. In the late 1960s Singapore entered teams in the World Cup without significant success, but the city played host to the 1969 World Cup and the team of Phua Thiu Kiay and Alvin Liau finished in 25th place.

In the 1970s Singapore continued to compete in the World Cup, with a best finish of 23rd in 1975.

However, in the 1980s Singapore improved considerably, finishing 17th in 1984 and tied for tenth in 1984 with Lim See Wah finishing seventh in the individual competition.

The Singapore Open is, interestingly, not a part of the Asian Tour but rather the Australasian Tour, and thus attracts perhaps a stronger field at the present time than other tournaments in the region—but at present Singapore does not have any native-born players in the Sony 200 rankings.

SLOVENIA

No. of Players (Rank): 980 (54)
No. of Courses (Rank): 4 (58)
Players/Course (Rank): 245 (35)
World Cup results 1995: Did not compete.
Prominent Players: Rafael Jerma, Slavko Vodnjov, Marko Vovk.
Prominent Courses: Bled, Golf Lupica
Golf Professionals: 11
National Golf Association: Golf Association of Slovenia c/o Golf Club Bled Svbode 1364260 Bled Yugoslavia 38 (64) 78282

History: Slovenia formed the heart of what used to be the Yugoslavian golf scene, with four courses—the oldest of which, Bled Golf Club, is considered first-rate and which dates back to 1938.

The former country of Yugoslavia entered several teams in World Cup competition during the mid-to-late 1970s without notable success. Today, Slovenia is the home of the Slovenian Open which attracts an international field and which this year was won by a native Slovenian, Urban Lega.

SOUTH AFRICA

No. of Players (Rank): 250,000 (10)
No. of Courses (Rank): 441 (8)
Players/Course (Rank): 567 (56)
World Cup results 1995: 8th. Retief Goosen finished fifth in the individual competition.
Prominent Players: De Wet Basson, John Bland, Tienie Britz, Bobby Cole, Ernie Els, Retief Goosen, Dale Hayes, Harold Henning, Bobby Locke, Gary Player.
Prominent Courses: Durban, Glendower, Kempton Park, Lost City, Mobray, Roodeport, Royal Johannesburg, Sun City, Wanderers, Wingate Park, Zwartkop.
National Golf Association: South Africa Golf Union, P.O. Box 1537, Cape Town 8000, South Africa

History: South Africa has a long and successful association with golf, but there is some confusion over whether seniority belongs to the Cape Golf Club founded at Wynberg in 1885, or Maritzberg Golf Club in Natal Province, which was either founded in 1886 or 1884. Certainly they were the first two clubs, with Harrismith founded shortly thereafter.

The 1890s were a time of great expansion due to the increasing commercial viability of the Cape Colony, and because of the increasing numbers of British troops stationed in South Africa due to tensions with the Boers. The game was primarily played by British regimental officers quartered in the Cape Colony and other provinces. Bleomfontein had a six-hole course as early as 1888. Klerksdorpf dates to 1889, while Port Elizabeth, Mermiston, Uitenhage, Johannesburg and Maseru date back to the 1890s.

Following the granting of independence to South Africa in 1911, golf languished somewhat due to the difficulty of maintaining turf in the sun-baked conditions that the nation expanded into. The first great South African golfers were active after the Second World War, beginning with Bobby Locke's runner-up finish to Sam Snead in the 1946 British Open. Locke won many tournaments in the late 1940s and early 1950s in an astonishing array of countries, including Britain, South Africa and the United States, culminating in three great British Open victories in 1949, 1950 and 1952. Locke's career provided a prototype for modern "world tour" golfers such as Gary Player in the 1960s and 1970s and Greg Norman today.

Gary Player emerged as Locke's successor during the mid-1950s, pairing with Locke to finish second in the 1955 Canada Cup. Player was the first in a long line of first-class players out of South Africa in the 1960s, the most prominent of which were Bobby Cole, Harold Henning, and Retief Waltman. Player was by far the most successful, winning nine major championships over a span of 21 seasons, beginning with the 1959 British Open. In the 1960s Player was one of golf's Big Three along with Jack Nicklaus and Arnold Palmer and he became only the second player to win each of golf's four major championships. In addition to his personal achievements, Player was a regular in the Canada and World Cups in the 1960s and led South Africa to many top-three finishes and a victory in 1965. He also was a multiple winner of the World Match Play title. But his services were not indispensable, as seen when in 1974 the team of Dale Hayes and Bobby Cole won South Africa's second World Cup.

In the late 1970s and early 1980s the world of golf became increasingly closed to South Africa and South Africans as the protests against South African apartheid policies intensified and led to the breaking of sporting ties. Golf had been exempted for many years because it is largely an individual sport, but South Africa's final World Cup appearance came in 1980, and their final major amateur challenge (a runner-up finish in the Eisenhower Trophy) came that same year. During the 1980s South Africa was virtually cut-off from world golf, although spectacular purses and the spectacular golf complex at Sun City lured many foreign pros to the South African Open. Gary Player and Harold Henning both found success in this decade on the PGA Senior TOUR.

Since the modification of apartheid policies (and their eventual elimination) South Africa has undergone a transformation in golf, making strong runs at the World Cup, Dunhill Cup, and in major championship golf. Exciting new players such as David Frost and Ernie Els (who became the second South African to win the United States Open, in 1994) have emerged along with promising players such as Retief Goosen. Currently first-rank South African golfers are relocating full-time to the European and American Tours, but South Africa is also the home to most of the African Tour, and many exciting players such as Tony Johnstone play here in the South African summer and switch at mid-year to the Northern Hemisphere tours. Among senior golfers, John Bland has made a mark on the PGA Senior Tour with a victory in 1995.

SPAIN

No. of Players (Rank): 85,000 (16)
No. of Courses (Rank): 160 (13)
Players/Course (Rank): 531 (52)
World Cup results 1995: 15th. Santiago Luna finished eighth in the individual competition.
Prominent Players: Seve Ballesteros, Jose-Maria Canizares, Antonio Garrido, Santiago Luna, Angel Miguel, Sebastian Miguel, Jose-Maria Olazabal, Jose Rivero, Ramon Sota.
Prominent Courses: Club de Campo, El Prat, El Saler, Las Brisas, Puerto de Hierro Sotogrande (old), Valderrama
National Golf Association: Real Federacion Espanola De Golf, Capitan Haya, 9-5E-28020 Madrid, Spain, 34 (1) 555-2757

History: The story of Spanish golf begins in the Canary Islands, where the Real Golf de Las Palmas was founded in 1891 by a group of British expatriates. Golf arrived on the mainland in 1904 with the building of Puerta de Hierro in 1904 in the Madrid vicinity. But the real expansion of Spanish golf happened on the north coast, where several courses were built near the French-Spanish border near the French resort town of Biarritz, favored by the European aristocracy (especially England's King Edward VII) in the years prior to the First World War. In the 1920s a few courses were built in the Barcelona vicinity.

Following the Second World War course construction was sluggish, but Spain entered teams in the early Canada Cups and did surprisingly well, finishing as runner-up in 1958, 1963 and 1965 with key players such as Angel Miguel, Sebastian Miguel, and Ramon Sota. Classic golf courses were laid out during this era in golf, including El Prat near Barcelona in 1956 and Sotogrande, the prototypical Costa del Sol course opening near Gibraltar in 1964.

With the 1970s came a significant boom in Spanish golf—courses were built in relatively large numbers, and at the same time Spanish golfers began achieving world class tournament victories and results. Jose-Maria Canizares, Manuel Pinero and Seve Ballesteros formed the nucleus of the Spanish renaissance. Spanish teams won the 1976, 1977, 1982 and 1984 World Cups, and individual players began to win frequently on the European and American tours, culminating in Seve Ballesteros' extraordinary 1979 Open victory at Royal Lytham, the first major ever won by a Spaniard. In fact it was primarily the success of Spanish golfers that led to the expansion of the Ryder Cup format to include a European rather than a Great Britain & Ireland team—and the Spaniards responded with tremendous success, particularly in the 1985 matches.

The 1980s were an auspicious time for Spanish golf—excellent courses continued to be developed, and Ballesteros matured into the world's leading player with two victories at Augusta and two more in the British Open.

The 1990s have been witness to the rise of a new Spanish star, Jose-Maria Olazabal, who experienced great success in Europe while also playing a limited schedule in the United States. Olazabal crowned his as-yet-young career by winning the Masters in 1994. Spain continues to contribute key players to the Ryder Cup team, and will host the Ryder Cup matches at Valderrama in September 1997. In addition Spain is host to several key events on the European PGA Tour, and fields a formidable amateur team which finished runner-up in the 1983 European Amateur Team Championship. The women's amateur teams are also quite successful, finishing runner-up in the 1975 and 1977 European Team championships as well as winning the Women's World Amateur Team Championship in Caracas in 1986. Regrettably, Spain has been in the news lately because of bickering between Seve Ballesteros and Spanish golf authorities over the actual site of the Ryder Cup matches.

SRI LANKA

No. of Players (Rank): 700 (59)
No. of Courses (Rank): 66 (22)
Players/Course (Rank): 350 (41)
World Cup results 1995: Did not compete.
Prominent Players: H.L. Premedasa, W.P. Fernando.
National Golf Association: Ceylon Golf Union, P.O. Box 309, Model Farm Road, Colombo 8, Sri Lanka

History: The history of golf in Sri Lanka dates back far indeed, back to the founding of the Colombo Club in 1881. Lacking a large population however, Sri Lanka has not made a great impact on the international game. Sri Lanka did field a team in the 1975 World Cup played in Bangkok—the team of Premedasa and Fernando finished 36th.

SWEDEN

No. of Players (Rank): 360,000 (7)
No. of Courses (Rank): 365 (10)
Players/Course (Rank): 952 (67)
World Cup results 1995: 9th. Jesper Parnevik finished tenth in the individual competition.
Prominent Players: Helen Alfreddson, Ake Berquist, Anders Forsbrand, Joakim Haeggman, Per-Ulrik Johannson, Harry Karlson, Matts Lanner, Gunnar Malmar, Liselotte Neumann, Jesper Parnevik, Magnus Persson, Ove Sellberg, Jan Sonnevi, Annika Sorenstam, Sven Tumba, Arne Werkell.
Prominent Courses: Barsebacks, Falsterbo, Forsgardens, Haninge.
Golf Professionals: 800
Golf Schools: 2
Prominent Publications: Svensk 205,000; Golf Digest 20,000.
National Golf Association: Svenska Golfforbundet, Box 84 (Kevingestrand) S182 11 Danderyd

History: Sweden has had a long association with golf, dating back to a six-hole course built in 1888 at Ryfors. The members of Gothenburg Golf Club, however, were primarily responsible for the development of Swedish golf after the club's establishment in 1891. Several clubs were built before the First World War, notably Stockholm Golf Club in 1904, Falsterbo in 1909, and by the end of the Second World War Sweden had one of the most extensive array of courses in Europe outside of Great Britain.

The Swedish Golf Federation was organized in 1904, and the country has long been active in world amateur competition and in the Canada Cup throughout the 1950s and 1960s, but the best the Swedes could manage was an 18th place finish in 1956. It wasn't until the 1970s when Gunnar Mueller finished fifth in the 1978 World Cup, that Sweden posed a credible threat in first-class competition, although the amateurs managed to finish runners-up in the 1963 European Amateur Team Championship played at Falsterbo.

With the 1980s Swedish golf hit new heights with high achievement in practically every competitive level. The Women's Amateurs managed victories in the 1981 and 1987 European Amateur Team championships, while the Amateur men finished runner-up in 1985 in the same European Team championships at Halmstad, before winning the Eisenhower Trophy in 1990 at Christchurch.

The professional women's outlook also brightened considerably in the 1980s with the rise of international star Liselotte Neumann, who won the 1988 U.S. Women's Open in addition to several other titles internationally. Teamed with rising star Helen Alfredsson, she took home the Sunrise Cup (the women's equivalent to the World Cup) in 1992. Alfredsson won her own first major in 1993 with a victory in the Dinah Shore. Annika Sorenstam continued the trend with an outstanding season in 1995, leading the LPGA in official money as well as winning the 1995 U.S. Women's Open.

The Swedish men have yet to win a major championship, but players such as Anders Forsbrand, Mats Lanner, Magnus Persson and Per-Ulrik Johannsen, in addition to newcomers Joakim Haeggman and Jesper Parnevik make up one of the strongest international contingents. The Swedes scored a victory in the 1991 World Cup at Rome with the team of Forsbrand and Johannsen, and reached the semifinals of the Alfred Dunhill Cup in 1993.

In the 1990s Sweden continues to move from strength to strength, with Joakim Haeggman becoming the first Swede selected to the Ryder Cup team (in 1993), while Jesper Parnevik made a bold run at the British Open before faltering on the final hole. The Swedish women form a dependable part of the surprisingly strong European team in the Solheim Cup. The Swedes host annual events on the European PGA Tour, the European Senior Tour, and the European Women's Tour, and participation in golf continues to build strongly in part due to the continuing success at the professional level.

SWITZERLAND

No. of Players (Rank): 23,000 (24)
No. of Courses (Rank): 47 (25)
Players/Course (Rank): 489 (46)
World Cup results 1995: 12th. Andre Bossart and

Paolo Quirici finished tied for 19th in the individual competition.
Prominent Players: Patrick Bagnoud, Jacky Bonvin, Andre Bossert, Bernard Codonier, Robert Lanz, Paolo Quirici, Franco Salmina, Otto Schoepfer, Ronald Tingley
Prominent Courses: Crans-sur-Sierre, Geneva, Lausanne, Montreux
National Golf Association: Association suisse de golf, En Ballque, Case Postale, 1066 Epalinges

History: Switzerland had its first course as far back as 1893, a course built on the initiative of the Hotel Kulm at St. Moritz. Montreux dates back to 1900, and the Association suisse de golf to 1902. Switzerland maintained one of the most complete golfing calendars in the pre-Second World War era, with the annual match-play national championship dating back to 1907.

Switzerland has placed teams regularly in Canada and World Cups since 1954, but without particular success since the stunning fourth place finish of Andre Bossert in 1991 at Rome elevated the Swiss to an 11th place finish. Switzerland continues to host many Tour events and international tournaments, the most prominent of which are the Senior Zurich Pro-Am and the Canon European Masters.

TAIWAN

No. of Players (Rank): 400,000 (6)
No. of Courses (Rank): 29 (34)
Players/Course (Rank): 13,793 (74)
World Cup results 1995: Did not compete.
Prominent Players: Chen Ching Po, Hsieh Yung Yo, Kuo Chie Hsiung, Li Wen-Shen, Lin Wen Li, Lu Hsi Chuen, Lu Ling Huan, Mei Yun Wang.
Prominent Courses: Chang Gung, Sunrise, Taiwan.
National Golf Association: Golf Association of the Republic of China 71, Lane 369 Tunhua South Road, Taipei, Taiwan (106)

History: Taiwan has an extremely successful golfing record, second only to Japan, among Asian nations, and the record is particularly strong when the small number of available courses is considered. The Shanghai Club, founded in 1896, was the first Chinese golf club, and after the Chinese Nationalists fled to Taiwan in 1949, golf followed and met up with the course established by American occupying forces. Shortly afterwards Taiwan (sometimes referred to as the Republic of China, or Chinese Taipei) established itself as one of the major forces in international golf.

From the late 1950s Taiwan has had particular success in the World Cup, rarely finishing out of the top ten and scoring a victory in 1972 when Hsieh Mon Nam took the individual trophy and Lu Liang Huan finished fourth to defeat the Japanese and South Africans at Royal Melbourne. Lu had made a huge impression on the golfing world a year earlier when he finished second in the British Open to Lee Trevino at Royal Birkdale.

Throughout the remainder of the 1970s Taiwan remained a perennial threat in the World Cup, with six more top-five finishes and a second-place finish in the 1976 individual competition from Kuo Chie-Hsiung.

In the 1980s the Taiwan team disappeared from international competition for political reasons, and since returning in 1987 the team has been less of a threat although still typically finishing in the top ten. Taiwan currently hosts several Tour events on a variety of tours, and players such as Chen Tze Chung are perennial title favorites, with Chen holding the lone Sony Top 100 ranking among Taiwan professionals.

TANZANIA

No. of Players (Rank): 350 (65)
No. of Courses (Rank): 5 (55)
Players/Course (Rank): 70 (4)
World Cup results 1995: Did not compete.

THAILAND

No. of Players (Rank): 10,300 (32)
No. of Courses (Rank): 19 (41)
Players/Course (Rank): 542 (53)
World Cup results 1995: 26th.
Prominent Players: Uthai Dabphavibul, Suthep Messawud, Sukree Oncham, Sareh Sangsui, Samsadi Srinagar.
Prominent Courses: Panya Resort, The Royal Gems, Royal Thai Army
National Golf Association: Thailand Golf Association Railway Training, Centre Vibhavadee Rangsit Road, Bangkok Thailand

History: Golf in Thailand stretches back to 1890, with the founding of the Royal Bangkok Club which had a temple for its clubhouse. Since Siam maintained its independence throughout the 19th-20th centuries, the earliest courses were built by British engineers working in Siam rather than the British military occupying the country.

Thailand has competed quite successfully in the

Canada and World Cups since 1957, with solid performances occasionally broken by flashes of brilliance such as the fourth place finish in 1969 at Singapore, when Suchee Onchum finished 3rd in the individual competition. Navantnee, in Bangkok, played host to the 1975 World Cup and the Thai team finished a quite credible seventh. Since then, however, the team has finished no better than 19th, although a Thai team competed in the final sixteen of the Alfred Dunhill Cup in 1992.

Today Thailand plays host to international tournaments on the Women's Asian Tour and the Asian PGA Tour.

TRINIDAD & TOBAGO

No. of Players (Rank): 3,100 (41)
No. of Courses (Rank): 10 (46)
Players/Course (Rank): 310 (40)
World Cup results 1995: Did not compete.
Prominent Players: Peter Singh, Lennox Yearwood.
National Golf Association: Trinidad & Tobago Golf Association, 7A Warner Street, New Town Port of Spain, Trinidad

History: Trinidad's lone foray into major world competition was the 1974 World Cup, in which the team finished a respectable 20th place. Since then, Trinidad has been principally known in golf as a winter destination, with the Mount Irvine Bay course on Trinidad the most popular.

UNITED STATES

No. of Players (Rank): 24,563,000 (1)
No. of Courses (Rank): 14,000 (1)
Players/Course (Rank): 1,754 (71)
World Cup results 1995: 1st. Davis Love finished 1st in the individual competition; Fred Couples finished eighth.
Prominent Players: Amy Alcott, Paul Azinger, Jim Barnes, Patty Berg, Jane Blalock, Julius Boros, Pat Bradley, Jack Burke, Jr., Donna Caponi, JoAnne Carner, John Cook, Fred Couples, Ben Crenshaw, Beth Daniel, Jimmy Demaret, Judy Dickinson, Leo Diegel, Olin Dutra, Chick Evans, Doug Ford, Ed Furgol, Hubert Green, Ralph Guldahl, Walter Hagen, Chick Harbert, Dutch Harrison, Sandra Haynie, Ben Hogan, Jock Hutchinson, Juli Inkster, Hale Irwin, Bobby Jones, Betsy King, Tom Kite, Lawson Little, Gene Littler, Nancy Lopez, Davis Love III, John McDermott, Charles Blair Macdonald, Meg Mallon, Lloyd Mangrum, Carol Mann, Laurie Merten, Cary Middlecoff, Johnny Miller, Dottie Mochrie, Orville Moody, Byron Nelson, Jack Nicklaus, Andy North, Francis Ouimet, Arnold Palmer, Henry Picard, Jerry Pate, Judy Rankin, Betsy Rawls, Paul Runyan, Gene Sarazen, Patty Sheehan, Denny Shute, Horton Smith, Sam Snead, Hollis Stacy, Payne Stewart, Dave Stockton, Louise Suggs, Jerome Travers, Lee Trevino, Sherry Turner, Lanny Wadkins, Tom Watson, Tom Weiskopf, Kathy Whitworth, Craig Wood, Mickey Wright, Babe Zaharias.

Prominent Courses: Aronimink, Atlanta Athletic Club, Augusta National, Baltimore, Baltusrol, Barton Creek, Bay Hill, Bellerive, Bethpage, Black Diamond, Blackwolf Run, Brooklawn, Butler National, C.C. of Detroit, C.C. of Indianapolis, Camargo, Canterbury, Cascades, Castle Pines, Cedar Ridge, Champions, Charlotte, Cherry Hills, Chicago, Cog Hill, Colonial, Congressional, C.C. of North Carolina, The Country Club (Mass.), The Country Club (Ohio), Crooked Stick, Crystal Downs, Cypress Point, Del Paso, Desert Forest, Desert Highlands, Desert Mountain, Doral, Double Eagle, Dunes Club, Eugene, Firestone, Firethorn, Fishers Island, Forest Highlands, Garden City, The Golf Club, G. C. of Georgia, Grandfather, Greenville, Haig Point, Harbour Town, Hazeltine National, High Pointe, The Honors Course, Indianwood, Interlachen, Inverness, Jupiter Hills, Kahkwa Club, Kauai Lagoons, Kiawah, Kittansett Club, La Grange, Lake Nona, La Quinta, Laurel Valley, The Links at Spanish Bay, Long Cove, Los Angeles, Maidstone, Mauna Kea, Meadow Brook, Medinah, Merion, Milwaukee, Montclair, Muirfield Village, Muskogee, NCR, National Golf Links of America, North Shore, Northwood, Oak Hill, Oakland Hills, Oakmont, Oak Tree, Ohio State, Old Marsh, Old Tabby, Old Warson, Olympia Fields, Olympic, PGA National, PGA West, Pasatiempo, Peachtree, Pebble Beach, Pinehurst, Pine Tree, Pine Valley, Plainfield, Point O'Woods, Prairie Dunes, Princeville, Pumpkin Ridge, Quaker Ridge, Richland, Ridgewood, Riviera, Rolling Green, Sahalee, St. Louis, Salem, San Francisco, Saucon Valley, Scioto, Shadow Creek, Sherwood, Shinnecock Hills, Shoal Creek, Shoreacres, Skokie, Somerset Hills, Southern Hills, Spyglass Hill, Stanford University, Stanwich Club, Sycamore Hills, TPC at Sawgrass, Tanglewood, Troon, Troon North, Valhalla, Valley Club of Montecito, Wade Hampton, Wannamoisett, Waverly, Wild Dunes, Wilmington, Winged Foot, World Woods, Wynstone.

National Golf Association: United States Golf Association, Golf House, Far Hills, NJ 07931, (708) 234-2300.

History: Aside from Scotland and England, no country has had a greater impact on the history of golf than the United States: its effect on the modern game, its popularity and rules is simply incalculable.

Golf had somewhat humble origins in the United States, for like Scotland the first appearance of golf in the public records is by way of banning it, in this case a ban applying to the streets of Albany, New York issued in 1659.

Golf disappeared for over a century until the formation of the South Carolina Golf Club in 1786 in Charleston, which was the first golf club formed outside of the United Kingdom. Golf flourished in South Carolina for a short period of time, but then again died out—the primary connection of the USA to golf throughout the 19th century was the hickory exported from America to construct good club shafts.

Golf was permanently established in 1884 in Virginia, with the first surviving course constructed for the St. Andrews Club (New York) which was founded in 1888. In the 1890s the popularity of golf increased rapidly, helped by the efforts of Charles Blair Macdonald, a former pupil of Old Tom Morris who was instrumental in the foundation of the Chicago Golf Club and, in 1895, the United States Golf Association. The USGA immediately established both Amateur and Open Championships; the Open was in particular dominated by foreign-born players for two decades. In addition the Western Golf Association was founded and staged the annual Western Open which in its first decades had quasi-major status and was, as a PGA TOUR event today, the first tournament with ties to the present TOUR.

The early 1900s were a time of great expansion of the game to the Southeast and Western States. The era of the great amateur course architects was in early flower, yielding courses such as Oakmont and the National Golf Links. English stars such as Harry Vardon made their first visits to the United States, and Donald Ross began his pivotal tenure at Pinehurst.

The 1910s proved to be a time of even greater expansion, with courses such as Pebble Beach, Merion, Oakland Hills, San Francisco Golf Club, Scioto, and Inverness opening for play. John J. McDermott became the first American-born player to win the U.S. Open, and in 1913 Francis Ouimet defeated heavy favorites Harry Vardon and Ted Ray to win the Open in the championship that first brought large-scale national attention to the game. During the decade the careers of Walter Hagen and Bobby Jones first got underway, and in 1910 the USGA took the momentous decision to issue Rules of Golf separately from the Royal & Ancient Golf Club, beginning a period of eighty years in which two different rules systems were in force. The Professional Golfers Association of America was founded and began staging the PGA Championship in 1916.

The 1920s are known as the Golden Era of American golf, for the massive national popularity of champions such as Jones, Hagen and Gene Sarazen and the abundance of outstanding courses opened, including Pine Valley, Cypress Point, Winged Foot, Olympic, Seminole, Medinah, Oak Hill, Los Angeles, and Quaker Ridge. Jones in particular reached heights of popularity unmatched by golfers until the 1960s, and thousands of new golfers flocked to the game nationwide. During this decade tournaments such as the Texas Open, the North & South, the Western Open, and several winter tournaments in Florida provided the beginnings of a men's professional circuit. The Ryder Cup and Walker Cups also date back to this decade, which marked the first real beginnings of worldwide golf with the leading players regularly crossing the Atlantic to play in the major championships and Cup matches.

The Great Depression ended the golf boom and the 1930s were a time of retrenchment for the game, but the work of enterprising individuals ensured that the popularity of the game continued to increase even if the capital to bankroll flocks of new courses and tournaments was lacking. Augusta National, Shinnecock Hills, Pinehurst No. 2, Southern Hills and Prairie Dunes were the great new courses of the era, which also saw the rise of the professional golf architect in Robert Trent Jones. The increasing number of professional tournaments led to the formation of a PGA Circuit in 1933 and The Masters also dates to that year. Only a few players could (or were willing to) support themselves via the professional tournament Circuit, but in the mid-1930s Lawson Little became the first prominent amateur to switch over the the touring pro side, a milestone in the growth of the TOUR. Another TOUR tradition, the pro-am, found its beginnings in the 1930s at the Bing Crosby National Pro-Am. The late 1930s also marked the emergence of Byron Nelson, Sam Snead and Ben Hogan, who would become golf's second generation of dominating players.

Golf went into a state of hibernation during the early 1940s due to World War Two, with the fledgling PGA TOUR reduced to a few dates which paid prize money in War Bonds, and the major championships and international matches sharply curtailed. However, the TOUR came back to life in 1945 with Byron Nelson winning eleven consecutive tournaments and 17 for the year to become the Associated Press' Athlete of the Year (the first golfer to win the honor since Bobby Jones). The TOUR reached new heights of popularity in the post-war years and in 1947 golf was first televised with a local St. Louis station providing limited coverage of the U.S. Open. The LPGA dates to the late 1940s due to the efforts of a forceful group of women golfers led by Babe Zaharias.

Golf boomed anew in the 1950s in part due to its popularity with leading entertainers such as Bing Crosby and Bob Hope as well as President Dwight Eisenhower who joined Augusta National and was popularly associated with the game. Ben Hogan won three legs of the modern Grand Slam in 1953 and become the decade's leading player, while the PGA TOUR as a whole was able to expand to a nearly full annual schedule of events, one of which (the World Championship of Golf) offered the first $100,000 purse. Aggressive course-building resumed in the 1950s and it was the era of Robert Trent Jones and Dick Wilson, with courses such as Point O'Woods, Bellerive, Firestone, and Meadow Brook opening during the decade.

During the 1960s golf experienced its greatest boom to date, as the growth of television and televised sports coincided with the emergence of Arnold Palmer, Jack Nicklaus, and Gary Player as golf's Big Three. Palmer in particular captured the public's fancy in a way no golfer has before or since, and millions of Americans took up the game at courses built around the new suburban communities that were being developed. PGA TOUR purses skyrocketed during the decade and golfers such as Palmer had an international schedule of endorsements, exhibitions, and tournaments that catapulted them to the top-rank of American sportsmen. Their success led them to break away from the PGA of America and form the PGA TOUR as an independent organization with Joe Dey as the first Tour commissioner. The LPGA also expanded significantly in this decade with the dominating play of Mickey Wright and Kathy Whitworth. Architects such as Pete Dye, Ed Seay, Tom Fazio and Ted Robinson did their early work in this decade, with courses such as Harbour Town, Spyglass Hill, Mauna Kea, The Golf Club and Doral showing new design ideas to golfers.

In the 1970s the career of Jack Nicklaus, Lee Trevino, Johnny Miller, and Tom Watson ensured even greater popularity for professional golf, which now had become a big business under the direction of administrators such as Deane Beman and super-agents like Mark McCormack. The LPGA likewise flourished with popular new players such as Jane Blalock, Judy Rankin, JoAnne Carner and Nancy Lopez, and in the late 1970s the establishment of the Legends of Golf tournament presaged the launch of the PGA Senior TOUR. Courses such as Jupiter Hills and Muirfield Village were the highlights of a decade of decline in the opening of new courses.

Prosperity and the emergence of new stars and the Senior TOUR made the 1980s a decade of huge growth for the game both at the professional and amateur level. The PGA TOUR went to an all-exempt list of 125 players in 1981 and also launched the Tournament Players Clubs, an ambitious plan for a network of "stadium" design courses that would host PGA Tournaments across the country, beginning with The Players Championship at the TPC at Sawgrass. Television also became a backbone of TOUR revenues as virtually every date on the TOUR calendar was televised, and several made-for-television events such as the Skins Game debuted. The LPGA and the PGA Senior TOUR flourished, although the LPGA to a lesser degree due to the lack of good television and print exposure. The emergence of top-flight foreign players such as Greg Norman, Seve Ballesteros, Bernhard Langer and Nick Faldo ensured a greater rivalry in the Ryder Cup matches and major championships, thus further stimulating interest in the game and in a world tour. While the business of golf was booming in the sales of equipment, real estate, apparel, and resort vacations, late in the decade several conflicts over the legality of high-tech equipment prompted several lawsuits between companies and the governing bodies in the game. With players flocking to the game, courses were opened at a record pace in the 1980s, including classics such as Black Diamond, Haig Point, Desert Highlands, Lake Nona, PGA West and the TPC at Sawgrass, although some designs were considered overly radical and often overly penal.

In the 1990s a new generation of leading professionals led by Fred Couples, Paul Azinger and Davis Love III has emerged, and interest in the game (stimulated also by the rivalries created by the rise of golf stars in other nations) has heightened interest in golf as never before. The LPGA has also experienced rapid growth, as well as mini-tours such as the NIKE TOUR launched in 1990 by the PGA TOUR and the Ben Hogan Company. A new level of variety and creativity is evident in course design with new courses such as the World Woods, Old Tabby, The Ocean Course, Sandhills, Sandpines, Shadow Creek and Pumpkin Ridge. Formation of The Golf Channel, a cable network, as well as many home pages on the World Wide Web, provides evidence that golf will continue to grow in popularity and exposure in the U.S. in the foreseeable future.

URUGUAY

No. of Players (Rank): 500 (60)

No. of Courses (Rank): 4 (58)
Players/Course (Rank): 125 (15)
World Cup results 1995: Did not compete.
Prominent Players: Juan Dapiaggi, Juan Esmoris, Enrique Fernendez, Clever Menendez, Juan Sereda, Pascual Viola
Prominent Courses: Club de Golf del Uruguay

History: Uruguay first appeared on the international golf scene in 1961, fielding a team which finished 25th in the Canada Cup. Juan Sereda and Jose Esmoris went on to finish 13th in the 1962 event, which remains the high point in Uruguay's competitive record, but the Uruguayans continued to field teams throughout the 1960s and early 1970s with some success. The Uruguayan Open played at Club de Golf del Uruguay in Montevideo is a regular stop on the South American tour and continues to attract a strong regional field.

VENEZUELA

No. of Players (Rank): 4,000 (36)
No. of Courses (Rank): 23 (38)
Players/Course (Rank): 174 (23)
World Cup results 1995: 28th.
Prominent Players: Manuelo Bernardez, Francisco Gonzalez, Ramon Munoz, Teobaldo Perez, Angel Sanchez.
Prominent Courses: Lagunita.
National Golf Association: Federacion Venezolana de Golf Unidad Comercial "La Florida," Local 5, Avenida Avila La Florida Caracas 1050 Venezuela

History: Venezuela was the second South American country, after Argentina, to prove to be a force in international golf, fielding Canada Cup teams since 1958 and finishing in the top ten on two occasions (1958 and 1974), while playing host to the World Cup at Lagunita in 1974. Lagunita also was the site of a South American tour stop, and hosted the Eisenhower Trophy competition in 1986.

VIRGIN ISLANDS

No. of Players (Rank): 500 (64)
No. of Courses (Rank): 4 (58)
Players/Course (Rank): 125 (15)
World Cup results 1995: Did not compete.
Prominent Courses: Carambola, Mahogany Run.
National Golf Association: United States Golf Association, Golf House, Far Hill, NJ 07931

History: The Virgin Islands have been known largely as a popular golfing destination more than as a source of international golfers, due to the small population base and generally spotty economic progress. Carambola and Mahogany Run are the best known of the resort courses (Carambola on St. Croix, and Mahogany Run on St. Thomas).

WALES

No. of Players (Rank): 35,000 (18)
No. of Courses (Rank): 119 (18)
Players/Course (Rank): 294 (38)
World Cup results 1995: 16th. Mark Mouland finished 19th in the individual competition.
Prominent Players: Craig Defoy, Harold Gould, Brian Huggett, David Llewellyn, Sid Mouland, Mark Mouland, Philip Parkin, Dai Rees, Dennis Smalldon, Dave Thomas, David Vaughan, Ian Woosnam.
Prominent Courses: Royal Porthcawl.
National Golf Association: Welsh Golfing Union Powys House, Cwmbran Gwent, NP44 1PB Wales 44 (633) 870261

History: Golf arrived comparatively late in Wales with the oldest club, Pontnewydd, dating back to 1875. Development was rapid, with many clubs dating back before the turn of the century, most notably Royal Porthcawl which is the only Welsh club given the "royal" honorific.

The Welsh national team has yet to succeed in the home internationals against Ireland, Scotland, and England, but the Welsh team has fared extremely well in Canada Cup and World Cup team competitions with eighteen top-ten finishes since 1954, including eight consecutive top-eight finishes between 1956 and 1963 when Dai Rees and Dave Thomas were at the height of their careers. Rees also served as Captain of the British Ryder Cup squad.

Leading players emerging in the 1960s were Brian Huggett and Sid Mouland, and Wales managed a fifth-place finish in the 1970 World Cup. During the 1970s Wales produced David Vaughan, David Llewellyn and Craig Defoy, but struggled to reproduce the results of the past until 1979, when the Welsh team placed second in the European Amateur Team Championship.

In the 1980s Ian Woosnam, David Llewellyn and Mark Mouland raised the profile of Welsh golf to its highest-ever level, Llewellyn and Woosnam combining for a victory in the World Cup and Woosnam and Mouland subsequently teaming for several top-five finishes. Woosnam became the first Welshman to win a major championship in 1992 with a victory in The Masters, and he remains Wales' number-one golfer although he has slipped far from the number-one world ranking he held briefly in 1991.

In 1995, Wales hosted the Walker Cup matches at Royal Porthcawl, the most prestigious international ever staged in the country. The stunning upset victory of the Great Britain & Ireland team fueled speculation that Porthcawl will be added to the rotation for future Cup matches.

ZAMBIA

No. of Players (Rank): 4,000 (38)
No. of Courses (Rank): 20 (39)
Players/Course (Rank): 200 (26)
World Cup results 1995: Did not compete.
Prominent Courses: Lusaka.

History: Zambia has yet to be considered one of the major players in the international arena—however, 1994 U.S. Senior Open champ Simon Hobday is a veteran of the Zambian national amateur team from the 1960s. In addition, the country hosts the annual Zambian Open at Lusaka Golf Club in the capital city, which has attracted an international field including past winners Ian Woosnam, David Llewellyn and Gordon Brand. Golf in Zambia dates back to 1908 and the founding of Livingstone by the British colonists.

ZIMBABWE

No. of Players (Rank): 35,000 (18)
No. of Courses (Rank): 62 (23)
Players/Course (Rank): 565 (55)
World Cup results 1995: 10th.
Prominent Players: Antony Edwards, Leon Evans, Donald Gammon, William Koen, Mark McNulty, Nick Price, Tim Price.
Prominent Courses: Chapman, Royal Harare.
National Golf Association: Zimbabwe Golf Association, P.O. Box 3327, Harare, Zimbabwe

History: Golf arrived in Zimbabwe (then known as Rhodesia) in 1895 with the founding of Bulawayo. Royal Salisbury (now Royal Harare), the most prestigious course in the country, dates from 1899. Zimbabwe arrived late as a leading golfing nation, but has hosted a regular stop on the African Tour for years in the Zimbabwe Open, which is usually staged at Royal Harare.

As Rhodesia, Zimbabwe competed in the 1971 World Cup with a respectable 21st place finish behind the outstanding play of Donald Gammon, but has emerged as a leading golf nation only in the late 1980s with the emergence of Nick Price and Mark McNulty as world-class golfers. Price and McNulty both cracked the top-twenty in the Sony Rankings during 1992 with Price reaching eighth. Both improved in 1993 and the two combined in the 1993 World Cup to finish second behind the United States.

Nick Price had perhaps the finest season ever recorded on the PGA TOUR by a non-American in 1994, winning the British Open and PGA Championship as well as taking two other tournaments, winning every player of the year award, and taking first place in the Sony Rankings from Greg Norman. Price had a very successful campaign in 1995 and held on to second place in the Sony Ranking, but did not win a tournament. Zimbabwe cracked the top-ten at the World Cup again in 1995.

GOLF, BY U.S. STATE

OVERVIEW: *Key statistics, history, prominent players, tournaments, and courses, plus a census of golfers.*

ALABAMA

No. of Players (Rank): 247,000 (31)
Participation Rate (Rank): 7.1% (44)
Percentage of Female Players (Rank): 12.9 (47)
Percentage of Senior Golfers (Rank): 23.5 (15)
Prominent Golfers: Glen Day, Gardner Dickinson, Buddy Gardner, Hubert Green, Steve Lowery, Larry Nelson, Dicky Pride, Nancy Ramsbottom, Mike Smith.
Major Golf Companies: Burton.
Prominent Courses: Shoal Creek, Grand National, Birmingham C.C.
State Golf Association: Alabama Golf Association, P.O. Box 20149, Birmingham, AL 35216—(205) 979-1234.

Highlights: Alabama has been in the news in recent years primarily for the controversy at Shoal Creek Golf Club, the highly-ranked Jack Nicklaus-designed private club that was accused of race discrimination just prior to hosting the 1990 PGA Championship. In 1992 the State embarked on the remarkable development of the Robert Trent Jones Golf Trail, seven 36- and 54-hole golf centers situated throughout the state combining low fees and quality courses from Robert Trent Jones, Inc.

Prior to the 1980s, Alabama had hosted the Montgomery and Mobile Opens on the PGA TOUR as early as 1946, but the tournaments did not last. The 1974 and 1986 Senior Women's Amateurs were staged in Point Clear. Ironically, it was the highly successful staging of the PGA Championship at Shoal Creek in 1984 that led to the controversies of 1990 when the Championship returned.

ALASKA

No. of Players (Rank): N/A
Participation Rate (Rank): N/A
Percentage of Female Players (Rank): N/A
Percentage of Senior Golfers (Rank): N/A
Prominent Golfers: Danny Edwards.
Prominent Courses: Eagle Glen.
State Golf Association: Anchorage Golf Association, P.O. Box 112210, Anchorage, AK 99511—(907) 349-4653.

Highlights: Alaska has yet to host a prominent tournament, but has the advantage of offering over 18 hours of sunshine during the peak summer months. Several courses, such as Eagle Glen at Elmendorf Air Force Base, come highly recommended.

ARIZONA

No. of Players (Rank): 437,000 (19)
Participation Rate (Rank): 13.5% (15)
Percentage of Female Players (Rank): 21.6 (22)
Percentage of Senior Golfers (Rank): 30.2 (4)
Prominent Golfers: Todd Barranger, Amy Fruhwirth, Robert Gaona, Dick Lotz, Billy Mayfair, Deborah Parks, Don Pooley, Howard Twitty.
Major Golf Companies: Antigua Sportswear, Arizona Manufacturing, Karsten Manufacturing, Royal Grip.
Prominent Courses: Desert Forest, Desert Highlands, Desert Mountain-Cochise, Desert Mountain-Renegade, Forest Highlands, La Paloma, Troon, Troon North, Ventana Canyon-Canyon.
State Golf Association: Arizona Golf Association, 11801 North Tatum Blvd., Suite 247, Phoenix, AZ 85028—(602) 953-5990

Highlights: Arizona is far too hot to host USGA Championships, but the state has played host to both the Phoenix Open and the Tucson Open since the close of the Second World War, as well as the Skins Game in recent years. But it is more as a golfing destination for amateur players and retirees that Arizona has made its mark, with its sparkling array of desert courses. It was the tight restrictions on water usage and irrigation (usually limiting new golf courses to 80 acres of grass) that led architects to develop the "target golf" design approach in the early 1980s where grassed tee-to-green areas are replaced by small, pocketed landing areas. This type of design has become associated with Arizona and in particular the designs of Jack Nicklaus.

In addition to its excellent courses, Arizona is the long-time home of Karsten Manufacturing Co., makers of PING clubs, and thus has benefited greatly from the golf equipment boom of the 1980s and 1990s. Due to the strict water-usage restrictions, Arizona has also been a leader in golf-oriented environmental testing and innovation.

ARKANSAS

No. of Players (Rank): 123,000 (37)
Participation Rate (Rank): 6.1% (46)
Percentage of Female Players (Rank): 19.7 (29)
Percentage of Senior Golfers (Rank): 30.6 (2)
Prominent Golfers: Bill Hall, Paul Runyan, John Daly.
Prominent Courses: Texarkana, Hardscrabble.
State Golf Association: Arkansas State Golf Association, 2311 Biscayne Drive, Suite 308, Little Rock, AR 72207—(501) 227-8555

Highlights: Arkansas is known as the home of John Daly, as well as the home of several outstanding courses. The state was home to the Ozark Open, which briefly graced the PGA TOUR in the late 1940s, but since then the state has seen little of major golf tournaments until the 1990s, when the Texarkana Open became a regular stop on the Hogan and later NIKE TOUR. Chenal Country Club in Little Rock was recently named the third best new private golf course by Golf Digest, while several retirement communities such as Hot Springs Village, Bellas Vista and Cherokee Village have proved popular for year-round golfers.

CALIFORNIA

No. of Players (Rank): 2,782,000 (1)
Participation Rate (Rank): 10.9% (28)
Percentage of Female Players (Rank): 20.3 (25)
Percentage of Senior Golfers (Rank): 25.9 (10)
Prominent Golfers: Amy Alcott, George Archer, Brandie Burton, Billy Casper, John Daly, Al Geiberger, Juli Inkster, Gene Littler, Nancy Lopez, Gary McCord, Phil Mickelson, Johnny Miller, Corey Pavin, Loren Roberts, Bob Rosburg, Scott Simpson, Craig Stadler, Dave Stockton, Ken Venturi, Mickey Wright.
Major Golf Companies: Aldila, Ashworth, Belding Sports, Callaway, Cleveland, Cobra, Ray Cook, Cubic Balance, Daiwa, Fila, Founders Club, Garfalloy, Kunnan, Langert, Lyle & Scott, Lynx, Mitsushiba, Odyssey, Plop Putter, Rawlings, Slotline, Stan Thompson, Taylor Made, Tiger Shark, Yamaha, Yonex.
Prominent Courses: Carmel Valley Ranch, Cypress Point, Del Paso, Haggin Oaks, Half Moon Bay, La Quinta-Mountain, Links at Monarch Beach, Links at Spanish Bay, Los Angeles (North), PGA West (Nicklaus Private), PGA West (Stadium), Pasatiempo, Pebble Beach, Riviera, San Francisco, Sherwood, Silverado, Spyglass Hill, Stanford University, Valley Cub of Montecito.
State Golf Association: (Northern) California Golf Association, P.O. Box NCGA, Pebble Beach, CA 93953—(408) 625-4653

Highlights: While California was not the first Pacific Coast state in which golf was played, Californians have taken to the game with great zeal over the past 70 years, and since 1919 California has been home to Pebble Beach, universally recognized as one of the five greatest courses in the world. Cypress Point, also considered in that group, dates from 1929.

The first courses in the state date back to the 1890s, and a Pacific Coast Golf Association staged an annual open championship from 1901. The primary development of the game occured in the Bay Area, with clubs established early at Oakland and San Francisco as well as the Monterey Peninsula. California was home to the first work of Alister MacKenzie in this country, with Cypress Point, Pasatiempo and the Valley Club of Montecito among others still offering testament to his genius.

From the early 1920s California anchored the first weeks on the PGA tournament circuit, with the Los Angeles Open and later the Bing Crosby National Pro-Am on the Monterey Peninsula offering excellent courses, top fields, and good purses. California, in fact, is the birthplace of the pro-am—an idea which grew out of the Crosby.

There are several regular major tour tournament stops today in California including the Mercedes Championships (La Costa), the AT&T National Pro-Am (Pebble Beach et al), the Bob Hope Chrysler Classic (several Palm Springs area courses), the Buick Invitational of California (Torrey Pines), the Nissan Los Angeles Open (Riviera), the Shark Shootout (Sherwood Oaks), the Skins Game (Bighorn), Inamori Classic (StoneRidge), The Transamerica (Silverado), Ralph's Senior Classic (Rancho Park), and the Raley's Senior Gold Rush (Rancho Murieta).

The PGA Championship was held at Pebble Beach in 1929, and since then California has hosted many major championships of golf, including acting as the permanent home of the Dinah Shore, a major championship on the LPGA Tour.

California is home to many famed golf resorts, including PGA West, La Quinta, Silverado, La Costa,

Rancho Bernardo, and the complex at Pebble Beach comprising Pebble Beach, Spyglass Hill, and the Links at Spanish Bay. In addition, California is home to many golf-oriented residential and retirement communities of the first rank.

The state is headquarters for many of golf's best known manufacturing concerns, and has played host to the National Golf Foundation's Golf Summit. The PGA West Coast Show was held in Anaheim for many years before moving to Las Vegas in 1995.

COLORADO

No. of Players (Rank): 372,000 (22)
Participation Rate (Rank): 12.6% (22)
Percentage of Female Players (Rank): 23.8 (14)
Percentage of Senior Golfers (Rank): 22.8 (22)
Prominent Golfers: Tommy Armour III, Lori West.
Major Golf Companies: Descente.
Prominent Courses: Bear Creek, Broadmoor-East, Castle Pines, Cherry Hills, C.C. of the Rockies, Keystone Ranch, Telluride.
State Golf Association: The Colorado Golf Association, Suite 101, 5655 South Yosemite, Englewood, CO 80111—(303) 779-4653

Highlights: Colorado offers 300 days of sunshine, breathtaking mountain vistas, and thin air that allows the ball to travel 8-15 percent farther than at sea level. With over 175 courses, Colorado is home to one of the most extensive collections of courses in the nation. Cherry Hills and Castle Pines are perennials in the top-100 rankings, while courses such as Arrowhead, Hyland Hills, Pole Creek, and Riverdale Dunes grace the public course rankings and Keystone, Singletree, Broadmoor and Tamarron are always present in golf resort rankings. Colorado has been known as a skiing mecca but increasingly attracts out-of-state golfers.

Colorado was the first western state to host a United States Open (1938—Cherry Hills) and the state hosted the Denver Open in the early days of the PGA TOUR. Recently Colorado has been home to The International at Castle Pines, the only TOUR event employing a modified Stableford system.

Colorado leapt into golf history in 1960 with the electrifying final round of the U.S. Open at Cherry Hills, when Arnold Palmer swept the field with a final round 65. The 1960 Open is generally regarded as the beginning of the Palmer era in golf—although it also featured the last final round challenge from Ben Hogan, as well as the first challenge from Jack Nicklaus. Colorado continues to host major championships in addition to TOUR Events—the 1978 U.S. Open won by Andy North, the 1993 U.S. Senior Open at Cherry Hills and the 1995 U.S. Women's Open at The Broadmoor in addition to the U.S. Amateur and Women's Amateur. The Sprint Championship, held at Castle Pines each September, provides the only opportunity to see the world's leading professionals playing a modified Stableford event.

In 1982 the Colorado Golf Association became the first state to rate courses for the USGA Slope system, and the state's successful experience prompted the USGA to extend the concept nationwide.

CONNECTICUT

No. of Players (Rank): 380,000 (21)
Participation Rate (Rank): 13.8% (14)
Percentage of Female Players (Rank): 17.1 (39)
Percentage of Senior Golfers (Rank): 22.2 (19)
Prominent Golfers: Julius Boros, Doug Ford, Ken Green, Joan Joyce, Glenna Collett Vare.
Major Golf Companies: BJ Designs.
Prominent Courses: Brooklawn, Stanwich, Yale University.
State Golf Association: Connecticut State Golf Association, 35 Cold Spring Road, Suite 212, Rocky Hill, CT 06067—(203) 257-4171

Highlights: Connecticut has a long association with the game, with the state golf association dating back to 1899. Connecticut's most prominent tournament is the Canon Greater Hartford Open, which is one of the steadiest dates on the PGA TOUR calendar with a continuous history stretching back to 1952. Sammy Davis was for many years associated with the event. In 1979 Brooklawn became the first Connecticut course to host a major championship by staging the U.S. Women's Open. Subsequently Brooklawn also hosted the 1987 U.S. Senior Open won by Gary Player. The outstanding Yale University course is home to the annual Connecticut Open on the NIKE TOUR.

DELAWARE

No. of Players (Rank): 50,000 (47)
Participation Rate (Rank): 8.6% (40)
Percentage of Female Players (Rank): 10.6 (49)
Percentage of Senior Golfers (Rank): 23.5 (15)
Prominent Golfers: Jim Woodward.
Prominent Courses: Biderman, Wilmington-North, Wilmington-South.
State Golf Association: Delaware State Golf Association, 100 Greenhills Avenue, Suite D, Wilmington, DE 19805

Highlights: The tiny state is home to only 22 golf clubs and public courses, but among them are Wilmington and the Dupont Country Club, two of the best courses in the country. Wilmington was the site of the 1971 U.S. Amateur won by Gary Cowan over Eddie Pearce, as well as the annual home of the McDonald's LPGA Championship.

DISTRICT OF COLUMBIA

No. of Players (Rank): 19,000 (49)
Participation Rate (Rank): 3.8% (49)
Percentage of Female Players (Rank): N/A
Percentage of Senior Golfers (Rank): N/A
Prominent Golfers: Michell Mackall.
State Golf Association: Washington Metropolitan Golf Association, 8012 Colorado Springs Dr., Springfield, VA 22153

Highlights: Washington, DC, and the District of Columbia proper are home to just four golf courses—the District is closely associated in the public's mind with the Congressional, which hosted the famed 1964 U.S. Open won by Ken Venturi in record heat, and the 1976 PGA Championship. East Potomac Park hosted the Publinx in 1923, and Columbia Golf Club was the site of the 1955 Canada Cup (now the World Cup). Major championship golf returned to Congressional in 1995 with the staging of the U.S. Senior Open.

FLORIDA

No. of Players (Rank): 1,168,000 (7)
Participation Rate (Rank): 10.0% (34)
Percentage of Female Players (Rank): 23.9 (15)
Percentage of Senior Golfers (Rank): 42.3 (1)
Prominent Golfers: Laura Baugh, Guy Boros, Michael Bradley, Tom Garner, Scott Gump, Mark McCumber, Shaun Michael, Charles Raulerson, Larry Rinker, Colleen Walker.
Major Golf Companies: Boast, Golden Bear, LPGA, National Golf Foundation, Nicklaus Equipment, PGA of America, PGA Tour, Palmer Course Design Company, Tail, Toney Penna.
Prominent Courses: Bay Hill, Black Diamond-Quarry, Bonita Bay, Doral-Blue, Fiddlesticks, Foxfire, Hammock Dunes, Innisbrook- Copperhead, JDM, Jupiter Hills, Lake Nona, Long Point, Loxahatchee, Mayacoo Lakes, Old Marsh, PGA National Champions, Pine Tree, Sawgrass, Southern Dunes, TPC at Sawgrass, Walt Disney World-Osprey Ridge, World Woods-Pine Barrens.
State Golf Association: Florida State Golf Association, 5710 Draw Lane, Sarasota, FL 34238—(813) 921-5695.

Highlights: Florida was far from the first home of American golf, but since the introduction of the game in the early 20th century golf has sunk deep roots, and today there are over 1,000 courses in the Sunshine State. The Florida land boom of the mid-1920s and the winter holiday opportunities led to the staging of many winter golf tournaments in Florida from the 1920s onward, from *mano-a-mano* matches, such as the famed Bobby Jones/Walter Hagen 72-hole match in 1926 won by Hagen 12 and 11, to standard stroke play events. By the 1940s Florida was the home of several annual stops on the PGA Tour and in the 1950s the fledgling LPGA also had a Florida-heavy schedule. Both Robert Trent Jones and Dick Wilson constructed a number of their best-known courses in Florida during the 1950s and 1960s as Miami and the east coast became established as the leading winter vacation destination.

By the 1970s large numbers of touring pros made Florida their home base, as did the PGA of America and the PGA Tour, the National Golf Foundation, the famed PGA Merchandise Show—and thus Florida has been able to claim truthfully that it is the home base of American golf. Due to summer weather conditions the state has rarely hosted major national championships; nevertheless the 1969 U.S. Women's Open and the 1971 and 1987 PGA Championships were staged in the state. In the amateur ranks the 1987 U.S. Amateur (at Jupiter Hills) was played at Jupiter Hills, while in team events Florida has hosted the 1990 Solheim Cup, the 1990 and 1993 World Cups, and the 1983 Ryder Cup matches. With the relocation of the LPGA to Florida, the World Golf Hall of Fame and Museum scheduled to open in 1996, and with the launch of The Golf Channel from Orlando in 1995, there are even more reasons to regard Florida as the epicenter of American golf.

GEORGIA

No. of Players (Rank): 458,000 (18)
Participation Rate (Rank): 8.1% (42)
Percentage of Female Players (Rank): 12.7 (48)
Percentage of Senior Golfers (Rank): 23.0 (20)
Prominent Golfers: Tommy Aaron, Andy Bean, Jim Dent, Bobby Jones, Kenny Knox, Steve Melnyk, Larry Mize, Jerry Pate, Doug Sanders, Gene Sauers, Cindy Schreyer, Hollis Stacy, Louise Suggs.
Major Golf Companies: Bridgestone, Cayman Golf, Club Car, Divots, E-Z-Go, Kasco, Macgregor, Merit, Mizuno, Sporthompson
Prominent Courses: Atlanta A.C., Atlanta C.C., Augusta National, Callaway Gardens (Mountain View), G.C. of Georgia, Peachtree, Reynolds Plantation.
State Golf Association: Georgia State Golf Association, Building 9, Suite 100, 42200 Northside Parkway, Atlanta, GA 30327—(404) 233-4742

Highlights: Georgia has played a central role in American golf since the era of Bobby Jones. Jones' establishment of the Augusta National Golf Club and The Masters Tournament gave American golf a much-needed shot in the arm in the throes of the Great Depression, and by the 1940s the tournament was firmly established at the pinnacle of championship golf. After the war Jones was associated with the construction of Peachtree G.C. in 1948 which helped enhance the prestige of Georgian golf. Since then a steady flow of outstanding courses from resorts such as Reynolds Plantation to private clubs such as the Atlanta A.C. and the Golf Club of Georgia have solidified this reputation.

In addition to the Masters, Georgia has hosted the U.S. Open (1976), the PGA Championship (1981), the U.S. Women's Open (1951 and 1990), and the 1950 and 1971 Women's Amateur. In addition the 1963 Ryder Cup matches were staged at East Lake, which was Bobby Jones' home club. In addition to staging major tournaments, Georgia has become known as a home of golf manufacturing concerns, with a number of key manufacturers based in-state. In 1994, Georgia played host to the 1994 Senior Women's Amateur at Sea Island G.C., as well as a large number of TOUR, Senior TOUR, LPGA and NIKE TOUR events. Due to controversy surrounding venues and eligibility, a plan foundered to include golf as a competitive or demonstration sport at the 1996 Olympics in Atlanta.

HAWAII

No. of Players (Rank): N/A
Participation Rate (Rank): N/A
Percentage of Female Players (Rank): N/A
Percentage of Senior Golfers (Rank): N/A
Prominent Golfers: David Ishii, Ted Makalena.
Major Golf Companies: Tall-Sax.
Prominent Courses: The Experience at Koele, Kapalua-Plantation, Kauai Lagoons (Kiele), Ko Olina, Mauna Kea (Jones), Mauna Lani (South), Princeville-Prince, Royal Kaanapali (South), Turtle Bay.
State Golf Association: Hawaii State Golf Association, 3221 Waialae Avenue, Suite 305, Honolulu, HI 96816—(808) 732-9785.

Highlights: Hawaii first began to boom as a golfing state in the late 1940s, when postwar travel to the islands grew and led to the staging of the first PGA TOUR events in the islands, the 1947-48 Hawaiian Opens. But Hawaii became firmly established as a golf mecca beginning in the 1950s, when commercial airlines were first able to offer non-stop jet service to the islands. With the addition of the Hawaiian Open to the PGA TOUR calendar in the early 1960s, the allure of Hawaii and courses such as Kaanapali and Mauna Kea beckoned in annual telecasts. Due to the travel distance (not to mention time-zone difference) Hawaii has to date staged only the 1960, 1975 and 1985 Publinx and the 1983 Women's Publinx in the USGA rota, but Hawaii has hosted the World Cup on three occasions (1964, 1978 and 1987), as well as annual events on all of the major tours. The Publinx returns to Wailua G.C. on Kauai in 1996. Interestingly, Hawaii was allowed to field its own team (separate from the regular American contingent) in the Canada Cup during the 1960s! Today, Hawaii is better recognized as a part of the United States and has a reputation as one of its prime golfing meccas, with many nationally-ranked resort courses and good year-round golfing weather.

IDAHO

No. of Players (Rank): 141,000 (36)
Participation Rate (Rank): 15.9% (9)
Percentage of Female Players (Rank): 33.1 (5)
Percentage of Senior Golfers (Rank): 20.1 (36)
Prominent Golfers: Don Bies.
Major Golf Companies: Henry-Griffits.
Prominent Courses: Coeur D'Alene, Elkhorn, Sun Valley.
State Golf Association: Idaho Golf Association, P.O. Box 3025, Boise, ID 83703.

Highlights: Idaho has enhanced its golfing profile in recent years with the opening of the Coeur D'Alene resort and the annual staging of the NIKE Boise Open. Prior to the 1990s, Idaho had an LPGA event briefly in the 1960s but overall was not a major player on the national golf map, despite a high participation rate in the amateur ranks. The Sun Valley resort area has grown considerably in popularity as a summer golfing destination in recent years.

ILLINOIS

No. of Players (Rank): 1,491,000 (3)
Participation Rate (Rank): 15.5% (10)
Percentage of Female Players (Rank): 25.2 (12)
Percentage of Senior Golfers (Rank): 23.0 (20)
Prominent Golfers: Jerry Barber, Jill Briles-Hinton, Bob Goalby, Gary Hallberg, John Huston, David Ogrin, Nancy Scranton, D.A. Weibring.
Major Golf Companies: Tommy Armour, Hyatt Golf Resorts, Northwestern, Pro-Select, Ram, Wilson.
Prominent Courses: Bob O'Link, Butler National, Chicago, Cog Hill (No. 4), Kemper Lakes, Knollwood, La Grange, Medinah (No. 3), North Shore, Olympia Fields, Shoreacres, Skokie, Wynstone.

Chicago Golf Association: Chicago District Golf Association 619 Enterprise Dr, Oak Brook, IL 60521 Tel: (708) 954-2180 Fax: (708) 954-3650.

Highlights: Illinois has been central to the American golf story since its earliest years, since Charles Balir Macdonald was a founding father of the Chicago Golf Club and it was at his instigation that the United States Golf Association was founded. In fact Illinois has hosted 45 national championships to date through the USGA including 12 U.S. Opens, the latest the heart-stopping victory of Hale Irwin over Mike Donald in 1990 at Medinah. Illinois has also been the site of four PGA Championships, the latest in 1989 at Kemper Lakes, as well as four PGA Grand Slam of Golf events from 1986-89. In 1996 the Spencer T. Olin Community G.C. in Alton will host the U.S. Women's Publinx.

In addition to national championships, Chicago was from the start the capital of Western golf, as suggested by the establishment of the Western Golf Association at Chicago in 1899, which led directly to the institution of the Western Open, a tournament which in its heyday had quasi-major status and today (known as the Motorola Open) remains a key event on the PGA TOUR. The Western Open was staged throughout the Western U.S. in its early years but now is a Chicago event.

Charles Blair MacDonald and the Chicago Golf Club were instrumental in the founding of the USGA in 1895 and MacDonald himself won many converts to golf through his efforts to popularize the game. For many years his Chicago G.C. was considered the finest course in the country until Pebble Beach, Shinnecock Hills and Pine Valley opened after the First World War. But Illinois had perhaps its greatest impact on American golf in the 1940s and 1950s, when events such as the All-America Open, the Tam O'Shanter, and the World Championship took PGA TOUR purses to new heights and did much to establish a foundation for the explosive growth of golf in the 1960s. In 1954, for instance, the winner of the World Championship banked $50,000, while the next most lucrative tournament (the Tournament of Champions) paid $10,000 to the winner.

In addition to its many tournaments, Illinois is home to several of the most prestigious clubs in the country and also several major golf manufacturing concerns, notably Wilson Sporting Goods and Ram Golf Corp. With the Cog Hill complex, Chicago is home to the best public golf courses of any major city.

INDIANA

No. of Players (Rank): 605,000 (12)
Participation Rate (Rank): 12.8% (19)
Percentage of Female Players (Rank): 20.2 (25)
Percentage of Senior Golfers (Rank): 27.5 (8)
Prominent Golfers: Alice Dye, Pete Dye, Chick Evans, Jackie Gallagher-Smith, Lori Garbacz, Cathy Gerring, Herb Graffis, Sandra Spuzich, Mike Sullivan, Fuzzy Zoeller.
Major Golf Companies: Sansabelt.
Prominent Courses: C.C. of Indianapolis, Crooked Stick, Meridian Hills, Sycamore Hills.
State Golf Association: Indiana Golf Association, 111 East Main Street, Carmel, IN 46032—(317) 844-7271

Highlights: By hosting the 1991 PGA Championship and the 1993 U.S. Women's Open, Indiana emerged from under the shadow of several more traditionally prominent golfing states of the Midwest—and with the launching of tournaments such as the Brickyard Crossing, it looks as if Indiana plans to stay on centerstage for a few years.

Crooked Stick was, of course, the host of the famed 1991 PGA Championship in which John Daly, gaining entrance to the tournament as the ninth alternate with less than 24 hours' notice, went on to win the tournament. Crooked Stick is also known for a top-100 ranking from several golf magazines, the hosting of the 1989 Mid-Amateur and as one of the earliest courses designed by Pete Dye. But other courses in the state have hosted PGA TOUR, LPGA, Senior PGA TOUR and NIKE TOUR events as well as the Girls' Junior Amateur, the Publinx, and the PGA Championship.

For all these recent developments, prominent golf tournaments have been staged in Indiana for many years, beginning in 1926 when the Western Open visited the state. Ft. Wayne was the site of a PGA TOUR event as early as 1951, while three of the first six LPGA Championships were played here in 1955 and 1958-59.

IOWA

No. of Players (Rank): 388,000 (20)
Participation Rate (Rank): 16.7% (8)
Percentage of Female Players (Rank): 30.3 (5)
Percentage of Senior Golfers (Rank): 17.8 (44)
Prominent Golfers: Jack Fleck, Sean Murphy, Tom Purtzer, Dave Rummells, Clifford Roberts, Barb Thomas.
Major Golf Companies: AER, Inc.
Prominent Courses: Wakonda, Des Moines (Red).
State Golf Association: Iowa Golf Association, 1930 St. Andrews Court NE, Cedar Rapids, IA 52402—(319) 378-9142

Highlights: Although Iowa does not command a high

profile on the national golfing scene, Iowans such as Jack Fleck and Cliff Roberts have played a major role in the development and popularization of the game—and Iowa has hosted several tournaments of national import since it first hosted the Western Open in 1936 and an annual PGA TOUR event, the Cedar Rapids Open, first staged in 1949. The Waterloo Open was a fixture on the LPGA TOUR in the late 1950s and early 1960s, while Wakonda Club hosted the 1963 Amateur won by Deane Beman. Today, Iowa is home to the Nike Hawkeye Open played in Iowa City.

KANSAS

No. of Players (Rank): 286,000 (28)
Participation Rate (Rank): 13.9% (13)
Percentage of Female Players (Rank): 18.0 (34)
Percentage of Senior Golfers (Rank): 21.0 (33)
Prominent Golfers: Dick Goetz, Steve Gotsche, Bruce Lietzke, Tom Shaw, Tom Watson.
Major Golf Companies: Excelerator, Gear for Sports.
Prominent Courses: Prairie Dunes, Wolf Creek.
State Golf Association: Kansas Golf Association, 3301 Clinton Parkway Court, Suite 4, Lawrence, KS 66047—(913) 842-4833

Highlights: Golf in Kansas dates back to the first decade of the century, with the Kansas Golf Association being formed in 1908. The construction of Prairie Dunes in 1937 gave Kansas a focus of state golfing pride and the course continues to be regarded as one of the all-time great national courses, and indeed has hosted several major national and international tournaments, notably the Women's Amateur, the Mid-Amateur and the Curtis Cup. Major championship golf returned to Kansas in 1995 with the staging of the Senior Amateur at Prairie Dunes. Kansas has also hosted the U.S. Women's Open (1955), the Senior Amateur, the Women's Publinx, and both the Girls' Junior and the Junior Amateur. Kansas played host to the historic upset by Great Britain & Ireland in the 1986 Curtis Cup matches, marking the end of a 28 year old American victory streak. The Kansas City Open, first staged in 1949, also gave Kansas exposure on the PGA TOUR. Today, Kansas is home to the Wichita Charity Classic on the NIKE TOUR.

KENTUCKY

No. of Players (Rank): 337,000 (24)
Participation Rate (Rank): 10.7% (30)
Percentage of Female Players (Rank): 20.5 (24)
Percentage of Senior Golfers (Rank): 20.5 (35)
Prominent Golfers: Russ Cochrane, Brad Febal, Larry Gilbert, Jodie Mudd, Bobby Nichols, Kenny Perry, Joey Sindelar, Ted Schulz, DeWitt Weaver, Bob Wynn.
Major Golf Companies: H&B/Powerbilt.
Prominent Courses: Idle Hour, Louisville, Persimmon Ridge, Valhalla.
State Golf Association: Kentucky Golf Association, P.O. Box 20146, Louisville, KY 40250—(502) 499-7255

Highlights: Kentucky first hosted a national championship when Shawnee G.C. was the site of the 1932 Publinx—the Publinx returned in 1950 and the PGA Championship was played in Louisville in 1952, firmly establishing Kentucky as a championship golf state. While the Kentucky Derby Open faltered after a few years on the PGA TOUR calendar in the late 1950s, the Bluegrass Invitational was a fixture for years on the LPGA from the 1960s into the 1970s. Recently, Valhalla Golf Club reached the top-100 rankings, and in 1996 it will host the PGA Championship, the first major championship to be staged in the state. At present, though, Kentucky's leading tournament is a date on the T.C. Jordan-Hooter's Tour.

LOUISIANA

No. of Players (Rank): 182,000 (33)
Participation Rate (Rank): 5.3% (47)
Percentage of Female Players (Rank): 15.8 (43)
Percentage of Senior Golfers (Rank): 21.3 (30)
Prominent Golfers: Miller Barber, Kelly Gibson, Jay Hebert, Lionel Hebert, Mike Heinen, Gary Koch, Tommy Moore, Deb Richard, Hal Sutton, Doug Tewell, Rocky Thompson, David Toms.
Major Golf Companies: River City Trading Co.
Prominent Courses: C.C. of Louisiana, English Turn, Oakbourne.
State Golf Association: Louisiana State Golf Association, 1305 Emerson Street, Monroe, LA 71201—(318) 342-1967.

Highlights: Louisiana has maintained a consistent presence on the PGA TOUR since the 1938 campaign via the Greater New Orleans Open (now known as the Freeport McMoRan Open). The tournament has always been well regarded but is especially so since moving to the Jack Nicklaus-designed English Turn course, one of the most difficult on the TOUR, in addition to landing the coveted slot a week prior to the Masters, a date which ensures a quality field.

In addition to the annual PGA tournament, Louisiana has had LPGA tournaments (most prominently the Baton Rouge Ladies' Invitational in the mid-1960s) and the 1966 Senior Women's Amateur.

MAINE

No. of Players (Rank): 98,000 (43)
Participation Rate (Rank): 9.6% (36)
Percentage of Female Players (Rank): 22.6 (17)
Percentage of Senior Golfers (Rank): 29.7 (5)
Prominent Golfers: Laura Kean, David Peoples.
Prominent Courses: Sugarloaf, Portland.
State Golf Association: Maine State Golf Association, 40 Pierce Street, Gardiner, ME 04345—(207) 582-7130

Highlights: With a short summer golf season, Maine has had limited opportunities to stage tournaments and build resorts that bring national golfing attention to the state—nevertheless, the 1978 Publinx was staged in Bangor at Bangor Municipal G.C.

MARYLAND

No. of Players (Rank): 348,000 (23)
Participation Rate (Rank): 8.4% (41)
Percentage of Female Players (Rank): 18.0 (34)
Percentage of Senior Golfers (Rank): 23.5 (15)
Prominent Golfers: Tina Barrett, Mark Carnevale, Fred Funk, Donnie Hammond, Katie Peterson-Parker, Mike Reid, Tina Barrett.
Major Golf Companies: Head Golf Co.
Prominent Courses: Baltimore - Five Farms, Congressional-Composite, Columbia, Burning Tree.
State Golf Association: Maryland State Golf Association, P.O. Box 16289, Baltimore, MD 21210.

Highlights: The Maryland State Golf Association was formed in 1921 and since then Maryland has hosted many national championships and tournaments, foremost among them the 1964 U.S. Open and 1976 PGA Championship at Congressional. Five Farms has been the site of both the Walker Cup and the 1988 U.S. Women's Open, while courses such as Burning Tree have some of the most exclusive membership lists in the country. In recent years both the Kemper Open and the LPGA Championship have been located in Maryland, and the Senior Open was played at Congressional in 1995.

MASSACHUSETTS

No. of Players (Rank): 588,000 (13)
Participation Rate (Rank): 11.8% (24)
Percentage of Female Players (Rank): 15.7 (45)
Percentage of Senior Golfers (Rank): 24.8 (13)
Prominent Golfers: Billy Andrade, Paul Azinger, Michelle Bell, Pat Bradley, Fred Corcoran, Paul Harney, Meg Mallon, Francis Ouimet, Bob Toski, Richard Tufts.
Major Golf Companies: Acushnet, Dexter, Etonic, Reebok, Spalding, Textron.
Prominent Courses: Brae Burn, The Country Club, Kittansett, Myopia Hunt Club, Pleasant Valley, Salem.
State Golf Association: Massachusetts Golf Association, Golf House, 190 Park Road, Weston, MA 02193—(617) 891-4300

Highlights: Massachusetts played a critical role in the development of the game in the United States—with The Country Club in Brookline becoming a charter member of the United States Golf Association. Massachusetts clubs have subsequently hosted 41 national championships through the USGA, as well as numerous Tour events, PGA Championships, and the initial Ryder Cup match in 1927.

Massachusetts has hosted nine U.S. Opens beginning with the 1898 Open at Myopia Hunt Club. Perhaps the best-known of these was the 1913 Open where Francis Ouimet scored his historic upset over Harry Vardon and Ted Ray. Walter Hagen won the 1919 Open here and Bobby Jones the 1928 Amateur at Brae Burn.

Three Walker Cups and three Curtis Cups have been held in Massachusetts as well as nine Women's Amateurs. In addition the 1956 PGA Championship was held at Blue Hill in Canton.

The PGA TOUR has been represented in the state by the New England (now Ideon) Classic, Kemper Open, and the Carling Open. Women's professional golf has maintained an even more consistent presence in the state—two U.S. Women's Opens (1954 and 1984) and seven LPGA Championships (1967-68, 1970-74), as well as regular tour events such as the Lady Carling, the Boston Five Classic, and the World Championship of Women's Golf. In 1995-96 the state was well represented on the USGA's championship roster: in 1995 Massachusetts hosted the 1995 Women's Mid-Amateur, the 1995 Publinx, the Girls' Junior Amateur and the Women's Amateur, while in 1996 the Senior Amateur comes to Williamtown and Taconic G.C.

In addition to tournament play, Massachusetts is notable for the concentration of major golf manufacturers in the state, notably Spalding and Acushnet.

MICHIGAN

No. of Players (Rank): 1,323,000 (6)
Participation Rate (Rank): 17.0% (7)
Percentage of Female Players (Rank): 27.9 (8)
Percentage of Senior Golfers (Rank): 23.4 (18)
Prominent Golfers: Mike Donald, Nolan Henke, Dave Hill, Mike Hill, Lon Hinkle, Ed Humenik, Debbie Massey, Calvin Peete, Dan Pohl, Chris Tschetter, Tom Wargo.

Major Golf Companies: Ball-o-Matic.
Prominent Courses: The Bear, Boyne Highlands-Composite, C.C. of Detroit, Crystal Downs, Grand Traverse, High Pointe, Indianwood, Oakland Hills (South), Point O'Woods, Shanty Creek, Treetops, Warwick Hills.
State Golf Association: Golf Association of Michigan, 37935 Twelve Mile Road, Suite 200, Farmington Hills, MI 48331—(313) 553-4200

Highlights: Despite its northern location, Michigan has the third highest number of golf courses of any state in the U.S., and has been a mainstay of both the professional tours and national championships since early in the century. The state has hosted 23 national championships since the Country Club of Detroit first hosted the Amateur in 1915, and five U.S. Opens and two U.S. Women's Opens have been played here to date between 1924 and 1989, as well as five PGA Championships and the 1956 LPGA Championship.

Oakland Hills, designed by Donald Ross, is considered the leading championship course, but fifteen other courses have hosted national championships to date. In addition, Michigan has hosted many PGA TOUR events dating back to the Western Open which was staged in Grand Rapids in 1904. The best known professional tournament today is the Buick Open, which dates back on the PGA TOUR to 1958, although the Motor City Open was a PGA TOUR event in the late 40s and early 50s. The LPGA arrived in Michigan with the Wolverine Open in 1955, and today stages the Oldsmobile Classic in Detroit. The Senior PGA TOUR also stops in Michigan, giving the state an unusually strong tournament line-up. In 1996 the U.S. Open will return to Oakland Hills where it has been played on five previous occasions.

In recent years Michigan has grown significantly in stature as a golfing destination with the continuation of development of public and resort courses in the Boyne area in the north of the state. Complexes such as Grand Traverse have vaulted Michigan into the top five among golf vacation states, despite the short golfing season.

Michigan is also home to one of the true hidden-gem private courses in Crystal Downs.

MINNESOTA

No. of Players (Rank): 743,000 (10)
Participation Rate (Rank): 20.2% (2)
Percentage of Female Players (Rank): 27.4 (9)
Percentage of Senior Golfers (Rank): 21.1 (32)
Prominent Golfers: Patty Berg, Jerilyn Britz, Lee Janzen, Howie Johnson, Tom Lehman, Mac O'Grady, Becky Pearson, Cindy Rarick, Karen Weiss.
Major Golf Companies: Munsingwear.
Prominent Courses: Hazeltine, Interlachen, Minikahda, Minneapolis, Rochester.
State Golf Association: Minnesota Golf Association, 6550 York Avenue South, Suite 405, Edina, MN 55435-2383—(612) 927-4643

Highlights: Enthusiasm for golf has been strong and consistent through the years since the first course—Town & Country Club—opened for play in 1888 as the first golf course west of the Mississippi. Today Minnesota has over 400 courses and the highest number of golfers per capita of any state in the Union.

The state has hosted 28 national championships to date, the eighth largest number among all the states. Four U.S. Opens have been staged here, including the 1930 Open that was the first leg of Bobby Jones' Grand Slam, as well as two U.S. Women's Opens and two Walker Cups. The first national championship staged in the state was the 1916 Open and the most recent was the 1993 Walker Cup and the 1993 Women's Mid-Amateur. Minnesota has also played host to three PGA Championships, the most recent in 1959. In 1995 Somerset C.C. in St. Paul hosted the Senior Women's Amateur.

The professional tours have frequently staged tournaments in Minnesota, dating back to the 1914 Western Open at Interlachen, although there has not been a regular PGA TOUR stop in Minnesota since the demise of the Minnesota Classic after the 1969 season. The LPGA arrived with the American Women's Open in 1958 and continues today with the Minnesota LPGA Classic.

Minnesota is not a major player in the golf manufacturing economy, but the revenues generated by the daily fee golfers and private clubs, as well as by the small but vibrant group of in-state resorts, makes Minnesota a key state in the national golf economy.

MISSISSIPPI

No. of Players (Rank): 109,000 (39)
Participation Rate (Rank): 5.1% (48)
Percentage of Female Players (Rank): 17.0 (41)
Percentage of Senior Golfers (Rank): 22.8 (22)
Prominent Golfers: J.R. Richardson.
Prominent Courses: Annandale, Laurel, Hattiesburg, Old Waverly.
State Golf Association: Mississippi Golf Association, P.O. Box 684, 515 Central Avenue, Laurel, MS 39441—(601) 649-0570

Highlights: Mississippi golf dates back to the early part of the century with the construction of the Laurel Country Club in 1917 from a design by Seymour

Dunn. The Mississippi Golf Association was formed in 1925 and in the early days of the PGA Circuit Mississippi played a somewhat prominent role due to the warm winters providing good weather for winter tournaments. The Gulfport Open was staged on the TOUR as early as 1946. During the late 1960s the PGA TOUR experimented with satellite events—non-official tournaments that would be staged the same week as limited-field events such as the Tournament of Champions and the Masters, and Mississippi's Magnolia State Classic was born. After years of non-official status, it moved to Annandale G.C. in 1994 and became an official PGA TOUR event. The USGA staged the Mid-Amateur at Annandale in 1986, which to date has been Mississippi's lone opportunity to host a national championship.

With the expansion of gambling and resort development in the Gulfport and Biloxi areas on the coastline, Mississippi seems poised for considerable golf expansion in the late 1990s.

MISSOURI

No. of Players (Rank): 557,000 (15)
Participation Rate (Rank): 12.9% (18)
Percentage of Female Players (Rank): 20.5 (24)
Percentage of Senior Golfers (Rank): 19.3 (38)
Prominent Golfers: Jay Delsing, David Edwards, Robin Freeman, Jay Haas, Hale Irwin, Jeff Maggert, Judy Rankin, Horton Smith, Payne Stewart, Tom Watson, Larry Ziegler.
Major Golf Companies: Intec Laboratories.
Prominent Courses: Bellerive, Old Warson, St. Joseph, St. Louis.
State Golf Association: Missouri Golf Association, P.O. Box 104164, Jefferson City, MO 65110—(314) 636-4225

Highlights: Missouri was one of the first states west of the Appalachians to embrace golf, with the 1904 Olympic Games in St. Louis featuring golf on the program, and the 1908 Western Open played in St. Louis as well. The first national championship staged in the state was the 1921 Amateur, followed by the 1925 Women's Amateur. The St. Louis Country Club hosted the 1947 U.S. Open, which was the first ever televised, and the Open returned to the state in 1965 where Gary Player completed his career Grand Slam. In addition the 1948 and 1992 PGA Championships plus the 1971 Ryder Cup matches were played here.

After hosting the 1938 Western Open, St. Louis acquired a PGA TOUR stop of its own in 1950, but today Missouri is host to the Southwestern Bell Classic in Kansas City and a NIKE TOUR event, the Greater Ozarks Open.

MONTANA

No. of Players (Rank): 89,000 (45)
Participation Rate (Rank): 13.0% (17)
Percentage of Female Players (Rank): 38.5 (1)
Percentage of Senior Golfers (Rank): 16.1 (46)
Prominent Golfers: Bob Betley, Alice Ritzman.
Major Golf Companies: Sun Mountain Sports.
Prominent Courses: Briarwood, Buffalo Hill, Eagle Bend.
State Golf Association: Montana State Golf Association, P.O. Box 3389, Butte, MT 59701—(406) 782-9208.

Highlights: Due to a short golfing season and a small resident population, Montana has lacked the essentials for a vibrant national golfing presence, but in recent years there have been some very good courses built, such as Eagle Bend, which in 1994 hosted Montana's first-ever national championship, the Publinx. Montana combines low green fees and spectacular scenery around its courses, and the state has thus one of the highest per-capita participation rates for golf in the country, despite the short golf season.

NEBRASKA

No. of Players (Rank): 225,000 (32)
Participation Rate (Rank): 17.2% (6)
Percentage of Female Players (Rank): 16 (6)
Percentage of Senior Golfers (Rank): 29 (29)
Prominent Golfers: Mark Calcavecchia, Tom Sieckmann, Val Skinner.
Prominent Courses: Firethorn, Happy Hollow, Highland, Sandhills.
State Golf Association: Nebraska Golf Association, 6001 South 72nd Street, Lincoln, NE 68516—(402) 486-1440

Highlights: Recent golf course openings such as Firethorn and the much-awaited opening of Crenshaw and Coore's Sandhills complex have considerably raised Nebraska's profile in golfdom. Prior to the 1990s, Nebraska has hosted the occasional tournament, such as the 1941 U.S. Amateur at Omaha Field Club, but the professional tours and the major championships have eluded the state.

NEVADA

No. of Players (Rank): 157,000 (35)
Participation Rate (Rank): 13.4% (16)
Percentage of Female Players (Rank): 22.0 (20)
Percentage of Senior Golfers (Rank): 28.8 (6)
Prominent Golfers: Robert Gamez, Deborah McHaffie.

Major Golf Companies: Carsonite International.
Prominent Courses: Desert Inn, Edgewood Tahoe, Las Vegas, Shadow Creek.
State Golf Association: Nevada State Golf Association, P.O. Box 5630, Sparks, NV 89432—(702) 673-4653

Highlights: Nevada's intimate involvement with golf stems from the Tournament of Champions which was first staged as a PGA TOUR event in 1953 and offered at the time the second-highest purse on the Tour. Las Vagas still hosts an annual event, the Las Vegas Classic, on the PGA TOUR calendar.

By the 1980s, Nevada's profile as a golf state had increased considerably, as the result of population growth, the construction of top-ranked courses such as the Edgewood Tahoe in the north and the TPC at Summerlin near Las Vegas, plus the addition of Senior PGA TOUR and LPGA events to the golf calendar. Nevada hosted the 1980 Publinx and the 1985 U.S. Senior Open at the Edgewood Tahoe.

Nevada was in the news during the 1990s when Chip Beck tied the all-time 18-hole record with a 59 in the 1991 Las Vegas Invitational—and also for the awarding of a top-10 ranking to the brand-new Tom Fazio course at Shadow Creek. Shadow Creek has since fallen back a few places, but it remains the highest-ranked course designed in the 1990s.

NEW HAMPSHIRE

No. of Players (Rank): 94,000 (44)
Participation Rate (Rank): 10.2% (33)
Percentage of Female Players (Rank): 29.1 (6)
Percentage of Senior Golfers (Rank): 18.4 (41)
Prominent Golfers: Jane Blalock.
Prominent Courses: Manchester, Portsmouth.
State Golf Association: New Hampshire Golf Association, 45 Kearney Street, Manchester, NH 03104—(603) 623-0396

Highlights: A short playing season and a limited base of golfers has prevented New Hampshire from achieving status as a major golf state, but nevertheless there are several very scenic courses, such as the Balsams Grand Hotel and the Mount Washington Hotel, which combined with the mild summer climate draws a number of visitors northward.

NEW JERSEY

No. of Players (Rank): 677,000 (11)
Participation Rate (Rank): 10.2% (32)
Percentage of Female Players (Rank): 17.4 (38)
Percentage of Senior Golfers (Rank): 25.7 (11)
Prominent Golfers: Jim Colbert, Brad Faxon, Jim McGovern, Karen Noble, Walt Zembriski.
Major Golf Companies: Le Coq Sportif, United States Golf Association.
Prominent Courses: Baltusrol-Lower, Balt-usrol-Upper, Pine Valley, Plainview, Ridge-wood (East & West), Somerset Hills.
State Golf Association: New Jersey State Golf Association, 1000 Broad Street, Bloomfield, NJ 07003—(201) 338-8334

Highlights: New Jersey has played an integral role in American golf since before the turn of the century, hosting the Women's Amateur in 1896, the Amateur in 1898, and staging its first U.S. Open at Baltusrol in 1903. The state is tiny in area but large in the number of courses—over 250—and 16 of those courses have hosted 45 national championships to date including eight U.S. Opens. Seven of those Opens were held at Baltusrol, the latest in 1993 won by Lee Janzen.

In addition, New Jersey played host to the 1942 PGA Championship and the 1935 Ryder Cup matches at Ridgewood Country Club.

Despite Baltusrol's seven U.S. Opens, the most revered course in the state is in fact Pine Valley, in Clementon, widely regarded as the finest golf course ever built. The course has never hosted a major tournament except for the Walker Cup (in 1936 and 1985), but it is consistently ranked number one by the leading golf publications.

New Jersey has hosted professional tournaments since the early days of the PGA Circuit, from the Atlantic City Open of the 1940s to the Shoprite LPGA Classic today. New Jersey is also home to a first-class golf resort in the Marriott Seaview. Golfers in the Garden State also take advantage of the United States Golf Association's Golf Museum, featuring regular and special exhibits.

The highlight on the 1995 calendar was the staging of the Women's Publinx at Hominy Hill G.C.

NEW MEXICO

No. of Players (Rank): 158,000 (34)
Participation Rate (Rank): 12.2% (23)
Percentage of Female Players (Rank): 18.6 (31)
Percentage of Senior Golfers (Rank): 27.4 (9)
Prominent Golfers: Ronnie Black, Steve Jones.
Major Golf Companies: New Mexico State University golf management program, Resortowels.
Prominent Courses: Inn of the Mountain Gods, Picacho Hills.
State Golf Association: Sun Country Amateur Golf Association, 10035 Country Club Lane NW, Suite 5, Albuquerque, NM 87114—(505) 897-0864

Highlights: New Mexico is home to only 88 golf courses and has yet to host a national championship event, but it is home to several very testing courses including the Inn of the Mountain Gods resort. Albuquerque briefly had a PGA TOUR stop in the late 1940s, and had an LPGA event in the early 1960s known as Bill Brannin's Swing Parade, the Albuquerque Swing Parade, and finally as the Albuquerque Professional Amateur. In recent years noted designers such as Jack Nicklaus have been active in the state, raising the possibility that the professional tours will return.

NEW YORK

No. of Players (Rank): 1,722,000 (2)
Participation Rate (Rank): 11.3% (25)
Percentage of Female Players (Rank): 22.7 (16)
Percentage of Senior Golfers (Rank): 25.7 (11)
Prominent Golfers: Jim Albus, Danielle Ammaccapane, George Burns, Jane Geddes, Dudley Hart, Walter Hagen, Mike Hulbert, Brian Kamm, Larry Laoretti, Wayne Levi, Dottie Mochrie, Bob Murphy, Gene Sarazen, Jeff Sluman, Jerome Travers.
Major Golf Companies: Adrienne Vittadini, Bobby Jones, Quantum, Titleist by Corbin.
Prominent Courses: Bethpage (Black), Concord Hotel, Fishers Island, Garden City, Maidstone, National Golf Links of America, Oak Hill, Quaker Ridge, Shinnecock Hills, Westchester (West), Winged Foot (East), Winged Foot (West).
State Golf Association: New York State Golf Association, P.O. Box 3459, Elmira, NY 14905—(607) 733-0007

Highlights: New York was the site of the first 18-hole golf course, St. Andrews, and provided the bulk of the founding membership of the United States Golf Association; therefore, it would be fair to dub the state "The Cradle of American Golf." New York has been home to 54 national championships to date plus nine PGA Championships and, in 1995, its first Ryder Cup (at Oak Hill). Oak Hill, Winged Foot, and Shinnecock Hills are considered a firm part of the Open rota and a total of 13 U.S. Opens have been staged here beginning in 1896 and continuing through 1995 at Shinnecock Hills. In addition to the Open, the Ryder Cup matches were staged in New York (at Oak Hill in Rochester) in 1995, making the state the epicenter of championship golf for the year.

Many PGA, LPGA and Senior PGA events have been held in New York over the years, of which perhaps the Buick Classic (formerly the Westchester Classic) is the best known. New York's connection with the PGA TOUR goes back before the Second World War, to the Rochester Times-Union Open. The LPGA had a New York date on the calendar in its first season and continues today with the JAL/Big Apple Classic.

New York is home to some of the most revered public and resort courses in the country, principally Bethpage on Long Island and En-Joie and the Concord Hotel in the Catskills. But it is the private clubs such as Shinnecock, National Golf Links, and Garden City on Long Island, plus Winged Foot and Quaker Ridge in Westchester and Oak Hill in Rochester that have secured New York its place in history. Laurie Auchterlonie, Bobby Jones, and Gene Sarazen are among the winners of U.S. Opens in New York, along with Walter Hagen, Tommy Armour, and Jack Nicklaus in the PGA Championship.

NORTH CAROLINA

No. of Players (Rank): 577,000 (14)
Participation Rate (Rank): 9.9% (35)
Percentage of Female Players (Rank): 15.8 (43)
Percentage of Senior Golfers (Rank): 22.7 (24)
Prominent Golfers: Chip Beck, Lennie Clements, Jim Ferree, Marlene Floyd, Ray Floyd, Scott Hoch, John Inman, Neal Lancaster, Davis Love III, Mark O'Meara, Charlie Sifford, Leonard Thompson, Jim Thorpe.
Major Golf Companies: Cross Creek, Golf Pride, Kangaroo Motorcaddies.
Prominent Courses: Cape Fear, Champion Hills, Charlotte, C.C. of North Carolina, Elk River, Grandfather Mountain, Linville Ridge, Mid Pines, Mt. Mitchell, Nags Head, Oyster Bay, Pinehurst (No. 2), Pinehurst (No. 5), Pinehurst (No. 6), Pinehurst (No. 7), Pine Needles, The Pit, Tanglewood, Wade Hampton.
State Golf Association: Carolinas Golf Association, P.O. Box 428, West End, NC 27376—(919) 673-1000

Highlights: North Carolina is central to the American golf story because of the village known as Pinehurst, the American alternative to St. Andrews, and the impact that the Pinehurst development and its employees and owners have had on American golf.

Pinehurst was founded as a health resort, but added golf in 1900 and hired Donald Ross as greenkeeper and professional. Ross' design work included five courses at Pinehurst, including the famed No. 2 course, and he took on additional work originally in the Pinehurst area but eventually across the entire United States, contributing greatly to the Golden Age of course architecture of the 1920s and 1930s. Pinehurst has hosted the Ryder Cup, the Amateur, the Women's Amateur, the Eisenhower Trophy, the Women's World Amateur, the World Senior Amateur, the PGA Championship, the TOUR Championship, and in 1999 will host the United States Open for the first time, making it perhaps the most widely employed course in the United States for championship golf. In addition to national championships, Pinehurst was the host of the North and South Open, one of the earliest annual professional tournaments and one which provided the season finale in the earliest days of the PGA Circuit. The North and South Amateur is still played today and is one of the most prestigious amateur events.

The success of Pinehurst spawned a tremendous amount of quality golf development in North Carolina over the years, and five other courses to date have hosted national championships beginning with the 1955 Women's Amateur at Myers Park and continuing through the 1996 U.S. Women's Open at Pine Needles.

In addition to a host of national and world events, North Carolina has been home to a great number of touring professional events owing to the state's mild winters and convenience to both northern and southern states. The K-Mart Greater Greensboro Open, for instance, dates back to 1938, and at one point in the early 1940s North Carolina hosted four PGA TOUR tournaments. The LPGA had its first tournament in state in 1957 and the Senior PGA TOUR is playing annually at Piper Glen.

In addition to coastal communities and the Pinehurst-Raleigh-Durham triangle, North Carolina features a number of private and resort courses in the Great Smoky Mountains near Asheville that are hugely popular with both southerners and northerners—chief among these are Grandfather Mountain and Wade Hampton Golf Club.

NORTH DAKOTA

No. of Players (Rank): 113,000 (38)
Participation Rate (Rank): 22.1% (1)
Percentage of Female Players (Rank): 30.8 (4)
Percentage of Senior Golfers (Rank): 27.9 (7)
Prominent Golfers: Pat McGowan.
Prominent Courses: Fargo, Minot.
State Golf Association: North Dakota Golf Association, P.O. Box 452, Bismark, ND 58502—(701) 255-0242.

Highlights: North Dakota ranks first in the nation in golfers per capita population—rates are low and land is plentiful. But North Dakota has been hampered by a tiny population base and national championship or professional golf had eluded the state until 1995 when the Junior Amateur was held at Fargo C.C.

OHIO

No. of Players (Rank): 1,341,000 (4)
Participation Rate (Rank): 14.6% (11)
Percentage of Female Players (Rank): 22.6 (17)
Percentage of Senior Golfers (Rank): 20.1 (36)
Prominent Golfers: Gay Brewer, John Cook, Marty Dickerson, Judy Dickinson, Dow Finsterwald, Robert Lohr, Dick Mast, Jack Nicklaus, Muffin Spencer-Devlin, Tom Weiskopf.
Major Golf Companies: The Golfworks, Medicus, Ryobi-Toski.
Prominent Courses: Camargo, Canterbury, Coldstream, The Country Club, Double Eagle, Firestone-South, Firestone-North, The Golf Club, Inverness, Muirfield Village, NCR-South, Ohio State Univ. (Scarlet), Scioto, Shaker Run.
State Golf Association: Northern Ohio Golf Association, 17800 Chillicothe Road, Suite 210, Chagrin Falls, OH—(216) 543-6320; Toledo District Golf Association, P.O. Box 6313, Toledo, OH 43614—(419) 866-4771; The Greater Cincinnati Golf Association, P.O. Box 317825, Cincinatti, OH 45231—(513) 522-5780; Columbus District Golf Association, 437 Pamlico, Columbus, OH 43228—(614) 274-5441

Highlights: Ohio first leapt into national prominence as early as 1902 when the Euclid Club hosted the Western Open (the U.S. Amateur followed five years later), but the state's reputation was significantly bolstered after the First World War, when courses such as Inverness and Scioto hosted U.S. Opens and the Western Open made several stops in the state. The addition of Canterbury to the Open rota in the 1940s added considerably to the state's luster, but it was the building of the golf complexes at Firestone and Muirfield Village in the 1950s and 1970s that firmly established Ohio as one of the handful of leading golf states.

29 national championships to date have been played in Ohio as well as nine PGA Championships and the 1931 and 1987 Ryder Cup matches. The 30th championship will be staged in 1996 when the Senior Open is held at Canterbury G.C. in Cleveland. In addition, quasi-majors The Memorial and the World Series of Golf are annual PGA TOUR stops, and the LPGA Championship was held four consecutive years in Ohio in the mid 1980s.

Ohio native Jack Nicklaus is still closely associated with the state through Muirfield Village and the Jack Nicklaus golf complex at Kings Island. Pete Dye's work was also seen here quite early in his career, as was Donald Ross'—and thus Ohio is also quite a showcase for golf course architecture.

In addition to the World Series and the Memorial, Ohio is also home to annual events on the Senior PGA TOUR and the LPGA Tour, as well as the NIKE TOUR.

OKLAHOMA

No. of Players (Rank): 290,000 (27)
Participation Rate (Rank): 10.9% (27)
Percentage of Female Players (Rank): 21.8 (21)
Percentage of Senior Golfers (Rank): 20.6 (34)
Prominent Golfers: John Adams, Tommy Bolt, Bob Dickson, Dale Douglass, Bill Glasson, Mark Hayes, Gil Morgan, Orville Moody, Ron Streck, Bob Tway.
Major Golf Companies: Swingtrac.
Prominent Courses: Cedar Ridge, Muskogee, Oak Tree, G.C. of Oklahoma, Southern Hills, Twin Hills.
State Golf Association: Oklahoma Golf Association, P.O. Box 449, Enid, OK 73083—(405) 340-6333.

Highlights: Oklahoma is rarely on the short list of great golfing states, but in fact the state has hosted 15 national championships including three U.S. Opens, four PGA Championships, has several top-ranked courses and a long list of native Oklahomans who have gone on to great success in the professional ranks.

Perry Maxwell is the architect most closely associated with the state, beginning with Dornick Hills in 1919 and going on to design both Twin Hills and Southern Hills. Twin Hills hosted the state's first PGA Championship in 1935.

After the Second World War Southern Hills became the best-known course in the state and it was the site of the 1958 Open, the 1970, 1982 and 1994 PGA Championships, the 1995 TOUR Championship and the 1977 Open. Oak Tree, a Pete Dye design, has also hosted the 1984 Amateur and the 1988 PGA Championship. The PGA TOUR stopped in Tulsa as early as 1945, but has been absent most years with the major exception being the Oklahoma City Open played in the early 1960s.

OREGON

No. of Players (Rank): 284,000 (29)
Participation Rate (Rank): 11.2% (26)
Percentage of Female Players (Rank): 26.4 (11)
Percentage of Senior Golfers (Rank): 22.5 (25)
Prominent Golfers: Bob Gilder, Fred Haas, Peter Jacobsen, Susan Sanders, Mark Wiebe.
Major Golf Companies: Nike.
Prominent Courses: Columbia-Edgewater, Eugene, Pumpkin Ridge, Salishan, Sandpines, Sunriver, Waverly.
State Golf Association: 8364 S.W. Nimbus Avenue, Beaverton, OR 97005—(503) 643-2610.

Highlights: Oregon had a limited exposure as a golfing state prior to the Second World War because of the time involved in traveling to the state. Nevertheless the 1933 Publinx and the 1937 Amateur were held in Oregon.

The war years were crucial to Oregon golf because the key role played in the war by the West Coast port cities put Portland in a position to stage golf tournaments like never before. In 1944 Portland had its first PGA TOUR event; in 1946 the city hosted the PGA Championship; in 1947 Oregonians made perhaps their most important contribution to golf by rescuing the Ryder Cup from its WWII hiatus, staging the matches in Portland and going considerable lengths to aid the British team in making the voyage to the West Coast. But by the late 1950s Oregon had slid back into the second rank of golfing states.

In recent years, however, Oregon has been undergoing a renaissance based on the development of new resort and public courses such as Sandpines, and building new metropolitan golf clubs of the first rank such as the Oregon Golf Club and Pumpkin Ridge. Interest in Oregon has been renewed, with the Mid-Amateur and the Junior Amateur both staged in the state in 1993, and Pumpkin Ridge will host the 1997 U.S. Amateur.

PENNSYLVANIA

No. of Players (Rank): 1,092,000 (8)
Participation Rate (Rank): 10.8% (29)
Percentage of Female Players (Rank): 17.6 (37)
Percentage of Senior Golfers (Rank): 21.2 (31)
Prominent Golfers: Missie Bertiotti, Jim Furyk, Jim Gallagher Jr., Betsy King, Rocco Mediate, Arnold Palmer, Jay Sigel, Mike Souchak, Ted Tryba, Art Wall Jr.
Major Golf Companies: Adidas, Izod, Aureus/Aurea.
Prominent Courses: Aronimink, Hershey, Kahkwa, Laurel Valley, Merion-East, Moselem Springs, Oakmont, Philadelphia, Philadelphia Cricket Club, Rolling Green, Saucon Valley-Grace.
State Golf Association: Pennsylvania Golf Association, 700 Croton Road, Wayne, PA 19087—(215) 687-2340

Highlights: Pennsylvania, along with Massachusetts, Illinois, New Jersey and New York, was the site of some of the earliest organized golf in the Union, with a rich golf history stretching back into the 19th century and 63 national championships completed here beginning in 1904.

Some of the earliest of the great American golf courses were built in the state with the help of amateur golf architects—including Oakmont, Merion and Philadelphia Cricket Club. The U.S. Open was first staged in Pennsylvania in 1907, and a total of 14 Opens and nine PGA Championships have been played here in total, including seven Opens at Oakmont alone. The first PGA Championship was played at Oakmont in 1922. Bobby Jones, incidentally, completed his Grand Slam in the U.S. Amateur at Merion in 1930.

In addition to USGA-conducted national events, Pennsylvania has hosted a number of international events including the 1960 Eisenhower Trophy and 1954 Curtis Cup at Merion, and the 1975 Ryder Cup matches at Laurel Valley.

In professional tour events, the Hershey Open was the first PGA TOUR event sponsored by a corporation, and Pennsylvania hosted at least one tournament annually from the late 1930s until the early 1980s. The state has no PGA TOUR event at present but hosts several Senior PGA TOUR and LPGA stops.

Today, Pennsylvania is home to over 600 courses and remains one of the largest bases for American golf, both at the public-golf level and at the championship level with five of Golf Digest's top-100 ranked courses within state borders.

RHODE ISLAND
and Providence Plantations

No. of Players (Rank): 108,000 (40)
Participation Rate (Rank): 12.8% (20)
Percentage of Female Players (Rank): 19.2 (30)
Percentage of Senior Golfers (Rank): 21.6 (29)
Prominent Golfers: Bob Eastwood, P.H. Horgan III, Ed Kirby, Lawson Little.
Prominent Courses: Newport, Rhode Island, Wannamoisett.
State Golf Association: Rhode Island Golf Association, 10 Orms Street, Suite 326, Providence, Rhode Island 02904—(401) 272-1350

Highlights: The tiny state of Rhode Island has a small base of golfers and golf courses—just 40 in all—but a history closely intertwined with golf ever since the first U.S. Open was played at Newport Country Club in 1895. The Amateur was also played at Newport that year and Newport hosted the Amateur in 1995 to celebrate the centennial of the event and the USGA.

A large percentage of Rhode Island's courses were designed by famed architect Donald Ross, owing to the fact that Ross had his summer house in Rhode Island—the Women's Amateur has been played three times at his Rhode Island Country Club, and his Wannamoisett hosts a prestigious amateur event, the Northeast Amateur Invitational as well as the 1931 PGA Championship.

Rhode Island has hosted several tour events over the years dating back to the Providence Open in 1948. Most recently the state hosted the PGA Senior TOUR's Newport Cup through the 1992 season.

SOUTH CAROLINA

No. of Players (Rank): 318,000 (26)
Participation Rate (Rank): 10.6% (31)
Percentage of Female Players (Rank): 20.2 (25)
Percentage of Senior Golfers (Rank): 30.4 (3)
Prominent Golfers: Beth Daniel, Dillard Pruitt, Betsy Rawls.
Major Golf Companies: Maxfli, Slazenger, Zett Golf.
Prominent Courses: Callawassie, Colleton River, Dataw Island, Dunes, Greenville, Haig Point, Harbour Town, Kiawah-Ocean, Kiawah (Turtle Point), The Legends-Moorland, Long Bay, Long Cove, Old Tabby, Tidewater, Wild Dunes.
State Golf Association: South Carolina Golf Association, 145 Birdsong Trail, Chapin, SC 29036—(803) 781-6992

Highlights: South Carolina was home to the first chartered golf club in the Western Hemisphere, the South Carolina Golf Club at Harleston Green which was organized in the late 18th century and continued for several years.

Golf was reinstituted in the state at the turn of the century, but golf did not achieve its present prominence until after the Second World War and the expansion of major resorts such as Myrtle Beach and Hilton Head Island. Florence Country Club hosted the Girls Junior Amateur in 1955 and the LPGA's Peach Blossom Invitational was held in the western part of the state during the early 1960s, but it was the PGA TOUR's Heritage Tournament on Hilton Head Island, and the golf explosion at Myrtle Beach that put South Carolina on the national map. Hilton Head hosted the Senior Amateur in 1974 and Myrtle Beach the U.S. Women's Open in 1962 and the LPGA Championship in 1977. Subsequently Harbour Town has hosted the Nabisco Championships (now the TOUR Championship), while Kiawah Island hosted the famous 1991 "War by the Shore" in the Ryder Cup matches that year. Various PGA TOUR, Senior PGA TOUR and LPGA events have been played in the state during the 1980s and 1990s, notably the Heritage, the Wendy's Three Tour Challenge, and the Hilton Head Seniors International. The Dunes Club in Myrtle Beach is scheduled to host the Senior TOUR Championship for several years beginning in 1994.

In addition to the various championship events, South Carolina is now considered one of the leading golf destination states in the country, with extensive golf offerings in the Charleston, Hilton Head Island, and Myrtle Beach areas. In addition, the state has become a major center for golf-oriented planned communities.

SOUTH DAKOTA

No. of Players (Rank): 107,000 (41)
Participation Rate (Rank): 18.5% (3)
Percentage of Female Players (Rank): 33.4 (2)
Percentage of Senior Golfers (Rank): 12.4 (48)
Prominent Golfers: Curt Byrum, Tom Byrum, Marlene Hagge.
Prominent Courses: Dakota Dunes, Meadowbrook, Minnehaha.
State Golf Association: South Dakota Golf Association, 509 South Holt, Sioux Falls, SD 57103—(605) 338-7499

Highlights: South Dakota hosted its first national championship in 1984 when Meadowbrook in Rapid City played host to the Women's Publinx. The Girls Junior is slated for Westward Ho C.C. in Sioux Falls in 1996. South Dakota is also home to a NIKE TOUR event, the Dakota Dunes Open, and the future looks promising for the state after many years without major golf events on the calendar.

TENNESSEE

No. of Players (Rank): 321,000 (25)
Participation Rate (Rank): 7.5% (43)
Percentage of Female Players (Rank): 12.9 (47)
Percentage of Senior Golfers (Rank): 23.1 (19)
Prominent Golfers: Bruce Fleisher, Gibby Gilbert, Lou Graham, Cary Middlecoff.
Major Golf Companies: Johnston & Murphy.
Prominent Courses: Belle Meade, The Honors Course, Memphis, Richland.
State Golf Association: Tennessee G.A., 4711 Trousdale Drive, Nashville, TN 37220—(615) 833-9689

Highlights: Tennessee first reached the mainstream as a golfing state in the late 1930s when Memphis Country Club hosted the Women's Amateur in 1937. Subsequently the state hosted the PGA TOUR in several stops in the early years of the TOUR, beginning with the Knoxville War Bond and the Nashville Open as early as 1944, and including the Memphis Invitational and the Memphis Open along the way. The LPGA followed suit in the late 1950s with a Memphis Open of its own. National Championships continued to return with the Amateur in 1948, the Senior Amateur in 1955 and 1959, the Women's Amateur in 1979 and the U.S. Women's Open at Richland Country Club in 1980. In the past decade, the LPGA's Sara Lee Classic has been played in the state, along with the FedEx-St. Jude Classic on the PGA TOUR. Tennessee has become the home of one of the most highly-regarded courses in the country with the construction of The Honors Course in the early 1980s, from a Pete Dye design, and the course hosted the Amateur in 1991; recently the PGA TOUR-developed TPC at Southwind was constructed in Memphis.

TEXAS

No. of Players (Rank): 1,334,000 (5)
Participation Rate (Rank): 9.1% (38)
Percentage of Female Players (Rank): 18.3 (33)
Percentage of Senior Golfers (Rank): 18.8 (39)
Prominent Golfers: Frank Beard, Homero Blancas, Ben Crenshaw, Charles Coody, Jimmy Demaret, Lee Elder, Ralph Guldahl, Sandra Haynie, Ben Hogan, Don January, Tom Kite, John Mahaffey, Byron Nelson, Sandra Palmer, Lee Trevino, Scott Verplank, Kathy Whitworth, Babe Zaharias.
Major Golf Companies: American Ball Manufacturing Corp., Hogan, Nitro, Pro-Gear, Sahara, Tempo, Texace, Wood Brothers.
Prominent Courses: Austin, Barton Creek, Champions (Cypress Creek), Colonial, Home-stead Bay, TPC at Las Colinas, TPC at The Woodlands.
State Golf Association: Dallas District Golf Association, 4321 Live Oak, Dallas, TX 75204—(214) 823-6004; Houston Golf Association, 1830 South Millbend Drive, The Woodlands, TX 77830—(713) 367-7999; San Antonio Golf Association, 70 N.E. Loop 410, Suite 370, San Antonio, TX 78216—(512) 341-0823

Highlights: Texas, along with California and Florida, was one of the early hotbeds of professional golf, and from the late 1910s has been one of the major centers of the game. The Texas Open is, next to the Western Open, the oldest PGA TOUR event with a history that stretches back into the Golden Age of golf in the 1920s, with winners such as Walter Hagen and Mac Smith on the victory roll. The PGA Championship arrived as early as 1927, when Hagen recorded his fourth consecutive win, and the U.S. Open was played at the brand-new Colonial C.C. in 1941. Colonial subsequently became the host site of the prestigious Colonial Invitational on the PGA TOUR, while Texas continued to add tournaments until today eight PGA, LPGA, and Senior PGA TOUR events are played in the Lone Star State.

National championships were plentiful in Texas during the 1960s, with two PGA Championships and the 1969 U.S. Open. Weather conditions have subsequently hampered efforts to bring the majors to Texas. But in the last decade the 1991 U.S. Women's Open was played at Colonial and the 1993 Amateur at Champions. In addition, Texas hosted the 1967 Ryder Cup matches, the 1975 TPC, and the 1986-87 TOUR Championship (then known as the Nabisco Championships).

In addition to hosting numerous distinguished tournaments, Texas is known as a state that has for several generations produced many of golf's greatest players on the extensive collection of municipal courses, as well as several of the best-known golf writers and broadcasters. The state is also known increasingly as a golf resort destination since the construction of the Las Colinas complex, as well as The Woodlands and Barton Creek.

UTAH

No. of Players (Rank): 259,000 (30)
Participation Rate (Rank): 18.3% (4)
Percentage of Female Players (Rank): 22.2 (19)
Percentage of Senior Golfers (Rank): 18.3 (42)
Prominent Golfers: Jay Don Blake.
Major Golf Companies: Carbon Fiber.
Prominent Courses: Park Meadows, The Country Club.
State Golf Association: Utah Golf Association, 1512 South 1100 East, Salt Lake City, UT 84105—(801) 299-8421

Highlights: Utah has not promoted itself as a leading golf state—nevertheless there are several outstanding courses and resorts and not a little golf history. There have been no national championships staged in the state, but Utah did have a PGA TOUR event as early as the 1948 Utah Open, which did not survive but was briefly revived in the late 1950s and early 1960s. The Salt Lake City Open was also briefly played on the LPGA Tour in the early 1960s. In recent years Utah has been known more for a Senior PGA TOUR event played at the Park Meadows complex, and a NIKE TOUR event.

VERMONT

No. of Players (Rank): 43,000 (48)
Participation Rate (Rank): 9.0% (39)
Percentage of Female Players (Rank): 16.2 (42)
Percentage of Senior Golfers (Rank): 23.7 (14)
Prominent Golfers: Patty Sheehan.
Major Golf Companies: Bogner of America.
Prominent Courses: Ekwanok, Rutland.
State Golf Association: Vermont Golf Association, P.O. Box 1612, Station A, Rutland, VT 05701—(802) 773-7180

Highlights: Vermont's involvement with golf on a national scale dates back to the 1914 Amateur which was played at Ekwanok, and which provided Francis Ouimet with a worthy follow-up to his triumph in the 1913 U.S. Open. Subsequently, Vermont has not been able to maintain a high profile due to the short summer golf season and the small number of local golfers, but the state has an excellent resort at Stratton Mountain which is the host of an LPGA event, the McCall's LPGA Classic.

VIRGINIA

No. of Players (Rank): 510,000 (17)
Participation Rate (Rank): 9.4% (37)
Percentage of Female Players (Rank): 17.1 (39)
Percentage of Senior Golfers (Rank): 22.1 (27)
Prominent Golfers: Donna Andrews, Joe Dey, Page Dunlap, Vinny Giles, Bill Kratzert, Kathy Postlewait, J.C. Snead, Sam Snead, Ed Sneed, Curtis Strange, Bobby Wadkins, Lanny Wadkins, Robert Wrenn.
Major Golf Companies: Hi Tech Golf.
Prominent Courses: C.C. of Virginia, Cascades, Golden Horseshoe-Gold, The Homestead, Kingsmill, Lower Cascades, Robert Trent Jones.
State Golf Association: Virginia State Golf Association, 830 Southlake Boulevard, Suite A, Richmond, VA 23236—(804) 378-2300

Highlights: The Oakhurst Golf Club, built in 1884, represented the first identifiable golf course built in the United States. The course is currently undergoing restoration, but the next instances of golf occur in the western part of the state where the Virginia Hot Springs G.C. was built—the first tee there, built in the early 1890s, remains open today and is the oldest tee in continuous use in the Union.

Despite these early golfing roots, Virginia found itself outside the mainstream of golf development—both the Amateur game which was centered on the Northeast and Midwest, and the professional game which centered on Florida, Texas, and California. The state did not host its first national championship until 1928 when the Virginia Hot Springs course hosted the Women's Amateur. The center of Virginia moved eastward in the 1940s as Richmond was the site of a PGA TOUR event in the mid-1940s and hosted the PGA Championship at the Hermitage in 1949. Richmond also hosted an LPGA event, the Richmond Open, in the mid-1950s, as well as the 1955 Amateur, while Virginia Beach briefly became home to another PGA TOUR event. In the 1960s the western part of the state saw the Hot Springs Open and two major women's events, the 1966 Curtis Cup and the 1967 U.S. Women's Open. Amateur golf was also fiercely contested in the 1960s and early 1970s with amateurs such as Vinny Giles, Lanny and Bobby Wadkins, and Curtis Strange.

In the 1980s the PGA TOUR returned to Virginia with the Anheuser-Busch Classic in Williamsburg, sparking off a tremendous rush of golf development in the Williamsburg area that continues today. The LPGA staged its Crestar Classic in Virginia from the mid-1980s through 1992, while the 1991 Publinx and the 1993 Senior Amateur were held in the Charlottesville area and the 1988 Amateur at Virginia Hot Springs. Perhaps the highlight on the Virginia calendar today is the President's Cup, which debuted at the Robert Trent Jones G.C. in Manassas in 1994.

WASHINGTON

No. of Players (Rank): 557,000 (16)
Participation Rate (Rank): 12.8% (21)
Percentage of Female Players (Rank): 21.4 (23)
Percentage of Senior Golfers (Rank): 17.8 (44)
Prominent Golfers: Rick Acton, JoAnne Gunderson Carner, Fred Couples, Bing Crosby, Rick Fehr, Mary Bea Porter-King, Anne Sander, Bill Sander, Ken Still, Kirk Triplett, Audrey Wooding, Mark Wurtz, Kermit Zarley.
Major Golf Companies: G. Loomis.
Prominent Courses: Canterwood, Harbour Pointe, Indian Canyon, Port Ludlow, Seattle, Semi-ah-moo.
State Golf Association: Washington State Golf Association, Northgate Executive Center #1, 155 NE 100th Street #302, Seattle, WA 98125—(206) 526-1238
Highlights: While the Tacoma Golf Club, founded in 1904, was the one of the first West Coast golf clubs to attract national attention, Washington has lagged behind other Pacific states in golf development over the years—due in part to the short golfing season and often-inclement weather. Clubs such as Seattle G.C. were the site of a significant number of exhibitions in the 1920s and 1930s, and Washington produced a number of fine amateurs in the pre-Second World War era. But during and after the war golf boomed significantly—Spokane hosted the 1941 Publinx and the 1944 PGA Championship, while in 1945 alone two PGA TOUR events were played in the Puget Sound area. Tacoma subsequently hosted the occasional PGA TOUR event in the 1950s while Seattle played host to the 1952 Amateur and the 1953 Publinx.

In the 1960s Washington's economy boomed with the growth of the aerospace industry, and both eastern Washington (hosting an LPGA TOUR event) and in particular Western Washington (hosting the Seattle Open and the 1961 Walker Cup, and the 1961 Women's Amateur) were experiencing dramatic surges in golf interest. Seattle's first top-100 ranked course, Sahalee, also dates from the 1960s.

In the 1970s golf did not experience the excitement of the 1960s, with Washington hosting only the 1974 Women's Amateur, but the 1980s brought a revival with the Senior PGA TOUR and the LPGA hosting events, and the Senior Amateur, Women's Amateur and the Publinx coming to the state. Resort development also began to grow in Washington state in the 1980s such as the Resort Semiahmoo, taking advantage of the excellent turf-growing conditions. The culmination of these developments will come in 1998 when the PGA Chanpionship is scheduled to be contested at Sahalee.

WEST VIRGINIA

No. of Players (Rank): 102,000 (42)
Participation Rate (Rank): 6.7% (45)
Percentage of Female Players (Rank): 18.6 (31)
Percentage of Senior Golfers (Rank): 18.0 (43)
Prominent Courses: Greenbrier-Greenbrier, Greenbrier (Old White), Pete Dye, Sheraton Lakeview.
State Golf Association: West Virginia Golf Association, P.O. Box 8133, Huntington, WV 25705-0133—(304) 525-0000

Highlights: West Virginia golf has until recently largely revolved around the golf at The Greenbrier, site of the 1922 Women's Amateur and a brief PGA TOUR event in the late 1950s. The Greenbrier also hosted the 1979 Ryder Cup Matches in which the combined European team played for the first time. Also in the 1970s Guyan Golf and Country Club hosted the 1977 Girls' Junior Amateur. The LPGA staged the West Virginia LPGA Classic in Wheeling during the early 1980s. The Solheim Cup was staged at The Greenbrier in 1994, marking the return of championship golf to the area—while quality golf development is growing as indicated by the construction of the Pete Dye Golf Club in the state.

WISCONSIN

No. of Players (Rank): 752,000 (9)
Participation Rate (Rank): 18.2% (5)
Percentage of Female Players (Rank): 28.7 (7)
Percentage of Senior Golfers (Rank): 22.1 (27)
Prominent Golfers: Bob Brue, Stephanie Farwig, Dan Forsman, Skip Kendall, Laurie Merten, Martha Nause, Andy North, Sherri Steinhausen, Steve Stricker.
Major Golf Companies: Hornung.
Prominent Courses: Americana Lake Geneva, Blackwolf Run, Geneva National, Milwaukee.

State Golf Association: Wisconsin State Golf Association, P.O. Box 35, Elm Grove, WI 53122—(414) 786-4301

Highlights: Championship golf arrived in Wisconsin as early as 1933 when Gene Sarazen won the PGA championship at Blue Mound in Milwaukee. Subsequently the LPGA staged the Milwaukee Jaycee Classic in the state during the 1960s, while the Milwaukee Country Club hosted the 1969 Walker Cup. The event that the state is best known for, the Greater Milwaukee Open, debuted in 1968 on the PGA TOUR. Among national championships both the Publinx and Women's Publinx were held in the state in 1977, while the Women's Publinx returned in 1986. The Senior Amateur was also staged in Wisconsin in 1986. Wisconsin has been long noted for having one of the most enthusiastic golfing populations in the country, with a high per-capita participation rate and a surprisingly strong number of out-of-state visitors.

WYOMING

No. of Players (Rank): 52,000 (46)
Participation Rate (Rank): 13.9% (12)
Percentage of Female Players (Rank): 24.3 (13)
Percentage of Senior Golfers (Rank): 14.3 (47)
Prominent Golfers: Jim Benepe.
Prominent Courses: Jackson Hole, Old Baldy.
State Golf Association: Wyoming Golf Association, 1808 Kit Carson, Casper, WY 82604—(307) 265-3216

Highlights: Wyoming has an enthusiastic golf population, but only a small number of courses. A short golf season hinders golf development in most parts of the state. Nevertheless the state has a top-100 ranked course in Old Baldy, an outstanding resort at Jackson Hole in the western part of the state, and a small number of national championships to its credit in recent years. The first national played in Wyoming was the 1988 Publinx, played at Jackson Hole—the Women's Publinx was also played there in 1993.

ECONOMICS AND DEVELOPMENT

OVERVIEW: *Key industry statistics from the National Golf Foundation and industry sources regarding course and facility construction, fees, spending trends, employment, TOUR finances, corporate sponsors, charitable donations, and a census of golfers since 1945.*

American Professional Tour Purses

Sources: PGA TOUR, LPGA, Senior PGA TOUR, and Nike TOUR. All figures in thousands.

Year	PGA	LPGA	Sr. PGA	Nike	TOTAL	%+(-)	PGA share
1938	158	—	—	—	158	—	100.0%
1939	121	—	—	—	121	(23.4)	100.0
1940	117	—	—	—	117	(3.3)	100.0
1941	169	—	—	—	169	44.4	100.0
1942	117	—	—	—	117	(30.8)	100.0
1943	17	—	—	—	17	(85.5)	100.0
1944	151	—	—	—	151	788.2	100.0
1945	435	—	—	—	435	188.1	100.0
1946	412	—	—	—	412	(5.3)	100.0
1947	353	—	—	—	353	(14.3)	100.0
1948	427	—	—	—	427	21.0	100.0
1949	338	—	—	—	338	(20.8)	100.0
1950	460	50	—	—	510	50.9	90.2
1951	460	70	—	—	530	3.9	86.8
1952	498	150	—	—	648	22.3	76.9
1953	563	120	—	—	683	5.4	82.4
1954	601	105	—	—	706	3.4	85.1
1955	782	135	—	—	917	29.9	85.3
1956	847	140	—	—	987	7.6	85.8
1957	820	148	—	—	968	(1.9)	84.7
1958	1,006	159	—	—	1,165	20.4	86.4
1959	1,225	203	—	—	1,428	22.6	85.8
1960	1,335	187	—	—	1,522	6.6	87.7
1961	1,462	289	—	—	1,751	15.0	83.5
1962	1,790	338	—	—	2,128	21.5	84.1
1963	2,045	345	—	—	2,390	12.3	85.6
1964	2,301	351	—	—	2,652	11.0	86.8
1965	2,849	356	—	—	3,205	20.9	88.9
1966	3,704	510	—	—	4,214	31.5	87.9
1967	3,979	435	—	—	4,414	4.7	90.1
1968	5,078	550	—	—	5,628	27.5	90.2
1969	5,466	597	—	—	6,063	7.7	90.2
1970	6,752	435	—	—	7,187	18.5	93.9
1971	7,116	559	—	—	7,675	6.8	92.7
1972	7,597	988	—	—	8,585	11.9	88.5
1973	8,657	1,471	—	—	10,128	18.0	85.5
1974	8,166	1,753	—	—	9,919	(2.1)	82.3
1975	7,895	1,742	—	—	9,637	(2.8)	81.9
1976	9,158	2,527	—	—	11,685	21.3	78.4
1977	9,689	3,058	—	—	12,747	9.1	76.0
1978	10,337	3,925	—	—	14,262	11.9	72.5
1979	12,801	4,400	—	—	17,201	20.6	74.4
1980	13,372	5,150	250	—	18,772	9.1	71.2
1981	14,175	5,800	750	—	20,725	10.4	68.4
1982	15,090	6,400	1,372	—	22,862	10.3	66.0

Year	PGA	LPGA	Sr. PGA	Nike	TOTAL	%+(-)	PGA share
1983	17,588	7,000	3,365	—	27,953	22.3	62.9
1984	21,251	8,000	5,156	—	34,407	23.1	61.8
1985	25,291	9,000	6,076	—	40,367	17.3	62.7
1986	25,442	10,000	6,300	—	41,742	3.4	61.0
1987	32,106	11,400	8,700	—	52,206	25.1	61.5
1988	36,959	12,510	10,500	—	59,969	14.9	61.6
1989	41,289	14,190	14,195	—	69,674	16.2	59.3
1990	46,252	17,100	18,323	3,050	84,725	21.6	54.6
1991	49,628	18,435	19,788	3,625	91,476	8.0	54.3
1992	49,387	21,325	21,025	4,200	95,937	4.9	51.5
1993	53,204	20,400	26,250	4,975	104,829	9.3	50.8
1994	56,416	21,975	28,850	5,675	112,916	7.7	50.0
TOTAL	894,038	214,781	170,900	21,525	1,031,244	—	60.5

Speed Of Play

Source: 1989 PGA Cost/Revenue Survey. 18 hole Regulation Length Courses.

Group or Facility type	4 hrs or less	4 to 4-1/2 hrs.	More than 4-1/2 hrs.	Average Round
All Facilities	44.2%	19.4%	36.4%	4 hrs 15 min
Municipal	27.8	19.1	53.1	4 hrs 27 min
Daily Fee	34.1	15.6	50.3	4 hrs 23 min
Private Non-Equity	46.5	25.5	27.9	4 hrs 11 min
Private Equity	58.2	19.5	22.3	4 hrs 06 min
Men	59.8	24.7	15.5	3 hrs 59 min
Women	58.9	14.5	26.6	4 hrs 04 min
0-9 handicap	67.7	14.6	17.7	3 hrs 49 min
10-19 handicap	62.2	27.6	10.2	3 hrs 52 min
20-29 handicap	55.3	27.1	17.6	4 hrs 05 min
30-49 handicap	54.5	19.8	25.7	4 hrs 14 min
50+ handicap	42.1	26.3	31.6	4 hrs 22 min

Course and Facility Development, 1981-94

Year	Courses Opened	Year	Courses Opened	Year	Courses Opened
1981	149	1986	131	1991	342
1982	140	1987	145	1992	351
1983	104	1988	211	1993	340
1984	136	1989	290	1994	381
1985	109	1990	351		

Source: National Golf Foundation

PGA TOUR Charitable Contributions, 1977-1994

Year	Total Contributions	Year	Total Contributions
1977	$3,300	1986	$16,100
1978	$4,300	1987	$17,600
1979	$4,400	1988	$18,390
1980	$4,500	1989	$19,779
1981	$6,800	1990	$20,161
1982	$7,200	1991	$19,534
1983	$7,800	1992	$22,223
1984	$9,400	1993	$22,752
1985	$11,300	1994	$24,701

Source: PGA TOUR. Figures in thousands.

Growth in the Golf Facility Supply, by Facility Type, 1931-1994

Source: National Golf Foundation

Year	Total	Private	Daily Fee	Muni.	Year	Total	Private	Daily Fee	Muni.
1931	5,691	4,448	700	543	1968	9,615	4,269	4,110	1,236
1934	5,727	4,155	1,006	566	1969	9,926	4,459	4,192	1,275
1937	5,196	3,489	1,070	637					
1939	5,303	3,405	1,199	699	1970	10,188	4,619	4,248	1,321
					1971	10,494	4,720	4,404	1,370
1941	5,209	3,288	1,210	711	1972	10,665	4,787	4,484	1,394
1946	4,817	3,018	1,076	723	1973	10,665	4,787	4,484	1,394
1947	4,870	3,073	1,061	736	1974	11,134	4,715	4,878	1,541
1948	4,901	3,090	1,076	735	1975	11,370	4,770	5,014	1,586
1949	4,926	3,068	1,108	750	1976	11,562	4,791	5,121	1,650
1950	4,931	3,049	1,141	741	1977	11,745	4,847	5,203	1,695
					1978	11,885	4,872	5,271	1,742
1951	4,970	2,996	1,214	760	1979	11,966	4,848	5,340	1,778
1952	5,026	3,029	1,246	751					
1953	5,056	2,970	1,321	765	1980	12,005	4,839	5,372	1,794
1954	5,076	2,878	1,392	806	1981	12,035	4,789	5,428	1,818
1955	5,358	2,801	1,692	865	1982	12,140	4,798	5,494	1,848
1956	5,358	2,801	1,692	865	1983	12,197	4,809	5,528	1,860
1957	5,553	2,887	1,832	834	1984	12,278	4,831	5,566	1,881
1958	5,745	2,986	1,904	855	1985	12,346	4,861	5,573	1,912
1959	5,991	3,097	2,023	871	1986	12,384	4,865	5,587	1,912
					1987	12,407	4,898	5,583	1,926
1960	6,385	3,236	2,254	895	1988	12,582	4,897	5,748	1,937
1961	6,623	3,248	2,363	912	1989	12,658	4,862	5,833	1,963
1962	7,070	3,503	2,636	931					
1963	7,477	3,615	2,868	994	1990	12,846	4,810	6,024	2,012
1964	7,893	3,764	3,114	1,015	1991	13,004	4,686	6,272	2,046
1965	8,323	3,887	3,368	1,068	1992	13,210	4,568	6,552	2,090
1966	8,672	4,016	3,483	1,173	1993	13,439	4,492	6,803	2,144
1967	9,336	4,166	3,960	1,210	1994	14,939	4,792	7,032	2,415

Census of U.S. Golfing Population and Rounds Played, 1960-1994

Source: National Golf Foundation. Figures in thousands.

Year	Golfers	Rounds	Rounds/Golfer	Year	Golfers	Rounds	Rounds/Golfer
1960	5,000	N/A	N/A	1985	17,500	415,000	23.7
				1986	19,900	419,000	21.1
1970	11,200	266,000	23.8	1987	21,200	431,000	20.3
				1988	23,000	484,000	21.0
1975	13,000	309,000	23.8	1989	24,200	469,000	19.4
1980	15,100	358,000	23.7	1990	27,800	502,000	18.1
1981	15,600	368,000	23.6	1991	24,800	479,000	19.3
1982	16,000	379,000	23.7	1992	24,800	505,000	20.4
1983	16,500	391,000	23.7	1993	24,500	499,000	20.4
1984	17,000	403,000	23.7	1994	24,300	464,800	19.1

DIRECTORY OF ASSOCIATIONS AND GOVERNING ORGANIZATIONS OF GOLF

OVERVIEW: *Addresses, telephone numbers and fax numbers (if available) for the leading international, national, province, country and state golfing organizations.*

INTERNATIONAL GOLF ASSOCIATIONS

Asia-Pacific Golf Confederation
52,1st Floor, Jalan Hang,
Lekiu 50100
Kuala Lumpur

European Golf Association
En Ballgue, Case Postale CH-1066,
Epalinges, Lausanne,
Switzerland
Tel: 010-4l-21-784-3532 Telex 450804
Golf Fax: 41-21-784-3536.

Royal & Ancient Golf Club,
St. Andrews, Fife, Scotland
Tel: (0334) 72112 Fax: (0334) 77580

United States Golf Association
Golf House, Liberty Corner Rd.,
Far Hills, NJ 07931
Tel: (201) 624-8400

International Golf Association
P.O. Box 176, Greenwich, CT 06831-0876
Tel: (203) 531-1113 Fax: (203) 531 4373

South American Golf Federation
Avda. Brasil 3025, Rib 50, Montevideo, Uruguay

NATIONAL GOLF ASSOCIATIONS
ARGENTINA

Asociacion Argentina de Golf
Calle Corrientes 538 - piso 11
1043 Buenos Aires
Argentina
Tel: 54-1-325-7498

AUSTRALIA

Australian Golf Union
155 Cecil Street
South Melbourne
3205 Victoria
Australia
Tel: 61-03-699-7944

Australian Ladies' Golf Union
22 McKay Road,
Rowville 3178, Victoria
Tel: (03) 764-4019 Fax: (03)764-5219

**Australian Professional Golfers'
Association - PGA Tour**
4/140 George Street,
Hornsby 2077 New South Wales
Tel: (02) 477-6333 Fax: (02) 477-7625

Victorian Golf Association
15 Bardolph Street,
Burwood,Victoria.
Tel: (03) 296731 Fax: (03) 291077

New South Wales Golf Association
17 Brisbane Street,
Darlinghurst, New South Wales.
Tel: (02) 264-8433 Fax: (02) 261-4750

Tasmanian Golf Council
2 Queen Street
Bellerive, Tasmania 7018
Tel: (002) 44-3600 Fax: (002) 44-3201

Queensland Golf Union
Cur Wren Street & Walden Lane,
Bowen Hills, Queensland 4006
Tel: (07) 854-1105 Fax: (07)257-1620

Western Australian Golf Association
Suite 14, 49 Melville Parade
South Perth 6151 Western Australia
Tel: (09) 367-2490 Fax: (09) 368-2255

South Australian Golf Association
249 Henley Beach Road
Torrensville 5031 South Australia
Tel: (08) 352-6899 Fax: (08) 352-3900

Victoria Women's Golf Association
598A Glenliuntly Road,
Elsternwick 3185, Victoria
Tel: (03) 523-8511 Fax: (03) 528-1056

Western Australian Women's Golf Association
Unit 3, 66 Mill Point Road,
South Perth 6151, Western Australia
Tel: (09) 368-2618

South Australian Women's Golf Association
2 Marshall Street
Glengowne 5044 South Australia
Tel: (08) 294-7838

Tasmania Women's Golf Association
86 Roslyn Avenue
Kingston Beach 7050 Tasmania
Tel: (002) 296222

AUSTRIA

Osterreichischer Golf-Verband
Prinz-Eugen Strasse 12, A-1040 Vienna
Austria
Tel: 43-222-505-3245

THE BAHAMAS

Bahamas Golf Federation
P.O. Box N 4568
Nassau
The Bahamas

BELGIUM

Federation Royale Belge de Golf
Chemin de Baudemont, 23, B-1400 Nivelles
Belgium
Tel: 32-67-220440

BERMUDA

Bermuda Golf Association
Box HM BX-433, Hamilton
Bermuda

BOLIVIA

Federacion Boliviana de Golf
Casilla de Corree 6130, La Paz
Bolivia

BOTSWANA

Botswana Golf Union
P.O. Box 1033, Galoorone
Botswana

BRAZIL

Confederacao Braseleira de Golf
Rua 7 de Abril 282- s/83
01044 Sao Paulo
Brazil

BURMA

Burma Golf Federation
c/o Aung San Stadium, Rangoon
Burma

CANADA

Canadian (Royal) Golf Association
Golf House, RR No. 2
Oakville, Ontario L6J 4Z3

Canadian Ladies' Golf Association
1600 James Naismith Drive, Gloucester, Ontario
KlB 5N4. Tel: (613) 748-5642

Canadian Professional Golfers' Association
69 Berkeley Street, Toronto M5A 2W6.
Tel: (416) 368-6104

British Columbia
Room 22,1675 West 8th Ave,
Vancouver, BC V6J 1V2

Alberta
200-H Haddon Road
Calgary, Alberta T2V 2Y6

Saskatchewan
205 Victoria Ave.
Regina, Saskatchewan S4P 0S4

Manitoba
1700 Etlice Ave.
Winnipeg, Manitoba R3H 0B1

Ontario
400 Esna Park Drive, Unit 11
Markham, Ontario L3R 1H5

Quebec
3300 Cavendish Blvd, Sinte 250
Montreal, Quebec L4B 2M8

New Brunswick
3 Sunset Lane
St. John, New Brunswick E2H 1GB

Nova Scotia
4 Lanardo Drive
Dartmouth, Nova Scotia 3A3X4

Newfoundland/Labrador
PG Box 5361
St. Johns, Newfoundland

Prince Edward Island
PG Box 51
Charlottetown, PEl C1A 7K2

CHILE

Federacion Chilena de Golf
Vicuna Mackenna 40, Casilla 13307 Santiago
Chile

CHINA (TAIWAN)

Professional Golfers' Association
of the Republic of China
2nd Floor, No. 196 Pei Ling 5th Road
Taipel, Taiwan
Republic of China
Tel: (02)822-0318 822-9684

COLOMBIA

Federacion Colombiana de Golf
Carrera 7a N. 72-64, Of. Int. 26
Apartado Aereo 90985
Bogota, D.E. Columbia

COSTA RICA

Costa Rica Golf Association
c/o ANAGOLF, P.O. Box 2041-1000, San Jose
Costa Rica

CYPRUS

Cyprus Golf Union
c/o JSGC Dhekelia, BPPO 58
Cyprus

CZECH REPUBLIC

Czech Golf Federation
Na porici 12, CS-11530, Praha 1
Czech Republic
Tel: 42(2) 2350065-84

DENMARK

Danish Golf Union
Golfsvingt 2, 2625 Vallensbaek
Denmark
Tel: 45-4-264-0666

DOMINICAN REPUBLIC

Dominican Golf Association
P.O. Box 641
Santa Domingo
Dominican Republic

ECUADOR

Federacion Ecuatoriana de Golf
Baquerizo Moreno 1120
P.O. Box 521
Guayaquil
Ecuador

EGYPT

The Egyptian Golf Federation
Gezira Sporting Club
Gezira, Cairo, Egypt
Tel: (2) 80 6000

EL SALVADOR

Asociacion Salvadorena de Golf
Apartado Postal 631, San Salvador
El Salvador

ENGLAND

Amateur Golf Championship
Royal & Ancient Golf Club, St. Andrews
Tel: (0334)72112 Fax: (0334) 77580

Association of Public Golf Courses
35 Sinclair Grove, Golders Green,
London NW11 9JH
Tel: 081-4585433

British Assoc. of Golf Course Architects
5 Oxford Street, Woodstock,
Oxford GX7 lTQ.
Tel: (0993) 811976

British Assoc. of Golf Course Constructors
Tellford Farm,
Willingale, Ongar
Essex CM5 OQE
Tel: (0277) 896229 Fax: (0245) 491620

British & Int'l. Golf Greenkeepers' Assoc.
Aldwark Manor, Aldwar
Alne, York Y06 2NF
Tel: (03473) 5812 Fax: (03473) 8864

British Professional Golfers' Association, Apollo
House, The Belfry, Sutton Colfield,
West Midlands,B76 9PT
Tel: (0676) 70333 Fax: (0675) 70674

Golf Foundation
57 London Road, Enfield,
Mliddlesex EN2 6DU. Tel: 081-367 4404

Golf Society of Great Britain
Southvlew, Warren Road,
Thurlestone, Devon
TQ7 3NT Tel: (0548) 560630

Ladies' Golf Union
The Scores,St. Andrews, Fife KYl6 9AT Tel:
(0334)75811

The Professional Golfers' Association
National Headquarters
Apollo House, The Belfry, Sutton Coldfield,
West Midlands, B76 9PT
Tel: (0675) 70333 Telex 338481
Fax: (0675) 70674

PGA European Tour
The Wentworth Club,
Wentworth Drive, Virginia Water,
Surrey GU25 4LS
Tel: (0344) 842881 Fax: (0344) 842929

**Women Professional Golfers'
European Tour**
The Tytherington Club, Macclesfield,
Cheshire SK1O 2JP
Tel: (0625) 611444

Sports Turf Research Institute
Bingley, West Yorkshire BDl6 lAU
Tel: (0274) 566131 Fax: (0274) 561891

Bedfordshire County Golf Union
8 Galusborough Avenue, St. Albans, Bedfordshire
ALl 4NL Tel: (0727) 67834

**Bedfordshire Ladies'
County Golf Association**
3 Sherbourne Avenue, Luton,
Bedfordshire LU2 7BB Tel: (0582) 675883

**Berks, Bucks and Oxon
Union of Golf Clubs**
Leyscre, Lodersfield, Lechlade
Gloucestershire GL7 3DJ Tel: (0637) 52926

**Berkshire, Buckinghamshire and Oxfordshire
Golfers Alliance**
Wayside, Aylesbury Road, Monks Risborough
Aylesbury, Bucks

**Berkshire Ladies' County Golf
Association**
Hon Sec, Mrs BE Band, 11 Lynton Green, College
Road, Maldenhead
Berkshire SL6 6AN Tel: (0628) 21462

**Buckinghamshire Ladies' County Golf
Association**
Springfield Bungalow, Butlers Cross, Aylesbury
Buckinghamshire
Tel: (0296) 624376

Cambridgeshire Area Golf Union
2a Dukes Meadow, Stapleford,
Cambridgeshire CB2 6BH Tel: (0223) 842062

**Cambs and Hunts Ladies'
County Golf Association**
The Paddock, 14 Mingle Lane, Stapleford Carobs
CB2 6BG Tel: (0223) 843267

Channel Islands Ladies' GA
Oakertbilch, Park Estate, St Brelade, Jersey
Tel: (0634) 42072

Cheshire County Ladies' Golf Association
12 Higher Downs, Knutsford
Cheshire WA1 6 8AW

Cheshire Union of Golf Clubs
4 Curson Mews, Wimislow
Cheshire SK9 6A1 Tel: (0626)632866

Cornwall Golf Union
8 Lydcott Crescent, Widegates, Looe, Cornwall PL13
lOG

**Cornwall Ladies'
County Golf Association**
Hain Walk, St. Ives, Cornwall
Tel: (0736) 796392

**Cumbria Ladies'
County Golf Association**
Cawdor, Garth Heads Road, Appleby Cumbria CA6
6DD Tel: (07683) 61672

Cumbria Union of Golf Clubs
Thorn Lea, Lazouby Penrith, Cumbria
Tel: (0768) 83231

Derbyshire Alliance
c/o Buxton & High Peak CC, Fanfield, Buxton,
Derbyshire Tel: (0298) 3112

Derbyshire Ladies' County Golf Association
11 Pine Close, Smalley,
Derbyshire DE7 6EH Tel: (0332) 880929

Derbyshire PGA
Erewash Valley Golf Club
Stanton-by-Dale, Derbyshire
Tel: (0662) 324667

Derbyshire Union of Golf Clubs
67 Portland Close,
Mickleover,
Derbyshire DE3 6BR
Tel: (0332) 612466

Devon County Golf Union
Appledowne, Keyberry Park,
Newton Abbot,
Devonshire TQ12 lDF
Tel: (0626) 62999

Devon County Ladies' Golf Association
The White House, Hansford,
Sidmouth, Devonshire

Devon Professional Golfers' Alliance
Surthaven, 2 Landscore Close,
Devonshire Tel: (03632) 3146

Dorset County Golf Union
38 Carlton Road, Bournemouth BH1 3TG
Tel: (0202) 290821

Dorset Ladies' County Golf Association
4 Egdon Glen Crossways, Dorchester, Dorsetshire
DT2 8BQ Tel: (0306) 862647

Durham County Golf Union
Iliginiam Lodge, Park Mews, Harilepeol, Cleveland
T526 ODX Tel: (0429) 273186

Durham County Ladies' Golf Association
107 Hartsey Road, Harthurn,
Stockton-on-Tees

English Golf Union
1-3 Upper King Street, Leicester LEt 6XF
Tel: (0633) 663042 Fax: (0633) 471322

Midland Group
Chantry Cottage, Friar Street, Droitwich, Worns
WR9 8EQ Tel: (0906) 778660

Northern Group
7 Northbrook Court, Harilepool, Cleveland TS26
ODJ Tel: (0429) 274828

South Eastern Group
22 Wye Court, Malvern Way, Ealing, London W13
BFA Tel: (081) 9977466

South Western Group
Hariland, Potterne, Devizes,
Wills SNIU 6PA Tel: (0380) 3936

English Ladies' Golf Association
Edgbaston Golf Club, Church Road, Birmingham
B16 3TH Tel: (02) 466 2088

Northern Division
10 Cleehill Drive, North Shields, Tyne & Weir
NE29 9EW Tel: (091) 267 6926

Midlands Division
3 Leanolme Gardens, Pedmore, Stourbridge,
West Midlands DY9 OXX Tel: (0662) 884682

South-Eastern Division
71 Parkanaur Avenue, Thorpe Bay Essex SSl 3JA
Tel: (0702) 688336

South-Western Division
19 Ferndown Close, Kingsweston, Bristol
Tel: (0272) 683643

Essex County Amateur Golf Union
9 Willow Walk, Hadleigh,
Benfleet, Essex SS7 2RW Tel: (0702) 669871

Essex Ladies' County Golf Association
1 The Paddocks, Stock, Essex
Tel: (0277) 810466

**Gloucestershire and Somerset
Professional Golfers' Association**
Cotswold Hills CC Tel: (0242) 616263

Gloucestershire Golf Union
2 Hartley Close, Sandy Lane,
Chariton Kings, Cheltenham CL63 9DN
Tel: (0242) 614024

**Gloucester Ladies'
County Golf Association**
1 Avon Crescent, Cumberland Road, Bristol BS1
6XQ Tel: (0272) 264606

**Hampshire Ladies'
County Golf Association**
182 Bassett Green Road, Southampton
Hampshire S02 3LW Tel: (0703) 789273

**Hampshire, Isle of Wight and
Channel Islands Golf Union**
Glyngarth, Tower Road, Hindhead
Surrey CU26 6SL Tel: (042 873) 4090

**Hampshire Professional
Golfers' Association**
3 Lily Close, Kempshott Down,
Basingstoke, Hants
RC22 6NT Tel: (0266) 466070

**Hertfordshire County
Professional Golfers' Alliance**
1 Field Lane, Letchworth
Hertfordshire SC6 3LF Tel: (0462) 682266

**Hertfordshire County
Ladies' Golf Association**
22 The Avenue, Radlett
Hertfordshire WD7 7DW Tel: (0923) 867184

Hertfordshire Golf Union
2 The Heath, Radlett
Hertfordshire WD7 7DF Tel: (0923) 867184

Isle of Man Golf Union
22 Mount View Road, Onchan,
Isle of Man Tel: (0624) 622991

Isle of Wight Ladies' Golf Association
Rosloing, Solent View Road
Seaview, Isle of Wight PO34 6HY Tel: (0988) 613266

Kent County Golf Union
62 Queens Road, Littlestone, New Romney, Kent TN28 8LY Tel: (0679) 63613

Kent County Ladies' Golf Association
Colleton House, North Road, Hythe, Kent CT21 4AS Tel: (0303) 66286

Kent Professional Golfers' Union
20 The Grove, Baritham, Kent
Tel: (0227) 831666

Lancashire Ladies' County Golf Association
26 Park Road, Colborne, Warrington,
Cheshire WA3 3PU

Lancashire PGA
32 Pembridge Road, Blackley
Manchester M9 2IE Tel: (061) 7968647

Lancashire Union of Golf Clubs
4 Cedarwood Close
Lytham Hall Park,
Lytham, Lancashire FYB 4PD
Tel: (0263) 733323

**Leicestershire and Rutland Ladies'
County Golf Association**
4 Bailey's Lane, Burton Overy
Leicestershire LE8 0DD Tel: (063) 769 2697

Leicestershire and Rutland Golf Union
187 Leicester Road, Groby, Leicester
Tel: (0633) 873676

Leicestershire Professional Golfers' Association
218 Hamilton Lane, Scraptoft, Leicester
Tel: (0633) 414736

Lincolnshire Ladies' County Association
86 South Parade, Boston
Lincolnshire PE2l 7PN Tel: (0206) 69948

Lincolnshire Professional Golfers' Association
Seacroft CC, Skegness, Lincolnshire
Tel: (0764) 3020

Lincolnshire Union of Golf Clubs
Allenby Ores, Fotherby Nr Louth
Lincolnshire, LNl 1 OLl Tel: (0607) 604298

Middlesex County Golf Union
36 Grants Close, Mill Hill
London NW7 1DD Tel: (081) 3490414

Midland Golf Union
Chantry Cottage, Friar Street
Droitwich, Worcestershire WR9 8EQ
Tel: (0905) 778560

Norfolk County Golf Union
2a Stanley Avenue, Norwich, Norfolk
Tel: (0603) 31026

Norfolk Ladies' County Association
17 Taylor Avenue, Cringleford
Norfolk NR4 6XY Tel: (0603) 56049

Northamptonshire Golf Union
10 12 Edge Hill Road, Duston, Northampton INS 6BY Tel: (0604) 51031

**Northamptonshire Ladies'
County Golf Association**
534 Wellingborough Road
Northampton NN3 3HZ Tel: (0604) 09298

Northamptonshire PGA
Ivycroft, Back Lane, Chapel Trampton
Northamptonshire Tel: (0605) 843305

**Northumberland Ladies'
County Golf Association**
23 Mast Lane, Ullercoats,
North Shields NE30 3DK Tel: (091) 252 5382

Northumberland Union of Golf Clubs
5 Calthurst Drive, Kenton Ark, Gosforth
Newcastle-upon-Tyne NE3 4J5

**Nottinghamshire County
Ladies' Golf Association**
Cranmer Lodge, Maln Steet,
Kinoulton, Notts, NA12 3EL Tel (0949) 81201

Nottinghamshire PGA
52 Barden Road, Mapperley
Nottingham NG3 5QD Tel: (0602) 269635

Nottinghamshire Union of Golf Clubs
48 Weaverthorpe Road, Aroodthorp
Nottinghamshire NG5 4NB

Oxfordshire Ladies'
County GolfAssociation
532 Banbury Road, Oxford OX2 BEG
Tel: (0865) 58300

Sheffield PGA
Hillsborough CC, Worrall Road
Sheffield S6 4BE Tel: (0742) 332666

Sheffield Union of Golf Clubs
8 Newfield Court, 186 Fulwood Road, Sheffield
S1O 3QE

Shropshire and Herefordshire
Union of Golf Clubs
23 Poplar Crescent, Bayston, Shrewsbury
SY3 0GB Tel: (0743) 722655

Shropshire and Herefordshire PGA
Bridgorth Golf Club, Stanley Lane, Bridgnorth
Shropshire Tel: (07462) 2045

Shropshire Ladies' County Golf Association
122 Fieldhouse Drive, Muxton, Telford, Shropshire
TF8 8BB Tel: (0952) 604522

Somerset Golf Union
Longwood, Grange Road, Salford
Bristol BS1B 3AC Tel: (0225) 872166

Somerset Ladies' County Golf Association
Tresausen, Mill Lane, Corfe
Taunton TA3 7AH

South-Western Counties Golf Association
Hartland, Potterne, Devizes, Wiltfordshire SN1O
SPA Tel: (0380) 3935

Staffordshire Ladies'
County Golf Association
11 Westhill, Finchfield Hill, Wolverhampton WV3
9HL Tel: (0902) 753279

Staffordshire and Shropshire
Union of Professional Golfers
22 Wyan Road, Penn, Wolverhampton

Staffordshire Union of Golf Clubs
19 Broadway Walsall
West Midlands WSl 3EX Tel: (0922) 24988

Suffolk County Golf Union
2 Barton Road, Felixstowe
Suffolk WU 7JH Tel: (0394) 286429

Suffolk Ladies' County Golf Association
20 Meadowside, Snowdon Hill
Wickman Market, Woodbridge, Suffolk
Tel: (0728) 747609

Suffolk PGA
Bury St Edmunds CC,
Forubam All Saints, Bury St Edmunds
Suffolk W28 2LG Tel: (0284) 755978

Surrey County Golf Union
Rushmoor Cottage, Rushmoor Close
Fleet, CU13 9LD Tel: (0252) 614078

Surrey Ladies' County Golf Association
Tel: (0883) 723163

Surrey PGA
27 Lower Wood Road, Claygate, Surrey
Tel: (0372) 63882

Sussex County Golf Union
12 Redmell Avenue, Saltdean, Brighton, Sussex BN2
8LT Tel: (0273) 304415

Sussex County Ladies' Golf Association
Flat 1, 22 Granville Road, Eastbourne,
East Sussex BN2O 7HA Tel: (0323) 28452

Sussex Professional Golfers' Union
96 Cranston Avenue, Bexhill-on-Sea, Sussex
Tel: (0424) 221298

Warwickshire Ladies'
County Golf Association
57 White House Green
Solihull, W Midlands 831 lSP
Tel: (021) 705 8062

Warwickshire PGA
5 Church Lane, Stoneleigh, Warwickshire
Tel: (0203) 418113

Wiltshire County Golf Union
10 Priory Park, Bradford-on-Avon, Wiltshire BA1S 1QU Tel: (022 16) 6401

Wiltshire Ladies' County Golf Association
South Lodge, Northleigh
Bradford-on-Avon, Wiltshire Tel: (02216)3387

Wiltshire PGA
Marlborough CC, The Coramon, Marlborough
Wiltshire Tel: (0672) 512493

Worcestershire APG
Droitwich CC, Ford Lane Droitwich
WR9 0BH, Worcestershire Tel: (090S) 770207

Worcestershire County Ladies' Golf Association
12 Russeil Road
Kidderminster, Worcestershire DY1O 3UT

Worcestershire Union of Golf Clubs
70 Cardinal Drive, Kidderminster, Worcestershire
DY1O 4RY Tel: (0562) 823109

Yorkshire Ladies' County Golf Association
Ingle Court, Lepton, Huddersfield, Yorkshire
Tel: (0484) 602011

Yorkshire Professional Golfers' Association
1 Summerhill Gardens, Leeds
Yorkshire LS8 2EL Tel: (0532) 664746

Yorkshire Union of Golf Clubs
50 Bingley Road, Bradford
West Yorkshire BD9 6HH Tel: (0274) 542661

FIJI

Fiji Golf Association
PO Box 177, Suva
Fiji

FINLAND

Finnish Golf Union
Radiokatu 12, SF-00240 Helsinki
Finland
Tel: 358 (0) 158-2244

FRANCE

Federation Francaise de Golf
69 Avenue Victor Hugo, F-75783,
Paris Cedex 16
France
Tel: 33 (1) 4-502-1355

French Professional Golfers' Association
69Victor Hugo 75116 Paris 16
France
Tel: Paris (1) 500-4372

GERMANY

Deutscher Golf Verband
eV Postfach 2106, Wiesbaden D-6200
Germany
Tel: 49 (6121) 526-041

Deutscher Golfiehier Verband (PGA)
Eberlestrasse 13, 89 Augsburg
Germany
Tel: 010 49 (821) 628900

GHANA

Ghana Golf Association
PO Box 8, Achimola
Ghana

GREECE

Hellenic Golf Federation
PO Box 70003, GR 166 10 Athens
Greece
Tel: 30 (1) 894-1933

GUATEMALA

Federacion Guatemalteca de Golf
3a Avenida Finca, El Zapote Zona 2
Guatemala

GUYANA

Guyana Golf Union
c/o Demerara Bauxite Co Ltd, Mackenzie
Guyana

HONDURAS

Asociacion Hondurena Golf
Apartado Postal No 68-C
Tegucigalpa, DC
Honduras

HONG KONG

The Golf Association of Hong Kong
GPO Box 9978 Room 110
Yu To Sang Building, 37 Queens Road
Central Hong Kong

Hong Kong Professional Golfers' Association, PG Box 690, Hong Kong
Tel: (5) 222111 Telex lX73751

HUNGARY

Hungarian Golf Federation
c/o Rodata RT, Budapest 1028
Hungary
Tel: 36 (1) 176-6722

ICELAND

Golfsamband Islands
PO Box 1076, Reykjavik IS-101
Iceland
Tel: 354-168-6686

INDIA

The Indian Golf Union
43 Chowringhee Road, Calcutta 700-071
India

INDONESIA

Indonesian Golf Association
J1 Rawamangun Muka Taya, Jakarta 13220
Indonesia

IRELAND

Irish Golf Union
Glencar House, 81
Eglinglon Road, Donnybrook, Dublin 4
Tel: (0001) 694111

Ulster Branch
High Street, Holywood
Co Down, BTl8 9AE Tel: Holywood 3708

Leinster Branch
1 Clonskeagh Square, Clonskeagh Road, Dublin 14
Tel: (0001) 696977 / 696727

Munster Branch
Sunvilte, Dromshgo, Mallow Co, Cork
Tel: (22) 221123

Irish Ladies' Golf Union
1 Clonskeagh Square,
Clonskeagh Road, Dublin 14
Tel: (0001) 696244

Northern District
1 4D Adelalde Park, Belfast BT9 6FX
Tel: (0232) 682152

Southern District
11 Baritead Drive,
Church Road,
Blackrock, Cork Tel: (21) 291698

Eastern District
4 Castletown Court, Colbridge, Co. Kildare

Western District
Dooney Rock, Cleveragh Drive, Sligo
Tel: Sligo (71) 62351

Midland District
Glena Terrace, Spawell Road,
Wexford Tel: Wexford (53) 22866

ISRAEL

Israel Golf Federation
PO Box 1010, Caesarea
Israel
Tel: (972) 6-361172

ITALY

Federazione Italiana Golf
Via Flaminia 388,
Roma 1-00196
Italy
Tel: 39 (6) 394641

IVORY COAST

Federation Nationale du Golf
08 BP 1297, Abidjan 08
Cote D'Ivoire
Tel: 22-521-3874

JAMAICA

Jamaica Golf Association
PO Box 743, Kingston 8
Jamaica

JAPAN

National Golf Foundation Japan
3-3-4 Sebdagaya Shibuya-ku, Tokyo
Japan
Tel: 81 (03) 478-4355

Japan Golf Association
606-6th Floor, Palace Building,
Marunouchi
Chiyoda-ku, Tokyo
Japan
Tel: (3) 215 0003

Japan Ladies' Professional Golfers' Association
Kuranae Kogyo Kalkan 7E
Slanbasi 2-19-1, Minato-ku, Tokyo,
Japan
Tel: (3) 571 0928

Japan Professional Golf Association
Thmin-Ueno Building,
4F, 1-7-15,
Higashi-Ueno, Talto-Ku, Tokyo 110
Japan

KENYA

Kenya Golf Union
PO Box 49609 Nairobi
Kenya
Tel: (2) 720074

Kenya Ladies' Golf Union
PO Box 45615 Nairobi
Kenya

KOREA

Korea Golf Association
Room 18 - 13 Floor Manhattan Building
36-2 Yeo Eui Do-Dong, Yeong Deung Po-Ku, Seoul
Korea
Tel: 82 (02) 783-4748

LIBYA

Libyan Golf Federation
PO Box 3674, Tripoli
Libya

LUXEMBOURG

Luxembourg Golf Club
Grand Ducal 1, Route de Treve
L-2633 Senningerberg, Luxembourg
Tel: (352) 34090

MALAWI

Malawi Golf Union
PG Box 1198, Blantyre
Malawi

Malawi Ladies' Golf Union
PG Box 5319, Inmbe
Malawi

MALAYSIA

Malaysian Golf Association
No 12-A Persiaran Ampang, 55000 Kuala Lumpur
Malaysia

MEXICO

Federacion Mexicana de Golf
Cincinati No. 40-104, Col Napoles, 03710
Mexico
Tel: (5) 563-9194

MOROCCO

Federation Royale Marociane de Golf Royal
Golf Rabat dar es Salam,
Route des Zaers, Rabat
Morocco

NETHERLANDS

Nederlandse Golf Federatie
PO Box 221, 3454 PV De Meern
Netherlands
Tel: (31) 34-06-21888

NEW ZEALAND

New Zealand Golf Association
Dominion Sports House, Mercer Street
PO Box 11842, Wellington
New Zealand

New Zealand PGA
PO Box 27337, Wellington
New Zealand
Tel: (04) 722687 Fax: (04) 712152

New Zealand Ladies' Golf Union
PO Box 13-029, Wellington 4
New Zealand
Tel: (04) 793868

NIGERIA

Nigeria Amateur Golf Association
National Sports Commission
PO Box 145, Lagos
Nigeria

NORWAY

Norwegian Golf Association
Hauger Skolevie 11351 Rud, Oslo
Norway

PAKISTAN

Pakistan Golf Federation
PO Box 1295, Rawalpindi
Pakistan

PANAMA

Panama Golf Association
PO Box 8613, Panama 5
Panama

PAPUA NEW GUINEA

Papua New Guinea Amateur Golf Association,
P.O. Box 382, Lao
Papua New Guinea

Papua New Guinea Ladies' Golf Association
P.O. Box 1256, Port Moresby
Papua New Guinea
Tel: 675214745

PARAGUAY

Asociacion Paraguaya de Golf
Casilla de Correo 1795, Asuncion
Paraguay

PERU

Federation Peruana de Golf Estadio
Nacional Puerto 4, Piso 4, Casilla 5637 Lima
Peru

PHILLIPINES

Republic of the Philippines Golf Association
Rm 209 Administration Building
Rizal Memorial Sports Complex, Vito Cruz, Manila
The Philippines

PORTUGAL

Federacao Portuguesa de Golf
Rua Almeida Brandao, 39 P-1200 Lisboa
Portugal
Tel: 351 (1) 661121

PUERTO RICO

Puerto Rico Golf Association
GPO Box 3862, San Juan 00936
Puerto Rico
Tel: (809) 781-2070

SCOTLAND

Scottish Golf Union
The Cottage, 181a Whitehouse Road, Barnton,
Edinburgh EH4 68Y Tel: 031-339 7546

Scottish Golfer's Alliance
5 Deveron Avenue, Gifinock
Glasgow G48 6NH

Scottish Ladies' Golfing Association
Chacewood, 49 Fullarton Drive
Troon KA1O 6LF Tel: (0292) 313047

Scottish Ladies' Golfing Association-County Golf
Straibdon, Nelson Street, Dumfries
Tel: (0387) 54429

Scottish Schools' Golf Association
Grangemouth High School, Grangemouth, Central Region

West of Scotland Girls' Golfing Association
7 Gardenside Avenue, Uddingston, Glasgow G71 7BU

Aberdeen Ladies' County Golf Association
9 Earlsweil Place, Cults,
Aberdeen AB1 9LG
Tel: (0224) 861502

Angus Ladies' County Golf Association
The Hawinorns, 1 Grange Avenue,
Mocifieth Dundee Tel: (0382) 532799

Ayrshire Ladies' County Golf Association
8 Station Road, Prestwick KA9 1AG
Tel: (0292) 77330

Border Counties' Ladies Golf Association
Fultarton, Darnick, Metrose, Roxburghshire
Tel: (089682) 2962

Dumfriesshire Ladies' County Golf Association
Strathdon, 10 Nelson Street, Dumfries
Tel: (0387) 54429

East Lothian Ladies' County Association
Glenlair, Main Street, Gullane
Tel: (0620) 842534

Fife County Ladies' Golf Association
Greyfriars, Greyfriars Garden
St Andrews Tel: (0334) 72639

Galloway Ladies' County Golf Association
3 Seggies, Kirkcudbright Tel: (0557) 30542

Lanarkshire Ladies' County Golf Association
76 Kenmure Gardens, Bishopbriggs, Glasgow G64 2BZ Tel: (041) 772 1720

Midlothian County Ladies' Golf Association
37 Thomson Drive, Currie
Midlothian EH14 5EY Tel: 031-4493441

Perth and Kinross Ladies' County Golf Association
Broom, Caleclonian Crescent, Auchierarder Perthshire
Tel: (0764) 62254

Renfrewshire Ladies' County Golf Association
21 Holmnead Road, Glasgow G443AS
Tel: (041) 637 1307

Stirling and Clackmannan Ladies' Golf Association
7 Craighorn Drive, Falkirk 1KI 5NX
Tel: (0324) 29672

SIERRA LEONE

Sierra Leone Golf Federation
Freetown Golf Club, PO Box 237, Lumley Beach,
Freetown
Sierra Leone

SINGAPORE

Singapore Golf Association
c/o CL Loong & Company
4 Battery Road #12000
Bank of China Building, Singapore 0104
Singapore

SLOVENIA

Golf Association of Slovenia
c/o Golf Club Bled, C Svbode 13, 64260 Bled
Slovenia
Tel: 38 (64) 78282

SOUTH AFRICA

South Africa Golf Union
PO Box 1537, Cape Town 8000
South Africa

South African Ladies' Golf Union
PO Box 135, 1930 Vereeniging, Transvaal
South Africa

South African PGA
PO Box 55253, Posbus Northlands
2116 Johannesburg
South Africa
Tel: (011) 884 3404 Fax: (011) 884 3436

Border Golf Union
Box 1773, East Lendon 5200 CP
Tel: (0431) 403899

Eastern Province Golf Union
Box 146, Port Elizabeth 6000, OP
Tel: (041) 21919

Northern Cape Golf Union
Box 517, Bloemfontein 9300, OFS
Tel: (051) 470511

Natal Golf Union
Box 1939, Durban 4000, Natal
Tel: (031) 223877

Transkei Golf Union
Box 210, Umtata, Transkei

Transvaal Golf Union
Box 391661, Bramley 2018, Transvaal
Tel: (011) 6403714

Western Province Golf Union
Box 153, Howard Place, 7450,
Orange Province
Tel: (021) 536728

Spain

Real Federacion Espanola De Golf
Capitan Haya, 9-5, E-28020 Madrid
Spain
Tel: 34 (1) 555 2757

Sri Lanka

Ceylon Golf Union
PO Box 309, Model Farm Road, Colombo 8
Sri Lanka

Swaziland

Swaziland Golf Union
S Mabuza, PO Box 1739, Mbabane
Swaziland

Sweden

Svenska Golfforbundet
Box 84 (Kevingestrand)
A-182 11 Danderyd
Sweden
Tel: 46 (8) 753-0265

Swedish PGA
PO Box 35, S-181 21, Lidingo
Sweden
Tel: Stockholm (8) 767 83 23

Switzerland

Association Suisse de Golf
En Ballque, Case Postale,
1066 Epalinges
Switzerland
Tel: 41 (21) 784-3531

Swiss Professional Golfers' Association
Perrelet 9, 2074, Marin
Tel: (038) 33 23 79

Tanzania

Tanzania Golf Union
PG Box 4879, Dar-es-Salaam
Tanzania

Thailand

Thailand Golf Association
Railway Training Centre,
Vibhavadee Rangsit Road, Bangkok,
Thailand

Trinidad & Tobago

Trinidad & Tobago Golf Association
7A Warner Street, New Town, Port of Spain
Trinidad

UGANDA

Uganda Golf Union
Kitante Road Box 2674, Kampala
Uganda

UNITED STATES

Professional Golfers' Association of America
100 Ave of the Champions
Palm Beach Gardens, FL 33418
Tel: (407) 624-8400

United States Golf Association
Golf House, Liberty Corner Rd
Far Hills, NJ 07931
Tel: (201) 624-8400

Wood Brothers Gulf Coast Scratch Series
Tel: (904) 941-2031

Emerald Coast Senior Scratch Series
Tel: (904) 243-4836

Hooters/Jordan Tour
Tel: (800) 992-8748

Senior Series
Tel: (910) 940-6400

Western States Tour
Tel: (602) 331-8020

Golden State Tour
Tel: (619) 742-1461

Moonlight Tour
Tel: (813) 393-8531

Gulf Coast Tour
Tel: (904) 234-8453

Gold Coast Tour
Tel: (800) 345-5066

South Florida Tour
Tel: (800) 383-9737

40-Plus Tour of Florida
Tel: (407) 333-2000

Emerald Coast Tour
Tel: (904) 862-0803

North Atlantic Tour
Tel: (508) 352-9719

Carolina Mountain Tour
Tel: (704) 252-7442

Triangle Tour
Tel: (919) 596-2473

Powerbilt Tour
Tel: (910) 579-9904

Lone Star Tour
Tel: (214) 484-7270

Futures Tour
Tel: (813) 385-3320

Players West
Tel: (415) 962-1267

American Junior Golf Association
Tel: (404) 998-4653

Plantation Junior Tour
Tel: (803) 875-2054

STATE AND LOCAL ASSOCIATIONS

Alabama Golf Association
1025 Montgomery Hwy, Ste 210
Birmingham, AL 35216
Tel: (205) 979-1234 Fax: (205) 979-1602

Anchorage Golf Association
PO Box 112210
Anchorage AK 99511
Tel: (907) 349-4653

Arizona Golf Association
7226 North 16th Street, Suite 200
Phoenix, AZ 85020
Tel: (602) 944-3035 Fax: (602) 944-3228

Cactus & Pine Superintendents Association
7418 Helm Dr, Suite 227, Scottsdale, AZ 85260
Tel: (602) 998-9059 Fax: (602) 951-9756

Junior Golf Association of Arizona
5040 E Shea, #250, Scottsdale, AZ 85254
Tel: (602) 443-9009 Fax: (602) 443-9006

Arkansas Seniors Golf Association
7002 Lucerne Dr, Little Rock, AR 72205
Tel: (501) 666-0951

Arkansas State Golf Association
2311 Biscayne Dr, #308,
Little Rock, AR 72207
Tel: (501) 227-8555 Fax: (501) 227-8234

LA Junior Chamber of Commerce
404 S Bixel St, Los Angeles, CA 90017
Tel: (213) 482-1311

N California Golf Association
3200 Lopez Rd, Pebble Beach, CA 93953
Tel: (408) 625-4653 Fax: (408) 625-0150

San Diego City Junior Golf Association
Jack Murphy Stadium
9449 Friars Rd, San Diego, CA 92108-1771
Tel: (619) 280-8505 Fax: (619) 281-7947

San Diego City Women's Golf Association
3102 Lavante St, Carlsbad, CA 92009
Tel: (619) 436-0266

S California Pub Links Golf Association
7035 Orangethorpe Ave, Ste E,
Buena Park, CA 90621
Tel: (714) 994-4747

Colorado Golf Association
5655 S Yosemite, Ste 101,
Englewood, CO 80111
Tel: (303) 779-4653 Fax: (303) 220-8397

Connecticut State Golf Association
35 Cold Spring Rd, #212, Rocky Hill, CT 06067
Tel: (203) 257-4171 Fax: (203) 257-8355

Connecticut Women's Golf Association
183 Plagler Ave, Cheshire, CT 06410

Delaware State Golf Association
7234 Lancaster Pike, #302B,
Hockessin, DE 19707-9273
Tel: (302) 234-3365 Fax: (302) 234-3359

Dade Amateur Golf Association
1802 NW 37th Ave, Miami, FL 33159
Tel: (305) 633-4563

Florida Golf Republic Association
PO Box 2280, Boca Raton, FL 33427
Tel: (407) 391-3292

Florida State Golf Association
PO Box 21177, Sarasota, FL 34276
Tel: (813) 921-5695 Fax: (813) 923-1254

Florida Turfgrass Association
302 S Graham Ave
Orlando, FL 32803-6399
Tel: (407) 898-6721 Fax: (813) 923-1254

Pensacola Sports Association
201 E Gregory St, Pensacola, FL 32501
Tel: (909) 939-4455

**Georgia Golf Course
Superintendents Association**
1141 Station Dr,
Watkinsville, GA 30677
Tel: (706) 769-4076 Fax: (706) 769-4076

Georgia State Golf Association
121 Village Parkway, Bldg 3
Marietta, GA 30067
Tel: (404) 955-4272 Fax: (404) 955-1156

Hawaii Golf State Association
3599 Waielae Ave #PH
Honolulu, HI 96816-2759
Tel: (808) 732-9785

Idaho Golf Association
PO Box 3025, Boise, ID 83703
Tel: (208) 342-4442 Fax: (208) 345-5959

**Central Illinois
Golf Course Superintendents Association**
5350 Old Jacksonville Rd
Springfield, IL 62707
Tel: (217) 787-7750

Chicago District Golf Association
619 Enterprise Dr
Oak Brook, IL 60521
Tel: (708) 954-2180 Fax: (708) 954-3650

Illinois Junior Golf Association
2100 Clearwater Dr, Suite 206
Oak Brook, IL 60521
Tel: (708) 368-0000 Fax: (708) 990-7864

Western Golf Association
1 Briar Rd, Golf, IL 60029
Tel: (708) 724-4600 Fax: (708) 724-7133

Indiana Association of Nurserymen
2635 Yeager Rd, Ste,
West Lafayette, IN 47906
Tel: (317) 497-1100 Fax: (317) 463-0190

Indiana Golf Association
PO Box 516, Franklin, IN 46131
Tel: (317) 738-9696 Fax: (317) 738-9436

Indiana Junior Golf Association
PO Box 4454, Lafayette, IN 47903
Tel: (317) 447-1992 Fax: (317) 448-9969

Iowa Golf Association
1930 Saint Andrews Ct NE
Cedar Rapids, IA 52402
Tel: (319) 378-9142 Fax: (319) 378-9203

Kansas City Golf Association
9331 Ensley Lane, Leawood, KS 66206
Tel: (913) 649-8872 Fax: (913) 842-3831

Kansas Golf Association
3301 Clinton Parkway Ct #4, Lawrence, KS 66047
Tel: (913) 842-4833 Fax: (913) 842-3831

Kentucky Golf Association
4109 Bardstown Rd #5A, Louisville, KY, 40261
Tel: (502) 499-7255 Fax: (502) 499-7422

Louisiana Golf Association
1305 Emerson St, Monroe, LA 71201
Tel: (318) 342-1968 Fax: (318) 342-1989

Maine State Golf Association
11 Cook St, Auburn, ME 04210
Tel: (207) 582-6742 Fax: (207) 582-6743

Maryland State Golf Association
PO Box 16289, Baltimore, MD 21210
Tel: (410) 467-8899

Massachusetts Golf Association
190 Park Rd, Weston, MA 02193
Tel: (617) 891-4300 Fax: (617) 891-9471

Golf Association of Michigan
37935 12 Mile Rd, Ste 200,
Farmington Hills, MI 48331
Tel: (313) 553-4200 Fax: (313) 553-4438

Michigan Publinx Sr Golf Assoc
43525 W 6 Mile Rd, Northville, MI 48167
Tel: (313) 349-2148

Minnesota Golf Association
6550 York Ave S, Ste 211, Edina, MN 55435
Tel: (612) 927-4643

Trans-Mississippi Golf Association
240 Minnetonka Ave S, #212
Wayzata, MN 55391
Tel: (612) 473-3722 Fax: (612) 473-0576

Mississippi Golf Association
1019 N 12th Ave #3, Laurel, MS 39441
Tel: (601) 649-0570 Fax: (601) 649-1737

Missouri Golf Association
PO Box 104164, Jefferson City, MO 65110
Tel: (314) 636-8994 Fax: (314) 636-4225

St Louis District Golf Association
537 N Clay, Kirkwood, MO 63122
Tel: (314) 821-1511

Montana State Golf Association
PO Box 2289, Butte, MT
Tel: (406) 723-4312 Fax: (406) 782-9551

Nebraska Golf Association
5625 O Street, Suite Fore
Lincoln, NE 68510-2149
Tel: (402) 486-1440

Nevada State Golf Association
PO Box 5630, Sparks, NV 89432-5630
Tel: (702) 673-4653 Fax: (702) 673-1144

Southern Nevada Golf Association
1434 Cottonwood
Las Vegas, NV 89104
Tel: (702) 382-6616

New Hampshire Golf Association
45 Kearney St, Manchester, NH 03104
Tel: (603) 623-0396

New Jersey State Golf Association
1000 Broad St, Bloomfield, NJ 07003
Tel: (201) 338-8334 Fax: (201) 338-5525

Southern Jersey State Golf
277 Mayflower Dr, Buena, NJ 08310
Tel: (609) 697-9318

Trenton District Golf Association
7 High Acres Rd, West Trenton, NJ 08628
Tel: (609) 771-2191

Sun Country Amateur Golf Association
10035 Country Club Ln NW, #5
Albuquerque, NM 87114
Tel: (505) 897-0864 Fax: (505) 897-3494

Buffalo District Golf Association
PO Box 19, Cheektowaga, NY 14225
Tel: (716) 632-1936

Metropolitan Golf Association
125 Spencer Pl
Mamaroneck, NY 10543
Tel: (914) 698-0390

Rochester District Golf Association
1106 Long Pond Rd Ste 190
Rochester, NY 14626
Tel: (716) 227-4053

Syracuse District Golf Association
2205 W Genesee St
Syracuse, NY 13219-1617
Tel: (315) 488-7391

Westchester Golf Association
106 N Broadway, Irvington, NY 10533
Tel: (914) 591-4970

Carolinas Golf Association
PO Box 428, West End, NC 27376
Tel: (910) 673-1000 Fax: (910) 673-1001

Turfgrass Council of N Carolina
231 W Pennsylvania Ave
Southern Pines, NC 28387
Tel: (910) 695-1333 Fax: (910) 695-1222

North Dakota State Golf Assoc
PO Box 452, Bismark, ND 58502
Tel: (701) 223-2770 Fax: (701) 223-6719

Northern Ohio Golf Association
17800 Chillicothe Rd, Ste 210
Chagrin Falls, OH 44023
Tel: (216) 543-6320

Ohio Assoc of Public Golf Courses
5874 Morray Ct, Dublin, OH 43017
Tel: (614) 761-1527

Ohio Golf Association
5300 McKitrick Blvd
Columbus, OH 43235
Tel: (614) 457-8169 Fax: (614) 457-8211

Toledo District Golf Association
Southwyck Blvd, Ste 204, Toledo, OH 43614-1505
Tel: (419) 866-4771 Fax: (419) 866-0388

Oklahoma Golf Association
PO Box 449, Edmond, OK 73083
Tel: (405) 340-6333 Fax: (405) 340-6333

Oregon Golf Association
8364 SW Nimbus Ave #A1, Beaverton, OR 97005
Tel: (503) 643-2610 Fax: (405) 340-6333

Erie District Golf Association
1223 Jonathan Dr, Erie, PA 16509
Tel: (814) 838-8524

Golf Association of Philadelphia
PO Drawer 808, Southeastern, PA 19399
Tel: (215) 687-2340 Fax: (215) 687-2082

Keystone Public Golf Association
2186 Locust St, Export, PA 15632
Tel: (412) 468-8880 Fax: (412) 468-8897

Western Pennsylvania Golf Association
1360 Old Freeport Rd Ste. 1BR
Pittsburgh, PA 15238
Tel: (412) 963-9806 Fax: (412) 967-0612

Rhode Island Golf Association
10 Orms St, Ste 326,
Providence, RI 02904
Tel: (401) 272-1350

South Carolina Golf Association
PO Box 286, Irmo, SC 29063
Tel: (803) 781-6992 Fax: (803) 781-6992

Women's South Carolina Golf Association
10638 Two Notch, Elgin, SC 29045
Tel: (803) 736-0081

South Dakota Golf Association
509 S Holt, Sioux Falls, SD 57103
Tel: (605) 338-7499 Fax: (605) 334-3447

Dallas District Golf Association
4321 Live Oak, Dallas, TX 75204
Tel: (214) 823-6004

Houston Golf Association
1830 S Millbend Dr,
The Woodlands, TX 77380
Tel: (713) 367-7999 Fax: (713) 363-9888

San Antonio Golf Association
70 NE Loop 410, Ste 370
San Antonio, TX 78216
Tel: (512) 341-0823 Fax: (512) 340-1625

Utah Golf Association
1110 E Englewood Dr.
N Salt Lake City, UT 84054
Tel: (801) 299-8421

Vermont Golf Association
PO Box 1612, Stn A, Rutland, VT 05701
Tel: (802) 773-7180 Fax: (802) 773-7061

Virginia State Golf Association
830 Southlake Blvd, Ste A
Richmond, VA 23236
Tel: (804) 378-2300 Fax: (804) 378-2369

Washington Metro Golf Assoc
8012 Colorado Springs Dr.
Springfield, VA 22153
Tel: (703) 569-6311 Fax: (703) 569-6332

Pacific Northwest Golf Association
155 NE 100th St, #302, Seattle, WA 98125
Tel: (206) 526-1238 Fax: (206) 522-0281

Washington Junior Golf Assoc
633 Mildred, Ste C, Tacoma, WA 98406
Tel: (206) 564-0348 Fax: (206) 564-2602

West Virginia Golf Association
PO Box 8133, Huntington, WV 25705-0133
Tel: (304) 525-0000

Golf Course Assoc of Wisconsin
PO Box 65, Mauston, WI 53948
Tel: (608) 847-7968

Wisconsin State Golf Association
PO Box 35, Elm Grove, WI 53122
Tel: (414) 786-4301 Fax: (414) 786-4202

Wyoming Golf Association
501 First Ave S, Greybull, WY 82426
Tel: (307) 568-3304

URUGUAY

Asociacion Uruguaya de Golf
Casilla de Correo 1484, Montevideo
Uruguay

VENEZUELA

Federacion Venezolana de Golf
Unidad Comercial "La Florida,"
Local 5 Avenida Avila,
 La Florida, Caracas 1050
Venezuela

WALES

Welsh Golfing Union
Powys House
Cwmbran, Owent NP44 1PB

Welsh Ladies' Golf Union
Ysgoldy Gynt, Llanhennock
Newport, Gwent NP6 1LT
Tel: (0633) 420642

Anglesey Golf Union
20 Gwelfor Estate
Cemaes Bay, Anglesey
Tel: (0407) 710755

Caernarvonshire and Anglesey Ladies' County Golf Association
Deunant, Llangefni
Anglesey LL7 7YP
Tel: (0248) 722338

Caernarvonshire and District Golfing Union
23 Bryn Rnos, Rhosbodrual
Caernarfon, Owynood UL55 2BT
Tel: (0286) 3486

Dyfed Golfing Union
55 Clover Par
Haverfordwest, Dyfed

Flintshire Golfing Union
Cornist Lodge, Cornist Park
Flint, Clwyd
Tel: (03526) 2186

Glamorgan Ladies' County Golf Association
19 Trem-y-Don, Barry, South Glamorgan
Tel: (0446) 734866

Mid Wales Ladies' County Golf Association
Ael-y-Byrn, Pontfaen Road, Lampeter, Dyfed
Tel: (0570) 422463

Monmouthshire Ladies' County Golf Association
Flat 2, 405 Chepstow Road, Newport, Gwent
Tel: (0633) 279638

South Wales PGA
St. Mellons Golf Club, Mid Glamorgan
Tel: (0633) 680101

ZAIRE

Zaire Golf Federation
Tshitol, BP 1648 Lubumbashi
Zaire

ZAMBIA

Zambian Golf Union
PG Box 37446, Lusaka
Zambia
Telex: ZA 40098

Zambia Ladies' Golf Union
PG Box 32150, Lusaka
Zambia
Tel: Lusaka (1) 251668,

ZIMBABWE

Zimbabwe Golf Association
PO Box 3327, Harare
Zimbabwe

Zimbabwe Ladies' Golf Union
PG Box 3814, Harare
Zimbabwe

EASY GUIDE TO GOLFING TERMINOLOGY

OVERVIEW: *Simple definitions and explanations of golf's sometimes arcane and always unique vocabulary.*

Ace. Holing the ball on the first stroke. Also HOLE-IN-ONE.

Action. A strong backspin on a shot, usually a wedge or short iron to the green. Also JUICE.

Address. The position of the player immediately before commencing the backswing.

Albatross. (Rare) Three strokes under the PAR score for a hole; i.e. A hole-in-one on a par-four, or a two on a par-five. Also DOUBLE EAGLE.

Alternate Shot. A match format in which two players on one team play one ball, alternating shot for shot. Also FOURSOME, SCOTCH FOURSOME.

Approach. A stroke aimed to finish on the putting surface and close to the hole.

Apron. The area of close-cropped grass surrounding the putting surface. Also FRINGE or FROG HAIR.

Arnie. Making PAR after missing the fairway with the drive.

Baffie. An older golf club, now seldom in use, similar in design to the modern 3-iron. From the Scottish word "baff," to put a ball in the air.

Balata. A by-product of the rubber-tree used to make a golf-ball cover material which spins faster than other cover materials, although it tends to fly a shorter distance and cut easily.

Banana Ball. See CUT SHOT.

Barkie. Making PAR after hitting a tree on the approach shot.

Baseball Grip. See GRIP.

Best Ball. A team scoring format in which the team records only the lowest score among all the team members (sometimes the two lowest, as in "two best balls".).

Birdie. Holing the ball in one stroke under the PAR score.

Bisque. A handicap stroke that may be freely employed at any time during a match.

Blade. 1: The leading edge of an iron. 2: A narrow, forged iron favored by lower handicap players. 3: (Verb) To scull a ball, usually across and over the putting surface.

Blast. A lofted recovery from a greenside bunker, typically struck with the flanged-sole sand wedge and often accompanied by terrific backspin. Also EXPLOSION.

Bogey. Holing the ball in one stroke over the par score. Originally conceived as the average score by the mythical expert player, it has come to represent a mediocre effort in light of modern improvements in technique and equipment. A double-bogey is two over the par score, a triple-bogey is three over, &c.

Brassie. A golf club used prior to 1945, similar to the modern two-wood, so named because of a distinctive brass plate on the sole of the club.

Bump-and-run. A short (20-60 yard) shot in which the player employs a short, flattened backswing to produce a low, running ball which bounces rather than flies into the green. Used most effectively on windy or dry courses.

Bunker. A scrape or swale in the ground filled with sand, usually placed near the green to perplex the player. Also SAND TRAP.

Caddie. The associate who carries the player's clubs, cleans his equipment, and is the only person allowed under the rules to offer advice or information to the player during a round. Often an expert golfer, caddies have often formed life-long associations with top clubs or top professionals. The word comes from the French *cadet*, after the French pages brought to Scotland by Mary, Queen of Scots, who was a keen golfer.

Calcutta. An auction of players before a match—bettors bid for players and the resulting sum of wagers is put into a pool distributed to the winning players and bettors.

Callaway System. A scoring system used for players lacking formal HANDICAP ratings.

Captain's Choice. See SCRAMBLE.

Cast Irons. A technology for casting irons from a mold (rather than forging individually), which introduced the era of cavity-back irons. With weight re-distributed to the perimeter, cavity-back irons have enlarged Sweet Spots and provide more control and distance for off-center hits.

Casual Water. Collections of dew, rainfall, or ground moisture not considered a part of the course; a player is allowed a free drop away from casual water.

Cayman Ball. A ball developed for use on short golf courses which travels significantly less far than the modern golf ball while retaining its spin and control characteristics.

Chili Dip. The clubhead striking the ground well behind of the ball, resulting in a very weak and short shot, as well as an especially impressive DIVOT.

Chip. A shot around the green in which the player employs a putting stroke with a lofted iron; the result is a shot which flies a short distance before rolling toward the hole.

Cleek. (Rare) A golf club similar to the modern 4-wood.

Closed Face. Rotation of the golf club-face in a counter-clockwise direction to produce less loft, more overspin, and a more pronounced DRAW.

Closed Stance. A stance in which a right-handed player's body is aligned right of the target.

Course Rating. The average score of a scratch handicap player on a course, as sanctioned by the United States Golf Association, the Royal & Ancient, or its designated representatives. See SLOPE RATING.

Cross-bunker. A typically narrow and wide bunker which stretches across the fairway, rather than parallel to it. A typical design feature in PENAL ARCHITECTURE.

Cut, The. The reduction of the field, typically after the second day's play, to the low 40-90 contestants. In pro events, only those players who make the cut earn prize money.

Cut Shot. A ball that spins for the right-hander from left to right. The cut shot typically travels a shorter distance than the DRAW, but is easier to control. Also FADE or, in severe and uncontrolled cases, SLICE or BANANA BALL.

Dance Floor. (Slang) The putting surface.

Dimple Pattern. The design of the small indentations in the golf ball that help lengthen its flight and control its spin.

Divot. The turf freed by a golf club when it strikes the ground. Making a DIVOT behind the ball produces a CHILI DIP; hitting after the ball produces backspin.

Dormie. A position in match play where one player is far enough ahead that he cannot be beaten, but has not yet achieved victory. E.g. five holes up with five to play.

Double Eagle. See ALBATROSS.

Drainpipe. A narrow, lightweight golf bag suitable for walking the course.

Draw. A ball that for the right-hander spins from right to left. The draw shot typically travels further than the FADE, but is less subject to precise control. Also known as a HOOK or, in severe and uncontrolled cases, as a DUCK HOOK. "You can't talk to a hook."—Lee Trevino.

Drive. An initial stroke on a hole, when played with a DRIVER. The stroke produces the longest shots in golf, at the risk of some loss in accuracy.

Driver. The longest, least-lofted club in the modern golf bag, almost exclusively used for tee shots, particularly where distance is a factor. Originally known as the PLAY-CLUB.

Duck Hook. See DRAW.

Eagle. Two strokes below the PAR score for a hole. E.g. A HOLE-IN-ONE on a par-three, two strokes on a par-four, and three strokes on a par-five.

Equitable Stroke Adjustment. An adjustment made in a player's score (for handicap purposes only), which limits the maximum score a player can record for an individual hole. The rule was established to prevent players inflating their handicaps with deliberately poor play. See SANDBAGGING.

Explosion. See BLAST.

Face. The front part of the clubhead.

Fade. See CUT SHOT.

Fairway. Short-cropped grass, usually in the 30-50 yards on either side of the center line of a hole, which is the preferred landing point of the player off the tee.

Fat. Hitting significantly behind the ball, resulting in a short hit best distinguished by a rather timid thump coming off the club face.

Feathery. One of the most ancient types of golf balls, it consisted of feathers tightly packed inside a leather cover. Costly and not particularly lively, the ball was superceded in the mid-19th century by the GUTTIE.

Flop Shot. A shot, typically employed in heavy rough, where the player opens the club face so that it is almost parallel to the ground, to reduce resistance and allow the club to move through heavy grass without digging into the turf.

Forged Irons. See CAVITY-BACK IRONS.

Fourteen-Club Rule. The rule instituted in the 1930s limiting a player to carrying a maximum of fourteen golf clubs in a round.

Forecaddie. A player's associate who does not carry the clubs, but in other ways fills the role of the CADDIE.

Four Ball. A match between two teams of two players each.

Foursome. In the United States, any grouping of four golfers. In the rest of the world, a foursome is a match format pitting four players in two-man teams in an ALTERNATE SHOT format. Also SCOTCH FOURSOME.

Fringe. See APRON.

Frog Hair. See APRON.

Frosty. See SNOWMAN.

Gimme. A putt conceded to a player by his opponent, typically a putt of less than two feet, or less than the length of a putter from the sole to the base of the grip.

Grain. The angle at which the grass is growing. Proper allowance for the "drag" caused when putting against the grain is an essential part of READING a green.

Green. Originally, the entire golf course, hence the design principle of "flow through the green," or the "greenkeeper." The modern definition is confined to the putting surface.

Greenie. A bonus bet won by the player who is closest to the pin on a par-three hole (and on the putting green).

Grip. The position of the hands on the shaft. The TEN-FINGER GRIP (also BASEBALL GRIP) is the oldest form, in which the hands work independently. The OVERLAPPING or VARDON GRIP has the little finger of the right hand (for a right-hander) overlapping the index finger on the left. The INTERLOCKING GRIP, popularized by Jack Nicklaus, has the little finger of the right hand interlocked between the index and middle fingers of the left hand, and is used primarily by players with small hands.

Gross Score. A player's actual score, before deductions for HANDICAP and EQUITABLE STROKE ADJUSTMENT.

Ground Under Repair. Ground usually defined as part of the golf course which, due to ground conditions, is ruled unplayable. Players who land here are allowed a drop without penalty.

Guttie. The gutta-percha ball, a solid rubber ball developed in the mid-19th century, superceded the FEATHERY and preceded the HASKELL ball. The Guttie had a tendency to fly quite low, and was difficult to control.

Halve. A tie between two players or two teams in a hole or match.

Handicap. An average of scores, expressed in strokes over par, for the individual player. E.g., a player who averages a score of eighteen strokes over par is said to have a handicap of 18. Handicaps were developed in the stroke play era to allow players of different abilities to compete in "NET SCORE" competitions.

Haskell Ball. The first modern rubber-cored golf ball, invented in 1902.

Hazard. A position within the course boundaries, such as a pond, where the ball is typically unplayable; the player may under penalty of one stroke drop the ball behind the point where the ball entered the hazard. See LATERAL HAZARD.

Heel. The edge of a clubhead nearest the shaft.

Heroic Architecture. A philosophy of course design, most closely associated with the designs of Robert Trent Jones, that presents golfers with difficult or "heroic" shots that, if risked and carried off, make eagle or birdie scores possible. The Heroic style flourished after the Second World War but has in recent decades been superceded by STRATEGIC ARCHITECTURE, which is closely related.

Hole-in-One. See ACE.

Honor. The player who recorded the lowest score on the preceding hole is said to have "the honor," and tees off first on the next hole.

Hook. See DRAW.

Horseshoe. A putted ball which spins around the entire rim of the cup without falling into the hole. Also PAINT JOB.

Hosel. The point at which the shaft joins the clubhead.

Initial Velocity. The speed of a golf ball struck by the USGA's Iron Byron machine, when it first leaves the club-face. Golf balls which exceed the initial velocity specified by the United States Golf Association and the Royal and Ancient Golf Club are not recognized as legal for the purposes of competition.

Interlocking Grip. See GRIP.

Iron. The ancient Scottish word for "sword," it refers to the family of clubs, originally with iron clubheads, used for the short-to-medium length shots. Irons were first developed for use in unusual lies, but since Young Tom Morris demonstrated their ability to produce high, soft shots that stopped quickly (or, in modern times, backed up), they have been used anywhere from the tee to the green. Irons are numbered from 1 through 9; there are also several types of high-lofted or flanged irons known as Sand Wedge, Pitching Wedge, Lob Wedge, &c.

Juice. See ACTION.

Lag Putt. A long putt aimed to finish close to the hole for an easy tap-in.

Lateral Hazard. A water or other HAZARD area in which the player can take a penalty drop beside, rather than strictly behind, the hazard line.

Links. In the traditional sense, a course built atop land from which the ocean has receded, hence a course built on sandy soil. In practice, the term has expanded to include all seaside courses, and many Scottish-influenced designs. As a marketing term, it has been used to describe practically anything that resembles a golf course.

Marker. The score-keeper. Typically another competing player, although the Marker can either be a non-participant or a non-competing player.

Mashie. The old name for what is the modern 3-iron.

Match Play. A competition decided by the number of holes won. See MEDAL PLAY.

Medal Play. Competition decided by the total number of strokes taken, rather than holes won (as in MATCH PLAY).

Metal Wood. See WOOD.

Modified Stableford. See STABLEFORD.

Mulligan. Named for circa-1930s Winged Foot member David Mulligan, it is a replay of a shot without penalty. Forbidden under the Rules of Golf, the Mulligan is nonetheless universally, frequently, and cheerfully employed in amateur golf, particularly with novices. The original interpretation of a Mulligan was a replay of the first tee shot of the day, but the term has since grown to include any replay without penalty granted by a playing partner during the round.

Nassau. A match between two teams in which one-third of the bet is placed on the outcome of the first nine holes, the second third on the second nine, and the final third on the round as a whole. The most popular and enduring of golf wagers.

Net. A player's GROSS score less adjustments for HANDICAP.

Niblick. A golf club similar to the modern five-iron. This was the highest-lofted club manufactured until the 20th century.

Opened Face. Rotation of the club face in a clockwise direction to produce more loft, more back-spin, or a more pronounced FADE.

Opened Stance. A position at address in which a right-handed player is aligned left of the target.

Out of Bounds. Outside the boundary of the course. Any ball hit "O.B." must be replayed from the original position under a penalty of one stroke.

Overlapping Grip. See GRIP.

Paint Job. See HORSESHOE.

Par. Of unknown origin, the term developed in the early 20th century to express the number of strokes the mythical expert player should take to complete a golf hole. Currently defined formally as: Under 225 yards, par 3; 225-474 yards, par 4; 475-575 yards, par 5; over 575 yards, par 6. Courses are not obliged to follow these USGA guidelines, and there are many exceptions. See BOGEY.

Penal Architecture. A philosophy of golf course instruction where errant shots are penalized with difficult lies and hazards. Pine Valley is one of the finer examples of the type. The penal architectural style flourished in the early 20th century but has fallen into disfavor.

Pitch Shot. A short (50-120 yards) shot typically played with a wedge in which the player lofts the ball high into the air to achieve a soft landing on the putting surface.

Play Club. See DRIVER.

Pneumatic Ball. An experimental ball from the early 20th century which, featuring a core of compressed air, had a reputation for flying great distances. When several competitors were injured by the ball exploding in warm temperatures, it was withdrawn from sale.

Pot Bunker. A small and typically deep bunker which is a common feature of Scottish and Scottish-influenced courses.

Pro-Am. A match format mixing professionals and amateurs in a team, often on the day before a professional tournament.

Punch Shot. A low-trajectory shot used in heavy wind or when the shot is crowded by trees. The classic stroke is played with a three-quarter swing and the ball aligned opposite the back foot.

Purse. The pool or prize-money in a professional tournament.

Putt. A stroke employed on the putting surface or close around the green in which the player rolls the ball along the ground instead of lofting it into the air.

Putter. The club employed typically for shots on the green, typically featuring a face with no loft.

Qualifying School. A qualifying tournament or series of tournaments in which professionals vie for a limited number of playing cards for professional tours.

Read. A player's estimate of the slope of the ground, an important factor in choosing the line for a putt.

Rough. Unmowed or heavy grass that is part of the golf course but off the FAIRWAY.

Rub of the Green. An element of good or bad luck. E.g. A ball which strikes the flagstick and, in the one case, drops into the hole, but in another case rebounds into a water-hazard.

Rules of Golf. The official Rules of the Game as codified by the United States Golf Association and the Royal & Ancient Golf Club of St. Andrews.

Rut Iron. A de-lofted club used to hit a ball from an embedded lie. In the modern game most embedded lies are allowed relief with a free drop, and the club has fallen out of use.

Sandbagging. (Slang) The practice of quoting a higher number than one's actual handicap in order to receive either more strokes in a tournament or match, or more favorable terms in a wager. Also refers to the practice of deliberately playing poorly to inflate one's handicap prior to a match or tournament.

Sandie. A ball holed in two shots ("up and down") from a sand-trap.

Scramble. A team format in which team members each hit a shot, choose the best result, and each drop a ball within a club-length and hit from that point. The routine is repeated until the ball is holed. The format, which often produces rashes of birdies and eagles and outrageously low scores, is usually employed with novice players or with groups of widely varying abilities; the format has become widely known through the annual Oldsmobile Scramble, a national amateur championship, which employs the format. Also CAPTAIN'S CHOICE.

Scratch Handicap. A handicap of zero. Hence SCRATCH player.

Scull. To hit the ball with the lowest edge of an iron, causing a low-flying and often wildly-errant shot.

Shamble. Related to a SCRAMBLE, a team format in which team members each hit a shot, choose the best result, and thereafter play their own ball in.

Shank. A ball which is hit off the HOSEL, causing the ball to fly in a low and wildly off-line trajectory.

Skins. A match format in which points or prizes are awarded ("Skins") only when one player wins the hole outright. The format is often played with "carry-overs," in which prizes not awarded because of a halve on one hole are carried over to the next.

Slice. See CUT SHOT.

Slope Rating. The average score of BOGEY golfers over a course, divided by the average score of SCRATCH HANDICAP golfers (COURSE RATING). The purpose of slope is to enable the comparison of scores made by golfers of any ability on differing courses. Using COURSE RATINGS alone offers an effective comparison only for low handicap golfers.

Snowman. (Slang) A score of eight on a single hole. Also FROSTY.

Sole. The bottom edge of a golf club.

Spin-rate. The number of revolutions per second of a golf ball hit by the USGA's "Iron Byron" ball-striking machine.

Spoon. An older term for the fairway wood, now the three-, four- or five-wood.

Square. An alignment of the player at ADDRESS, or the club face at impact, which is perpendicular to the target. Also, a position in a match where the players or teams are level.

Stableford. A scoring system which utilizes a points system, and which encourages bold play through heavy premiums placed on birdies and eagles. The Sprint International, a PGA TOUR event, uses a modified Stableford system.

Strategic Architecture. A philosophy of golf course design which emphasizes presenting options to the golfer, typically a safe route to PAR and a heroic route to BIRDIE or EAGLE. The Strategic style has become increasingly popular in the past twenty years, and is the dominant style in contemporary course design.

Stroke Play. See MEDAL PLAY.

Stymie. Until 1951, players could not mark and lift their balls on the putting surface, and a player whose path to the hole was blocked by another player's ball was "stymied." The stymie became increasingly unpopular with the introduction of greenkeeping and smooth putting surfaces in the 19th century. The subsequent development of the rolled putt (rather than the chipping style previously favored) created loud demand for marking of balls on the green. Such an amendment was made to the RULES OF GOLF in 1951, and since then the stymie has been obsolete.

Surlyn. A patented formula for a hard golf-ball cover which is resistant to scuffing and cutting, introduced by Spalding in 1972.

Sweet Spot. The center of gravity on a club FACE.

Target golf. The strategy of hitting highly lofted shots loaded with backspin that will hold on elevated, heavily watered greens. The strategy is most effective on American courses. In the rest of the world, drier and less elevated greens favor the BUMP-AND-RUN. Also refers to a style of architecture and play found in desert areas where, for water conservation purposes, there is a strict limitation on irrigated turf, and golfers play by hitting from target area to target area.

Tee. Originally a point one club-length or less from the hole where players would begin play on the next hole. The term still refers to the starting point for a hole, but in the modern game up to eight distinct teeing grounds may be designed for individual golf holes, to cut down on wear-and-tear as well as allowing for varying levels of ability or strength. The term also now commonly applies to the wooden pegs on which the ball is placed for the tee shot.

Ten-finger Grip. See GRIP.

Texas Wedge. A shot in which the player uses a putter to stroke the ball from a position off the putting surface. The shot is generally most effective on hard, dry courses.

Thin. Hitting slightly above the ball, producing a low-trajectory flight. A THIN shot in cold weather is one of golf's most memorable experiences.

Three-piece Ball. A ball with a cover, wound rubber strands and a solid rubber core.

Toe. The edge of a golf club farthest from the shaft.

Topper. A shot which catches only the top of the ball, causing it to fly only a short distance with tremendous overspin and a characteristically hopping motion.

Trap. See BUNKER.

Two-piece Ball. A ball with a cover and a solid core.

Unplayable Lie. A difficult lie in which the player, under penalty of one stroke, elects to take a drop within two club-lengths rather than attempting a stroke.

Vardon Grip. See GRIP.

Waggle. A part of the pre-shot routine, a to-and-fro motion utilized to set the tempo of the swing and build concentration for the shot.

Waste Area. A sandy area where the player is allowed to ground his club at address. Named after a bunker on the 16th hole at Harbour Town.

Whiff. A swing which misses the ball.

Winter Rules. Local rules imposed to protect turf during the off-season, allowing players to pick, clean, and place the ball on the fairway. Winter Rules are not endorsed in the Rules of Golf and, of course, by encouraging players to hit off the remaining undamaged turf can actually accelerate the deterioration of a golf course in the winter season. Winter Rules have nonetheless prospered because of their positive effect on scoring.

Wood. A club, originally with a large wooden clubhead, typically used for the longer distance shots in the modern game. Woods are numbered from 1 to 9, and since 1980 have been made with metal and ceramic heads in addition to the traditional persimmon wood.

Yips. A shaking of the hands experienced by older golfers trying to manipulate the small muscles in their hands, especially noticeable in the PUTTING stroke. Yips have destroyed many a fine golf round and even in some cases a career. The most famous example of yips is the WHIFF recorded by Harry Vardon while attempting to putt in the U.S. Open, which he went on to win anyway.

Zanesville Ceramics and other collectibles. A valuable series of ceramics depicting golf, created in the early 20th century. Golfers have been known to collect an astonishing range of useful and utterly useless items that have some remote connection with the grand old game. Collecting began in the late 18th century and encompasses books, clubs, balls, art, accessories, ceramics, toys and games, autographs, stamps, and the all-inclusive "ephemera."

GENERAL INDEX

AWARDS
  PGA TOUR PLAYER OF THE YEAR.....................249
  VARDON TROPHY..249
  PGA PLAYER OF THE YEAR................................249
  LPGA PLAYER OF THE YEAR..............................250
  VARE TROPHY..250
  RICHARDSON AWARD.......................................250
  BEN HOGAN AWARD..251
  CHARLIE BARTLETT AWARD..............................251
  JOE GRAFFIS AWARD..251
  HERB GRAFFIS AWARD.....................................251
  NGF/JACK NICKLAUS GOLF
     FAMILY OF THE YEAR AWARD.......................251
  PGA GOLF PROFESSIONAL OF THE YEAR.....252
  PGA CLUB PRO OF THE YEAR............................252
  HORTON SMITH TROPHY..................................252
  BOB JONES AWARD..252
  CARD WALKER AWARD....................................252
  LPGA TEACHER OF THE YEAR...........................252
  LPGA GOLF PRO OF THE YEAR..........................252
  PATTY BERG AWARD...252
  OLD TOM MORRIS AWARD...............................252

CALENDARS AND PREVIEWS
1995 PROFESSIONAL GOLF CALENDARS
  PGA TOUR...6
  LPGA..11
  SENIOR PGA...9
  EUROPEAN TOUR..13
1995 MAJOR CHAMPIONSHIP PREVIEWS............4

CHAMPIONSHIPS
JUNIOR GOLF
  U.S. JUNIOR AMATEUR.....................................246
  U.S. JUNIOR GIRLS' AMATEUR.........................246
COLLEGES
  NCAA DIVISION I MEN......................................237
  NCAA DIVISION I WOMEN................................237
AMATEURS
  U.S. AMATEUR...193
  U.S. WOMEN'S AMATEUR.................................198
  U.S. MID-AMATEUR..194
  U.S. WOMEN'S MID-AMATEUR.........................199
  U.S. SENIOR AMATEUR.....................................194
  U.S. WOMEN'S SENIOR AMATEUR...................199
  THE WALKER CUP...195
  THE CURTIS CUP..200

  U.S. PUBLIC LINKS..194
  U.S. WOMEN'S PUBLIC LINKS..........................199
OPEN—MEN'S
  AUSTRALIA..52
  CZECH REPUBLIC...51
  ECUADOR...53
  ENGLAND...50
  EUROPE..51
  GERMANY...51
  HOLLAND (NETHERLANDS)...............................51
  HONG KONG..55
  IRELAND...50
  JAPAN..55
  THE PHILIPPINES...54
  SCOTLAND...50
  SPAIN..50
  UNITED KINGDOM..50
  UNITED STATES...31

DIRECTORIES
LEADING GOLF CLUBS
  UNITED STATES
    ARONIMINK..321
    ATLANTA ATHLETIC CLUB.................................321
    ATLANTA..322
    AUGUSTA NATIONAL..322
    BALTIMORE (FIVE FARMS)................................322
    BALTUSROL..322
    BARTON CREEK..322
    BAY HILL CLUB...322
    BELLERIVE..322
    BETHPAGE..322
    BLACK DIAMOND...322
    BLACKWOLF RUN...322
    BROOKLAWN..322
    BUTLER NATIONAL..323
    CAMARGO...323
    CANTERBURY..323
    CASCADES...323
    CASTLE PINES...323
    CEDAR RIDGE...323
    CHAMPIONS...323
    CHARLOTTE...323
    CHERRY HILLS..323
    CHICAGO...323
    COG HILL...323
    COLONIAL..324

General Index

CONGRESSIONAL	324
C.C. OF DETROIT	324
C.C. OF NORTH CAROLINA	324
THE COUNTRY CLUB	324
THE COUNTRY CLUB (OHIO)	324
CROOKED STICK	324
CRYSTAL DOWNS	324
CYPRESS POINT	324
DEL PASO	325
DESERT FOREST	325
DESERT HIGHLANDS	325
DESERT MOUNTAIN	325
DORAL	325
DOUBLE EAGLE	325
DUNES CLUB	325
DUPONT	325
EUGENE	325
FIRESTONE	325
FIRETHORN	325
FISHERS ISLAND	325
FOREST HIGHLANDS	326
GARDEN CITY	326
THE GOLF CLUB	326
THE GOLF CLUB OF GEORGIA	326
GRANDFATHER	326
GRAND NATIONAL	326
GREENVILLE	326
HAIG POINT	326
HARBOUR TOWN	326
HAZELTINE NATIONAL	326
HIGH POINTE	326
THE HONORS COURSE	326
INDIANWOOD	326
INTERLACHEN	326
INVERNESS	326
JUPITER HILLS CLUB	327
KAUAI LAGOONS	327
KIAWAH	327
KITTANSETT CLUB	327
LA GRANGE	327
LAKE NONA	327
LA QUINTA	327
LAUREL VALLEY	327
LONG COVE	327
LOS ANGELES	328
MAIDSTONE	328
MAUNA KEA	328
MEDINAH C.C.	328
MERION	328
MILWAUKEE	328
MISSION HILLS	328
MONTCLAIR	328
MUIRFIELD VILLAGE	328
MUSKOGEE	328
NCR	328
NATIONAL GOLF LINKS OF AMERICA	328
OAK HILL	328
OAKLAND HILLS	328
OAKMONT	328
OAK TREE	329
OHIO STATE	329
OLD MARSH	329
OLD TABBY	329
OLD WARSON	329
OLD WAVERLY	329
OLYMPIA FIELDS	329
OLYMPIC	329
PGA NATIONAL	329
PGA WEST	329
PASATIEMPO	330
PEACHTREE	330
PEBBLE BEACH	330
PINEHURST	330
PINE TREE	330
PINE VALLEY	330
PLAINFIELD	330
POINT O'WOODS	330
PRAIRIE DUNES	330
PRINCEVILLE	331
PUMPKIN RIDGE	331
QUAKER RIDGE	331
RICHLAND	331
RIDGEWOOD	331
RIVIERA	331
SAHALEE	331
ST. LOUIS	331
SALEM	331
SAN FRANCISCO	331
SAUCON VALLEY	331
SEMINOLE	331
SCIOTO	331
SHADOW CREEK	331
SHADOW GLEN	331
SHERWOOD	332
SHINNECOCK HILLS	332
SHOAL CREEK	332
SHOREACRES	332
SKOKIE	332
SOMERSET HILLS	332
SOUTHERN HILLS	332
SPYGLASS HILL	332
STANWICH CLUB	332
SYCAMORE HILLS	332
TPC AT SAWGRASS	332

General Index

TPC OF MICHIGAN..................................332
TROON 333
TROON NORTH 333
VALHALLA 333
VALLEY CLUB OF MONTECITO..........333
WADE HAMPTON 333
WANNAMOISETT 333
WILD DUNES 333
WILMINGTON 333
WINGED FOOT......................................333
WYNSTONE 333

AUSTRALIA
THE AUSTRALIAN 333
COMMONWEALTH................................334
KINGSTON HEATH................................334
NEW SOUTH WALES............................334
ROYAL ADELAIDE..................................334
ROYAL MELBOURNE..............................334
VICTORIA..334

CANADA
ASHBURN G.C. 334
BANFF SPRINGS G.C. 334
BRANTFORD G. & C.C. 334
CAPILANO 334
CHERRY HILL 334
GLEN ABBEY..334
THE HAMILTON....................................334
LONDON HUNT....................................334
MAYFAIR 334
MISSISSAUGUA......................................334
THE NATIONAL 334
THE ROYAL COLWOOD........................334
THE ROYAL MONTREAL........................334
ST. GEORGE'S..334

COLOMBIA
EL RINCON..334

DOMINICAN REPUBLIC
CASA DE CAMPO..................................334

ENGLAND
ALWOODLEY..334
THE BELFRY 334
BERKSHIRE 334
FORMBY 334
GANTON 334
HILLSIDE 334
LINDRICK 334
LITTLE ASTON......................................334

NOTTS..336
ROYAL BIRKDALE..................................336
ROYAL LIVERPOOL (HOYLAKE)..........336
ROYAL LYTHAM & ST. ANNE'S..........336
ROYAL ST. GEORGE'S............................336
ROYAL WEST NORFOLK......................336
SAUNTON 336
SUNNINGDALE......................................336
SWINLEY FOREST..................................336
WALTON HEATH..................................336
WENTWORTH..336
WOODHALL SPA..................................336

FRANCE
CHANTILLY..337
LE TOQUET 337
MORFONTAINE 337
SEIGNOSSE 337

GERMANY
CLUB ZUR VAHR..................................337
HAMBURGER..337

HOLLAND
KENNEMER 337
NOORDWIJK 337

INDONESIA
JAGORAWL..337

IRELAND
BALLYBUNION 337
COUNTY LOUTH..................................337
COUNTY SLIGO 337
LAHINCH 338
PORTMARNOCK 338
ROYAL COUNTY DOWN....................338
ROYAL PORTRUSH................................338

ITALY
MILANO..338
PEVERO 338

JAPAN
HIRONO..338
KASUMIGASEKI 338
KAWANA 338
TOKYO..338

MOROCCO
ROYAL DAR-ES-SALAAM......................338

NEW ZEALAND
PARAPARAUMU BEACH.....................338

PORTUGAL
QUINTO DO LAGO..............................338
SAN LORENZO....................................339
VILAMOURA...339

SCOTLAND
BLAIRGOWRIE.....................................339
CARNOUSTIE.......................................339
CRUDEN BAY......................................339
GLENEAGLES.......................................339
MUIRFIELD...339
ROYAL DORNOCH.............................339
ROYAL TROON...................................339
ST. ANDREWS.....................................339
TURNBERRY..339

SOUTH AFRICA
DURBAN...340

SPAIN
CLUB DE CAMPO...............................340
EL PRAT..340
EL SALER..340
LAS BRISAS...340
PUERTO DE HIERRO..........................340
SOTOGRANDE....................................340
VALDERRAMA.....................................340

SWEDEN
FALSTERBO..340
HALMSTAD..340

SWITZERLAND
LAUSANNE..340

WALES
ROYAL PORTHCAWL.........................340

DIRECTORY OF ASSOCIATIONS................359
DIRECTORY OF GOLF SCHOOLS..............340

ECONOMICS AND DEVELOPMENT
AMERICAN PRO TOUR PURSES.......355
SPEED OF PLAY..................................356
PGA TOUR CHARITY CONTRIBUTIONS........357
GROWTH IN GOLF FACILITY SUPPLY............357
CENSUS OF U.S. GOLF POPULATION.............356
U.S. GOLF POPULATION 1995..........353

GOLFING TERMINOLOGY.........................378

HISTORY
PROFESSIONAL TOUR EVENT HISTORIES
PGA TOUR...................................204
LPGA...226
SENIOR PGA................................231
MEMORABLE DATES IN GOLF HISTORY........253

INTERNATIONALS
THE PRESIDENTS CUP..................189
THE RYDER CUP............................185
THE SOLHEIM CUP........................187
THE WORLD CUP..........................187

MAJOR CHAMPIONSHIPS
MEN
BRITISH OPEN...............................17
THE MASTERS...............................16
PGA CHAMPIONSHIP...................18
U.S. OPEN......................................16
WOMEN
DINAH SHORE..............................19
DUMAURIER CLASSIC..................22
LPGA CHAMPIONSHIP.................20
U.S. WOMEN'S OPEN....................21
SENIORS
SENIOR PGA CHAMPIONSHIP......24
SENIOR TPC..................................25
THE TRADITION............................23
U.S. SENIOR OPEN.......................24

THE NATIONS OF GOLF
ANTIGUA AND BARBUDA............272
ARGENTINA....................................272
AUSTRALIA......................................272
AUSTRIA..273
THE BAHAMAS...............................273
BARBADOS.....................................273
BELGIUM...274
BERMUDA.......................................274
BOTSWANA....................................274
BRAZIL...274
CANADA..275
CAYMAN ISLANDS........................275
CHILE...276
CHINA..276
COLOMBIA......................................276
COSTA RICA...................................276
CZECH REPUBLIC..........................278
DENMARK.......................................278

DOMINICAN REPUBLIC..................278
EGYPT..279
ENGLAND..279
FIJI..279
FINLAND..279
FRANCE..279
GERMANY..280
GREECE..280
GUADALOUPE....................................281
HONG KONG......................................281
ICELAND..281
INDIA..281
INDONESIA..282
IRELAND..282
ISRAEL..283
ITALY..283
JAMAICA..284
JAPAN...284
KENYA..285
KOREA..285
MALAWI...285
MALAYSIA...285
MEXICO..286
MOROCCO..286
NETHERLANDS..................................286
NEW ZEALAND..................................287
NORWAY...288
PAKISTAN..288
PANAMA..288
PARAGUAY..288
PERU...289
THE PHILIPPINES..............................289
PORTUGAL..289
PUERTO RICO....................................290
ST. MAARTEN.....................................290
SCOTLAND...290
SINGAPORE..292
SLOVENIA...292
SOUTH AFRICA.................................292
SPAIN..293
SRI LANKA..294
SWEDEN..294
SWITZERLAND..................................295
TAIWAN...295
TANZANIA..296
THAILAND..296
TRINIDAD & TOBAGO....................296
UNITED STATES................................297
URUGUAY...299
VENEZUELA.......................................299
VIRGIN ISLANDS..............................300
WALES..300
ZAMBIA..300
ZIMBABWE...301

PEOPLE
PGA TOUR PERSONALITIES
  FULTON ALLEM................................70
  BILLY ANDRADE...............................70
  PAUL AZINGER..................................70
  DAVE BARR..71
  CHIP BECK...71
  JAY DON BLAKE................................71
  GUY BOROS..71
  BRAD BRYANT...................................73
  MARK BROOKS..................................73
  MARK CALCAVECCHIA...................73
  BRIAN CLAAR.....................................73
  LENNIE CLEMENTS..........................74
  RUSS COCHRAN................................74
  JOHN COOK..74
  FRED COUPLES..................................75
  BEN CRENSHAW................................75
  JOHN DALY...75
  GLEN DAY...76
  JAY DELSING.....................................76
  ED DOUGHERTY...............................76
  DAVID EDWARDS.............................76
  STEVE ELKINGTON..........................76
  BOB ESTES...77
  NICK FALDO.......................................77
  BRAD FAXON.....................................77
  RICK FEHR...77
  BRUCE FLEISHER..............................78
  DAN FORSMAN.................................78
  DAVID FROST.....................................78
  FRED FUNK...79
  JIM GALLAGHER, JR.........................79
  ROBERT GAMEZ...............................79
  BOB GILDER.......................................79
  BILL GLASSON..................................80
  KEN GREEN...80
  JAY HAAS...80
  GARY HALLBERG..............................80
  DONNIE HAMMOND.......................81
  MIKE HEINEN....................................81
  NOLAN HENKE.................................81
  BRIAN HENNINGER.........................81
  SCOTT HOCH....................................82
  MIKE HULBERT................................82
  JOHN HUSTON..................................82
  HALE IRWIN.......................................82
  PETER JACOBSEN..............................83
  LEE JANZEN..83

TOM KITE..83
GREG KRAFT..84
NEAL LANCASTER...................................84
TOM LEHMAN..84
WAYNE LEVI...85
BRUCE LIETZKE.......................................85
ROBERT LOHR..85
DAVIS LOVE III...86
STEVE LOWERY.......................................86
ANDREW MAGEE....................................86
JEFF MAGGERT..86
ROGER MALTBIE......................................86
BILLY MAYFAIR..87
BLAINE McCALLISTER............................87
MARK McCUMBER..................................87
JIM McGOVERN.......................................88
ROCCO MEDIATE....................................88
PHIL MICKELSON....................................88
LARRY MIZE...88
GIL MORGAN...89
GREG NORMAN......................................89
BRETT OGLE...90
JOSE MARIA OLAZABAL........................90
MARK O'MEARA.....................................90
CRAIG PARRY...90
STEVE PATE...91
COREY PAVIN..91
KENNY PERRY...91
NICK PRICE...91
DICKY PRIDE..92
TOM PURTZER...92
LOREN ROBERTS.....................................92
GENE SAUERS..92
SCOTT SIMPSON.....................................93
VIJAY SINGH..94
MIKE SPRINGER......................................94
JEFF SLUMAN...94
CRAIG STADLER......................................94
MIKE STANDLY..95
PAYNE STEWART 95
CURTIS STRANGE...................................95
STEVE STRICKER.....................................95
HAL SUTTON...96
DOUG TEWELL..96
KIRK TRIPLETT...96
BOB TWAY..96
HOWARD TWITTY..................................97
LANNY WADKINS...................................97
GRANT WAITE...97
DUFFY WALDORF...................................97
TOM WATSON...97
D.A. WEIBRING.......................................98
IAN WOOSNAM......................................98
FUZZY ZOELLER.....................................98

LPGA PERSONALITIES
KRISTI ALBERS...99
HELEN ALFREDSSON..............................99
DANIELLE AMMACCAPANE.................99
DONNA ANDREWS................................99
TINA BARRETT..99
AMY BENZ..100
MISSIE BERTEOTTI................................100
PAT BRADLEY...100
BARB BUNKOWSKY..............................100
BRANDIE BURTON...............................101
JOANNE CARNER..................................101
DAWN COE-JONES...............................101
JANE CRAFTER......................................102
ELAINE CROSBY....................................102
BETH DANIEL...102
LAURA DAVIES......................................102
ALICIA DIBOS..102
JUDY DICKINSON.................................103
DALE EGGELING...................................103
JANE GEDDES..103
GAIL GRAHAM......................................103
TAMMIE GREEN....................................103
SHELLEY HAMLIN.................................104
JULI INKSTER...104
CHRIS JOHNSON..................................105
TRISH JOHNSON...................................105
ROSIE JONES...105
LISA KIGGENS.......................................105
BETSY KING...105
HIROMI KOBAYASHI............................106
NANCY LOPEZ......................................106
MEG MALLON.......................................107
MISSIE McGEORGE...............................107
MICHELLE McGANN............................107
LAURI MERTEN.....................................107
DOTTIE MOCHRIE................................107
KRIS MONAGHAN................................108
MARTHA NAUSE...................................108
LISELOTTE NEUMANN........................108
NANCY RAMSBOTTOM.......................108
CINDY RARICK......................................109
DEB RICHARD.......................................109
ALICE RITZMAN...................................110
KELLY ROBBINS....................................110
PATTY SHEEHAN...................................111
VAL SKINNER..112
HOLLIS STACY......................................112
SHERRI STEINHAUER...........................112

JAN STEPHENSON..................113
KRIS TSCHETTER....................113
LISA WALTERS........................114

SENIOR PGA TOUR PERSONALITIES

TOMMY AARON.....................115
JIM ALBUS..............................115
ISAO AOKI..............................115
TOMMY AYCOCK...................115
GEORGE ARCHER..................116
MILLER BARBER....................116
BOB BETLEY..........................116
DON BIES...............................117
BOB CHARLES.......................117
JIM COLBERT........................117
CHARLES COODY..................118
BRUCE CRAMPTON...............119
JIM DENT..............................119
DALE DOUGLASS..................128
JIM FERREE..........................120
RAYMOND FLOYD..................120
AL GEIBERGER......................120
GIBBY GILBERT....................121
LARRY GILBERT...................121
DICK HENDRICKSON.............121
HAROLD HENNING................121
MIKE HILL............................122
SIMON HOBDAY...................123
DON JANUARY......................123
JACK KIEFER........................124
LARRY LAORETTI.................124
DICK LOTZ...........................124
RIVES MCBEE......................124
ORVILLE MOODY..................124
LARRY MOWRY....................125
BOB MURPHY......................125
BOBBY NICHOLS..................126
JACK NICKLAUS...................126
GARY PLAYER.....................127
DICK RHYAN........................128
CHI CHI RODRIGUEZ............129
TOM SHAW..........................129
BEN SMITH..........................129
J.C. SNEAD..........................129
DAVE STOCKTON.................130
ROCKY THOMPSON..............130
HARRY TOSCANO.................131
LEE TREVINO.......................131
TOM WARGO........................131
DEWITT WEAVER.................131
TOM WEISKOPF...................132
KERMIT ZARLEY..................132

WALT ZEMBRISKI..................132
LARRY ZIEGLER....................132

FOREIGN PERSONALITIES

ROBERT ALLENBY................133
PETER BAKER......................133
SEVE BALLESTEROS............133
LUIS CARBONETTI................133
RODGER DAVIS....................133
ERNIE ELS...........................133
NICK FALDO........................134
ANDERS FORSBRAND...........134
JOAKIM HAEGGMAN.............134
MARK JAMES......................134
KANG-SUN LEE...................134
BARRY LANE.......................134
BERNHARD LANGER.............134
LIANG-HSI CHEN..................135
SANDY LYLE.......................135
MARK MCNULTY.................135
COLIN MONTGOMERIE..........135
TOMMY NAKAJIMA...............135
NAM-SIN PARK...................135
FRANK NOBILO....................135
JOSE MARIA OLAZABAL........136
MASASHI "JUMBO" OZAKI....136
RONAN RAFFERTY...............136
STEVEN RICHARDSON..........136
JOSE RIVERO......................136
COSTANTINO ROCCA...........136
EDUARDO ROMERO.............136
ANDERS SORENSEN.............137
STEEN TINNING...................137
SAM TORRANCE..................137
JEAN VAN DE VELDE............137
IAN WOOSNAM...................137
YU-SHU HSIEH....................137

HALL OF FAME PERSONALITIES

WILLIE ANDERSON................138
TOMMY ARMOUR.................138
JOHN BALL..........................138
JIM BARNES.......................138
PATTY BERG.......................138
JULIUS BOROS....................138
JAMES BRAID.....................138
MIKE BRADY......................138
BILLY BURKE......................139
JACK BURKE, JR..................139
JOANNE CARNER................139
HARRY COOPER..................139
HENRY COTTON..................139

General Index

BOBBY CRUICKSHANK.....................139
JIMMY DEMARET..............................139
ROBERTO DE VICENZO....................140
LEO DIEGEL.......................................140
ED DUDLEY..140
OLIN DUTRA......................................140
CHICK EVANS....................................140
JOHNNY FARRELL.............................140
DOUG FORD.......................................140
VIC GHEZZI..141
RALPH GULDAHL..............................141
WALTER HAGEN................................141
CHICK HARBERT...............................141
CHANDLER HARPER........................142
E.J. (DUTCH) HARRISON...................142
SANDRA HAYNIE...............................142
BEN HOGAN.......................................142
DOROTHY CAMPBELL HURD HOWE.....142
JOCK HUTCHINSON..........................143
BETTY JAMESON...............................143
ROBERT T. JONES.............................143
LAWSON LITTLE................................149
BOBBY LOCKE...................................144
NANCY LOPEZ...................................144
LLOYD MANGRUM............................144
CAROL MANN....................................144
JOHN MCDERMOTT..........................145
FRED MCLEOD...................................145
CARY MIDDLECOFF..........................145
TOM MORRIS, JR................................145
TOM MORRIS, SR................................145
BYRON NELSON.................................145
JACK NICKLAUS.................................146
FRANCIS OUIMET..............................146
ARNOLD PALMER.............................147
HENRY PICARD..................................147
BETSY RAWLS....................................148
JOHNNY REVOLTA............................148
PAUL RUNYAN...................................148
GENE SARAZEN.................................148
DENNY SHUTE...................................149
ALEX SMITH.......................................149
HORTON SMITH.................................149
MAC SMITH..150
SAM SNEAD..150
LOUISE SUGGS...................................151
JOHN H. TAYLOR...............................151
PETER THOMSON..............................151
JEROME S. TRAVERS.........................151
WALTER TRAVIS................................151
HARRY VARDON................................152
GLENNA COLLETT VARE.................152
JOYCE WETHERED............................152
KATHY WHITWORTH........................152
CRAIG WOOD.....................................153
MICKEY WRIGHT...............................153
BABE ZAHARIAS................................153

RANKINGS
AMATEURS...230
JUNIORS...245
LPGA PROS...59
PGA TOUR..61
SENIOR PGA...65
SONY RANKINGS.................................67
PING LEADERBOARD.........................68

STATE-BY-STATE GOLF SUMMARY
ALABAMA...302
ALASKA...302
ARIZONA..302
ARKANSAS...303
CALIFORNIA......................................303
COLORADO..303
CONNECTICUT..................................304
DELAWARE..304
DISTRICT OF COLUMBIA.................304
FLORIDA...305
GEORGIA..305
HAWAII...306
IDAHO...306
ILLINOIS...306
INDIANA...307
IOWA...307
KANSAS..307
KENTUCKY..308
LOUISIANA..308
MAINE..308
MARYLAND.......................................308
MASSACHUSETTS.............................309
MICHIGAN...309
MINNESOTA......................................309
MISSISSIPPI.......................................310
MISSOURI..310
MONTANA...312
NEBRASKA..312
NEVADA...312
NEW HAMPSHIRE.............................312
NEW JERSEY......................................312
NEW MEXICO....................................313
NEW YORK..313
NORTH CAROLINA...........................314
NORTH DAKOTA..............................314
OHIO...315

OKLAHOMA	315
OREGON	315
PENNSYLVANIA	316
RHODE ISLAND	316
SOUTH CAROLINA	317
SOUTH DAKOTA	317
TENNESSEE	317
TEXAS	318
UTAH	318
VERMONT	319
VIRGINIA	319
WASHINGTON	319
WEST VIRGINIA	320
WISCONSIN	320
WYOMING	320

STATISTICS
PGA TOUR

SCORING LEADERS	61
DRIVING LEADERS	61
DRIVING ACCURACY	61
GREENS IN REGULATION	61
ALL AROUND	61
TOTAL DRIVING	61
PUTTING LEADERS	62
BIRDIE LEADERS	62
EAGLE LEADERS	62
SAND SAVES %	62
PGA 1885 MONEY LEADERS	62
PGA TOUR CAREER MONEY	62

LPGA TOUR

SCORING LEADERS	58
DRIVING LEADERS	58
PUTTING LEADERS	58
BIRDIE LEADERS	58
PLAYER OF THE YEAR	58
ROOKIE OF THE YEAR	58
LPGA 1885 MONEY LEADERS	59
LPGA CAREER MONEY	60
PING LEADERBOARD—TOP 50	59

SENIOR PGA TOUR

SCORING LEADERS	62
DRIVING LEADERS	62
DRIVING ACCURACY	62
GREENS IN REGULATION	62
ALL AROUND	63
TOTAL DRIVING	63
PUTTING LEADERS	63
BIRDIE LEADERS	63
EAGLE LEADERS	63
SAND SAVES %	63
SENIOR 1885 MONEY LEADERS	64
SENIOR CAREER MONEY	65

EUROPEAN TOUR

MONEY LEADERS	78

TOURNAMENTS
PGA TOUR

ANHEUSER-BUSCH GOLF CLASSIC	32
AT&T PEBBLE BEACH NATIONAL PRO-AM	28
B.C. OPEN	33
BELL CANADIAN OPEN	33
BELLSOUTH CLASSIC	30
BOB HOPE CHRYSLER CLASSIC	28
BRITISH OPEN	32
BUICK CLASSIC	31
BUICK INVITATIONAL OF CALIFORNIA	28
BUICK OPEN	33
BUICK SOUTHERN OPEN	39
BYRON NELSON CLASSIC	30
CANON GREATER HARTFORD OPEN	32
COLONIAL NATIONAL INVITATIONAL	31
DEPOSIT GUARANTY GOLF CLASSIC	32
DINERS CLUB MATCHES	8
DORAL-RYDER OPEN	28
FEDEX ST. JUDE CLASSIC	33
FRANKLIN FUNDS SHARK SHOOTOUT	8
FREEPORT-MCMORAN CLASSIC	29
GREATER MILWAUKEE OPEN	33
HONDA CLASSIC	29
THE INTERNATIONAL	33
JC PENNEY CLASSIC	8
KEMPER OPEN	31
KMART GREATER GREENSBORO OPEN	30
LAS VEGAS INVITATIONAL	39
LINCOLN-MERCURY KAPALUA 'INT'L	8
THE MASTERS	29
MCI HERITAGE CLASSIC	30
MEMORIAL TOURNAMENT	31
MERCEDES CHAMPIONSHIPS	31
MOTOROLA WESTERN OPEN	32
NEC WORLD SERIES OF GOLF	33
THE NESTLE INVITATIONAL	29
THE NEW ENGLAND CLASSIC	33
NISSAN LOS ANGELES OPEN	28
NORTHERN TELECOM OPEN	31
PGA CHAMPIONSHIP	33
PHOENIX OPEN	31
THE PLAYERS CHAMPIONSHIP	29
QUAD CITIES OPEN	8
SHELL HOUSTON OPEN	30

General Index

SKINS GAME 8
TEXAS OPEN 39
THE TOUR CHAMPIONSHIP 39
UNITED AIRLINES HAWAIIAN OPEN 31
US OPEN 31
WALT DISNEY WORLD/OLDSMOBILE
    CLASSIC 8

SENIOR PGA TOUR

AMERICAN EXPRESS GRANDSLAM 9
AMERITECH SENIOR OPEN 38
BANK OF BOSTON SENIOR GOLF CLASSIC ... 39
BANK ONE CLASSIC 39
BELL ATLANTIC CLASSIC 35
BELLSOUTH SENIOR CLASSIC 10
BRICKYARD CROSSING CHAMPIONSHIP 9
BRUNO'S MEMORIAL CLASSIC 43
BURNET SENIOR CLASSIC 39
CADILLAC NFL GOLF CLASSIC 43
CHRYSLER CUP 41
DALLAS REUNION PRO-AM 42
DINERS CLUB MATCHES 49
THE DOMINION 9
EMERALD COAST CLASSIC 10
FHP HEALTH CARE CLASSIC 9
FIRST OF AMERICA CLASSIC 39
FORD SENIOR PLAYERS CHAMPIONSHIP ... 38
SENIOR TOUR CHAMPIONSHIP 10
GTE NORTHWEST CLASSIC 40
GTE SUNCOAST CLASSIC 40
HYATT REGENCY MAUI KAANAPALI
    CLASSIC 41
THE INTELLINET CHALLENGE 40
KROGER SENIOR CLASSIC 38
LAS VEGAS SENIOR CLASSIC 37
LIBERTY MUTUAL LEGENDS OF GOLF 37
NATIONWIDE CHAMPIONSHIP 43
NORTHVILLE LONG ISLAND CLASSIC 39
PAINEWEBBER INVITATIONAL 37
PGA SENIORS CHAMPIONSHIP 37
QUICKSILVER CLASSIC 40
RALEY'S SENIOR GOLD RUSH 41
RALPH'S SENIOR CLASSIC 41
ROYAL CARIBBEAN CLASSIC 40
SENIOR SKINS GAME 40
SENIOR SLAM OF GOLF 35
THE TRADITION 41
THE TRANSAMERICA 41
TOSHIBA SENIOR CLASSIC 9
US SENIOR OPEN 38
VANTAGE CHAMPIONSHIP 40
VFW SENIOR CHAMPIONSHIP 38

LPGA TOUR

CUP NOODLES HAWAIIAN LADIES OPEN 36
DINER'S CLUB MATCHES 49
DU MAURIER LTD. CLASSIC 22
GHP HEARTLAND CLASSIC 41
HEALTHSOUTH INAUGURAL 36
JAL BIG APPLE CLASSIC 39
JAMIE FARR TOLEDO CLASSIC 39
JCPENNEY CLASSIC 42
LPGA CORNING CLASSIC 38
MCCALL'S LPGA CLASSIC 40
MCDONALD'S LPGA CHAMPIONSHIP 20
NABISCO DINAH SHORE 19
NICHIREI INTERNATIONAL 42
OLDSMOBILE CLASSIC 38
PINEWILD WOMEN'S CHAMPIONSHIP 40
PING/WELCH'S CHAMPIONSHIP (AZ) 36
PING/WELCH'S CHAMPIONSHIP 40
PING-CELLULAR ONE LPGA GOLF
    CHAMPIONSHIP 41
ROCHESTER INTERNATIONAL 38
SAFECO CLASSIC 41
SARA LEE CLASSIC 37
SHOPRITE LPGA CLASSIC 39
SPRINT CHALLENGE 37
STANDARD REGISTER PING 37
STATE FARM RAIL CLASSIC 40
TORAY JAPAN QUEENS CUP 13
U.S. WOMEN'S OPEN 21
WORLD CHAMPIONSHIP OF WOMEN'S GOLF ... 41
YOUNGSTOWN-WARREN LPGA CLASSIC ... 39

EUROPEAN TOUR

BELL'S SCOTTISH OPEN 44
BENSON AND HEDGES OPEN 44
BMW INTERNATIONAL OPEN 44
BRITISH OPEN 44
EUROPEAN MASTERS 45
CZECH OPEN 45
DUBAI DESERT CLASSIC 44
DUNHILL BRITISH MASTERS 15
HEINEKEN DUTCH OPEN 44
JERSEY OPEN 44
GERMAN MASTERS 45
MURPHY'S ENGLISH OPEN 44
MURPHY'S IRISH OPEN 44
OPEN CATALONIA 14
PEUGEOT OPEN DE ESPANA 44
PORTUGUESE OPEN 44
SCANDANAVIAN MASTERS 44
EUROPEAN OPEN 15
TOURNOI PERRIER DE PARIS 44

TOYOTA WORLD MATCH PLAY
  CHAMPIONSHIP..................................15
TROPHEE LANCOME.............................45
TURESPANA OPEN DE CANARIES.......................44
TURESPANA OPEN MEDITERRIANIA...............44
GERMAN OPEN.......................................45
VOLVO MASTERS.. 15
VOLVO CHAMPIONSHIP.........................44

JAPANESE TOUR
ANA OPEN..49
ASAHI BEER GOLF DIGEST..................49
DUNLOP OPEN....................................49
JAPAN OPEN.......................................49
PGA MATCH PLAY CHAMPIONSHIP.................48
PGA PHILANTHROPY.........................48
SUNTORY OPEN..................................48
TOKEN CORPORATION CUP..............................48

ASIAN TOUR
BENSON & HEDGES MALAYSIA OPEN............48
VOLVO CHINA OPEN............................48
HONG KONG OPEN..............................49
MANILA SOUTHWOODS PHILIPPINE OPEN.....48

AUSTRALIAN TOUR
AIR NEW ZEALAND-SHELL OPEN...................46
AUSTRALIAN MASTERS........................46
AUSTRALIAN OPEN..............................46
CANON CHALLENGE.............................46
COOLUM CLASSIC................................46
GREG NORMAN HOLDEN CLASSIC................46
PLAYERS CHAMPIONSHIP......................46
VICTORIAN OPEN.................................46

SOUTH AMERICAN TOUR
ABIERTO DE LOS LEONES....................48
ABIERTO DE PRINCE OF WALES........................48
ABIERTO DE URUGUAY.........................48
T.C. ECUADORIAN OPEN......................47

PGA CLUB PROS
LANGERT PGA MATCH PLAY CHAMP............222
LANGERT PGA QUARTER CENTURY
  CHAMPIONSHIP.............................222
LANGERT PGA SENIOR-JUNIOR CHAMP......222

LANGERT PGA STROKE PLAY CHAMP.............223
LANGERT PGA SR. STROKE PLAY CHAMP.......222
PGA CLUB PROFESSIONAL
  TOURNAMENT...............................222
PGA CUP MATCHES................................223
PGA SENIOR CLUB PRO. CHAMP...................222
PGA TOURNAMENT SERIES.............................223
TITLEIST/FOOT-JOY PGA ASSISTANT PRO
  CHAMPIONSHIP.............................222

AMATEURS
MEN'S WORLD AMATEUR TEAM CHAMP........233
WOMEN'S WORLD AMATEUR TEAM
  CHAMPIONSHIP.............................239

JUNIORS
AJGA BOYS JUNIOR CHAMPIONSHIP............241
AJGA CAPE COD JUNIOR................244
ASPEN JUNIOR CLASSIC...................244
BLUEGRASS JUNIOR INVITATIONAL..........244
BUICK JUNIOR OPEN.........................244
CANON CUP......................................244
CLUBCORP JUNIOR CHAMPIONSHIP............244
CLUBCORP JUNIOR PLAYERS CHAMPIONSHIP.......244
FREEPORT-MCMORAN JUNIOR CLASSIC.....244
INDIGO RUN JUNIOR CLASSIC................244
KMART GREATER GREENSBORO JUNIOR....244
LAS VEGAS FOUNDERS' LEGACY JUNIOR...244
MARRIOTT AT SAWGRASS FIRST COAST JR. CLASSIC.....244
MISSION HILLS DESERT JUNIOR...................244
NORTHERN TELECOM JR. TEAM CHALLENGE......244
OKLAHOMA JUNIOR CLASSIC.........................244
PING MYRTLE BEACH JUNIOR CLASSIC......244
PING PHOENIX JUNIOR CHAMPIONSHIP.....244
RAY FLOYD TURNBERRY ISLE JUNIOR...........244
ROBERT TRENT JONES GOLF TRAIL JUNIOR CLASSIC....244
ROLEX TOURNAMENT OF CHAMPIONS........244
TAYLOR MADE PINELSLE JR. CLASSIC..............244
TAYLOR MADE WOODLANDS JR. CLASSIC......244
TEXACE SAN ANTONIO SHOOTOUT.............244
TODD MOORE MEMORIAL.............................244
SMITH CORONA APAWAMIS JUNIOR.............244
SOUTHWESTERN JUNIOR.............................244
WILSON GENEVA NAT'L JUNIOR CHAMP........244

Sources

The primary source for contemporary information in this guide has been releases received by The Complete Golfer's Almanac. The Almanac also includes much original material supplied by state, regional, trade, and national golf associations throughout the world. 20th-century historical material has been compiled from records supplied by the organizations named below, through surveys conducted by The Complete Golfer's Almanac, and/or from a variety of secondary information sources. The organizations named below are staffed by tireless individuals who labor, usually in anonymity, to preserve golf history and collect and share golf data. Each of them merits your support through membership, subscription, or volunteer activity.

PRIMARY SOURCES
1995 Golfer's Almanac Survey of States
1995 Golfer's Almanac Survey of Nations
1995 Golfer's Almanac Survey of Courses
1995 Golfer's Almanac Survey of Schools
1995 Golfer's Almanac Survey of Associations
1995 Golfer's Almanac Economic Survey
American Junior Golf Association
American Society of Golf Course Architects
Augusta National Golf Club
The Australian PGA
The Asian PGA Tour
The European PGA
Golf Course Superintendents of America
Golf Data Online
The International Golf Association
The Japanese PGA
The LPGA
National Collegiate Athletic Association
National Golf Course Owner's Association
The National Golf Foundation
The PGA of America
The PGA TOUR
The South American Tour
Sporting Goods Manufacturers Association
The United States Golf Association
The Women's Professional Golf European Tour

SECONDARY SOURCES
1993 Merchandise Show Directory & Buyer's Guide
1994 Golf Almanac (Publications International/Signet: 1994)
1994 Yellow Pages of Golf
Allen, Sir Peter—The Sunley Book of Royal Golf (Stanley Paul: 1989)
Baumgart, Ruth and the Editors of LINKS Magazine—LINKS Magazine's Property Lines (LINKS: 1995)
Borton, Brett and Cherry, Ed, and the Editors of LINKS Magazine —The Endless Fairway (Simon & Schuster: 1992-94)
Browning, Robert—A History of Golf (Dent: 1955)
Darwin, Bernard—The Golf Courses of the British Isles (Storey/Ailsa: 1988)
Golf Consumer Survey (National Golf Foundation: 1989)
Golf Digest
Golf Digest Almanac 1989
The Golfer's Handbook
Golf Magazine
Golf Magazine's Encyclopedia of Golf (HarperCollins: 1993)
Golf Participation in the United States (National Golf Foundation: 1988-1995)
Golfweek Magazine
Golf World Magazine
Golf Writers Association of America 1994 directory
Hobbs, Michael—The Golfer's Companion (Macdonald/Queen Anne Press: 1988)
Lane, James M.—The Complete Golfer's Almanac 1995 (Perigee: 1995)
Lane, James M.—Peterson's Golf Schools & Resorts (Peterson's: 1995)
LINKS Magazine
LPGA Media Guide
PGA of America Media Guide
PGA of America Slow Play Survey (1989)
PGA TOUR Media Guide
Macdonald, Charles Blair—Scotland's Gift-Golf (Ailsa, Inc.: 1985)
The National Golf Course Directory (Sports Directories: 1994)
The United States Golf Association Media Guide
The World of Professional Golf (IMG: 1990-95)

We welcome all suggestions, corrections, and new material for inclusion in future editions. Please contact us at:

THE COMPLETE GOLFER'S ALMANAC
E-Mail: Gymbabwe@aol.com

Acknowledgments

Any book of this size and scope requires some grateful acknowledgment to a number of key people who have worked behind the scenes to bring this book to you. Thanks to:

Sheila Curry, Steven Anderson, Julie Merberg, Hardy Justice, David Shanks, and the very patient crew of production staff including (notably) Bill Harris and Paul Winkler. Many thanks for another series of star performances and for a study in patience as we held the Almanac open for late-breaking results.

Alex Miceli, Ruth Baumgart, George Fuller, Brian Henley, Gary Galyean, Jim Carlin, Vic Oleson, Dean Christopher, Ann Lane, Adam Weisman, Rudy Marrocco, Geoff Shackleford, Lori Radcliff and Jeff Stern—for the jokes, endorsements, ideas, unbilled contributions, advice and occasional tee-times that kept the author going during the creation of this edition of the book.

Thanks also to:

My patient staff of dedicated non-golfers at JSA Publishing who are such a joy to work with—with special thanks to Michael Foti, Luciane Garbin, Julie Gillen, Howard Maat, Michelle Mendez, Betty Sedor, Joy Simon, Jeff Still and Jenny Sucov.

My wonderful and somewhat extended family for their continued support.

The following providers of raw data: Dave Lancer and staff at the PGA TOUR; Elaine Scott and the staff at the LPGA; Maxine at the USGA for many mad dashes for facts; the European PGA Tour; Augusta National Golf Club; Julius Mason and Sherry Major at the PGA of America; John Benda for some key assistance on South America; Mr. Sato at the Japanese PGA; Tom Place at the IGA; the staff at the Women's Pro Golf European Tour, the National Golf Foundation, the staff at iGOLF and NBC Golf Tour, and finally all the dedicated individuals who staff national golf associations around the world who took time to return surveys and provide background history.

Errata and amendments

In a book of this size, there is the possibility of a small error—no matter who the quoted source is for the material, the final responsibility rests entirely with me. Future editions of **The Complete Golfer's Almanac** will correct any and all errors which are detected.

James M. Lane
Los Angeles
January 1996

This book is dedicated to
Mum, Dad and Nancy
with love.

Walt Spitzmiller
is one of the world's foremost sporting artists.

He has dedicated some of his finest work to portraying the many aspects of the game of golf— from its rich traditions to its heroes and most memorable competitions. Walt was recently featured by The United States Golf Association Museum and Library with an exhibition showcasing his golf art.

Spitzmiller is perhaps best recognized for his many contributions to *Sports Illustrated, Golf* magazine, *Senior Golfer, Outdoor Life* and other popular magazines. His work is held in private collections throughout the world.

Corporate collections of Spitzmiller's portraits include CBS Sports, The PGA Tour, Titleist, Baseball Hall of Fame, and ABC Sports. Other collections are featured in the American Museum of Illustration, The National Art Museum of Sports, and The Professional Rodeo Hall of Champions Museum.

Readers of The Complete Golfer's Almanac 1996 are invited to purchase a print of Walt Spitzmiller's 1995 PGA Tour image, for $95. each, plus shipping and handling of $7.50 each, or $102.50 per print, by ordering by phone or mail from:
Walt Spitzmiller Prints
P.O. Box 905
Georgetown, CT 06829
1-203-938-3551

SPECIAL OFFER

The cover illustration for THE COMPLETE GOLFER'S ALMANAC 1996 was created by Walt Spitzmiller for the 1995 PGA Tour Poster Program. A limited number of fine prints is being made available to the readers of the ALMANAC for the price of $95., plus shipping and handling. This beautiful color print celebrating the great game of golf, and the PGA Tour, is already a much-sought-after collector's item by golf enthusiasts around the world. **The print is 21" by 30", on fine art paper that is acid-free neutral PH.**